EARLY CHILDHOOD EDUCATION

1900	1920	1940	1960	1980	1990

Susan Blow 1843-1916 William T. Harris 1835-1909 Patty Smith Hill 1868-1946 Rachel & Margaret McMillan 1860-1931	Harriet Johnson 1867-1934 Lucy Sprague Mitchell 1878-1961 Marie Montessori 1870-1952	Alfred Adler 1870-1937 John Dewey 1870-1937 Sigmund Freud 1856-1939 A.S. Hall 1844-1929	Benjamin Bloom 1911- Erik Erickson 1902- Anna Freud 1895-1982 J. McVicker Hunt 1906- Jean Piaget 1896-1980 B.F. Skinner 1904-1990	Millie Almy Barbara Biber Barbara Bowman Marian Wright Edelman Jimmy Hymes Constance Kamii Lillian Katz Bernard Spodek David Weikart Edward Zigler	

U.S. Children's Bureau 1912	**Works Progress Administration** 1935-1943 **Lanham Act** 1941-1945		**Project Head Start** 1965 **Bilingual Education Act** 1965, 1974 **Project FollowThrough** 1967	**Child Abuse & Prevention Act** 1973 **Education for All Handicapped Children (PL-94-142)** 1975 **Gifted & Talented Act** 1978 **Federal Preschool & Early Intervention Program Act (PL 99-457)** 1986	

World War I 1914-1918	The Great Depression	World War II 1939-1945	Civil Rights Movement	Vietnam War	New Wave of Immigration 1980-

RISE OF INDUSTRIAL DEMOCRACY TWENTIETH CENTURY 1900 - 1965		**AGE OF INFORMATION & TECHNOLOGY 1970 -**	

Early Childhood Education

An Introduction
Third Edition

Carol Seefeldt
University of Maryland
College Park

Nita Barbour
University of Maryland
Baltimore County

MERRILL, AN IMPRINT OF
MACMILLAN COLLEGE PUBLISHING COMPANY
  NEW YORK
MAXWELL MACMILLAN CANADA
  TORONTO
MAXWELL MACMILLAN INTERNATIONAL
  NEW YORK OXFORD SINGAPORE SYDNEY

Cover photo: Ron Rovtar
Editor: Linda A. Sullivan
Production Editor: Louise N. Sette
Art Coordinators: Lorraine Woost, Vincent A. Smith
Photo Editor: Anne Vega
Cover Designer: Cathleen Norz
Production Buyer: Patricia A. Tonneman
Artist: Jane Lopez
Electronic Text Management: Ben Ko, Marilyn Wilson Phelps, Matthew Williams

This book was set in Bookman by Macmillan College Publishing Company and was printed and bound by R.R. Donnelley & Sons Company. The cover was printed by Phoenix Color Corp.

Macmillan College Publishing Company
866 Third Avenue
New York, NY 10022

Macmillan College Publishing Company is part of the
Maxwell Communication Group of Companies.

Maxwell Macmillan Canada, Inc.
1200 Eglinton Avenue East, Suite 200
Don Mills, Ontario M3C 3N1

Library of Congress Cataloging-in-Publication Data
Seefeldt, Carol.
    Early childhood education : an introduction / Carol Seefeldt, Nita
Barbour. —3rd ed.
        p.   cm.
    Includes bibliographical references and index.
    ISBN 0-02-408452-2
    1. Early childhood education—United States. I. Barbour, Nita.
II. Title.
LB1139.25.S44   1993
372—dc20   93-24744
                                                          CIP

Printing: 1 2 3 4 5 6 7 8 9   Year: 4 5 6 7 8

Photo credits: Dan Floss/Macmillan, pp. 9, 18, 20, 23, 52, 72, 86, 99, 115, 126, 133, 135, 146, 154, 174, 189, 194, 222, 230, 243, 248, 284, 302, 305, 318, 363, 390, 400, 453, 460, 529, 557, 567, 578, 579; KS Studios, p. 537; Barbara Schwartz/Macmillan, pp. 276, 313, 355, 372, 499, 554; Anne Vega/Macmillan, pp. 34, 41, 46, 61, 93, 119, 184, 271, 296, 324, 332, 378, 394, 448, 475; Todd Yarrington/Macmillan, pp. xxii, 12, 14, 30, 56, 170, 179, 218, 237, 254, 260, 264, 267, 279, 308, 340, 349, 388, 397, 414, 420, 428, 432, 437, 457, 464, 469, 484, 486, 496, 513, 520, 524, 542, 548, 564, 573.

I dedicate this book to my family, Eugene, Paul, and Andrea, who believe women have the right and the responsibility to participate in the whole of life; and to my parents, George and Mary Wohanka, who taught me how to work.

Carol Seefeldt

I dedicate this book to my family, Chandler, Valerie, and Steven; to my friend Tupper Webster; and to the Early Childhood Education students at the University of Maryland–Baltimore County.

Nita Barbour

Preface

"Once I had a teacher," explained a famous surgeon when asked how she became so successful, "a teacher who, because of her love of children and her understanding of how they learned, changed the course of my life."

Nearly everyone can recall a special teacher, one who made a difference in their lives. The third edition of *Early Childhood Education: An Introduction* has been designed to prepare students to become one of those special teachers, who because of their knowledge, skill, and dedication to children and their learning will not only be remembered with fondness, but will have made a difference in the lives of many.

Written for the preservice early childhood teacher, the third edition of *Early Childhood Education: An Introduction* is based on the belief that teachers of young children must be highly skilled—knowledgeable about children, their parents, and the community in which they live, as well as the processes of teaching curriculum content.

A look at the content and features of the third edition of *Early Childhood Education: An Introduction* gives a sense of the comprehensive, integrated nature of the text and its usefulness in the preparation of teachers who really can make a difference in children's lives, now and in the future.

Content and Features

Comprehensive, Complete, and Current

Defining early childhood education as those years from birth through age eight, *Early Childhood Education: An Introduction* offers preservice teachers a complete, comprehensive, and current overview of the field. While the text focuses on children between the ages of three and eight, it also includes information on working with infants and toddlers because teachers must have an understanding of where children have been as well as where they will be going, in order to be effective.

Early Childhood Education: An Introduction is comprehensive in other ways. By balancing theory and research with the practical, students have a complete knowledge base on which to build their skills. Additionally, the processes of education—those of working with parents and other staff, planning, and guiding children—are balanced throughout with teaching strategies and methods of introducing curriculum content to young children.

With content in each chapter based on research and theory, as well as the most current position papers in the field of early childhood education and the curriculum content areas, this text offers students the most current information on teaching young children. Because of its comprehensiveness, completeness, and currency, students using this text should be well prepared to pass the *National Teachers' Examination*, but more importantly, to successfully teach young children.

An Open, Integrated Approach

Early Childhood Education: An Introduction, Third Edition, is based on an open, integrated approach to early childhood education, with both adult and child taking the initiative and responding. Other approaches, however, are not neglected. Effective teachers, who do make a difference in children's lives, must have a basic understanding of all approaches, not only to be current and able to articulate which approaches must be rejected and why, but to be able to meet the needs of all of today's children.

The text approaches early childhood education as an integrated experience, one that involves the school, parents, and community. Early childhood education is also presented as a continual experience, one that builds continuously as children move from the child-care center or preschool through kindergarten and the primary grades.

Rather than a teacher-directed, separate-subject approach, the text presents teaching and learning as an integrated activity taking place through children's play and activity. The curriculum areas of art, music, the language arts, science, math, health and safety, and the social studies, although appearing as separate chapters, are presented in a way that forms an integrated whole.

A thematic approach to curriculum content is present. Throughout the text, examples are given of how teachers can use children's literature to create themes for children's learning.

The text also presents an integration of care, nurture and love, and intellectual stimulation. Throughout, the text reinforces the constant needs of children for a nurturing, yet intellectually challenging environment; for continuity and stability in human relationships; and for warmth, responsiveness, and genuine commitment from their teachers.

Focus on Child Development

Based on theories of child development, *Early Childhood Education: An Introduction*, Third Edition, offers beginning teachers a solid foundation on which to develop their teaching skills. Based on a solid foundation of child growth, development, and learning, each chapter explains and expands on the concept of developmentally appropriate practices.

The chapter on child development makes child development come alive for students. Using anecdotes of individual children to illustrate normal stages of development, the text makes theories of child development real and accessible. The children in the anecdotes are referred to throughout the text, uniting the text, but also keeping students focused on principles of child growth and development.

Inclusion of children with special needs is featured in a separate chapter, and each chapter also includes suggestions and ideas for working with special needs children and their families.

Because our nation continues to welcome immigrants from all over the world, working with children from diverse cultural and ethnic backgrounds is also featured.

Play as the Integrator

Play, the integrator of the curriculum, is covered in depth in a separate chapter. However, because play is the integrator of the curriculum and viewed as the basic mode of children's learning, it is also featured in each of the chapters. Specific suggestions for teaching content through play are given in each of the curriculum content chapters. Not only does this enable students to be current, but it promotes their success as teachers. Teachers who do not have a solid understanding of children's play and its role in their growth, development, and learning can never be effective.

Reality Based

The fact that the entire text is reality based and practical yet theoretical is highly beneficial for students as they develop the skills of effective teachers. Each of the authors has been in the field of early childhood education for over 35 years. *Early Childhood Education: An Introduction*, Third Edition, is based on the combined experiences of both authors, who have taught at every age level in the period of early childhood education. Their experiences as leaders in the field are reflected in this edition.

Students are the beneficiaries of this extensive experience. Using this text, students will be in touch with the past, knowledgeable about the present, and prepared for the future in the field of early childhood education.

New to the Third Edition

Extensive revisions in each chapter reflect not only current references but the most current thinking in the field of early childhood education today.

Each chapter includes content from the position papers and guidelines of the National Association for the Education of Young Children and the Association for Childhood Education International. Each of the curriculum content chapters is based on the current guidelines and position papers from that area's professional association or organization.

A new section on **learning to observe young children** has been added. This section, found at the end of Chapter 2, encourages students to begin a case study. Information on how to learn to observe children, write complete anecdotes, and then compile these into a case study is presented. At the end of each chapter in the text, the feature ***Continuing Case Study*** offers suggestions for observing the child selected for the case study as that child plays, interacts with the learning environment and with others, and experiences curriculum content.

The chapter on planning to teach has been rewritten as planning for **thematic or project learning**. Planning is presented as a process that takes place between the child, the teacher, and the environment. This feature too is unique to the third edition.

In addition to a complete chapter on **parent involvement**, ideas for involving parents are given throughout the text. These appear in the chapters on working with children with special needs, planning, guiding young children, and most of the curriculum content areas.

Beginning with Chapter 1, the text includes the **primary grades** as a part of early childhood education. The history of the nongraded primary unit is included in Chapter 1, and the growth, development, and learning of primary-age children in Chapter 2. Arranging the learning environment in the primary grades, as planning in the primary grades, is included. Each of the curriculum content areas includes teaching in the primary grades.

Several **chapters have been rewritten** to reflect current research and theory. The chapter on play has been rewritten to illustrate how play is the integrator of the curriculum; the art chapter to present the perspectives of Reggio Emilia, Italy; and the chapter on guiding young children has been rewritten to make the process of guiding children's behavior more specific and usable.

The rich history of the profession of early childhood education is found throughout this third edition of *Early Childhood Education: An Introduction*. The **historical perspective** in the time line on the inside cover page offers students and their teachers a way to organize and think about the history of the field of early childhood education. This is followed with a description of the history of early childhood in our nation and with references to historical ideas throughout the text. The perspective of history prepares students to build on the past as they prepare to take their places in the field today.

Early Childhood Education: An Introduction, Third Edition, asks students to make a **commitment to teaching young children**. From the first chapter to the last, the preservice student is asked to examine the reasons they wish to become an early childhood educator and to continually reflect on this decision as they develop the skills, attitudes, and knowledge required to become an effective teacher, one who will be long remembered.

Acknowledgments

We wish to express our gratitude for the constant support and the willingness of Gene Seefeldt, Chandler Barbour, and Tupper Webster to give us their ideas and suggestions for improving this text. We also acknowledge the help of our editor, Linda Sullivan.

We are grateful to Dan Floss, Anne Vega, and Todd Yarrington for the photographs used in this book; to Janet Willen for her work in copy editing; and to Louise Sette for her work in the production of this book.

The insights, knowledge, and strategies of early childhood educators in child care, Head Start, preschools, kindergartens, and the primary grades recorded in the text must be recognized.

The following reviewers contributed insights and suggestions to this text: Martha Cray-Andrews, The College of Saint Rose; E. Anne Eddowes, University of Alabama at Birmingham; Noelle Greathouse, Eastern Illinois University; Teresa T. Harris, James Madison University; Alice Hosticka, Georgia Southern University; David L. Roland, The University of Mary Hardin-Baylor; and Timothy Wilson, University of Central Arkansas.

Brief Contents

Contents

Play: The Integrator of the Curriculum ...296
8

The Language Arts ...332
9

Art ...372

Music ...414

Commitment to Children

I will know about, abide by,
and advocate for laws and
regulations that enhance the
quality of life for young children.

I will support the rights of
children to live and learn in
environments that are responsive
to their developmental needs.

I will improve my competencies
in providing for children's needs.

I will appreciate each child's
uniqueness, thus enhancing
the child's self-respect.

NAEYC Governing Board Statement. Reprinted by permission from *Young Children* 35, no. 1 (November 1979): 17. Copyright © 1979 by the National Association for the Education of Young Children, 1834 Connecticut Ave. N.W., Washington, D.C. 20009.

Introducing Early Childhood Education

Early childhood is a diverse field.

After you read this chapter, you should be able to respond to the following questions:

1. How did early childhood education begin in our nation?

2. What forces led to the growth of the profession?

3. Why is the field of early childhood education considered a true professional field today?

4. How do administrative units and program approaches differ, and how are they alike?

5. What factors unify all early childhood programs?

6. Why do you want to join the profession?

Today early childhood education is on the threshold of maturity. It has passed a long period of infancy, a peaceful childhood, and a brief, if turbulent, adolescence. As the field approaches maturity, it has a store of knowledge on which to continue to grow and perfect itself. Never before in our history have we known so much about how children learn and grow. Never before have we had so much information about the process of teaching and about how we can foster children's growth, development, and learning.

It's a wonderful time for you to be entering the field because many of the challenges are yours. It is you who will take the next step over the threshold. Your personal knowledge, your emotional and intellectual commitment to the field, and your confidence in yourself will determine the future of early childhood education.

Early childhood stands on the threshold of maturity today not because of any one event or any one individual, but because of the idealism, vision, and work of many. No one person has had the greatest impact, "but the influence of many individuals has lived in endless progression, in chain reaction, as each built in his own way on what his predecessors had projected" (Snyder, 1972, p. 10).

Today, as you enter the field, you will have the opportunity and the responsibility to make your own contribution to the field of early childhood education.

History

Long Beginnings

Infancy is described as a time of dependence on others and of a slowly developing sense of self-awareness. The beginnings of the field of early childhood education were just like those of the human infant—slow, gradual, and dependent on the nurture and care of many individuals who fostered the profession's gradually developing sense of self-awareness (Bornstein & Lamb, 1992).

It is difficult to pinpoint just when early childhood education began. Perhaps the field's birth can be traced to the philosophers Plato (427–347 B.C.) and Aristotle (394–322 B.C.), who advocated that a child's education start well before age six, or to John Amos Comenius (1592–1670), a Czech educator and bishop who wrote *The School of Infancy* in 1628 and recommended that education begin on the mother's lap. Education for Comenius would be the same as play, as natural as life and growth itself.

Nevertheless, many cite Jean Jacques Rousseau (1712–1778) as responsible for the birth of early childhood education. In his book *L'Emile ou l'education* (1947) Rousseau stressed the importance of beginning a child's education at birth. He also believed that children's education should be based on the nature of children, not on adults' notions of what children are like or should be like. Rather than sending children to schools, he felt they should be raised in the country with their education left up to nature. There, unrestricted by the "depravity" of adult society, especially as found in cities, children would grow freely and fully. Rousseau abhorred strict lessons or strong discipline and believed that school should be based on children's interests. This ideal of naturalism continues to influence our thinking about the nature of children and their education (Rousseau, 1947).

Johann Pestolozzi (1746–1827) created schools based on this naturalistic philosophy. Pestolozzi thought that education begins in the home, through the child's play and sensory experiences. His school curriculum was based on children's natural development, and he believed that they learned best through their own self-discovery (Froebel, 1889, p. vii).

In 1837 Friedrich Froebel (1782–1852) opened a school for children under age six called the *kindergarten,* a German word meaning *children's garden.* After trying a number of occupations and teaching at several levels, Froebel concluded that the early years of life, those on which the foundation for later years was built, were the most critical. Play was education, and at the center of everything was the need to bring the child to unity with God (Froebel, 1889).

Froebel's kindergarten was designed to be a place where children could grow as naturally as flowers in a garden or the woods. Play, creative self-expression, sense perception, and harmonious living with one another formed the basis of the program. Froebel presented children with *gifts and occupations.* Some of the gifts were balls, blocks, and cubes; and the occupations were paper folding, perforating paper, weaving, and stringing beads. Songs, games, movement and dance, and plays were also a part of the gifts and occupations and like them were to help children achieve unity with God. The kindergarten flourished in Germany and elsewhere in Europe, and when it was introduced to the United States, it found fertile ground.

Froebel's careful design and sequence of materials along with explicit directions for their use probably contributed to the successful growth of the kindergarten in America. The materials formed a "kit" that could be taken and adapted anywhere. "The sense of unity with which Froebel's kindergarten curriculum was impregnated fostered its expansion as a totality. This is precisely the manner in which the kindergarten idea spread to the United States" (Weber, 1969, p. 17).

The Kindergarten in America

Perhaps the precise directions for kindergarten teaching and the "kit" of materials did contribute to the movement's growth in America. But the social forces in this new land, a land of ideas and ideals, were probably the major reason the kindergarten grew and flourished in America.

During the late 1800s, America was recovering from the Civil War and facing new crises. Thousands of immigrants from Ireland, Asia, and southern and eastern Europe poured into the United States. The population became increasingly heterogeneous, and instead of finding streets paved with gold, immigrants struggled to survive. Their lives were difficult, filled with both poverty and discrimination. "It was a time of strife. Yet then, as now, education was looked to as holding the potential for the solution of human problems for a better way of life" (Snyder, 1972, p. 14). And the kindergarten, with its basic idealistic philosophy, was seen as a vehicle to relieve the suffering of the immigrants.

Credit for establishing the first kindergarten in our country goes to Margarthe Meyer Schurz (1832–1876), who is traditionally known by her married name, Mrs. Carl Schurz. Mrs. Schurz, a German immigrant, decided she could best preserve her children's heritage by opening a kindergarten for them and the children of her German neighbors.

She opened the kindergarten in her home in Watertown, Wisconsin, in 1856 (Newell & Putnam, 1924). She held classes in her sitting room or parlor and sometimes on the broad porch that ran across the front of the house. Believing that the location of her home was inconvenient, Mrs. Schurz moved the kindergarten to a house in the center of town.

The kindergarten was a small program, never enrolling more than six children and lasting only a few years. Yet it had a great impact on the field of early childhood education.

Mrs. Schurz's pioneering work is commemorated at the Octagon House in Watertown. The Octagon House now stands as a museum, displaying Froebelian gifts and occupations. This monument to Mrs. Schurz illustrates how one person's contribution, though it appears minor at the time, can make lasting changes on a nation's way of life (Harrison, 1924).

A chance meeting between Schurz and Elizabeth Peabody (1804–1894) may have done much to spur the development of the kindergarten in America. Elizabeth Peabody, an idealistic and religious woman living in genteel poverty, was impressed by the precocity of Schurz's daughter. When she asked how this lovely child had been raised, Schurz described Froebel's kindergarten and sent Peabody a copy of his book, *The Education of Man*. After this encounter Peabody, then 55, decided that every child in America should have the benefits of the kindergarten because it embodied the ideals of a good, religious life and was a way to reach the immigrants. With missionary zeal, Peabody, nightgown under her dress and toothbrush in her pocket, was prepared to go anywhere to establish the kindergarten (Weber, 1969).

Succeed she did. All over the nation kindergartens were founded by church societies, missionary leagues, the Women's Christian Temperance Union, and settlement houses. The kindergarten was so popular that it soon became a part of the public school system. In 1873 Susan Blow (1843–1916), along with W. T. Harris, the superintendent of the St. Louis

Public Schools, opened the first public school kindergarten. The old Des Peres school, site of that first kindergarten, is now a museum honoring Blow's contributions (Harris, 1983).

As the kindergarten grew ever more popular and spread across the nation, it changed. Patty Smith Hill, Anna Bryan, and others found their views of the kindergarten more in harmony with the theories and philosophy of G. Stanley Hall and John Dewey than with those of Froebel (Hill, 1987). Instead of basing the kindergarten curriculum wholly on Froebel's prescribed gifts and occupations, the natural curiosity, activities, and interests of children became the foundation. The work of Blow, Hill, and many others made the kindergarten an accepted part of American education by 1935 (Shapiro, 1983).

The Primary School

Once the kindergarten became a part of the public schools, conflicts occurred. Many kindergarten teachers decried the public school's emphasis on neatness, discipline, and drill in the basic skills. Some were even said to succumb to the tyranny of the primary teacher (Hall, 1907). First-grade teachers, in turn, complained that children coming to them from the kindergarten could not pay attention or follow directions.

To help bring unity to the kindergarten and primary grades, Samuel Chester Parker and Alice Temple wrote *Unified Kindergarten and First-Grade Teaching* (1925). They claimed that the curriculum could become continuous and delightful.

> We wish to make it clear that we sympathize with the idealistic motives that actuated pioneering American kindergartners [the teachers not the children] into their efforts to ameliorate the conditions of young children and to bring more enjoyment and more socialized experience into their lives. At the same time we recognize the importance of the essential social skills which the primary school has historically emphasized. We see no necessary conflict between these two points of view but feel that both kindergarten activities and the essential social skills can be merged in the education of children from five to seven years of age in a manner completely in keeping with the mental ages of the pupils. (Parker & Temple, 1925, p. 2)

In the process, the first three grades became more centered as the play spirit of the kindergarten was introduced (Beatty, 1989). "Observational studies of kindergarten and primary teaching methods in the late 1920s and early 1930s documented evidence of the infiltration of child-gardening methods into the primary grades" (Beatty, 1989, p. 86).

The creation of the *nongraded* or *ungraded* primary unit in 1935 further supports the idea that the primary grade was becoming more child-centered. In 1935 Robert Hill Lane, a district principal in the public schools of Los Angeles, proposed establishment of a so-called Junior School. In this unit there would be no grades, and each child would be "passed" only once, when making the transition to the Upper School. Some children would be in the Junior School three years, others four, and others two.

The Nursery School

At the same time that the kindergarten was spreading across the country, the nursery school was growing for many of the same reasons. The concept of the nursery school is credited to the McMillan sisters, Margaret and Rachel, of London, who opened their school in the Deptford slums in 1910. The McMillan sisters recognized that their ideas were built on those of others. "It would be absurd to say that nothing has been discovered, nothing improved or invented" (McMillan, 1919, p. 13). But their school did present an idea unique to the field of early education. They called their establishment a nursery school to communicate this new idea. They chose the word *nursery* to represent the love, nurturing, and physical care children would receive in their school, and the word *school* to acknowledge that it was a place where children would learn as well as experience love. They saw their school as "urgent, not merely for a few children here and there but for hundreds of thousands of children in dire need of education and nurture in their first years. For the lack of it all the rest of their life is clouded and weakened" (McMillan, 1919, p. 7).

The nursery school had a slower beginning in our country than the kindergarten. Goodykoontz (1948) reports that there were only three schools in 1920 and 25 in 1924; most were supported by colleges for child study or by private citizens for profit. Many people, however, worked to establish the nursery school as a part of American education.

Patty Smith Hill, whose work helped revolutionize the kindergarten and first grade during the early 1900s, became interested in nursery schools and started them as part of her work at Columbia University Teachers College. Abigail Eliot, who worked with Margaret McMillan in her London Nursery School, is credited with popularizing the nursery school in the United States. She is considered one of the originators of the nursery school in the United States, together with Harriet Johnson (who opened a Bureau of Educational Experiments nursery school in 1919) and Edna White (who started a nursery school at Merrill Palmer in 1922) (Antler, 1987). The nursery school was based on the newer ideas of child growth, development, and learning of people like Freud, G. S. Hall, John Dewey, and Arnold Gesell.

Child Care

Child care, like kindergarten and nursery school, experienced a long infancy. Its beginnings are fuzzy and difficult to pinpoint. Programs were reported in Boston as early as 1828, in New York in 1854, and in

Philadelphia in 1863 (Ginsberg, 1978). Separating child care from the kindergarten and nursery school movement is also difficult because many of the child-care programs followed either the kindergarten or nursery school program.

In its early years, the major difference between child care and the nursery schools and the kindergartens was its purpose and hours. Even though adopting the program of the kindergarten or nursery school, the child-care centers served children during the entire working day. They often opened by 6 A.M. and remained open until 7 P.M. Some also provided care for children on the weekends or throughout the night to accommodate children whose parents worked different shifts; most were open the entire year.

There were spurts of activity and growth as social forces dictated provision and care for children. A child-care center in Philadelphia, for instance, was opened in 1863 in response to needs created by the Civil War to provide care for children of widows and to permit those whose husbands were at war to support themselves and their children. During and after the Civil War, the federal government even supplied funds for child care for children of soldiers' widows.

During the late 1800s and early 1900s, child-care centers were opened in factories and slums to provide care for children whose parents were employed outside the home. By 1892 there was a nationwide list of 90 organized group child-care programs, and there were more than 200 by the end of the century (Ginsberg, 1978). Then as now family child care appeared to be popular. The "tenement house nursery," as it was called, was popular with working parents.

Early Childhood Education

By the early 1900s, early childhood education was a part of American life. Nevertheless, it was still dependent on others and still searching for self-awareness. The field was established, yet there was no uniform approach or program for the care and education of the young. There was no concept of early childhood as a professional field, serving children from birth through eight years of age. There were divisions among those who worked in kindergartens, nursery schools, and child-care centers, and years of growth lay ahead before the field would have an identity of its own.

The Growing Profession

Childhood is a time of steady, progressive, even growth. It is a time for consolidation of skills, of learning new skills, and maturing. Early childhood education as a profession had just that—a quiet, even childhood, a time that permitted reflection, steady growth, and maturation from the early 1900s through around the mid-1950s. As with any maturation, there were changes. Some changes were inevitable as nursery schools and kinder-gartens reached more and more children in every part of the nation.

As early childhood educators tried to apply Froebel's rigid gifts and occupations to children from diverse cultures, communities, and backgrounds throughout the United States, changes occurred naturally. Other changes occurred, however, because of changing ideas.

Kindergarten teachers were also being introduced to the scientific method for studying children, to the field of psychology, and to changing philosophies. The study of children, not the writings of Froebel, became the basis of the curriculum. Anna Bryan, Patty Smith Hill, and Alice Temple were the acknowledged leaders in making the break with Froebelianism. As they studied with the psychologist G. Stanley Hall at Clark University and with the philosopher John Dewey at Teachers College, they became convinced that kindergartens needed to incorporate the scientific study of children and the new philosophies into their approach (Hall, 1907).

This break was not without conflict. Records of the meeting of the Kindergarten Union, a professional association, document the hurt feelings and betrayals between the traditional Froebel supporters and the new leaders who wanted to bring new ideas and thinking into the kindergarten (Newell & Putnam, 1924).

This break was inevitable because Dewey's writings and philosophy were becoming widely accepted. The key to his philosophy was that children should be prepared to become citizens of a democratic society. As such, he believed that they needed to learn to think, reason, and make decisions for themselves. Dewey (1916) advocated that through their play, activity, and interaction with their environment, children learned the skills that they needed in order to think. Real-life experiences, not secondhand information, were the preferred ways to learn.

A very different kind of teacher was needed to educate according to Dewey's philosophy (Biber, 1977). A teacher rigidly following Froebel's prescriptions would fail. Dewey envisioned teachers who were active scientists, constantly evaluating and diagnosing the children's learning and growth in order to put new learning activities into sequence. Like Froebel, Dewey also saw the teacher as a guide, one who monitored each child's experience and offered assistance, encouragement, and new directions.

These ideas were just what the new kindergarten leaders were seeking. They were familiar because they seemed similar to Froebel's ideas, which wanted children to be active and learn through their own activity. But Dewey's philosophy was broader. It offered early childhood educators an openness of thinking and teaching, one that would permit the flexibility required to meet the needs of children from diverse communities and cultures as well as the needs of a developing democracy (Greenberg, 1987).

In Italy, another concept of early childhood education was being developed. Maria Montessori had opened her Casa dei Bambini in the San Lorenzo slum district of Rome in 1907. The school attracted a great deal of

Dewey advocated that children learn through play and activity.

attention, for she taught manners, cleanliness, reading, writing, and mathematics to children who lived in the slums—all before the children had reached age five. Her major premise was that children learn largely through the senses, and for this purpose she designed special materials.

Many American educators traveled to Rome to visit the Casa dei Bambini. For the most part, however, Americans found the program and its basic philosophy at odds with their changing Froebelian beliefs and Dewey's theories. American educators believed their new perception of the kindergarten and early education was based on a much deeper and more accurate understanding of the child and the educative process than that achieved by Montessori.

In addition to the changing ideas of early childhood based on the works of Hall, Dewey, and others, two major events influenced this period of early childhood as a profession. The Great Depression of the 1930s and the Second World War helped early childhood educators to realize the power of their profession and bring status to the field.

During the 1930s the government funded the *Works Progress Administration (WPA)*. One program under the WPA was the nursery school. WPA nursery schools were designed to provide employment for unemployed teachers and other school staff as well as to help families facing unemployment and poverty. WPA schools were full-day, comprehensive programs, with the major goal of helping those affected by the depression.

WPA nursery schools had a lasting impact on the growth of early childhood education (Steiner, 1976, p. 16). Nursery school and kindergarten teachers were hired as consultants, wrote curricula, and retrained upper-grade and secondary-school teachers to work with young children. It was really the first time in the history of early childhood education that many children in every part of the nation had a chance to attend a nursery school (Hymes, 1978, p. 5).

Another milestone in the history of early childhood education came with the passage of the *Lanham Act* in response to the Second World War. This act provided federal funds to establish child-care centers in factories so that women could work for the war effort. About 300,000 children were enrolled in these programs. Once again, as during the depression, early childhood education had a chance to demonstrate its growing maturity, efficiency, and acceptability (Hymes, 1978, p. 5).

Both the WPA and Lanham Act programs were short-lived. Many of the individuals who worked in these programs and contributed to their success and acceptance are not remembered.

Yet their work had a lasting effect on the profession—just as yours will. With the ideas of Dewey, knowledge of children's growth and development, and the success of the WPA and Lanham Act programs, early childhood education had prepared itself for a period of peaceful, steady growth.

Throughout the 1930s and 1940s principles of child growth and development continued to influence the growth of early childhood education as a field. Based on the idea that children's growth and development directed the curriculum, the ungraded primary school was being developed in schools across the nation. The ungraded, or nongraded, primary unit was seen as "an administrative tool to encourage and promote a philosophy of continuous growth" (Milwaukee Public Schools [MPS], 1942). By removing rigid practices of age/grade placement and basing evaluation on each child's individual progress, "no child is asked to repeat what he had already learned but is helped to adjust his learning to his own growth pattern" (MPS, 1942, p. 3).

Turbulent Times

Adolescence is never an easy time. It is a time of searching, of shifting values and beliefs, of questioning and growth so rapid it disrupts and startles. Indeed, the profession of early childhood education experienced just that during its adolescence. Perhaps its preadolescence began when Sputnik circled the Earth in 1957, and educators were called upon to prepare children for survival in a hostile, competitive world. But its true adolescence began in the 1960s, when the field was thrust into a time of challenge, change, questioning, and unparalleled growth.

"Now and then, in the complicated affairs of Man, the factors in a situation arrange themselves in such a way as to accelerate the development of some service or institution so that it makes a generation's normal growth [happen] in a few short years" (Goodykoontz, 1948, p. 44). Perhaps never again will circumstances arrange themselves in such a way as to permit the profession to achieve as much growth as it did during the 1960s.

The 1960s were a time of social unrest. Civil rights leaders made it clear that inequalities of opportunity existed between rich and poor as well as African-American and white segments of the population. The president declared a War on Poverty, and the federal government focused its energy on programs to break the poverty cycle.

At the same time, ideas in psychology were changing. A cogent, convincing case was being made for the idea that intelligence is malleable and susceptible to change. Research was showing that children reared in nonstimulating early environments were likely to score lower on intelligence tests than those in more stimulating environments. The idea that an environment such as that found in a good preschool could increase the intellectual functioning of children born in poverty was being accepted.

Hunt (1961) and Bloom (1964) described how enriching early experiences might work to increase intelligence. The work of Piaget and Inhelder (1969) was becoming accepted in the United States. Piaget made it clear that children learn through direct experiences and social interaction with peers. Play and activity, according to Piaget, were equated with intellectual growth.

Conceived by the Office of Economic Opportunity, a federal agency at the time, in the fall of 1964 as a military strategy in the War on Poverty, *Head Start* was implemented in the summer of 1965. Called a miracle of instant organization (Hymes, 1978), Head Start received a welcoming response in every community. Implemented as a program of education, health, nutrition, psychological services, career development, and parent and community involvement, Head Start was comprehensive. "It was thought that healthy, well-nourished children would have a better chance of doing well in school than sickly hungry ones. A transition program in which children and teachers could become acquainted with each others' widely different worlds would somewhat ameliorate the destructive cultural collision that often occurs in the classroom, with children inevitably the losers" (Greenberg, 1990, p. 41).

Like the first nursery schools and the WPA program, parents of Head Start children were seen as key players and were expected to participate in their child's education and make decisions about the program and their own welfare. In fact, approximately thirty years after it began, more than 443,000 Head Start parents have reported volunteering in schools for young children. Successful Head Start programs continue to view the child as a part of a family and the family as a part of the neighborhood and community, and they continue comprehensive services to children and families (Shorr, 1989).

Piaget made it clear that children learn through direct experience.

In 1967, *Follow Through* was launched. Follow Through expanded the ideas, ideals, and practices of Head Start to include the kindergarten and primary grade programs. Initiated under the Office of Economic Opportunity, Follow Through brought resource specialists, aides, and educational innovation to the primary grades through a plan for alternative model programs.

Once again it was a time of conflict. Competition between those endorsing differing philosophies and programs was keen. The ideas of Piaget and Dewey were rediscovered and translated into open education. The *British Infant School,* based on the philosophies of both Dewey and Piaget, became a popular model. Others believed a more structured approach was the answer, and the *DISTAR* program of Carl Bereiter and Siegfried Engelmann, then professors at the University of Illinois, attracted a great deal of attention. At the same time, the Montessori program enjoyed renewed enthusiasm not only because of Montessori's ideas of sensory learning, but also because of the focus on learning early reading and writing skills.

Other controversies centered around control of early childhood programs. While some believed the church or public school should control programs, others suggested that parents and the community have the major role in decisions related to early education. Traditional early childhood educators found themselves challenged by psychologists to identify their goals, describe their methods, and document success. New challenges arose daily.

Early childhood educators did become more articulate about their goals and techniques. They tried new methods and ideas and experimented and responded to community and parental needs. They continued to analyze their methods and theories and to revise their practices.

The Head Start program can be credited with bringing early childhood education into full adolescence. Head Start can document its ability to break the poverty cycle. Although a single year's enrichment cannot undo all the damage inflicted by poverty, children who have participated in the program do better in school, repeating fewer grades than those outside the program. Fewer of these children are institutionalized or placed in special education classes than those who did not attend model Head Start programs. Adults who attended Head Start as children hold jobs and go to college, demonstrating that the theories of the psychologists who claimed that early, enriching educational experiences could ameliorate the effects of poverty were correct (Mallory & Goldsmith, 1990).

At the end of the 1960s, the field of early childhood education was growing so rapidly that no one was sure what age group or class of children it was for. Some believed, because of the Head Start program, that early education was only for economically disadvantaged children. Others believed that early childhood education was reserved for children under age four and didn't include the kindergarten and primary grades. In spite of the confusion, the field expanded. The civil rights movement included women's rights, and demands for child care increased. Kindergarten programs were mandated in states that had not formerly provided preschool education, and parents sought nursery school experiences for their children.

The questions of what methods, how much structure, or what approach to use in the different programs disrupted the field. As in the past, each period of growth was used by early childhood educators to consolidate knowledge and to demonstrate once again that early childhood education is of benefit to children, families, and society.

Maturity

Early childhood education is now a bona fide profession. It is fully developed, recognized by the National Council for Accreditation of Teacher Education as a separate field, and distinguished from elementary education or any other type of education. The field has clarity of purpose and a clear definition. The National Association for the Education of Young Children defines early childhood education as "services for children from birth through age eight in part-day and full-day group programs in centers, homes, and institutions; kindergartens and primary schools; and recreational programs" (National Association for the Education of Young Children [NAEYC], 1982, p. 1).

The field of early childhood education continues to grow.

The field continues to grow. In 1915 only 12 percent of children five or under attended an early childhood program, but in 1991, 71 percent of all children in first or second grade attended a child-care center or nursery school program—including prekindergarten or Head Start—on a regular basis before starting first grade (U.S. Department of Education, 1991). Nearly 95 percent of all five-year-olds are enrolled in kindergarten programs (Sava, 1987), making universal education for five-year-olds a virtual reality, and nearly all children in the United States attend a primary school (Williams & Fromberg, 1992).

Increased enrollment and recognition of the benefits of early childhood education are not the only evidence of maturity. Today the field of early childhood has documented its maturity by defining itself, influencing policies, and setting professional standards.

Defining Ourselves

Early childhood educators have defined their own field. Not only has the National Association for the Education of Young Children defined the field of early childhood as those years between birth and age eight, but it has also defined the diverse settings, roles, and responsibilities of staff in programs serving children during early childhood in the *Position Statement on*

Nomenclature, Status, Salaries, and Working Conditions (1984) and the paper *Accreditation Criteria & Procedures* (1991).

The *Encyclopedia of Early Childhood Education* (Williams & Fromberg, 1992) further defines the field of early childhood education. It does so against the background of historical, political, economic, sociocultural, intellectual, and educational influences on early childhood education.

Influencing Policies

By taking positions on current issues facing the field of early childhood education, the professional organizations in the field of early childhood education are influencing policies for young children. The following papers and publications have influenced policies and practices affecting young children and their families: the Association for Childhood Education International's position paper *On Standardized Testing* (Perrone, 1991), the National Association for the Education of Young Children's *Developmentally Appropriate Practice in Early Childhood Programs Serving Children From Birth Through Age 8* (Bredekamp, 1987), *Testing of Young Children: Concerns and Cautions* (National Association for the Education of Young Children [NAEYC], 1988), *Appropriate Education in the Primary Grades* (NAEYC, 1989), and the *Guidelines for Appropriate Curriculum Content and Assessment in Programs Serving Children Ages 3 Through 8* (NAEYC, 1990).

Using these position papers as a guide, many school systems have abolished the use of standardized tests for young children and are in the process of changing curricula and programs to conform to stated developmentally appropriate practices. In turn, these position papers have been the basis for other position papers. The National Association of State Boards of Education, for instance, based its report *Right From the Start* (1988) on NAEYC's statement of *Developmentally Appropriate Practice in Early Childhood Programs Serving Children From Birth Through Age 8* (Bredekamp, 1987).

Setting Professional Standards

Through the National Academy of Early Childhood Programs, the NAEYC offers a voluntary program of accreditation for programs serving children from birth through age eight. The purpose of the program is to improve the quality of care and education provided for young children in group programs in the United States by administering a national, voluntary accreditation system for early childhood programs.

Any program that meets the following criteria may apply for accreditation. It must serve a minimum of ten children within the age group of birth through five in part- and full-day programs and/or school-age children before and/or after school; have at least two adults present; and have been in operation for at least one year. The process of accreditation begins with a self-study, which is followed by an on-site visit by validators. Based on the findings of the self-study and validators' reports, an accreditation commission of three people decides whether to grant accreditation.

To ensure that all young children receive high quality care and education, the NAEYC has established a National Institute for Early Childhood Professional Development. Based on a systems approach, the institute articulates a system of professional development "serving two purposes: every child—regardless of the setting—will have access to high-quality services that reflect professional knowledge, and the current inequities in status and compensation among early childhood professionals will be corrected" (Bredekamp & Willer, 1992, p. 50).

The NAEYC has also established standards for teacher education. By administering the Child Development Associate program, NAEYC enables those teachers who do not seek a baccalaureate degree to obtain a Child Development Associate (CDA) National Credential. Through *Guidelines for Early Childhood Education Programs in Associate Degree Granting Institutions* (1985) and *Early Childhood Teacher Education Guidelines: Basic and Advanced* (1991), NAEYC sets standards for two- and four-year university and college teacher-education programs.

Early Childhood Education Today

As early childhood education approaches maturity, it includes diverse administrative units, sponsors, and program types. Some programs are sponsored by the public schools, while others are supported with local, state, or federal funds. Nonprofit as well as for-profit programs are run by parents, churches, or other agencies to meet a community's needs. Units include primary grades, kindergarten, nursery schools, child care, Head Start, and others.

Administrative Units

Primary Grades.   Grades one, two, and three are for children between ages six and eight, and they are usually a part of the public school system or a private school. Their major goal is to teach children academic skills and provide for cognitive, social, emotional, and physical growth. Children receive instruction in the arts, sciences, health, physical education, reading, and math.

Many school systems are eliminating specific grade designations and implementing nongraded primary units. As in the past, these units permit children to move from kindergarten through grade three at their own pace by removing rigid age-grade boundaries.

Kindergarten.   Kindergartens are usually sponsored by a school system and are designed for five-year-olds. In some public school systems, however, three- and four-year-olds are now attending prekindergarten programs. The kindergarten program may run for a half or a full day. Its goal is usually to offer children opportunities for academic, intellectual, social, emotional, and physical growth through a well-rounded program of activities; it is not to provide total care for the child or comprehensive services (Willer & Bredekamp, 1992).

Nursery Schools. Today, nursery schools are usually for children between ages two and five. They may be half day, full day, or two or three days a week. Some are sponsored by church groups, others by parents or civic organizations, and still others are private, profit-making establishments. The parent cooperative nursery school, uniquely American in origin, is popular. Parents work part time in the cooperative school or contribute in some other way to defray the cost (Taylor, 1978).

The goal of the nursery school is to provide nurture and education for children under age five. Play, songs, games, and other activities are planned to meet children's social, emotional, physical, and intellectual needs.

Head Start. Head Start is a comprehensive program for children between ages two and five that is sponsored by the federal government for children under a certain income level. The program focuses on increasing children's mental skills, self-concept, social and emotional development, and on readiness for school. There is a heavy emphasis on parent and community involvement. Health, nutrition, and psychological services for children and their families are a part of the program.

Home Start is a variation of Head Start. It is based on the principles of Comenius who believed that education begins in the home. The focus of the program is on the parent, and a home visitor works with parents in their homes developing and reinforcing parenting skills.

The Transition Demonstration, a program that follows former Head Start children through grade three, with Head Start like services and curriculum, is now taking place in thirty-two states.

Child Care. Child care is designed to provide care for children when parents work full or part time. Some programs offer 24-hour care for children whose parents work night shifts. There is a diversity of child-care programs, and parents select a program suited to their needs. Whether a program is for profit or nonprofit and sponsored by local, state, or federal agencies, churches, or parents, its focus is on care for the child and provision for educational, social, emotional, and physical growth.

Family child care is one form of child care. Care is provided in a home by a parent or other adult. Usually a limited number of children are permitted in a group family day-care program. This program is often more informal than other types of day care, because it is in a home and has a small number of children, and may be well suited for children who find a large group situation difficult or for those with special needs.

Child-care programs provide care for young children for a full day.

Program Variations

Diversity exists not only in administrative units but in basic program approaches as well. Different models, or alternative programs, have been developed. These programs, models, and differing approaches can be categorized by the role assumed by the child and the teacher (Weikart, 1971).

In a teacher-directed model or approach, the teacher is the initiator. In that case, the curriculum is teacher-planned and teacher-directed, and the children respond to the teacher's directions. When the approach is child-centered, the child is the initiator. In this approach, the children are trusted to initiate their own learning, and the teacher is responsive, following the children. When both teacher and child take the initiative, both teacher and child direct and respond. This is termed the *interactionist,* or *constructionist,* approach.

Teacher-Initiated Approaches.   Some educators believe that the best program approach, whether in a day-care center, a nursery, or a primary grade school, is one in which the adult is the initiator and clearly in charge. In the *teacher-initiated approach,* goals and activities are predetermined by the adult, and specific tasks are assigned to children. Achievement of the tasks is assessed and evaluated. Packaged curriculum kits, programmed materials, or curriculum guides may be used.

"This means that educational planning is essentially a 'top down' experience. Broadly defined adult goals and values form the basis of a formal K–12 span of educational requirements. Early childhood curricula, as preschool-kindergarten, are conceived to facilitate successful adaptation to existing primary programs and so on" (Evans, 1983, p. 110).

Highly structured, programmed curricula and materials, such as DISTAR, are presented to children; goals and activities are predetermined and structured, and the teacher follows these, presenting them to children. Academic content often falls into two main areas, language arts and mathematics. Direct instruction teaches sound-to-symbol relationships and a wide variety of mathematics skills (Gersten & George, 1990). A prime example of this approach is the DISTAR model.

Child-Initiated Approaches.   An opposing approach views the child as the initiator. In the *child-initiated approach*, the teacher responds to cues from the child. Children are trusted to initiate their own activities and do their own learning and evaluating. The teacher's role is to provide an enriched, safe, and stimulating environment in which children are free to play, select activities and materials, and determine their own goals. Creative self-expression and growth through play are valued, and children's emotional and social growth, along with their intellectual growth, are emphasized. Mental growth is believed to arise from children's activity, and teachers are to guide it. Some examples of programs based on this approach are the Bank Street College Model and programs, the Tucson Early Education Model, and Nimnicht's Responsive Program.

Teacher-Child-Initiated Approaches.   A third approach to early childhood programs is an open framework in which both child and adult initiate learning activities—*teacher-child-initiated approaches*. At times, the teacher directs the activities, usually by structuring experiences and the environment; at other times, children direct the curriculum. It is like a ballet between a sensitive adult and the child: Both are in control, both initiate, both respond, and both take cues from the other.

Based on interactionist or constructionist theories of Dewey, Piaget, and Vygotsky, those endorsing teacher-child-initiated approaches believe children construct their own knowledge. Teachers do lead; they set objectives, guide children, and teach. In doing so, however, teachers respond to the children, their interests and individual abilities, intelligence, and backgrounds. As in the child-initiated approach, play is seen as a vehicle for learning. But this play is used more actively by the teacher to stimulate children's thinking and is exploited for learning opportunities. Children's cognitive growth is fostered by a variety of opportunities to have direct contact with people and processes in their environment (Vygotsky, 1986). Examples of the open approach are found in the British Infant and Primary schools and in Weikart's Cognitively Oriented Curriculum.

Constructionists believe both children and teachers initiate, both respond, and both take cues from each other.

Unified by Democracy

A democratic society demands diversity and, at the same time, unity. All early childhood programs, regardless of administrative type or program approach, are unified by the needs of our democratic society. All citizens of a democratic society must achieve certain skills. They must be able to make decisions, be knowledgeable, have confidence in themselves, be able to respect the rights of others, and assume responsibility for themselves and the group. These principles are reflected in all early childhood programs of quality.

1.   All quality programs provide children with a foundation for learning. "At whatever age the child starts school, his beginning school years are critical for what he learns and will continue to learn" (Association for Childhood Education International, 1983, p. 1). Every program offers children a foundation for learning.

2.   All quality programs help children build a strong sense of self. Everyone needs self-confidence. Without confidence in themselves, children will fail to learn. Learning involves risk taking; there is always a challenge to learning something new. Children who believe they are not capable will not

be able to take the risk involved in learning. Children in all programs should have the opportunity to develop self-confidence, esteem, and understanding.

3.   All quality programs help children develop physically. Physical growth and health are as important as intellectual and emotional growth. Every program for young children is designed to meet children's physical needs for safety, comfort, nutrition, and health as well as to provide opportunities for the development of large and small muscles.

4.   All quality programs help children learn to relate effectively with others. Children must be able to demonstrate concern for others and learn to relate with them. Just as children develop an awareness of themselves, developing understanding of their own feelings and emotions, they must learn that others have these same feelings. Programs are designed to enable children to grow in the ability to adjust their own thinking as they take the thinking of others into account (Greenberg, 1992).

Finding Your Place

All early childhood programs, regardless of administrative type or approach, are unified by the teacher's commitment and the goals and values of this democratic society.

Making a Commitment

In reality, teachers use parts of each approach as they work with children. Even though programs may be based on a specific approach, what actually happens between teacher and child often reflects several approaches. The critical factors for success as a teacher involve enthusiasm for teaching and ability to communicate deep affection and personal concern for each child. This point is aptly illustrated by the case of Ms. D., a kindergarten teacher.

Ms. D. was introducing the project of making valentine cards for family members to a group of kindergarten children. She decided to begin by asking the children if they knew someone who was very special to them, a parent, brother or sister, or grandparent who cared about them a great deal, who really loved them, and whom they loved in return. The children named their parents, grandparents, siblings, and other relatives. Then Ms. D., whose recent marriage had been witnessed by the children, said that she too knew someone she would make a valentine for. This person was someone very special to her, someone who loved her, and whom she loved in return. She asked the children if they knew who that was, thinking they would, of course, name Mr. D., her new husband. The children in unison responded, "Oh yes, we know, we know, it's us! We're special to you, we're your special people." They nodded and giggled, agreeing with one another, secure in the knowledge that Ms. D. couldn't possibly know anyone else more precious to her than they.

This kind of emotion transcends any specific approach. All children, regardless of the approach their teachers adopt, need teachers who communicate their commitment to the children.

Joining the Profession

"History is not events, but people" (Bronowski, 1973, p. 438). As you enter the field of early childhood education, you will be joining those dauntless men and women—those pioneers and giant thinkers—who took early childhood education from infancy to the threshold of maturity (Snyder, 1972). Like the pioneers of the past, you must be willing to commit yourself fully to the profession. Being an early childhood educator is not an easy task. It is physically, emotionally, socially, and intellectually draining. More than ever before, today's early childhood educator must be able to dare to innovate and experiment.

These very challenges make the profession rewarding and satisfying. Because of the challenges, you as an individual can make a real and lasting contribution. Each day, as you face and master challenges, you know you count. You're secure in the knowledge of the power of your work.

Early childhood educators can gain more power by joining professional associations. The Association for Childhood Education International, National Association for the Education of Young Children, The Southern Early Childhood Association, and other professional associations and organizations enable early childhood educators to build on their own strengths while contributing to their community.

Before making the decision to become an early childhood educator, ask yourself these three questions:

1. Why do I want to work with young children?
2. What personal qualities and abilities do I possess that will make me successful in working with children?
3. What degree of involvement with children is best for me? (Seaver, Cartwright, Ward, & Heasley, 1979).

Why Do You Want to Work with Children?

Become familiar with the nature of young children before entering the profession. Young children are messy, their "I wanna's" are exceeded only by their "I don't wanna's," and their needs are constant and immediate. If you envision yourself as an authority figure, standing in front of a group of quiet, listening children, imparting knowledge and wisdom, then perhaps you might want to reconsider your decision. Preschool-primary children learn by doing, through their own activity, and your role is to provide experiences, not to lecture.

Begin by observing children. Make it a habit, as you shop, ride the bus, or walk through your neighborhood to observe children. Or volunteer to work in a child-care center, baby-sit, or get a job working in an after-school program for primary children. Experience children for yourself, firsthand, and then decide whether you really enjoy being with them.

Know the joys of working with children. Young children are fun to be with. They're inventive and full of expressive creativity. They're active and eager to find out more about the world in which they live. You'll be able to laugh with them and share some of the excitement of their young lives. As you work with children, you will actually see the difference you make in their lives. Others, perhaps those working in offices or behind the scenes, may never directly witness the effects of their work. You will observe daily the growth, learning, and development of children.

Some elect to become teachers of young children because they don't want to work with adults. Their belief is a fallacy. "Adults who work in careers

Know the joys of working with young children.

involving young children will always experience some form of contact with the children's family" (Seaver, Cartwright, Ward, & Heasley, 1979, p. 5). Working with children means working with their parents. Parents act as volunteers in classrooms, and you will also have contact with them as you join advisory boards, attend parent meetings, and have individual conferences.

Then too, it's rare for today's teachers to work in isolation in their classrooms. More and more, teaching is a team activity. Be prepared not only to work with parents in your classroom, but also with other staff members. In addition, as you work with children who have special needs, you will be working with representatives of other agencies serving children and their families.

What Personal Qualities and Abilities Do I Possess That Will Make Me Successful in Working with Young Children?

Everyone has certain qualities, abilities, and characteristics that contribute to success as a teacher. Self-understanding permits you to use your uniqueness to benefit children, as in the following case.

Darian, a first-grader, finally read an entire page without a single error. Mr. K. said nothing, but looked at Darian and rolled his eyes upward. Darian cocked his head, smiled at him, and said, "I really like it when I can see the whites of your eyes." Mr. K. often showed a special warmth and responsiveness to the children through the use of his expressive eyes.

Becoming aware of the effect your personality has on children doesn't always mean that you can or should change that trait. Some teachers have used videotapes of their interactions with children to enable them to reflect on which traits they wish to change and to recognize those contributing to success as a teacher. Understanding yourself, however, enables you to understand the dynamics of teaching and the role your uniqueness plays in the teacher-child relationship.

What Degree of Involvement Do You Want with Children?

The pioneers of early childhood education might be surprised at the number and type of early childhood positions available for today's educator. In the past, an early childhood educator had one choice, that of working in close contact with children. Although most positions involve direct contact with children, there are many other possibilities for careers in early childhood education.

You probably will begin your career working directly with children. You might be employed by a school system, or in a nursery school, Head Start program, or child-care center. There are other career choices, however. You might find that you are particularly adept at working with parents. If you decide to work with parents directly, you probably will need additional training; on the other hand, there are positions open in Head Start and child care that permit you to work through parents to help children, and to focus on developing the parents' potential (Seaver et al., 1979, p. 27).

Organizing services for children and their families is another potential field. You might obtain a position as a director of a child-care or nursery program, or become a curriculum specialist, team leader, or model specialist to a program. Many early childhood educators go into business for themselves, opening up their own nursery schools, or preschools, child-care centers, or early childhood programs. Usually these leadership positions require some experience working directly with children, as well as advanced degrees or special training in administration, supervision, or curriculum design.

Your knowledge of young children and curriculum may also prepare you to consult with agencies, organizations, or the government. Toy companies, the media, department stores, museums, park services, and city, state, and federal governments all provide services for children and families. They often require assistance in deciding how best to provide these services, what types of experiences are best for children, and how to deliver services.

Licensing agencies, health departments, and other organizations find a need for people who understand the complex issues involved in working with young children and their families. Teachers have been hired by such groups as consultants. A broad range of programs and positions are available to you in early childhood education.

Summary

It is a wonderful time for you to be entering the field of early childhood education. You will take your place among the giant intellectual thinkers and doers who made early childhood education the power it is today.

Early childhood is a diverse field. You may want to work in child care, preschool, or kindergarten, or the primary grades. Or you may associate with a program like Head Start or Follow Through or with a transition program. Regardless of which area of early childhood you choose, you will know that your work builds on the work of others and will create the future for the children whose lives you touch.

Take your decision seriously. This is not a field for the weak. You will need a great deal of intellectual strength as well as the personal qualities and abilities necessary to work with young children, their parents, and the other adults who care for them.

Projects

1. Interview a long-time director of a Head Start center, nursery school, or child-care program and a long-time principal of an elementary school. Ask each how their programs have changed over the years. Write a summary of their responses and compare the changes they have identified. As a class, discuss the changes in the field that you have learned about from your interviews.
2. Examine the diversity and variety of preschool programs by researching your class. Ask each member in your group to describe his or her preschool or primary school experience. Make a graph or chart of the variety of administrative units and program approaches represented by your group. Discuss why there is a variety of programs, the goals of each program, and the differences in approach.
3. Read the Sunday classified advertisements in your local newspaper. List all of the positions early childhood educators might fill. Locate those that require work with children, those that require work with adults, and the positions for consultants or specialists in the field.
4. Ask yourself the three questions listed under the heading "Joining the Profession." Write your answers down and decide why you want to become a teacher of young children. List the personal qualities you have that might enhance your ability as a teacher.

Resources

Professional organizations offer services, information, and the opportunity to meet and work with other early childhood educators. Joining and becoming an active member of professional organizations promotes your own growth and development. Send a postcard requesting information about services, membership, and free or inexpensive materials. Inquire about affiliates or local branch groups that may be active in your area.

Association for Childhood Education International
11501 Georgia Avenue, Suite 315
Wheaton, MD 20902

Children's Defense Fund
122 C Street, NW
Washington, DC 20001

Child Study Association of America
50 Madison Avenue
New York, NY 10010

ERIC Clearinghouse on Early Childhood Education
805 West Pennsylvania Avenue
Urbana, IL 61801

National Association for the Education of Young Children
1509 16th Street, NW
Washington, DC 20036-1426

National Black Child Development Institute
1463 Rhode Island Avenue, NW
Washington, DC 20005

The following publication may be useful for those wanting to learn more about the history of early childhood education and the nature of the field today.

The *Encyclopedia of Early Childhood Education* (1992), edited by Leslie R. Williams and Doris Fromberg, offers a complete and extensive overview of the history and current status of the field of early childhood education. It is the most comprehensive resource available to students of early childhood education.

References

Antler, J. (1987). *Lucy Sprague Mitchell: The making of a modern woman.* New Haven: Yale University Press.

Association for Childhood Education International. (1983). *Association for Childhood Education International's Guidelines for Teacher Preparation.* Bethesda, MD: Author.

Beatty, B. (1989). Child gardening: The teaching of young children in America. In D. Warren (Ed.), *American teachers: Histories of a profession at work* (pp. 65–98). New York: Macmillan.

Biber, B. (1977). Cognition in early childhood education: A historical perspective. In B. Spodek & H. Walberg (Eds.), *Early childhood education: Issues and insights*. Berkeley, CA: McCutchen.

Bloom, B. (1964). *Stability and change in human characteristics*. New York: John Wiley.

Bornstein, M. C., & Lamb, M. E. (1992). *Developmental psychology: An advanced textbook*. Hillsdale, NJ: Lawrence Erlbaum.

Bredekamp, S. (1987). *Developmentally appropriate practice in early childhood programs serving children from birth through age 8*. Washington, DC: The National Association for the Education of Young Children.

Bredekamp, S., & Willer, B. (1992). Of ladders and lattices, cores and cones: Conceptualizing an early childhood professional development system. *Young Children, 47*(3), 47–50.

Bronowski, J. (1973). *The ascent of man*. Boston: Little, Brown.

Bryant, D. M., & Clifford, R. M. (1992). 150 years of kindergarten: How far have we come? *Early Childhood Research Quarterly, 7*, 147–155.

Dewey, J. (1916). *Democracy and education*. New York: Macmillan.

Evans, E. (1983). Curriculum models and early childhood education. In B. Spodek (Ed.), *Handbook of research in early childhood education*. New York: Free Press.

Froebel, F. (1889). *The education of man*. New York: D. Appleton. (Original work published 1826)

Fromberg, D. (1992). Constructivist/intellectual curriculum. In W. R. Williams and D. P. Fromberg (Eds.), *The encyclopedia of early childhood education* (pp. 313–314). New York: Garland.

Gersten, R., & George, N. (1990). Teaching reading and mathematics to at-risk students in kindergarten. In C. Seefeldt (Ed.), *Continuing issues in early childhood education* (pp. 245–257). Columbus, OH: Merrill/Macmillan.

Ginsberg, S. (1978). The child care chronicle. In J. L. Hymes, Jr. (Ed.), *Living history interview: Book 2. Care of the children of working mothers* (pp. 1–15). Carmel, CA: Hacienda.

Goodykoontz, B. (1948). Recent history and present status of the education of young children. In N. B. Henry (Ed.), *The forty-sixth yearbook of the national study for the science of education: Part II. Early childhood education* (pp. 124–136). Chicago: University of Chicago Press.

Greenberg, P. (1987). Lucy Sprague Mitchell: A major missing link between early childhood education in the 1980s and progressive education in the 1890s–1930s. *Young Children, 42* (5), 70–84.

Greenberg, P. (1990). Head Start—Part of a multi-pronged anti-poverty effort for children and their families . . . Before the beginning: A participant's view. *Young Children, 45* (6), 40–52.

Greenberg, P. (1992). Why not academic preschool? Part 2. Autocracy or democracy in the classroom? *Young Children, 47* (3), 54–65.

Hall, G. S. (1907). *The content of children's minds*. Boston: Ginn.

Harris, N. (1983). "The Carondelet historic center and Susan E. Blow." *Childhood Education, 59*, 336–338.

Harrison, E. (1924). The growth of the kindergarten in the United States. In International Kindergarten Union: Committee of Nineteen (Eds.), *Pioneers of the kindergarten in America*. New York: Century.

Hill, P. S. (1987). The function of the kindergarten. *Young Children, 42* (5), 12–20.

Hunt, J. McVicker. (1961). *Intelligence and experience*. New York: Ronald.

Hymes, J. L., Jr. (1978). *Living history interviews*. Carmel, CA: Hacienda Press.

Hymes, J. L., Jr. (1983). The satisfactions. In *Annual editions: Early childhood education—1983–1984* (pp. 37–43). Guilford, CT: Duskin.

Lazar, I. (1977). *The persistence of preschool effects: A long term follow up of fourteen infant and preschool experiments.* Washington, DC: Administration for Children, Youth, and Families.

McMillan, M. (1919). *The nursery school.* London: J. M. Dent.

Mallory, N. J., & Goldsmith, N. A. (1990). Head Start works! Two Head Start veterans share their views. *Young Children, 45* (6), 36–40.

Milwaukee Public Schools. (1942). *Curriculum guide for kindergarten primary.* Milwaukee, WI: Author.

National Association for the Education of Young Children. (1982). *Early childhood teacher education guidelines.* Washington, DC: Author.

National Association for the Education of Young Children. (1984). *Position statement on nomenclature, status, salaries, and working conditions.* Washington, DC: Author.

National Association for the Education of Young Children. (1985). *Guidelines for early childhood education programs in associate degree granting institutions.* Washington, DC: Author.

National Association for the Education of Young Children. (1988). *Testing of young children: Concerns and cautions.* Washington, DC: Author.

National Association for the Education of Young Children. (1989). *Appropriate education in the primary grades.* Washington, DC: Author.

National Association for the Education of Young Children. (1990). *Guidelines for appropriate curriculum content and assessment in programs serving children ages 3 through 8.* Washington, DC: Author.

National Association for the Education of Young Children. (1991a). *Accreditation criteria & procedures.* Washington, DC: Author.

National Association for the Education of Young Children. (1991b). *Early childhood teacher education guidelines: Basic and advanced.* Washington, DC: Author.

National Association of State Boards of Education. (1988). *Right from the start.* Alexandria, VA: Author.

Newell, B. B., & Putnam, A. (1924). *Pioneers of the kindergarten in America.* New York: Century.

Parker, S. C., & Temple, A. (1925). *Unified kindergarten and first-grade teaching.* Boston: Ginn.

Perrone, V. (1991). *On standardized testing: A position paper.* Wheaton, MD: Association of Childhood Education International.

Piaget, J., & Inhelder, B. (1969). *The psychology of the child.* New York: Basic Books.

Rousseau, J. (1947). *L'Emile ou l'education.* In O. E. Tellows & N. R. Tarrey (Eds.), *The age of enlightenment.* New York: F. S. Croft. (Original work published 1762)

Sava, S. G. (1987). Development, not academics. *Young Children, 42* (5), 15.

Schweinhart, L. (1992). Sociocultural studies of the effectiveness of early childhood education. In L. R. Williams and D. P. Fromberg (Eds.), *Encyclopedia of early childhood education* (pp. 187–188). New York: Garland.

Seaver, J. W., Cartwright, C. A., Ward, C. B., & Heasley, C. A. (1979). *Careers with young children: Making your decision.* Washington, DC: National Association for the Education of Young Children.

Shapiro, M. S. (1983). *Child's garden.* University Park, PA: Pennsylvania State University Press.

Shorr, L. B. (1989). Commentary. Future choices. *Toward a National Youth Policy, 1*(3), 83.

Snyder, A. (1972). *Dauntless women in childhood education.* Washington, DC: Association for Childhood Education International.

Steiner, G. Y. (1976). *The children's cause.* Washington DC: Brookings Institution.

Taylor, K. W. (1978). Parent cooperative nursery schools. In J. L. Hymes, Jr. (Ed.), *Living history interviews: Book I. Beginnings* (pp. 1–7). Carmel, CA: Hacienda.

U.S. Department of Education (1991). *National Household Education Survey.* Washington, DC: Author.

Vygotsky, L. (1986). *Thought and language* (rev. ed.). Cambridge, MA: The MIT Press.

Weber, E. (1969). *The kindergarten.* New York: Teachers College Press.

Weikart, D. (1971). *Early childhood special education for culturally different children.* Ypsilanti, MI: High Scope.

Williams, L. R., & Fromberg, D. P. (Eds.). (1992). *Encyclopedia of early childhood education.* New York: Garland.

2 Child Growth and Development

"Study your children, for assuredly you do not know them."

(Rousseau, 1947)

After you read this chapter, you should be able to respond to the following questions:

1. What are the major theories of human growth and development, and who are some of the people associated with these theories?

2. Different theorists suggest that children normally progress through various stages of development. Name some of the theorists, and describe the stages they discuss.

3. What are some of the important children's behaviors that mark development as children grow from infancy to being sophisticated eight-year-olds in the areas of:

   a. Physical development

   b. Social development

   c. Emotional development

   d. Cognitive development

Rousseau's statement "Study your children, for assuredly you do not know them" (1947) is as important for us today as it was for his audience during the eighteenth century. Rousseau, like other philosophers, was fascinated with the nature of children. This fascination continues for today's psychologists, biologists, sociologists, linguists, anthropologists, and educators who engage in the study of children and have advanced differing theories to explain what children are like and how they mature. Researchers in different fields and with different perspectives continue to examine not only children's development but also the circumstances that enable them to thrive as they face an ever changing environment. As you learn about these theories and research, you'll gain insights into various views of how children learn, the different stages of their development, and the influences of their environment. These insights will help you as you begin your own study of children.

Theories of Development

Historically, two contrasting views of human nature developed, and the polarization of these views is called the nature-nurture controversy. Theories of child growth and development today still reflect aspects of the two opposing theories. The *nativist* interpretation stems from philosophers like Rousseau, who view children as unfolding like flowers in a natural, logical way, according to some innate plan. Studies in genetics affirm the hereditary determinants in development. The *nurturist* view, set forth by John Locke (1623–1704), maintained that humans are essentially passive and receptive; learning is the result of the mind's receiving stimuli from others and from the environment. Much of behaviorism today derives from such a viewpoint.

A third way of looking at the nature of human development is an *interactionist/constructivist* perspective. These theorists emphasize that learning takes place as a result of interactions between the child's natural unfolding or maturational development and environmental influences or stimuli. This means that, as children develop and mature, they construct their own inner knowledge by acting upon stimuli from the environment.

More recently constructivist researchers have maintained that individual differences are accounted for by the different ways that individuals, at different developmental stages, act upon events and respond to people in their environment. Indeed, "in this view human experience is the construction of reality" (Scarr, 1992, p. 5), and this reality is influenced by the cultural and societal conditions into which children are born and raised.

During the last fifty years considerable research in child development has resulted in a better understanding of children's behavior, but these basic theoretical ideas about development are still the background for most specific and focused research on child development (Horowitz, 1987, p. 8). Even though the nature-nurture controversy has not been completely resolved, most psychologists view learning as a result of some combination of hereditary and environmental influences (Dworetzky, 1990, p. 37).

No one of these theories can explain all of human growth and development. Nevertheless, looking at children from the viewpoints of the different theories will enable you to have a broader perspective of children as you observe how they function in a classroom.

Behavioristic Theories

Behavioristic theory has its roots in the philosophy of John Locke, who viewed children as arriving in the world as a blank slate. The slate would be written on by those educating a child by a series of rewards and punishments.

Historically, behaviorists have believed that learning comes about because a person receives a reward, or reinforcement, for an action or a correct response to a particular stimulus (Skinner, 1974). Children are conditioned by a series of stimuli and responses, and learning results from the conditioning provided by adults and the environment. They learn from having their needs satisfied—or not satisfied—by another person or environmental factors.

Other behaviorists, called *associationists*, see learning as the result of associations between events. To these theorists, children's learning becomes generalized. A young child who has received milk as the result of saying "mk" at first may say "mk" for anything to drink. As adults shape the response, the child learns to distinguish between milk, water, orange juice, and so on. The process is gradual; children do not receive rewards when their request for "mk" is directed toward juice or water, only when it is directed toward milk.

Not all learning is believed to result from this direct conditioning. Children can observe behavior and form mental pictures of it. Later they will try to imitate the observed behavior, especially if they believe it will be rewarded or reinforced (Bandura & Walters, 1969). As their responses are reinforced in a number of ways, the behavior becomes stronger.

Behaviorists also show how to extinguish behavior. Inappropriate or undesirable behavior in children can be eliminated simply by ignoring it. The child not receiving a response for running away from her father in the supermarket soon learns to stop running because there are no payoffs, no father running after her screaming demands, no reinforcement for the behavior.

Behaviorists use carefully controlled experimental approaches to test their theories. The results of their research have been used to develop pro-

Children observe behavior and try to imitate it.

grams for children and strategies for teachers. In many instances the research has led to the development of schedules of reinforcement designed to help children develop specific skills and change undesirable behaviors. These programs have the support of educators who favor teacher-initiated approaches to education, in which teachers determine and initiate the goals and objectives of the program and select curriculum activities designed to foster achievement of those goals.

Nativistic Theories

Rousseau admonished his contemporaries to love childhood, to take advantage of its play, its pleasures, and its admirable spirit (Rousseau, 1962, p. 558). In *L'Emile* he recommended that children be left to ripen like a piece of fruit on a tree so that the natural and lovely character in the child would flower without adult direction. Gesell, Ilg, and Ames (1974), following the work of G. S. Hall, documented that children's growth and development occur as naturally as a flower grows, buds, and blossoms. They say children's growth is the result of "laws and sequence of maturation which account for the general similarities and basic trends of child development" (Gesell & Ilg, 1940, p. 7). Though Gesell recognized that environment played a role in the child's behavior, he believed that the basic progression of development was inherent and due to the process of maturation—continuous and spiral. Each child goes through similar stages, but according to his or her own developmental clock.

Linguists like Lenneberg (1967), Slobin (1966), and Chomsky (1965) support this notion that development is the result of maturation, at least in language. Their explanations for the rapid growth of grammar, similarities in stages of language development among children in differing cultures, and the novel sentences children produce is that children are "prewired" for language.

This theory leads to a faith that the child *will* learn, given proper time to develop. Therefore children's outward behaviors indicate readiness. Hastening the process would be undesirable and detrimental, if not impossible. When teaching, the adult assumes the role of supporter of children's development, rather than controller. This translates into the program approach where the child is the initiator and the adult the responder. The teacher, or adult, provides a child-centered learning environment organized in relation to children's levels of readiness and takes cues for introducing content and experiences from the children.

Psychoanalytic Theories

Freudian Theory

Sigmund Freud's (1856–1939) *psychoanalytic* theories of human personality concerned emotion, motivation, and personality development. He viewed children as having human sexual energy and believed that as they grew and developed, this energy was invested in different ways.

Freud stated that the three basic drives that the infant possesses are the sexual drive, survival instincts, and the drive of destructiveness. He defined three structures to explain a person's personality. The *id* is the instinctive structure that infants possess and that drives them to seek satisfaction. As they come in conflict with reality, as they grow and develop, the *ego*, their rational part, emerges. Finally the *superego*, or moral or ethical part, develops.

Freud (1949) wrote that children go through distinct developmental stages. The particular stages, called *psychosexual stages*, reflect the development of gratification zones. The *oral stage* (first year of life) reflects the infant's need for gratification from the mouth. An infant's eating, sucking, spitting, and chewing are not only a need to satisfy hunger, but also provide pleasure. The *anal stage* (second to third year) reflects the toddler's need for gratification from the rectal area. The *phallic stage* (four and five years) reflects the preschooler's gratification from the genitals. The *latency stage* (middle years) is a repression of sexuality ending during the preadolescent years.

During the *genital stage* (beginning at puberty), adolescents develop an awareness of their own sexuality and need for gratification. As love relationships develop and mature, pleasure derives from giving as well as receiving gratification.

The child moves from one stage to the next partly as a result of physical development, but also because at each stage parental expectations change. Changes and expectations result in conflicts in the child as he or she is torn between seeking gratification and meeting parental expectations that require its denial. As these pleasure urges are repressed, anxiety develops. Because the child needs to relieve that anxiety, he or she develops different defense mechanisms. In normal development, children gain control of inner conflicts and reduce anxiety by using some of these defense mechanisms. But even though these inner conflicts may seem under control, feelings that have been repressed recur. Freud believed that such long-term personality traits or problems as stinginess, compulsiveness, alcoholism, depression, and promiscuity develop from the need to control these recurring feelings.

Though there has been much criticism of Freud's views and methods of research, Gleitman (1986) cites two major reasons for his continuing influence on psychology: (1) Freud was the first to point out that children's inner conflicts have a major influence on their development; and (2) Freud's view of human nature was all-encompassing, for he saw humans as biological, social, emotional, and rational beings to be understood through their psychology.

Erikson's Theory

A follower of Freud, Erik Erikson (1902–) focused his theory on the ego and what it meant for human development. Erikson (1963) theorized that there were eight psychosocial stages.

1. Basic trust vs. mistrust
2. Autonomy vs. shame and doubt
3. Initiative vs. guilt
4. Industry vs. inferiority
5. Identity vs. role diffusion
6. Intimacy vs. isolation
7. Generativity vs. stagnation
8. Ego integrity vs. despair

Each of the eight psychosocial strengths exists at all eight stages and is related to every other. However, each strength has a critical period for development, and the eight stages follow a proper sequence and structure. Cultural and social values, according to Erikson, also affect how people construct and maintain progress from one of these phases to another (Levine, Jakubowski, & Cote, 1992). For a child to develop a normal pattern of behavior, the positive attribute of the stage needs to be satisfied at the critical period before the next stage develops. The person's development from a trusting infant to an old man or woman with ego integrity depends on successful integration of all stages.

The stages most pertinent for early childhood educators are basic trust vs. mistrust, autonomy vs. shame, initiative vs. guilt, and industry vs. inferiority.

Basic Trust.   For *basic trust* to develop, infants, between birth and eighteen months, must gradually develop a sense of "inner goodness" because they have determined that there is an "outer predictability." Their environment has provided consistency, continuity, and sameness of experiences (Clarke-Stewart & Freidman, 1987). Without this, a child will develop a basic mistrust and hostility toward others and the world.

Autonomy.   Between nineteen months and three years of age, toddlers develop a sense of *autonomy.* As they start to walk, they develop a desire to let go as well as a need to hold on. Children begin to develop a sense of self and pride in their achievements. If they are shamed because of their attempts at letting go and their experiments with the world, they'll develop a sense of shame about themselves and self-doubt as they function in the world.

Initiative.   At age three or four, a new stage, *initiative,* unfolds. At this stage, children are able to undertake and plan their own activities and do them in cooperation with other children. If the adult world does not offer proper regulations, a child may undertake more than he or she can achieve, and this develops into a sense of guilt or failure. On the other hand, if the adult world doesn't permit practicing developing skills, children live with a sense of failure.

Industry.   From about six years of age until puberty, children are developing a sense of *industry.* At this stage they become producers of things and users of tools, not the least being reading, writing, and mathematics. Children become socially adept as they work beside and with others. One problem that can occur in this stage is that children may develop a sense of inadequacy in using the "tools" of their world or see themselves as inferior to others. Another danger is overwork, which makes the child a "conformist or thoughtless slave of his technique" (Erikson, 1963, pp. 247–274).

Interactionist/Constructivist Theories

Piaget's Theory

Jean Piaget (1896–1980) spent a lifetime studying and interpreting the growth of children. His work was influenced by Rousseau, who saw the child as active; however, Piaget (1952) extended this concept of natural unfolding by maintaining that knowledge is created as children interact with their social and physical environment. Piaget calls this interaction *assimilation* and *accommodation,* and *equilibration.* As children interact with their environment, they form *schemata,* or organizational patterns. These are the bases for more complex structures as mental activity develops. Children use assimilation and accommodation to organize their experiences into increasingly complex structures.

Assimilation is the process of absorbing new material into an already existing structure or schema. For example, a child, having been given a whole orange for the first time and told it was a fruit, grasped it and bit into it as she would an apple. She was familiar only with fruit that didn't need peeling. She was assimilating the orange into an already existing pattern, or schema, for fruit.

Accommodation is the act of changing the already existing structures to include a new situation. The child must accommodate the structure that some fruit needs peeling into an already existing structure that allowed this understanding of fruit through a series of assimilations and accommodations as she experienced the new fruit, orange. Assimilation and accommodation happen at the same time and are intertwined.

Equilibration is the organism's tendency to bring about a dynamic balance between already existing structures and new events. Children devise ways that are more effective in dealing with their environment. As they gain more experiences they acquire more structures, and thus can deal with more and more complex situations.

Piaget maintains that the infant, the child, and the adult all adapt, but adaptation is different at different times. Thus the schemata or structures that one uses vary during a lifespan in fairly regular sequences. These variations represent developmental stages, and each stage is distinct from the others. The stages reflect the interaction of maturation and experience upon the already existing mental structures. Children develop these stages of thinking in the same sequence and at approximately the same time, although the exact age differs from individual to individual and among cultures. Piaget's four major periods of intellectual development are *sensorimotor, preoperational, concrete operational,* and *formal operational.*

Sensorimotor Period (Birth to Two Years).   During the *sensorimotor period,* children develop from newborns, whose interactions with the environment are based on reflexes, to toddlers who can interact well with people, walk and run, and manipulate things in their environment for their own purposes. The basic mode of operating is through senses and muscles. Children learn their world by manipulating and exploring through the use of their bodies. Through interactions with the environment, as well as innate maturation, children begin to understand the concept of *object permanence,* that objects exist even if they cannot actually see them. They are also able to decenter, seeing themselves as separate from others and from objects in the environment.

Preoperational Period (Two to Seven Years).   The *preoperational period* is characterized by children's learning to use mental symbols or imagery. Language develops rapidly, from using words for immediate things or actions to beginning steps in reasoning. Play takes on symbolic forms, with children playing as if a block were a truck, or as if they were the teacher, parent, or doctor.

Concrete Operational Period (Seven to Eleven Years).   The *concrete operational period* is characterized by children's ability to do logical thinking as long as they are able to manipulate the objects from a base of concrete reality. During this stage children develop and refine abilities to classify, seriate, decenter, and mentally reverse a process, and to deduce new relationships.

Formal Operational Period (Eleven Years Through Adulthood).   The *formal operational period* is characterized by movement from concrete manipulations to abstract thinking. At this highest level of thinking the adolescent can form abstract ideas, formulate and test hypotheses, and engage in reflective thinking.

   Piaget's work is characterized by age-related stages of development. Many research studies from various cultural settings have corroborated his findings. Today researchers, building on Piaget's work, are examining separate aspects of development like creativity, memory, and problem solving, rather than broad developmental changes. As they explore these domains, they are finding that changes from one stage to the next may be less even than previously thought. Change is normally gradual and not abrupt, and some evidence shows that the quality of environmental interactions can affect the time that changes will occur for some children (Chance & Fischman, 1987).

Vygotskian Theory

In more recent years, early childhood educators have found that the theories of the Russian psychologist and philosopher Vygotsky (1896–1934) have implications for working with young children. Vygotsky and Piaget were contemporaries and knew about each other's work, and there are similarities in their viewpoints.

Vygotsky, like Piaget, believed development could not be explained by a single factor, such as biological and maturational influences or environmental and social factors, but that development depended on the interaction of these two factors. Vygotsky's and Piaget's views of development differ in the way each emphasizes the relationship between the internal organism and the social milieu. Piaget's emphasis was on the individual's accomplishment while interacting with the external environment. Vygotsky's emphasis was the effect the sociocultural process had in stimulating an individual's development (Biddell, 1992).

Fundamental to Vygotsky's view of development is that there is not a single explanatory principle for all development but that explanations for development have to change as development progresses. At certain points in a child's development, biological factors may be the primary force of change, but as the child develops and changes, there are new influences that affect the change. Varying social factors become the predominate influence for development and thus offer better explanations of changes. However, development still operates within a given biological framework and must be accounted for (Wertsch, 1985).

Vygotsky maintained that higher mental processes develop as children develop their speech in context with practical activities. Before they acquire speech, children use tools to accomplish tasks in a similar manner to apes. As children acquire speech, however, they incorporate it into their activities, and their action becomes transformed. They are able to plan and master their surroundings with the help of verbalizations. A preverbal child will bring an object placed on a blanket closer to her by pulling the blanket toward her. A child beginning to talk may draw a picture and jabber while making the swirls on the paper in rhythm with her sound. She may even point to the picture and say "pretty." As children develop, at first they must do an action before they can describe it. For example, a child may not be able to tell you what she is drawing until after it is drawn. But by four or five years of age, children can look at a situation, describe it, and play out the solution as they are carrying out the activity (Vygotsky, 1978).

Learning and development are not the same thing, but they are interrelated from the very earliest moment of a child's life. At different developmental stages, children learn different things as they independently act on and interpret their environment, but also other people interact with the child and affect the course of that learning. Children respond differently to different adults, and how that interaction progresses determines both children's learning and development. Vygotsky suggested that there are two developmental levels at which children operate. One level of operation is the stage at which children can do problem-solving tasks independently—actual developmental level. The second level of operation is when children can do the same task under the guidance of an adult or a more skilled peer—potential developmental level. As children mature, the potential level becomes the actual level, when the child can perform the task indepen-

How other people interact with the child can affect the course of learning, according to Vygotsky.

dently. The distance between these two levels is called the *zone of proximal development* (Vygotsky, 1978, pp. 84–91). Vygotsky maintains "that an essential feature of learning is that it creates the zone of proximal development, that is, learning awakens a variety of internal developmental processes that are able to operate only when the child is interacting with people in his environment and in cooperation with his peers. Once these processes are internalized, they become part of the child's independent developmental achievement" (Vygotsky, 1978, p. 90).

Vygotsky was concerned that so much emphasis is placed on children's actual level of development. He urged that children should be "tested" more often to determine their potential level. Without the adult encouraging higher levels of achievement, he believed, the internal forces would not be activated to enable the child to progress in learning and development.

Piaget's work and, more recently, Vygotsky's work have had a profound influence on early childhood education. Their ideas support the premise of the importance of the early years of life for later intellectual development. Further, they made clear the connection between children's physical and mental activity and intellectual growth. Because Piaget and Vygotsky were so clear about the importance of the child's interaction with and manipulation of the environment to intellectual growth, early childhood educators found in their work support for many of the principles that had guided their practices throughout the years. The theories of these two men offer guidance especially for those endorsing an open framework as a program approach. The idea of teacher and child both initiating and responding, the necessary interaction between adult and child as well as between child and other children, and the environment are all congruent with Piaget's and Vygotsky's theories.

Piagetian and Vygotskian theories give credence to a program that emphasizes the following principles:

1. Play is the basic mode for young children's thinking.

2. The teachers's role is to exploit daily encounters, both physical and social, as ways to stimulate the thinking process.

3. The cognitive search for relationships should be stimulated by providing varied opportunities for children to have direct contact with the people and processes of their environment. (Biber, 1977, p. 47)

Normal Growth and Development

Early childhood educators need to understand theories of development as well as stages of development. From different theorists you will grasp how children's behavior is explained and understand how development in one area interrelates with development in another area. Children do not develop physically in isolation from their social, emotional, and cognitive development. Each aspect of development will greatly influence other areas of development (Berk, 1991). In order to affect children's learning and enhance their development, you need to know when to expect children to be able to complete particular tasks without guidance or help and when you need to provide them with information, directions, or encouragement to try something new.

Infancy (Birth to Twelve Months)

Vicki is a delightful ten-month-old. She is twenty-seven inches tall and weighs eighteen pounds. She has seven teeth, two new ones having appeared in her tenth month. She has learned to creep and delights in exploring the large recreation room at her community center. She has only gradually been willing to move from her mother's lap when "strangers" come into the room. Some of the older children have come in and are playing on the piano. Vicki creeps rapidly to her mother, stands up beside her, and begins to move her little bottom and hands rhythmically. Then she sits down and begins to wave her hands, still in time to the music. She makes babbling and tonal sounds that rise and fall with the music. The older girls approach and prepare to play with Vicki; she jabbers at them excitedly, waving her hands and arms about. Susan, one of the girls, bends down and picks up Vicki, but Vicki resists. She frowns, grunts, and pushes against Susan until she wiggles free. She then starts to creep rapidly across the rug toward the open window. Her mother gasps, Vicki stops, turns briefly toward her mother and then turns back, picks up speed, and arrives in time to grab a tiny butterfly that has flown into the room through the open window and is now resting on the rug. Vicki pops the butterfly into her mouth. Her mother grabs her and attempts to remove the butterfly, saying "No, no, dirty, dirty." But Vicki clamps her mouth shut tight and shakes her head from side to side as she swallows the butterfly. Her mother continues to try to open Vicki's mouth, but Vicki squirms from her mother's grasp and creeps away to the middle of the rug, where she turns and sits. She begins to wave her arms about and jabbers at her mother. The mother picks Vicki up again, saying "Naughty, naughty, you shouldn't put things in your mouth." Vicki waves to the girls, smiling happily and saying "bye, bye" as the somewhat distressed mother carries her from the room.

Though it begins in complete dependency, infancy is a period of rapid growth for humans. Most infants arrive in the world with some reflexes and all sensory organs ready to grow and develop. They appear small and helpless, especially if they are as tiny as Vicki, who weighed five pounds at birth and was seventeen inches long. Their body muscles are limp, and they do not really hold themselves up well. The noises they hear tend to frighten or soothe them, and they can make their needs or wants known only by crying.

Infants sleep most of the time, waking only to satisfy their hunger, usually with a three-to-four hour sleep-and-waking pattern. By the end of their first year, they are getting about well, crawling and creeping. Some are even walking. They can spot things, as Vicki did, and sometimes grab them, seeming to move faster than an adult.

They understand many of the common noises and words and respond to them as Vicki did to the music. The one-year-old doesn't use many words, but has vocal, body, and facial expressions that communicate likes or dislikes to others. Vicki didn't want to be picked up. She made it clear to the friendly girls by her scowl and the noises she made, and by using her body to resist. At the end of the first year, many children are awake most of the day except for one or two naps. They usually sleep through the night.

Physical Development.   The infant's *physical development* is rapid, although there are great variations in rate and style. At birth, infants have a grasping reflex. At first they grasp and release things that they accidentally touch as they wave their arms and legs about. These movements become refined as they begin to gain control over eye, hand, and leg muscles and movement.

They are also learning to raise their heads, arch their bodies, and flex their legs. At two to five months, babies can be propped up in a sitting position. By four to six months, they roll over, and between six and eight months, they can sit up unattended. Crawling and creeping usually begin between seven and ten months. Vicki was just beginning to creep at 10 months, but she made rapid progress once she started. Some babies will begin to stand when held by the adult, and take their first steps alone at around eleven or twelve months. Variations are great; some babies start walking with a parent's help by seven months (Bayley, 1969, p. 90).

Babies have a sucking reflex at birth, and their first diet is liquid. By six months teeth usually appear, and the baby begins to eat solid food. These foods are explored by squeezing, squishing, and smearing food on faces, chairs, trays, and any nearby object. When solids are started, babies like to pick up the food and feed themselves.

This rapid growth is intertwined with other types of development because now the baby can use hands, eyes, ears, mouth, and body to explore and test the environment. Vicki's curiosity about the butterfly was satisfied by an amazing combination of the skills of creeping, grasping, listening, and tasting. This period is Freud's oral stage of development. Freud (1949) maintained that the greater part of children's energy at this stage is spent exploring the world through oral activities like tasting, biting, and spitting.

Social Development.   Newborns are not truly social beings. They spend most of their time sleeping and eating, yet they are in a state of readiness to respond to the touch, sight, and sound of another human being. Their *social development* starts early. Babies, for survival, need not only to receive care for their physical well-being, but they must also get attention, stimulation, and interaction from a loving adult for their social/emotional/intellectual development.

Infants' first social interactions come about as parents and other caregivers respond to their vocalizations and movements as if they intended to communicate (Meadows, 1986). Thus they grow quickly from an asocial being to a smiling, wiggling social being. They begin to notice their mother and other familiar caretakers at about four months. By six months, they enjoy being played with. They enjoy games like peek-a-boo, "This Little Piggy," and others. At around six to ten months, the once very social infant may suddenly become wary of strangers. Vicki was skeptical at ten months, but when given time, she was willing to move out to be sociable and even wave "bye-bye."

Emotional Development.   Newborn infants demonstrate *emotional development* when they cry from pain or discomfort. Crying is differentiated to indicate hunger, wetness, and cold. Babies show their emotions by kicking, arm waving, and facial expressions as they begin to hug, kiss, and chew or even bite on something to show their affection. They also show their fear or dislike for people or things by cringing, pulling away, or biting.

Emotions are temporary and change suddenly. Vicki first clung to her mother as visitors appeared and later pushed them away as they tried to pick her up. Later, safe in the arms of her mother, she could smile and wave happily.

Cognitive Development.   Babies' *cognitive development* begins as they learn to trust the world. At about four months they develop *intentionality,* the ability to make things happen, and object permanence.

Intentionality gradually develops as babies experience their ability to make things happen. Babies learn that when they cry, their mother will come; when hungry, they'll be fed; and when they let go of the rattle, it bangs. Infants are so delighted with the ability to make things happen that they'll become tyrants, banging their high chairs to hear the noise or throwing all the toys out of the playpen, protesting loudly until an adult picks them up. Then they can start the game all over again.

Object permanence is gradually learned as infants become more and more aware of objects and people. At some point they'll start protesting the disappearance of people. At about six months of age, infants become aware that an object still exists even if it is not in view. At first, they'll hunt for the object where it was last seen, but as they develop their abilities, they'll begin to remove obstacles to find it and look in other places for it. In a primitive game of hide-and-seek, the baby finds Daddy behind the door. At a year, babies will surprise their parents by finding yesterday's bottle left under a blanket in the playpen.

The infant's language is mostly nonverbal, with some distinctive types of vocalizations. For example, newborns wiggle their bodies, arms, and legs to express pleasure or pain. As they begin to move, they lift their arms to be picked up, get their coats to indicate they want to go out, or bring Mommy's purse as if to ask "Where is Mommy?" The game of language has begun. At two or three months infants smile, frown, and scowl. They babble, coo, and gurgle. These vocalizations take on phonemic sounds: first vowels, then consonants. At six months, parents are sure their child is saying "ma ma" (Stone & Church, 1984, p. 228).

Babies even imitate sounds from the environment. Vicki, at about eight months, would only stare as her mother would say "doggie" to animals or pictures of a dog. But when one day Vicki and mother were out walking, a large dog came by, sniffed Vicki, and barked. Later that day, as Vicki's mother was reading a book to her, Vicki pointed to a picture of a dog and said "wow-wow" in nearly perfect imitation of the dog's sound.

Vicki points to a picture of a dog and says, "Wow-wow."

By six months of age babies begin to jabber, producing a flow of nonsense words with a reasonable intonation pattern. Words usually do not appear until near the end of the first year; however, children have receptive language and understand a great deal more than they can say. Indications of this understanding start early, and the baby will turn her head at the sound of a familiar voice or quiet down as she hears her father's footsteps as he comes to feed her. By the end of the first year, babies will point to familiar objects when asked, "Where is the ball?" and may even go to get it. Vicki indicated her response to environmental sounds when she swayed to the music and began to "sing."

The adult plays a key role in language development, often quite unconsciously. The way adults talk to babies, known as "motherese," is characterized by slower speech, special pitch and tonal qualities, and simpler language patterns, even sometimes using one- or two-word phrases (Blewitt, 1983; Ratner & Pye, 1984; Fernald & Simon, 1984). Motherese seems to attract and hold the baby's attention. Vicki's mother used such abbreviated speech as she reprimanded her for eating the butterfly: "No, no, dirty, dirty." As children's speech increases and develops, adults' manner of speaking to them also changes (Biehler & Hudson, 1986).

Toddler (One to Three Years)

Brian, eighteen months, is sitting quietly in the kitchen as his mother is cooking. He is surrounded by several pots and pans that he previously dug out from the cupboard. He has dumped out the remains from the Cheerios box onto the floor beside him and is busily engaged in picking up each piece and dropping it into the pan beside him. At times he holds the piece over the pan and then suddenly lets it go and waits, almost as if to hear it hit bottom. Occasionally he pops one into his mouth.

After a few moments his mother turns, notices what he is doing, and exclaims, "No, no, Brian." She scoops up the cereal and dumps the pans into the cupboard as Brian helps. She then turns and says, "Brian, go find your blocks and bring them out." She turns back to cooking. Suddenly there is a loud howling from upstairs. She runs to find Brian at the top of the stairs, looking down. When Brian sees his mother he cries, "Mommy down! Mommy down!" Ms. T. says, "Oh, Brian, you want to come down? You climbed too far, I'll help you."

She then goes up the stairs and stands just one stair below as Brian creeps down the stair backwards, secure in the knowledge that his mother is there. When he reaches the bottom, Brian starts to climb up again. Ms. T. says, "That's far enough." Brian then backs down. He repeats the procedure three or four times until Ms. T. exclaims, "Brian, I need to finish my work. Here, come to your table and draw a picture." Ms. T. then gets a crayon and some paper, and Brian turns and backs into his chair, balancing himself with both hands on the side of the chair as he does so. He then picks up the crayon in his right fist in an overhand grasp and begins to scribble vertically. "Mommy do, Mommy do," he jabbers away in singsong fashion. Suddenly he drops the crayon, slaps his hands, and jumps off his chair. He picks up his picture and takes it to his mother, saying, "pretty?"

Brian is well into the toddler stage. It is a time of tremendous growth in general body control. Children advance from beginning to walk to running, jumping, and climbing. Brian, like many toddlers, is able to climb upstairs but still is uncertain about getting down. He can crawl down backwards, but wants the security of his mother nearby. He likes to practice new skills, but under "safe" conditions.

Brian can sit down in a child-size chair by backing into it. His fine motor control is improving. He can pick up small objects like Cheerios and put them into a pot. He can grasp a crayon, but does it in fistlike fashion. Brian is still developing motor abilities at a rather rapid pace. His oral language is not extensive, though he responds to the simple commands his mother gives. He jabbers away in a singing fashion as he draws, seemingly saying "mommy do" just to hear the sounds. He uses the word "pretty" almost as if he were asking, "It's pretty, isn't it?" He uses the two-word phrase "mommy down" to mean "please help get me down these stairs."

Physical Development.   Toddlers start to walk between twelve and fifteen months of age and usually retain a rather wobbly gait until eighteen months. By the end of two years, they are able to walk without assistance and run. They develop climbing skills and can climb up and down stairs, holding onto the railing and advancing the same foot one step at a time.

At eighteen months, toddlers can stack two blocks, and by two years, six blocks. They can grasp pencil and crayons to scribble. Hand preference starts to emerge about this time. Toddlers, if permitted, can do some parts of dressing themselves, and like to try.

They now have a full complement of teeth and are eating three meals a day, with additional snacks of milk or crackers. At eighteen months they start to use a spoon. They are more adept with a spoon at two years, though they still like to use their fingers.

At two, daytime bladder control is beginning. Children become interested in eliminating and in the whole process of this bodily function. Toddlerhood reflects the Freudian anal developmental stage and Erikson's stage of autonomy. Freud (1949) suggests that the energy children expend at this stage is related to the anal area and is manifested by their fascination with their ability to hold on or to let go, thus beginning control over bodily functions. Erikson (1963) defines the stage as one of autonomy, emphasizing the social aspects of development. Children want to move out and let go of their secure environment, but they still want to cling to that security.

Social Development.   Socialization skills develop during this period from a meager sense of self to separating self from others. At eighteen months toddlers begin to separate themselves from others, and by two they have even become rather possessive of their toys, parents, and things that are *their own*. They are happy to play by themselves and can be quite self-absorbed, as was Brian when putting cereal into the pot or scribbling away. Toddlers will obey commands, but they're often distracted by the motor activity involved. Brian went to get some toys, but noticed the stairs on the way and busied himself climbing up and down. The toddler wants to do things by himself, but in a safe way. Brian's mother was wise in permitting him to climb down the stairs by himself while she stood nearby for safety.

By two, toddlers are ready to give up their mother as a playmate and are delighted to play beside a child of their own age. This play tends to be side by side rather than social, with each child having his or her own toys and playing happily without interacting, but enjoying the company of another child. This pleasant interaction can be disrupted should one child take the belonging of another. Sharing is not what toddlers are about.

Emotional Development.   One-year-olds seem rather amiable, whereas eighteen-month-olds begin to resist events, and twos express strong wishes and preferences. Emotional development is uneven during this time. Emotions go from one extreme to another. Toddlers can be exuberant one moment, laughing or showing affection, and the next moment hitting and kicking. Suddenly the eighteen-month-old will not let his mother out of sight. By two—the "terrible twos"—there are often a great many "nos" as well as negative behavior and willfulness.

It is almost as if toddlers' developing sense of autonomy needs an outlet. Other emotions are beginning to develop. Toddlers begin to show pity, sympathy, and a growing sense of caring. Two-year-olds don't like to see another cry, and will often put their arms around the baby they have just walloped, saying "Don't cry, don't cry." At eighteen months there is no sense of guilt, but by two, a child may have a look of being sorry. Twos judge their crime by whether or not they will be punished for "making a puddle" rather than whether it was an accident or not.

The need for autonomy is characterized by a dependent-independent stance. One moment toddlers want to move out and try things; the next they need to know their mother is near. Brian wanted to practice climbing the stairs—but with the security of his mother nearby.

Cognitive Development.   As toddlers take on the world, cognitive development expands. Mental imagery and deductive reasoning start to develop. The eighteen-month-old will look for things that are hidden and search in more than one place. Brian went to get his toys because he knew where they were kept in his playroom.

By eighteen months, object permanence is established. Toddlers remember the actions of others, and delayed imitation occurs frequently and becomes elaborated. Toddlers remember past events and figure things out. Brian, at twenty months, watched his mother and father cutting stencils and making pictures one evening. They put the cutting tools in a jar on top of the china closet, safely out of his reach. The next day, he found a footstool in the kitchen, pushed it into the dining room beside the china closet, and climbed up. He reached up with his right hand to get the tools, but couldn't reach them. He climbed down, went to the playroom, and got a cardboard box. He took that to the stool, placed it bottom side up on the stool. He again climbed on the stool, then onto the box. Again he reached to the top of the closet, but he couldn't reach the tools.

He climbed down a second time, and went to the kitchen for the yard-stick. Back he went again, and with the stick in his hand, he climbed up, carefully reached over, and with the stick succeeded in pulling the tools to the edge of the cabinet. He was just about to reach the tools, only to be "rewarded" by his mother grabbing him and the tools.

Toddlers have a sense of time, because they can remember past events, as Brian did. They may not know such terms as *today, yesterday*, or *tomorrow*, but they do recognize the passage of time. Toddlers are learning color names and may be able to distinguish one or two colors accurately. Two-year-olds love to count and can do so in rote fashion to three or beyond, but they get confused after that. Rarely can they count objects correctly or rationally. They are more likely to count five objects as "1, 2, 3, 8, 9, 4, 10."

Language development from age one to three grows by leaps and bounds. At age one, children may know a few words, but most of their communication is jargon and gesturing. From this point on, they add to their vocabularies about five to eight words each day. Though new word acquisition is slower from twelve to twenty-four months, vocabulary development increases dramatically after that; by age five children can produce between 8,000 and 14,000 words (Stroufe, Cooper, & Marshall, 1988, p. 267). During the early part of toddlerhood, children use two- or three-word sentences, but the development of *syntax* has started, and they use "I" and "mine" correctly. By the end of the second year the pronouns are in place, and they use past and future tense, though often with mistakes. Two-year-olds are aware of the patterns and sounds of the language and will play with language; they will talk to hear themselves talk. Brian's "mommy do, mommy do, mommy do" contains real and nonsense words, and he says them with no apparent desire to communicate.

Preschooler (Three to Four Years)

Lisette, an exuberant three-and-a-half-year-old, is one of the first children to arrive at the child-care center. This morning one of the teachers has brought her dog to share with the children. Lisette arrives at the door holding her mother's hand, spots the aide, drops her mother's hand, and runs across the room. She stops abruptly just in front of the aide, who doesn't seem to notice her.

Lisette frowns, stomps her foot, puts her hand on her hip, then smiles as the aide turns to her. She takes a step forward and throws her arms around the aide. Just as quickly she lets go and runs over to the doll corner, where Shona is playing. Lisette puts both arms around Shona and says "I gotcha!" She laughs abruptly, lets go, spins around once, and runs to the door as Mark arrives. She bends over toward Mark and shouts, "Go away Mark!" She then straightens, laughs, spins about again, and runs over to the table under which the dog is lying. Lisette gets down on her hands and knees and crawls under the table. "Come outa there," she says. Lifting her head and spotting the teacher, she shouts, "He's under the table." She crawls further under the table, saying "Come out, come out." Then she crawls out and walks over to the teacher. "Him under the table," she exclaims, turning and pointing toward the dog. The teacher looks at Lisette, smiles, and says, "I know, he'll be all right. . . ."

Lisette straightens up, smiles, and hugs the teacher. She spins around again, spots the puzzles, and selects one. She takes it to the table and dumps out the pieces. Picking up a piece in her right hand, she tries it in every place around the puzzle, until she finds the place it fits. She tries to fit a second piece in the corner. The aide comes by and suggests she try it in another place. Lisette glares at the aide and tries to fit the piece in another spot. Then she bangs it with her fist when it doesn't fit. "I don't think it's going in there . . . turn it around and try it here," the aide suggests, pointing to another place. Lisette successfully places the puzzle piece. She picks up a third piece: "Where this one go?" she asks as she tries to fit it in. The aide points. "Now this one?" persists Lisette. "Try it over here," the aide responds. As Lisette fits the piece in correctly, the aide leaves the table. Lisette picks up the next to last piece, and turning it around and around in each remaining slot, successfully fits it in. She does the same with the last piece.

Then she picks up the puzzle and starts to get up from the table. Instead she sets the puzzle down and takes out each piece. After all are out she picks up the first piece and on the first try successfully fits it in. The third piece is in her left hand, but with her right hand she takes it out, fits it in again, and then takes it out. She continues, fitting the other pieces on the first or second try. When the puzzle is complete, she dumps it out and then rapidly puts it together, frowning as she does so. With a huge sigh, she picks up the puzzle and with both hands, puts it back on the shelf.

Preschoolers move from the home to experience life in a sociable way with other children. They are willing to leave the parent if the new environment is one in which they feel safe or secure, as the child-care center apparently was for Lisette. At this age, exuberance abounds, and children can be loving and rude almost simultaneously. Lisette hugged the aide and Shona, but told Mark to go away. Language is developing rapidly. Preschoolers may make grammatical errors one moment, yet use correct English the next. Lisette asks, "Where this one go?" but the next minute says, "Where does it go?" Children of three or four are rapidly developing fine-motor and gross-motor skills and practice them over and over. They are perfecting their

Lisette picks up a puzzle piece and asks, "Where this one go?"

competencies as they progress through Erikson's stage of initiative. Lisette ran and spun, ran and spun, then practiced with the puzzle until she could do it to her satisfaction.

Physical Development.   Preschoolers have an extremely high energy level. They are developing and refining their gross- and fine-motor skills. They can run smoothly, stop easily, spin about, climb, and jump. They advance in ability to maintain body balance and equilibrium and can walk a wide balance beam. Preschoolers are improving their ability to toss a ball and often are able to throw a ball overhand with some force. Three- and four-year-olds enjoy riding tricycles and pushing and pulling cars and wagons.

Fine-motor development is nearly complete. Preschoolers can build with blocks, building tall towers and connecting their vertical buildings with roadways. Coloring, painting, and tearing and folding paper are intriguing to the children as they develop increasing control over fine muscles. For three-year-olds, scissors can often be frustrating, but by four, children are able to make cuts into paper. Their paintings and crayon drawings consist of long, short, or circular brush strokes. Often colors are juxtaposed, but at times they blend them all together. Drawings begin to be representational, and children name them.

Although hand dominance is established by this time, some children use both hands with ease. Lisette mostly used her right hand to work her puzzle, but she used her left one time. Subsequently, she took out that piece, as though putting it in with her left hand was wrong.

Social Development.   Three- and four-year-olds can be loving and cooperative one minute, bossy and resisting the next. They are aware that they are growing and changing, and sometimes wish the growth process would hurry up. When Lisette was nearly four, she could hardly wait for her birthday. She was sure she would have hair under her arms when she was four in spite of the fact that everyone told her she would not. She was crushed when her fourth birthday came and went, and no hair appeared.

At this age, children are happy to play side by side with others. Sometimes they cooperate in their play, but often they do not. In one preschool, the entire group of three-year-olds gathered in the block area where roadways were being built. Two or three children would run the cars over the roadway, messing it up, while one child, protesting loudly, spent her time straightening it out. Towers were built and knocked down, and trucks were being driven about, over, under, and into things. Children protested others' intrusions, but kept on about their own tasks. On another day, only two of the children used the block area. They built a roadway together, but afterward played with their own cars, up and down the roadway.

By three, night-time bladder control is usually accomplished. By four, most children can manage their toileting, needing help only with difficult clothing.

Emotional Development.   Emotions for threes and fours are largely on the surface. Lisette laughs as she runs about the room from person to person. She shows her excitement for life. Threes and fours are beginning to develop a sense of humor. They will watch adults and often laugh as they do. They may laugh simply to make others laugh.

At this age, children often begin to have fears. Monster books, such as *There's a Nightmare in My Closet* by Mercer Mayer and *Where the Wild Things Are* by Maurice Sendak, are appealing to them. The books affirm what children already know, "that monsters are really there," but through the books, the children are able to keep them in their place. Some children find it helps to have the light on in the closet or bedroom.

Threes and fours are curious and generous, and these traits sometimes get them in trouble. One little boy picked all the rosebuds from his neighbor's bush because they were pretty and he wanted them for his mother.

At this age, children are beginning to realize that others have feelings also. Lisette, when told that she must be careful or a block would fall on Tom's head, asked why. The teacher replied that it would hurt Tom. Lisette looked startled and said, "hurt him?" The teacher replied, "Yes, it would hurt you if it fell on your head, wouldn't it?" Lisette touched her head and said, "Yes." Then Lisette continued with a surprised look, "It would hurt you?" The teacher again nodded yes. Lisette summed it all up by saying "I would cry." Lisette is beginning to understand that others can be hurt just the same as she. She is beginning to decenter, to see herself as separate from others, but to understand that others have feelings, opinions, and ideas just as she does.

Cognitive Development.   Threes and fours manipulate their environment and make discoveries about it. They begin to generalize from one situation to another. One four watched her mother nurse the new baby for the first time, and asked what the baby was doing. The mother explained that the baby was getting some milk so she could grow. The child stood back, looked at the mother's other breast, and asked if "coffee came out of that one." She had recently been to a self-service restaurant and had seen her mother get milk from one spout for her and coffee from the other for herself. The generalization that she was making was logical to her: if there are two sources of drink, one will have milk in it, the other coffee.

Preschoolers are able to add and subtract one or two objects when they are personally and concretely involved. One four-year-old, when told to put the silverware out for dinner, got two spoons to put on the table. She placed one at her place and the other at her mother's, then looked around and said, "Mommy, I need two more, one for daddy and one for Stevie." Children also begin very rudimentary *classification* using one attribute alone. From experience they can clean up the room after play and put dishes in the cupboard, the silverware together, and the dress-up clothes in the clothing box. The classification may start out with one attribute and then suddenly switch. Lisette was arranging the hats, gloves, and shoes on shelves in the housekeeping area. She had two hats on one shelf, and two shoes on the next. On the third shelf she put one white glove and a white hat. When asked about it, she replied, "The hats go here, the shoes go here, and the whites go here." When asked where the gloves went, she merely shrugged.

Vocabulary and sentence structure are developing very rapidly. By the fifth birthday, the normal preschooler has mastered 90 percent of her language, although she may continue to make grammatical errors forever (Lenneberg, 1967, p. 229). Lisette has not yet completely distinguished subject and object, "he" and "him." One time she tells the teacher "He's under the table," and the next she reverts to the younger pattern of "Him under the table." She does the same thing when dropping the helping verbs, as in "Where this one go?" then "Where does it go?"

Threes and fours talk as they act, and they act out their thoughts. The language is often a monologue. At times it's almost as if they are trying to put words to what their muscles are doing or to explain their actions to themselves. Mark is talking to himself as he is playing with a play school bus and toys. He moves the bus and closes the door. "Close the door, close the door to the bus," he says. He reopens the door, takes out a little man, and puts him on the seesaw, which starts to swing. "He's swinging, look he's swinging, look he's swinging."

Early Primary Years (Five to Six Years)

Bob is six years old and is enjoying his first-grade experience. Today he has brought the tooth he lost the day before to school. It is carefully wrapped in tissue and placed in a box that fits handily into his pocket. During writing period, with his tooth displayed before him, he composes a letter to the tooth fairy. In composing his letter, he asks for help with the word "gymnastics." The teacher asks him to sound out the word. He succeeds, except for "tics," which he wants to spell "tiks." The teacher then gives him the correct spelling. This is Bob's letter.

> Dear Tooth Fairy
>   I lost my tooth in gymnastics. When I got home I opened the case and I lost my tooth. Mom and I looked all over for it but we didn't find it then, but when Mom was tieing her shoe to go to the middle school, she found it. So my tooth had a rough time getting here.
>   Happy valitim day,
>   Love, Bob

At math time the teacher had taken the children outside with meter sticks, paper, pencil, and assignments to measure specific things on the playground. Bob and Jim worked together industriously, carefully measuring the distances between the bases of the big slide and the big tree. When they finished their assigned measurements, the teacher suggested that they measure something of their choosing until the others had finished. Bob suggested the slide, and he and Jim ran over to it. Bob agilely and quickly climbed to the top of the slide; Jim was at the bottom. Both extended their sticks, but they didn't meet. Jim said, "I'll come up." He grabbed the side of the slide with both hands and walked up the front of the slide. He then lay down and held on, yelling, "Sue, pass me the meter stick." Sue did, and Jim abutted it to Bob's stick. Still the entire length of the slide wasn't measured. Bob ran down from the slide, but Jim lost his grasp before Bob could get to him and slid down, Jim said, "Let's try again, but you take both sticks and then run fast when I get up there." The performance was repeated, but this time Bob quickly slid the first stick to Jim. When Jim had it in place, Bob let go of the stick and ran quickly to the front of the slide. He had just got the stick in place when Jim came crashing down. Bob said, "We almost got it. I bet I could ran faster next time."

In the first years of school, five- and six-year-olds are expanding their knowledge of the world and the universe. Certainly their language grows, but more in terms of vocabulary and discovering that words have more than one meaning. Physically, their bodies develop less rapidly, though physical strength and prowess have increased. Bob and Jim are agile as they use their bodies for climbing the slide. Jim shows considerable strength in his arms and legs as he climbs up the face of the slide and holds on. They are willing to persist in the task and get better at doing it. The boys elected to do this project together, and it is not uncommon for children of this age to prefer to play with other children of their own sex. They can plan cooperatively and figure out things as long as they are acting on them. Events that happened in the past are remembered. Bob recaptures an event that happened the day before in his letter. He uses complex language even in writing.

Physical Development.   Children at this age vary greatly in height and weight, but all fives and sixes are agile. They continue to refine fine- and gross-motor skills. They can hop, skip, climb, jump, run, and dance, and some begin participating in sports like bicycling, skiing, swimming, skating, and gymnastics. Bob and Jim both manage the big slide with ease and agility. Sixes are quite willing to try things out, even if they stumble a bit. Jim, without regard for falling, tackled climbing up the front of the slide. Both stopped only when they'd completed the task to their satisfaction.

Fives and sixes are agile and are continuing to refine large and small motor skills.

Five- and six-year-olds' fine-motor skills are developed so they can write, although not necessarily on the line or in a restricted space. Letters are not uniform, and reversals are still common.

Five- and six-year-olds now draw the human figure, though the range in ability is wide. In one first grade, the teacher asked children to draw themselves. The pictures ranged from that of a child who drew a huge head, a triangular body with arms and legs protruding, round hands, and stick fingers to that of one who drew herself in excellent proportions with hands in pants pockets, curly hair, glasses tinted brown, and wearing her favorite Superwoman shirt.

Social Development.   Fives and sixes, as they start school, become increasingly social. They form friendships. Five-year-olds tend to move in and out of small groups and are usually cooperative and helpful. Fives still enjoy interacting with both sexes. They can assume and carry out small tasks in maintaining both the home and the classroom. Sixes become more assertive and sometimes seem bossy. They like to make rules and are rather dogmatic about having them obeyed. They also change the rules frequently and become tattletales if the rules aren't obeyed.

In one first grade, children made a class rule that only two people could write on the chalkboard at a time. Most of the time the girls used the chalkboard. One day when two boys started to write, two girls came to take over, insistent that only girls could write on the chalkboard because only boys could use the carpentry table. They were very sure of the two rules and insisted that the rules be obeyed. When the teacher stepped in, saying that the rules stated only the number of given children in an area and did not specify the gender, the girls wanted to change the rule to make chalkboards for girls only. Gender role identity and gender role stereotyping are becoming more evident. By the end of age six, depending on many societal, situational, cognitive, and biological factors, girls and boys may insist that certain behaviors are not appropriate for the other sex, as the girls in this class did. These children often choose to be with their own rather than the opposite sex. Freud called this period the latency period and maintained that it lasts until puberty (Clarke-Stewart & Freidman, 1987, pp. 337–338).

Children are eager to participate in games, but they have a strong need to win. It's not unusual that halfway through a game that they are losing, they'll suddenly change the rules. Though they enjoy team games, they like to be first and will pout if they lose. They're likely to blame their loss on someone or something else. Nevertheless, they soon recover from their disappointments and go on to play again. Fives and sixes tend to be outgoing, self-assured, and socially conforming.

Emotional Development.   Fives and sixes go through periods of ups and downs emotionally. Five-year-olds are beginning to be able to express their feelings in socially accepted ways. They're expanding their understanding of the emotions they are experiencing and are able to attach words to express them. They may even do so in rather poetic terms, as one boy did when riding in a car on a beautiful autumn day. The family was listening to bright, spritely music from the radio, when the child leaned against his mother and exclaimed, "Oh Mommy, we're so lucky to have music to match the color of the leaves."

By six, the rather placid five-year-old may have turned into a child in emotional ferment, capable of wild outbursts of joy and sudden shifts to tears. Parents may be startled to have a child come home from school and scream, yell, and storm about for five minutes and then come to the kitchen, hug them, and chatter away about the wonderful day at school. Sixes often have stormy relations with their parents and threaten to run away. They also enjoy humor, and giggle, whisper, and act silly at times.

Children are beginning to be aware of their emotions and are sometimes alarmed and puzzled by the conflicting feelings they have. They may love their parents one minute and hate them the next. Then they worry that their feelings may hurt the other person. Children at this stage are forced to learn to wait their turn, share, and lose in games they so desperately want to win. They are having to learn to control these feelings and to wait to have their needs met.

Cognitive Development.   During the kindergarten and first grade, early primary children acquire a great many intellectual and academic skills. They become aware that symbols have meanings and that there is a technique for figuring out these symbols. In two years, many children (although not all) master the rudimentary skills of reading and writing words that they've heretofore heard and spoken.

As they become more skilled in *decoding* and *encoding* skills, they begin to learn new concepts from the printed page. The normal rate and manner in which children learn these skills varies greatly. A few five-year-olds can read beyond their experiential background, while others are eight years old before they are comfortable with reading.

Reading for many six-year-olds involves physical as well as mental activity. Many need a finger or a marker to follow the line of text. They need to say the words out loud to understand what they mean. Bob, as indicated in the vignette, has mastered many of the beginning skills. He can also write a story that has a beginning and an end. He can listen to the sounds of letters and then reproduce them in writing, as he did with the word "gymnastics."

The early primary children are interested in numbers and can do concrete types of similar problems. They can and do memorize number facts, although they still need a great many concrete examples before developing more abstract numerical concepts.

Concepts of time and space are difficult, but these children do have a sense of their own past and future. Six-year-olds are especially interested in their parents' past, although they might confuse it with ancient history.

Sequences of historical time and large numbers do not have much meaning. One five-year-old, during a reenactment of the Thanksgiving story, related that "about 100 years ago, God was born, and about twenty hundred years ago Indians was born, and about two hundred years ago there was cowboys and Indians out in the West."

Children still believe (or pretend to) in Santa Claus, the Easter bunny, and the tooth fairy. Fantasy may be fun, but Bob seemed quite serious about the tooth fairy.

Language development is nearly complete for six-year-olds. New words and complexity of language continue to develop, however. Vocabularies increase, and children become aware that words have more than one meaning. Sometimes they get confused and even frightened because of misunderstandings. Often the misunderstandings are amusing to the adult. Bob told his teacher that he would be going into the hospital and wouldn't have a good Thanksgiving vacation. (He had a middle ear infection and needed to get some small drainage tubes replaced.) When the teacher asked why he was going to the hospital, he replied, "I got to get my tubes tied."

Later Primary Years (Seven to Eight Years)

Jenny is a very alert and active seven-and-a-half-year-old. She is sitting at the kitchen table doing her homework. She is very intent upon her task and seems oblivious to her parents washing dishes and a friend who is copying recipes. Jenny quickly glances about the room, and she starts to shuffle her feet back and forth underneath the table.

She is bent forward at the waist, sitting near the edge of her chair. Her complete attention seems to be focused on a piece of lined writing paper. She holds a wide green pencil in her right hand. It seems that all of her muscles in her right arm and especially her fingers are strained as she attempts to make the letter *L*. Her right hand squeezes the pencil hard, almost as if she is afraid someone will snatch it from between her fingers.

All of Jenny's attention is focused on her effort in writing the cursive capital letter *L*. Her left arm and hand are positioned so as to hold her piece of paper correctly. Jenny's shuffling of her feet continues. She viciously erases her writing and attempts another *L*, then erases this letter. Suddenly her bottom lip protrudes in a pout. She bites into it with her upper teeth as if in deep concentration. Her facial muscles tense. Her feet are still. She writes another *L* and then slumps back in her chair, letting her arms relax while her legs go limp.

Jenny's father pulls up a chair next to her while she sighs in discouragement. "How do you make a capital *L* in writing?" she asks. As she speaks, she seems to relax. Jenny's father looks at the *L* Jenny has made, which looks more like a *T*. Jenny watches her father intently as he takes a piece of paper from her writing table. She props her head on bent elbows. Her father begins to demonstrate making the *L* saying, "You see what I'm doing?" "Here, don't lift your pencil from the paper," and "understand now?" Jenny's body relaxes; she smiles and nods as her father continues to show her how to make the letter. Suddenly Jenny sits bolt upright and protests. "Tracy says that *this* is how you make an *L*," indicating with her right forefinger the *T*-like letters she had written earlier.

Jenny sits back in her chair, folds her arms, and awaits her father's response. Her father stands up and says, "Perhaps Tracy is right." Then he leaves the room. Jenny sits straight up in her chair, resumes the "proper" writing position, and writes one of Tracy's *T*-like letters. Quickly she erases it and glances over to the paper where her father has written a few letters. The tension disappears from her facial muscles, although she still squeezes her pencil tightly. She seems relaxed as she makes and practices several of the letters that her father has made (Ashford, 1980).

Seven- and eight-year-olds are expanding their horizons and in many ways are pleasant and fun to be with. They are curious about their world and at times enter into conversations in an adult fashion. Subtle body changes are taking place. Facial features and body physique are altering. Sevens and eights are independent and industrious. They are still asking for help or advice, but sometimes refuse to accept it when it's contrary to the peer group.

Jenny wants her father to help her, but when his letter didn't conform to her perception of what her friend said, she refused his help. When he left, however, she was willing to try it his way. Jenny kept at the task, struggled with it, and finally settled down to practice the skill. The seven's body movement is contained. Jenny shows her tension, but in a contained way, by shuffling her feet, tightly holding her pencil, and pursing her lips. When she isn't happy with her work she erases it to try again.

Physical Development.   During this period, children are making steady and regular progress in both fine-motor and gross-motor skills. Jenny grasps her pencil tightly, but in the proper way. She holds the paper as she was instructed and can control where the letters go on the page.

Interest and opportunity give rise to a wide variation in abilities and types of skills. Children have more consistent energy at this point and usually are willing to try out new skills and to practice and perfect them. Jenny attempting her *L* in *cursive writing* is an example.

Now children can ride, run, jump, and climb with greater fluidity and accuracy. They can throw a ball better and farther. Their writing improves, as do their drawing and painting. Artistic endeavors become more elaborate. Team as well as individual sports are pursued. Children have devel-

Sevens and eights are independent and industrious.

oped laterality. They can identify not only their own left and right hands and feet, but also the left and right sides of others.

Social Development.   Just as the seven- and eight-year-olds make steady progress in physical capacities, they also make progress in social interactions. Friendships form; close pals appear; and by the end of the period strong association with peer groups has started to form. Children take on the modes of dressing, walking, and talking as well as the values and habits of the peer group. Jenny shows some inkling of that when she wants to model her *L* after her friend's. However, at seven, the peer group influence is still fluid. (Jenny eventually accepts her father's advice.) Rejecting and making fun of the odd one often begins as groups start to form.

This period is the time when children start collecting things, show an interest in belonging to clubs, and become avidly interested in playing table games. They become interested in childhood rituals, such as not stepping on cracks, walking under ladders, or wishing on chicken bones.

Awareness of gender-related activities starts with the six-year-olds as they seek gender identity. They can be rigid in their ideas of what girls and boys can and cannot do. By eight, however, children seem more secure in their sexual identity and are willing to agree that many activities can be appropriate for people of either sex. These attitudes are greatly influenced by societal, parental, social class, and peer mores and expectations.

Emotional Development.　　Emotionally the seven- and eight-year-olds are separating from family. As they make new friends and acquaintances, they form new attachments. They're developing the ability to see things from another perspective and are able to be more emphatic. At the same time, they're very sensitive and get their feelings hurt easily. They find it hard to take criticism and feel slighted or dejected when classmates scorn or ridicule them.

Sevens and eights are delightful to be with as their sense of humor is expanding. They seem possessed with telling jokes and riddles. Elephant jokes abound and are told as if they were original and newly invented.

Sometimes these children have difficulty starting activities. Once under way, however, they can and will persist to the end. Jenny has trouble practicing her *L* and erases a great deal. She is dissatisfied with her own work, gets help, and rejects it, but still persists until she's achieved her goal to her own satisfaction.

Since children of this age are collectors, they begin to develop a sense of possessiveness and will take care of their own belongings. They can and do assume responsibilities for home and school tasks. Certainly there are different personality traits and a variety of responses in assuming responsibility for self.

Now a sense of conscience develops. Children distinguish between good and bad, and may be rigid about the terms being absolute. Fantasy and fairy tales are still reassuring because in them good is rewarded and evil punished. At seven, children define a rule as something that one is not to do. They obey because of concern with future punishments. By eight, some children may be moving toward defining a rule as something you are supposed to do (Mussen, Conger, & Kagan, 1980, p. 294).

Sevens and eights want to please and be good. They're ready to take responsibility and accept the consequences of their actions, but they do alibi and blame others for what happened. They may even begin to fabricate stories about their actions (Gesell, Ilg, & Ames, 1974).

Cognitive Development.   Sevens and eights are in the concrete operational period of development, the time when new ways of thinking arise. Children of this age are able to use the understandings gained at earlier ages and apply them to a wide range of problems. Though some evidence suggests that preschoolers can conserve a small number of objects or, due to extraordinary environmental conditions, can conserve quantity, there is definitely a qualitative difference in the seven- or eight-year-olds' ability to conserve (Gleitman, 1986, pp. 484–485). By seven or eight children are beginning to realize that two balls of clay can change shape and still have the same amount of clay. They know that objects can be put into classes by specific attributes and that they can belong to more than one class at a time. Children see relationships between objects and put them in order from bigger to smaller or brighter to darker. They can conduct these operations as long as they are dealing with the concrete or familiar world, but they are not yet able to hypothesize or conjecture about what might be.

Because of this ability to think logically, children are rapidly expanding their knowledge about their world. They are aware of time and how slowly or quickly it passes. They learn to tell time and to understand the calendar in terms of weeks, months, and years. They become interested in historical events.

Their interest in the world community is expanding, and they begin to understand human contributions and destructiveness in terms of the universe. They can make judgments and decisions relative to the community as well as themselves, though often these decisions are intuitive rather than reasoned.

Eights enjoy doing projects. Their attention span is much longer, and they can plan, stay with, and carry out a project, sometimes over weeks. Basic skills of reading, writing, and computing are being mastered. Many now read for enjoyment and can solve mathematical problems of increasing difficulty.

Chomsky (1970) maintains that language continues to develop through age ten. Seven- and eight-year-olds certainly can express themselves well. They may make grammatical errors but can and do correct themselves as well as others. They become better listeners and can relate stories and events in a logical sequence. They take an interest in poetry as a form of literature as well as a means of expressing feelings and thoughts. Children at this age are intrigued with the meter, metaphor, and imagery of language. As they grow to understand that words have more than one meaning, they delight in using language in a humorous way. When they are exposed to a rich language background, their own expressive language expands.

Becoming familiar with the way children grow and develop and the basic characteristics of children of different ages permits you to better understand and plan for their growth. Figure 2–1 summarizes children's normal growth and development, from infancy through late primary years, and charts the hallmarks of different ages.

Infancy (Birth through Twelve Months)

Physical

Development rapid.

Sleeping patterns change from sleeping and waking due to hunger and distress to sleeping through the night with two naps.

Eating patterns change from eating every three hours to eating regular meals three times a day.

Head-controlling muscles develop. By four months baby enjoys holding up head.

Eyes begin to focus and baby begins to visually explore the environment.

Grasps objects beginning about sixteen weeks. Can grasp and let go by six months.

Holds own bottle (six to eight months).

Rolls over intentionally (four to six months).

First tooth may appear around six months. Baby has about twelve teeth at age one.

Sits well alone, can turn and recover balance (six to eight months).

Raises self up at nine months. May even be able to pull self up to a standing position.

Starts to crawl at six months and to creep at nine to ten months.

May begin walking.

Social

First four or five months smiles socially.

Enjoys jostling and being frolicked with.

Recognizes mother or significant other.

Notices hands and feet and plays with them.

Recognizes self in mirror.

By six months likes to play alone but also likes company.

Begins to be wary of strangers.

Cooperates in games like peek-a-boo and pat-a-cake.

Imitates actions of others.

Emotional

Differentiates crying because of discomforts such as being hungry, cold, or wet.

Shows emotions by overall body movements such as kicking, arm waving, facial expressions.

Begins to show pleasure when needs are being met.

By six months shows affection by kissing and hugging.

Shows signs of fearfulness.

Pushes away things he or she doesn't like.

Cognitive

Discriminates mother from others first, later discriminates familiar faces from strangers (five – eight months).

Explores world through looking, mouthing, grasping.

Inspects things a long time.

Figure 2–1

Chart of developmental characteristics, birth through eight years of age

First signs of awareness of objects as he or she protests their disappearance.

Discovers ability to make things happen and delights in doing so by repeating the action several times.

Between six and twelve months beginning of object permanency develops as baby recognizes an object has been taken away and looks for a hidden object in place where it was hidden.

Beginning of intentionality occurs. Baby can get an object by pulling it toward himself or herself and will remove an obstacle to get an object.

Becomes increasingly curious about surroundings.

Language

At two to four months coos, chuckles, babbles, and gurgles.

Vocalizes a variety of vowel and consonant sounds as well as sounds of the environment.

Around six months, first "ma ma" or "da da" appears.

Begins to jabber and to imitate words and intonation patterns.

Waves "bye-bye."

Understands common objects and looks to them when person says words.

Appears to understand simple requests.

Responds to music with body movements (nine–twelve months).

Toddlers (One- and Two-Year-Olds)

Physical

Beginning to develop many motor skills.

Teething continues to about eighteen months, all twenty teeth by two years.

Large muscles develop. Can crawl well, stand alone (at just about a year), and push chair around.

Starts to walk about fifteen months, may be still wobbly at eighteen months.

Places ball in and out of box.

Releases a ball with throwing thrust.

Creeps downstairs backwards.

Fine-motor skills develop. Can stack two blocks, pick up a bean, and put objects into a container. Starts to use spoon.

Puts on simple things, such as an apron over head.

By end of eighteen months scribbles with a crayon in vertical or horizontal lines.

Turns pages of a book.

During second year, walks without assistance.

Runs, but often bumps into things.

Jumps up and down.

Walks up and down stairs with one foot forward.

Holds glass with one hand.

Stacks at least six blocks and strings beads.

Opens doors and cupboards.

Scribbles look like spirals, loops, and rough circles.

Hand preference starts to emerge.

Starts day control of elimination.

Social

At one year meager sense of differentiation between self and other.

Approaches mirror image socially.

By eighteen months distinguishes between the terms *you* and *me*.

Spontaneous play, self-absorbed play, but notices newcomers.

Imitative behavior becoming more elaborate.

Identifies body parts.

Responds to music.

By two socialization buds. Is less interested in playing with parent and more with a peer.

Parallel play begins.

Learns to distinguish between self and others.

Ambivalent about moving out and exploring.

Becomes aware of owning things and may become very possessive.

Emotional

At one year is amiable.

At eighteen months is resistant to change. Often suddenly won't let mother out of sight.

Tends to rebel, resist, fight, run, and hide.

No sense of guilt.

Perceives emotions of others.

Humor begins—will laugh at mislabeling of objects or events (like eye for mouth).

By two beginning to experience guilt. Beginnings of a conscience.

Negative—says *no* emphatically. Shows willfulness.

Exuberant in laughing and jumping.

Cognitive

Mental Imagery: looks for things that are hidden, recalls and anticipates events, moves beyond here and now, begins a temporal and spatial orientation.

Deductive Reasoning: searches for things in more than one place.

Memory: deferred imitation—sees an event and imitates it later. Remembers names of objects.

Object permanence completed by end of period.

By two to three distinguishes between black and white and may use color names.

Distinguishes one from many.

Uses 1, 2, 3 in rote counting but often not in rational counting.

Thinks through muscles—acts out what he or she says and talks as he or she does things.

Takes apart things and tries to put them back together.

Has sense of time in remembering events and knows terms *today* and *tomorrow*, but mixes them up.

Figure 2–1 *(continued)*

Language

Talks in fluent and inflected jargon.

Jargon disappears (twenty-four months).

Words accompany or replace gestures to express wants or needs.

Responds to simple requests.

By eighteen months has mastered four-fifths of English phonemes.

Has vocabulary between twenty and fifty words at eighteen months.

At eighteen months has "one-word sentence" and begins to put two words together.

Between two and three years rapid growth of language. Knows 300 to 1,000 words. Beginning grammar. Basic pronouns *I* and *mine*.

Develops two- to three-word sentences.

Becomes aware of language and plays with it, repeating new words and phrases as if practicing.

Enjoys rhythm and patterns of language and will repeat nursery rhymes and jingles.

Likes to hear same story over and over again.

Preschooler (Three- and Four-Year-Olds)

Physical

Expansion of physical skills.

Rides a tricycle.

Pushes a wagon.

Runs smoothly and can stop easily.

Climbs jungle gym ladder.

Walks stairs with alternating feet.

Can jump with two feet.

Has high energy level.

By four can do a running broad jump.

Begins to skip pushing one foot ahead of another.

Can balance on one foot.

Keeps relatively good time in response to music.

Expanding fine-motor skills for dressing: works zippers, maybe even buttons.

Developing control with scissors—cuts paper in half.

Holds paper with one hand while writing with the other.

Some may be able to cut paper on a line.

Night control of elimination.

Social

Becoming more social.

Moving from parallel play to beginning associative play. Does joint activities.

Awareness of racial differences and sexual differences.

Helpful mainly because of interest in matching words to actions.

Beginning of independence.

By four growing sense of initiative and self-reliance.

Becoming aware of basic sex identity.

Imaginary playmates not uncommon (may appear as early as two-and-a-half).

Emotional

Growing inner control over own behavior.

Expanding humor. (Laughs when adults laugh or over an incongruous event (like the dog scolding you for misbehaving).

Less negativism.

Beginning of phobias and fears that may continue until age five.

At four years intentional lying may begin, but child outraged by parents' white lies.

Cognitive

Beginning problem-solving skills. Stacks blocks and may kick them down to see what happens.

Learns to use listening skills as a means of learning about world.

Drawings at three still scribbling but in one direction and less repetitive.

At four drawings represent what child knows and thinks is important.

Thinking is perceptually bound to one attribute and characteristic. "Why?" questions abound.

Everything in the world has a reason but in accordance with child's own knowledge.

Egocentric thinking persists.

Begins to sort out fantasy from reality.

Language

Rapid language growth by end of year. Uses well-formed sentences and complex grammar.

At three talks in a monologue as if practicing own language as acts out adult roles and while carrying out own activities.

By four child has mastered about 90 percent of phonetics and syntax of language but still may overgeneralize verb tenses, plurals, pronouns.

By four can engage in a conversation by taking turns at speaking

Has discovered bathroom words and enjoys using them to shock.

Early Primary (Five- and Six-Year-Olds)

Physical

Well controlled and constantly in motion.

Often rides a bicycle as well as a tricycle.

Can skip with alternating feet and hop.

Greater control of fine-motor skills. Beginning to use tools, such as toothbrush, saws, scissors, pencils, hammers, needles for sewing.

Handedness well established—can identify hand used for writing or drawing.

Can dress self but may still have trouble tying shoe laces.

At six beginning to lose teeth.

Social

Very social—visits with friends on one's own.

Very self-sufficient.

Persists longer at a task. Can plan and carry out activities and return to project next day.

Figure 2–1 *(continued)*

Plays with two or three friends often just a short time only and then switches play group.

Beginning to conform. Is very helpful.

By six becoming very assertive. Often bossy, dominating a situation and ready with advice.

Needs to be first—has difficulty losing.

Possessive and boastful.

Craves affection. Often has a love/hate relationship with parents.

Sex roles becoming more refined. Has tendency to sex-type.

Becomes clothes-conscious.

Emotional

Sense of humor continues.

Learns right from wrong.

At five begins to control emotions and is able to express them in socially approved ways.

Quarrels frequently, but quarrels are of short duration.

At six often there is shift in emotions and child seems to be in an emotional ferment. New tensions appear with attending school all day.

Temper tantrums or angry outbursts may appear.

Giggles over bathroom words.

Develops a conscience at five, but actions seen as all good or bad. At six acceptance of rules develops and often a rigid insistence that they be obeyed (at least by others).

May become a tattletale.

Cognitive

Beginning of conservation of amount and length.

Interested in letters and numbers. Some begin printing or copying letters and numbers. Counts.

Knows most colors.

Recognizes one can get meaning from the printed word.

Has a sense of time but mainly child's own time. Knows when events take place in child's day or week.

Recognizes own space and can move about by self in familiar territory.

At the end of six years has begun reading, writing, and calculating. Range of ability in these areas is great.

Even at end of six years some may still need to vocalize when reading and may still make some reversals both in reading and writing.

Language

Very articulate (over 2,500 word vocabulary).

Sometimes *l*, *r*, or final *sh* may still be difficult to pronounce.

Often misunderstands words and uses them in a humorous manner.

Moving from fantasy to reality.

Uses language to control others.

Incessant talker.

Late Primary (Seven- and Eight-Year-Olds)

Physical

Great variation in height and weight, but rate of growth slows.
Masters physical skills for game-playing and enjoys team sports.
Is willing to repeat a skill over and over to mastery.
Increases in fine-motor performance—can draw a diamond correctly and form letters well.
Has sudden spurts of energy.
Loss of baby teeth continues and permanent teeth appear.
Physique begins to change. Body more proportionately developed and facial structure changes.

Social

Beginning to prefer own sex—has less boy/girl interaction.
Peer groups begin to form.
Security in sex identification.
Self-absorption.
Begins to work and play independently.
Can be argumentative.
Seven still not a good loser and often a tattletale.
By eight plays games better and not as intent on winning.
Conscientious—can take responsibility for routine chores.
Less selfish. Able to share. Wants to please.
Still enjoys and engages in fantasy play.

Emotional

Difficulty in starting things but will persist to end.
Worries that school might be too hard.
Beginning of empathy—sees others' viewpoint.
Sense of humor expressed in riddles, practical jokes, and nonsense words.
Discriminates between good and bad, but still immature.
Is sensitive and gets hurt easily.
Has sense of possession and takes care of possessions (makes collections).

Cognitive

Attention span is quite long.
Can plan and stay with a task or project over a long period.
Interested in conclusions and logical ends.
Aware of community and the world.
Expanding knowledge and interest.
Some sevens read well and by eight really enjoy reading.
Can tell time—aware of passage of time in months and years.
Interested in other time periods.
Conscious of others' work and their own. May comment "I'm good at art, but Sue is better at reading."
Differences in abilities widening.

Figure 2–1 *(continued)*

Language
   Good listener.
   Makes conversation and running comments on what he or she is doing.
   Can express self orally and in writing, even rather poetically.

Sources for Chart
ASCD Developmental Characteristics of Children and Youth. Washington,
Association for Supervision and Curriculum Development, 1975.
Bayley, Norma. *Bayley Scales of Infant Development.* New York: Psychological
Corporation, 1969.
Gesell, Arnold. *The First Five Years of Life: A Guide to the Study of the Preschool
Years.* New York: Harper and Row Publishers, 1940.
Gesell, Arnold, Ilg, Frances L., & Ames, L. B. *Infant and Child in the Culture of
Today.* New York: Harper and Row Publishers, 1974.
Linder, Toni W. Transdisciplinary *Play-Based Assessment: A Functional Approach to
Working with Young Children.* Baltimore, MD: Brookes, 1990.
U. S. Department of H. E. W. *Day Care Serving Infants.* Washington: Author, 1971.

Learning to Observe

Children at different ages exhibit behaviors similar to those discussed in this chapter, but children's development is not linear and children do not exhibit the same behaviors at the same ages. Generalizations have been made about children because of the vast research that has been done through both experimental and ethnographic studies. Careful observations and recording of behaviors by researchers have led to our understandings of what infants, toddlers, preschoolers, and schoolchildren are like at different ages. By understanding children's abilities and potentials, we are better able to interact with them to assist them in reaching new levels of achievement.

Studying what others have discovered is important, but in order to truly understand children, you must also study children. Undoubtedly you do observe what children do, but it is important to go beyond the normal kind of observing and train yourself to become a careful observer who has studied the theorists and is able to observe how the children you are working with are both like others yet unique in their development. By developing such a skill, you then become skilled in understanding the children you teach. You are better prepared to change children's lives by helping them to reach higher levels of learning and development. A teacher who knows how to observe and connect those observations to that knowledge of child development can:

- Appraise children's behavior, understand their thinking and feelings, in order to make wise decisions about how and what to teach
- Judge children's progress and the effectiveness of their own teaching

All children go through similar stages, but each is a unique individual.

- Help solve children's problems by identifying the source or reasons for a child's behavior or learning difficulty
- Test out hunches or ideas in order to either confirm or reject records, judgments of others, or standardized scores.

Beginning

To *observe* means to perceive, to notice, to watch carefully in order to see or learn something. Obviously we perceive and notice all of the time without even being aware.

Think of the observing that takes place while driving. We attend to and notice other cars, the speed limit, pedestrians, and traffic signals. Once in the parking lot, observing continues. Now we not only note and attend to traffic, but we also focus our attention on empty parking spaces and on people exiting the building with car keys in their hands, all in an attempt to try to learn where a parking space is likely to be.

In a college classroom observing may become more deliberate. We note and attend to the instructor, listening to directions, lectures, or discussions. Deliberately, our observation focuses on specific things: when the exam will be, what is likely to be on it, how the other students act and respond.

When observing children in order to know and understand them, our observations become more deliberate, focused, and formal. Now observing is not tacit, as when driving, or even deliberate, as it is during a class, but it is focused, systematic, and guided by specific questions, hypothesis, or ideas.

Is Shashana really as well-adjusted and socially adroit as she seems, or is her behavior an act?

Why does Susan sit alone with her thumb in her mouth so much of the time? Why isn't she able to enter into a play group or find something to do?

Is Kim really going to be able to make it in kindergarten? What can I tell the kindergarten teacher about her strengths? Weaknesses?

What's wrong with Bryan? Why doesn't he like school? His father says it's a struggle each morning to get him from the car to the school and says he's always complaining that he "hates" school.

To learn from children by observing them takes more than informal, spontaneous observations. To study children requires the ability to be able to:

- Conduct objective observations that are free from your own feelings and are detailed.
- Conduct multiple observations in a variety of settings, using program goals as a guide, as well as event and time sampling.

Objectivity

Observing is not a precise, objective act. No two people will ever see the same thing. Watching a kindergarten child splashing bright paints randomly at the easel, one teacher observed that the child had a great deal of motor dexterity and excelled in the ability to express herself freely and creatively. Another teacher, observing the same scene, reported that the child had poor eye-hand-motor coordination, and lacked the ability to express herself symbolically.

One sees a five-year-old boy dressed in a small suit, vest, and bow tie as well-behaved, extremely polite, and coming from a fine family. Another observes a child too preoccupied with keeping clothes clean and who is restrained, inhibited, and can't enjoy being a child because of his clothes.

You only have to recall three people who witnessed the same event but described different versions of it. All of them witnessed a traffic accident, but one reported that it was caused by an absent-minded driver, another attributed it to a dog running along the road, and the third person said it was caused by a truck swerving into the wrong lane.

It is a fact. Observing can never be totally objective or independent of the observer. Whatever is observed passes through the filter of the observer's beliefs, biases, assumptions, history, understanding, and knowledge. The individual observer's biases, beliefs, and ideas dictate what is observed, how, when, and where. The individual always brings his or her own perception and interpretation to the observation.

Because observations are so dependent upon the individual, they are considered subjective in nature. The objectivity necessary for scientific evidence is not possible. How can one person's observations and perceptions of a child or a given incident be considered either valid or reliable evidence?

Accepting the fact that observations will always be subjective, effective teachers learn the skills necessary to observe more objectively. Effective teachers learn to decrease subjectivity and increase their ability to observe objectively by:

- Becoming aware of and admitting to their own feelings about situations
- Developing techniques of observing details and describing events in non-judgmental terms
- Avoiding making judgments on one or two observations by observing over time, accumulating multiple observations, and checking out hunches by making additional observations.

Becoming Aware of Your Feelings.   A student, Ms. G., was given the assignment of conducting an observation. She decided to focus on Juanita. Ms. G. observed that Juanita is very nervous and told the teacher, "Juanita is anxious and always uncomfortable in a group. She's nervous when completing any task, and is very nervous as she interacts with other children, even while playing."

The supervisor questioned the student, asking why she had made these judgments. She asked the student to repeat the observation, but this time to focus only on Juanita's behaviors, describing them without making any inferences.

This time the student observed that Juanita's hands shook as she poured the juice. She said that when juice spilled on the table, another student, Aliki, giggled and Juanita's face twitched and hands shook as she put the pitcher back on the table.

Later, the supervisor explained to Ms. G. that Juanita had a physical problem that resulted in muscle spasms and twitching. The problem had nothing to do at all with Juanita being nervous.

When observing, try to separate yourself, your own ideas, your past, and your biases from the situation. After discussing Ms. G.'s observation, the supervisor asked her how she felt when she first observed Juanita.

Ms. G. said, "I felt embarrassed, I was empathic toward Juanita." She added, "You see, my mother didn't let me play with other children when I was little. She said I would catch too many things from them, not just germs, but bad habits. As a result, when I got to kindergarten, I didn't know how to act with other children. I was always very nervous and, being nervous, always spilled things and made mistakes."

When observing, ask yourself how you really feel about the situation and why. The teacher who saw the child splashing paints at the easel as a sign of creativity had always wanted to be an artist. To her, the ability to splash paints randomly was expressing oneself creatively. The other teacher admitted to enjoying representational art, saying, "I never understood Picasso or any other impressionistic art works. It's hard for me to even like children's scribbles or make sense of them."

Once you've identified your own feelings, try to put them aside and focus attention only on the child's behaviors. Observing only the behavior will add a measure of objectivity. The student who observed Jenny writing the letter *L* at the kitchen table focused fully on Jenny's behaviors without trying to interpret them or judge them. She wrote, "She is sitting at the kitchen table doing her homework . . . she starts to shuffle her feet back and forth underneath the table. She is bent forward at the waist, sitting near the edge of her chair."

Observing Details and Describing Events in Nonjudgmental Terms. Learn to observe details. All of the details. Training yourself to observe details, really learning to look, helps avoid interpreting behaviors. Recall the details in the observation of Brian, the eighteen-month-old. "Brian backs into his chair. He then picks up the crayon in his right fist in an overhand grasp and begins to scribble vertically. Suddenly he drops the crayon, slaps his hands, and jumps off his chair." Rather than observing that the child dashed to the crayons and made a scribble, the details in this observation let the reader really come to know and understand the nature of toddlers.

Observe a child doing something as simple as walking into the room. Focus on the details. How does the child hold her shoulders? What is her facial expression? What is she wearing? How does she use her hands and arms as she walks? Does she say anything?

One person observed Alberto walking into the classroom. "Alberto was angry when he came into the classroom this morning." Another wrote, "Alberto stomped into the classroom, stamping each foot as he walked across the floor. His face was red. He frowned, wrinkling his forehead making his eyes appear as slits. His hands were clenched. He pulled his chair out from under the table with such force that the table slid across the floor. Slamming himself in the chair, he pulled himself to the table and put his hand on it."

The first observer interpreted Alberto's behaviors, the second described the behaviors in detail. Mood cues, facial features, and other details were described. While the interpretation of both observations may be that Alberto was angry when he walked into the classroom, the second observation, by describing details, avoided a premature conclusion.

By noting details and describing behavior in objective terms, you have better information that will enable you to check your observations with others. Many scholars in the field of early childhood have made detailed descriptions of behaviors, such as Gesell, Piaget, and Chomsky. Consult their descriptions and determine if the child you are observing is exhibiting similar behaviors. Try to determine their interpretations of the behavior and compare your own reactions to theirs. Ask teachers and students who are attuned to making good observations for their perceptions. Becoming objective does not mean always accepting the views of others, even those more expert than you. Instead, it is important to check your perceptions and biases in relation to others. It keeps you more open and allows you to consider alternative explanations.

Conducting Multiple Observations

One observation, no matter how detailed and complete, can never offer enough evidence to enable a teacher to know a child. If one observation were sufficient, then the conclusion would be that Alberto was truly an angry child. Which was not the case at all.

Setting.   Before reaching a conclusion, a number of observations, conducted over time, and in a variety of settings and situations, must take place. You might observe children:

- As they say goodbye to their parents in the morning
- When they enter the classroom
- On the play yard
- During circle time
- During the routines of dressing, washing, toileting, eating, and resting
- While they play by themselves
- Interacting with peers
- Interacting with adults
- During a directed activity
- Reacting or responding to other children
- At the end of the day, greeting parents as they leave the school
- In their home and neighborhood

Development.   Observations can focus on all aspects of the child's growth and development. Some might focus only on the child's physical growth, fine- and large-motor skills, or physical health. Others could focus on language development, describing receptive and expressive language usage or on the child's cognitive development. Children's social and emotional growth might serve as the focus of yet other observations.

Program Goals.   At other times, observations may revolve around the goals and objectives of the program. For instance, can behaviors be observed that indicate children are learning to solve problems, to observe their environment, to express doubts and ask questions? Is there evidence in children's behaviors that they are thinking about their experiences and using past experiences to help them solve problems? Are they exhibiting any behaviors that might be illustrative of their developing ability to use symbols?

Event Sampling.   Specific events or situations might also be observed. A specific behavioral problem, such as aggressive behavior, might be observed. One child-care center had a rash of biting behaviors. It wasn't just one child accidentally biting another but a number of children biting many times in any given period. The director hired a student to observe only the event of biting. The student noted when and where the biting occurred and gave all the details of what was happening when it took place, who was involved, and what happened after each incident. Based on the observations, it was concluded that biting behavior increased during transition times for the staff or when children were over tired. Extra staff was added, and the incidents of biting stopped.

The events sampled need not be negative. Teachers in one kindergarten program documented the success of their newly implemented program of cooperative learning by taking time to observe and make note of any cooperative behaviors the children exhibited. The two teachers involved each had a notebook full of observations of children initiating cooperative behaviors. Others have used event sampling to observe children's use of toys, sharing behaviors, interaction with adults, or peer interactions.

Time Sampling.   Another way to ensure that your observations are objective is to sample a child, or the group, using time sampling. Psychologists often observe behavior using a preset time schedule to make observations. This way, a measure of objectivity is guaranteed because when and what are observed are dictated by the time, not by the observer.

For example, if you are interested in understanding how a particular child is adjusting or learning, you might decide to observe the child, noting what she or he is doing, once every five or ten minutes. At those intervals, you would then look up from what you were doing and observe the child and record what she or he is doing.

Time sampling can be used to observe the entire group of children as well. The observer would, using a time schedule, observe the nature of the group activity throughout the day, week, or month. Observing individuals at the beginning of the school year, in the middle of the year, and near the end of a year, helps you to understand and know their growth and learning over the year.

The point of frequent observations is to gain a good description of a cross section of a child's life in your program so that you will really come to know each child as an individual by observing how the child acts in a variety of situations, over a period of time.

Guidelines for Recording Observations

Anecdotal Records.   Try to recall last week's class. Do you remember what the professor said? Wore? What was discussed? How the other students reacted? What you said and did?

It's easy to forget what one has observed. Because the purpose of observing children is to gain a better understanding of each child, you will need some type of record or notation to help you remember what you observed. Recording observations in the form of anecdotal records is a way of ensuring that your observations will be remembered. They can also serve as evidence or data that will be helpful in developing knowledge of each individual child you will teach.

The anecdotal records of the observations of Brian, Lisette, and other children in this chapter were written by Dr. Nita Barbour. Under her direction, one of her students wrote the observation of Jenny writing the letter *L*. These are examples of anecdotes that are useful in developing an understanding of children, their growth, development, and learning. They are vignettes of a behavioral moment in the life of a child. They describe complete episodes in detail using concrete language, like adjectives, adverbs, and action verbs, to describe the setting and behavior, and they include quotes of the child's conversation during that behavior moment.

The Setting.   An anecdote should give a description of the setting. It should include the date and time of the event and should describe the place, situation, people present, and the setting in which the action occurred.

Mood Cues.   You should also include mood cues, which are indications of how the other person might be feeling. Examples are descriptions of facial expressions, hand gestures, and voice inflections. These mood cues do not provide interpretations of feelings, but only describe the behaviors of the children.

Language Usage.   The way language is used affects the usefulness of an anecdote. An elephant, cat, and child each walk. The word *walk* is rather generic. Think of words that communicate more accurately. An elephant might lumber, a cat stalk, and a child skip. Use adverbs and adjectives to capture the nature of a child's walk. The child walked quickly, quietly, gently, hastily, loudly, into the room. Remember to use vivid language to describe the details: The child walked with head held high, arms swinging, fists clenched at sides, or with drooping shoulders.

Describe an Episode.   The anecdote should be extensive enough to cover the episode. The action is not left incomplete and unfinished, but is followed through to the point where a vignette of a behavioral moment in the life of a child is supplied. Every behavior has a beginning, middle, and end. Look back to the observation of Lisette, and you'll find several behavioral episodes fully described, each with a beginning, middle, and end. The first episode describes Lisette's arrival at school; the next, her interaction with two children, then with the dog, and finally the puzzle episode.

Each of these episodes is complete. How the behavior was initiated, who was involved, the actions of the child, reactions of others involved, and what happened as a result of the behavior are fully described.

Use Quotes.   When you use direct quotes in writing anecdotes, you allow people to speak for themselves rather than through your interpretations of what you think they said. If you quote people accurately, then you will not have to make inferences or judgments. Instead of writing "Judy was too tired to participate," which is an inference, it's more accurate and objective to write, "I can't do it," said Judy. "We went to Grandma's last night, and I didn't get home till late and I'm just too tired to build with you." To quote a child yelling at her mother, "I hate you!" is clearly more objective than writing, "Ingrid has difficulty relating with her mother."

Give Details.   Objectively writing and describing all of the details of a behavior without interpreting or making value judgments will help an anecdote meet the criteria of objectivity. Instead of writing, "Katrina doesn't get along well with other children," which is an interpretation of her actions, write "Katrina stood at the edge of the housekeeping area. Thumb in mouth, she hummed to herself as she bounced from one foot to the other. She cautiously moved toward the children, still humming and stood closer to them. Now she took her thumb from her mouth and smiled at Aleatha. Then still smiling, she made a grab for the doll Aleatha was carrying." A detailed anecdote avoids premature conclusions, that Katrina doesn't get along with others, with a more objective description of the behavior.

How to?   When learning to observe and write anecdotes or trying to improve observational skills, it is a useful exercise to practice writing complete anecdotes like the ones given in this chapter. These have been written by people who had the time and opportunity to sit and observe children, and they are complete, even extensive.

It is not realistic, however, to think that beginning teachers who struggle to keep everything running smoothing will have the luxury of sitting and only observing or the time to transfer their observations into complete anecdotal records. Experienced teachers, though, will still observe children and keep anecdotal records. Each teacher will find his or her own way of doing this.

One useful technique is to make a habit of keeping note cards and a pencil in a pocket or somewhere handy. Then as you observe a child, you can quickly jot down telegraphic notes on one of the cards. One teacher watched Aliki as she climbed up a slide, sat at the top calling, "Come and catch me, who will come and catch me?" When no one responded, Aliki carefully, slowly, and holding tightly to the sides of the slide, let herself slide down. The pride Aliki felt at her accomplishment showed all over her face and in her posture. She smiled broadly, holding her body straight and tall, full of confidence. She went back up the steps of the slide and this time let herself slide down quickly and with joy. The teacher observing Aliki wrote on a note card: "3/4/93 Aliki at slide . . . calling who come catch me . . . sliding down, confidence in face, smile, body."

Later the teacher transcribed her telegraphic record into a complete anecdote on her computer. Keeping a file on each child in her class, she used her anecdotal records when conferring with parents, and to make judgments regarding the curriculum.

To ensure that all children were observed, this teacher kept a box of file cards with each child's name at the top of the cards. Each day she would select two or three of the named cards from the file and several blank cards to carry with her during the day. In this way, she would focus on one or two observations of the named children. The blank cards were useful for recording incidents, like Aliki at the slide, that would be useful evidence of a child's growth, learning, or problems.

The idea of writing anecdotes on note cards is to collect a large number of short anecdotal records, which will, over time, provide an objective description of a child. At the end of a period of time, the anecdotes can be compiled and serve to report a child's progress, growth, development, and learning.

Recording Observations for a Case Study

The Case Study.   A case study is an intensive investigation conducted on the life of one child. The purpose is to gain a better understanding of the actual and potential adjustment, learning, and growth of a child. The heart of the case study is the anecdotal records collected on the child over a period of time and in a variety of settings and situations.

At the end of each of the following chapters in this text, you will find suggestions for conducting observations and recording anecdotes for a *Continuing Case Study* on a child. Even if you are not required to do so, select a child and begin a case study of one child's curriculum experiences in an early childhood program. After reading each of the chapters, use the suggestions in the *Continuing Case Study* to observe your selected child's behavior, adjustment, and achievement in each of the areas of school.

You may also want to conduct some time sampling observations to note the general adjustment of the child over a day or so. Time sampling has the advantage of providing an objective picture of a child's functioning in the school setting independent of observer biases or preconceived ideas. Or you may observe events, perhaps recording every instance of aggressive or cooperative behavior exhibited over a period of time. Or use your own ideas to conduct a case study of your child in school.

If you were to conduct a complete case study, other sources of evidence would also be collected. As the purpose of a case study is to come to know and understand the nature of an individual child, you need more evidence than just the observations of a child in a school setting.

The major source of evidence collected will be the anecdotal records of the child at home, school, and in the community. In addition, a case study requires sources of information such as:

• Cumulative records
• Home visits
• Life-space description
• Sample of the child's work
• Conferences with colleagues
• Interviews with the child

These are only examples of the sources of information that you could use to obtain a minimum understanding and a record of the child's adjustment and progress at school and at home. Information might be obtained from the child, other teachers, parents, and peers, or from existing records and files.

Before Beginning.   Before beginning to conduct a case study, realize that the basic purpose of the study is to understand and really know an individual child as that child reacts to the total environment at school and at home. Because the assumption is that you will be developing a very personal knowledge of a child, you will have to be aware of the need for confidentiality and informed consent. Informed consent is the agreement of the subject—or in this case, the subject's parent or guardian—to participate in the study after being fully informed of what it involves.

Informed consent implies that whenever human subjects are studied as closely as they are during a case study, they have the right to know they are being observed and to be guaranteed confidentiality. If you are conducting a case study as a part of a school program, either public or private, ask the teacher, principal, or director of the program if the school has previously collected parental consent permitting their children to be studied as a part of the regular school program. If this has not been done, or does not apply to students, then you will want to obtain consent from the child's parents before beginning.

Analyzing and Using Anecdotes or the Case Study

Once collected, all of the evidence is treated scientifically—reviewed, analyzed, and interpreted. Read through the collected anecdotes and other information. Now analyze your anecdotes. Try to find indications of the child's interaction with peers, adults, curriculum content, and the total environment. Look for recurring patterns of behavior in a variety of settings and situations. Can you see patterns of behavior regardless of setting? Do you see growth or lack of growth? What strengths in which areas of the child's life at school do you find? Areas of weakness? Are there areas of extreme behavior? Extreme achievement or failure?

Now write a final summary of the child, giving your interpretation of the child as you have come to know her or him through your continuing observations. You will want to reach tentative conclusions about the child's adjustment and adaptation in school. These conclusions, however, must remain tentative. No study, whether it involves numbers and tight controls or is more subjective, as are observations, can ever *prove* anything. Your summary, referring to actual observations, only offers suggestions, indications, or hypotheses of the nature of this child at the time he or she was being observed.

Through conducting a case study of one child in an early childhood program, by following the suggestions of the *Continuing Case Study* boxes, and by reaching some tentative conclusions, you will come to know an individual child intimately. You will come to know more than just this one child, however. You also will have gained invaluable insights and understanding of the growth and development, adjustment, and adaptation of all children, as well as knowledge about how to guide and teach them.

Summary

If you want to become a teacher who really cares and who can make a difference in children's lives, you will want to study children and come to know them. Just as the theorists of the past observed children and developed an understanding of their growth and development, so you will want to observe and study children. By becoming familiar with the hallmarks of growth and development that are characteristic of infants, toddlers, preschoolers and kindergartners, and primary-age children, you will be developing your own theories of children and understanding of their growth and development.

This understanding is the foundation from which your skills and abilities as a teacher will stem. The effectiveness of your interactions with children, your planning, and every curriculum experience you have with children will be based on your knowledge and understanding of the children.

Conducting a case study is one way to strengthen your understanding of children. As you begin your case study, relate your observations and findings to those of Freud, Erikson, Piaget, and Vygotsky.

Projects

Continuing Case Study

Begin a case study of one child. As you read each chapter, you will collect different types of evidence about how this child is functioning in his or her environment. After each observation you should write your percep-

tions of the way the child functions in relationship to the "textbook" view. Your first observation will be in relation to impressions of general growth and development. Throughout the day of this first observation, note the following: (a) physical characteristics; (b) movements, such as how the child walks, sits, and grasps objects; (c) people with whom the child interacts and the form the interaction takes; (d) involvement in classroom events, such as which ones, for how long, and with how much interest; and (e) a sample of the child's language.

1. Record the speech of a two-year-old for a period of at least five minutes. How does the child use speech to communicate needs? What words appear most frequently? What kind of sentences does the two-year-old create?
2. How do preschoolers use language and communicate with one another? Observe in a preschool setting and record preschoolers' language use during a free play situation for a five-minute period. How does the preschooler's language differ from the two-year-old's?
3. Observe children writing in a primary classroom. How many of the children look tense? What physical cues tell you they might be tense? How do they sit or grip the pencil? How many erase frequently in a five-minute span?
4. Ask a group of five-year-old children to draw a picture of a man. Collect the drawings and note their differences. How many children drew a man consisting of a circle, without trunk, and arms and legs coming from the circle? How many drew a trunk? Neck? Feet and hands? Can you draw any conclusions about variations in normal growth and development?
5. Preschoolers are developing social skills. Observe a group of three- and four-year-olds to note any times they demonstrate dawning social awareness, as in the case of Lisette. Now observe a group of five-year-old children and note what overall differences you see in social skill development between those two age groups.

Resources

Learning about normal children's growth and development is a lifetime project. This chapter provides a brief introduction to theories of children's growth and gives some of the hallmarks of normal development. To become better acquainted with human growth and development, you might read and study some of the psychology books found in the references, as well as the following texts.

Allen, K. E., & Marotz, L. (1989). *Developmental profiles: Birth to six*. Albany, NY: Delmar.

Ames, L. B., Gillespie, C., Haines, J., & Ilg, F. L. (1980). *The child from one to six: Evaluating the behavior of the preschool child*. London: Hamish Hamilton.

Beaty, J. J. (1994). *Observing development of the young child* (3rd ed.). New York: Merrill/Macmillan.

Garvey, C. (1984). *Children's talk*. Cambridge, MA: Harvard University Press.

Hendrick, J. (1992). *The whole child* (5th ed.). New York: Merrill/Macmillan.

Morrison, G. S. (1990). *The world of child development: Conception to adolescence*. Albany, NY: Delmar.

Piaget, J., & Inhelder, B. (1969). *The psychology of the child*. New York: Basic Books.

Schiamberg, L. B. (1988). *Child and adolescent development*. New York: Macmillan.

Webb, P. K. (1989). *The emerging child: Development through age twelve*. New York: Macmillan.

References

Ashford, C. (1980). *An observational assignment*. Unpublished course project, University of Maryland, Baltimore County, Baltimore, MD.

Bandura, A., & Walters, R. H. (1969). *Social learning and personality development*. New York: Holt, Rinehart & Winston.

Bayley, N. (1969). *Manual: Bayley scales of infant development.* New York: Psychological Corporation.

Berk, L. E. (1991). *Child development.* Boston: Allyn & Bacon.

Biber, B. (1977). Cognition in early childhood education: A historical perspective. In B. Spodek & H. J. Walberg (Eds.), *Early childhood education: Issues and insights* (pp. 41–65). Berkeley, CA: McCutchen.

Biddell, T. R. (1992). Beyond interactionism: Contextualist models of development. *Human Development, 35*(5), 306–315.

Biehler, R. R., & Hudson, L. M. (1986). *Developmental psychology: An introduction* (3rd ed.). Boston: Houghton Mifflin.

Blewitt, P. (1983). Dog versus collie: Vocabulary in speech to young children. *Developmental Psychology, 19,* 602–609.

Chance, P., & Fischman, J. (1987). The magic of childhood. *Psychology Today, 21*(5), 48–51, 55–58.

Chomsky, C. (1970). The acquisition of syntax in children from five to ten. In *MIT research monographs, vol. LVII.* Cambridge, MA: The MIT Press.

Chomsky, N. (1965). *Aspects of the theory of syntax.* Cambridge, MA: MIT Press.

Clarke-Stewart, A., & Freidman, S. (1987). *Children: Development from infancy through adolescence.* New York: John Wiley.

Dworetzky, J. P. (1990). *Introduction to child development* (4th ed.). New York: West.

Erikson, E. H. (1963). *Childhood and society* (2nd ed.). New York: Norton.

Fernald, A., & Simon, T. (1984). Expanded intonation contours in mother's speech to newborns. *Developmental Psychology, 20,* 104–113.

Freud, S. (1949). *An outline of psychoanalysis.* New York: Norton.

Gesell, A. (1940). *The first five years of life: A guide to the study of the preschool years.* New York: Harper & Row.

Gesell, A., & Ilg, F. L. (1940). *The child from five to ten.* New York: Harper & Row.

Gesell, A., Ilg, F. L., & Ames, L. B. (1974). *Infant and child in the culture today.* New York: Harper & Row.

Gleitman, H. (1986). *Psychology* (2nd ed.). New York: Norton.

Horowitz, F. D. (1987). *Exploring developmental theories: Toward a structural behavioral model of development.* Hillsdale, NJ: Lawrence Erlbaum.

Lenneberg, E. (1967). *Biological foundations of language.* New York: John Wiley.

Levine, C., Jakubowski, L., & Cote, J. (1992). Linking ego and moral development: The value consistency thesis. *Human Development, 35*(5), 286–301.

Linder, T. W. (1990). *Transdisciplinary play-based assessment. A functional approach to working with young children.* Baltimore, MD: Brookes.

Locke, J. (1969/1690). *Some thoughts concerning education* (4th ed.). New York: Dutton.

Maslow, A. H. (1968). *Toward a psychology of being.* New York: Van Nostrand Reinhold.

Mayer, M. (1969). *There's a nightmare in my closet.* New York: Dial.

Meadows, S. (1986). *Understanding child development: Psychological perspectives in an interdisciplinary field of inquiry.* London: Hutchinson.

Mussen, P. H., Conger, J. J., & Kagan, J. (1980). *Essentials of child development and personality.* New York: Harper & Row.

Piaget, J. (1952). *The origins of intelligence.* New York: International Universities Press.

Ratner, N. B., & Pye, C. (1984). Higher pitch in BT is not universal: Acoustic evidence from Quiche Mayan. *Journal of Child Language, 11,* 515–522.

Rousseau, J. J. (1947). *L'Emile ou l'education.* In O. E. Tellows & N. R. Tarrey (Eds.), *The age of enlightenment.* New York: Crofts. (Original work published 1762)

Scarr, S. (1992). Developmental theories for the 1990s: Development and individual differences. *Child Development, 63*(1), 1–19.

Sendak, M. (1963). *Where the wild things are.* New York: Harper & Row.

Skinner, B. F. (1974). *About behaviorism.* Princeton, NJ: Alfred A. Knopf.

Slobin, D. (1966). The acquisition of Russian as a native language. In F. L. Smith & G. A.

Miller (Eds.), *The genesis of language: A psycholinguistic approach* (pp. 129–248). Cambridge, MA: MIT Press.

Stone, L. J., & Church, J. (1984). *Childhood and adolescence: A psychology of the growing person* (5th ed.). New York: Random House.

Stroufe, L. A., Cooper, R. G., & Marshall, M. E. (1988). *Child development: Its nature and course*. Princeton, NJ: Alfred A. Knopf.

U.S. Department of Health, Education and Welfare. (1970). *Day care serving infants.* Washington, DC: Author.

Vygotsky, L. S. (1978). *Mind in society.* Cambridge, MA: Harvard University Press.

Wertsch, J. V. (1985). *Vygotsky and the social formation of mind*. Cambridge MA: Harvard University Press.

3

Individual Differences: The Effects of Diversity

How can humans be so alike and yet so different? Each child has his or her own unique way of developing and growing. One infant may approach the new environment with seriousness, taking it all in, quietly settling down to the business of nursing. Another will nurse only sporadically and squalls, fusses, and tenses up while adults try to comfort him.

After you read this chapter, you should be able to answer the following questions:

1. What factors contribute to differences in humans?

2. What rights has legislation provided for children with special needs?

3. What behavioral characteristics of children might suggest to you that they are gifted, bilingual, handicapped, or abused and have a right to special services under the law?

4. What are some considerations or strategies you could make in order to provide for different special needs children in your classroom?

Reasons for Diversity

A group of student teachers has returned from its first week of student teaching. The student teachers have been placed in suburban, city, and rural schools.

Clarence bursts out, "I have two Japanese students in my class, and one of them can't speak English at all. Although the other child speaks fluently in both English and Japanese, he gets real impatient having to translate for Yoshiko all the time. I don't know how I'm going to communicate with Yoshiko or get her not to depend on Haga."

"You think that's bad," Tanya pitched in. "We have five new kids, all of whom speak different languages at home. One speaks Spanish, another is Vietnamese, one, I think, is Hungarian, and the other two are Cambodian—but they don't seem to be able to speak very well even to each other. Some of the kids speak English, but not much, and I gather the parents speak a limited amount of English."

"My teacher is having real discipline problems," offers Janine. "We've got two kids on Ritalin, and she thinks more of the kids ought to be. They have real learning problems. They can't pay attention and are moving all over the place."

Jorge exclaims, "I think maybe one of my kids has been abused, and I'm in one of the wealthier schools in the district. She has been complaining about being hungry every day, she looks dirty and unkempt, and today she had two fingers that were badly burned and only a small Band-Aid. These poor little kids, what do you do?"

"It seems like we're going to be teaching kids who come from really different backgrounds. Somehow individual differences are suddenly taking on a whole new meaning," says Brenda.

The experiences of these student teachers are not unique. Individual differences are readily apparent in all schools in this country. Like this class of early childhood student teachers, teachers are being challenged with wide diversity in their classrooms. There will be children with very different background experiences, like the children above. Some like Haga may be fluent in two languages, and others like the Cambodian children may use different dialects of their native tongue. Some children will come from secure, safe homes, and others may come from families that are struggling to function. Coping abilities will vary, so that some children will find it easy to adapt to classroom rules. Other children will find it difficult to attend and adjust to so many new stimuli and regulations.

Children develop physically and intellectually in unique ways. One child may be reading at four years of age but be unable to run without stumbling. Others may not talk until age three but then do so using complete sentences and abstract language. One child may be able to manipulate blocks, climb to the highest rung of the jungle gym, or get enough plates to set a table for four. Another of the same age and sex will have difficulty completing any of these tasks.

Some characteristics are a matter of genetics. Chromosomes, the physical carriers of hereditary material, govern development and are responsible for some differences. The genetic makeup of a person accounts for a wide range of individual differences, including sex and eye and hair color, as well as color blindness, hemophilia, and other hereditary diseases or conditions that may result in birth defects or retardation.

Yet heredity alone doesn't account for all individual differences. Environment appears to be responsible for many traits and characteristics. Social class and education, environmental factors that are not genetically determined, have been related to individual differences in intelligence, as well as to physical, social, and emotional characteristics (Kagan, 1978).

While genetics are responsible for some individual differences and environment for others, they interact to produce a great many characteristics. Although how the interaction occurs is not entirely clear, we do know that the influence of either genetics or environment on development is not constant but changes over time. The development of individual differences is best explained by a number of genetic and environmental events that affect one another (Santrock & Yussen, 1984). For example, individuals inherit their stature, a physical characteristic, but because of the environmental condition of improved nutrition, they may be taller than their parents or grandparents. Similarly, the mother's emotional state, physical health, nutritional intake, and personal habits, such as smoking or drinking during pregnancy, can interact with genetics to affect the baby she is carrying.

Characteristics influenced by heredity may be modified by the environment. In one situation, a baby who is passive by nature may be left alone a great deal and thus not receive much stimulation. In another situation, a passive baby may receive reinforcement for even the weakest response to some stimulus and thus develop into a more gregarious person than the first infant. Children are not completely malleable, however, and the second infant would probably not be as outgoing as an infant predisposed to gregariousness and reinforced for her reaching-out behaviors (Berk, 1991, p. 119). Although a child's development can be enhanced, there are so many factors that determine the direction of that development that diversity among any group of similar age children should be considered normal and valued.

Society recognizes each individual's characteristics, but norms have been determined for human development. These norms are standards against which children are judged (Bergan & Henderson, 1979). To construct norms, researchers select a large sample of individuals representing different ages. Then the characteristics that are being studied are assessed for each child.

Scores are then used as standards. Scores that a child receives on one assessment can be compared to those of children in the norming group. Thus society determines how normal people function, and people who do not function easily in that range are labeled either *gifted* because they surpass that range or *disabled* because they are unable to meet it. Some children may be ahead or behind in all areas of development. Others may have only one or two areas of development that do not fit the normal range and are able to function very well in most situations.

Laws Regarding Special Needs Children

America, though predominately white, has always been a nation of racial diversity. Demographers predict that this racial mix will change in the twenty-first century, and that by 2024 our school-age population will be 46 percent minority (Banks, 1993b). America's continued success in a global society requires that our educational systems constantly change and improve instruction for all children whatever their abilities or background. Research has provided an understanding of the many ways that children differ—different learning styles, different cultural experiences and values, and different developmental variations. To ensure equity for all citizens, laws have been enacted that require school personnel, including teachers, to provide appropriate educational opportunities for all children. In meeting these requirements, experimental programs have been designed for children of diverse backgrounds, and some general principles of management have been established in most areas that enable teachers to meet the needs of individual children.

As you prepare to teach a diverse group of students, you will need to know about these laws and how they relate to specific populations of children.

The move to expand services for children with special needs within the public schools began in 1950, with the organization of the National Association for Retarded Citizens (NARC), an advocacy group.

By the 1960s, our nation was attempting to guarantee the civil rights of all persons. NARC, along with the Council for Exceptional Children and others, fostered the creation of the Division of Handicapped Children and Youth within the Office of Education in 1963. After this, laws were passed guaranteeing basic educational opportunity for all children regardless of special need. These included three laws in 1965: Title I/Chapter I of the Elementary and Secondary Education Act (ESEA), Project Head Start, and the Bilingual Education Act. Other laws and their years include the Child Abuse Prevention and Treatment Act, 1973; the Education for All Handicapped Children Act, 1975; the Gifted and Talented Children's Education Act, 1978; the Federal Preschool Program and Early Intervention Program Act, 1986; and the Americans with Disabilities Act (ADA), 1990.

Laws Regarding Handicapped Children

Education for All Handicapped Children Act

Public Law (PL) 94–142, the Education for All Handicapped Children Act, enacted in 1990, states that all "*handicapped* children have the right to a free education that provides services and an environment suitable to their needs." The definition of *handicapped* used in the legislation includes those who have been designated as "mentally retarded, hard of hearing, deaf and speech impaired, visually handicapped, health impaired, deaf-blind, multi-handicapped; as having specific learning disabilities who because of their impairments need special education and related services" (*Federal Register*, 1977, p. 42478). The act has four major purposes.

1. To insure handicapped children free, appropriate public education
2. To protect the rights of handicapped children and parents
3. To assist states and localities in providing services for handicapped children
4. To assist in and insure the effectiveness of efforts to educate handicapped children

The following five major components of the law ensure the rights to:

1. A free appropriate public education
2. Nondiscriminatory evaluation
3. Procedural due process
4. An individualized education program
5. *Mainstreaming* into the regular classroom under the least restrictive environment

To ensure a free, appropriate public education in the *least restrictive environment*, children with special needs have been placed in the regular classroom, a process called mainstreaming. You may very well be working with children with special needs, designing individualized education programs *(IEPs)* for each, working with a team of specialists in evaluating the needs of each child, and following the due process procedures guaranteed in the law.

PL 94–142 also helps state and local governments to develop child-find agencies, whose responsibility is to reach out into communities to locate and identify handicapped children. As these children are located, they and their families receive appropriate educational, health, and social services.

Federal Preschool Program and Early Intervention Program Act

Public Law 99–457, the Federal Preschool Program and Early Intervention Program Act, passed in 1986, extends rights and services from handicapped children to handicapped infants, toddlers, and preschoolers. Until 1986, children between the ages of three and five received services only at each state's discretion. The Federal Preschool Program mandated that, as of 1990, states must provide appropriate public education for these children. It also makes instruction available for parents, if they so desire. Parents may elect part- or full-day care as well as home-based care.

The Early Intervention Program provides for services to handicapped children from birth to age two who show signs of developmental delay in intellectual, physical, and language areas; have identifiable physical or mental conditions like Down's syndrome or cerebral palsy; or are at risk because of medical or environmental problems. Medical services and therapy as well as counseling services and family training are included.

Americans with Disabilities Act

The Americans with Disabilities Act (ADA), signed into law in 1990, requires that intervention services for infants and toddlers be provided, as appropriate, in "natural settings"—settings that are provided for normally developing children (Surr, 1992). Organizations such as the National Association for the Education of Young Children, the Association of Childhood International, the Council for Exceptional Children, and the Association for Persons with Severe Handicaps urge support for the act through their statements and position papers stating the rights of all handicapped persons to be provided with opportunities to be fully integrated into society (Sexton, Snyder, Sharpton, & Stricklin, 1993).

With such laws being implemented and published statements being made, pressure is on the schools to provide for the education of handicapped children along with other children in the classroom to give them the same opportunities as other children but adapting to their special needs. In the preschool or primary classroom, provisions can be made for various disabilities within the mainstream of the school society.

Working with Handicapped Children

Under PL 94–142 children who have some physical or intellectual disability have the right to be placed in the least restrictive environment, the one best suited to meet their needs. Often the least restrictive environment is the preschool or primary classroom. There provisions can be made for the disability within the mainstream of the school society. Children who are hearing or visually impaired, have some physical disability or health-related

All children have the right to the least restrictive educational environment.

problem, speech impairment, mental or learning disability, or are emotionally disturbed may be mainstreamed into the regular classroom.

Hearing-Impaired Children

Hearing-impaired children are often mainstreamed into an early childhood program. A number of strategies are helpful in working with children with a hearing loss. Speak directly to the child using normal, well-articulated speech. Exaggerations can be confusing. The child should sit where he or she can see you, the other children, and the materials you use.

The hearing-impaired child will probably be able to participate in the majority of early childhood education activities. The many sensory experiences they have in the classroom foster concept formation. The social activities of play, such as working with other children, building with blocks, or creating a store, foster social skills and other learning. And even if they cannot hear the full range of sounds in music or songs, they will still be able to move to the vibrations, dance, and take part in the physical activity.

Attention should be given to the specific mode of communication the individual child uses. If children wear hearing aids, you'll need to learn how to care for them. They may have to be removed so the child can participate in specific activities, like playing in a sprinkler on a hot day, so the aid won't get wet.

Other children will probably be curious about the aid, and the teacher can help them learn about it by making constructive use of it for the whole class. An audiologist, parent, or other person might demonstrate the use of the aid and show children how they can test and change the batteries. Or the audiologist might have children practice using the aid. The class could participate in having a hearing test, observing the audiometer, and learning something of their own hearing and how to protect it (Reynolds & Birch, 1977, p. 525).

Other hearing-impaired children may read lips or use cued speech or sign language. Learn something about each of these modes of communication and introduce them to the other children.

Because there is such a wide variation in hearing impairments, and some may not be noticeable until children are older, part of your responsibility is to be alert to indications of hearing loss in young children. If you have children who do any of the following, you may want to talk with parents about having the child's hearing tested or correcting some problem to prevent hearing loss:

- Appear to strain to hear
- Ask to have comments or questions repeated
- Have speech inaccuracies
- Seem confused during discussions, even though trying to participate
- Have running ears, soreness, or aches, and frequently rub and scratch ears

Visually Impaired Children

Visual impairments, like any physical disability, vary widely in type and severity. Children whose only disability was visual impairment were among the first to be mainstreamed into the regular classroom (Gearheart, Weishahn, & Gearheart, 1992) because, for the classroom teacher, these children are frequently the easiest to assimilate, especially if the impairment is partial. Also, the child with severe disabilities is normally diagnosed early and will already have made some adaptations to cope with the environment.

Curriculum activities for children with visual impairment do not differ from those for other children in the group. Mode of presentation, however, does. It may be necessary to have a specialist work with the child to read

Braille or teach other skills. Special materials for you and the child may be required.

A consistent and predictable room arrangement is crucial. The other children may have to be more careful to keep furniture, equipment, and other obstacles out of the pathways. Sighted children can be encouraged to direct and help the visually disabled child when appropriate. In one group of four-year-olds, a sighted child was playing with blocks and wanted the visually disabled child to come and join her. She successfully directed the blind child around the blocks to where she was playing by a series of "go a little more that way, no the other way, back this way, OK, now you're here where I'm here."

Although most visually impaired children are identified early, as a preschool teacher, you may be able to identify children whose faulty vision hasn't been detected. Gearheart, Weishahn, and Gearheart (1992) list several signs that a teacher might note. If children exhibit any of these in a consistent or prolonged way, they should be referred for testing and evaluation:

- Rub eyes a great deal
- Hold book or written materials close to eyes
- Eyes that are crossed or move about excessively, or have uneven pupils
- Complain of headaches or nausea after attending to details in pictures or other work
- When looking at pictures in books or at small objects, squint or scowl

Physically Disabled or Health-Related Problem Children

There are more than two hundred categories of physical disabilities and health-related problems. The conditions may range from hyperactivity in children on special medication to cerebral palsy and a need for such special equipment as braces, wheelchairs, or stand-up tables. The range of physical disabilities is so broad that it is impossible to give a detailed list of the characteristics of physically disabled children who may be mainstreamed into the early childhood program. Many children with a physical disability will function very well in the classroom and should have the same experiences as any other children; however, adjustments, determined by the nature of the physical disability, may have to be made for some children.

Certain children have difficulty focusing attention and require a less stimulating environment; others require special equipment—typewriters and special desks and chairs. For children on medication or special diets, you may want to be alert to changes in behavior that may be due to a changed prescription or to the need for a change.

Orthopedically disabled children may be limited physically but should be encouraged to do what they can and given the independence to do so. Emphasize the areas in which these children excel, just as you would for any child.

Medical science and technology have prolonged life for more and more children who have chronic and life-threatening illnesses like leukemia, liver or kidney dysfunction, or congenital heart defects. Many of these children are part of regular school programs. Their needs vary according to their illnesses, but keeping certain considerations in mind and being in communication with parents should make the children's experiences successful. Because of their illnesses, these children may have restrictions on activities; like all children, however, they need firm but gentle guidance. When special privileges must be granted because of a special condition, other children can be helped to understand why and to cooperate. Special efforts may need to be made to inform the parents of any changes in routines or about special projects. The event may mean partial involvement for the chronically ill child. Parents need to be encouraged to keep you informed of treatment, medication, and required hospital visits, for these experiences may alter the child's in-class behavior (Faure, 1988).

HIV (AIDS) Infected Children

You may not have any children in your classroom who have *AIDS* (acquired immune deficiency syndrome), but you may have children who know about or have relatives affected with the virus. Learn the facts about AIDS and keep abreast of the research. The U.S. Department of Health and Human Services publishes current reports and recommendations about this disease.

The AIDS virus is transmitted by certain bodily fluids. Because of this, centers and schools must have high hygienic standards. Recommendations have been made that teachers and caregivers wear disposable gloves when changing children's diapers and when handling cuts or other secretions of any child (Raper & Aldridge, 1988). In 1986 the surgeon general of the United States called for mandatory AIDS education for children eight years and older (U.S. Department of Health and Human Services, 1986). It is important that younger children be protected from risk of the disease without being frightened by information that they cannot understand or assimilate. Skeen and Hodson (1987) suggest that young children who ask about the disease should be given sufficient information accompanied by reassurances that they are safe. Children should understand that the disease is a very serious one, but there are safeguards taken by the adults in their world that can protect them from being infected (pp. 69–70). Margaret Merrifield (1990) has written a children's book, *Come Sit by Me*, explaining in terms they can understand how they can be safe and still associate with people who may be infected with HIV. Her explanation for adults is straightforward, and she recommends an honest but assuring approach to answer children's questions.

Children Prenatally Exposed to Drugs or Alcohol

Prenatal exposure to drugs is not a new health problem, but it was not until the 1980s that fetal alcohol syndrome was described. This discovery resulted in a general awareness of the devastating effects on children prenatally exposed to tobacco, alcohol, and drugs, such as cocaine, heroin, and marijuana. It has been estimated that 18 percent of all newborns in recent years have been exposed to drugs or alcohol and in many instances to more than one drug (Tyler, 1992).

The problems of infants exposed to drugs or alcohol are compounded by the fact that they may return to dysfunctional homes where both drug and physical abuse continues. Because of the widespread use of certain drugs, like crack, in recent years, large numbers of drug-exposed children began entering public and private schools in the United States in the early 1990s. The abnormalities that they are displaying range from neurological impairments to physical and emotional impairments, such as autism, blindness, hyperactivity, learning disabilities, and attention deficit disorders (Sautter, 1992). Although all drug-exposed children will show some signs of neurobehavioral deficiencies as infants, many will be able to function intellectually, socially, and emotionally at a normal level if they receive consistent and loving support (Sautter, 1992, p. K4). Others will exhibit such extreme behavioral and attention disorders that they will require a lot of individualized care if they are to thrive and develop.

Drug-exposed children will not all exhibit the same symptoms because of the varying conditions of prenatal exposure and the environments in which they are raised. However, there are some similarities in cognitive and social behaviors of these children. These characteristics include:

- Inability to attend to given task
- Aggressive behavior
- Nonresponsiveness to teachers' expectations
- Loss of control often due to too much stimuli or a specific stimulus
- Inability to relate to peers
- Receptive and expressive language delays
- Poor communication skills
- Inability to organize thoughts or experiences
- Difficulty in seeing cause and effect relationships (Greenspan, 1991; Graham, Harris, & Reid, 1992)

These children typically need a caring adult who can respond directly to their needs. So that they can keep focused on a task or have demonstrated the coping mechanisms for controlling their own behavior, they may need direct intervention and physical proximity to an adult (Bredekamp, 1987; Cohen and Taharally, 1992). When these children are in classrooms with large numbers of children, they are often unable to receive the consistent care that they require. If you have several of these children in your class, you must pressure for small class size and support in the classroom, in order to meet your students' needs.

At times, too much stimuli can be a problem, so there needs to be a place in the classroom with few distractions where the drug-exposed child can go. One teacher had a special area that was partially enclosed. When Jake became overwhelmed with too many choices, Mr. J. helped him to select an activity that he could do in that enclosed space. At times, Jake was able to play/work there with one or two other children.

Drug-exposed children need the consistency of routines. When a disruption of the day's schedule is to take place, these children need to be reminded that the class will be doing something different today but assured that the regular routine will be followed the next day. Writing the schedule on the board provides security for some of these children.

Because children need the experiences of communicating with others and developing social relationships, play needs to be an integral part of the curriculum. For some drug-exposed children, however, other children themselves can be too much stimuli, and the drug-exposed children may need help to enter into dramatic play. If they seem unsure of what to do, it might help to model some appropriate interactions, such as "Because I'm the grocer, I'll need to stack these groceries here. Come help me and when Jane comes, we'll ask her what she wants and then get it for her." They need help in understanding and remembering that there are rules to be followed even in play.

Like all children, these special needs children need to have choices, but they may need to be given fewer choices. If they make unwise choices and there are negative results, they may need repeated explanations as to what caused those results.

Often drug-exposed children are unable to sit or work "quietly." Some of them seem to be in perpetual motion. Ways need to be found so that they can have some movement and not disturb others. Rewarding them for even small gains in self-control is important.

Because these children may regress and appear to have made little progress, you will need to document the progress that the child *is* making and congratulate the child, the parents, and yourself.

Speech-Disabled Children

The normal three- or four-year-old is very verbal. Preschoolers still, however, encounter some consonants that are hard to pronounce, such as *r*, *sh*, *l*, or *th*, and they may mix up tenses or misuse pronouns. But some children have delayed speech or have speech patterns so far behind the norm that it is difficult to understand them. Deiner (1983, p. 54) has identified three types of disorders:

1. Poor articulation (mispronunciation)

2. Difficulties with phonation (vocal malfunctions)

3. Stuttering (rhythm patterns)

Language-delayed children may also exhibit immature speech. Their vocabularies may be limited, grammatical usage may be simplistic and with many errors, and children may have difficulty communicating with other children (Dumtschin, 1988).

If you note consistent irregularities in a child's speech, you or a speech therapist can check the child's speech patterns against the developmental norms. Check with parents and with people in the school who come in contact with the child about their observations. Different speech problems require different strategies for improvement.

Extreme problems in speech are obvious, and you can work with a therapist to establish what you can do to follow up on the exercises or therapy. Some exercises foster children's use of lips, tongue, breathing, and vocal cords in ways that enhance correct speech. Speech therapists can determine which of these will help specific children and can train you to use them.

Teachers encourage children to talk to one another and make their needs known without adult help.

The entire early childhood program is full of opportunities to use language. Having children with speech disabilities join in repeating finger plays, singing songs, or speaking parts in puppet shows or dramatic presentations is encouraged.

A child with a speech problem requires the same explanations, clarifications, and poetic language experiences as a child without one. All young children are expanding their receptive as well as their oral language. They respond to expressive language and may even try to imitate it. One three-year-old with phonation problems talked in complete and complex sentences with proper intonations, although most of the words were incomprehensible. His phonation was faulty, but he understood very complex language patterns and attempted to respond to requests in complete sentences.

Like other children, he would talk in a monologue to himself as he carried out his activities. The teacher took time to talk with him, was patient as he responded, and tried to understand his particular language patterns. She also encouraged and supported interactions with other children, so that the child could establish the ability to communicate with others.

As children play with others, opportunities to use oral language arise, as in this example.

One four-year-old girl whose parents were deaf did not use oral language in the home but did use it at school in a type of echolalia [repeating sounds and words]. She would repeat sounds in intonations of the last words someone said, but when she wanted something, she used body language. Even when she had a temper tantrum, it was all through body movement, with no sound.

One day at the center, she had a truck that another child grabbed. She looked at him, then started to jabber in an angry tone. The startled child quickly returned the truck. The speech-delayed child was astonished. She looked at the truck, at the other child, and at the teacher as if to say, "It worked, he gave me the truck!" The teacher replied, "See, Nancy, you get things by asking for them." The teacher then played a game with Nancy. The teacher would gently take the truck, and when Nancy tried to say "truck," or "give me the truck," she would give it to her. Speech wasn't accomplished overnight, but from that point on, she showed steady progress and began to interact with the other children using language.

It may be that you can structure experiences for speech-delayed children that will encourage them to ask for objects, as this teacher did for Nancy. Change is slow, however, and you should be ready to accept the child's improvement in the desired speech pattern and not expect perfection.

Reward improved speech patterns with recognition, a smile, a nod, or some other form of praise.

Mentally Disabled Children

Children with mild retardation, who can gain from the usual early childhood program, may also be mainstreamed. Children with mild mental retardation may exhibit one or more of the following characteristics:

- Poor sensory and motor coordination skills
- Poor attention span
- Low frustration level
- Difficulty in generalizing
- Play interests that are immature for their age
- Language ability below their age group
- Poor self-concepts because they've been unable to master simple self-help skills (Gearheart, Weishahn, & Gearheart, 1992)

Usually the retarded child has been tested and diagnosed. A team may have developed a special IEP for the child. The teacher is responsible for seeing that the child gets the help specified in the IEP.

Most early childhood program experiences are suitable for children with mild retardation. Sensory and motor experiences are most valuable. Providing materials for children to taste, touch, smell, and hear offers them several modalities through which to learn concepts. For example, the word *ball* has more meaning if children can touch one, put their arms around a big ball, toss a small one, or select a white one to pass to a friend.

These children may need extra time and help in developing skills. Breaking down the skill into smaller parts and letting the child practice each part gives an important sense of accomplishment. The child might pull the zipper the last inch, pull the button through the rest of the way, or push the belt end through the final loop. Some Montessori equipment or homemade materials for tying, buttoning, and zippering can be fun as well as useful in helping children develop special skills.

Encourage retarded children to enter into play activities by teaching them specific skills. Show them how to enter a play group: "When you want to play with the blocks, say . . ." or "This is the way to ask to play house . . ." The other children may be taught techniques for playing with children who have special needs.

Children with mild retardation respond well to stories and poetry and should be encouraged to develop this interest. They can tell a story even if it's only the first part or the end. They can be encouraged to become involved in nursery rhymes and can take small parts in choral work and other language experiences.

Learning-Disabled Children

Learning-disabled children are of normal intelligence but have difficulty in school. The difficulty may be in one of four areas of learning: *(a)* receiving information for the brain; *(b)* organizing this information so that it is understood; *(c)* remembering the information, if it is understood; *(d)* communicating or acting on the information, if it is remembered (Silver, 1991).

Learning-disabled children are often thought to be lazy or to have a poor attitude rather than being recognized as having a learning difficulty. They may show immature behavior for a much longer time and in greater intensity than children without learning disabilities. They may make reversals when writing, forget what they've learned, and stumble going up stairs. They often display athletic prowess, but only in one area. "This is the distractible child who tends not to look, who tends not to listen, who tends not to remember, who tends not to do what he's supposed to do" (Smith, 1978, p. xiii). Often diagnosing the learning-disabled child is difficult because many of the characteristics may be similar to those of other handicapping conditions. When children are labeled incorrectly because of a misdiagnosis, all too often they end up in an inappropriate placement.

There are no easy ways to remediate the situation for these children. They need time to grow and develop while learning to cope with their disability. They need to recognize that they may have to work harder than others. Theorists in perceptual-motor development like Kephart (1960), Getman (1963), Frostig (1964), and Furth and Wachs (1974) recommend many types of fine- and gross-motor activities to help develop children's attending behaviors and other thinking abilities.

Learning-disabled children need to feel that they are good, cared for, and appreciated for what they can do well. Like all children, they need acceptance from their peers. Their chances for success are greatest when school, child, and parents work together. An example of this working together follows.

Laura insisted on trying to read Marguerite Henry's *Misty of Chincoteague* even though it was beyond her reading level because "that's what all my friends are reading." Finally, upon urging from her mother, she took a considerably easier book, Anderson's *Billy and Blaze*, to share with her class. After her report, the best reader in the class asked if he could borrow the book because he thought her report was so "neat." The wise teacher commented later to Laura on how marvelous it was that she had brought a book for Tom because he was so hard to please and usually had already read all of the books anyone else brought in. Laura's reading skills began to improve as she read other Anderson works. With the support of all, Laura's self-concept took a giant step forward that day.

Emotionally Disturbed Children

We all have emotional outbursts, show signs of fear and anger, and are hostile and aggressive at times. Sometimes children lose control as a result of the stress of the school day. At other times, a change in behavior may stem from an unusual or unexpected event at home, such as a new baby or a parent's leaving for some reason.

There are some children, however, whose actions go beyond the normal outbursts. For them frustrations build, and outbursts of uncontrollable behaviors are extreme and consistent. This type of disturbance ranges in type and cause.

Children displaying outbursts or hostilities in consistently deviant patterns may need to be referred for diagnosis and appropriate treatment. The American Psychiatric Association has identified four categories of behaviors of emotionally disturbed children: aggressiveness, withdrawal, unrealistic fears and phobias, and shyness or overdependence (American Psychiatric Association, 1987).

The hostile, aggressive child usually comes to the attention of the teacher, but withdrawn, depressed, too shy, and perfection-conscious children may easily be overlooked. You'll want to spend time observing all children so you don't miss the needs of a quiet child who may be living with emotional trauma.

Ask for help in observing. Careful observation is important if you're going to be able to determine how consistently some of these perplexing behaviors are being exhibited by children. Ask your principal, school psychologist, or counselor to come into your classroom to make observations of these children, as well as provide information on how to help them.

Emotionally disturbed children may not feel good about themselves. They desperately need to be accepted for who they are and what they can do, and they do not need the negative aspects of their behavior emphasized. Emotionally disturbed children will need help in accepting themselves, as you and the other children learn to accept them (Deiner, 1983, p. 219).

You will need professional help and guidance as you work with emotionally disturbed children in the classroom. You will be learning the specifics of how to deal with each child as an individual, and many of the strategies that are helpful with other children are helpful with these children. However, they will need individual attention and a large share of consistent love. As you help them to build self-esteem, provide them with realistic expectations for the skills they need to acquire and praise them for the growth they show. These children need a structured and consistent environment, an opportunity to play safely with peers, and a chance to receive information about their behavior and to role play different solutions (Webb, 1989, pp. 421-436).

Attention Deficit-Hyperactivity Disorder

The learning-disabled child, the emotionally disturbed child, or the child exposed to drugs prenatally may exhibit behaviors that are similar to those of children with attention deficit-hyperactivity disorder (ADHD). The term *attention deficit-hyperactivity disorder* was coined to reflect the nature of this neurologically based problem. Three types of behavior typify this condition—hyperactivity, distractibility, and impulsivity. A child might exhibit one, two, or all three behaviors (Silver, 1991).

Hyperactivity relates to ADHD children's inability to remain still for very long. They seem to be in constant motion, tapping fingers, scooting about on the floor, wiggling while sitting in their seats.

Distractibility refers to their inability to filter out sounds, impressions, or movements that are unnecessary for gaining particular information. Children who are easily distractible have difficulty paying attention to the task at hand. They react to almost any stimulus and have trouble concentrating.

Impulsivity means that children react suddenly and without thinking. They are easily upset, get angry over seemingly nothing, and can't wait their turn to say something. They are unable to reflect on the consequences of their actions, so they often get into trouble.

Hyperactivity, distractibility, and impulsivity are also found in children who are not ADHD. The difference is not in the actions but in the cause. ADHD children are hyperactive, impulsive, or distractible because of neurological disorders. When children are exhibiting such behaviors, it is important that they be seen by trained professionals to determine the causes of the behaviors. If the problems are neurologically based, then medicine may be prescribed. However, there is some controversy about the use of such drugs especially when the behaviors are not neurologically based and because of the possible harmful side effects if the drug is not carefully selected (Divosky, 1989).

If children in your classes do receive medical treatment, then you as the teacher will need to monitor them and report to the parents any significant changes in behavior that may indicate side effects.

ADHD children need regular routines, spaces where they can play/work without too many distractions, consistent directions, and reminders of changes in routines or during transition times. Because these children may have trouble remembering the rules and the consequences for not obeying the rules, you will need to be consistent with them. You may want to try having them set some of the rules and post them as reminders. When a rule is broken, ask the child to repeat the rule and firmly and immediately establish the punishment (Buchoff, 1990).

As is true of all special needs children, ADHD children may have trouble developing positive images of themselves. They need to be singled out for recognition, as all children do. All children feel prized when a classroom environment and a curriculum are designed so that all children can be successful.

Laws Regarding Abused Children

Definitions of child abuse are plentiful, but there is no consensus of what constitutes abuse. Usually *child abuse and neglect* refer to maltreatment of children that can include deliberate physical injury or sexual abuse, as well as failure to provide sustenance, clothing, shelter, medical attention, or other care necessary for a child's well-being.

The Child Abuse Prevention and Treatment Act, passed in 1973, established the National Center on Child Abuse and Neglect, which provided a national focus for children requiring protection. The center offers coordination, integration of services and activities for children and families, and assistance in the identification, prevention, and treatment of child abuse and neglect.

By 1973, all fifty states had child abuse legislation. The legislation varies from state to state because there is no consensus on how to prevent child abuse and neglect or how to treat the abusing parent or child. The following are essential to effective child protection:

- A reasonably accurate knowledge of the incidence of child abuse in the community
- An effective central register of reports on child maltreatments
- A specially trained child protective service
- Treatment and rehabilitative facilities and programs for parents and children
- A court system capable of dealing quickly, effectively, and fairly with families
- Interdisciplinary exchanges and cooperation at all levels so that the most effective services may be developed

Working with Abused Children

Teachers and other professionals are required by law to report cases of suspected child abuse. You are given confidentiality when reporting suspected cases; nevertheless, to report a case is not an easy decision. What if you make a mistake? What if your fears about the child's treatment are unfounded? Or what if your suspicions are confirmed but make the parent increase the abusive behavior toward the child? Not reporting a suspected case of abuse or neglect is just as dangerous, however, for the data suggest that a child who has been abused or neglected is at great risk of being reinjured and abused (Gil, 1970). It is a serious moral issue not to report such cases, and recently lawsuits have been brought against educators for negligence in reporting such cases (Hendrick, 1992, p. 172).

Seek support from your school system, child-care director, supervisor, or principal. Follow the procedures outlined by these authorities. Ask someone else, a school nurse, director, or counselor, for assistance if you suspect abuse. If you suspect a case of abuse, many others do also. Usually a parent, neighbor, or someone close to or in the family will report the case at the same time.

Physical abuse will most likely be noticed. Other types of abuse, such as nutritional deprivation, lack of medical care, or sexual or emotional abuse, are less easy to spot. In general, children who are abused or neglected exhibit some or more of these traits:

- Cry for no apparent reason, frequently and repeatedly
- Are afraid of everyone and everything, or may be bullies terrifying others
- Have unexplained lacerations and bruises
- Do not want to go home after school
- Are unclean, smelling of urine or feces
- Withdraw from adult contact
- Exhibit destructive behavior
- Smell of alcohol
- Are below normal height and weight
- Are afraid of their parents and fear other adults
- Withdraw from peer interaction
- Are hyperactive or aggressive
- Are sick and absent from school frequently
- Have short attention spans and lack interest in school
- Exhibit sudden and dramatic changes in behavior
- Are tired and often fall asleep in class (Gil, 1970)

Certain behaviors of a child's caregiver may indicate that the caregiver, purposely or inadvertently, is endangering the child's physical or emotional well-being. Meddin and Rosen (1986) suggest that when you are trying to determine if the caregiver may be abusing the child, you should consider whether any of the following descriptions apply to that person:

- Substance abuse
- Unrealistic expectations for child's intellectual or social behavior
- Lack of skill or knowledge about child-rearing practices
- Expectations that child meet adult emotional needs
- Sudden or undue stresses in the home

You will need to observe suspected cases carefully in order to determine if patterns of behavior in either the children or the adults suggest abuse. Reports of abuse should be made in accordance with state or school policies. Social agencies will then determine what action must be taken.

After you have submitted a report, the child will still be in your classroom, and you'll have to find ways to be supportive of both the child and the parents. Take time to observe the child and note the things that the child finds pleasing or upsetting. Build a sense of security in the classroom. Perhaps a volunteer could be assigned to work with the child, building a sense of safety and security. Use caution in making advances to the child.

The child may be afraid of adults and need time to understand that you are not hurtful. Find ways for the child to express feelings, whether they are fear, sadness, or anger.

Abused children often suffer educational setbacks. Because of the manner in which they have been treated, they often view themselves as helpless in any situation and unable to prevent things from happening to them. They become passive to learning. If they are to assume responsibility as students for their own learning, they will need to learn that what they do can affect their lives (Craig, 1992). For children to become active learners, you may have to structure the environment so children can see immediate results of their interactions. They may need you to demonstrate appropriate actions, so that they realize what they do does change what happens.

Supporting parents who want help can be both tricky and hindered by your natural anger toward them. Parents who are under stress may talk with you about their concerns and inability to cope. You can help them by listening and by referring them to the proper support agencies. Later, discussion about their children's needs in relation to both your and their expectations of children that age may be helpful. In some instances, you may serve as a model. Therefore it is important that your behavior toward their children be one of acceptance and firm guidance.

Laws Regarding Gifted and Talented Children

Legislative attention has also focused on the gifted. In 1978, as a part of the Education Amendments, Congress passed Title IX, Part A, the Gifted and Talented Children's Education Act. The act was to provide for and improve progress for the special educational needs of the gifted and talented. Gifted and talented children are those who have "high performance capability in areas such as intellectual, creative, specific academic, or leadership ability or in the performing and visual arts, and who by reason thereof, require services or activities not ordinarily provided by the school" (Ehrlich, 1982, p. 186).

The Office of Gifted and Talented Children was a force in developing state and national programs for the gifted and talented (Clark, 1992). In the early 1980s, federal support was terminated, and the Education Consolidation Act of 1982 eliminated the federal Office of Gifted and Talented but merged funding for gifted and talented students with other programs. States now receive money in terms of block grants for all types of special education programs. The states then decide what funding to provide for the gifted and talented. In 1988, the Jacob K. Javits Gifted and Talented Student Education Act was passed as part of the Elementary and Secondary Education Act. Some monies were allocated for identification of and services for gifted children (Heward & Cavanaugh, 1993).

Working with Gifted and Talented Children

Why do you need to give special attention to gifted children? These are the children who can go it alone, succeeding under any circumstances. They have the skills, talents, and high intellect that ensures achievement and success. Ehrlich (1982) points out that the gifted are normally "a law abiding, conforming group that contributes comparatively few offenders to any social order" (p. 41). Nevertheless, just as there is diversity in any group of children, there is diversity among those who are talented and gifted.

The very definition of talented and gifted suggests diversity. It includes children who have high intelligence, who have special talents in art and music, and even those who excel in leadership (Sisk, 1979, p. 527). Identification of gifted and talented children is not always easy because of the wide diversity among the gifted and talented as well as the broad definition of the group. In the past, identification was less problematic. The earlier definition of gifted included only those who scored above average on an intelligence test (Wood, 1992). Intelligence tests can be used to identify those children who have above average intelligence. On IQ tests, only 1 in 10,000 score 160 or above and 7 in 1,000 between 140 and 159. A child whose IQ is 136 is equal to or excels 99 percent of children of the same age (Mussen, Conger, & Kagan, 1980, p. 259).

Although IQ is relatively stable, in many instances IQs have fluctuated because of emotional problems or other factors. Then, too, many children who have outstanding ability in mathematics, for instance, are unable to read and score low on intelligence tests. Albert Einstein had problems learning to read. IQ alone is not sufficient to predict even intellectual giftedness, much less gifts and talents in other areas.

In studying the characteristics of gifted and talented children, Ehrlich (1982) and Clark (1992) listed a number of traits they seem to have in common. All gifted and talented children do not have all of these, and nongifted children frequently exhibit a number of them. But this list can help supplement an IQ score. A few of the more prominent traits of gifted children are:

- Verbal facility
- Ability to grasp ideas well beyond chronological age
- Avid interest in knowing about things
- Originality of thought
- Creativity in endeavors
- Curiosity about the world that exceeds the normal curiosity of a child that age
- Flexibility of thought
- Ability to predict
- Special response to the beauty and order around them
- Interest in the future

- Unusual ability to lead others
- Unusual empathy and concern for people

A variety of tests and other measures, such as systematic observations of children, are used to identify gifted children. Tests of creativity, problem solving, musical, or artistic talent can be employed.

Programs for the gifted have often been of three types: separation, acceleration, or enrichment. Separation involves isolating the gifted from others in a distinct classroom within a school or in a separate "gifted" school in a county. The theory is that in isolation they'll have a better opportunity to face challenges they couldn't find in a regular classroom or school. The curriculum employs a variety of approaches designed to foster children's gifts and talents.

Enrichment is a well-accepted approach to providing for the special needs of gifted and talented children. Enriching experiences are provided either in the classroom or in a pullout program (with the gifted pulled out of the classroom for a special project). The enriching experience can be anything from visiting an art museum to listening to concerts or working with a mathematician.

Usually the early childhood educator can arrange for enriching experiences in the classroom for all children. One kindergarten teacher managed to have a rich classroom environment by having most of the children's learning experiences evolve around projects and by designing a completely individualized reading readiness program.

All children were permitted to study a topic of their choice in depth, either alone or with others interested in the same topic. One child became an expert on dogs. He talked with dog fanciers, had his parents and the teacher read books to him about dogs, and visited a veterinarian and a dog breeder. Not only did he know about the characteristics of different breeds of dogs, but he also knew the subtypes of dogs of several breeds. He became intrigued with the various intellectual levels of different species of dogs. His interest and enthusiasm displayed the traits of above-average curiosity, avid interest in knowing all about a topic, persistence, and originality of thought. The teacher provided for his unique characteristics without labeling the child or isolating him.

Acceleration programs can work in two ways. One is to have the gifted skip grades or move ahead in specific subject matter by working with older children for instruction in that subject. Johns Hopkins University runs an acceleration program in mathematics for children who have special gifts and talents in the field. Children attend Saturday classes taught by mathematicians and move forward at their own speed.

Another method of acceleration is to provide gifted children with more advanced materials in the regular classroom setting and allow them to progress at a rapid rate. This provision would mean instruction is individualized so that each child can work at his or her own pace. Flexible grouping allows you to group children with similar skills and interests to work on projects together. Volunteers might be asked to work with a particular group. If the program is flexible and has large blocks of time set aside for activity or project work, you would be able to work with the gifted children.

In seeking community support for schools, you may find community persons who would be willing to provide tutoring. In one community where there were active retirees, talents and interests of these retirees were matched with those children who showed unusual interests or abilities in specific areas. Some of the retirees worked with children in languages or math for an hour each day. In other instances, the retirees volunteered their time to work on a specific project that the children wished to pursue. Many of these projects included children from differing age groups who had a special interest or talent.

Both enrichment and acceleration can work within the classroom if you provide books and materials that range in difficulty. It may mean having a variety of projects that gifted children may work on along with others or a project they can complete at their own pace on an individual basis. It may even mean providing some out-of-class tutoring and seeking community support (Fowler, 1990).

Laws Regarding Bilingual Education

Other laws have been passed to provide for the special needs of children who enter school without fluency in English. There has been a long history of legislation regarding bilingual and bicultural education, and there is concern about the child who comes to school fluent in a language other than English. Nevertheless, there is no agreement as to the type of education this child should receive.

Regulations and programs have proliferated since the mid-1960s, when the Bilingual Education Act of 1965 was passed in an attempt to provide educational programs to meet the needs of students with limited English proficiency *(LEP)*. In the 1970s many schools developed *bilingual* and English as a second language *(ESL)* programs for the LEP student. When the Bilingual Education Act was reissued in 1974, transitional bilingual education programs increased greatly in number. These programs allowed instruction to be given either in the child's native language or in English. The purpose of instruction was to allow a child "to progress effectively through the educational system" (Bilingual Education Act of 1974, §703a[4]A). In effect this act was interpreted to mean that children should be educated to function in more than one language and culture.

As a result, controversy has raged over whether America should be *multicultural* and multilingual or whether the "melting-pot" concept should be reinstated. Advocates of the melting-pot view have argued that bilingual education delays the acquisition of English and causes divisiveness in society (Wong Fillmore, 1985). As the controversy continued in the 1980s and states struggled with implementation of appropriate educational programs for children of differing cultural backgrounds, the Bilingual Act of 1978 was clarified. Bilingual programs were for children with limited English and were to be designed to improve their English proficiency. Education in a foreign language was permitted only if it helped the child learn English (Barry, 1983, pp. 58-59). However, the Secretary of Education, William Bennett (1986), instituted changes in the federal role in bilingual education, permitting states to determine the extent of native language instruction.

Working with Bilingual Children

Immigrants in the United States have played a major role in shaping the structure of American society. After the early settlements by Europeans and the forced immigrations of blacks in the 1600s and 1700s came three major waves of immigration. The first wave, in the 1800s, brought people mainly from northern Europe; the second, in the early 1900s, was dominated by people from central and southern Europe; and the third, beginning in the 1960s and increasing greatly in the 1980s, has brought both legal and illegal immigrants from Latin America, Asia, and the Caribbean. As a result, we now have the most ethnically diverse population in our history (Seefeldt, 1983; Kellogg, 1988).

Like their earlier counterparts, the latest immigrants have affected the makeup and complexity of American society. Immigrants come to America for a better chance at life. How we succeed in helping their children to adapt the dominant U.S. culture to their primary culture and to thrive in American schools will greatly affect our future.

One of the greatest barriers to immigrant children's success is language. Though some immigrants arrive in this country fluent in or speaking some English, many do not. And while some of the children come from families who are educated in their own language and culture, others are not literate even in their own language. The challenge to schools and to classroom teachers is great. Any one school may have children from several different cultures all speaking different languages or dialects.

Programs have been designed to meet the needs of children who have varying degrees of English-language skills. Some schools have bilingual programs in which children can learn academic concepts in their own language as they also learn English. Other students are placed in a classroom with their age group but are pulled out for lessons in English as a Second Language (ESL). In a few classrooms the classroom teacher has had ESL training and works individually to help non-English-speaking children acquire English. Many children are totally immersed in the American classroom and are expected to learn English from their peers.

In each of these groups children come with a range of abilities and capacity to learn. Some non-English-speaking children quickly learn the basic communication skills and in one or two years become conversant in English; to be really fluent for academic achievement, however, may take five to seven years (Soto, 1991; Urza, 1992). Others have greater difficulty adjusting to the new language. Environment, intellectual ability, motivation, quality and length of English instruction, and the age when children begin to learn English are all factors.

As a teacher, you must understand that these children are not only confronted with a different language but they also are faced with a confusing and bewildering world. Many have emotional and health problems from the traumatic experiences of escaping war-torn countries or because of severe economic deprivation.

As you work with non-English-speaking children, the following guidelines may help:

1.   Children are eager to learn English or any new language when there is an openness and an acceptance of them, their culture, and their native language.

2.   Language should not be taught in isolation from school activities but as a part of the total, integrated program that includes focus on language development. Listening, speaking, reading, and writing are part of mathematics, social studies, art, and science, not just "English."

3.   Children learn through their senses, including their muscles. Concepts and new words and phrases are learned better when children can participate in some action. They need to examine and explore real objects, to act out new expressions. Pictures can help, but action imprints the message more strongly (Gonzalez-Mena, 1976).

4.   Children need to build the new language on their knowledge of how their native language works. Ask children to share their terms for certain objects or certain actions as you are supporting their efforts to use the English words.

5.   Curriculum should be designed around a central idea or theme that allows inclusion of the immigrant child's culture and experiences.

6.   Storybooks and nonfiction stories that depict positive images of children of different cultures in various settings should be included regularly as part of the classroom environment and events.

7.   Children learn from one another. Cooperative activities permit each child to contribute as well as to get help from peers.

8.   The classroom climate should reflect respect for diversity.

9.   Children are more successful when parents can be helped in finding support services they need.

10.   The most successful programs are those in which the school develops a partnership with parents and the ethnic community (First & Carera, 1988).

You should also become aware of some of the different cultural and familial learning expectations of non-English-speaking children. Providing experiences that build on native cultural experiences makes instruction more meaningful for immigrant children, and it creates a rich and varied experience for other children in your classroom (Chamot, 1988).

Nonverbal behaviors and children's learning strategies indicate cultural differences, too. For example, admitting that one does not understand a teacher's comment may cause embarrassment for children from some cultures or even imply disrespect for the teacher (Kasper, 1988).

Parents with limited English skills may be confused by an educational system that is strange to them. They may be reluctant to ask questions, for to do so in their culture would be to challenge the teacher's authority. Or they may be confounded by the role of play in young children's learning, especially if the schools they were familiar with emphasized rote learning (Olsen, 1988). It is impossible to know all the cultural differences that are likely to cause problems, but by being alert to possible ones, you can help children bridge the gap between home and school.

Laws Regarding Children of Poverty

In 1965 President Lyndon Johnson declared a War on Poverty. Two major laws were enacted and continue to be funded in order to provide resources so that children of poverty could be more equitably served in this country.

Project Head Start, enacted in 1965, is an educational program with comprehensive services for children two to five years of age whose parents are below the poverty line. The program provides experiences that support children's social, emotional, physical, and intellectual development. A key feature of this program is that Head Start staff is required to involve parents and community leaders in their programs. Health, nutrition, and psychological services are also provided for participants. Children of poverty need the comprehensive services provided by programs such as Head Start, and for those who receive such services, their chances of success as adults are greatly enhanced (Lazar, 1977).

In 1965 the federal government also enacted Title I/Chapter 1 of the Elementary and Secondary Education Act to provide extra instruction in reading, writing, and mathematics to low-achieving children in low-income neighborhoods. The law had two major components: *(a)* comparability of services whereby Chapter 1 students received more funds and thus more services, and *(b)* to "supplement not supplant" programs whereby Chapter 1 students were to receive extra help but not replace the teaching of the classroom teacher (Fagan & Heid, 1991).

In 1984 a study was conducted to determine the effectiveness of the program before the 1988 scheduled reauthorization of the bill. It was found that children receiving the services from Chapter 1 did indeed improve, but the gap between the disadvantaged and more advantaged children had not lessened. With the reauthorization of the act in 1988, the quality of the program was stressed. Programs were required to set high standards for outcome and to measure the effectiveness of these programs (Fagan & Heid, 1991). The intent of the law is to provide better programs to increase students' learning, but some criticisms of Chapter 1 programs in the past have been that they are designed to "facilitate monitoring rather than to maximize student learning" (LeTendre, 1991, p. 580). The impact of the reauthorization should be that personnel will search harder to find innovative programs or techniques that are best for the students.

Working with Children of Poverty

Children of poverty may live in desperate conditions, but they have only their poverty in common. Some of these children may function within a normal range of development and achievement in spite of hunger, poor health services, or even homelessness. Others may be among the special needs children listed above, including the gifted and talented. As a classroom teacher, you may need to be sensitive to the economic needs of your children to be sure that they receive the services to which they are entitled and that their special talents and skills are not overlooked because of their poor economic condition. Some lower-income families often do not have the physical or emotional resources to help them seek appropriate services for their children. You may need to recommend community resources that they could use to provide needed services.

When children are hungry, cold, or tired, it is difficult for them to do their best academically. Because of their insecure conditions, many of them will lack the self-esteem or the self-confidence to succeed. You may be able to find some assistance for them in and around the school. Some schools have early morning breakfast programs for children who do not receive breakfast at home. If this program is not available, PTAs often will provide you with money so that you can have nutritious snacks available if children arrive at school hungry.

If your classroom is arranged so there are spaces for quiet activities, you may be able to let a child who is too tired to function have a brief nap before the intensive part of the program begins.

Like many others, children of poverty need a caring teacher who provides structure and consistent routines, but who has a flexible curriculum where all children can succeed. The special qualities that each child brings to the classroom need to be recognized and prized. You will need to coordinate services of Chapter 1 personnel so that these children are not denied your teaching talents but are receiving extra help as needed.

General Guidelines of Working with Special Needs Children

The children who come into your classroom are very likely to be from a diverse population. In order to provide them with appropriate services, it is often necessary to determine which category these children fall under. However, it is important not to let the labels determine the intervention strategies. What is important is each child's abilities and needs and that each child be helped to develop to his or her potential. There are some guidelines that will enable you to provide a more individualized program in your classroom.

The physical environment communicates to children the type of emotional and academic environment in the classroom. It is important that your classroom be arranged to accommodate the special children. There need to be spaces where the entire class can meet together as well as arrangements so that children who have difficulty sitting still can move but also be a part of the group. Children will need private spaces where too much stimuli can be sorted out. As children learn to work together more productively, they need space to do so. Materials need to be orderly but inviting for children to explore. To help children build self-concept and self-esteem, their work needs to be valued. Displays should reflect the special accomplishments of all the children not just the quickest and brightest. The

Children come from diverse backgrounds.

books, materials, and displays need to reflect the diversity of cultures in your own classroom and in the world.

A curriculum reflecting diversity teaches concepts that take into account different viewpoints. For example, in a study about coming to America, the celebration of the Pilgrims landing at Plymouth would only be one part of a greater story. You would need to integrate into the curriculum these and other people's struggles and search for freedom in this country: the Native Americans' loss of land and struggle to keep their culture and freedom; the African Americans who were brought against their will into slavery and their struggle to regain freedom and dignity; the Asian American arrival in California to search for the golden opportunities that were often dashed in racist struggles; and the immigrants who have come from all over the world to escape famine, despotism, and war. Each culture's contributions to society should be reflected throughout the curriculum. Children's self-esteem is enhanced when they realize that they are a part of an important heritage. Sharing your own cultural heritage will provide a model for children's examination of their own (Banks, 1983a, p. 211).

Establishing a consistent schedule and structure provides children with a sense of security. Within this structure it is important to identify what strategies enable children to function better. Are there children, events, or materials in the classroom that will trigger a certain child's unruly behavior and that can be changed? Can schedules be arranged so children who take more time or who need nurturing can get it before entering into more rigorous academic activities? Are activities structured so that children unable to monitor their own behavior receive the guidance they need and at the same time provide for their developing independence? (Stevens and Price, 1992).

Developing cooperative learning strategies allows children to learn important social skills while learning academic skills, and it also provides for differences. Cooperative learning groups may be formed so that brighter students can work as peer tutors. The brighter students gain in ability to explain and in clarifying their own understanding. Other cooperative groups can be formed that consist of students with similar interests or abilities working together on projects ranging from drilling each other on needed skills to designing a geographic area that contains a quicksand trap (Barbour, 1990). In any group there are specific roles that members must take. Taking responsibility at different times for leading, monitoring, or reporting for a group gives each child a sense of well-being and teaches different ways of operating within a group setting. Encouraging children to establish the rules of behavior for each of the positions enables them to make sense of rules and understand the consequences of not responding.

One third-grade teacher had a group of children who had a great deal of difficulty paying attention, keeping on task, and sticking to an assignment until it was completed. Their disruptive behavior was affecting the entire class's productivity. She decided to experiment by putting each of these boys and girls in charge of a separate cooperative group and then giving them special awards when their group performed well or met established criteria. Periodically the students in each group would assess the things that worked well for them and those things they needed to change in order to complete tasks. The rewards were simple ones that all could achieve, such as having a special lunch with the principal or a pizza or popcorn party, or selecting a special video to watch. At one point, one group decided that their reward should be celebrating individual successes within the group and asked to be given class time and bulletin board space to present "themselves." The class liked the idea so much that they instigated a plan to select periodically different "success stories" to present to the entire school. Not only did the disruptive children's academic skills and behavior patterns improve, but they also became integrated into the entire fabric of the school.

Individualizing the instruction for all children can be accomplished when the curriculum is theme based and integrated. Differentiated and self-paced learning are accomplished when there are many self-selected activities that can appeal to diverse interests and talents. Math games requiring different skills, science projects requiring different levels of involvement, and differentiated reading and writing assignments can be available in learning centers around the classroom. Developmentally appropriate practice means that instruction is presented in a way that every child, no matter what the special need is, can assimilate information and develop important skills.

In a second-grade classroom, one teacher used trade books exclusively to teach reading. She made lists of books that were of varying levels of difficulty. Sometimes the books reflected a variety of genres or themes, and at other times, they reflected particular ones. Children were encouraged to select their own book by picking up the book and reading one page. If they had difficulty reading five words, then they might want to try a new book. However, if they found the book interesting and wanted to continue, the teacher offered to work with them individually to assist them when they got stuck. Children put their initials on the list beside the book title that they were reading, and the teacher had an instant record of the books the children were selecting.

In addition, children always read with a partner, and partnerships changed from time to time. Sometimes partners read the same book together, first one reading a page and then the other. Sometimes partners read different books silently. The children always helped each other when they came to difficult words. Strategies for figuring out unknown words were a regular part of children's discussions with each other and with the teacher. Each day children were to read and to share some aspect of their book with their partner. At times, the teacher selected what was to be shared; other times each team decided. Reading to find out specific things, such as what your favorite character is like or how you know when and where the story takes place, could be accomplished even with children reading at different levels. Total class sharing was always a part of the reading period time. When one child was especially excited about a particular book, that often sparked the interest of another child.

In teaching writing, you also can individualize the program. One way to do that is by writing for authentic purposes. Hadaway (1992) describes how letter writing between bilingual/ESL students and native English speakers provides children the opportunity to write for real purposes and to authentic audiences. Correspondence can be set up within the school or community with schoolchildren in another part of the country. Children write about things that interest them in seeking to build a bond with their pen pals, and that structure allows for diverse abilities and interests. Children control what is being written about, so that they begin writing within their own level of linguistic accomplishments. As the correspondence continues, however, their language development expands.

Learning to deal with your own feelings will sensitize you to your own attitudes and feelings toward children with special needs. It will help you to avoid making statements that may unwittingly hurt a child already badly hurt. It is natural to have emotions of sadness, anger, guilt, overprotection, frustration, or exhaustion. Looking at these emotions honestly, discussing them with others, and striving to look at your day-to-day accomplishments and successes will help you to grow professionally (White & Phair, 1986).

Summary

It's true that all children are special, but many have needs that require special attention. It may seem overwhelming to think about meeting all the special needs of children in any one group. Yet teachers have found that the special needs children are basically the same, except in degree, as all other children.

By taking time to observe the special needs of children, using skills of observations and the results of testing and consulting with the children's parents, specialists, or other staff members, teachers are able to plan the best classroom spaces and programs to meet the needs of all children.

Implementing the mandates of federal and state laws to provide the least restrictive educational environment for all children offers you an exciting and challenging opportunity to use your creativity and intelligence in order to teach all children.

Projects

Continuing Case Study

From the first observation that you made of your case study child, draw up a list of behavioral characteristics. Observe your child as he or she interacts with a special needs child, if possible. Using your list, note

Take time to observe special needs children on the play yard, with others, and in the classroom.

similar behaviors in the second child. In your report compare similarities and differences in the two children's behaviors. Describe how your perceptions of both children relate to behaviors of special needs children, as described in this or another textbook.

1. Examine your own feelings about children with special needs. Did you ever know a person with a handicap? How did you feel about that person? Do you believe that all children should have the same educational experiences? Why and why not? Who do you think is responsible for paying for the education of special needs children—parents, the local community, or state or federal government?

2. Observe four children of the same sex and age. Try to identify how these children are alike and different.

3. Create your own chart of individual characteristics. List those characteristics that you believe are the result of genetics, such as eye or hair color, those that are the result of environment, and those that might be the result of an interaction between environment and genetics.

4. In your own family, identify individual differences in development between you and one of your siblings or other relatives. When did you first talk? What was your first word? When did you first begin to walk? How long were you afraid of strangers? How old were you when you

first began to alternate feet going up and down stairs? Now compare your growth record with your relative's.

5. Contact a local chapter of an association concerned with the welfare of children who have special needs. See if you can talk with a parent of a child who has special needs. Find out what parents expect of teachers and how teachers can help support the family.

Children's Books

Aseltine, L., Mueller, E., & Tait, N. (1986). *I'm deaf and it's okay*. Illustrated by H. Cogancherry. Niles, IL: Whitman. (A deaf child faces the frustrations, challenges and successes of everyday life.)

Baker, P. J. (1986). *My first book of sounds*. Illustrated by P. B. Gillen. Washington, DC: Gallaudet University. (A book about signing with excellent and clear illustrations of how to sign.)

Brightman, A. (1976). *Like me*. Boston: Little Brown. (The story of a retarded child.)

Cairo, S. (1985). *Our brother has Down's Syndrome*. Photographs by I. McNeil. Toronto, Canada: Annick. (A family gives and receives love from a Down's Syndrome child.)

Caudill, R. (1965). *A certain small shepherd*. Illustrated by William Pene du Bois. New York: Holt, Rinehart & Winston. (A child who doesn't speak is portrayed.)

Delton, J. (1985). *I'll never love anything ever again*. Chicago: Whitman. (A child who discovers that he is allergic to animals must get rid of his dog.)

Dodge, N. C. (1975). *Morning arrow*. Illustrated by J. Lunge. New York: Lothrop, Lee & Shephard. (A story of a Native American child who has a blind grandmother.)

Fanshawe, E. R. (1975). *Rachel*. Illustrated by M. Charlton. Scarsdale, NY: Bradbury. (Relates the life of a child in a wheelchair.)

Gaes, J. (1987). *My book for kids with cansur*. Illustrated by Tim Gaes & A. Gaes. Pierre, SD: Melus & Peterson. (A young child writes his own story about cancer.)

Girard, L. W. (1990). *Alex, the kid with AIDS*. Illustrated by B. Sims. Chicago: Whitman. (Alex has AIDS and the class must learn to understand.)

Gold, P. (1975). *Please don't say hello*. Photographs by C. Baker. Boston: Houghton Mifflin. (This story deals with the disability of autism.)

Goodsell, J. (1965). *Katie's magic glasses*. Illustrated by Barbara Cooney. Boston: Houghton Mifflin. (Katie's magic glasses help her to see.)

Heide, F. (1970). *Sound of sunshine, sound of rain*. New York: Parents Magazine Press. (Sounds are meaningful to a blind child.)

Keats, E. J. (1971). *Apt. 3*. New York: Macmillan. (A blind, elderly man is the character in this story.)

Kraus, R. (1973). *Leo the late bloomer*. Illustrated by Jose Aruego. New York: Dutton. (Children who have been "slow developers" will find this story is for them.)

Lasker, J. (1974). *He's my brother*. Niles, IL: Whitman. (The story of a retarded child.)

Litchfield, A. B. (1976). *A button in her ear*. Photographs by E. Mill. Niles, IL: Whitman. (To help children understand the use of a hearing aid.)

Martin, B., & Archambault, J. (1987). *Knots on a counting rope*. Illustrated by Ted Rand. New York: Holt. (A young blind Native American boy reminisces about his birth and gains strength from his grandfather.)

Merrifield, M. (1990). *Come sit by me*. Illustrated by H. Collins. Toronto, Canada: Women's Press. (Karen's new friend at school has AIDS and Karen's parents help her and the class understand the disease.)

Peet, B. (1969). *Fly, Homer, fly*. Boston: Houghton Mifflin. (An accident disrupts life in this story.)

Peter, D. (1977). *Claire and Emma*. Photographs by J. Finlay. New York: Day. (Hearing impaired children are portrayed.)

Powers, M. E. (1986). *Our teacher's in a wheelchair*. Chicago: Whitman. (The class learns to help and function well.)

Rankin, L. (1991). *The handmade alphabet*. New York: Dial. (Exquisitely illustrated book that introduces children to American sign language.)

Raskin, E. (1972). *Spectacles*. New York: Macmillan. (Nearsighted Iris sees things differently until she finally gets glasses.)

Silverstein, A., & Silverstein, V. (1988). *Learning about AIDS*. Hillsdale, NJ: Enslow. (Though written for children ages 9 and up, can be helpful for teachers in answering questions younger children ask about AIDS.)

Simon, N. (1975). *See the first star*. Illustrated by J. Lasker. Niles, IL: Whitman. (A visually impaired child is portrayed.)

Sobol, H. L. (1977). *My brother Steven is retarded*. Photographs by P. Ayre. New York: Macmillan. (Steven is retarded and the family learns to cope.)

Stanek, M. (1983). *Don't hurt me, mama*. Illustrated by H. Cogancherry. Chicago: Whitman. (A young child finally tells of her mother's abuse, and the mother gets help.)

Stein, S. B. (1974). *About handicaps: An open family book for parents and children together*. Photographs by D. Frank. New York: Walker. (A child with cerebral palsy affects family life.)

Vigna, J. (1988). *I wish my daddy didn't drink so much*. Niles, IL: Whitman. (Lisa's father can't take her sledding Christmas Day because he is drinking, and Lisa must learn to cope.)

Williams, J. (1979). *Stupid Marco*. Illustrated by F. Henstra. New York: Parents Magazine Press. (Marco is a slow learner.)

Wolf, B. (1977). *Don't feel sorry for Paul*. New York: Lippincott. (Paul wears a prosthesis.)

Yolen, J. (1977). *The seeing stick*. Illustrated by R. Charlip & D. Maraslis. New York: Crowell. (An Asian blind child is the character in this story.)

Resources

The following texts are additional resources for teaching special needs children.

Benya, R., & Muller, K. E. (Eds.). (1988). *Children and languages: Research, practice, and rationale for the early grades*. New York: The American Forum.

Children's Defense Fund. (1989). *A children's defense budget. An analysis of our nation's investment in children*. Washington, DC: Author.

Derman-Sparks, L., & the ABC Task Force. (1989). *Anti-Bias curriculum: Tools for empowering young children*. Washington, DC: National Association of Education for Young Children.

Hakuta, K. (1986). *Mirror of language: The debate of bilingualism*. New York: Basic Books.

Hale-Benson, J. E. (1986). *Black children: Their roots, culture and learning styles*. Baltimore: Johns Hopkins University Press.

Helfer, R. E., & Kempe, R. S. (Eds.). (1987). *The battered child* (5th ed.). Chicago: University of Chicago Press.

Heward, W. L., & Orlansky, M. D. (1992). *Exceptional children: An introductory survey of special education* (4th ed.). New York: Merrill/Macmillan.

Hobbs, N., Perrin, J. M., & Ireys, H. T. (1985). *Chronically ill children and families*. San Francisco: Jossey-Bass.

Karu, D., Reed, R., & Krebs, E. (1987). *Teaching about AIDS: A teacher's guide*. Saratoga, CA: R. E. Publishers.

Peterson, N. L. (1986). *Early intervention for handicapped and at-risk children: An introduction to early-childhood-special education*. Denver, CO: Love.

Ramsey, P. G. (1986). *Children's understanding of diversity: Multicultural perspectives in early childhood education*. New York: Teachers College Press.

Stevens, L. J., & Price, M. (Eds.) (1992). A Special Section on Children At-Risk. *Phi Delta Kappan*, 74(1), 15-40.

Tower, C. C. (1988). *Child abuse and neglect: A teacher's handbook for detection, reporting, and classroom management*. Washington, DC: National Education Association.

Tower, C. C. (1984). *Secret scars: A guide for survivors of child sexual abuse*. New York: Viking Penguin.

Townley, R. (1985). *Safe and sound: A parent's guide to child protection*. New York: Simon & Schuster.

Whitmore, J. R. (1987). *Intellectual giftedness in young children: Recognition and development*. New York: Haworth.

The following national organizations offer resources and assistance in helping you meet the needs of all children. Drop a postcard requesting information about the association and its resources.

Association for Children with Learning
    Disabilities
    5225 Grace Street
    Pittsburgh, PA 15236

Closer Look
    National Information Center for the
    Handicapped
    1201 Sixteenth Street, NW
    Washington, DC 20037

The Council for Exceptional Children
    1201 Association Drive
    Reston, VA 22091

Gifted Child Society, Inc.
    59 Glen Gray Road
    Oakland, NJ 07436

The Guild for the Blind
    180 N. Michigan Avenue
    Chicago, IL 60601

National Association for Retarded Citizens
    2709 Avenue E, East
    Arlington, TX 76011

National Center on Educational Media and
    Materials for the Handicapped
    The Ohio State University
    Columbus, OH 43210

National Easter Seal Society for Crippled
    Children and Youths
    2023 West Ogden Avenue
    Chicago, IL 60612

National Foundation of March of Dimes
    Division of Health Information
    and School Relation

    1275 Mamaroneck Avenue
    White Plains, NY 10605

United Cerebral Palsy Association
    66 East 34th Street
    New York, NY 10016

We Are People First
    P.O. Box 5208
    Salem, OR 97304

References

American Psychiatric Association (1987). *Diagnostic and statistical manual of mental disorders* (3rd ed.). Washington, DC: American Psychiatric Association.

Anderson, C. W. (1936). *Billy and Blaze*. New York: Macmillan.

Banks, J. A. (1993a). Approaches to multicultural curriculum reform. In J. A. Banks & C. A. M. Banks (Eds.), *Multicultural education: Issues and perspectives* (2nd ed.) (pp. 195-214). Boston: Allyn & Bacon.

Banks, J. A. (1993b). Multicultural education: Characteristics and goals. In J. A. Banks & C. A. M. Banks (Eds.), *Multicultural education: Issues and perspectives* (2nd ed.) (pp. 1-28). Boston: Allyn & Bacon.

Barbour, N. (1990). Flexible grouping: It works! *Childhood Education 67*(2), 66-68.

Barry, J. E. (1983). Political, bilingual education and the curriculum. *Educational Leadership, 40*, 56-60.

Bennett, W. J. (1986). *The condition of bilingual education in the nation, 1986*. A report from the Secretary of Education to the President and the Congress. Washington, DC: Department of Education.

Bergan, J. R., & Henderson, R. W. (1979). *Child development*. Columbus, OH: Merrill.

Berk, L. E. (1991). *Child development*. Boston: Allyn & Bacon.

Bilingual Education Act (1974). PL 93-380 (21 Aug. 1974). 88STAT.503.

Bredekamp, S. (Ed.), (1987). *Developmentally appropriate practice in early childhood education programs serving children from birth through age 8*. Washington, DC:

National Association of Education for Young Children.

Buchoff, R. (1990). Attention deficit disorder: Help for the classroom teacher. *Childhood Education 67*(2), 86-90.

Chamot, A. U. (1988). Bilingualism in education and bilingual education: The state of the art. *Journal of Multilingual and Multicultural Development, 19,* 11-35.

Clark, B. (1992). *Growing up gifted in the classroom* (4th ed.). New York: Merrill/ Macmillan.

Cohen, S., & Taharally, C. (1992). Getting ready for young children with prenatal drug exposure. *Childhood Education, 69*(1), 5-9.

Craig, S. E. (1992). The educational needs of children living with violence. *Phi Delta Kappan, 74*(1), 67-71.

Deiner, P. L. (1983). *Resources for teaching young children with special needs.* New York: Harcourt Brace Jovanovich.

Divosky, D. (1989). Ritalin: Education's fix-it drug? *Phi Delta Kappan, 70*(8), 599-605.

Dumtschin, J. U. (1988). Recognize language development and delay in early childhood. *Young Children, 43*(3), 16-24.

Ehrlich, V. I. (1982). *Gifted children: A guide for parents and teachers.* Englewood Cliffs, NJ: Prentice Hall.

Fagan, T. W., & Heid, C. A. (1991). Improving Chapter 1 programs: We can do better. *Phi Delta Kappan, 72*(8), 582-585.

Faure, M. (1988). Including young children with "new" chronic illnesses in an Early Childhood Education setting. *Young Children, 43,* 71-77.

Federal Register, Vol. 42, No. 163, 23 August, 1977.

First, J. M., & Carera, J. W. (1988). *New voices: Immigrant students in U.S. public schools.* Boston: National Coalition of Advocates for Students.

Fowler, M. (1990). Gifted education: Some considerations. *Childhood Education, 66*(5), 320-322.

Frostig, M. (1964). *The Frostig program for the development of visual perception.* Chicago: Follett.

Furth, H. G., & Wachs, H. (1974). *Thinking goes to school: Piaget's theory in practice.* New York: Oxford University Press.

Gearhart, B. R., Weishahn, M., & Gearhart, C. J. (1992). *The exceptional student in the regular classroom* (5th ed.). New York: Merrill/Macmillan.

Getman, G. N. (1963). *How to develop your child's intelligence.* La Verne, MN: Hanover Press.

Gil, D. G. (1970). *Violence against children: Physical child abuse in the United States.* Cambridge, MA: Rand McNally.

Gonzalez-Mena, J. (1976). English as a second language for preschool children. *Young Children, 32,* 14-20.

Graham, S., Harris, K. R., & Reid, R. (1992). Developing self regulated learners. *Focus on Exceptional Children,* February, 1-16.

Greenspan, S. I. (1991). Regulatory disorders I: Clinical perspectives. In M. Kilbey & K. Asghare (Eds.), *Methodological issues on controlled studies on effects of prenatal exposure to drug abuse* (pp. 165-172). Rockville, MD: National Institute on Drug Abuse.

Hadaway, N. L. (1992). Letters to literacy. Spurring second language development across the curriculum. *Childhood Education, 69*(1), 24-28.

Hendrick, J. (1992). *The whole child* (5th ed.). New York: Macmillan.

Henry, M. (1947). *Misty of Chincoteague.* New York: Rand McNally.

Heward, W. L., & Cavanaugh, R. A. (1993). Educational equality for students with disabilities. In J. A. Banks & C. A. M. Banks (Eds.), *Multicultural education: Issues and perspectives* (2nd ed.) (pp. 239-261). Boston: Allyn & Bacon.

Kagan, J. (1978). The child in the family. In A. S. Rossi, J. Kagan, & T. V. Havreven (Eds.), *The family* (pp. 33-56). New York: Norton.

Kasper, G. (1988). Bilingual education and bilingualism in education: A comment. *Journal of Multilingual & Multicultural Development, 9,* 37-42.

Kellogg, J. B. (1988). Faces of change. *Phi Delta Kappan, 70,* 199-204.

Kephart, N. C. (1960). *The slow learner in the classroom*. Columbus, OH: Merrill.

Lazar, I. (1977). *The persistence of preschool effects: A long term follow up of fourteen infant and preschool experiments*. Washington, DC: Administration for Children, Youth and Families.

LeTendre, M. J. (1991). Improving Chapter 1 programs. We can do better. *Phi Delta Kappan, 72*(8), 576-581.

Meddin, B. J., & Rosen, A. (1986). Child abuse and neglect: Prevention and reporting. *Young Children, 41*, 26-30.

Merrifield, M. (1990). *Come sit with me*. Toronto, Canada: Women's Press.

Mussen, P. H., Conger, J. J., & Kagan, J. (1980). *Essentials of child development and personality*. New York: Harper & Row.

Olsen, P. (1988). Crossing the schoolhouse border: Immigrant children in California. *Phi Delta Kappan, 70*, 211-219.

Raper, J., & Aldridge, J. (1988). AIDS. What every teacher should know. *Childhood Education, 64*, 146-149.

Reynolds, M. C., & Birch, J. W. (1977). *Teaching exceptional children in all America's schools*. Reston, VA: The Council for Exceptional Children.

Santrock, J., & Yussen, S. (1984). *Children and adolescents*. Dubuque, IA: Wm. C. Brown.

Sautter, R. C. (1992). Crack. Healing the children. *Phi Delta Kappan, 74*(3), K1-K12.

Seefeldt, C. (1983). The new arrivals. *Childhood Education, 60*(2), 74-76.

Sexton, D., Snyder, P., Sharpton, W. R., & Stricklin, S. (1993). *Infants and toddlers with special needs and their families. Position Paper*. Wheaton, MD: Association for Childhood Education International.

Silver, L. B. (1991). *ADHD. Attention deficit-hyperactivity disorder and learning disabilities. Booklet for the classroom teacher*. Summit, NJ: CIBA-GEIGY.

Sisk, D. (1979). Need for gifted programs. *Educational Leadership, 36*, 527-529.

Skeen, P., & Hodson, D. (1987). AIDS: What adults should know about AIDS (and shouldn't discuss with very young children). *Young Children, 42*, 65-72.

Smith, S. L. (1978). *No easy answers: The learning disabled child*. Rockville, MD: National Institute of Mental Health.

Soto, L. D. (1991). Understanding bilingual/bicultural young children. *Young Children, 46*(2), 30-36.

Stevens, L. J., & Price, M. (1992). Meeting the challenge of educating children at risk. *Phi Delta Kappan, 74*(1), 18-23.

Surr, J. (1992). Early childhood programs and the Americans with Disabilities Act (ADA). *Young Children, 47*(5), 18-21.

Tyler, R. (1992). Prenatal drug exposure: An overview of associated problems and intervention strategies. *Phi Delta Kappan, 73*(9), 705-708.

Urza, C. (1992). "You stopped too soon." Second language children composing and revising. *TESOL Quarterly, 21*(2), 279-304.

U.S. Department of Health & Human Services. (1986). Surgeon General's report on Acquired Immune Deficiency Syndrome. Washington, DC: U.S. Government Printing Office.

Webb, P. K. (1989). *The emerging child. Development through age twelve*. New York: Macmillan.

White, B. P., & Phair, M. A. (1986). "It'll be a challenge!" Managing emotional stress in teaching disabled children. *Young Children, 41*(2), 44-48.

Wong Fillmore, L. (1985). Teaching bilingual learners. In M. C. Wittrock (Ed.), *Handbook of research on teaching* (3rd ed.)(pp. 648-686.). New York: Macmillan.

Wood, J. W. (1992). *Adapting instruction for the mainstream and at-risk students*. New York: Merrill/Macmillan.

4 Relating with Parents and Other Adults in School and Community

"We cannot afford to sequester parents on the periphery of educational enterprise. Parent involvement is neither a quick fix nor a luxury. It is absolutely fundamental to a health system of public education."

(Henderson, 1988. p. 153)

After you read this chapter, you should be able to answer the following questions:

1. In what ways have family patterns changed in the last 35 years?

2. What impact do socioeconomic factors, attitudes and beliefs, and technology have on differences in children's development and learning?

3. What are some ways to establish effective communication with parents?

4. Why is it important for a teacher to establish autonomy in the classroom, and how might one proceed?

5. What are some ways a teacher might involve other adults in enriching children's learning experience?

6. Describe different ways that community resources could be tapped to enhance children's learning?

Children and Families Today

Ms. Robin is reading *Goodnight Moon* by Margaret Wise Brown to a group of five-year-olds. At the end, she asks, "When you go to bed, to whom do you say goodnight?" The children raise their hands, but they speak out eagerly one after another.

"I say goodnight to my mom and nana."
"I say goodnight to my mom, my stepdad, and my real dad."
"I say goodnight to my dad, Aunt Marilyn, and Uncle Joe."
"I say goodnight to my mom, my dad, my sister, my brother, and my dog, Molly."
"Well, I say goodnight to my mother, my father, my sister, my brother, gramma, and grampa, Aunt Helen, Uncle Phil, my cousins, John, Susie, and Louise, and my dog, and my canary, and. . . ."
"How about you, Tommy?" Ms. Robin asks, trying to include a child who doesn't speak up and call out.
"I just have my two dads. I say goodnight to them."

In any classroom today, the family unit reflects as great a diversity as shown by the perceptions the children in Ms. Robin's class have of their families. If children are to grow and to develop skills, attitudes, and characteristics that enable them to live productive and satisfying lives, they must be supported by a society dedicated to meeting their needs. The school cannot provide for all needs; no institution can. In conjunction with other agencies in the community, schools and families must find ways to cooperate in providing the nurturance necessary for productive educational experiences for all children. Adversarial roles between home and school do great harm to children's learning, but when there is effective parental involvement in schools, children learn better (Comer and Haynes, 1991; Schorr, 1988; Henderson, 1988).

The structure of the American family is diverse. As an early childhood educator, you will need to become familiar with the status of children and their families and adept at developing positive relationships with children's families. Only then can you share in creating a society that makes the needs of children and families a top priority.

Changing Family Patterns

In this century the family unit has undergone rapid and drastic changes. Change started when our society moved from being agrarian to industrial. In an agrarian society, children were valued because they were an economic blessing. At a very early age, they assumed an important role in the household work, on the farm, or in the family business. As they worked beside adults, they learned important skills as well as something about their place in the larger society and their own self-identity.

After the Industrial Revolution, work was no longer a family enterprise but something that men and women went out of the family to do. During the 1920s and 1930s, labor-saving devices became common. Freed from hard physical labor both at work and at home, parents no longer needed to teach their children a great many homemaking skills or a trade. Today the focus is more often on parents as providers of a foundation that enhances intellectual and social development.

Structural and sociological changes in American society are taking place as the information age takes hold. Many higher paying manufacturing jobs are disappearing and are being replaced by less well paid retail and service jobs or higher paid jobs requiring more education. As a result, a larger portion of American society is poor; one in five children today lives in poverty (Children's Defense Fund, 1989). The number of homeless families is growing. Nearly one-third of all the homeless have children (Children's Defense Fund, 1989; Hodgkinson, 1992). These children and parents need help and support.

Changing job structures create many societal problems that, in turn, affect children. To receive better paying jobs, teenagers need to continue and extend their education. Yet, teenage pregnancy is on the rise, and teenage mothers are keeping their babies and attempting to raise them alone with minimal financial support or education to assist them in getting decent jobs (Frost, 1986).

Drug and alcohol abuse in our society is affecting all Americans no matter what their economic, social, or ethnic background might be. It has been estimated that as many as 18 percent of newborns are born to drug- and alcohol-addicted mothers. Too many of these children will not receive the adequate medical and familial support necessary for healthy growth (Sautter, 1992). Inadequate health insurance and housing contribute to the poverty conditions in which children are raised. These children and their parents need help and support not only from schools but from the larger community as well.

Family units in our country have changed. In 1955, 60 percent of all households consisted of a working father, a housewife mother, and two or more school-age children. By 1985, only 7 percent of households had such a makeup (Georgiades, 1988). In Ms. Robin's class, only one child of the six suggested such a family unit. The number of mothers who have preschool and school-age children and work outside the home is increasing. It is estimated that by 1995 two-thirds of all preschoolers and four-fifths of school-age children will have working mothers (Children's Defense Fund, 1989, p. 175). Another change is the dramatic rise in the number of single-parent homes. Sixty percent of today's two-year-olds will have lived in a single-parent home before they reach 18 years of age (Frost, 1986). Many children will be raised without the ongoing support of a male figure.

But where fathers are present, they are taking a more active role in child rearing. Many fathers are gaining full or partial custody of their children in divorce cases. And both single men and women, as well as gay and lesbian couples (Clay, 1990), are adopting children.

Remarriage is common for divorced parents, and these remarriages mean different or shifting life-styles for many children. New expectations and role models emerge from such *blended families.* These shifting relationships may affect children's functioning in school. Teachers need to be sensitive to the period of change in a family's life.

The number of children of interracial parentage and the number of adopted minority children have increased in the past decade. Some of these adopted children are African-Americans being brought up in Euro-American homes, and others are minority children who have been adopted from foreign countries. These interracial children and parents will need the emotional and psychological support of schools as they seek their special ethnic identity (Wardle, 1987, 1990).

Today families live in isolated units, with relatives having less impact on children's upbringing than they once did. In the latter half of this century, Americans have tended to segregate themselves according to age, so children have fewer and fewer contacts with older relatives or others of different age groups.

Family units are also smaller, so children have fewer siblings with whom to interact. Contact with children of other ages is also limited by large school systems that segregate children into classes of a single chronological age. Even recreational facilities are age-segregated, preventing interactions among older and younger children.

With the number of extended families decreasing and with more public information available to all, parents tend to seek help from the outside rather than the family for the child's physical and emotional well-being and intellectual development. They often turn for help to doctors, teachers, social workers, and the mass media. Thus many people outside the family today share child-rearing responsibilities with parents.

The School's Role

If so many people in the society share in child rearing, obviously children and families need support from schools. Part of your plans and work with children must take into account the changes in families and the variety of family styles. Because more children are being reared in single-parent households, you can help children by extending opportunities for adult-child interactions in the classroom by inviting adults, especially elders, from the community to work with you as aides or volunteers.

For children reared in female-headed households, it might be helpful to provide more contact with males. Furman (1992) suggests that these children often have unexpressed needs and interests in examining their feelings about their absent fathers. It is important that they have opportunities to discuss their feelings and attitudes about fathers and that they have male role models. You might arrange to have men volunteer in the classroom and find curriculum materials that show men in a variety of roles, especially nurturing ones.

Taking children out of the classroom and into the community gives them opportunities to see both men and women at work and to observe how adults function in the world. Or perhaps you can invite a resource person from the community to visit the school to bring the world of work to the classroom. Adding materials to the dramatic play area in the classroom that reflect various parental and community workers' roles enables children to express their reactions and feelings regarding these people.

You might also consider a variety of activities that bring your students together with both older and younger children. The exchange needs to be ongoing and consistent if all parties are to benefit from the experience.

No one is suggesting that the school or the teacher will be able to solve all the problems facing today's changing family, but you can become sensitive to the needs of individual children and their families and try to meet some of these needs in the classroom. Awareness and acceptance of each child's unique family situation are perhaps the most important ways you can support children and their families.

Become aware of the language you use in the classroom. Referring to children whose parents have divorced as coming from "broken homes" is insensitive. "Often those homes are more 'whole' than they were before the parents separated" (Clay, 1980, p. 42). When making gifts for Mother's Day or Father's Day or when inviting parents in for special occasions, children from single-parent homes can be a part of the activity if invitations or gifts are for the special adults in children's lives. Sometimes children whose family patterns are different are reluctant to invite other significant adults to school for various reasons (Furman, 1992). It is important that you be sensitive to children's reactions and help them to express their concerns.

Socioeconomic Factors and Parental Style of Interaction

The dramatic social changes taking place in our society put pressures on families that influence how they rear their children. We know that the greatest influence on a child is the family unit, whatever form it may take (Radin, 1982, p. 61). Children's socialization, learning, growth, and development depend on the family. Within that unit, a process of mutual interaction is established whereby the child's emerging behavior depends upon the temperament of both parents and child.

Radin (1982, pp. 62-64) believes that at least six different processes in child-parent behavior influence children's development.

1.   Parents influence their children by modeling. Children are great imitators so they respond to the adult model whether the adult intends them to or not.

2.   Parents tell or explain to children what they are or are not to do. Sometimes it is an elaborate explanation, while at other times it may be a series of dos and don'ts.

3.   Parents may state certain household rules. These rules indicate expected behavior. Some parents are more consistent in following through with rules than others.

4.   Parents use a system of rewards and punishments. Parents may not always be aware of how they reward or punish.

5.   Parents may use a series of techniques that label the child's action. They may try reasoning with the child to change behaviors, or they may try to shame a child or arouse guilt.

6.   Parents provide an environment that intellectually influences children. Toys, clothes, food, and learning materials influence not only the children's learning but also the way they view themselves. Self-image is particularly molded by children's comparisons of their environment with their peers'. The space where children live and play, how they are allowed to use and explore that space, and trips or other extensions of their environment all contribute to the child's social, emotional, and cognitive development.

Although these six processes always seem to be used at some level between parent and child, it is not clear how each works for different children and parents.

Some researchers (Bernstein, 1970; Kagan, 1978) have suggested that poverty may be related to the way parents talk with their children. Other researchers have found that, though parenting styles result in a marked difference in children's achievement, all styles exist across ethnic groups, levels of education, and family structures (Dornbusch, Ritter, Leiderman, Roberts, & Fraleigh, 1987).

Both groups of researchers have noted that some parents are more authoritarian in their treatment of children. They do not give explanations for their actions but make statements like "Stop it," "Don't," or "Do it because I said so." Other parents may be firm in their approach but more open to discussion, explanation, and negotiation. They are more likely to give reasons for or elaborate on their requests, saying "Please go outside and play now," "Don't touch the stove, because it's hot, and you could burn yourself," or "Put your seat belt on, it will help protect you if we have an accident."

Research indicates that effective parents, no matter what their life-style, have developed a positive self-image, have established meaningful relationships and communication patterns with their children and with another adult, and have acquired a sense of belonging to a larger community. Such parents believe that they are basically in control of their lives and have various options when making decisions (Swick & Graves, 1986).

These interaction patterns have an effect on how children learn in school. Children from less authoritarian homes and from homes where parents feel in control tend to be reared in such a way that they have developed a large vocabulary, understand the consequences of their acts, and solve their own problems. Because schools tend to use the more open interaction pattern, children from such environments tend to do better in schools, and teachers may consider children who do not automatically respond to this pattern incompetent.

The School's Role

Children first learn who they are from their parents and home. They develop a sense of how their parents view them and who their parents are. When children move out into the neighborhood and the school, they begin to compare their life-style with their peers'. They get messages from both peers and adults they encounter.

Children first learn who they are from their parents.

Because schools tend to reflect middle-class values, children raised in a different value structure may begin to believe that the qualities they have and the values they have learned are not those accepted by the school. Some children gradually come to believe that they cannot achieve and must not be worthy of acceptance (Kenniston, 1977, p. 46).

As a teacher, you must recognize each child's worth regardless of the parenting style or socioeconomic situation at home. Learn to see how these factors work both to enhance and to negate children's development. Learn not to make value judgments about the child's family background, but work to see that each child views himself or herself as a capable, worthy human being—one who can and will succeed. Remember, too, that all families, no matter how poverty-stricken, want their children to succeed. Teach every child, plan for each one to learn, and support and prize the positive effects of each child's home background.

Attitudes and Beliefs

Each family has its own distinct culture, set of values, and mode of rearing children. Parents rear children according to their beliefs and in relation to the attitudes they have about themselves.

Parents are influenced in their child-rearing practices by the way in which they were reared. Current theories and practices also influence child rearing. Books, magazine articles, and radio and television programs bombard parents with instructions about raising their children.

Some parents admire or reject characteristics they see in themselves and other people. Parents may emulate the dress and traits or characteristics they prefer. At times, they may admonish or attempt to have their children be like them or behave like those they admire. For example, the father who admires baseball heroes may push his child to excel in sports, or the mother who admires the success of a woman legislator may encourage and reward assertive behavior in her daughter (Margolin, 1982, p. 14).

Children do not always respond in the same way to these pressures. A great deal depends on the child's temperament. Some children who strive to acquire these characteristics are rewarded and feel a sense of self-worth. Others, unable or unwilling to meet these expectations, acquire a sense of failure and reject the parent's views, setting up conflicts between themselves and their parents.

Technology

Family life has been affected by rapidly advancing technology. The television has been a mainstay of family life for approximately forty years. The computer, a far more recent addition, is increasingly becoming an integral part of the family.

We are moving from a "culture organized around typography to a culture based on the electronic image" (Postman, 1983, p. 311). Families watch television a great deal, with children between the ages of six and eighteen averaging about 16,000 hours of television viewing and only 13,000 of schooling in that twelve-year period (Postman, 1983).

Some people are concerned about the possible negative effect television has on family interactions. Television is believed to limit conversations and family activities. Postman (1983) sees television as "present centered, emotion centered, image centered, attention centered, and largely incoherent" (p. 316).

In the past, some effort has been made to limit types of programming during prime time for children's viewing. But since 1982, when the Federal Communication Commission decided to deregulate children's commercial television, violent acts in children's programs have greatly increased (Gerbner and Signorelli, 1990). Many children see the same programs and advertising as adults. Violence, free sexual activity, and social aberrations are part of some children's steady diet. Advertisements aim at the viewer's need or desire for immediate gratification (Notar, 1989). With the increase in the amount of violence and in the toys of destruction shown on TV, the National Association of Education for Young Children issued a position paper calling for more responsible actions of adults in controlling the exposure of young children to such violence (National Association of Education for Young Children [NAEYC], 1990). The statements serve to remind adults of responses they need to make to their children's requests to watch television, to advertisers who promote violent products on children's shows, and to legislators to restrict programming.

When children view television, some form of adult guidance will be required.

Young viewers need adult supervision to discover ways to solve problems without resorting to violence. It takes experience to realize that wonderful things do not happen as a result of some advertiser's product (Isenberg, 1987). Many professionals who work with children believe that television has a negative effect on children's total development. Rather than producing a family-centered culture, it is producing now-oriented, violence-immune, and television-centered children who are intellectually inert.

Others, who also work with children, maintain that television viewing isn't all that passive. Some believe that children bring their own experiences and understanding to the content and do experience cognitive processing as they watch (Anderson & Collins, 1988). In any case, watching television is less passive when children can interact with adults and get help in interpreting some of the events they see. Television watching may have benefits if children have someone who can question them and help interpret the behaviors of the characters they see. When children have adults who will talk with them about the programs and instruct them in the customs, mores, knowledge, and understanding of adult society, television may be a teaching tool (Winick & Wehrenberg, 1982).

Computers are another form of technology that have become a part of our daily lives, and many homes now have them. Some educators claim that children as young as eighteen months of age can be taught to use a computer (Zeiser & Hoffman, 1983). It is not so much the age of the child, however, as it is use of *developmentally appropriate* software that makes the most impact on children's lives (Haugland & Shade, 1988). The computer may be used to support children's social, intellectual, and language development when adults select quality software for children and are involved in encouraging, questioning, and interpreting children's responses (Clements, 1987). Because software quality differs significantly, it is important to encourage parents to select programs that are developmentally appropriate, allow children to be actively involved in its use, and permit both independent and trial-and-error explorations (Haugland & Shade, 1988, p. 39). When adults allow children to explore, practice acquired concepts, write or tell stories, and review their creations, the computer can be a powerful learning tool.

Families tend to use the computer in several ways. Some use the computer to play games, and others to help with family bookkeeping or as a means of teaching children programming skills. Weyer (1983) has suggested that computers might serve to bring families closer together as parents and children become involved in computer-related activities.

The School's Role

You'll be challenged as a teacher to build on the best of the television and computer culture in your classroom. You might suggest ways children and families can interact with one another and with the television and the computer. Identify programs designed for children's viewing, and send information home on how parents can use these programs to increase interactions of parent and child as well as to foster intellectual growth.

For instance, you could have parents show children how the images they see on television compare with actual experiences: "How is the grocery store on TV just like or different from the one we go to?" and "Do the real clerks ever ask you the questions asked by the TV clerks?"

The computer offers other challenges. Some children may be familiar with computers and be able to complete simple programs. Others may have little or no experience with the computer. Plan to provide equal access to skill development for all children and to expand on their experiences with the classroom computer.

Offer assistance to parents as they work with their child and the computer at home or work with individuals in the classroom to help children translate the electronic image to their own environment.

Relating with Parents

Americans are disturbed about their schools. Parents are frightened at the rising cost of education and disappointed by their children's lower test scores. Americans have demonstrated their displeasure with the schools by voting for tax cuts and against school bonds, by taking their children out of school, and by supporting a voucher system.

Some educators believe that these actions may have resulted because parents lack a sense of ownership in the schools. This hasn't always been the case. "The history of American education reflects that the roots of the public schools are deeply tied to the neighborhood, the community, and the home" (Gordon & Breivogel, 1976, p. 1). At one time, parents not only hired and fired the teachers, but they also told them what and how to teach, how to behave, and even which church to attend.

Schools today are far removed from this period of involvement. Parents and teachers probably do not live in the same neighborhood, and they may not share the same community experiences. Schools are large and may be intimidating to parents. When most mothers and fathers are employed outside the home, it is increasingly difficult to arrange for contacts between parents and teachers.

Yet the need to involve parents in the education of their children continues. We know that a child's learning is greatly enhanced when there is an understanding of the parental and teaching roles in the child's life. Umansky (1983, pp. 262-264) clarifies these roles in today's society.

Much learning today occurs outside formal educational settings. Whereas the home and religious sanctuary were once the predominant sources of learning, schools have emerged to share this function. Today, peers and media also play a significant role in education. In this division of labor, the school assumes primary responsibility for transmitting to children academic knowledge and skills to apply new technology. Parents retain responsibility for transmitting values and standards to their children. The linkage among home, school, and community, so necessary if this formula is to work, must be strengthened.

Perhaps early childhood educators have always recognized this. The young child is so closely tied to the home that it would be impossible not to involve parents, and as a result early childhood educators have developed a number of established methods to build a strong school-home relationship. These are based on the understanding that:

- Parents have expectations from the school.
- Parents are busy whether their family is traditional, single-parent, or blended.
- Teachers and parents share a love and concern for the child.

Parents' Expectations

Teachers are authority figures for both children and parents. No matter how young or inexperienced you are, parents may look to you as all-knowing because you are the teacher and have had courses in psychology and learning. You are in charge of their child, and they expect you to have answers for all their questions and concerns.

- "Tim has a terrible temper, what can I do?"
- "How do I get Susie to stop sucking her thumb?"
- "Jackie has become terrified of the banging of the radiator. . . . I've tried everything. Do you think we'll have to move?"
- "Clare makes me so angry at times, I hit her. I'm afraid I may really hurt her one of these days. What should I do?"

One teacher of four-year-olds was overwhelmed by the personal questions asked by parents who were all older than he. "They look to me as the expert, and I've never even had a child," he said. Even if you *have* had a lot of experience or had your own children, you will not have all the answers. But you should have a sympathetic ear, offer support and understanding, and guide parents to resources. You might keep handy pamphlets from the U.S. Government Printing Office, a list of books on child-rearing available at the library, or other resources that you can give to parents. Or you could arrange to have a child psychologist or pediatrician speak at a parents' meeting or guide parents to other resources either within the school or in the community.

Some parents may not have had pleasant experiences themselves with school. They may come to school expecting you to criticize them or their children. It may take time for you to build up trust with these parents. Promote their cooperation by asking for their opinions and then acting on them, complimenting the achievements of their children, and showing genuine respect for the family.

Parents of special needs children will have many of the same expectations as other children's parents, but because of handicapping conditions, extreme poverty, homelessness, or limited English ability, they will have other needs and expectations too. You can guide these parents to resources that will provide them with information about available services. They may want information about day care or respite care or about availability of funding and special transportation for their children (McCormick & Holden, 1992). Availability of special classes in English or topics related to their children's needs can be posted on a parents' bulletin board. And since they may need information about their child's particular condition, you can have a library that contains books or articles that would assist your parents. Also share with them the many children's books about special needs children that you use in your classroom. Videotapes could be made available for parents to take home, too (Brantlinger, 1991).

Regardless of their socioeconomic background, all parents are concerned that their children succeed in school. They expect you to be able to tell them how their child is doing in terms that are understandable to them. You should be prepared to explain each child's strengths and areas where you think improvement can realistically be made.

Because parents are so concerned about their children's achievements, you can show them how they can reinforce the school's work at home. You might have games and books they can borrow, or you could send home ideas they can use to help their children practice special skills. These don't have to be formal homework assignments but ways parents can informally teach children at home. You might tell them how letting children help put away groceries will help teach them about classification or letting them weigh vegetables or fruits at the supermarket provides experiences with measurement and numbers.

Many parents will also want you to describe their own child's attitudes toward learning and his or her ability to socialize with peers. You should be able to state the school's expectations and values and explain the rationale for them. Be able to articulate the children's skills in these areas as well. Understand that you build support and trust if you can share with parents the similarities and differences between their expectations and those of the school.

Parents expect confidentiality. Teachers share much of children's lives and receive a lot of confidential information about their families. Parents expect you to be discrete, and they have the right to do so. If you expect parents to respect and work with you, to share their hopes and disappointments, their joys and tribulations for their children, then you must be most careful how you discuss their children's background, achievement, or failings with anyone else. This sounds like common sense, but it is an area where professionalism can break down.

Involving Parents

Schools work best when parents are involved. Many informal and formal ways exist to involve parents in the school program, and you will develop a wide repertoire as you work with parents. What succeeds in one neighborhood with one family will not necessarily work in another place with another. Effective teachers use a variety of methods to involve parents successfully. They may only be involved as they interact with you regarding their children's developmental progress, or they may be actively involved in tutoring children, working on fund-raising events, or in many other different activities in the school. In some schools, parents assist in staff hiring and grant writing, and some schools have a special parent liaison. Successful programs depend upon how the principal and staff welcome the parents and respond to their needs (Bloom, 1992).

Conferences

Conferences are a traditional method of involving and informing parents. The intent of the formal conference should be to inform parents how their children's progress and performance stand in relation to the school's expectations.

Before you plan the conference, consider the time, place, general purpose, materials, and agenda. In scheduling conferences, time and place are critical because they must be convenient to both you and the parents. With the large number of single-parent households, and those where both parents work outside the home, scheduling may be a problem. If you show a willingness to adjust your schedule, however, parents are often willing to do so as well. If conferences are scheduled one after the other, then a comfortable waiting place is important for those parents who arrive early.

A half hour of time per conference is usually sufficient if you have carefully planned your agenda. If some parents need more time, then it is best to schedule another appointment. Try to arrange for a conference room that's comfortable, and make parents feel welcome in some way, perhaps by providing light refreshments or having a photo album with pictures and captions of the children at work in school.

Think about the goals and objectives of the conference and the procedures you'll use to achieve them. Usually the major objective is to give information and get it from parents so you can better meet the child's needs.

Plan to start and end the conference on a positive note. Structure your comments so parents can enter comfortably into the discussion. Ask questions such as "What does Tom like best about preschool?" "I've noticed Mary stays longer to hear a story. What are her favorite stories?" "Aletha was so excited about the trip to the zoo. What did she tell you about it?" Ask parents questions that can be answered with more than a yes or no in order to foster discussion. Even if their response is "I don't know," "yes," or "no," you have demonstrated your care and concern for them and their child.

Prepare a written agenda that you can use to discuss the child's progress. Give the parents a copy so they can follow your discussion. You might even send the agenda home or give it to them when they arrive so they can think about it before the meeting. Rutherford and Edgar (1979) suggest that you give general impressions of a child on the agenda, such as "Bill is a quiet, industrious child. He seems to prefer to work alone, but I've been encouraging him to develop projects with other children." General statements can be followed by more specific comments describing a child's performance in all major areas of development and curriculum.

Even though preparing an agenda for each child is time consuming, it establishes your procedures, gives assurance to you and the parents, and serves to prepare both of you for the conference. Along with the agenda, have samples of each child's work ready to document performance. These could include materials from more than just one area of the curriculum and can represent work over a period of time so the parents can see their child's progress. Be sure to stress areas of growth and progress, and be frank about the areas in which the child needs improvement.

In addition to samples of work, you might be able to share results of standardized testing with the parents. Often, too, the conference is used as the forum for interpreting the child's report card. The grading system and standardized test scores can be explained and discussed.

Invite parents to share with you things that they have observed at home about their child's learning. They might tell you about the books their child reads at home, about the ways their child has become more independent in doing tasks about the house, about building or art projects done with the parent or independently, or about trips they have taken as a family. In sharing such events, you can get a larger picture of the child's interests and activities and can help the parent realize the skill and intellectual potential of such tasks. You also give parents an important message, which indicates that you and they together are cooperating and facilitating their child's development.

At some point in the conference, you should ask parents if they have any questions or concerns. If you have parents who seem uncomfortable with posing questions, you might share with them questions that other parents have asked and that reflect the important goals of your program. Coleman (1991) suggests that parents be helped to ask questions that include such concerns as:

- Progress that their child is making not only academically but socially and how such progress is assessed
- Rules for behavior in the classroom, how teachers reinforce these rules, and how their child is responding
- Different ways that schools keep parents informed of their child's progress
- Parental involvement and available resources at home, in the community, and at school that will assist them in helping their child

Plan ahead to think of a positive way to end each conference. You might ask parents if they have any other questions or concerns and recap the major points of the conference, stressing the fact that you have gained a better understanding of the child through the meeting. Express the hope that they've also increased their understanding of the child. Always thank the parents for coming, and let them know how appreciative you are of their interest in your work, the school, and their child's progress.

Home Visits

In recent years there has been an increase in the number of home visiting programs, especially for young children in Head Start, Home Start, and Even Start programs as well as in day-care, nursery schools, and public school four-year-old programs. The purpose of these programs varies, and although some are operated by school systems, others are operated by health departments and mental health agencies (Powell, 1990). Program designs and goals vary. Some programs are designed to provide children and parents with educational experiences that focus on children's intellectual, social, physical, and nutritional needs. These programs are not the responsibility of the classroom teacher but are managed by specially trained home visitors.

In other programs, teachers make home visits at least once or twice a year. In most situations, the initial visit is to acquaint the parents with the program and for the teacher to get a clearer understanding of the developmental level of the children who will be attending the program. A major goal of any home visit should be to begin to establish good communication links between school and home.

Home visits can be threatening for both teacher and parent. Parents often fear that teachers are snooping; teachers fear a slammed door or cold shoulder when they approach. These fears are usually ungrounded, however, and most home visits are pleasant and appreciated. Hymes (1974) assures teachers that if they approach the home visit in the same manner they would any new acquaintance, there will be no problem. Don't try to change your style of relating with people or your personality when you make home visits. Be yourself and follow your own instincts and style. You should, however:

1. *Call ahead of time*. Don't drop in on people. Set up a time that is mutually convenient for you and the parents, and tell the parents how long you expect the visit to last.

2. *State the purpose of your visit*. Even if it's just "to get to know you and Moritz better" so you can better plan to meet his needs and interests, build on his strengths, and meet the family's desires.

3. *Bring an icebreaker with you*. It may be a finger puppet; a short, quick, and catchy game you can play with the children in the home; or something for the parents. Experienced home visitors find it useful to have several ideas ready in case the child rejects your first idea. You might bring crayons and paper for the children or a pamphlet for the parents. Or you may not have anything concrete at all but just a plan for breaking the ice with something to talk about, like "Are you going to the picnic Sunday?" or "What in the world are they doing to the street?"

4. *Be on time and leave close to the time you said you would*. Be prepared to leave sooner if family interruptions occur.

5. *Encourage parents to let the child stay for the visit*. Two reasons you want to visit the home are to understand better how the child interacts with adults and peers in the home setting and to let the parents see how you and the child interact.

6. *Discuss positive aspects of the child's school behavior*. Talk about what the child will be doing and learning during the year.

7. *Try to be an active listener as parents discuss concerns or satisfactions with the child's schooling*. Don't let yourself be drawn into family controversies, but ask questions and respond to the parents' discussions, letting them know you are sincerely interested in them and their child.

Informal Contact

It is hard for parents to think about taking one more night away from home to go to a school conference when they work outside the home, have meals and the care of children to worry about, struggle to provide even the bare necessities, or struggle with communicating in English. In today's busy and complicated world, informal contacts between home and school become even more critical. Often the informal, spontaneous communications between you and parents do the most to build effective school-home relationships. This does not mean that you give up formal conferences or home visits but that you become committed to establishing communication with parents through daily school events.

It is especially important to organize your schedule to permit you to greet children in the morning. Then you can learn briefly from the parent how the child's evening went or perhaps comment on what you'll be doing during the day. "We're going to make bread today. We'll save a piece for you" or "The dentist is coming today."

Reserve time at the end of the day to share something special about the child's day with the parent. If you are unable to be present when parents pick up their children, you might leave a message with the person who will be seeing the parents at the end of the day.

Telephone calls are effective. It is rewarding to the family to have the teacher call, "just to let you know that Paul told us about his trip to his grandparents. He remembered everything that happened on the plane; it must have been a very special time for you. We enjoyed hearing about it." Take as much care and thought when telephoning as you do for conferences. Parents' time is valuable, so keep the conversation short and to the point. Make clear to parents that telephoning is a way for them to keep in touch with you as well.

Informal notes are another means of cementing parent-teacher relationships, but a flood of notes is counterproductive. If notes go home all the time and are vague general approvals, they lose effectiveness. The notes need to communicate a child's important accomplishment, some changed behavior, or a special thank you for the child's cooperation.

Bulletin boards communicate as well. The bulletin board is placed somewhere parents will be sure to see it when they enter the school. Care should be taken that notices are important, that the board is changed frequently, and that it is attractive and intriguing. One school posts the children's daily activities for interested parents. Another reserves a bulletin board for pictures taken during special events, such as a trip to the duck pond, the birth of guinea pigs, or a visit by firefighters. The pictures and titles used to describe them should communicate something about school activities.

Another teacher used the idea of an "artist of the week" bulletin board, displaying different students' artwork. A bulletin board that attracted a great deal of attention from parents, teachers, and children was one titled "GUESS." Each teacher and other adults working in the school placed one of their baby pictures on the board. The purpose was to guess which baby picture belonged to which teacher or other staff member. Children brought their own baby pictures to the school, and the guessing game continued.

If you have space, the bulletin board concept could be extended to a Parents' Corner or Parents' Room. The corner can have not only a bulletin board but also books, magazines, and other pamphlets and materials that parents can look through or borrow. Special issues of magazines on sex education, parenting, or computers in the home might be available. Keep the place attractive and the materials up-to-date. Toys, games, children's books, or even a clothing exchange might be a part of the parents' space.

Newsletters are another means of keeping parents informed of school activities. These vary in tone and intent. Some report special events, others list poems and songs enjoyed by the children, and others contain news items concerning the faculty, children, and school staff. At other times, you might include notices of special television shows that parents can watch with their children, educational events that will occur in the community and be of interest to children and families, or other resources. Annotated lists of books and articles relating to child-rearing practices or other concerns could be included. Encourage parents to help you find materials, events, and books to share with other parents.

One kindergarten teacher sent home a weekly newsletter in which he told about the goals for the week, why certain activities were planned, and how parents could support the lessons at home. For instance, in September he was concentrating on children's safety in walking to and from school. He included a description of what he would be doing and teaching in school to promote safety on children's trips to and from school. He provided suggestions for parents, such as to take time to find the safest route to school and to walk this route with their child, pointing out stop signs and obeying safety rules.

Parents in the Classroom

Keeping parents informed is vital, but involving them as active partners in the classroom provides an even stronger base of support for school and families. If parents are on site, they benefit by getting firsthand information about the school's functioning and the teacher's interactions with the children. Immediate feedback is available, and they have an opportunity to compare their values and expectations with the school's.

In Head Start and other federally funded school programs, parents are often hired as aides in the classroom or asked to serve as volunteers. Whether aides or volunteers, parents need to be used in ways that capitalize on their skills. Written guidelines for parents involved in classroom activities might be useful. Reviewing responsibilities with the parents beforehand and allowing time for evaluation after the day is over help communicate patterns of expected adult behavior.

For parents who volunteer regularly, training or some form of orientation is required. It is unfair to expect anyone to assume a productive role who does not understand the way the early childhood program functions, his or her role in it, and something about the children they will be working with. Training or orientation to the program should provide the parents with this understanding and build a sense of security.

You should give parents who volunteer on a regular basis a schedule indicating their days for volunteering. Parents who are free to volunteer on an irregular basis can also be part of a wholesome classroom environment. Some parents will find themselves with unexpected free time, so be welcoming and encouraging to them to approach the school and participate. With such an open policy, it is important that parents understand the different ways they can help you in the classroom.

You can inform parents about how to assist in your classroom by posting the kind of help you can use on a bulletin board, describing the roles parents can play in the classroom at general meetings, and informing parents in the newsletters of how children have gained from parental help. Children who are accustomed to volunteers in the classroom are often very comfortable with requesting appropriate help from other adults.

If parents are unable to work as paid aides or volunteers on a regular basis, they may be willing to help in other ways. Parents can share their special talents or occupations at school functions and classes. A concert pianist, bluegrass singer, male nurse, and female police officer are just a few examples of adults who visited one school during a "career week." Parents of differing ethnic heritages may describe their experiences, customs, and family life with the children.

Others might help out by making materials for the classroom. One parent made stuffed Winnie the Pooh characters. These animals reinforced the stories of *Winnie the Pooh* in the kindergarten, served as comforters for a few troubled children, and became friends for others during nap time. Helping out on trips, providing refreshments, or coming to school to read a special story are other ways parents can take part in school activities.

Volunteering in an early childhood program is intrinsically rewarding. When parents see children grow and recognize their contribution to this growth, no other form of recognition is necessary. Yet no matter how fulfilling their role is or how important the volunteer perceives the task, outside

Parent volunteers can help in a variety of ways.

recognition is important. A certificate of appreciation, perhaps presented at a formal end-of-the-year ceremony, is meaningful as well.

Rewards and recognition are continual. They need not be formal. A teacher's thank you at the end of the day, a hug from a child, or recognition of a special task completed successfully are examples of rewards. Courteous treatment, respect, and compliments given throughout the day let volunteers know they are making important contributions.

An open-door policy is necessary so that parents should be allowed to observe in the classroom whenever they are able to. Observing a regular school day gives parents a clear picture of what school is like for their children.

Whether parents are actively involved in the classroom or observing, you are still responsible for setting the objectives and ground rules for the visit. Parents need to know the school's policies and regulations as well as their responsibilities and standards of ethical behavior when in the school. When parents are in the school, they need to know, for example, that they are to respect the confidentiality of their experiences and the welfare of all children.

Parent Education

Parents have skills, talents, and expertise. They know a lot about raising their own children; nevertheless, many do look to the early childhood program for help in continuing their own education about child development and rearing. Sometimes formal meetings are held about topics that interest parents. These will vary from school to school. Some are held monthly and others when special needs dictate. Parents can be polled to determine topics and speakers that will be of most benefit to them.

A coffee and dessert night with school staff was successful in one primary school. Families were invited to the school to meet informally with the teachers over coffee to discuss educational issues. Weekend workshops were effective in another school. At this school, workshops were held to provide information on topics of concern to several parents.

In another school, the principal was concerned that no matter what the topic or outreach program, a group of parents remained leery of even entering the school and appeared uncomfortable when they did come. They seemed to feel that school offered them and their children little chance of success. This principal finally succeeded in involving particular parents when she encouraged one of them to get two or three other parents who would be willing to help design and carry out programs of interest to uninvolved parents. This nucleus group began to plan programs that they called "Hot Tips for Parents." The programs include such topics as "The One-Minute Parent" (easy ways to communicate with your children), "Improving Your Image" (assertiveness in dealing with everyday situations without feeling negative about yourself), "Turning Point: How to Reenter the Work Force," and "Community Services" (where to turn when you need help). These programs not only drew many previously uninvolved parents to the school but also attracted friends and relatives who had a stake in the child's future. Parents designed incentives to encourage others to attend, trained parent leaders, planned trips to the community, and held occasional social affairs. Meetings took place at different times during the day and evening to allow for different work schedules, and baby-sitting was always provided. The program's success was not just greater involvement; but also parents demonstrated greater self-confidence, more positive attitudes toward their children, and a pride in being part of the school environment (Shafer, 1988).

The most successful parent programs are those in which *all* parents feel they have contributions to make to the schools and in which they have a sense of ownership in the planning and execution of the programs. Research and common sense indicate that involving parents in school programs has many beneficial effects. Henderson (1988) points out some of these benefits:

- Children whose parents are involved in their formal education have greater academic achievement.
- Well-planned and comprehensive parent involvement has the most lasting effect.
- Children from minority and low-income families benefit the most from parental involvement.
- Parents of all educational levels can assist their children through school involvement.
- Students' positive attitudes about self and sense of control over the environment are greatly enhanced by parental school involvement.

Relating with Others in the School

Many people within the school and community significantly affect the quality of instruction you are able to give children. Some of these persons work outside the classroom, like the principal, center director, curriculum supervisor, cook, custodian, librarian, and secretary. Others will work with you in the classroom—an aide, a specialist who works with children with special needs, or a consultant who conducts lessons from specific curriculum areas.

When you enter a new situation, take some time to observe how people function and the roles that they assume. Find out what people expect of you. What type of behavior does the principal or director expect? Does the principal want daily lesson plans posted? Does your director expect you to represent the center within the community or want you to be solely responsible for this role? What behaviors are expected of the children? How should they walk through the building? What behaviors are accepted on the playground, waiting for the bus, or in the lunchroom?

One early childhood program may operate under a set of specific rules and regulations, with the principal or director running a "tight ship." In another program, a more relaxed atmosphere may prevail. In either case, you'll want to determine your autonomy and authority. If the director doesn't clarify this for you, ask for a conference. Find out what you can and cannot do, the parents' role in the program, how you are to handle specific problems with children, to whom you report, what kind of reporting is desired, and what rules and regulations you should know about.

Understanding which areas you will be expected to be in charge of and which the director or others will handle gives you a measure of security, as well as autonomy, as a new teacher.

Establishing Your Autonomy

Teachers and child-care workers are faced with from sixty to one hundred decisions in each hour of any classroom day (McNergney, Lloyd, Mintz, & Moore, 1988). Some decisions are made automatically but others will demand skill and foresight. How you make these decisions and your sense of freedom to choose a course of action based on your knowledge and expertise, rather than on what someone expects of you, reflect the amount of autonomy you have in your setting. Effective decisions depend upon teachers' skill in applying to any situation their knowledge about children's needs and developmental levels, about appropriate content, about appropriate teaching strategies, and about effective climates. Such skill and expertise are gained through continual learning and experience.

A certain amount of autonomy and authority will be yours at the beginning of your teaching career, but establishing your authority and autonomy is an ongoing project.

Circumstances change, you change, and the early childhood program changes. Ideas of how things are run also change. Periodically you'll need to assess these changes and the effects they have on you, your teaching, and the children.

The principal or director is not the only person in the program who might influence your autonomy and teaching. Other teachers, cooks, custodians, and secretaries can influence them as well. Often the de facto person in charge of the program isn't the principal or director at all but one of the teachers, perhaps someone who has been with the program for years or who has some other perceived authority in the community.

In some programs, a teacher or group of teachers may be in control. They may have taught at the school for years and have survived many changes of directors or principals. They may be the ones who inform the new director of the school's standard procedures and who take the new teacher in hand, believing they are in charge of any new staff member. Take time to observe teachers as they work together and see if this may be the case in your program.

Watch the teachers as they work with the children and communicate with one another. Is there an easy sharing of information and responsibility? Are there cliques? Do the teachers want you to do things the way they have always been done, or are they open to new ideas and change? Establishing a good rapport with other teachers is important because you will work together as a team to identify and solve problems and to provide the best for the children.

Good relationships with others in the school, such as the cooks, custodians, and secretaries, are also critical. You may wish to cook in the lunchroom, take the children to the library for a special research project, or paint in the hall. To do so without first checking with the people in charge is not only rude but could be disastrous.

- -

Ms. R. and the children were trying out some science ideas through cooking experiences. They needed more space than they had in the classroom. It was afternoon, and the lunchroom next door to the kindergarten class was empty. Ms. R., the kindergarten children, and the aides moved into the lunchroom. Just as things were really popping, an angry cook brought in a startled and dismayed principal. The explosion that followed wasn't due to the chemistry of the physical elements but to personal conflicts.

- -

You should always be careful to respect the domains of others in the school. If you don't know whom to ask about using an area or its equipment, check with your principal or director. Consideration for others will bring support for your work instead of hostility. Explaining your objectives to the cook or your plans for cleaning up after the experiences could bring about a willingness to help rather than bad feelings and resentment.

Secretaries, nurses, bus drivers, and custodians all affect the quality of school life. To ensure that early childhood programs function for children rather than for the convenience of adults, establish communication with each of these persons. Tell them about the goals you have for the children and some of your specific learning objectives. Let them know how important they are to the children's welfare. Thank them formally through notes or letters for the work they do. Involve them in special events, perhaps a Halloween or birthday party. Remember them when children make gifts, perhaps having children make a greeting card for each of them or giving them a bag of the bean sprouts you've grown in class.

Ride the school bus with the children to get to know the drivers and find out something about their job. Find out how they want the children to behave on the bus. Perhaps they allow the children to sing songs while riding on the bus, and you could supply a list of songs children enjoy. Give the secretary a list of the names of children in your class. Always inform the secretary ahead of time of your needs to have materials duplicated. If you are planning messy projects, protect the table and floor with discarded plastic shower curtains or paper, and let the custodians know that you and the children will be responsible for cleaning up your share of the mess.

Respect for existing lines of authority in the early childhood program will enable you to develop your own autonomy in a cooperative way. In this way you become a part of a team with a common aim—providing the best for children. You will usually work with other adults in your room. Aides, supervisors, and specialists may be a part of the team working with you and the children.

The Aide

"Every teacher, no matter what the grade level, should have an aide, a helper, or a co-worker with her in the classroom" (Hymes, 1968, p. 3).

Having an aide is valuable in numerous ways. First, it obviously benefits the children. An aide provides an extra pair of hands and another sensitive, caring adult with whom children can interact. The aide is another person who talks with children, listens, and promotes cognitive and academic skills. Every classroom is bound to have at least one child with special needs, who has trouble controlling emotions, or is gifted and needs additional challenges. With an aide, it is possible to meet individual needs while enriching the classroom experiences for all.

Teachers benefit from having an aide as well. In one classroom in which there wasn't an aide, one of the children had banged his head on a post and was bleeding profusely. In this case, an aide would certainly have taken the child to the director's office. Without one, the teacher had to line up all twenty children and march them to the director's office, where she carried the badly bleeding child. The teacher was concerned about the injured child and was also unable to leave frightened children alone. If you work with older children, one can be sent for help. But when you're working with very young children—children who may be new to the program and do not know their way around the school—you cannot give them responsibilities beyond their capabilities.

Aides can also share some of the load of the clerical, technical, and housekeeping duties. Because aides often live in the community, they can help interpret the values of the parents to you. They serve as a link between the school and parents and can help you understand and communicate with parents and others in the community. The insights aides have about the community will be invaluable in addressing problems and determining strategies.

Aides may be trained or untrained, paid or volunteers. They may be a part of your program, or you may have to recruit and train them yourself. You can recruit aides from parents or church and community groups. Some may be recruited from universities or museums to provide specific talents or expertise, like working with disabled children or playing the piano.

Orientation for the Aide

Regardless of the aides' backgrounds or prior training, some orientation will be necessary. Even though the aides may be unpaid or lacking in professional training in early childhood education, they will be assuming professional roles in the school. Aides will be working closely with children, have access to records, and be expected to behave like a professional. The rules and regulations of the school and the tasks the aides can and cannot perform must be made clear. For instance, aides will be expected to protect the confidentiality of children and their families, just as you and the other professionals within the program do.

Take some time to explain your own philosophy and techniques. Describe your goals and the types of learning activities and experiences you believe essential for children. Discuss how you expect to work with the aides and how you will both interact with the children.

Lines of authority must be established. Sometimes it is hard to give directions to aides. They may be older than you or may have been in the program longer than you have. Nevertheless, you are in charge of the group of children and the people who work with them. When you fully respect the work the aides do and take the time to explain how you will be teaching children, your authority is established. Productive relationships can be developed when it is clear that you do not consider the aides servants and that although you are in charge, you will both share in the routines of cleaning up, dressing children, and so on.

Responsibilities of Aides

Aides can assume various tasks in the classroom. Ideally, you will want to make use of their services in ways that best match their skills, interests, and the needs of the children. If your program receives federal funding, however, there may be restrictions on the kinds of duties the aides may perform as well as on the children with whom they may work. It is important to check with the principal or the director about the role of the aide in your classroom.

Discussion and planning with the aides are ongoing. It is important that the aides share with you their background, work with children, special interests and talents, and confidence level in working on any of the important classroom tasks. The extent of their involvement will depend on these factors and should change as they gain more skill and as children's needs change.

Tasks may be technical, supervisory, or instructional. Technical tasks include such things as making materials, running audiovisual equipment, collecting money, arranging field trips, or preparing snacks. Supervisory tasks occur throughout the day as aides monitor children's activities, giving help as needed and interacting with children in the classroom and on the play yard. If aides are trained and experienced, they may supervise a small group of children working on a special project or take a small group to another part of the building to listen to a story or for some similar experience.

Supervision is a tremendous help during arrival and departure times. When an aide can supervise some of the children, you're free to greet parents and to take the time to talk with them. You can also greet the children in the morning or give some individual attention to them as they leave the program for the day.

Mature and trained aides may conduct instructional tasks as well. They may take the responsibility to listen to children read, take a group for story hour, or work with the total group singing songs. When aides have special talents, say, doing ceramics, then their instructional role is to transmit them to the children.

After you and an aide have worked together for a time, evaluate your experiences. How does the aide feel about his or her role? Is the aide learning new skills, and if so, is he or she ready to try them in the classroom? Discuss concerns with the aide. Analyze situations together, thinking of alternative ways to deal with problems or concerns. Although some of this evaluation will take place informally, try to schedule regular sessions with the aide devoted entirely to work, growth, development, and the relationship with the children and you.

Specialists

You'll be relating with a number of specialists as well. Some may be special educators, English as a second language teachers, or curriculum area specialists. These specialists are as valuable as aides, once communication has been established.

When working with other specialists and professionals involved in children's education, you'll want to become familiar with the language they use and clarify and interpret your own terminology. The Council for Exceptional Children's book *Teaching Exceptional Children in All America's Schools* offers a glossary of terms that will help you communicate with some specialists. When working on teams to meet the needs of special children, a medical dictionary may be useful. Don't be intimidated by specialists. Ask them to explain their terminology and keep asking until you have a clear understanding.

Some specialists can work with children in the classroom without pulling them out for services.

Sometimes specialists will ask you to follow up on specific types of treatment or experiences in the classroom. You are the team's expert on the normal growth and development of children in your classroom. If specialists ask for treatment for a child that is beyond the normal expectation for a group setting, you'll need to tell them so and develop alternative strategies. You see the child every day and must consider the special needs child in relation to the total group.

When you have children who are bilingual in your class, you may also work with the English as a second language (ESL) teacher. It is helpful to discuss the child's progress with the ESL teacher. The ESL teacher may wish to work with the bilingual child outside the classroom, but this may be counterproductive, causing the child to feel even more isolated and to miss out on language-rich activities. You must ensure that the child's total educational needs are met and at the same time establish good communication with those who share this responsibility.

Some programs provide area specialists, such as music, art, and physical education teachers. Without question, these are important for children's intellectual and physical growth and development. But all too often this separate-subject approach to the curriculum "splinters the child's day" (Hymes, 1968, p. 143).

You may have no choice in having these specialists work with the children in your classroom, but you can be a part of the experience and interpret any misconceptions the specialists may have of your children's abilities. Or you can work with the specialists to coordinate unit or lesson plans so that the activities they introduce are coordinated into the children's day and not splintered from it.

Specialists offer you insights into special subjects and can support you in your efforts to provide appropriate educational experiences for young children. You might form a team to reeducate those who do not understand how basic art, music, dance, and physical education are important to a child's total growth and development and how they are integrated with the children's concepts of reading, mathematics, and science. Consider, for example, the teacher in the following episode:

The teacher was criticized when she suggested to Billy, a first grader, that he use his art skills to communicate instead of completing the prescribed reading ditto sheet. Billy observed the fish tank and was drawing his impressions of the fish rather than filling out the prescribed worksheet. The principal entered the room as Billy was drawing and severely reprimanded the teacher for allowing Billy to draw "during reading time." Moreover, Billy was using art paper, which was permitted only in the art room! Over the semester, this teacher, with the help of the art teacher, communicated to parents and the principal the value of art in fostering reading skills. Together, they conducted a number of workshops for parents titled "Help Your Child Read." They invited the principal to open each meeting or to assume some other role during the workshops. During the workshops, the art teacher and the first-grade teacher described how art can foster reading as well as other academic skills. The next semester, the principal encouraged all teachers to make room for more art in their program.

Supervisors

You establish relationships with your immediate supervisor as well. You'll be continually learning and developing right along with the children, and supervisors should help you achieve your full potential by offering various types of training and other experiences. Katz (1977) has suggested that there are stages of development for teachers, just as there are for children. At each stage teachers need specific types of support. Supervisors help teachers move through these stages (Katz, 1977, p. 13).

Table 4–1 How supervisors provide support to teachers through developmental stages

Developmental Stage	Supervisors Provide
Stage 1 Survival	On-site support and technical assistance
Stage 2 Consolidation	On-site assistance, access to specialists, colleague advice, consultants
Stage 3 Renewal	Conferences, professional associations, journals, magazines, films, visits to demonstration projects
Stage 4 Maturity	Seminars, institutes, courses, degree programs, books, journals, and conferences

The supervisor "assumes that teachers are professional adults who move from the short-term concern with immediate self-preservation to universal concern for humanity" (Hegland, 1984, p. 5). Good supervisor-teacher relations are promoted when both agree on the goals for the program and respect each other. Once basic trust and respect have been established, you and your supervisor can work together to promote your growth as a teacher.

Relating with the Total Community

Children do not live in a vacuum. They are a part of the total community. They have had experiences with religious congregations, hospitals, social welfare agencies, recreational services, and in some cases courts. From living in a community, children have acquired some knowledge of their world and many of the community's values and social skills. In different cultures there are different expectations for children's behaviors and the socializing agencies in which the parents participate and which play a role in molding the children's behaviors (Heath, 1983). If these values and skills do not coincide with school values or modes of interaction, then children may not achieve the intellectual skills of which they are capable (Barbour & Seefeldt, 1993).

The resources of the community continue to influence children even as the school exerts efforts in the educational process. Part of your responsibility is to integrate children's experiences in the community with those in the school.

First, you will need to understand the nature of the community and assess its resources. If schools are to serve the needs of all children, then school personnel will need to join forces with other agencies in the community. Schools are the one agency with whom all parents must relate; therefore, schools must become the "broker of multiple services" for children rather than the "deliverer" of academic learning and skills (Heath & McLaughlin, 1989). If you want to be a part of a society committed to providing for its children, you'll join forces with other community groups and become a "broker" who advocates for children. You'll become informed about the community, the values of those living in that community, available resources, and services for families. You'll keep the community informed of the school's activities and keep yourself informed of political issues in the community affecting children.

Assessing the Community

Each community has its own characteristics. In order to understand some of the knowledge, values, and social skills children have already acquired, you will need to determine the type of community your school or center is a part of. Assessing the community is a continuing process. Walks through some of the neighborhoods can give you an idea of the community's racial, socioeconomic, and cultural components.

Visits to the local library can reveal information about the location of the community's special features—parks, museums, zoos, recreational areas, shopping plazas, business districts, industrial areas, churches, and transportation depots. The library can also provide details of the community's topology and ecology.

Make an effort to visit places of interest in your community and to talk with the people there about the services they provide. These experiences will help you build a sense of the community and, at the same time, make you aware of resources. When the resources you use are familiar to children, the content from the curriculum-guide units or themes you have devised makes more sense to them. Start your lessons with materials in the children's immediate environment, and then help them to discover and explore more resources in their own community and experiences.

Every community has natural resources, people resources, and material resources. By becoming better acquainted with all of these, you become a collector of ideas and materials. You get some answers to questions like "What materials can I get free from commercial establishments?" "What places in the area would be good for a field trip?" "Which people would be useful visitors to the classroom?"

Insights into children's background of experience can be gathered as well. What knowledge or materials do children pick up when they play in the community? What trees, flowers, and insects are children likely to notice? Are there shop windows they might look in on the way to school? Are there signs that they might read? Smells to notice? Sounds besides those of traffic? Knowing about the community, with its sights, sounds, and smells, will help you plan your curriculum, building on children's prior knowledge and experiences. Table 4–2 suggests resources you might look for.

Table 4–2 Community resources

I. Natural Resources
Woods, trees, plants, ponds, streams, lakes, beaches, animals, birds, insects, fish, rocks, seashells, minerals

II. Services
Educational Services: Libraries; parks; museums; zoos; other types of schools, including colleges and universities

Communication Services: Post office, radio/television stations, newspaper offices, print offices

Transportation Services: Airports, bus stations, taxi depots, gas stations, train stations

Entertainment Services: Concert halls, theaters, movie theaters, restaurants, entertainment on college and university campuses

Recreational Services: Public playgrounds, church or community clubs with facilities for athletics and art programs, fairs, festivals, art shows, circuses

Professional Services: Doctors' offices, dentists' offices, lawyers' offices, clinics, hospitals, courts, funeral homes, fire stations, police stations

Commercial Services: Grocery stores; specialty shops (clothing, pets, hardware, toys, music, bakery, ice cream parlors, barbers, beauticians); department stores, pharmacies; factories; farms, including dairies and fruit orchards; fish farms; artists or craft workshops; business enterprises

Living Environments: Children's homes, apartment complexes, new home sites, nursing homes, real estate offices

III. Materials
Materials might be available from any of the before-mentioned services, and could include:

Printed Materials: Books, pamphlets, magazine articles, and brochures that tell about the community

Audiovisuals: Films, filmstrips, slide-tape shows, videotapes, TV presentations relating to the community, exhibits, or models

Collections of Discardibles: Wood chips or scraps, carpet samples, ice cream cartons, boxes, wire, large and small spools, cloth samples, wallpaper samples, buttons, bottles, cans, certain medical supplies, ribbon, styrofoam, and paper

---

Establishing a community connection is a gratifying experience for all concerned. It works in all communities, from the wealthiest to the most impoverished, as well as for children at all ability levels. As people in the community contribute to children's learning, a new sense of pride in the school springs up (Borden, 1987). Not only do children gain by learning more, but also community people become friends and advocates for schools.

Businesses in some communities are becoming more involved in lending support to schools. Some contribute money for supplies and equipment, others provide initiative programs for improving academic skills. You can suggest or encourage such support through your principal, PTA groups, or school management teams. You could volunteer to visit a business enterprise to understand their goals and to see if there is some project your school and the company could undertake together. You might volunteer to invite the chief executive officer of some business to visit your classroom to get acquainted with the needs of the children in your school. Successful business/schools partnerships result from establishing programs with mutual goals in a collaborative effort rather than one institution imposing its objectives on another (MacDowell, 1989).

Understanding Public Policy

The political climate in any society has an impact on children's development. Laws that are passed affect all children and families. For some, laws are beneficial, although the effect may be indirect. Laws that provide special types of education directly affect children who are recipients of the programs. They affect others in more indirect ways. For example, a classroom in which a physically disabled child is mainstreamed provides opportunities for all children to gain new insights and understandings about themselves and others.

Local, state, and national economic policies affect the quality of life that families can provide for children. Health, medical services, income maintenance, day-care services, and child-abuse laws can provide needed services and support for parents at all income levels. Everyone concerned with children's growth and development should be aware of public policy and how it affects family life. You will have the responsibility as a teacher to become an advocate for children and families. Know what legislation is being considered and how it will affect children, especially directly. Acquire information regarding the local, state, and national mandates and determine how local interpretations of legislation relate to the intention of the law. Most legislation is passed with the intent of providing better services for children. When applications of mandates negate quality education for children, point out the discrepancies and urge reconsideration of how the mandate is met (Seefeldt & Barbour, 1988).

Be an advocate for policies that have the potential to sustain and support families. Protest legislation intended to deny families and children decent living conditions or that will affect children's development and learning in negative ways.

Being an Advocate for Children

Teachers must serve as advocates for children. One way to do this is to relate and communicate with representatives from the wider community. People in the community will not support the school or its programs if they are unaware or misinformed. Nor will they vote for legislation to benefit children if they do not feel a part of children's lives or have any knowledge of their needs.

People in the community form opinions about schools from stories their children tell about their teachers, from newspapers, from national television coverage of what is happening in the nation's schools, and from what they know of children. These opinions may be positive or negative, depending on what people hear or how it relates to their own value system. It is vital, therefore, that you find ways of communicating the positive aspects of school as well as what early childhood programs need to provide quality educational experiences for young children.

Direct contact is believed to be most efficient in communicating the positive aspects of early childhood programs. Community members are more supportive, financially and in other ways, when they have direct contact with schools through volunteering in the classroom, having children visit their establishments, or sharing their talents with children, both in and out of school (Gray, 1984).

Other forms of community involvement have been implemented in an attempt to promote better understanding of schools and the community. Business in some areas, working individually or in groups, provide assistance to early childhood programs. In what is called an "adopt-a-school model," specific businesses adopt a program and help with budgeting, management, or other special services (Timpane, 1984).

The faculty of your program, or perhaps your entire school system or association of child-care programs, might design a promotional campaign. In some areas of the nation, representatives from various businesses, agencies, media groups, government, and senior citizen groups are invited several times a year to spend a day touring the school system or observing the program in action. These days are carefully organized and usually begin with a brief description of the program and its benefits, as well as budgeting needs.

Because most adults have not been in an early childhood setting since they or their children were young, visitors are usually amazed, enthusiastic, and interested. Tours make people from the community aware of what early childhood education is like today, what it has to offer, and what it costs.

Communicate with the community by letting the local newspaper know something about your program. It is often eager for human-interest stories and will print information about special events in your school. It also often will print appealing photographs of very young children with their pets, hugging a senior volunteer, or working together to bake cakes for a holiday celebration.

Alert the press to what you're doing, and interpret how the activity is related to the education process. Explain what children are learning as they care for animals or interact with an elder. Describe the goals of your program and the benefits to children, families, and the community.

Fairs and festivals may be another means of advertising and educating the public about your program. Prepare printed materials relating to the philosophy and goals of the center or school as well as photographs and examples of children's artwork to display at a booth at the fair or festival. In the booth, you can show posters you have made that list the goals of the program and describe the benefits of early childhood education.

The National Association for the Education of Young Children (NAEYC) sponsors a yearly Week of the Young Child. The week is designed to make people aware of community programs that benefit young children. It also raises awareness of children's needs. The week's activities vary from community to community. In Baltimore one year, a balloon festival was held in a downtown area. Representatives from a variety of agencies set up booths illustrating and describing their program or services. As the mayor opened the festivities, hundreds of balloons were released into the sky. Entertainers, clowns, and folk singers volunteered their time to attract citizens to the booths and exhibits.

Make your services available to community agencies and organizations. Many service clubs and social groups are eager for speakers for their meetings. Sign up at the chamber of commerce for the speakers' bureau, and let people know you'd be willing to volunteer to speak to their organization about your program and early childhood education. A short slide show is easy to prepare and interesting to citizens.

Your efforts to be in touch with the community can result in positive changes that will affect the quality of life for children. Grass-roots efforts were responsible for the passage of PL 94–142, the Education for All Handicapped Children Act. In Mississippi, parents who had been denied education for their handicapped children became determined to do something. They asked for help from a local civil rights organization, which in turn contacted the Children's Defense Fund, an organization created to provide a long-range, systematic lobby on behalf of the nation's children. The battle was long and hard, but the children won the right to go to school. As this battle raged, so did others with a similar focus throughout the nation. Finally, in 1976, PL 94–142 was passed (Children's Defense Fund, 1981).

The efforts of concerned educators and parents helped establish bilingual programs as well as the Elementary and Secondary Education Act, which provided major breakthroughs in federal support of the schools, particularly programs serving disadvantaged children and youth.

In some local areas, parents and other concerned citizens have succeeded in stopping unpopular school closings or in keeping the child-teacher ratio in their schools at 25 to one. In other areas, community preschool programs have been implemented by concerned citizens, parents, and teachers.

Teachers have become leading advocates for children in a number of communities. A crossing guard at a busy intersection was obtained through the efforts of teachers in one early childhood program. In another area, signal lights were installed at an intersection as the result of teachers' efforts. Parks, after-school playground time, and before- and after-school child care have all resulted from efforts by individual teachers.

Early childhood educators must learn to be advocates for children. You must assume the responsibility of speaking effectively for children at all levels of political life—local, state, and national. Teachers today can and must stay abreast of the issues affecting the lives of young children. As a teacher, you can:

1. Be informed.
2. Contact your representatives.
3. Vote.
4. Inform others.
5. Join organizations.

Be Informed

Be aware of legislation before your local and state legislatures that could affect the lives of children and their families. Speak out either for or against this legislation. You can write to your local legislator asking for complete copies of all bills concerning children. After becoming familiar with the bills, express your opinion about them. In each issue of the NAEYC journal *Young Children,* the association publishes Policy Alerts, which informs readers of national legislation under consideration and interprets how this legislation might affect children. The Children's Defense Fund publishes an annual report on the status of children in our society and on the national budget that supports children's welfare.

Contact Your Representatives

Use the knowledge you've gained about legislation to urge your representatives to support issues that will improve the quality of life for children. Letters, telephone calls, and telegrams influence votes and legislation. When you write:

- Spell your representative's name correctly—don't guess the spelling or the initials.
- Address the letter properly.
- Use personal or plain stationery, not form or mimeographed letters or printed postcards.
- Support your opinion with facts, stating them precisely and concisely. Be sure you're accurate.
- Write a letter of appreciation when your representative's position meets your approval.
- Request a response, using such language as "May I count on your support for. . . ." This poses a question to which a response is indicated.
- Sign your name legibly, and include your address on the letterhead so your representative knows you are one of her or his constituents.

Vote

Ask your representatives at the local, state, and national levels for their positions on bills and legislation affecting the lives of children. Keep a record of your candidates' voting, then support those who have voted positively on issues affecting children. Let your candidates know your reaction to their votes.

Inform Others

Let your friends and neighbors know about the issues affecting children. You can ask them if they know of specific legislation and how it will affect the children you work with as well as those in the community or the nation as a whole. Often those who do not have direct contact with early childhood education are unaware of the needs of children and of legislation affecting them. Alert other community groups and organizations to bills relating to children, and ask them to support or oppose the legislation through a writing or telephone campaign.

Involve your local politicians and state representatives with your program. Invite them to have lunch with the children or to attend a parent get-together so they'll know more about early education and the needs of children.

Join Organizations

Join local chapters of national advocacy groups. These might include NAEYC, Association for Childhood Education International, Action for Children's Television, Council for Exceptional Children, Black Child Development Institute, and the National Center on Child Abuse and Neglect.

Summary

Some people may elect to teach young children because they enjoy being with and working with children rather than with adults. When you teach young children, however, you will be working with as many adults as children. First, because young children are still so closely dependent on their parents for their very life, it will be your responsibility to find effective ways of involving parents, ensuring that they truly are equal partners in their children's education.

Parents may be involved through social groups, policy-making groups, home visits, conferences, and by volunteering in the classroom. As you continue your studies in early childhood education, continually try to build your skills of communicating, relating, and working with parents.

Then, too, there are many other adults you will be working with on a daily basis. Many teachers have aides or work with resource people within the school. Finally, as a teacher of young children, you will want to involve others from the community, whether representatives of community-based agencies, businesses, or politicians, in the education of all of our children.

Projects

Continuing Case Study

After reviewing the section "Assessing the Community" in this chapter, walk through the community and neighborhood where your case study child lives to get acquainted with the child's milieu. Interview the parents, if possible, to determine what other community resources they use. Visit these establishments with an eye to what the child might encounter. Ask the child what happens when he or she goes to visit any of these places. In your report give your perceptions of the impact these resources seem to have on the child's learning.

1. Ask an early childhood teacher if you may observe a parent-teacher conference. Note the teacher's preparation and how the conference begins and ends.
2. Begin a collection of free or inexpensive booklets or pamphlets on education and child-rearing that can be given to parents when you begin teaching.
3. Interview a number of early childhood teachers to find out how they involve parents. Ask them which techniques they feel are most valuable and which they have found to be of less value.
4. Identify the agencies in your community serving children and families. Describe the types of services each agency provides and how these can be used as resources by early childhood programs and parents.
5. Design a publicity release for an early childhood program for the local newspaper. Imagine you are holding a special festival for Thanksgiving. Write the release to inform the community about the event as well as telling how the event will promote children's learning.

Children's Books

Children may find support and understanding from books that present differing life-styles. The following list contains only a few of the children's books that deal with the theme of differing family life-styles.

Adolf, A. (1973). *Black is brown is tan.* Illustrated by E. A. McCully. New York: Harper. (A white father and a black mother enjoy warm relationships with their children.)

Baum, L. (1986). *One more time.* Illustrated by Paddy Bouma. New York: Morrow. (When it is time to go back after visiting with his dad, Simon wants to do things one more time.)

Boegehold, B. (1985). *Daddy doesn't live here anymore.* Illustrated by Deborah Borgo. New York: Golden. (Case comes to realize that her parents love her even though they don't live together anymore.)

Bosche, S. (1983). *Jenny lives with Eric and Martin.* London: Gay Men's Press. (Jenny has two fathers who live together, take very good care of her, and love her very much.)

Bunting, E. (1990a). *Fly away home.* Illustrated by Ronald Himler. Boston: Houghton Mifflin. (A little boy lives with his father in an airport because they have no other place to live. They move from terminal to terminal, learning how to act.)

Bunting, E. (1990b). *The wall.* Illustrated by Ronald Himler. Boston: Houghton Mifflin. (A little boy visits the Vietnam Veterans' Memorial in Washington, D.C., with his father in order to find the name of his grandfather who had been killed in the Vietnam War.)

Caines, J. (1973). *Abby.* Illustrated by Steven Kellogg. New York: Harper & Row. (Abby is adopted but needs reassurance that her older brother loves her.)

Caines, J. (1977). *Daddy*. Illustrated by Ronald Himler. New York: Harper & Row. (A child enjoys visiting her father and his girl friend.)

Caseley, J. (1986). *When Grandpa came to stay*. New York: Greenwillow. (A special relationship develops as Grandpa must live with the family now that Grandma has died.)

Clifton, L. (1978). *Evertt Anderson's nine month long*. Illustrated by Ann Grifalconi. New York: Holt, Rinehart & Winston. (Evertt is excited about his mother's and stepfather's new baby.)

Crews, D. (1991). *Bigmamma's*. New York: Greenwillow. (The children love to visit with Bigmamma and hear her stories of days gone by.)

Dorros, A. (1991). *Abuela*. Illustrated by Elisa Leven. New York: Dutton. (A little girl enjoys going to the park with her *abuela* [grandmother] where they enjoy flying around and seeing the world from above. Spanish words are used in a way that children can understand their meaning.)

Drescher, J. (1986). *My mother's getting married*. New York: Dial. (A story of blended families.)

Friedman, I. (1987). *How my parents learned to eat*. Boston: Houghton Mifflin. (A Japanese American tells how her American father and Japanese mother met and learned to eat in the manner of the other one's culture.)

Jukes, M. (1984). *Like Jake and me*. New York: Alfred A. Knopf. (A boy and his stepfather develop a warm relationship.)

Lexau, J. (1975). *Emily and the klunky baby and the dog next door*. Illustrated by Martha Alexander. New York: Dial. (Emily decides to go and live with her father when mamma doesn't have time for her.)

Lexau, J. (1970). *Benjie on his own*. Illustrated by Don Bolognese. New York: Dial. (Benjie lives with his grandmother.)

Lobel, A. (1981). *Uncle Elephant*. New York: Harper & Row. (Uncle Elephant cares for the elephant child when the parents are lost at sea.)

MacLachlan, P. (1982). *Mama one, mama two*. Illustrated by Ruth Lercher Bornstein. New York: Harper & Row. (Warm relationships between foster child and foster mother.)

Mahy, M. (1986). *Jam, a true story*. Illustrated by Helen Craig. Boston: Atlantic. (The house husband/father makes jam.)

Newman, L. (1990). *Heather has two mommies*. Illustrated by Diana Souza. Boston: Alyson. (Heather's mommies live together and do many special things with Heather.)

Simon, N. (1975). *All kinds of families*. Illustrated by Joe Lasker. Niles, IL: Whitman. (Families are depicted in all the various compositions, but love and a sense of belonging are common to all families.)

Simon, N. (1983). *I wish I had my father*. Illustrated by Arieh Zeldich. Niles, IL: Whitman. (A little boy still longs for his father, who never calls or writes.)

Steptoe, J. (1980). *Daddy is a monster . . . sometimes*. New York: Lippincott. (Life with just Daddy sometimes creates a monster daddy especially when the children are monsters.)

Turner, A. (1990). *Through moon and stars and night skies*. Illustrated by James Graham Hale. New York: Harper Trophy. (An Asian child listens to his adopted mother tell how he came over land and through the skies to find a special spot in this American home.)

Van Leeuwen, J. (1974). *Too hot for ice cream*. Illustrated by Martha Alexander. New York: Dial. (Father doesn't show up on visiting day.)

Vigna, J. (1982). *Daddy's new baby*. Niles, IL: Whitman. (Adjusting to a new baby is doubly difficult when it is daddy and his wife's new baby, and you don't live with them.)

Vigna, J. (1980). *She's not my real mother*. Niles, IL: Whitman. (Miles has a hard time being nice to his stepmother, until he gets lost.)

Waybill, M. (1974). *Chinese eyes*. Illustrated by Pauline Cutrell. Scottsdale, AZ: Herold. (An adopted child appreciates her own special beauty when her adopted mother helps her.)

Williams, V. (1982). *A chair for my mother*. New York: Greenwillow. (Life with mother and grandmother.)

Resources

The following books are useful resources as you develop your skills in relating effectively with parents.

Berger, E. H. (1991). *Parents as partners in education* (3rd ed.). New York: Merrill/Macmillan.

Brandt, R. S. (Ed.). (1989). Strengthening partnerships with parents and community. *Educational Leadership, 47*(2), 4-67.

Cataldo, C. Z. (1987). *Parent education for early childhood: Child rearing concepts and program content for the student and practicing professional*. New York: Teachers College Press.

Campbell, P. F., & Fein, G. G. (1986). *Young children and microcomputers*. Englewood Cliffs, NJ: Prentice Hall.

Coleman, J. (1991). *Policy perspectives. Parental involvement in education*. Washington, DC: U.S. Department of Education, Office of Educational Research and Improvement.

Galinsky, E. (1987). *The six stages of parenthood*. Reading, MA: Addison-Wesley.

Henderson, A. (1987). *The evidence continues to grow: Parent involvement improves student achievement*. Columbia, MD: National Committee for Citizens in Education.

Hoffman, S. (Ed.). (1991). Educational partnerships: Home-school-community. *Elementary School Journal, 91*(3), 193-320.

Kagan, S. (Ed.). (1987). *America's family support programs: Perspectives and prospects*. New Haven: Yale University Press.

Lightfoot, S. L. (1978). *Worlds apart: Relationships between families and schools*. New York: Basic Books.

National Association of Elementary School Principals. (1986). *Report to parents: A collection*. Alexandria, VA: Author.

Neugebauer, B. (Ed.). (1987). *Alike and different: Exploring our common humanity with young children*. Redmond, WA: Exchange Press.

Papert, S. (1980). *Mindstorms*. New York: Basic Books.

Stone, J. G. (1987). *Teacher-parent relationships*. Washington, DC: National Association for Education of Young Children.

Winn, M. (1977). *The plug-in drug*. New York: Viking Press.

York, S. (1991). *Roots and wings: Affirming culture in early childhood programs*. St. Paul, MN: Toys 'n Things Press.

The following are national organizations devoted to advocacy for children:

Action for Children's Television
46 Austin Street
Newtonville, MA 02160

Association for Childhood Education International
11501 Georgia Avenue, Suite 315
Wheaton, MD 20902

Children's Defense Fund
122 C Street, NW
Washington, DC 20001

Council for Exceptional Children
1920 Association Drive
Reston, VA 22091

Council on Interracial Books for Children
1841 Broadway
New York, NY 10023

National Association for the Education of Young Children
1834 Connecticut Avenue, NW
Washington, DC 20005

National Center on Child Abuse and Neglect
Department of Health and Human Services
Washington, DC 20201

National Black Child Development Institute
1463 Rhode Island Avenue, NW
Washington, DC 20005

References

Anderson, D., & Collins, P. (1988). *The impact on children's education. Television's influence on cognitive development.* Washington, DC: U.S. Department of Education, Office of Educational Research and Improvement.

Barbour, N. H., & Seefeldt, C. (1993). *Developmental continuity across the preschool and primary grades: Implications for teachers.* Wheaton, MD: Association for Childhood Education International.

Bernstein, B. (1970). A sociolinguistic approach to socialization with some references to educability. In F. Williams (Ed.), *Language and poverty* (pp. 25-50). Chicago: Markham.

Bloom, J. (1992). *Parenting our schools.* Boston: Little Brown.

Borden, E. J. (1987). The community connection—It works. *Young Children, 42*(4), 14-24.

Brantlinger, E. (1991). Home-school partnerships that benefit children with special needs. *Elementary School Journal, 91*(3), 249-259.

Children's Defense Fund. (1981). *How to help handicapped children get an education: A success story.* Washington, DC: Author.

Children's Defense Fund. (1989). *A children's defense budget: FY 1989. An analysis of nation's investment in children.* Washington, DC: Author.

Clay, J. W. (1990). Working with lesbian and gay parents and their children. *Young Children, 45*(3), 31-35.

Clay, P. L. (1980). The schools and single parents. *NASSP Bulletin, 1,* 40-43.

Clements, D. H. (1987). Computers and young children: A review of research. *Young Children, 43*(1), 34-41.

Coleman, M. (1991). Planning for the changing nature of family life in schools for young children. *Young Children, 45*(4), 15-20.

Comer, J. P., & Haynes, N. M. (1991). Parent involvement in schools: An ecological approach. *Elementary School Journal, 91*(3), 271-277.

Dornbush, S. M., Ritter, F. L., Leiderman, P. H., Roberts, D. F., & Fraleigh, M. J. (1987). The relation of parenting styles to adolescent school performance. *Child Development, 58,* 1244-1257.

Frost, J. L. (1986). Children in a changing society: Frontiers of challenge. *Childhood Education, 62,* 242-250.

Furman, E. (1992). Thinking about fathers. *Young Children, 47*(4), 36-37.

Georgiades, W. (1988). The new America for the third millennium. In D. E. Orlosky (Ed.), *Society, schools and teacher preparations* (pp. 25-30). Washington, DC: American Association of College Teachers of Education.

Gerbner, G., & Signorelli, N. (1990). *Violence profiles, 1967 through 1988-89. Enduring trends.* Philadelphia: University of Pennsylvania, Annenberg School of Communication.

Gordon, I. J., & Breivogel, W. F. (1976). *Building effective home-school relationships.* Boston: Allyn & Bacon.

Gray, S. T. (1984). How to create a successful school/community partnership. *Phi Delta Kappan, 65*(6), 405-410.

Haugland, S. W., & Shade, D. D. (1988). Developmentally appropriate software for young children. *Young Children, 43*(4), 37-43.

Heath, S. B. (1983). *Ways with words: Language, life, and work in communities and classrooms.* Cambridge, MA: Cambridge University Press.

Heath, S. B., & McLaughlin, M. W. (1989). A child resource policy: Moving beyond dependence on school and family. *Phi Delta Kappan, 68*(8), 576-581.

Hegland, S. M. (1984). Teacher supervision: A model for advancing professional growth. *Young Children, 39*(4), 3-15.

Henderson, A. T. (1988). Parents are a school's best friends. *Phi Delta Kappan, 70,* 148-154.

Hodgkinson, H. L. (1992). *A demographic look at tomorrow.* Washington, DC: Institute for Educational Leadership, Inc., Center for Demographic Policy.

Hymes, J. L., Jr. (1968). More help for teachers. In S. Sunderlin (Ed.). *Aids to teachers and children*. Wheaton, MD: Association for Childhood Education International.

Hymes, J. (1974). *Effective home school relations*. (rev. ed.). Sierra Madra, CA: Southern Association for the Education of Young Children.

Isenberg, J. (1987). Societal influences on children. *Childhood Education, 63*, 341-344.

Kagan, J. (1978). The child in the family. In A. S. Rossi, J. Kagan, & T. K. Hareven (Eds.), *The family* (pp. 33-56). New York: Norton.

Katz, L. (1977). *Talks with teachers*. Washington, DC: National Association for the Education of Young Children.

Kenniston, D. (1977). *All our children*. New York: Harcourt Brace Jovanovich.

MacDowell, M. A. (1989). Partnerships: Getting a return on the investment. *Educational Leadership, 47*(2), 2-15.

Maroglin, E. (1982). *Teaching young children at school and home*. New York: Macmillan.

McCormick, L., & Holden, R. (1992). Homeless children: A special challenge. *Young Children, 47*(6), 61-67.

McNergney, R. M., Lloyd, J., Mintz, S., & Moore, J. (1988). Training for pedagogical decision making. *Journal of Teacher Education, 39*(5), 37–45.

National Association for the Education of Young Children. (1990). NAEYC position statement on media violence in children's lives. *Young Children, 45*(5), 18–21.

Notar, E. (1989). Children and TV commercials: "Wave after wave of exploitation." *Childhood Education, 66*(2), 66–68.

Postman, N. (1983). Engaging students in the great conversation. *Phi Delta Kappan, 64*, 310-317.

Powell, D. R. (1990). Home visiting in the early years: Policy and program design decisions. *Young Children, 45*(6), 65-72.

Radin, N. (1982). The unique contribution of parents to child rearing: The preschool years. In S. G. Moore & C. R. Cooper (Eds.), *The young child: Reviews of research, Vol. 3* (pp. 52-66). Washington, DC: National Association for the Education of Young Children.

Reynolds, M. C., & Birch, J. W. (1977). *Teaching exceptional children in all America's schools*. Reston, VA: Council for Exceptional Children.

Rutherford, R., & Edgar, E. (1979). *Teachers and parents: A guide to interaction and cooperation* (abridged ed.). Boston: Allyn & Bacon.

Sautter, R. C. (1992). Crack. Healing the children. *Phi Delta Kappan, 74*(3), K1-K12.

Schorr, L. B. (1988). *Within our reach: Breaking the cycle of disadvantage*. New York: Anchor/Doubleday.

Seefeldt, C., & Barbour, N. (1988). "They said I had to . . ." Working with mandates. *Childhood Education, 43*(4), 4-8.

Shafer, K. G. (1988, Fall). Parent involvement programs for at risk students. Paper presented at the Maryland Association of Supervision and Curriculum Development Conference in Ocean City, MD.

Swick, K. J., & Graves, S. B. (1986). Locus of control and interpersonal support as related to parenting. *Childhood Education, 63*, 41-51.

Timpane, M. (1984). Business has rediscovered the public schools. *Phi Delta Kappan, 65*(6), 389-394.

Umansky, W. (1983). On families and the revaluing of childhood. *Childhood Education, 59*, 257-266.

Wardle, F. (1987). Are you sensitive to interracial children's special identity needs? *Young Children, 42*(2), 53-59.

Wardle, F. (1990). Endorsing children's differences: Meeting the needs of adopted minority children. *Young Children, 45*(5), 44-46.

Weyer, S. (1983). Computers for communication. *Childhood Education, 59*, 232-237.

Winick, M. P., & Wehrenberg, J. S. (1982). *Children and T.V.: Mediating the medium*. Washington, DC: Association for Childhood Education International.

Zeiser, E. L., & Hoffman, S. (1983). Computers: Tools for thinking. *Childhood Education, 59*, 251-255.

5 Planning

Driven by the innate desire to know and understand and a never-ending curiosity, children learn. But you don't want to leave all learning up to chance encounters between the children and their environment.

After reading this chapter, you should be able to respond to the following questions:

1. What do you want children to be like? What goals will you establish for their growth and learning?

2. How will the children achieve these goals and objectives?

3. How will you design the daily schedule to meet your goals and objectives?

4. What knowledge of children, their community, and cultural values must you have in order to plan a curriculum that will enable you to achieve these goals and objectives?

5. What will you consider when selecting content to teach?

6. Why do effective teachers plan for thematic, project, or unit learning?

7. Describe how you would plan a project or unit for young children.

8. How does a lesson plan differ from that of a unit plan?

9. Describe the tools of evaluation, discussing the strengths and weaknesses of each.

Planning to Teach

It seems impossible. How can you make plans and follow them when teaching young children? Children are too spontaneous, too absorbed in living in the here and now, and their interests are too fleeting to permit teachers to make plans days, weeks, or months ahead of time and then expect to follow them.

Planning to teach anyone of any age is a complicated and involved process. Philosophy and theory, however, guide teachers through the complexities of planning. A teacher who endorses the philosophy of behaviorism plans very differently from one who believes learning and teaching depend on the interactions of children and their physical, social, and intellectual environments.

Behaviorist Plans

If you endorse the theories of behaviorism, planning may not be all that complicated. Believing that the teacher is in control and the initiator of children's learning, behaviorists feel secure about being clearly in charge. Even before meeting the children they will teach, behaviorists feel comfortable deciding what they will teach and when. They analyze the things they want children to learn and then identify the specific skills, tasks, or concepts that are necessary to learning these things. They design a schedule of direct instruction, including drill and practice, along with a schedule of reinforcement and rewards they will give for correct responses.

Assessment is integral to the teaching/learning process and begins prior to instruction. Before presenting a lesson, a teacher would assess the children's knowledge of the content of the lesson. Based on the results of the assessment, plans may be revised. After the lesson is presented, children's learning is again assessed. If children have not attained the skill or knowledge presented, then the teacher begins again. The teacher may repeat the lesson or back up and present a prerequisite to success. When children demonstrate success, the teacher would move on and present the next skill or concept identified in the plan.

It is a time-consuming process to identify what children are to learn, break the learning down into small steps or stages, and then design a way to assess this learning. So a lot of planning may be completed by someone other than the teacher. The developers of scope and sequence charts and the authors of curriculum kits, programmed learning materials, and computer-assisted instruction are often the ones who identify what will be learned, the steps or stages, and the assessment. All the teacher has to do is to follow these prepared plans meticulously.

Constructionist Plans

On the other hand, if you believe that children learn as they live, that they construct their own knowledge, that learning is whole and integrated, then planning is a great deal more complicated. Those endorsing interactionist or constructionist theories believe that children must initiate a great deal of their own learning because learning is a do-it-yourself project. No one can teach another anything or learn by being told or through rote drill, recitation, or practice. Each individual constructs his or her own understanding and knowledge.

Constructionists do not believe that children should be left alone to construct their own knowledge and make sense of their buzzing, confusing world. As Froebel conceptualized, teachers identify goals for children's learning. Then internalizing these goals, they structure the learning environment, scheduling abundant time for children to explore and experiment within the environment, and they plan learning experiences designed to enable children to achieve the goals.

The learning experiences are planned around children's interests and needs as well as the goals of the program. They may stem from any discipline—language, literature, music, mathematics, science, social studies, the visual arts—but all are designed to involve children in social, physical, and mental activity.

Instead of testing children, teachers observe them and enter into a dialogue with them in order to better understand what children are thinking and learning. Based on these interactions, teachers may structure additional experiences, offer information, or instruct a child or group of children as they guide them to achievement.

The constructionists place a lot of responsibility on the teacher. The teacher is the decision maker, the one who decides the goals and objectives for children's learning. It is the teacher who decides what and how children will learn, based on knowledge of the children, the community in which they live, and the subject matter.

Setting Goals and Objectives

In many ways those who endorse the constructionist approach to teaching and learning are right. Absorbed in life and living, children do learn.

Yet, if we want children to live fully today and at the same time be prepared to live fully throughout their entire life, then their learning cannot be left up to chance encounters with the environment. The adults who care for, guide, and teach children will want to have clear goals and objectives for children's learning. Teachers need to consider the following:

- What do I really want the children to learn?
- How do I want them to grow?
- How will they learn, grow, and achieve?
- What experiences will extend and expand their innate, personal ideas of the world?
- How can I tell when a child has learned something?

What Are Your Goals?

The song "Happy Talk" from *South Pacific* says it well. To paraphrase: If you don't have a dream, how will you ever make a dream come true? The goals and objectives you set for children embody your dreams for them. What are your dreams for the children you teach? What do you want them to be like? How do you want them to change, learn, and grow? What do you want them to learn?

*What are your goals for the children **you** will teach?*

Identifying goals and objectives for your teaching and their learning does not constrain you or restrain children's spontaneity or their instantaneous and ever-changing interests. Rather, goals and objectives act like a compass and free teachers. Goals and objectives guide you, provide direction for selecting activities, determine your interactions with each child, and enable you to work with clarity of purpose and communicate this purpose to others.

General Goals

The term *goals* is used to describe the broad, overall aims of your program. Goals are usually stated generally and serve as a framework for more specific objectives. The goals you select will be based on the nature of the children you teach, the values and goals of the community in which the children live, and your own values. Some general goals for children are

To enable them to experience intellectual growth and educational stimulation, by aiding them in

- Developing a positive attitude toward learning
- Making discoveries and solving problems
- Sharpening sensory awareness by learning about the environment: exploring, observing, listening, touching, tasting, and smelling
- Expressing themselves verbally; communicating with others; increasing speaking, listening, and reading vocabulary; gaining skill in enunciation and pronunciation; developing auditory discrimination
- Developing concepts and understanding of the world through mathematics, science, social science, language arts, and other curriculum areas

To help them to become emotionally sound, by aiding them in

- Building a positive self-concept; valuing themselves as unique individuals
- Becoming independent and self-reliant
- Developing confidence in others
- Persisting in their efforts and experiencing success
- Accepting and adjusting to opposition and lack of success
- Expressing emotions in positive ways

To help them become socially well-adjusted, by aiding them in

- Building positive relationships with other children and adults
- Understanding and accepting the life-styles of others
- Experiencing recognition of their own rights as humans in a democratic society
- Participating as a leader as well as follower

- Accepting the responsibilities and limits involved in living in a democracy

  To enable each child to acquire physical well-being, by aiding them in

- Developing muscular control and coordination
- Establishing desirable health habits
- Developing wholesome attitudes toward the body and bodily functions
- Practicing safety procedures
- Experiencing a balanced program of rest, activity, and relaxation
- Accepting and understanding disabilities in self and others

Specific Objectives

Goals are general, broad statements that provide an overall description of your program's major purposes. They are not specific enough to guide your daily interactions with the children, however, and do not permit you to determine when the children have reached them. More specific statements, *instructional objectives,* are often used, especially by those endorsing behavioral theories.

Instructional objectives are so specific that they name the behavior you want the children to exhibit. In writing these objectives, you avoid general terms like *know*, *understand*, *appreciate*, *enjoy*, *gain*, and *increase* and focus instead on exactly what behavior children will exhibit. Some examples of the terms you will use are *name*, *identify*, *construct*, *solve*, *select*, and *compare*.

An example of a broad goal statement is "Following a visit to a farm, children will have gained an understanding that there are many kinds of animals." An instructional objective for the same visit might be "After visiting the farm, children will be able to name four animals that live on a farm." Because the instructional objective specifies the behavior the children will exhibit, evaluation follows naturally. You will be able to determine when children have achieved the objective by observing their behaviors.

Working with Mandated Goals and Objectives

Today, teachers are often given programs, plans, and goals and objectives that they must follow. Your school system or child-care or nursery program might have a prepared curriculum guide that you are mandated to follow. Or you may be given a list of competencies that children are expected to achieve. Some school systems may expect you to use preselected reading, mathematics, or other content textbooks or to follow a curriculum kit purchased for the program.

The key to incorporating these mandated programs into your program lies in your ability to state your own goals and objectives for the children's learning and to articulate them to others. When you are clear about your own goals and objectives, you have the means to incorporate any mandate into your program (Seefeldt & Barbour, 1988).

Mr. B. was given a commercial curriculum kit to use in his class of four-year-olds. This kit requires that the teacher use a puppet to shake hands and say "good morning" to each child in the group. Realizing that the children would never sit still long enough for the puppet to shake hands with each of them, he used songs and games to call each child's name and say good morning in a way that actively involved each of the children. When his supervisor challenged him, asking, "Where is the puppet, and why aren't you following the kit?" Mr. B. was able to describe and then demonstrate how the same goals (those of having the children say good morning and learn one another's names) were being met. He was just using a different method that was more suited to his own enthusiastic personality and the nature of the children.

Presented with a list of competencies and the activities that were mandated to enable each child to achieve them, another teacher took her own list of goals and objectives and matched them to the stated competencies. Thus she was able to document how her goals and objectives were congruent with those of the system. From the mandated activities, she selected ones that she knew were appropriate for the children and substituted some other experiences and activities for those that were inappropriate. She, too, was able to articulate and demonstrate how the experiences and activities she planned were similar to the mandates, and that she was successful in accomplishing the same ends.

One first-grade teacher was required to have two reading groups. She had tested the children and found that there were actually three distinct levels rather than the mandated two. She worked with three reading groups for most lessons but put the children into two groups for other activities. She was able to demonstrate how her class functioned with three as well as two groups.

Teachers may have to make hard choices when faced with other mandates.

Ms. S. was mandated to have every child in her kindergarten on a specified page of a workbook by a given date. Aware of her own value system and the needs of the children, many of whom were immigrants and just learning English as a second language, she discussed the mandate with her principal. He refused to bend, on the grounds that parents, community, and school board demanded accountability. Ms. S. could not accept this position and asked for a transfer to another school where the principal held values more like hers.

Like Ms. S., all teachers must feel satisfied, content, and secure in order to work effectively with children.

Achieving Goals and Objectives Through the Daily Schedule

Now that you have decided on the general goals for learning, growth, and development of the children in your class and on some specific instructional objectives, you can plan for ways for children to attain these ends. You can achieve both broad and general goals and very specific objectives through the general routines of the day, week, month, and year; the planned activities; specific lessons; and the projects and themes for children's learning.

Planning Routines and Schedules

The Daily Schedule

The daily schedule reflects your goals and objectives as well as the needs of all children. Daily schedules differ depending on the program, the ages of the children involved, whether the program is full or half day, and whether it continues year-round. All daily schedules include the components described below.

Arrival.   Whether working with infants or primary-grade children, set aside time to greet the children and their parents and to give children time to settle in. It is an informal yet important time that sets the tone for the rest of the school day. Have your daily materials ready so that you will be free to talk with children in a relaxed, attentive manner.

Preschool, kindergarten, and primary-grade children all need to be greeted individually. Have some quiet games and activities ready. As children enter the room, they can talk informally with one another, assume responsibility for pets, or care for plants. Some children might select games or another individual or group activity as they begin their day. One primary teacher used this time for committees of children to collect milk money, take the lunchroom count, and do other bookkeeping activities that teachers sometimes spend much of the morning completing.

Planning.   Involve the children in some form of planning. Infants will not enter into the planning, but their parents might by requesting an activity, special food, or rest.

Planning with toddlers is often done on a one-to-one basis. As children arrive, ask them what they think they'll be doing: "Today you could begin painting or working with clay," or "Don't forget, this is the day we're going to the farm." It is a time for you to describe the choices available and to help each child clarify his or her own goals for the day. Some children as young as three might be ready with their plans, but some children won't be ready with ideas at all. You can help them make a decision by saying something like, "Start with the clay, and then you can think about what else you'll do during the day."

Children over age four will meet together as a group to discuss the plans for the day. This gives them a sense of unity and security as the group is informed of the choices available; they can receive guidance in making indi-

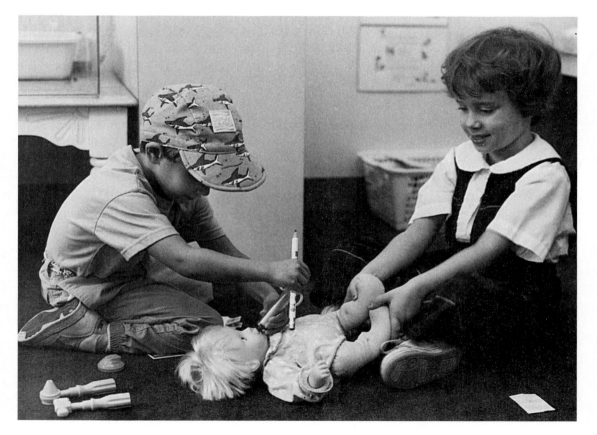

A large block of time is set aside for center work.

vidual plans. This time might also include such group activities as reading stories, poems, or singing together.

In the primary grades, children feel secure when the daily schedule is posted. Children need to know when they will be working as a total group, when their specific small-group skill lessons will take place, and when they will be free for individual projects or work.

Activity Time.   The heart of any early childhood program, whether in the infant center or primary grade, is the large block of time in the middle of the morning (and in full-day programs, again in the afternoon) that is reserved for work and play activities. This is when children engage in individual activities or work in small groups. It is the time when you can circulate among the children, working with individuals or groups, interacting and relating in ways that promote growth and learning.

In the primary grades, this time is usually reserved for reading and mathematics instruction. While the teacher works with small groups on reading, mathematics, or other skill development, the other children may be engaged in projects. Projects are designed to correlate with the mathematics, reading, and other skill activities and might involve such activities as building bridges in the sandbox or using mathematics and reading skills to construct a playhouse or block building.

During this activity time, children are responsible for their own toileting needs, rest, and food. Some teachers use this for snack time as well. During open snack time, small pitchers of juice or milk and a basket of crackers or a plate of snack foods are set on a table. When children feel hungry, they go to the table, pour a glass of juice, select a snack and napkin, and go to a quiet area of the room to eat.

At the end of the activity period, everyone participates in cleanup. Giving specific directions, such as "Vanessa, put the blocks on this shelf," permits even toddlers to take an active part in cleaning up and helps them to gain a sense of accomplishment. A song might help speed the time. Using any tune, you might sing, "picking up blocks, putting them on the shelf, now it's cleanup time."

Children in kindergarten and primary grades need little direction in cleaning up. A reminder that in a minute or two it will be cleanup time and perhaps suggestions for how to begin cleaning up are all that is required.

Group Sharing.   Following the active morning work, children need a time to relax, reflect, and come together as a group. This time may be used to discuss the morning activities, share experiences of the past day, listen to a story, or sing songs. It is a time for children to receive recognition for accomplishments and build feelings of togetherness through group activities.

Outdoor Activity.   All children need time outdoors. Some programs are able to combine outdoor and indoor activity times by opening sliding doors.

Other programs are unable to do this and must schedule a time for active play outdoors.

Lunch or Dismissal. If your program is half day, you'll next prepare the children for dismissal. They'll collect their work and wrap things up. A discussion of the morning's events, preliminary planning for the next day, and singing, storytelling, or special activities may take place.

In full-day programs, this time is devoted to group activity as well as preparation for lunch. As some children prepare themselves for lunch by washing their hands and faces, others will be setting tables and helping to prepare food. At the same time, group activities may be taking place, with children singing, listening to stories, or putting on a puppet show.

Ideally lunch will be family style. When meals are served in the classroom with small groups of children eating together and serving themselves under the guidance of an adult, lunch is a pleasant time for nourishing the body as well as learning.

Nap or Rest. Infants and children under age two require full naps. Children between three and five still require a quiet time, but individual differences will dictate its form. The opportunity for each child actually to sleep should be available; however, children who are not nappers should feel free to select a quiet activity they can take to their cots or conduct without disturbing the nappers. When children are in a group for a full day, even those who do not actually sleep need a time to rest on a cot alone.

In kindergarten and primary grades, children may find that a quiet time following lunch is good for completing projects, doing individual or small group work, or engaging in another relaxing activity.

Afternoon Activity Time. After children take their naps or rest for a period, afternoon activity time takes place. For preschoolers, activities could include another period of outdoor play, a trip to a place of interest, or a special event like cooking or science. Children in the primary grades use this time as another work period. A light snack may be served.

Evaluation and Dismissal. Following this large block of time for activity and work, the day ends with evaluation and dismissal. As in half-day programs, children gather their work together, meet for reflection on the day, or sing, tell stories, or play games. Then they prepare to go home.

Including the Spontaneous

Teaching young children is never predictable. Even the best of daily schedules can be derailed by the spontaneity of young children. Although you want to have clear goals and objectives and a routine that children are able to depend on day after day, you still will need to consider the spontaneous nature of young children.

As children work and play together, their interests and needs will change. Be ready to change plans and routines and make new ones to follow these interests. If children are absorbed in sociodramatic play when it is time for their snack, make the snack a part of their play. One group of children became involved in building a large fort on the play yard. Rather than stopping their play to return to the classroom, the primary teacher arranged an open snack on a picnic table in the yard.

This teacher recognized the potential for using math knowledge in building the fort. She also canceled her scheduled math time and permitted the children to continue outdoor fort building all morning. When the principal questioned her judgment, she detailed all of the math concepts and skills the children used as they measured materials for the fort and solved problems. At times, you will want to follow children's spontaneous interests by changing your own plans. Many teachers keep plans ready for events that they know will happen and that will be of high and immediate interest to the children. These can be computer lesson or unit plans or a plan for some activity. For instance, you know that at one time or another young children will probably argue over the use of equipment, materials, and toys. Before the start of the school year, you can identify a book, poem, or game that pertains to the topic of sharing and keep it ready to use when an argument occurs.

Keep plans ready for other things that you know will happen. These might include the following:

- The first snowfall and other seasonal changes
- Mathematics counting in one-to-one correspondence, such as counting the number of napkins needed at snack time
- The study of insects, plants, and animals common to the area
- The diversity of jobs within the school

You can keep many other plans ready to build on the spontaneous or incidental. One teacher prepared "concept boxes." In shoe boxes, she stored note cards with goals and objectives, materials, suggested activities, and even copies of poems and the titles of books that focused on a given concept. She had boxes on insects, birds, sharing and cooperating, clothing, rain, snow, wind, water, magnets, and many other topics. When she observed children's interest in a topic or event, she had boxes of materials ready on a variety of topics that she knew would spontaneously grab children's interests.

Achieving Goals and Objectives Through Curriculum

Years ago Lucy Sprague Mitchell said that each teacher was responsible for creating the curriculum. She wrote in *Young Geographers* (1934) that teachers create the curriculum anew for each group of young children taught. The tasks of the teacher, Mitchell claimed, were to study children, to understand their interests and abilities, and to study the environment in which they were born, "to watch the children's behavior in their environment, to note when they first discover relations and what they are. On the basis of these findings each school will make its own curriculum for small children" (p. 12).

Today, it is recognized that teachers do have a great deal of responsibility for creating curriculum. To create curriculum anew for each group of young children, teachers

- Must be familiar with the nature of the total group of children and each individual child within that group
- Have knowledge of the community in which each child lives
- Be competent in every subject-matter discipline and knowledgeable of the content from every field
- Understand the strategies for introducing this content to young children
- Be able to plan for thematic, integrated learning

Knowledge of Children

With the publication of *Developmentally Appropriate Practice in Early Childhood Programs Serving Children from Birth Through Age 8* (Bredekamp, 1987), the National Association for the Education of Young Children, which published it, challenged the field of early childhood education to base curriculum and programs for young children on knowledge of children's growth, development, and learning. This means that curriculum is planned to be both age appropriate and appropriate for each individual.

1. *Age Appropriateness.* Knowledge of the predictable changes that occur in all domains of development—physical, emotional, social, and cognitive—is the framework from which teachers prepare the learning environment and plan appropriate experiences.

2. *Individual Appropriateness.* Each child is a unique individual with an individual pattern and time of growth and an individual personality, learning style, and family background. Both the curriculum and adults' interactions with children should be responsive to these individual differences (Bredekamp, 1987, p. 2).

Planning begins with knowledge of children's growth and development as well as of their abilities and capabilities. Basing plans on both the universal characteristics—those that make all young children alike—and on those characteristics that make each an individual is one way teachers can contribute toward helping children live their lives fully each day and preparing them to take their place as citizens of a democratic society.

So Alike–So Different.   Children, so alike, are also so different. Each child grows and learns according to an individual internal plan. Each brings different experiences, interests, abilities, and needs to school.

Experiences.   Most children enter school with a full, rich background of experiences. Many children have had opportunities to explore their immediate neighborhoods, to become familiar with others who are younger and older than they, and have discovered relationships of things in their environment. Teachers who are knowledgeable about children's experiences can better plan learning experiences that will enable them to achieve goals and objectives. Teachers could

Developmentally appropriate means knowledge of predictable changes for all children and the uniqueness of each.

- Visit children's homes and talk with their parents about the things the children have done and experienced
- Walk around children's neighborhoods to see what the community offers children in the way of experiences
- Interview the children, asking them to tell about the things they have done, like to do, and would like to do

With some understanding of children's experiences at home and in the community, you will have a better sense of how to build on them and support them with experiences at school. New activities can be planned to clarify and expand on children's experiences, and new goals and objectives for children's learning may be determined.

Interests.   Research suggests that when children, as all humans, are interested in something, learning not only has more meaning, but is more efficient. "Interest-based activities (whether playing with a toy or reading on a topic of interest) are seen as highly motivating and involve attention, concentration, persistence, increased knowledge, and value" (Hidi, 1990, p. 554).

Fortunately children are interested in learning about everything. They enter school interested in "ants, worms, cars, boats, water, air, space, foreign countries, letters, machines, cosmic forces, good and evil" (Martin, 1985, p. 396). To plan a curriculum, you will need some idea of what interests the group and each child within the group. You might begin by

- Talking with children informally, as they work and play, asking them what they would like to know more about, what they would like to do, or what they already know a lot about
- Observing children as they play, noting the things they play with, how they use materials, what they play, talk about, and whom they select to play with
- Noting the books they choose, the songs they like best, and the materials and toys they select
- Discussing children's interests with their parents, asking what the children like to do at home

Abilities.   Not only do children bring a wide range of experiences and interests to the classroom, but they also bring great differences in social, emotional, physical, and intellectual abilities. These differences in abilities form the basis of other goals and objectives for the group and individual children. To determine the abilities of children, you might do the following:

- Review past records of health and physical growth
- Observe them at play and note social skills and the nature of their interactions with others

- Structure some task for them to complete, observing how successful each child is
- Review results of standardized measures or plan to administer a standardized assessment of abilities

Special Needs.   All children are special, with individual needs, strengths, and weaknesses. Some children, however, have needs and individual characteristics that require special planning and care. Planning involves meeting the special needs of these children. You might

- Ask the parents, who are most knowledgeable of the needs of their child, how you can best plan to meet these needs in school
- Listen to the parents' agendas and wishes for their child
- Plan with professionals and others who have expertise in meeting the special needs of children
- Take time to observe special needs children as they interact with others, work, and play

Knowledge of the Community

Knowledge of child growth and development is not the only foundation on which plans are made (Bredekamp, 1991). First, as Lucy Sprague Mitchell (1934) suggested, teachers must become aware of the nature of the "here and now" world in which children live. Then they must develop knowledge of the culture and values of this world.

The Child's Physical World.   Years ago teachers were a part of children's communities. Living in the same neighborhood, shopping in the same stores, and attending the same church or synagogue as the children, teachers had intimate knowledge of the children's world. Today, however, teachers and the children they teach are separated. Because they live in communities that may be very different from those of the children they teach, teachers will need to become knowledgeable of the nature of their students' community. Effective teachers study the physical nature of the children's community. Some teachers drive or walk around the children's neighborhood. One teacher asked a parent to guide her through the neighborhood of the school. As they walked and talked together, they noted the following:

- The physical nature of the area
- Places children enjoyed going
- Places for children's play
- Historical aspects of the neighborhood
- Neighbors with special skills or resources
- Places of business
- Other resources for children's learning

One day after school, the teacher walked through the neighborhood again. This time she noted where children played, the pathways they took on their way home, and the way they interacted with peers, parents, and other adults. She also noted how people functioned in the neighborhood, gaining insights into the nature of the children's world that affected her plans for the coming school year.

Cultural Knowledge and Values.   Less concrete, but perhaps even more important than understanding the nature of children's physical environment, is knowledge of the culture and values of the community. Teachers try to become acquainted with each child's ethnic and cultural backgrounds as well as the culture and values of the community as a whole. This can be done through various sources.

1.   *Informal Conversations.* Early in the school year, teachers can talk informally with parents and children. They can ask them what they do on weekends, in the evenings, before school starts, or on vacations. They can note the traditions, customs, language, special foods, items of dress, and types of celebrations mentioned by the children or their parents during these conversations.

2.   *Resource Persons.* A resource person might be able to inform teachers about the traditions, history, and meaning of a group's practices. When teachers are committed to learning about other cultures and are sincere in their interest, parents are generally open to describing their cultural values.

3.   *Formal In-Service Activities.* Teachers and administrators can initiate a variety of activities and programs designed to acquaint other teachers with different cultures and values. One school enrolled a large number of children from Cambodia. A resource person who knew about the Cambodian culture and its roles for children and their families was invited to talk with the teachers. In a short period of time, the resource person was able to provide the teachers and administrators with a base of knowledge that they could use in understanding and teaching the Cambodian American children in their school.

Other meetings might be sponsored by community organizations or local businesses and could involve parents and other community residents. Slides, videos, and photographs of the community are helpful in illustrating the culture of a community.

Knowledge of Content

What knowledge of content do teachers of young children need? Ruth Stanton reportedly answered this question in the early 1990s by saying teachers first needed a doctorate in psychology and medicine and then four years of study of astronomy, biology, economics, geography, mathematics, and so on through to zoology. By the time she is eighty-three, she said, she'll be ready to teach young children (Beyer, 1968).

Obviously, it is laughable to think that any one person could become knowledgeable of all content from every discipline. Yet teachers of young children do need a basic familiarity with content from every discipline in order to make it accessible to young children.

A child was examining seashells left on the science table in a kindergarten. She asked the teacher, "Where did the animal go?" The teacher replied, "Oh, the animal that once lived in that shell went off to find another home, a prettier one than this shell." When the teacher was asked why she elected to tell this to the child she said, "Well, that's how snails find homes, they crawl around on the ocean floor until they find a shell home."

The answer may seem laughable to us, but it is not laughable to think of a teacher who doesn't have knowledge of a subject responding inaccurately to children's spontaneous questions, interests, and ideas.

To make the vast and overwhelming amount of knowledge accessible to both teacher and child, authorities in content areas have identified key concepts, overriding principles, generalizations, or ideas from every subject matter to help the teacher organize discrete subject matter. Mitchell (1934) described how key concepts from the field of geography could unify geography curriculum and enable teachers to make it accessible to young children.

Starting with infancy and ending with the twelve-year-old, Mitchell specified the interests, drives, orientation, and tools of children and matched them with key content from geography. She observed how the infant, long before walking and talking, attends to and experiences the qualities of things and how the understanding of the relationship of self to not-self develops. The tools of the infant were the use of the senses and muscles in direct exploration of the environment. The content of geography was that of directly experiencing the immediate environment (Mitchell, 1934, pp. 18-21).

Bruner further articulated the idea. In *The Process of Education* (1960), he pointed out that each subject in every discipline has its own structure. This structure, illustrated with key concepts, can be used by teachers to organize and direct interactions with children.

Others, too, thought that if you could identify the big idea, or the organizational idea of a subject matter, then that subject could be taught to children with integrity. British educators wrote a series of science books called *Science 5/13*. In *Change* (Schools Council, 1973) British educators demonstrated how the concept of energy could be introduced to very young children. The educators defined the key idea of energy as "if material things are changed, energy is involved." The most elementary concepts of this concept are listed as specific knowledge, minor and major generalizations. For example, a specific concept is that "there are a number of forms of energy which are likely to be met with in everyday life;" an example of a major generalization or concept is "man uses energy" (p. 15).

To present the specific concept that we all encounter different forms of energy as we live, the very youngest of children are given toys that contain small electric motors to play with. The goal of the play is to become acquainted or aware of the idea that electric motors create motion. As children's interests dictate, they are encouraged to identify other electric motors in school and at home and are asked questions such as "What are they used for?" and "What makes the motor go?"

Fifth or sixth graders answer the question "What kind of things will conduct an electric current?" by testing a variety of solids to find out which ones act as conductors. The children perform these tests in small groups, and they diagram and list their results for the entire group.

Bredekamp and Rosegrant (1992) conceptualize the use of key concepts as a cycle of learning and teaching, as shown in Figure 5–1. They conceive of learning as a "process of movement from the more concrete, personalized understandings of very young children to the conventional understandings of society" (p. 32). They write:

> The cycle of learning begins in awareness. *Awareness* is broad recognition of the parameters of the learning—events, objects, people, or concepts; *aware-*

The cycle of learning begins with awareness.

Table 5–1 Cycle of learning and teaching

	What Children Do	What Teachers Do
Awareness	Experience Acquire an interest Recognize broad parameters Attend Perceive	Create the environment Provide opportunities by introducing new objects, events, people Invite interest by posing problem or question Respond to child's interest or shared experience Show interest, enthusiasm
Exploration	Observe Explore materials Collect information Discover Create Figure out components Construct own understanding Apply own rules Create personal meaning Represent own meaning	Facilitate Support and enhance exploration Provide opportunities for active exploration Extend play Describe child's activity Ask open-ended questions—"What else could you do?" Respect child's thinking and rule systems Allow for constructive error
Inquiry	Examine Investigate Propose explanations Focus Compare own thinking with that of others Generalize Relate to prior learning Adjust to conventional rule systems	Help children refine understanding Guide children, focus attention Ask more focused questions—"What else works like this?" "What happens if . . . ?" Provide information when requested—"How do you spell . . . ?" Help children make connections
Utilization	Use the learning in many ways; learning becomes functional Represent learning in various ways Apply learning to new situations Formulate new hypotheses and repeat cycle	Create vehicles for application in real world Help children apply learning to new situations Provide meaningful situations in which to use learning

ness comes from exposure, from experience. The next step in the process is exploration.

Exploration is the process of figuring out the components or attributes of events, objects, people, or concepts by whatever means available; young children activate all of their senses during exploration. While *exploring*, children construct their own personal meaning of their experiences.

Inquiry is the term we apply to the adaptation process during which children examine their conceptual understandings and compare them to those of other people or to objective reality. At this point in the cycle, the learner develops understanding of commonalities across events, objects, people, or concepts. Children begin to generalize personal concepts and adapt them to more adult ways of thinking and behaving.

Utilization is the functional level of learning, at which children can apply or make use of their understanding of events, objects, people, and concepts.

The learning cycle repeats because when the learner utilizes knowledge, skills, or dispositions, new awareness is created about what is not known or understood.

Table 5–1 illustrates the cycle of learning and teaching.

But What Content Will I Teach?

For teachers who support the interactionist theory, or constructionism, that children construct their own knowledge, Lucy Sprague Mitchell (1934) was correct: Teachers must plan their own curriculum. There will be guidelines from school systems, state departments of education, and curriculum planners, but it will be the teacher—with the knowledge of the children, their community, and their lives within the community—who will make the final decision. To undertake the planning, teachers might ask themselves the following:

1. From this body of knowledge and subject matter, what holds meaning for this group of children and for each individual child? The key concepts of any subject matter are developed gradually. With measurement, for example, preschoolers might sift sand and pour it from one container to another, while a group of second graders gets involved in weighing containers of sand to determine which holds the most.

2. What aspects of this concept or content can be introduced to children through their own firsthand experiences in the classroom or in the community? Many events in the classroom will allow children to expand their knowledge of a subject, and field trips can extend this understanding.

3. What ideas or understanding do children already have of this content or concept? Even though young children cannot define or describe a concept does not mean they have no understanding or knowledge of it. For example, children know about cooperation because they do cooperate, but few of them would be able to give a definition of the term. Six- or seven-year-olds draw maps and can use them to find a hidden treasure at a birth-

day party, but they will not be able to use and understand the abstract concepts involved in mapping, such as a scale dimension or key for map interpretation, until after eleven or twelve years.

4.   How could this concept or content be integrated with what children have already experienced or learned in the preschool, kindergarten, or a primary grade? Children in one school in a port city visited the harbor each year. Preschoolers watched the boats dock and went on a short ride around the harbor. In successive years, their teachers would ask what they remembered of the harbor and set up specific things to investigate. By third grade, these children had investigated such things as: types of ships using the harbor, products brought into the harbor, and jobs related to the harbor.

5.   What elements of this specific concept does a novice learner need to learn now? In other words, teachers make decisions between what a child can know, understand, or discover about a subject compared to an older more competent or proficient learner.

Long-Term Planning

Just as children cannot be separated into segments for social, emotional, physical, or intellectual development, so too content cannot be presented as separate and discrete subject matter. Identifying themes or units of study that emphasize key or major concepts has long been suggested as a means of unifying the curriculum. Planning around a theme or a unit is congruent with the belief that children are active and learn through their interactions with the social and physical environment. "The learning experiences in a unit of study allow children the opportunity to learn concepts as parts of an integrated whole, rather than isolated bits and pieces of information under a particular content area" (Raines & Canady, 1990, p. 12).

Units and projects organized around a theme accomplish a number of things, including the following:

1.   They offer opportunities for a group of children to build a sense of community by working together around a common interest over time. When children work together, they have the opportunity to learn more about each other and to develop relationships. They teach and check one another by spontaneously offering criticism and information as they exchange ideas and knowledge in a cooperative effort. Vygotsky saw this type of social activity as the generator of thought. He believed that individual consciousness is built from outside through relations with others: "The mechanism of social behavior and consciousness are the same" (Vygotsky, 1986, p. ii).

2.   When content is a part of an organized whole, children see it as useful and relevant to their daily lives. "Conceptual organizers such as themes,

units, or projects, give children something meaningful and substantive to engage their minds. It is difficult for children to make sense of abstract concepts such as colors, mathematical symbols, or letter sounds when they are presented at random and devoid of any meaningful context" (National Association for the Education of Young Children [NAEYC], 1991, p. 30).

3.   The projects and units provide for flexibility of teaching and learning by building on children's interests and experiences. Children's informal and spontaneous interactions with materials, blocks, toys, and books can take place, but there is also an active role for the teacher who guides and supports children's experiences. Katz and Chard (1989) believe that purposeful project work may even include some direct instruction if needed to guide and facilitate children's work.

Because units and projects are flexible, they can be planned for varying lengths of time. Some seem to end as quickly as they begin if children's interests are satisfied immediately. Others extend for several weeks or even months. As children's interests expand, new ideas are generated and new information sought.

4.   The units and projects can meet individual children's needs through a variety of learning experiences and opportunities offered over time. Children can pace themselves, staying with a specific activity for a long period of time in order to satisfy their interests or needs, or they can select tasks that permit them to practice skills or gain mastery over new ones.

In one kindergarten, a visit from a police officer turned into a semester-long project, which illustrates how units or thematic learning can offer children an opportunity to work together and build a sense of community, opportunities for meaningful learning, and flexibility. The police officer permitted children to sit in her police car. Following the visit, the children began building a police car out of large blocks. A sign was made to let others know the block structure represented a police car and was not to be disturbed. The teacher added a steering wheel, a piece that looked like an instrument panel, and some boards for the children to use however they wanted. The block structure expanded and became a more permanent "car" with seats, dashboard, horn, and gear shift.

As the children's interest continued to revolve around making the car more and more realistic, the teacher provided booklets so children could keep a record of their work on the car. She added books and read the children stories about cars. With a prop, the teacher demonstrated how an engine works. Videos of police cars in action were shown. With the aid of charts depicting a variety of cars and trucks, the teacher asked children to make comparisons on the basis of size, shape, and function. Finally, she added wires, bulbs, and batteries to the children's block structure. With the help of a volunteer, the children were able to connect the wires and turn the lights on and off.

Throughout the project, the teacher varied her involvement from that of direct instructor to unobtrusive observer. And although this unit lasted several months, not all of the children participated in the activities all of the time. One group of girls quickly lost interest in building the police car although they often "rode" in it. Noticing the girls' interest in an apple that had begun to rot and was covered with mold, the teacher directed their attention to molds. These girls focused their time on looking for moldy things, finding pictures of mold in an encyclopedia, and drawing their own "mold" pictures.

Planning for Unit, Project, or Thematic Learning

You will concentrate on the following as you write your plans for unit, project, or thematic learning: selecting a topic, specifying goals and objectives, identifying content, and deciding on procedures for introducing the unit, learning experiences, specific lessons, and a summary activity, and choosing a means for evaluating the unit or project.

Topic

The theme or topic of the unit or project can stem from a number of sources. In the child-care centers in Reggio Emilia, a city in northern Italy,

The theme of the unit can come from the group, the teacher, or some event in the community.

the selection of a project topic is a complex process, and the genesis can take a number of forms such as

1. The teacher may observe something of interest and importance to the children and introduce this for a topic.
2. A topic may stem from the teacher's interest or professional curiosity.
3. The topic might stem from some serendipity that redirects the attention of the children and the teacher to another focus (New, 1993).
4. Some topics may also be selected by the parents or some need of the community.

Specifying Goals and Objectives

Objectives direct the unit or project. They tell what the unit is to accomplish and how the children will change, and they lead to an evaluation of the unit. Objectives are flexible, however. At all times, teachers remain alert to children's interests and look for new objectives and ways to extend children's enthusiasm and curiosity for the theme or topic.

Content

You should list the content the unit or theme will cover. You will want to organize and specify the facts, information, and knowledge that will be presented. A list of available materials and possible field trips should be included.

Here, too, flexibility is key. Guided by the overall goals and objectives of the program, teachers select additional content to meet children's changing developmental and learning needs.

Procedures

The procedures consist of an introduction, a variety of learning experiences, and a summary or concluding activity.

Introduction.   Almost anything that serves to motivate and stimulate children's interest can be used to introduce the unit or project. The purpose of the introduction is to arouse children's curiosity by stimulating their interest in the topic. This could be

• A teacher-initiated discussion. You might ask the children some questions or make a statement to stimulate their thinking or interest. For example, a unit or theme on birds could begin with your saying, "On your way to school you see many things. As you walk home, see how many different birds you can observe."

- Incidental experiences. Sometimes a unit arises from unplanned experiences. The birth of a baby to one of the families might begin a unit on growth. Some event in the community—an election, fire-safety week, new construction—might initiate a unit.
- Audiovisual resources. A television show, filmstrip, record, or slides could serve to stimulate interest in a topic. You can make use of other media as well, such as newspapers, news magazines, or segments of TV news.
- Ongoing activities. Units can lead to other units. A study of the grocery store might lead to a unit on food, purchasers, consumers, or transportation. In one kindergarten, a unit on seashells led directly into a study of life in the sea, and then life on land.
- An arranged environment. To call children's attention to a topic and then stimulate questions and interest, you could display objects from another country, place, or time or a poster or an open book, or you could prepare a bulletin board. For example, you could place a branding iron on the library table along with a few books opened to pictures of cowhands at branding time to introduce a unit on this type of work.

Learning Experiences.   Learning experiences are the heart of a unit or project. Rather than a listing of isolated activities, these experiences are planned to foster the goals and objectives of the unit. You can plan some activities for individual children, others for small groups, and still others for the total group.

Because the purpose of a unit is to build a strong relationship between learning experiences and content, you will want to design the learning experiences so they work together to form a whole. You can plan a sequential presentation of learning experiences around the objectives of the unit. Analysis of each objective will suggest activities that would foster children's attainment of the objective. Ask yourself these questions: "What experiences will foster this goal? Which should come first and provide a base for further experiences? What will extend and clarify children's understanding?"

Learning experiences may come from any of the following content areas:

1. *Language Arts.* Some examples of activities in language arts that can be planned as part of the unit are oral discussions; listening to records; recording ideas in writing; dictating to a teacher or tape recorder; reporting to a group; and writing or dictating letters, booklets, or stories.

2. *Social Studies.* Field trips through the school, neighborhood, or community are considered a part of a unit plan. Or visitors from the school and community can be invited to the class. Films, filmstrips, slides, models, and pictures can supplement and complement field trips.

3. *Visual Arts.* Painting, constructing, drawing, modeling with clay, paper weaving, and many other art-and-craft activities can be coordinated throughout the unit.

4. *Mathematics.* Any unit presents opportunities to use math concepts. Children might measure, weigh, count, add, or classify objects as a part of

the unit. One unit, stimulated by the discovery of parsley caterpillars on the play yard, led to the children's determining how many days the caterpillars spent eating, how long they were, how many days it took for the chrysalides to form, and the number of days it took for butterflies to emerge.

5.   *Science.* Both the biological and physical sciences can be promoted through unit activities. By building a "police car," the children came into contact with the function of engines, wheels, and the concept of electricity.

Not all learning experiences are educational. "Experiences and education cannot be directly equated to each other" (Dewey, 1938, p. 14). In an early childhood program, whether in a child-care center or primary grade, learning experiences that are educational are the following:

- Firsthand
- Child initiated
- Meaningful
- Continuous
- Covered with language
- Those that involve others

Firsthand.   Children must be able to touch, handle, move, taste, pound, see, hear, and do something in order to learn from an experience. "When we experience something, we act upon it, we do something with it" (Dewey, 1944, p. 139). You can provide for firsthand experiences through the activity centers arranged throughout the room and by allowing time for children to explore them fully. With the time and freedom to explore, experiment, and engage in hands-on activity, children, alone or with others, will be able to find something to act on and something to do.

Child Initiated.   If children are to learn from their experiences, they must be able to initiate their own experiences. By letting children select whether to build with blocks and how to do so or to paint at the easel, teachers at least partially solve the problem of matching the circumstances of children's learning to their current intellectual growth (Hunt, 1961). When children select their own activities and experiences, they are in control and they gravitate toward that which fits their intellectual needs. They may choose to put the same puzzle together over and over to satisfy their need for mastery, or they may try to build an arch with blocks, challenging their current ways of knowing.

Children initiate their own learning by being involved in the planning process. Often child-initiated plans are informal and take place when three- and four-year-olds are asked to plan what they will do next or for the morning. Five-year-olds are able to make plans for a party the next week or for some event at the end of the month. Primary-age children are able to make more extensive and long-range plans.

More formal child-initiated planning can also take place. At the Center for Young Children at the University of Maryland, the kindergarten teacher sent letters of welcome to each child who would be in kindergarten in the fall. Included in the mailing was a postcard she had addressed to herself on which the children were to tell her the things they wanted to learn in kindergarten. The children were to send the postcard back to her. On the first day of school, the teacher categorized children's postcards by topics. The class then discussed, and later voted, on the topic they wished to begin studying.

Other teachers ask children what they know of a given topic, what they want to learn about the topic, and after they have had learning experiences, what they have learned. Children's responses are recorded and referred to as plans evolve. Some teachers ask children to make predictions before planning a lesson or unit. In New York City, a teacher asked a group to predict how many people would run in the New York marathon, how far the runners would run, how much time it would take the runners, and who would win. By recording their answers, and based on their predictions, she made decisions about specific topics that would be included in the unit and learning experiences.

All children should be asked to take part in making plans. Some may be too shy to speak in front of a group or not quick enough to take their turn; they will need opportunities other than group discussions to contribute their ideas. Some planning can take place by talking with individuals or small groups of children while they work and play.

Meaningful.   Children learn best when the content has meaning to them. Meaningful content is age appropriate. In one group, several of the families of the children had new babies. Two mothers brought their babies to visit the class, and the teacher read books on birth and growth. The children were fascinated and expressed interest in the books and in describing how the real babies were like those in the stories. Then the teacher used a strategy she had heard about from a friend who taught high school. Following the visit of the babies, the teacher presented each child with a raw egg; half of them had a blue dot, and the others a pink dot. She explained to the children that they were to take care of their eggs all day. She said, "Babies need a lot of care. It's a big responsibility to care for a baby. The egg is like your baby. Take care of it. If you desert it, your baby may be hurt."

The children went off to work in centers carrying their eggs. A group building with blocks soon tired of the eggs and put them in their cubbies. Later, when they put some of their work in the cubbies, they accidentally broke their eggs, which they had forgotten about. After the mess was cleaned up, the other teachers and the principal asked her why she had selected this particular activity. She explained that she wanted children to learn how much responsibility it takes to care for babies. Clearly, these young children, who needed to be cared for themselves instead of learning to be responsible for another, found no meaning in the activity. Without meaning, it was not a learning experience (Barbour & Seefeldt, 1993).

Continuous.   Experiences are not isolated. A thread of meaning should run through children's experiences, with one experience building on another. In one primary classroom, children's interest in a stray kitten on the play yard led the teacher to reading a story about kittens. Next, a veterinarian visited the class. She described how kittens grew and discussed her occupation. The class sorted and classified pictures of cats living in the wild, zoos, and homes, and took a trip to the zoo so the children could observe the big cats.

The children compared sizes and weights of cats, and they observed, discussed, and charted the likenesses and differences between cats and other animals. As the children's interest expanded, they consulted reference books and viewed filmstrips. They painted pictures of cats and other animals and created books. These experiences, presented as a continuous whole, gave children the opportunity to develop conceptual relationships between the separate subjects of biology, mathematics, language, and science.

Language.   Shared experiences and activities give children something to talk about. Given the freedom to talk, children's informal conversations and interactions "contribute substantially to intellectual development in general, and literacy growth in particular" (Dyson, 1987). Children converse informally as they work together on a puzzle, rotate the eggs in the incubator, or build with blocks.

More formal conversations take place during group times. Teachers encourage children to tell how they completed a project, found their way to the nurse's office, or why they think the fish died. They discuss plans for the day or the party next week.

Experiences demand expression. Langer (1942) believed humans were born with an urgent physiological need to express the meaning of their experiences in symbolic form—a need no other living creature has. As children think about their experiences, they develop ideas about them and feel the need to express them in some way. Expression of their ideas can take many forms. Children may draw or paint a picture about their experience or they may dance about it, or describe it in speech or writing.

Little by little, children take responsibility for their own writing. They begin by copying letters, words, and sentences, or by writing, figuring out and inventing their own spelling as they go.

Involve Others.   Children need to share an experience with others in order to learn from it. First, by sharing the same experience, children have a base for social activity and their play. In one classroom, a behind-the-counter trip to a fast-food restaurant resulted in sociodramatic play, with children taking on the roles of cooks, servers, and customers.

Summary Activity or Conclusion.   An experience is not educational unless there is time to reflect on it. After having an experience, children need some way to organize, present, or summarize their perceptions and ideas about it. In the British Infant Schools, children created displays that represented and summarized their experiences. One display, a table covered with a colorful cloth, consisted of seashells grouped by type, and mounted pictures and stories about seashells hung above the table. A few books were open to pictures of shells.

The child-care centers at Reggio Emilia also used displays as a means of helping children to summarize an experience. Following a trip to the park to gather leaves, children placed the leaves in plastic bags. The teachers then created a display of the bags, hanging them on the door frame.

Primary children may use graphs to organize an experience. The number of cardinals, blue jays, and other birds observed feeding at the windowsill bird feeder were charted as a graph in one classroom.

Individuals or groups may present their ideas or findings to the class. They may put on a play, acting out a story they've read or one they've created, or show and tell the group about their experiences. Other ways children can organize an experience are to draw or paint about it, dance, or write about the experience.

Evaluation

No unit is complete without an evaluation. The summary activities will provide an opportunity to evaluate the theme or project. Both the process and products that result from summary activities can be analyzed to determine whether or not children are achieving the goals of the program. How did the children work together? Do their activities show growth of knowledge from awareness to utilization? Are children moving to more sophisticated understandings, relating current experiences to previous activities?

You can get children to evaluate their own experiences by asking them to tell what they liked the best, what they know now that they didn't know before the project or unit, or what skills they gained. What knowledge or skills do they still want to know about?

Short-Term Planning: Lesson Plans

There will be times, perhaps during a unit or period, when you will want to achieve a goal or objective of the program through a specific lesson. Planned lessons differ from unit or project plans in length of time and in purpose. The planned lessons are part of a unit or project and may last ten or twenty minutes or for a morning or day. A lesson has very specific goals and objectives directing specific learning activities.

Beginning teachers find that writing lesson plans helps guide their thinking about what they will do. Even experienced teachers continue to write lesson plans and use them to help inform parents, administrators, and other teachers about what they are teaching and children are learning. Once you start writing a lesson plan for every lesson, planning becomes a habit or task that is done easily and facilitates your teaching.

Every lesson plan includes a statement of goals and objectives, a statement of procedures, and an evaluation.

Goals, Objectives, and Procedures

Go back to the general, broad goals of the program. Select one of them. Then plan one or two very specific instructional objectives for the lesson. An instructional objective, such as, "after listening to a story of the three bears, the children will be able to identify the biggest and smallest chairs in the room," describes the activity as well as very specifically what the children will be able to do after the learning activity.

Procedures are the activities you and the children will do to achieve goals and instructional objectives. They include your own preparation, some way of initiating the lesson, and the activities you will follow.

Always prepare yourself before a lesson by refreshing your knowledge of the topic. If you want to introduce children to the concept of shadows, you may read something about the rotation of the Earth or attend a lecture at a local college on the solar system. This ensures that you will present children with accurate information, gives you the knowledge necessary to answer questions, and allows you to arrange activities and experiences in the correct sequence.

Next, find out what the children know and understand about the topic. As you work with children, ask them what they know about shadows, the sun, and the Earth. Try to uncover their knowledge of the topic. This permits you to present children with experiences that build on their knowledge and provide a challenge without overwhelming them.

Locate resources and materials for the lesson. Identify possible resource people, library books, audiovisual aids, and any other materials you might need for art activities, dramatic play, and any other experiences you are planning.

Think of a way to initiate the lesson. You do not necessarily have to entertain children, but you should think of a way to interest them. You might introduce them to the game of shadow tag, put pictures of shadows around the room, or read Blaise Cender's *Shadow* (1982).

Now select the activities. In selecting activities, ask yourself, "How will this enable children to achieve the specified goals and objectives?" One teacher selected the activity of pasting cotton balls on cardboard in order to develop children's concepts of snow. When asked how this related to her goal of increasing children's knowledge of snow, she replied, "but it's so cute, and the children just love it." Obviously this activity did not aid in achieving her goal.

Select learning activities that

- Permit children to have an intense personal involvement in the experience. It should be of interest to them and relevant to their lives.
- Offer emotional satisfaction. The experience should offer a challenge but also be one that children can successfully achieve.
- Give children an opportunity to think. The experience will demand that they think. There should be consequences that children will have to relate to their experiences or future events, and they'll have to think about and reflect on the experience.

Evaluation

The final stage of lesson planning is deciding whether the goals and objectives for the lesson have been fulfilled. If you've stated instructional objectives, you have built *evaluation* into the lesson.

At this point, you want to evaluate only a specific lesson, not the entire program. Evaluation can include observations of the children during work and play and over a period of time. The teacher who developed the lesson on shadows observed children playing with their own shadows over a number of weeks. She noted how each one used vocabulary and how each one demonstrated knowledge of and interest in shadows.

Other lessons can be evaluated by asking children to draw, dance, or act something out. A learning station, game, or specific task can be designed to help you determine children's understanding of the goals and objectives of a specific lesson.

Figures 5–1 and 5–2 provide an example of a unit plan and a sample lesson plan, respectively.

The Final Step—Evaluation

You determine the worth or value of your teaching during the evaluation process. It is then that you judge whether the children have learned what you set out to teach. Careful planning is useless if you have no way of determining whether you have reached your goals.

Topic

Select a topic that reflects the interests, needs, and background experiences of the children, and fits the goals and objectives of the program. Ask children about the things they're interested in, or interview the parents to gain insights into children's interests. Observe children at play to determine their interests and thinking.

Goals and Objectives

Determine the general goal for the unit as well as specific objectives. Select one or two broad, general goals and a few specific objectives.

Content or Scope

Even though you're planning for the unit to be presented over a number of weeks, limit the scope of the unit. Select the points you want to cover and identify the facts and concepts you will present.

Materials and Resources

Identify available materials, possible field trips, and other resources you will use.

Initiating the Unit

The purpose of the initial activity is to arouse the children's curiosity by stimulating their interest. Some suggested activities might be audiovisual materials, an arranged environment—such as a branding iron and books on cowhands left on the library table for a unit on jobs of cowhands—or it may be teacher-directed, "Today we're going to learn about . . . ."

Learning Experiences

The learning experiences are the heart of the unit. Rather than a listing of isolated activities, these experiences are planned to foster the unit's goals and objectives and to support the content and theme. All learning experiences should work together to form a unified whole because the purpose of the unit is to build a strong relationship between experiences and content. A sequential presentation of learning experiences can be planned around the objectives. Ask yourself, "What experiences will foster this goal? Which should come first and provide a base for further experiences? What will extend and clarify children's learning?" Experiences will include those from the language arts, mathematics, science, music, or social studies.

Summary

A culminating activity provides time for review, closure, and reflection. It gives children an opportunity to tie concepts together. Units could end with children singing songs, acting out stories, dictating experience charts or thank-you letters, completing booklets, or sharing with others through a celebration. A "cowhand" day ended the unit on jobs of a cowhand, and the children made chili and took their "bedrolls" to the play yard for rest. They invited parents and siblings to join them in "cowhand" day and listen to them sing songs of cowhands, eat the chili, and describe the jobs of cowhands past and present.

Evaluation

Did the unit fulfill the goals and objectives? How successful was the total experience? Observe children and ask them to complete specific tasks. You might also ask children to evaluate their own experiences by asking them "What did you like the best?" "What do you know about cowhands that you didn't know before?" Or children could draw pictures of cowhands, dictate stories, or write about cowhands.

Figure 5–1
An example of a unit plan

A Visit Around the School and Retelling of the Events (Kindergarten)

Generalizations:
1. Events can be retold in sequence.
2. Printed words are symbols for speech.

Learning Environment:
The principal's office, library, cafeteria, music room, the first-grade room, the kindergarten room, and/or other rooms the children select. Chart paper, felt-tip pen, and pointer for the teacher at circle time.

Behavioral Objectives:
1. Children will be able to retell in order the events of the visit around the school.
2. Children will identify the room visited—"reading" from the chart made by the teacher and children.

Procedure:
1. At the beginning of the day the teacher announces that the children, in groups of five, will visit several other rooms in the school today.
2. The teacher elicits from the children names of different rooms and lets the children select five to visit.
3. The children and teacher take the trip, stopping at each room, and the teacher elicits from children what room it is, its function, and the order of visiting.
4. At circle time children retell the events of the trip in sequential order, while the teacher writes on the chart the rooms visited as children name them.
5. After the list is complete, the teacher uses the pointer and asks the children to name the rooms as he or she moves pointer from left to right under each room to be named.

Adjustments for Skill Levels:
1. The teacher asks children with fewer concepts first, accepting less advanced sentence structure or one-word answers.
2. The teacher asks the more advanced child afterward, requiring more complete sentences.

Evaluation:
1. Later, in an interview with each child, the teacher checks to see if the child can retell the visit in sequence.
2. By noting the ability of children to pick out room names from the chart, the teacher checks, by observation, the development of the generalization that printed words stand for speech.

Figure 5–2
A sample lesson plan

You need to know how far you have come in achieving the goals of the daily schedule, lessons, and units. Are you going to repeat these programs next year simply because you wrote them and they seemed to go reasonably well regardless of the children's achievement, growth, or learning?

Evaluation lets you make a judgment of the worth of your teaching, the program, and the children's learning. All evaluation should be authentic, that is, related to the ongoing activities and curriculum of the program. Authentic evaluation is a part of the program, adding or complementing what is already going on; it does not detract from the daily program, and it is not divorced from the daily activities of the center or school.

Authentic evaluation can be informal and ongoing; formative; or summative.

Informal and ongoing evaluation is common. All good teachers automatically judge the value of their teaching and program as well as the growth of the children at the moment of their teaching.

Teachers should informally reflect about the activities and experiences of the past day, week, or month. "Today went really well, didn't it?" "Alberto listened to the story today and answered two very involved questions." "Li is making progress; did you hear her playing with Emily?"

Feedback, given to children as they work, is one form of ongoing, continual evaluation. Children need to know how well they are doing in socializing, developing skills, and acquiring knowledge. Immediate feedback lets them know the progress they are making and gives information that enables them to continue working. Feedback isn't just praise; it offers children specific information about their current work and progress. "You can climb to the third rung." "You painted with three colors today." "You know all of the vowels." Some feedback helps children clarify their tasks. "Put this here, then try it this way." Other feedback permits them to analyze and evaluate their own work: "How did you think it went?" "What would happen if you . . . ?" When feedback is based on the child's individual work and progress, it helps the child feel worthy, respected, and valued.

Your program is also the focus of ongoing evaluation. Parents, other teachers, or supervisors may comment on the success of the total program. "The children seem to be doing very well." "Everyone is growing steadily in the program."

The term *formative evaluation* was first used to refer to curriculum improvement: "It involves the collection of appropriate evidence during the construction and trying out of a new curriculum in such a way that revisions of the curriculum can be based on evidence" (Bloom, Hastings, & Madaus, 1971, p. 117). Now the term is used for any evaluation of the teaching-learning process that leads to improving the curriculum, teaching, and children's growth and learning.

Formative evaluation, which helps you to formulate goals and objectives for your program and children's learning, is also ongoing and continual, but it is more formal. In formative evaluation, you systematically collect evidence that will be used to assess the worth of your teaching, the program, and the children's growth and learning. Then you use this evidence to make changes in the program, curriculum, goals and objectives, content, and teaching in order to improve the quality of children's experiences in the early childhood program.

Summative evaluation usually takes place at the end of a lesson, unit, or school year. It is often conducted by an unbiased outsider to provide an objective evaluation and judgment about the success of your teaching, curriculum, or program. Standardized tests are the most frequently used tool for summative evaluation. These tests determine how children stand in relation to children of the same age or level throughout the nation. Thus a judgment can be reached as to the program's value, the effectiveness of your teaching and the curriculum, and the nature of children's growth, development, and learning.

Because summative evaluation is frequently mandated by the funding agency, the school system, or the legislature, you probably will have little input into the decision to be a part of summative evaluation procedures. You can, however, familiarize yourself with the evaluation tools in order to be in a position to recommend appropriate measurement procedures.

Tools for Evaluation

By becoming acquainted with a variety of evaluation methods, including the use of standardized tests, you may be able to influence selection of measurement tools and procedures suitable to evaluating the growth of the children you teach and your program. A variety of measurement procedures can be used in both formative and summative evaluations. These include *systematic* observations of children's behaviors, structured interviews, records of children's work, checklists and rating scales, and standardized tests.

Observations

From the day the early kindergarten teachers heard G. Stanley Hall discussing the value of observing children, early childhood educators have used systematic observation of children as a means of evaluating their growth and achievement as well as a way to judge programs and teaching.

Scientific observations of children, unlike standardized testing, are authentic and unobtrusive; they do not interrupt the child or the activities of the day. They are natural and do not consist of contrived tasks, but instead they use children's natural environment and ongoing activities.

Observations that are collected and analyzed over time also yield a great deal of information about children. Raskin, Taylor, and Kerkhoff (1975) believe that behaviors that deviate from the norm can be accurately identified when children, especially those with handicapping conditions, are observed under similar conditions over time or while completing similar tasks.

It takes some time and training to learn to observe children objectively. Observations, unlike standardized tests, have the weakness of being open to different interpretations and the biases of the observer. If, however, you learn to focus on the behavior of the children you are observing and you describe it without drawing inferences, you'll have an accurate and objective evaluation method.

Structured Interviews

You can combine observational techniques with structured interviews. You might model these after Piaget's techniques as you interview children and record their responses. This will give you an objective perception of their developmental levels as well as of the progress they are making.

A specific task might be designed based on a program goal or objective. For instance, if you want children to learn to count using one-to-one correspondence, you might use a flannel board and cut-out trees and ask children to count the number of trees by placing them one at a time on the flannel board. Or you might arrange some cutouts, perhaps pumpkins, in groups on the flannel board and ask children to tell you which group has the most or least.

If your goals are to foster children's use of descriptive language, you could find a picture book and ask them to tell you about the pictures. Or you might show individuals a picture and have them tell you all they can about it.

Begin by establishing rapport with the children and by building security. Ask questions designed to probe the children's thinking, such as "Why does the sun come up?" Design the questions to relate to your goals and objectives.

When a child has answered, don't indicate whether the response is correct but probe for a deeper understanding of the child's thinking. Ask why, or say, "Tell me more . . . ," "Show me," "Another girl told me. . . . What do you think of that?" In this way, you'll be able to uncover more of children's thinking and ideas.

Give children plenty of time to respond. When giving standardized tests, time is limited; when administering an individual interview, you'll want to give children all the time they need to think and respond.

Interviews can be conducted during activity time or any time you and a child can get together for a few moments. As you interview children, look for the following:

1. *Consistency:* Does the child have a stable set of responses? Does the child reply in the same way to the same type of questions?

2. *Accuracy:* Are the child's answers correct? Is the response accurate even if it does not include all of the possibilities?

3. *Clarity:* Is the response clear and acceptable?

4. *Fullness:* How complete was the response? How many aspects of the concept were not covered by the response? How many illustrations of the concept were given?

Children may not be able to verbalize some of their concepts or understandings. Ask them to show you, draw, find an example of the concept, or act it out. They can also use pictures and manipulable objects (Darrow, 1964; Rogers & Stevenson, 1988).

Work Records and Portfolios

Interviews and observations are wonderful sources of information about children's progress, their strengths and weaknesses, and the concepts or skills they have or have not yet mastered. Another excellent and authentic way of illustrating children's progress is by collecting samples of their work over time (Grace & Shores, 1992). Teachers collect all types of work as examples of children's achievement (Meisels & Steele, 1991). In many classrooms children have their own math folders, reading folders, and science and social studies portfolios of projects.

Examples of samples that are included in portfolios are

- Children's drawings, paintings, scribbles, or other work
- Logs of books read to or by children
- Photos of children working, or of a special product
- Notes and comments from interviews with the child
- Copies of pages of journals with invented spelling preserved
- Tape recordings of children telling or reading a story, reciting a poem, or recording some special event
- Videos of children
- Dictated or written stories

Children, teachers, and parents all contribute to a portfolio. The child, as well as teachers and parents, should have the opportunity to select work samples to place in the portfolio. Meisels and Steele (1991) suggest that teachers guide the process of asking a child to contribute work samples to the portfolio. The teacher might ask the child to select something that was difficult to do, that illustrates a special accomplishment, or has special merit and meaning.

All materials should be dated and something should be recorded about when, how, and under what conditions that work was completed. Growth charts, checklists, standardized test scores, and observation information can be included.

When work in the portfolios is an accurate representation of children's growth and achievement, teachers can use the portfolio to evaluate their progress. The work is not to be compared with the work of other children, but rather each child's work should be analyzed and evaluated for progress toward a standard of performance. The standard is consistent with the teacher's curriculum and with appropriate developmental expectations (Grace & Shores, 1992).

Some teachers evaluate the portfolio with the child. Going through samples of work, the child or teacher enters into a dialogue about the work samples. The teacher can gain insights into the child's perceptions as well as the total worth of the program by learning the child's perspective of his or her work and progress.

In the primary grades, teachers, parents, and children can confer together over the portfolio. In one school, teachers ask the child to show and discuss the work samples in his or her portfolio with the parent before all of them meet. Then all of them have a conference to discuss the portfolio.

However the portfolio is used, the idea is to use samples of the work in order to reach conclusions about children's achievement, abilities, strengths, weaknesses, and needs. These conclusions can be the basis for planning to meet each child's needs and strengthening the total program.

Checklists and Rating Scales

Some teachers find checklists or rating scales convenient ways to evaluate children's progress. You can design and construct checklists to assess attainment of specific goals, skills, or concepts. Other checklists are based on more general goals of early childhood education and are provided by school systems or state departments of education. Figure 5–3 gives examples of a checklist and a rating scale.

Self-Evaluation

Even four-year-olds can begin to think of the ways they've grown and what they've learned. Self-evaluation is not only useful for you, but it also enables children to begin to monitor their own thinking and learning. Asking children to evaluate their growth gives you insights into the agreement between your goals and the children's expectations for themselves. The children also are given an opportunity to make decisions about their own learning.

You might ask children to describe their progress in a specific curriculum area. "What did you like best and why?" "What materials did you enjoy painting with?" "What did you learn today?" "What do you want to learn next?" "What is your hardest subject?" "How do you think you can learn to do that?" "How many things do you know now that you didn't know at the beginning of school?"

Older children can make booklets recording answers to these questions, dictating, writing, and illustrating what they've learned. Some teachers have found that checklists children complete for themselves foster self-evaluation.

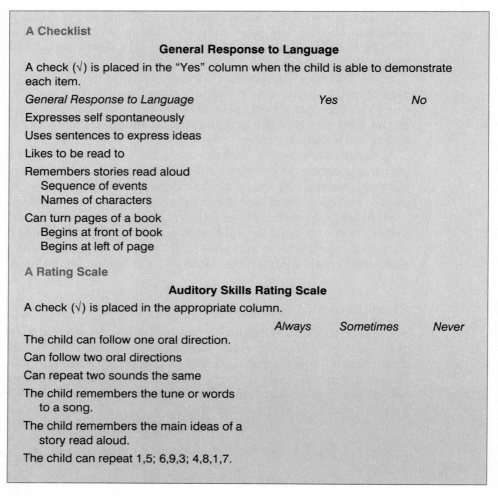

A Checklist
General Response to Language

A check (√) is placed in the "Yes" column when the child is able to demonstrate each item.

General Response to Language	*Yes*	*No*
Expresses self spontaneously		
Uses sentences to express ideas		
Likes to be read to		
Remembers stories read aloud		
Sequence of events		
Names of characters		
Can turn pages of a book		
Begins at front of book		
Begins at left of page		

A Rating Scale
Auditory Skills Rating Scale

A check (√) is placed in the appropriate column.

	Always	*Sometimes*	*Never*
The child can follow one oral direction.			
Can follow two oral directions			
Can repeat two sounds the same			
The child remembers the tune or words to a song.			
The child remembers the main ideas of a story read aloud.			
The child can repeat 1,5; 6,9,3; 4,8,1,7.			

Figure 5–3
Checklist and rating scale

In one third-grade classroom, children kept cards listing the books they were reading at school or home. At various times they wrote different information on the card, for example, characters (list major/minor ones, describe your favorite/least favorite one), setting (does it change), story events, and feelings about the book. By using their cards, the teacher could quickly see what books (level, type, number) the children were reading and how they were interpreting the stories (Barbour & Seefeldt, 1993).

After completing the social studies and science units, a first-grade teacher made lists with the children of the concepts they felt they had learned, and he posted these lists. At different times, he also asked children to write in their journals what they remember about a certain topic, as well as any skills they felt they had improved on. The lists served both to jog children's memories and to aid the children in spelling difficult words. Their responses were used by the teacher in planning follow-up lessons and as references for parent conferences.

Standardized Tests

Standardized tests are given under specific conditions and involve following a manual for exact directions and timing. Two kinds of standardized tests are available: norm-referenced and criterion-referenced. Standardized tests are not always appropriate; Figure 5–4 indicates purposes for which they must not be used.

Norm-Referenced Tests

A *norm-referenced* standardized test gives you a score that tells you how the child's performance on that test compares to that of other children of the same age and grade. Norm-referenced tests are used to assess a child's general readiness for a curriculum; to predict success; or to evaluate the success of a program, the curriculum, or your teaching. That they are standardized means you can take a child's test score and compare it to those of children across the nation. The raw score is also believed to be reliable and stable because of the standardization and norming procedures. This means that if you give the test several times to the same child, the child will probably perform at about the same level.

There are problems with using standardized tests with young children. First, young children are not good test takers (National Association for the Education of Young Children, 1988). Five-year-old Andrea delightedly informed her mother, "I'm the smartest kid in the class!" When asked why she thought this, Andrea replied, "We had a test today that would tell how smart we were, and I marked every answer even before the teacher handed the test out to the other kids!"

DANGER

Tests and Young Children

No Test Score Can Be Used To:
 Deny children access to an early childhood program
 Fail children
 Place children in remedial, developmental, or special classes

---

Figure 5–4
Tests can be dangerous.

Other children mark only items in the middle or to one side. Still others refuse to respond at all. Christie Marie told her mother, "I didn't tell the teacher anything. She's dumb. I answered all those questions when I was in kindergarten."

Then too, young children are growing rapidly. Developmental spurts and lags are common. What a child learned one day may not be revealed for weeks, as the child focuses on gaining some other skill. A single test given on one day may be a poor indicator of the child's growth, development, and potential.

Further, test bias is well documented. Some standardized tests are normed on groups of children that differ from those you are teaching. For instance, if a test has been normed on middle-class white children living in the suburbs, then it is unfair to use it to judge the growth of children who are bilingual or from a different cultural background by comparing their test scores to these children's.

Because norm-referenced tests tell you only how the child does in relation to others of the same age across the nation, they are often not very use-

---

Achievement Tests

Measure what children have learned. They are not intelligence tests.
If you want to find out what children have learned in the program, you might use an achievement test.

Intelligence Tests

Assess children's abilities.
When you want to know a child's capacity or ability, an intelligence test may be given.

Readiness Tests

"Assess the skills children have acquired so teachers can plan instruction accordingly" (NAEYC, 1988)
These tests, like achievement tests, can be used to help teachers plan instruction.

Developmental Screening Tests

Assess children's ability to acquire skills, rather than which skills they already have.
Screening can be used to identify children who need more diagnostic testing to help plan for remediation strategies.

Diagnostic Tests

Like screening tests, diagnostic tests may be used to uncover areas of growth or development in need of remediation.
They can be useful in determining the nature of a child's problem.

Figure 5–5
Types of tests and appropriate use
Adapted from *Testing of Young Children: Concerns and Cautions* by National Association for the Education of Young Children (NAEYC), 1988.

ful to you as a teacher. These tests do not offer you information on children's specific strengths and weaknesses and may just confirm what you already know about the child and his or her progress in your program. Before administering a standardized test to young children, NAEYC (1988) suggests you ask yourself: "What new information about the child will be gained by giving this test?" and "How else could I find out more about the child?" Figure 5–5 offers guidelines for test use.

Criterion-Referenced Tests

Criterion-referenced tests are designed to assess how well a child has mastered a set of instructional goals and objectives, with the criteria specified. Usually this is a teacher-made test. It can be designed to assess anything that determines whether a child has achieved the teacher's specific goals and objectives. Such tests are useful because you can determine criteria that are appropriate to your goals and objectives. The tests tell you how well the child has mastered material, not necessarily how well the child is doing in comparison to others of the same age.

Deciding on Tests

Standardized tests are often used in summative evaluation, in which an outsider evaluates your program and judges its worth or value. Because many standardized tests are not appropriate to use with young children and others do not reflect the goals and objectives of your program, be certain you can have some input into the selection of tests that will be used to evaluate you and the children.

1. *Be certain you can specify your goals and objectives.* When you have taken time and care to specify your goals and objectives, communicate them to the decision makers and make certain that the selected test is congruent with your goals. You cannot permit yourself, the children, or your program to be judged by a measure that bears no relation to your goals and objectives (Perrone, 1991).

2. *Ask how efficient the test is.* Examine the test to see how much time it takes to administer, the energy required from you and the children, and the amount of information the test will yield. With the increasing stress on accountability in most school systems, many programs require children to be subjected to a large number of tests. Many diagnostic tests require a great deal of your time and the children's energies, and they detract from your program. If tests demand too much time, show how you're able to obtain the same type of information through systematic observations of children, records of their work, or a structured interview or task (National Association of State Boards of Education, 1988).

3.   *Look at the validity of the test.* Find out how valid the test is. Does it measure what the publishers claim it does? Look the test up in a reference book, perhaps Buros' *Eighth Mental Measurements Yearbook,* to see what the experts think of the test and to find out about its validity.

4.   *Is the test reliable?* As you find out about the validity of the test, check to see if it's stable. Find out if children will score about the same way each time they take it.

5.   *The norming population.* It is important that any standardized test selected is developed and normed on children with backgrounds similar to those of the children you are teaching, and that special needs children can also respond to the test (Anastasi, 1976).

6.   *How will the test scores be used?* More and more frequently, standardized tests scores are being used to keep children from entering kindergarten or to place them in pre- or developmental kindergarten programs. The use of test scores to deny children access to an early childhood program or to fail children once they are in the program, is unethical and immoral (NAEYC, 1988).

Summary

Planning to teach young children is complex. It begins, perhaps, with deciding on whether you believe young children learn through direct instruction or are guided in constructing their own knowledge. If you accept the theories of the constructionists, then you will have to determine the broad goals of your program and the specific learning objectives, and you will have to plan a daily schedule that will foster children's attainment of these goals.

Curriculum experiences as well are planned around the idea that children construct their own knowledge. This takes a great deal of knowledge—of the child, the community in which the child lives, as well as of sub-ject matter content. It is also necessary to plan for unit, thematic, or project learning as well as planning specific lessons.

Finally, you will need to be able to evaluate children's learning, your teaching, and the program. An understanding of how to use authentic assessment and evaluation methods completes the planning process.

Projects

Continuing Case Study

Plan a lesson based on the information you have about your case study child and how he or she interacts with the environment. Conduct the lesson with your child. Note how spontaneous encounters with the environment affect your plans. Evaluate the success of the lesson, using some of the suggestions given in this chapter.

1. Collect daily schedules and lesson and unit plans from teachers in preschool and primary classrooms. Look at state department of education curriculum guidebooks or other curriculum books for lesson plans. Analyze and compare them, asking yourself:
a. How are the needs of individual children considered in these plans?
b. Is there a balance in the plans?
c. How do the plans reflect the values of the teacher, the school, or the system?
d. Which of these plans would you use, and why?
2. Suppose you wanted children to learn to distinguish between poisonous and nonpoisonous plants found in your community. Write a general goal, specific objective, and learning activity suited to two-, four-, and seven-year-olds.
3. Observe an early childhood setting. Note each time a child encounters a learning situation not previously planned by the teacher. Were these encounters used for learning?
4. Ask a teacher if you can see copies of the types of achievement tests used in your community to assess the achievement of young children. What do these tests measure? Are they valid? How and when are they used?
5. Observe as a teacher or staff member interviews children to assess their growth, development, and learning. How is the information used?

Resources

The journals of the National Association for the Education of Young Children, *Young Children*, and of the Association for Childhood Education International, *Childhood Education*, offer many articles and suggestions for planning and evaluating programs and curriculum for young children. As a student, you can subscribe to these at a very reasonable rate, or you can use them at your college or local library. They will be invaluable resources for you as you develop the skills of planning for and evaluating children's learning. Addresses for the associations are given in the resource section of chapter 1.

Sue Bredekamp and Teresa Rosegrant's book, *Reaching Potential: Appropriate Curriculum and Assessment for Young Children* (1992), published by the National Association for the Education of Young Children, is an outstanding conceptual description of how to plan and assess curriculum for young children. The National Association for the Education of Young Children, in Washington, DC, publishes the books and guides listed below.

Setting up for infant care: Guidelines for centers and family day care homes, by Annabelle Godwin and Lorraine Schrags (1988), offers a complete description of how to plan for and implement quality child-care programs.

Developmentally appropriate practice in early childhood education: Serving children from birth through age 8, edited by Sue Bredekamp (1988), provides everything anyone needs to know about planning appropriate practices in early childhood education. The videotape designed to accompany this book, *Developmentally appropriate practice: Birth through age 5* (1987; #854) is available from NAEYC for $39.00.

Accreditation criteria and procedures of the National Academy of Early Childhood Education (1984) describes criteria for quality early childhood programs.

What are appropriate activities and materials for children? How do children learn? The book *Curriculum Planning for Young Children*, edited by Jan Brown (1982), offers a wealth of information on building curriculum experiences and planning experiences for young children.

For curriculum guides for planning in the preschool and primary grades, write to your state department of education.

References

Anastasi, A. (1976). *Psychological testing.* 4th ed. New York: Macmillan.

Barbour, N., & Seefeldt, C. (1993). *Developmental continuity across the preschool and primary grades.* Wheaton, MD: Association for Childhood Education International.

Beyer, E. (1968). *Teaching young children.* New York: Pegasus.

Bloom, B. S., Hastings, J. T., & Madaus, G. F. (1971). *Handbook on formative and summative evaluation of student learning.* New York: McGraw-Hill.

Bredekamp, S. (1987). *Developmentally appropriate practice in early childhood programs serving children from birth through age 8: Expanded edition.* Washington, DC: National Association for the Education of Young Children.

Bredekamp, S. (1991). Redeveloping early childhood education: A response to Kendler. *Early Childhood Research Quarterly, 6,* 199–211.

Bredekamp, S., & Rosegrant, T. (1992). *Reaching potentials: Appropriate curriculum and assessment for young children.* Washington, DC: National Association for the Education of Young Children.

Bruner, J. (1960). *The process of education.* Cambridge, MA: Harvard University Press.

Bruner, J. (1968). *Man: A course of study.* Cambridge, MA: Educational Development Center.

Buros, O. K. (1980). *Eighth mental measurements yearbook.* Highland Park, NJ: Gryphon.

Cender, B. (1982). *Shadows.* New York: Macmillan.

Darrow, H. (1964). *Research: Children's concepts.* Washington, DC: Association for Childhood Education International.

Dewey, J. (1938). *Experience and education.* New York: Macmillan.

Dewey, J. (1944). *Democracy and education.* New York: Free Press.

Dyson, A. (1987). The value of time off-task. *Harvard Educational Review, 57,* 112–124.

Grace, F., & Shores, E. F. (1992). *The portfolio and its use: Developmental appropriate assessment of young children.* Little Rock, AR: Southern Association for the Education of Young Children.

Hidi, S. (1990). Interest and its contribution as a mental resource for learning. *Review of Educational Research, 60,* 549-573.

Hunt, J. M. (1961). *Intelligence and experience.* New York: Ronald.

Katz, L. G., & Chard, S. C. (1989). *Engaging children's mind.* Norwood, NJ: Ablex.

Langer, S. (1942). *Philosophy in a new key.* Cambridge, MA: Harvard University Press.

Martin, A. (1985). Back to basics. *Harvard Educational Review, 55,* 318-321.

Meisels, S., & Steele, D. (1991). *The early childhood portfolio collection process.* Ann Arbor, MI: Center for Human Growth and Development, University of Michigan.

Mitchell, L. A. (1934). *Young geographers.* New York: Bank Street.

National Association for the Education of Young Children. (1988). *Testing of young children: Concerns and cautions.* Washington, DC: Author.

National Association for the Education of Young Children. (1991). *Guidelines for appropriate curriculum control and assessment in programs serving children ages 3–8.* Washington, DC: Author.

National Association of State Boards of Education. (1988). *Right from the start.* Alexandria, VA: National State Boards of Education.

New, B. (1993). The integrated early childhood curriculum: New interpretations based on research and practice. In C. Seefeldt (Ed.). *The early childhood curriculum: A review of current research* (pp. 286-325). New York: Teachers College Press.

Perrone, V. (1991). On standardized testing. A position paper. *Childhood Education, 67,* 131-143.

Raines, S. C., & Canady, R. J. (1990). *The whole language kindergarten.* New York: Teachers College Press.

Raskin, L. W., Taylor, W. J., & Kerkhoff, F. G. (1975). The teacher as observer for assessment: A guideline. *Young Children, 30,* 339-345.

Rogers, V. R., & Stevenson, C. (1988). How do you know what the kids are learning? *Educational Leadership, 45*(5), 68-75.

Schools Council. (1973). *Change.* New York: MacDonald.

Seefeldt, C., & Barbour, N. (1988). They said I had to: Working with mandated plans. *Young Children, 43*(3), 4-9.

Vygotsky, L. (1986). *Thought and language.* Cambridge, MA: The MIT Press.

6 Creating the Learning Environment

"These classrooms teach lessons of their own; they tell the child who he is supposed to be (or at least who we think he is) and how he is supposed to learn."

(Getzels, 1975, p. 12)

After reading this chapter, you should be able to respond to the following questions:

1. How does the physical environment influence your behaviors?
2. What are the overall concerns for organizing the environment?
3. How are the program's goals and objectives related to the physical environment?
4. What health and safety concerns must be considered?
5. Is there balance in the environment as well as flexibility?
6. What kinds of materials are needed to develop interest centers for infants and toddlers, preschoolers and kindergarten children, and children in the primary grades?
7. What should be kept in mind when arranging spaces for outdoor learning?

Are you aware of how much your classroom environment teaches? Probably not. Most of us are no more aware of the effects of the physical environment than we are conscious of the surrounding air (Zimring, 1981). Nevertheless, the physical environment influences our behaviors and learning. Think of your own home and how the physical environment influences your behaviors. Do your behaviors differ when you are in the kitchen, the bedroom, and the family room?

Just as the physical arrangement of a home directs behaviors and interactions of family members, the environment of an early childhood program will affect the behaviors of children and adults (Greenberg, 1992; National Association for the Education of Young Children [NAEYC], 1991a). The idea that the physical environment can influence behavior isn't new (Barker, 1968). Rousseau even believed that a pure environment, such as that found in the woods or forests, was sufficient in and of itself to educate the child. Froebel, too, believed in the power of a prepared environment to educate children.

The pioneers of early childhood education had no doubt that the physical environment held great powers and could influence children's growth and learning. Harriet Johnson was firm in her belief that the environment must provide for children's basic need to interact with others and materials. "She was convinced that learning was soundest when the environment encouraged the child in his impulse to experiences" (Biber, 1972, p. viii). To the pioneers, the arrangement of space and the selection of materials were of the highest importance.

We know that children learn through interaction with the environment. In order for this learning to be productive, however, the classroom must be carefully arranged. It should be structured so that all children meet with success as they explore it and interact with others and with materials for learning. The environment is also arranged so that the group of children can function together in an orderly fashion—cooperating, communicating, learning, sharing, and working together.

Assessing the Learning Environment

"Hi there, let me show you to your room," the school director says to welcome you, the new teacher. She may lead you to a room specifically designed and created for young children's play and learning, or you may find yourself in a church basement, abandoned dormitory, dining hall, or hotel ballroom. You usually have little choice in the type of physical plant you'll be given to work in; you do have choices as well as a responsibility to organize the space effectively. You should select and arrange materials that will teach children that they are active humans who learn through interaction with their physical world and with others (Bredekamp, 1987). As you plan to organize and arrange an environment that provides for children's learning, take into account the following:

1. Your situation
2. Program goals and objectives
3. Health and safety concerns
4. Aesthetics, information, and stimulation

Your Situation

Perhaps in some future time, classrooms and outdoor play areas will be designed only for children's use. Every room will be bright and cheerful, full of open spaces, with doors and patios connecting the indoors with the outside. Bathrooms and sinks with hot and cold running water will be found in each room. There will be a separate room where teachers relax and refresh themselves, and another in which parents meet one another. Outdoor spaces will be as wondrous as those envisioned by Rousseau or Froebel—with trees for climbing, ponds to wade in and fish to watch, sand piles for playing, garden plots for planting, and pathways for bike riding.

That time is not now.

You'll have to make hard decisions about how best to work within a given space. Cornelia Goldsmith (1972) helped child-care directors in New York City see how they could make the most of whatever environment they had. She asked each teacher to:

1. Make a detailed floor plan of both indoor and outdoor spaces, noting where electrical outlets, doorways, built-in shelves, and windows were, and where fixed objects were located on the playground.
2. Write a statement of their goals and objectives.
3. Think about the nature of children.
4. Determine their budget for materials and supplies.

Using this information, she had teachers plan the best arrangement they could. Some of the questions she suggested that teachers think about were:

1. Can rooms be closed off, opened up, cleared of furniture for large-muscle activities or napping?
2. How can the rooms be divided to diminish discipline problems? How can screens or furniture be used to establish clearly defined pathways through the room and to separate specific activities?
3. How can more space be created for children in a small room? Could you use the hallway, take down a wall, or open up a closet or cloakroom?

4. Where can storage spaces be acquired and how?
5. What furniture do you have to work with? Which can be eliminated? What needs to be purchased? How can it be arranged or moved during the day to maximize children's learning?
6. How can the room be made aesthetically attractive to children and adults?
7. How is the environment arranged for children with special needs, including those in wheelchairs, with leg or body braces, or who have hearing or visual impairments?

Program Goals and Objectives

"To make space work for a program it is very important to have a realistic idea about the goals to be achieved" (Kritchevsky, Prescott, & Walling, 1969). Your overall goals and specific objectives will help you to determine how you'll arrange your environment. If you want children to learn specific skills through prescribed tasks, you'll probably arrange to have learning stations, cubbyholes for individual work, or desks and tables placed in rows.

Continually increasing in complexity, centers challenge children to new learning.

On the other hand, if your goals are to foster children's problem-solving abilities, you would arrange the room with centers of interest that demand physical and mental activity and present children with opportunities to identify and solve problems.

To develop social skills, you would provide spaces for small group work. A block area would attract a group of children, as would a dramatic play area, a housekeeping center, or an art materials table.

Daily lesson plans also affect space and materials arrangements. Each lesson plan is a type of organizational tool. You should make allowances in your plans for arrangements for special equipment, any necessary reorganization of space, positioning of children for different activities, and accessibility to materials.

Goals and objectives change as children grow and mature. As they change, so do the number and type of centers, the materials you will select for inclusion in the centers, and the arrangement of these materials. Continually increasing in complexity, centers challenge children to new learning.

Health and Safety Concerns

Planning for physical health and safety is a teacher's primary concern (Kendall & Moukaddem, 1992). Examine your classroom's lighting, heating, and ventilation. Look at the bathroom facilities and general sanitary conditions. If these are inadequate, bring the fact to the attention of your supervisor, director, or advisory board.

The school system will provide for repairs or corrections, perhaps by using volunteers to make the needed repairs. Check each piece of equipment for sharp edges, loose pieces that could cause accidents, or small parts that toddlers might swallow or stuff into their noses.

Plan for illness prevention as well. Potentially dangerous childhood diseases are spreading in today's child-care and preschool populations. These include Haemophilus influenza (H-flu), hepatitis, and measles (Centers for Disease Control, 1990). Sanitation must receive high priority in your preparation of the physical environment, especially when you work with infants and toddlers. Even if you're working with preschoolers or primary-grade children, you'll want to be able to disinfect equipment. Equipment can be disinfected by washing it in a detergent solution and drying in the sun. It can also be wiped with a bleach disinfectant solution. Steps for disinfecting follow.

1. Wash vigorously with detergent in water.
2. Rinse with clear water.
3. Wipe or spray with a solution of two tablespoons (15 ml) chlorine bleach and one gallon (3.785 l) water.
4. Sun or air dry. (Highberger & Boyton, 1983, p. 4)

Work with infants and toddlers requires additional caution. The diapering area should have a disposable covering, which should be changed after each child is diapered. The covering should be placed atop a washable surface, which should be cleaned any time a diaper leaks on the table but at least twice a day.

Handwashing is important. The Academy of Pediatrics states that the most effective way to prevent the spread of infections is washing hands both before and after diapering each child. Use soap in a dispenser, hold the faucet with paper towels, and have a trash container with a step-on lid (NAEYC, 1991a).

Adults, whether working with infants or primary-age children, must recognize their role in preventing the spread of disease. Careful attention to your own health and general hygiene is necessary.

When you work in a full-day facility, food preparation and service are other considerations. If children eat family style in their room, the table surface and the floor beneath the table must be kept thoroughly clean. Even if children clean up after lunch, you'll have to wash the table and floor with the disinfecting solution after they finish.

Keeping the physical environment safe and healthy takes time, but as Highberger and Boyton (1983) point out, it's time well spent. Children who are healthy are easier to care for, teach, and be with. Further, your own health is affected. "Some time spent each day on thoughtful attention to sanitation should yield more time for enjoyable learning activities . . . it can also make a difference in how caregivers feel about their own work, and in how often they become ill" (Highberger & Boyton, 1983, p. 7).

Aesthetics, Information, and Stimulation

Children's environments should be kept not only safe and clean, but aesthetically pleasing, informative, and stimulating as well (New, 1990). The child-care centers of the town of Reggio Emilia, Italy, illustrate the wonder and beauty of environments created with aesthetics in mind.

In Reggio Emilia, spaces are arranged to have visual appeal to both the children and adults who work with children, to give children something to ponder, and to inform both children and adults. This is "not the result of a higher-than-average budget for equipment and furniture, but of a creative, meticulous consideration of the potentials of the environment to meet program and curriculum goals" (New, 1990, p. 8).

Everything is arranged to be aesthetically pleasing everywhere. Mirrors of all types are found throughout the center. Bits of mirrors and colored glass hang from the ceilings to catch a sunbeam and bounce it back to children, and long, horizontal mirrors are mounted near the floor so children can watch themselves and others. In other places, square or triangle pieces of mirrors cover the walls.

Flowers, plants, mirrors, and art by children and others decorate the bathrooms and classrooms. Lunchrooms are places of beauty, arranged with small tables and spaces for relaxation. Displays of the food children will eat, as well as vivid close-up color photos of the foods, add color and beauty.

In the art room, the art supplies are arranged with aesthetics in mind, creating art shelves that themselves are stunningly beautiful works of art. Paints and papers are arranged by color, size, or texture. Found objects (leaves, fabric scraps, feathers) are "pleasingly arranged, often by color, on shelves within children's reach" (New, 1990, p. 8).

Everywhere you turn there is something else to ponder. Leaves and acorns found by the children are arranged in plastic bags along one wall. Large photos of children and displays of the children's artwork and image making are on another wall. Displays not only stimulate children to thought and to reflect on their past experiences, but also serve to inform others of children's work.

Some educators have attributed the emphasis on beauty in the Reggio Emilia child-care centers to the Italian culture. "The emphases on the arts and aesthetic sensibilities reflect an appreciation of detail and sensitivity to design consistent with the Italian cultural tradition of creative endeavors" (New, 1990, p. 10).

Nevertheless, all children everywhere, not just in Italy, deserve to live and learn in an environment that is aesthetically pleasing and visually appealing. All environments should be:

1. *Aesthetically pleasing with*
   a. prints or posters of real works of art instead of cartoon art
   b. plants and flowers strategically placed throughout the room, hallways, lunchrooms, office, even in the bathrooms
   c. children's art displayed and mounted
   d. things to look at and wonder about placed at all levels. Light-catching objects can hang from ceilings or walls, and other art or things that delight the eye can be placed at floor level, child height level, and at adult height level

2. *Cognitively stimulating with*
   a. displays that help children organize and think about their experiences
   b. group murals reminding children of the things they've done or learned
   c. child-created displays summarizing a group project
   d. bulletin boards or displays that introduce a new topic or theme

3. *Informative with*
   a. open books that might extend children's knowledge of a topic
   b. displays designed to reinforce a new concept
   c. pictures and objects chosen for their informational value

d. labels that explain the exhibit for adults, as well as simple labels children can read or make sense of

Organizing the Environment

The Needs of Special Children

You must also consider children with disabilities or special needs in arranging the environment. Special classroom organization is required if physically disabled children are present. To permit use of a wheelchair, remove physical barriers, provide wider paths for movement in the room, and arrange work spaces and activity units to offer shelter from intrusion or interference (Loughlin & Suina, 1982).

For visually impaired children, reduce the amount of visual information present in any one area. Patterned backgrounds on walls, display areas, or work mats should be removed. Small shelving units containing a few materials on each shelf, which offer little visual distraction, are recommended (Loughlin & Suina, 1982).

More visual stimulation and less auditory distraction are helpful for hearing-impaired children. These children learn through visual means and need less noise. Teachers can carpet shelves and other work surfaces, use felt pads on desktops, or place learning materials on clear display so choices can be made.

Loughlin and Suina (1982) do not believe that a teacher needs to reduce the amount and variety of learning materials within a classroom to accommodate the needs of children with physical disabilities. "Rather than reducing the amount and variety of learning materials, or simplifying their level to meet children's handicaps, the host teachers removed barriers for children with special needs by increasing the variation of materials, which also expanded learning possibilities for all children" (p. 211).

Flexibility and Change

Organizing the learning environment is an ongoing activity. Space arrangements should never be considered set. If the classroom isn't functioning smoothly, the teacher should reassess the arrangement of space. The environment will also change as children grow and mature or as their interests dictate new arrangements.

Children can be involved in changes. They may suggest ways of rearranging the room to eliminate problems or in a way that will permit them to follow up on a special interest or project.

In one kindergarten classroom, children were planning to make and paint a large rocket. The teacher realized that space would have to be allocated for the project, and either the dramatic play area or the block area would have to be disrupted. She discussed the problem with the children, and their consensus was to reduce the housekeeping area. The teacher was reluctant to eliminate this area because it was among the children's favorites. But by adding old boots, helmets, tools, work clothes, and mechanical pieces to the rocket area, she extended the rocket play to include a lot of the dramatic play that had occurred in the housekeeping area. She also fostered children's role-taking and use of language and symbols, which might have been lost by removing the housekeeping area.

The National Association for the Education of Young Children recommends having a minimum of thirty-five square feet of indoor space per child in the preschool and primary classrooms (NAEYC, 1991a). Less than thirty-five square feet of space per child causes crowding and limits children's opportunities to explore materials and experiment. It also presents difficulties for large group activities. When space is limited, children are less involved in activities and seem to withdraw socially. Physical aggression also increases as space decreases (Weinstein, 1979).

More space is not always desirable, however. When spaces are too large, children seem to get lost in the room. They are less likely to form small groups and to interact with one another. They may not do anything because they can't even see the choices available. Further, the open spaces encourage darting and dashing through the room, and discipline problems increase.

Too Large? Too Small?

If your room is too small, consider removing furniture, changing routines, or using platforms. Try to find additional space in the building or outdoors for specific learning activities. First, examine the furniture and its use. Note how frequently, when, and how each piece is used. Remove any piece that isn't being used, including your desk. A teacher's desk takes up a great deal of space and usually isn't necessary in an early childhood setting. Substitute a file drawer, the piano top, or a high shelf for your desk. Or move your desk into the hall, locking any drawers that contain confidential files or storing those files in the principal's or director's office.

Children in an early childhood program rarely need to be seated at the same time. They spend most of their day working on the floor or moving in

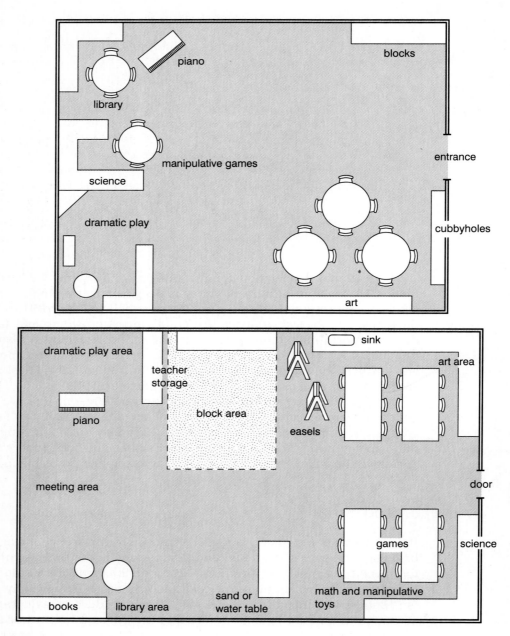

Figure 6–1
Two possible arrangements for indoor space

and out of groups. You can remove some tables and desks. If you do need to have all of the children seated at tables for a special activity, you can occasionally bring in folding tables and chairs.

Next think about the multiple uses of the furniture. A shelf can be used as a room divider or storage area or for activities like puppet shows. An upright piano with the back covered with paper can serve as a room divider and bulletin board. Rotate furniture and remove pieces that lose appeal during the year. Turn shelves against the wall to permit children to gather in large groups; when meeting time is over, turn the shelves back, providing spaces for interest centers and displays of learning materials.

Platforms can be used successfully to expand limited spaces. Volunteers may build a loft for your room. At the top of the loft children can find books and a quiet place for reading or studying. Underneath is a fine space for dramatic play. Climbing up and down gives children practice with large muscles and the opportunity to release pent-up energy.

When space is limited, good housekeeping practices become more important. Keeping everything in its place, moving trash, and keeping the room neat maximize use of small spaces. In coping with limited space, analyze your routines. How could a group be subdivided? Could you use the outdoors more often? Would a change in scheduling allow for more space? Would an additional staff member help by working with a group of children in a hall or outdoors, or would the staff member hinder by taking up more space?

A room that is too large needs to be divided. One part of the room could be equipped for large-muscle activity but be used only when outdoor play is not possible. You could create quiet areas by using existing furniture as dividers. If you are given a large gym or church meeting hall for a classroom, you might even want to divide the large space in half with shelves or cubbyholes and use part of it. Figure 6–1 shows two examples of how indoor space might be arranged. You should always remember that there is no "right" way to arrange indoor space, and feel free to use it in experimental and creative ways.

Indoor Spaces

Interest Centers

Children from infancy through age seven or eight can benefit from clearly delineated, organized, thematic work and play areas called *interest centers.* Centers are designed to foster the program's broad goals and to meet children's needs for activity, decision making, and interaction. They also add a certain amount of flexibility to the program.

Centers encourage children to make decisions. In a room with a variety of interest centers, children have to select the one in which they want to spend their time; then they must decide when they've completed their work in that center and are ready to move to another. Children can also participate in making a decision about which centers to include in the room.

Because children make the decisions, they may combine centers for specific types of play. Cass (1973, p. 142) says that "play and work spill over into each other and it's difficult sometimes to discover where one center begins and the other ends." Play may start in one center but move to another. One four-year-old "mother" was trying to get her "baby" to sleep in the housekeeping area. She suddenly asked, "Would a story help, honey?" She then went to the library corner, selected a book, and dragged the small library's rocking chair back to the housekeeping corner; she sat down, picked up her "baby," and started to read.

If children's interest in a specific center declines, it can be removed and replaced by something of greater interest. One group of children started to play fast-food restaurant in the housekeeping area. The play store next to the housekeeping area had gone untouched for days. The teacher, picking up on children's current interest, removed the store, replacing it with a fast-food restaurant. A small table, pencils, order pads, plastic food containers, and a check-out counter fostered this play.

Placing a noisy center next to a quiet area might be counterproductive.

The arrangement of the centers is critical if they are to fulfill children's needs for activity, decision making, and interaction with materials and with other children. Begin by making a floor plan of your room. On the floor plan, place the fixed items, such as electrical outlets, windows, and doors. Then try out various room arrangements by using pieces of paper to represent furniture and equipment. Plan for spaces for children to play on the floor or gather for large group meetings. Identify places for children to work alone, with others, and in both large and small groups.

Think about the arrangement of centers. Some centers are active and noisy, like the workbench or block area; others, like the listening or library area, are quiet and relaxed. Placing a noisy center next to a quiet area might be counterproductive.

Consider how children will move from one center to another. Pathways have two purposes. They facilitate movement through the room, and they have something interesting at their end, drawing children from one place to another.

> A path is the empty space on the floor or ground through which people move in getting from one place to another; it need be no different in composition from the rest of the surface; they are difficult to describe in words, but when they are well defined, they are easily seen. (Kritchevsky, Prescott, & Walling, 1969, p. 15)

If a child has to move through the library or housekeeping area to get to tables or blocks, you can expect trouble. Pathways between centers must be clear. Sometimes pathways seem clear to you, but when you stoop to a child's-eye level, you'll see that they're blocked by a piece of equipment, another attractive center, or a piece of furniture.

Children need somewhere they can go to be alone, so you should provide private spaces. A corner of the room with a beanbag chair, rocking chair, or just a strip of carpet protected from the room by a divider enables children to find shelter and privacy. They can get away from it all or work on some project without having others intrude (Loughlin & Martin, 1987, p. 53).

As you arrange the room, ask yourself if you'll be able adequately to supervise children as they work and move through the room. Can you see over the dividers and boundaries and into each space?

Infants and Toddlers

Centers in the infant and toddler rooms are concerned with caregiving and playing with a few infants and toddlers at a time. There will be an area for sleeping, with no more than five or six cribs. Cribs should be arranged informally rather than lined up institutionally against a wall. The crib room should be a quiet place away from other active areas or traffic patterns. Ideally the cribs should be in a separate room, but this is not always feasible.

Other caregiving areas include a place to feed infants and toddlers and a place for washing and diapering. Babies enjoy having a mirror that they can look at in the diapering and washing areas.

A large floor area, kept sanitized, should be available for crawling and floor play. This area offers space for movement as babies begin to raise their heads, roll over, and crawl. It also provides different textural experiences and a different view of the world.

The six- to nine-month-old is quite active when awake, so this space can also include pieces of stationary furniture on which children can pull themselves upright. Before reaching one year of age, some children will be completely mobile, walking while clinging to furniture, climbing on top of things, and crawling away with lightning speed to get something they see (Balban, 1992).

The infant room should be designed to meet babies' needs, just as every other room in early education programs should be designed for older children's needs. The infant room should be planned with flexibility in mind. Some babies and toddlers want to be held and cuddled for long periods of time; others enjoy the challenge of being placed on a blanket on the floor where they can raise their heads, roll over, and see the world from a different angle. Some like to sleep under a blanket; others kick off coverings. Some are awake for long periods; others sleep during much of the day. Some love to be near the bustling sounds and sights of other children and adults; others need to be alone in a quiet, serene atmosphere. You must structure an attractive, interesting, and comfortable room that meets the needs of each infant.

Because babies explore with their eyes, hands, and mouth, their play room and crib area should have pictures, mobiles, plants, or flowers in various places so the infants can examine them. Place pictures where they will catch the infants' eyes. Mobiles of all types and constructions can be hung over babies' cribs or from the ceiling. If plants and mobiles are placed so that they cast their shadows on the wall or floor, they will provide additional fascination.

Playpens, baby seats, bouncing seats, or port-a-cribs let infants observe and play with one another and with toys under the teachers' watchful eyes. Toys that babies enjoy and can play with in cribs and playpens or while on the floor include the following:

- Blocks inside a box
- Boxes with tissue paper inside (provided you can watch the children closely so the paper is only held and crumbled, not put into the mouth)
- Spill-and-fill toys like plastic cups, boxes, storage containers, and large wooden beads; clothespins and safety-proofed coffee cans; assorted shapes and sizes of cardboard boxes, and small wooden blocks
- Objects placed in a plastic dish, box, bowl, or bucket for banging together or putting in and taking out

- Discarded boxes covered with plastic, empty boxes with lids, discarded tin pie pans, coffeepots (with glass and sharp metal parts removed), and plastic reels from tape dispensers

Be certain that play objects are safe to handle, free from sharp or jagged edges, and large enough so they cannot be swallowed. They should be safe to taste or lick. Toys for infants should provide a variety of textures—soft and cuddly, hard, smooth, and rough.

Babies need objects of varying sizes and shapes. Some of the playthings they like are bracelets that can be put on an arm; cans that are round and long and can be rolled or used to put smaller toys in; boxes that can be stacked; pots, pans, wooden spoons, clear plastic containers, milk cartons, and keys that can be tied together to create intriguing noisemakers or trains. None of the toys for infants needs to be expensive; they just need to allow for baby's exploration of the world.

The toddler room needs equipment for caregiving, such as cribs, dressing tables, and playpens; but because toddlers are so active, they need more materials and equipment to explore than infants do. They enjoy objects to climb in and on, ride in, pull, and push. Toddlers can climb on benches, sturdy boxes or low walls, and up and down stairs.

Their sense of space develops as they crawl under, over, and through objects. A box with ends cut out makes a tunnel. An obstacle course of chairs, tables, large pillows, and tires provides for the experience of going under, on, and between both soft and hard objects. As toddlers develop the skills of pulling, pushing, and stacking, they'll construct some of their own "obstacle courses" by moving boxes, planks, pillows, and chairs around. Wagons are a big help for moving smaller items.

Toddlers need space where they can play alone or be onlookers as others play. Cubbyholes along the wall with a low shelf to sit on provide not only a space where they can keep belongings, but also a private place where they can watch others play or can cuddle with a favorite toy.

The toddler room may also contain

- Art materials
- Books (and a place to read them)
- Growing plants
- Animals like gerbils or fish to observe and care for
- Some dress-up clothes, toy dishes, and household items for *sociodramatic play*

Preschool/Kindergarten/Primary Classrooms

Preschool and primary rooms are filled with a wide variety of materials, supplies, and equipment. Children need space to begin to learn to play together: to construct large, complex buildings or to play house, office, store, and post office. The wider world of the community, the neighborhood, and all of the curriculum content areas assume greater importance. The centers and their materials permit preschoolers to understand new relationships, solve problems, and test their knowledge. Interest centers should vary from region to region because they should reflect the culture of the children involved as well as providing interests and insights into other cultures. In a Head Start center in coastal Maine, for example, the sand table was a clam flat, outfitted with

Figure 6–2
Possible indoor arrangement for kindergarten and primary classrooms

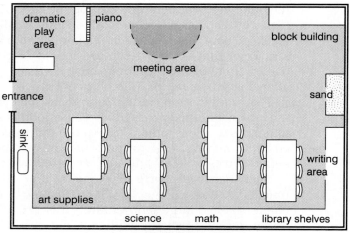

Primary classroom

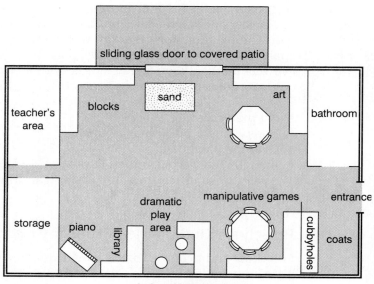

Indoor kindergarten

shells, hods, and hoes. It would be unlikely for a midwestern Head Start to have the same kind of interest center.

Primary classrooms are arranged much as preschool classrooms are, but the centers reflect older children's interests and their developing *symbolic* skills. They provide opportunities for children to practice academic skills. Written language is used to label centers in the primary grades, describe the centers, or present options for using them.

Primary age children, as children of any other age, need spaces arranged for small group work as well as for individual work (Gareau & Kennedy, 1991). As projects develop, children may find the space they need in the hallways or out of doors.

Centers should be flexible with materials displayed openly, inviting children to try activities for themselves. Centers common to all early childhood programs are

- Art
- Library
- Dramatic play
- Manipulative and mathematics play
- Science
- Block
- Audiovisual
- Writing
- Music

Figure 6–2 gives examples of possible arrangements of indoor space for kindergarten and primary classrooms. Remember to experiment for the best possible arrangement.

Art Center.   A popular area, the art center is really many centers, providing children with a variety of materials for experimenting, exploring, and creating. Each day children should have a choice of whether they want to draw, paint, model, construct, cut and paste, or do all or none of them.

Materials should be arranged on tables or low shelves easily accessible to the children. Scissors, including left-handed scissors, should be available and stored point down, possibly in empty egg cartons. Several types of paste should be available so children can do different kinds of projects.

Art activities often are spread out over several surfaces—tables, walls, easels, floor areas, or even into the hall. Locate painting activities near a water source if possible, or provide water for washing brushes in some other way. Plastic-covered cloth can be used for clay work or to cover other tables for messy art activities.

Library Center.   The library area should be located as far as possible from distractions and separate from other ongoing activities. Every library center should have bookshelves, at least one table, and a few chairs. In a small room, you may substitute pillows, sample carpet squares, or small footstools for the table and chairs.

Children's books may be displayed on the table and on shelves. Any arrangement that makes them difficult to see and select should be avoided. The local library is usually willing to lend you 30 to 40 books per month, so you can change the selection frequently.

In addition to children's books, add old catalogs (seed, flower, auto, and toy), parts of the Sunday newspaper, and some picture news magazines. Even three-year-olds enjoy "wishing" through a toy catalog, naming the things they see or want. Four- and five-year-olds play games with catalogs; for example, one child says "I'm looking at a toy, it's red and you can ride on it," and the other child either has to find the same picture in a duplicate catalog or guess the name of the toy or object the child is describing.

Some early childhood programs are fortunate to have listening stations or tape recorders with earphones attached. Favorite stories can be taped for children to listen to while they turn the pages of the book. Teachers in child-care programs have found they can foster parent involvement and increase children's motivation for books if they ask parents to record a story for the children to listen to during the day. It is a good idea to have flannel boards with cutout figures representing story characters, puppets, and other props in the area.

Kindergarten and primary children will begin to use reference books and materials. Although a complete encyclopedia need not dominate a library area, you can include a few volumes that contain information that children need for a given project or unit theme. Picture dictionaries may also be available.

Selected books may be organized in a take-home library. A simple check-out sheet can be mounted above the books with black and red crayons attached. The children place a red check by their name when they've taken a book and a black check when they return it.

Place books in other areas of the room too. You can store biographies, nonfiction, fiction, concept books, and poetry in separate plastic containers located throughout the room. For example, one teacher placed a container of books about building in the block area, a container of books illustrating spring near the art supplies to give children ideas for creating, and Mother Goose and baby poem books in the housekeeping area for children to use to help them get the babies ready to sleep.

Dramatic Play Center.   Children find a link between home and school in *dramatic play* areas. Children are free to find out how it would feel to be a teacher, doctor, mother, father, baby, witch, or king. There they explore roles they may someday assume as well as those that are make believe. Each dramatic play area should be representative of the child's community and home, so they will vary according to the region, culture, and characteristics of the neighborhood. Figures 6–3 and 6–4 list items that you might include in the center to promote development of both expressive and written language.

For example, children whose parents are migrant workers would need to find boxes and packing equipment that would enable them to act out moving from one picking area to another. Navajo children living in hogans would find props representing their hogan. In an urban area, subway tickets or tokens, subway and bus maps, taxi signs, or pretend elevators might be part of the dramatic play area.

The dramatic play area is located anywhere in the room that provides a feeling of closure for children. Low shelves or a rack for dress-up clothing can suggest separation, but the area should be open enough so you can observe and supervise. Children often extend their housekeeping play to other parts of the room as they leave the area to shop, go to work, or visit other children.

You can purchase or construct furniture for the area from heavy cardboard boxes, wooden crates, and discarded household items. The usual equipment includes a kitchen with table, chairs, stove, cabinet, sink, and refrigerator; a living room with a soft place to sit; and a bedroom with

In the dramatic play center, children find a link between home and school.

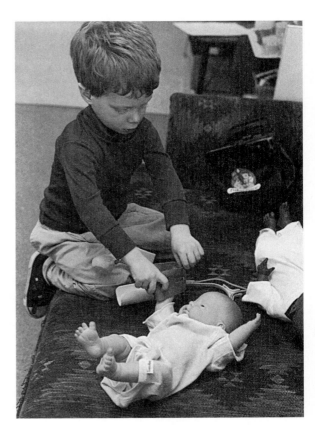

dressers and doll beds. Dolls of all sizes and diverse ethnic characteristics can be available.

Equipment bought at a local thrift shop or donated by parents or community groups for the center keeps this area fully supplied. You will need a variety of dress-up clothing, including all types of hats, boots, purses, wal-

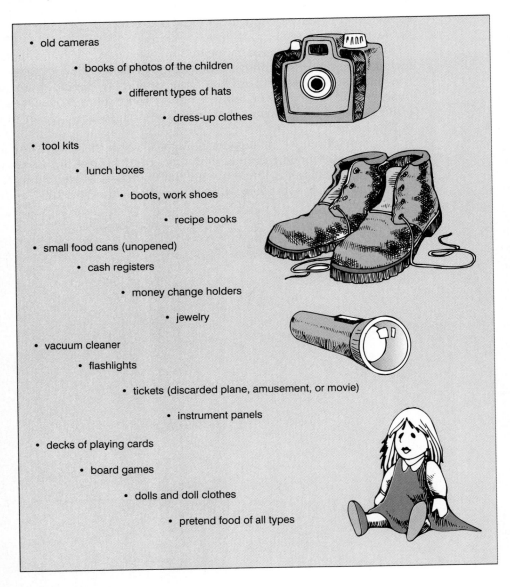

- old cameras
  - books of photos of the children
    - different types of hats
      - dress-up clothes
- tool kits
  - lunch boxes
    - boots, work shoes
      - recipe books
- small food cans (unopened)
  - cash registers
    - money change holders
      - jewelry
- vacuum cleaner
  - flashlights
    - tickets (discarded plane, amusement, or movie)
      - instrument panels
- decks of playing cards
  - board games
    - dolls and doll clothes
      - pretend food of all types

Figure 6–3
Props that encourage expressive language

lets, ties, and jewelry. A half slip, especially one with lace, is used for formal occasions, as are lace curtains that can be draped or pinned into king and queen's outfits.

Vocational aspirations are fostered by props representing different occupations. Briefcases, tool kits, and work clothing of all types permit children

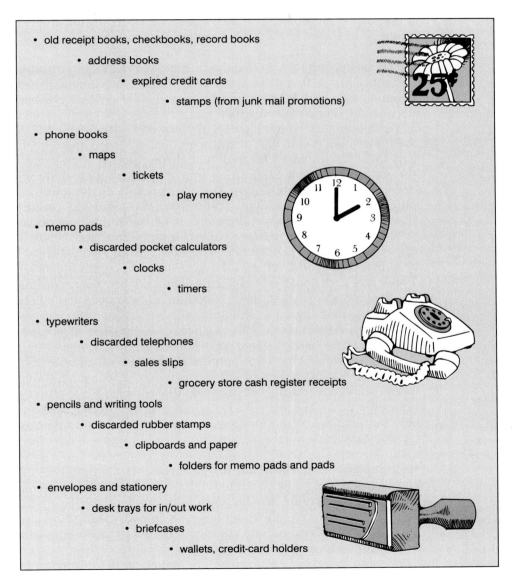

- old receipt books, checkbooks, record books
  - address books
    - expired credit cards
      - stamps (from junk mail promotions)

- phone books
  - maps
    - tickets
      - play money

- memo pads
  - discarded pocket calculators
    - clocks
      - timers

- typewriters
  - discarded telephones
    - sales slips
      - grocery store cash register receipts

- pencils and writing tools
  - discarded rubber stamps
    - clipboards and paper
      - folders for memo pads and pads

- envelopes and stationery
  - desk trays for in/out work
    - briefcases
      - wallets, credit-card holders

Figure 6–4
Props that encourage written language

to try out future careers. At the Center for Young Children at the University of Maryland, water and food are allowed in the dramatic play area. Small dishpans hold soapy water for washing dishes, and pitchers hold water for children to "cook" with. If water isn't available, children usually find some way to sneak it into the area. When you provide for water play, you assume control over the play and can keep it in bounds.

At times, simple recipes with words and illustrations, along with appropriate food items, are kept in the area for five- and six-year-olds. When this activity is part of the play, it is supervised fully by adults. Clean dishes and hands are required. Children with hands washed may produce snacks for the entire group in a disinfected area. Fruit kebabs, cheese and crackers, or peanut butter sandwiches can be served as a snack prepared by the children in the housekeeping area.

Dramatic play areas should include more than just the housekeeping area. For children in the primary grades, the need to reenact family life is less than for younger children. The dramatic play area more often reflects the older children's excursions into the community or themes that have developed in the classroom. You can provide these children with a play office, gas station, fast-food restaurant, plant nursery, store, or anything that offers them an opportunity to reenact their experiences.

Regardless of the nature of the dramatic play area, consider children's opportunities for language learning and growth. Keep books, newspapers, receipt books, and paper and writing tools available (Morrow, 1990). Typewriters, magazines, note pads, chalkboards for recording daily activities or a list attached to the refrigerator door replicate the literacy found in a middle-class home.

Integrate experiences with mathematics into the dramatic play area as well. Placing a pad of paper and pencils near the telephone, as well as a Rolodex or other type of telephone book, fosters number writing. Include old check books, notebooks, felt tip pens, crayons, and colored pencils. Blank books for journal keeping and diaries encourage other forms of writing in the housekeeping area. In equipping the dramatic play area for literacy, think of all of the language tools found in a middle-class home and include these.

Manipulative and Mathematics Centers.   A manipulative game center is highly interesting and valuable. There children find pegboards, nesting blocks, puzzles, table games, and other small-muscle equipment. The purpose of these is to build eye-hand-muscle coordination and specific visual or auditory discrimination skills; they also help develop attention span, memory, language skills, and concepts.

Wooden puzzles, pegboards, construction sets, small plastic blocks, wooden tiles, tinker toys, and erector sets should be available. A few sets of cards, whether regular playing cards or picture cards designed for children's games, are useful.

Materials for sorting and classification should be in the area. Objects to string, such as beads, macaroni, washers, and bottle caps with holes in them, can be placed on shoestrings, pipe cleaners, and other materials. Simple table games offer experiences in counting and facilitate learning to cooperate in a group. Matching games as well as commercial bingo and lotto games can be purchased or constructed. Children in the primary grades are especially interested in these games and will make up rules and change them to permit one or the other to win, as Bob and his friend did in chapter 2.

How you store games and items is crucial. The choices must be clear for children. If puzzles are stored in a rack, they're hidden from the children; boxes of games stacked one on top of the other permit only the top game to be visible. It's better to display a few items at a time, perhaps placing some on a nearby table.

Science Center.   Science centers are not just places to deposit fall leaves and old seashells. These are places in which children can actively explore. Balancing scales to weigh with, machines to take apart and put back together, seeds to plant and grow, and animals to care for can aid children.

An indoor place for water and sand should be provided. Select a place near the water source for water play. Some centers are equipped with low sinks that can be used for water play, but a dishpan set on a table or chair is sufficient. You can put coffeepots, plastic bottles, spoons, funnels, and walnut shells in the water to foster children's scientific exploration. If children lose interest, a bit of detergent initiates a different type of play—washing things and making bubbles. Food coloring provides additional fascination.

Sand can be placed in a purchased sand table, tin tub, bassinet, or wading pool. Keep water near the sand so children can moisten it as they build. Props like rocks, twigs, marbles, toy people, cars, or animals can be added. Toddlers and preschoolers enjoy sand and water play throughout the year. In primary classrooms, sand play becomes more sophisticated as children construct villages with ponds, streets, bridges, and hills.

For primary-age children, the sand table becomes a resource for language arts. Children create structures or scenes in the sand table inspired by books and stories they have read or have had read to them (Barbour, Webster, & Drosdeck, 1987). After hearing Byrd Baylor's *The Desert Is Theirs*, second-graders created a desert in their sandbox. Third-graders experimented with making quicksand, using Tomie de Paola's *The Quicksand Book* as their source (Barbour, Webster, & Drosdeck, 1987).

Block Center.   Blocks are essential for children of all ages. Every early childhood classroom should have large hollow blocks and unit blocks as well as bits of wood to build with. When well-chosen accessories are available, block play expands to rich dramatic play. "Instead of representational toys and hardware, use an abundant assortment of small unit blocks (only for accessories, not for building). These become cups, telephones, tools, sandwiches, machinery, flight controls—whatever. Crayons, paper, and masking tape should be on hand because children often need to make signs for their play" (Cartwright, 1990, p. 38).

Blocks belong in the kindergarten and primary grades as well. These might be stored on a roll-away shelf to be available when the need arises. In one school, the blocks were used to replicate the building of a new addition to the school. Using blueprints, the children constructed a block building to correspond to the building they observed being constructed. A group of second-graders found the blocks necessary to create castles and cathedrals after reading a book about life in the Middle Ages in Europe.

Another second-grade group found blocks useful after reading Munro's *The Inside-Outside Book of Washington, DC* (1987). After reading the book and visiting some of the places illustrated in the book, the group built their Washington out of blocks.

If the blocks are stored on a unit with wheels so that it can be rolled around, then they might be shared with other primary grades. One or two sets of unit blocks may be rotated through two or three primary classrooms.

Audiovisual Center.   Some provision for kindergarten and primary children to use audiovisual equipment is beneficial both to teach children how to manipulate the equipment and to show them slide shows, filmstrips, transparencies, or videotapes. Children can manage a slide projector with a minimum of direction and supervision. If you start filmstrip projects, children can usually manage to use them independently. A single-concept, 8-mm loop projector, although less common, is another piece of equipment children handle effectively. An overhead projector can be used with transparencies that either you or the children make or that you purchase. Videotapes are easily managed by children individually, or you can show them to the entire group.

A closed-off area of the room that can be semidarkened serves well as the audiovisual area. It may be set up during a specific unit and need not remain if space is a problem.

Writing Center.   Writing tools should be throughout the room, but a special place can be set aside as the writing center. Place different types of blank booklets, paper, pencils, and other writing tools in that center. Also store dictionaries there—picture dictionaries, box and file card dictionaries, and perhaps a list of words on a chart reflecting a recent experience of the children. Following a visit from a firefighter, for example, the list would include words like *firefighter, hat, hose,* and *fire truck.*

Music Center.   A quiet part of the room away from other activities can be set up as the music center. There a child can listen to a record, operate the phonograph independently, or experiment with musical instruments without damaging them or using them in ways that disturb other children. Using earphones might help in a small classroom, but usually children can listen to a record or experiment with musical sounds using low sound levels without disturbing others.

Computer Center.   Many early childhood programs now have computer centers. "We must think clearly how we want our children's education to improve, what computers can do to help, and how that assistance can, in fact, be accomplished and whether or not any of this is reasonably affordable" (Becker, 1983, p. 385). You will want children to become familiar with and competent in using the computer, just as with the telephone, television, or typewriter. There are a number of tasks preschoolers can accomplish with the computer. They can push keys to move objects; generate patterns, colors, letters, and numbers; compare and match objects; discriminate between items; create and recreate shapes; and figure out puzzles (Ziajka, 1983, p. 65). Children in the primary grades can use the computer to gain a new skill or obtain needed practice.

Software programs are becoming available to teach every subject. Teachers have also found they can adapt some computer games for classroom use. These programs have been integrated into the classroom to introduce a new unit, offer enrichment, and to regulate the pace of individualized work.

Software programs are becoming available to teach every subject.

Computers do not always offer the best method for instruction. Before using a program, ask yourself the following questions:

1.   Does this program teach something more effectively than traditional (and certainly less expensive) methods and materials? (Ziajka, 1983)

2.   Can more than one child use the computer or program at the same time?

3.   Will the computer or program be used only for computer-assisted instruction of the practice-rote learning type? How does the program differ from regular print or worksheet materials?

4.   Does it have the potential for helping children develop higher order thinking skills like judging, evaluating, analyzing, or synthesizing information?

You'll also want to examine the program for accuracy and for the value it presents. Emphases on war, violence, and discriminatory treatment of women and minorities have been found in many computer programs. The program's quality should also be judged in terms of color, voice, animation, and other technical elements (Becker, 1983, p. 385).

Using Centers

A teacher's responsibility does not end after interest centers have been arranged. First, centers are continually changed to reflect children's experiences and the themes that are developing in the classroom. Centers evolve to enable children to express their feelings, ideas, and develop new skills. "If you're doing a unit on a topic such as transportation or hospitals, set up for follow-up play" (Greenberg, 1992, p. 51).

Centers are never permitted to become cluttered or sloppy but are continually rearranged so children can see the choices available, discover relationships, and make decisions about what they are learning. Children are expected to help keep centers usable by putting blocks away, washing paint brushes and returning them to the easel, or displaying books on the library table.

Then, too, teachers teach, often by reviewing the choices of centers. A teacher may say, for example, "Today we have a table for clay and another for salt dough. There are puzzles and a new game that two can play at the third table. And of course there's the dramatic play area, blocks, books, easel painting, and art and writing area. The filmstrip projector is set up so you can watch *Caps for Sale*. You'll probably all have enough time to view the filmstrip if you want to, but we do not have to return it to the library until Friday. So if you don't view it today, you'll have another three days to do so."

Teachers also teach by asking children to make plans. "What will you want to accomplish today? What center do I want to begin working in?" asked one teacher. By the end of kindergarten children should be able to ask themselves three questions before they start an activity:

1. What is my goal?
2. What materials will I need?
3. What steps will I take to achieve my goals? (Casey & Lippman, 1991, p. 53)

Teachers need not prescribe rigid rules for what centers children will work in or how long they can stay in a center. They do, however, need to encourage children to expand their skills, "Alan, you haven't painted for a long time, would you begin with either easel or table painting?" and direct those who have difficulty making a choice. "Wanda, have you considered. . . ."

If everyone wants to begin the day by building with blocks, you can limit the number by saying something like, "Whoa—too many want to work with blocks first. Kim, Shawna, and Roberto, would you think of something else to begin with today?"

Supervise children's work in the centers. Give help to the children who need it. Do not permit any child to bully or threaten another. Offer suggestions. Teachers can work with individual children or with small groups, answering questions or posing new questions to challenge children's thinking.

Both teachers and children think and reflect on their activities in the centers. After work time, teachers find that children enjoy describing what they did or sharing what they constructed. They can tell the group how they solved some problem, found a relationship, or enjoyed some experience. Some teachers find that taking candid photographs of children as they work and play fosters children's ability to think about their work, learning, and growth.

Teachers reflect on their observations of children and their work with them. They can make anecdotal notes on children's progress, problems encountered, developing skills, or use of language. They note which children didn't participate with a group and which didn't attend to or stick with an activity for more than a moment.

A teacher's observations about work time are the basis for evaluation of individual children and of the total program (Hyson, Hirsh-Pasek, & Rescorla, 1990). Based on their observations, teachers change a center by adding some objects and materials and removing others. They may plan to remove an entire unused center and replace it with another that reflects a newly emerging theme.

Finally, teachers communicate to parents, other teachers, and administrators about the children's work in the center. They copy the photos and send them home. Other photographs of children's work are displayed in the hall with brief explanatory labels and titles. Teachers write notes to the parents describing their children's work and progress. From time to time, teachers can show principals and other administrators a scope and sequence chart that documents how children's work in centers fosters the goals of the school and system.

Learning Stations

Learning stations are not to be confused with interest centers. Centers are broad-based areas for learning organized around some theme and designed to foster the broad goals of the total early childhood program. Learning stations are much more specific and are designed to teach, reinforce, clarify, and extend specific learning objectives. Objectives are identified for each station.

Generally, learning stations should be

1. *Self-directing:* Directions should be obvious so children can use them independently.
2. *Self-correcting:* Children should be able to tell by the way they've completed the task whether or not they are correct.
3. *Activity-oriented:* Stations should be based on children's manipulation of materials, not just paper-and-pencil tasks.

Stations may be stored along with the manipulative games or placed around the room. Many of the manipulative items will become learning stations for children in the primary grades.

There are as many possibilities for learning stations as there are topics of interest and skills to learn. You can design stations that offer practice in the basic skills of reading, language arts, mathematics, science, the social studies, music, and art. They may be designed to reflect thinking skills such as observing, classifying, interpreting, or summarizing. Stations can be designed to be motivational, diagnostic, prescriptive, enriching, or evaluative (Thomas, 1975).

The following are examples of learning stations:

1.   *Alphabets (Kindergarten Through First Grade).* To foster visual discrimination, record the following on a tape recorder:

Look in the alphabet tray. Pick out all of the letters that are made with straight lines. Put these in the box lid marked "SL." Pick out all of the letters made with curved lines. Put these in the box marked "CL." Show me what you've done. If I'm busy, select another tape as you wait.

2.   *Comic Strips (First Through Third Grade).* Sequencing skills can be practiced with comic strips. The instructions are:

Below are several envelopes containing comic strips. The pictures are mixed up. Take the pictures from the envelope and arrange them in order to tell the story as it may have appeared. When you have decided on the arrangement, check the backs of the comics to see if the numbers are in order. When you've finished, take one of the sheets and answer the questions. (Ditto pages are next to the envelopes.)

—What makes the story funny?

—Do you know anyone like this?

— Who is Francis (or another character)? What kind of person is she or he?

— Could you change the story to make it funnier? How?

3. *Math Bingo (Kindergarten Through Primary Grades)*. Bingo promotes children's math skills. Construct a bingo board, put different numbers on each square, and cover the board with clear plastic paper. Draw one card at a time from a stack of cards that show math problems and cover the corresponding square with the correct answer. When you get three in a row, you've won. You can play with a partner, each one using a different board, and taking turns drawing answer cards. Check yourself by turning the cards over for the answers.

4. *Find the Parent (Preschoolers)*. Thinking skills are fostered at this station. You need one set of cards with pictures of adult and baby animals; two box lids, one with a picture of an adult animal and the numeral 1 written on it, the other with a picture of a baby animal and the numeral 2 written on it. Take the set of cards, and put the adult animals in the box lid labeled 1 and the baby animals in box lid 2. Check your answers by turning over the cards. All adult-animal cards have a red check on the back. Now take the cards and put the adult animal with the correct baby animal. You can tell when you are correct because the dots on the front of the cards will match.

5. *Classify Animals (Preschoolers)*. Classifying skills are fostered with this station. You need one set of cards with pictures of animals, reptiles, birds, insects, and spiders, and a board containing five squares labeled

No Legs   2 Legs   4 Legs   6 Legs   8 Legs

Sort the animals according to their number of legs.

6. *Idea Bucket*. This station is designed to be motivational. Place a bucket of ideas in a center with materials to match the ideas. Children draw a card from the bucket, pick the corresponding box of materials, and complete the task.

The bucket could contain such ideas as:

- What can you make with the clay and objects in box 1?
- Find out which of the materials in box 3 will float.
- List all of the people who might use the tools in box 4.
- Write a story about the objects in box 5.

Outdoor Spaces

More space is required for a successful outdoor play yard than for an indoor play area. Over 200 square feet of outdoor space per child is desirable, and 3,000 square feet for 15 children is optimum. The more space available, the greater the possibilities for children to have learning experiences. Still, successful play spaces have been created on rooftops, in vest-pocket parks, or in blocked-off church driveways.

In arranging outdoor play spaces, consider the following:

- Balance
- Pathways
- Selection of equipment
- The developmental level and needs of children

As with indoor play, you'll also plan and design interest centers that can be a part of the play yard.

Balance

It is important to consider balance between quiet and active areas. Some spaces should be set aside for boisterous running, jumping, and climbing, and others for quiet, small-muscle manipulative play with dolls, sand, or water. Boxes, plants, hills, or pieces of equipment can be used to separate active from quiet areas.

There should also be a balance between shady and sunny areas. If there is no shade from buildings or trees in the yard, construct retreats from the

There should be a balance between shady and sunny areas in the play yard.

sun using beach umbrellas or awnings, or create a chickechee, the thatched open-sided hut adapted from Seminole homes.

Look at the textures and surfaces in the yard and try to create a balance between soft and hard surfaces. Pine bark, cedar chips, or pine needles can be used to create a soft area, while other areas can be reserved for digging, gardening, and sand or water play. Still other surfaces can be covered with hardtop for playing organized games, riding bikes, or building with blocks.

A balance of levels can make the play yard attractive to children. Various levels of tree trunks, cable tables, boxes, or climbing bars offer a balance between high and low spaces. A hill bulldozed or shoveled onto a flat play area fosters a variety of play activities; children can become ship captains, mountain climbers, or space creatures. The muscular activities of climbing the hill and the feel of rolling down make even a small hill a valuable addition.

Pathways

In arranging outdoor play spaces, you'll want to plan for pathways. Outdoor pathways are more visible than those indoors and can direct children's movements through the yard. Paths can be created of cedar chips, stones, or cement. "A total absence of path, because of too much equipment placed too close together, is very disruptive. The adult cannot see a path, and neither can the children" (Kritchevsky, Prescott, & Walling, 1969, p. 16). Shift equipment or add pieces to create definite pathways throughout the yard.

Selection of Outdoor Equipment

A variety of play equipment should be available. Kritchevsky, Prescott, and Walling (1969) suggest thinking in terms of potential units and actual units. Potential units are those spaces that are surrounded, at least in part, by tangible boundaries and contain something to play with, such as a jungle gym or a slide. Actual units are discrete units, such as a sandbox or playhouse.

Units are classified as simple, complex, or super. Simple units are those that do not have parts and can be used for one activity, such as slides, swings, or tricycles. A complex unit has parts and can be used creatively for a number of activities by groups of children. A sand table, garden, playhouse, or art table is considered a complex unit. A complex unit has three or more play materials, such as sand, water, and plastic bottles; climbing boards and boxes; or large crates and boxes. Super units foster a great variety of creative and dramatic play.

Swings and other simple units are not that useful even when space is not limited. They are for one activity by one child and can't be exploited very creatively. Also swings are potentially dangerous because young children can't be expected to keep a safe distance away from a swing in use, and creative play on the swing might lead to an accident.

Most accidents in a play yard involve swings, slides, or stationary climbing equipment. Rather than purchasing such equipment, think about providing more complex units that can be used for climbing, balancing, pushing, pulling, and a combination of other physical activities.

Climbing.   Climbing equipment that comes in pieces that children can move about is recommended. Children of all ages can use the equipment, and they can change it to meet changing play interests. Even with movable equipment, however, be certain that wherever it is placed, it's sturdy and the surface underneath is cushioned with pine needles, sand, sawdust, cedar chips, or other soft material.

Some climbing equipment can be constructed. Trestle units, a gate to climb and swing on, or an A-frame unit are easily assembled by a person experienced in carpentry.

Cable tables, tree stumps planted firmly in the ground at differing levels, or existing trees can be made safe for children's climbing. Provide soft material underneath and around the climbing unit and establish clear rules such as

1. No climbing with something in your hands.
2. Only two children at a time on the unit.
3. No climbing above the red ribbon.
4. No ropes in the climbing area.

Balancing, a part of all motor activities, can be fostered by the addition of specific play yard equipment. The simplest yet most effective piece of balance equipment is a balance beam. This can be an old log, several logs placed end to end, a board on its side, or bricks partially buried in the ground. Stepping stones, patio stones, or old tires placed in a series offer another type of balancing experience as children jump from one to another.

Pushing and Pulling.   Through pushing and pulling, children experience a sense of controlling their environment as well as practice with large muscles. Large wooden boxes and planks require teamwork to push and pull into a desired location. Old tires can be pushed and rolled to a new place, stacked to make a tower, or arranged to build a fort. Small cable tables turned on end can be pushed around the yard. Barrels, heavy wood blocks, tree trunks, or even blocks of salt require group discussion and cooperation to move from place to place. Large cardboard boxes appeal to children of all ages and can be pushed and pulled even by the youngest.

Throwing and Catching.   The play yard should have a wide assortment of balls of various sizes and weights. Basketballs, large soft balls, and rubber balls, as well as those for skill games, should be available. Think in terms of providing more than one or two of any kind of ball so a number of children can be involved in the action.

Developmental Level and Needs of Children

Children of differing ages use outdoor play spaces. It is not unusual for a teacher to be asked to provide children's outdoor play space that can be safely used by both infants and third-graders. Scheduling time for different age groups to use the play yard is useful and necessary. Yet all equipment must be safe, intriguing, and challenging for children of all ages. If children of different age groups are to use the yard simultaneously, specific areas might be set up for use by the different groups and boundaries established with stationary equipment. Figure 6–5 gives three possible arrangements for outdoor play space, and Figure 6–6 suggests guidelines for planning spaces. Again, remember that these are only suggestions for the teacher to build on.

Infants and Toddlers.   Infants need their own time and space outside. Very young infants can be carried; older babies are taken in their strollers to play outdoors. One teacher put a baby outdoors in a bounce seat in a playpen. This gave the baby the pleasure of watching the older children at play, and the older children had the experience of observing the baby. But the baby was kept far enough away from the curious reach of the preschoolers.

Playpens, carriages, or strollers can be placed so that infants can experience the outdoors. They can watch the leaves move on the tree or the water drip from the roof after a light rain. Touching the tree bark, the soft grass, the hard sidewalk, or the building increases sensory awareness. There may be birds singing, traffic sounds in the distance, or just the sound of children's voices.

Infants may also practice crawling and pulling themselves up. A blanket on the ground or even a grassy space that's been made safe is enough. One of the best toys possible for toddlers is a cardboard box that is sturdy enough that they can both pull themselves up on it and push it around.

Once babies can walk, activities that let them develop their large muscles receive much of their attention and energy. Pull toys, wagons to sit in or pull, a kiddy car without pedals, and large wooden blocks are excellent toys for outdoor play.

Preschoolers and Kindergarten and Primary Children.   Room for large-muscle play and equipment should be arranged. A space just for running is wonderful. Plenty of equipment for climbing, jumping, and pulling oneself up is important as older children exercise large muscles. Places for primary-grade children to enter into group play and organized games are also necessary.

Figure 6–5
Three possible arrangements for outdoor play space

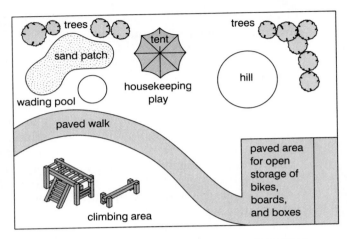

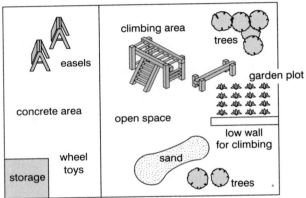

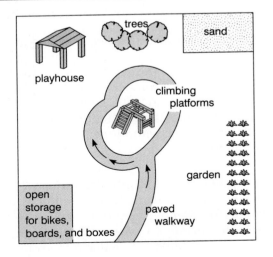

Think in terms of providing equipment for other than physical activity. Dramatic play can continue outdoors. "They play out their problems. One child's parents are divorcing. One child is moving. They practice being grown-ups" (Greenberg, 1992, p. 35). Add a platform or playhouse for housekeeping play, or simply put pots, pans, and tools in the sandbox. Maps and wallets or pocketbooks with tickets and play money encourage travel play. Tool kits, lunchboxes, packing boxes, and briefcases continue to attract children to dramatic play.

An old tube vacuum cleaner, hoses, flashlights, cameras, discarded instrument panels that have been made safe and discarded tools encourage children's mechanical play. Art activities can also take place outdoors. Each day think of providing an art activity that children can do outside. One day it could be clay; the next, paints or chalk.

Large wooden boxes, hammers and nails, saws, planks, and other lumber scraps allow children to build large complex structures with adequate adult supervision. The structures are added to throughout the year, and a variety of different types of play develop.

Science is natural outdoors. The plants and animals in the environment can be observed, a garden planted, or animals cared for. Sand and water play are abundant. A large sand area with water for moistening the sand should be

Figure 6–6

Guidelines for planning spaces

Adapted from slides for outdoor play spaces produced by L'Organization Mondiale de l'Education Préscolaire, 1970.

Do Your Play Spaces Show Thoughtful Planning For:

Safety for different age children?
Adequate supervision?
Care and storage of equipment?
Sheltered areas for peaceful pursuits?
Overall use of available space?

Does the Play Space Reveal:

Imaginative thinking?
Ingenious inventiveness?
Appealing colors, textures, sounds?
Development of potential beauty?

Do Your Play Spaces Have A Balance Of:

Textures
    soft—hard
    rough—smooth
Levels
    high—low
Colors
    bright—subdued
Shapes
    round—square
    rectangle—triangle

A space for just running is wonderful.

available. When weather permits, let children play in a sprinkler, wade in a pool, and paint a tree or sidewalk with a bucket of water and a paintbrush.

Children with Special Needs.   Outdoor play spaces need to be carefully planned to meet the needs of special children. An interview with parents or specialists can help you determine what arrangements to make. Often the equipment other children use is suitable for children with special needs. Nearly all children are able to use sand, mud, water, blocks, and wood. A different type of supervision, however, may be necessary when working with special needs children. You might have to teach one child how to use a specific piece of equipment, telling her to put her feet on the pedals, or show another how to climb. Often children with special needs find more active encouragement and supervision outdoors helpful.

For instance, children with poor muscle control or motor problems can ride tricycles if their feet are taped to the pedals or loosely attached to them with rubber bands. Children with large-muscle problems might find the following pieces of equipment useful:

- Irish mail—a ride-on toy operated with arm levers
- Platforms on wheels—to balance, lie on, and scoot around
- Scooter cars—for using legs and feet
- Rocking horses and boats—to gain balance and ability to push
- Chair swings—provide more control than a regular swing
- Large cardboard boxes and wooden blocks—to push, pull, and stack

Children with fine- or perceptual-motor problems might find the following pieces of equipment valuable:

- Large plastic nuts and screws to take apart and put back together
- Stacking toys
- Clothespins, boxes, and cans—children can place the pins along the edge of the can or exchange them from can to can
- Large beads and strings to practice eye-hand-muscle coordination
- Objects to push, such as sandbags in carriages and wagons

Children with visual problems may need toys that have sounding devices such as:

- Balls with bells inside or other items that make sounds to let the visually impaired child learn to bounce, catch, and throw a ball
- Push toys that make sounds, such as lawnmowers and carpet sweepers

Supervision and Safety

Supervision and safety should accompany outdoor play. Supervision begins before children enter the yard. Check to see that pathways are clear and equipment is spaced to avoid accidents. Conduct a safety check of the yard. Remove broken equipment, empty any water that is in tires or boxes, and oil toys with wheels. Be certain the sand area has been covered to prevent animals or insects from using it, and remove the cover before the children arrive. Disinfect any equipment that infants and toddlers will be using.

You'll have to be able to observe the entire yard when children are outdoors. Be certain you can see over barriers and into tunnels and playhouses.

Safety precautions are ongoing. You may have to remove a block from under the climbing gym or support a child having trouble climbing down. Reinforce the safety rules children have chosen. See Figure 6–7 for a safety checklist.

- A fence (minimum 4 feet high) protects children from potentially hazardous areas (e.g., streets, water).
- Eight to 12 inches of noncompacted sand, pea gravel, shredded wood, or equivalent material is in place under and around all climbing and moving equipment.
- Resilient surface is properly maintained (e.g., in place, noncompacted, free of debris).
- The equipment is sized to the age group served, with climbing heights limited to the reaching height of children standing erect.
- There are no openings that can entrap a child's head (approximately 4 to 8 inches).
- Swing seats are constructed of lightweight material with no protruding elements.
- Moving parts are free of defects (no pinch, shearing, or crush points; bearings are not excessively worn).
- Equipment is free of sharp edges, protruding elements, broken parts, and toxic substances.
- Fixed equipment is structurally sound—no bending, warping, breaking, or sinking.
- Large equipment is secured to the ground, and concrete footings are recessed in the ground.
- All safety equipment (e.g., guard rails, padded areas, protective covers) is in good repair.
- The area is free of electrical hazards (e.g., unfenced air conditioners and switch boxes).
- The area is free of debris (e.g., sanitary hazards, broken glass, and rocks).

Figure 6–7
Outdoor play yard safety checklist
From "The Evolution of American Playgrounds" by J. L. Frost and S. Wortham, 1988, *Young Children, 43*(5), pp. 19-28. Reprinted by permission.

Summary

If children learned from listening and sitting still, then arranging the physical environment of an early childhood program would not be very difficult. You could get individual desks, place them in rows, and put a teacher's desk in the front, where the teacher would sit or stand while telling the children what it is they were to learn.

But children, as all humans, do not learn this way. They learn through social and physical interactions with their environment. Because children must be active in order to learn, the nature of their physical environment is critical. Because the environment is so critical, it is carefully planned and arranged. Care is taken to meet the needs of each child, and to protect the health and safety of the group. Both indoor and outdoor spaces are thoughtfully arranged to promote active learning of individuals and groups.

Children change, the world changes. The physical environment of the early childhood program also changes. Daily, weekly, monthly, the environment changes to reflect the current interests, needs, and activities of the children.

A teacher's responsibility does not end, however, with the arrangement of safe, beautiful learning space for children. Continual supervision and teaching, both indoors and outdoors, is planned.

Projects

Continuing Case Study

Select an interest center and observe the child you are studying as she or he works there. Which materials does the child choose? How does the child use them? Which materials remain untouched? Which materials are used by more than one child? Can you note any behaviors of your child that could be attributed to the arrangement of the centers and the materials in them?

1. Observe a preschool and then a primary classroom. Make a floor plan of the room arrangements you've observed. Identify pathways and children's movement through space. Now redesign these spaces to maximize their use.
2. Pretend you have been given the job of equipping a classroom and outdoor play area for three- and four-year-olds. You have been given $500 to spend on equipment. How will you use this money? What toys and equipment will you have to purchase? Which can you obtain for little money?
3. Design your dream play yard and classroom. Money and space are no object. Design a dream play yard limited by this spatial arrangement.
4. Observe an infant room and preschool and primary classrooms. Describe how interest

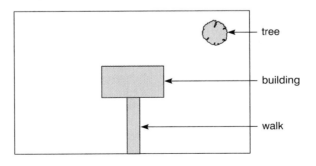

centers are available in each room and how they differ. As you observe, note specific arrangements for children with special needs. Make a list of toys and equipment for or especially useful to children with specific disabilities.

5. Visit a toy store. Identify equipment that could be used by children of differing ages. Also note toys that are useful for a variety of purposes and those that could only be used by children of a given age or for one purpose.

6. Review several computer software programs. Use the list of questions given in this chapter to evaluate them.

Resources

Useful guides for planning learning environments include the following:

Bredekamp, Sue (Ed.). (1983). *Developmentally appropriate practice in early childhood programs serving children from birth through age 8.* Washington, DC: National Association for the Education of Young Children.

Loughlin, Catherine E., & Suina, Joseph H. (1982). *The learning environment: An instructional strategy.* New York: Teachers College Press; and Loughlin, Catherine E., & Martin, Mavis D. (1987). *Supporting literacy: Developing effective learning environments.* New York: Teachers College Press. These two publications are musts for anyone who wants to plan effective learning environments in preschools and especially in kindergarten and primary classrooms.

Harms, Thelma, & Clifford, Richard M. (1980). *Early childhood environment rating scale.* New York: Teachers College Press. The scale is a research instrument designed to evaluate learning environments. As you plan spaces for children's learning, you can use the scale to check the quality of the environment you plan.

Esbensen, S. B. (1987). *The early childhood playground: An outdoor classroom.* Ypsilanti, MI: High Scope Press. This book covers the child/environment fit, including materials and arrangement within the play environment.

Moore, R. C., Goltsman, S., & Iacofano, D. S. (Eds.). (1990). *Play for all guidelines: Planning, design, and management of outdoor play settings for all children.* It is a complete guide to the planning, design, and management of outdoor play environments for all children, including those with special needs.

Greenman, J. (1990). *Caring places, learning spaces: Children's environments that work.* This book is an inspirational guide to facility design and arrangement. The book begins by looking first at the people who will live and work in the environments, then at the design of physical space.

References

Balban, N. (1992). The role of the child care professional in caring for infants, toddlers, and their families. *Young Children, 47*(5), 66–72.

Barbour, N., Webster, T. D., & Drosdeck, S. (1987). Sand: A resource for the language arts. *Young Children, 42*(2), 20-26.

Barker, R. (1968). *Ecological psychology.* Stanford, CA: Stanford University Press.

Baylor, B. (1975). *The desert is theirs.* New York: Scribner's.

Becker, H. J. (1983). Microcomputers: Dreams and realities. *Curriculum Review, 21,* 381-385.

Biber, B. (1972). Introductory essay. In H. Johnson, *The Nursery School* (pp. i–iv). New York: Schocken. (First published 1928)

Bredekamp, S. (1987). *Developmentally appropriate practice in early childhood programs serving children from birth through age 8.* Washington, DC: National Association for the Education of Young Children.

Cartwright, S. (1990). Learning with large blocks. *Young Children, 45*(3), 38-42.

Casey, M., & Lippman, M. (1991). Learning to play through play. *Young Children, 46*(4), 52-59.

Cass, J. (1973). *Helping children through play*. New York: Schocken.

Centers for Disease Control. (1990). *Day care contagion*. Atlanta: Author.

de Paola, T. (1978). *The quicksand book*. New York: Holiday.

Gareau, M., & Kennedy, C. (1991). Structure time and space to promote pursuit of learning in the primary grades. *Young Children, 46*(4), 46–52.

Getzels, J. W. (1975). Images and visions. In T. E. Davia & B. D. Wright (eds.). *Learning environments* (pp. 1–15). Chicago: University of Chicago Press.

Goldsmith, C. (1972). *Better day care for the young child*. Washington, DC: National Association for the Education of Young Children.

Greenberg, P. (1992). How much do you get the children out? *Young Children, 47*(2), 34.

Greenberg, P. (1992). Creating creative play opportunities. *Young Children, 47*(5), 52.

Highberger, R., & Boyton, M. (1983). Preventing illness in an infant/toddler day care. *Young Children, 38*, 3-11.

Hyson, M. C., Hirsh-Pasek, K., & Rescorla, L. (1990). The classroom practices inventory: An observation instrument based on NAEYC's guidelines for developmentally appropriate practices for 4- and 5-year-old children. *Early Childhood Research Quarterly, 5*(4), 475-495.

Kendall, E. D., & Moukaddem, V. E. (1992). Who's vulnerable in infant child care centers? *Young Children, 47*(5), 77-82.

Kritchevsky, S., Prescott, E., & Walling, L. (1969). *Planning environments for young children: Physical space*. Washington, DC: National Association for the Education of Young Children.

Loughlin, C. E., & Suina, J. (1982). *The learning environment: An instructional strategy*. New York: Teachers College Press.

Loughlin, C. E., & Martin, M. D. (1987). *Supporting literacy: Developing effective learning environments*. New York: Teachers College Press.

Morrow, L. M. (1990). Preparing the classroom environment to promote literacy during play. *Early Childhood Research Quarterly, 5*, 495-537.

Munro, R. (1987). *The inside-outside book of Washington, DC*. New York: Dutton.

National Association for the Education of Young Children. (1991a). *Accreditation criteria and procedures of the National Academy of Early Childhood Programs*. (rev. ed.). Washington, DC: Author.

National Association for the Education of Young Children. (1991b). Toward safer, exciting playground environments. *Young Children, 46*(6), 26.

New, R. (1990). Excellent early education: A city in Italy has it. *Young Children, 45*(6), 4-11.

Thomas, J. I. (1975). *Learning centers: Opening up the classroom*. Boston: Holbrook.

Weinstein, C. S. (1979). The physical environment of the school: A review of the research. *Review of Educational Research, 49*, 577–611.

Ziajka, A. (1983). Microcomputers in early childhood education? A first look. *Young Children, 38*, 57-61.

Zimring, C. M. (1981). Stress and the designed environment. *Journal of Social Issues, 37*, 145-171.

7 Guiding Children's Behavior

"Many people believe that autonomy is for adults, and that what is appropriate for young children is obedience."

(Kamii, 1984, p. 13)

After reading this chapter, you should be able to respond to the following questions:

1. Describe the major principles and techniques of modeling, behavior modification, psychoanalytic, and social-cognitive approaches to guiding children's behavior.

2. How will you balance your authority with the need for young children to develop autonomy?

3. Why is careful planning necessary as a part of the guidance process?

4. How would you apply a variety of approaches when working with individual children or groups of children?

Guiding

Everyone wants and needs discipline. Without discipline, children feel inse-cure and are unable to relate effectively with others.

Four-year-old Antonia was new to child care and to being in a group. On her first day, Antonia watched a group of children chatting together as they drew pictures with bright markers. She sat down with them and took a box of markers from Alberto together with the paper he was drawing on, and proceeded to begin her own drawing. Alberto screamed at Antonia and grabbed his markers and paper back. Antonia, in turn, started to pound on Alberto with clenched fists and began screaming. The others watching the scene joined in, grabbing one another's markers and paper. It was a mess.

Antonia and Alberto clearly needed discipline. Without discipline, they and the other children would be defenseless. All children need someone older who is clearly in charge to keep them safe and secure by setting lim-its, informing them of standards for their behavior, and guiding them through the complexities of living in a group.

Without discipline, children have only vague ideas of how to behave. Left on their own to make sense of living and working together, to learn to bal-ance their own developing autonomy with the skills of cooperating, children make too many mistakes. They will too often end up feeling inadequate, unworthy, and rejected.

As the teacher, you are in charge and responsible for guiding children's behavior in ways that will enable them to develop self-control and self-discipline.

There is a wide variety of theories and approaches to draw from. Some can be adapted to meet the needs of individual children, and others are useful in guiding the behavior of a group of children. With knowledge of the major approaches used to guide children's behavior, you will be able to develop a repertoire of skills and strategies of effective discipline.

Outstanding teachers are familiar with and proficient in using modeling, behavior modification, and psychoanalytic and social-cognitive techniques as they guide and discipline young children.

Modeling

Cindy's mother made a special trip to the child-care center. She told Ms. W., "I had to come see what kind of shoes you wear. We went to buy Cindy shoes Saturday, and none would do because 'they weren't like Ms. W's.' I thought I'd die! A whole Saturday spent trying to find shoes just like yours!"

Children who love and adore you want to be just like you. Not only do they want to dress like you, as did Cindy, but they want to incorporate your behaviors into their own repertoires.

A powerful theory of discipline is that of observational learning. "Most human behavior is learned by observation through modeling. By observing others, one forms rules of behavior, and on future occasions this coded information serves as a guide for action" (Bandura, 1986, p. 47). According to this theory, good manners, politeness, ways of interacting with others, and even what shoes are best to wear aren't taught or imposed on children, but are observed by children, imitated, and practiced, and soon they become a part of the children's own behavior.

Using this theory, Antonia's teacher might have prevented the tears and screams by inviting Antonia and her mother or father to first spend some time observing in the center before leaving Antonia on her own. The teacher might have modeled joining a group or asking others to share paper and crayons.

Modeling is a complex process. It's not as simple as it seems. A number of conditions must be present if children are to learn through modeling. The nature of the model, whether or not the model is reinforced, and the characteristics of the observer all affect the process of learning through modeling. Teachers can use the principles of modeling to increase desired behaviors and eliminate unacceptable behaviors.

The Model

Any person may serve as the model, but, not surprisingly, those whom the child views as having high prestige or importance are the most likely candidates (Bandura, 1986). Clearly, teachers are in positions of importance in children's lives, and children view them as prestigious.

Parents too are powerful in their children's lives, and children need to be like them. Children are vulnerable and need the acceptance, love, and protection of their parents. To gain acceptance, children model their parents, behaving like them and adopting the same values and attitudes.

Children are also models for other children. Alberto served as a model for Antonia when he began screaming. Antonia modeled the behavior by screaming back. And the other children modeled both Alberto and Antonia by joining in.

Parents are aware that children model other children. Who hasn't heard a parent lament, "He never used that word, hit, or screamed at me until he went to your school and learned this awful behavior from the other children." When classmates receive a great deal of attention, even negative attention like the screaming and hitting that occurred with Antonia and Alberto, they are viewed by others as somehow important and powerful, and their behaviors may be imitated.

Models can be symbolic as well. Television stars, even cartoon characters, sports heroes, and characters in books provide models for children. Clothing styles, behaviors, interpersonal relations, and the likes and dis-

Clearly, teachers are in positions of importance and likely to be modeled.

likes of even very young children can be the result of modeling a famous star or cartoon character.

Reinforcement

Models are more likely to be imitated when their behaviors are reinforced than when they are not reinforced or when there is no potential for reinforcement. When a teacher says to a group of children, "Look at George. George is doing it just the way I like it," then George's behaviors are likely to be modeled because George has received the praise of the teacher. Children are also likely to model famous sports figures who receive a lot of attention because they have heard other people speak admiringly of the athletes.

Reinforcement may also stem from the consequences of the behavior. If the behavior that is modeled is socially acceptable, so that others welcome the child because of it, it is likely that it will be repeated. The behavior will have been reinforced by its own consequences.

Any type of attention may be viewed as a reinforcement. If Antonia and Alberto's teacher scolded them or punished them in some other observable way because of their behavior at the drawing table, the other children would be likely to yell and hit one another the next time they wanted the teacher's attention.

The Observer

Bandura (1986) doesn't see modeling as mindless, with children blindly following the behaviors of prestigious people who receive attention. Children's standards, past reinforcement histories, and self-motivation determine which activities they will strive to model. As children develop cognitive skills, they can formulate solutions and evaluate probable immediate and long-range consequences of different courses of action. They do not always make the right decisions, but they do grow in ability to think and reason before blindly imitating the behaviors of others.

Increasing Desired Behaviors

Modeling can be used to increase desired behaviors. A teacher's enthusiasm for learning is modeled as is the way a teacher interacts with others.

Juan joined the class with the ability to speak Spanish fluently but with limited skills in English. The other first-graders began taunting Juan, calling him "funny talk." Instead of making an issue of the children's taunts and drawing negative attention to Juan, the teacher asked Juan to help her pronounce a word in Spanish and put him in the role of her teacher. The children stopped laughing and teasing Juan and began asking him to help them learn to roll *r*'s the way it is done in Spanish and to interpret and speak Spanish words.

Modeling is especially effective when you want children to learn a new response or strengthen one that occurs infrequently. In one preschool, children were observed spending little time in activities related to reading readiness. When the adults in the classroom began to model reading for the children, the children immediately increased the time they spent selecting books and library materials during their free time.

Sharing and other social behaviors are increased through modeling. A group of researchers tried to teach children social behaviors by telling them how they should behave and by asking the children to repeat rules for behaviors they had supposedly learned. The same children were then shown models who demonstrated social behaviors. The children's parents modeled social behaviors in their interactions with others and then explained why they behaved as they did. After children observed models, they, in turn, modeled social, altruistic behaviors (Yarrow, Scott, & Waxler, 1973).

Modeling can also be the source of unacceptable behaviors. Children attending a school located on a heavily traveled street had the habit of crossing in midblock, dashing and darting in traffic rather than walking to the corner and crossing with the assistance of the crossing guards and lights. The teachers wondered about the midblock crossings because they had "taught" children traffic safety each year. They decided to observe and try to identify the source of children's street crossing behaviors. To their surprise, they found that they themselves were serving as models for the children. They discovered that they crossed in the middle of the block to reach the school from the parking area across the street. When they took the time to walk to the corner and cross with the guards and told the children the reasons for doing so, the children changed their behavior.

Behavior Modification

A group of undergraduate students were complaining about yet to be written term papers due in a few days. One, however, said she had already turned in every paper. "How in the world did you manage to keep so far ahead?" another asked. "It's easy. I hate writing so much, I have to set up rewards for myself. Every time I finish one part of a paper, I reward myself with a frozen yogurt. I just love frozen yogurt," she explained.

It has long been known that any behavior followed by a pleasurable experience is likely to be repeated. Any behavior followed by unpleasantness is likely not to be repeated.

In this old principle of human behavior are found the roots of behaviorism. The behaviorists believe that you can guide children's behaviors by reinforcing those that are desired and ignoring those that are unacceptable.

Following these principles, children who complete work are given stars. Those who sit quietly or cooperate with the teacher may be given stickers. Others who raise their hands before speaking are rewarded with raisins or candy.

Behaviorism is a powerful tool for guiding children's behaviors. It really works. It is an effective and efficient way of modifying behavior. Because it is such a powerful strategy, everyone needs to understand the concepts of behaviorism. You probably will reject the idea of bribing children with stars, stickers, or candy, but you will want to develop an understanding of behaviorism. If you do not fully understand the techniques of using behaviorism to modify children's behavior, you may end up mistakenly reinforcing behaviors you do not find acceptable or ignoring those that are desirable.

For example, one teacher, after attending a workshop on techniques of behavior modification claimed she would never use these strategies. "They may work, but it's too mechanical." She was later observed in her classroom attempting to stop children from throwing sand at one another. She walked over to the sand throwers, saying "Stop that now!" When they didn't stop, she repeated, "Didn't you hear me. I said STOP!" When the children continued, she grabbed them and pulled them over to chairs at the side of the room. She then scolded, "You don't throw sand here. Sit and think about what you did."

At the same time this commotion was going on, two other children at the sand table were working together cooperatively, sharing, talking, and effectively negotiating for the use of trowels and other sand tools.

This teacher was, in effect, using principles of behaviorism, although she didn't understand the principles. She may have reinforced the behavior of the children who were throwing sand by paying so much attention to them while ignoring the children who were cooperating.

Receiving attention, even though it is negative, may be quite rewarding, especially if other children view the misbehavior and reprimand as having some type of status. If the other children see the misbehaving children as leaders, they will imitate their behavior and you will have established a schedule of reinforcing disruptive behaviors.

Establishing a Program

If you want to use behavior modification either to increase desired behaviors or to eliminate undesirable ones, you must establish a program. The

The first step is to observe children's behavior to obtain a baseline.

first step is a pretest. You observe children by keeping a record of their disruptive and nondisruptive behaviors and describing the conditions under which each occurs. This record is called the *baseline*.

Graphing the behaviors gives you a picture of how often, when, and why the disruptive behavior occurs. Often the very act of observing and graphing disruptive behaviors will serve to decrease inappropriate behavior. Observation focuses attention on the child, making the cause of the behavior clear.

Clifford was considered the class bully. He pushed, hit, and shoved children to get his way. His acting out and total disruption of the class had to be addressed. Mr. M. had tried a number of approaches with Clifford—reasoning, giving him special attention, and suggesting positive methods of interacting with other children. Nothing seemed to help Clifford change his negative behaviors. Mr. M. decided to try behavior modification and set up a schedule for observing Clifford throughout the week. At the end of the week, it became clear that other children precipitated Clifford's hitting, pushing, and kicking and that Clifford was reacting. Mr. M., in the process of observing, stopped the others from taking objects away from Clifford or ostracizing him from the group. Mr. M. decided not to set up a schedule to modify Clifford's behaviors. Instead he focused on the behaviors of other children and taught Clifford some positive ways of reacting to their teasing.

If observation doesn't eliminate disruptive behavior, then the next step in designing a behavior modification program is to pinpoint the specific behaviors you wish to change. It's not enough to say, "I want two-year-old Susan to stop being so dependent on me in the morning." You must describe the particular behaviors you want to eliminate: "I want Susan to stop crying when her mother leaves; stop hanging onto my leg; stop sucking her thumb." Then you set up realistic goals for eliminating these behaviors. "The first week my goal is to stop Susan from clinging to my leg."

Next, design and carry out a program by rewarding or reinforcing the desired behaviors and ignoring those you want to eliminate. You first determine the reinforcers the child values. Reinforcers can be anything—candy, toys, or tokens that can be collected and later traded for a privilege, or even a hug, wink, smile, or words of praise.

With Susan, every time she would cling to your leg, you would ignore her; when she moved away, even a small move, you would reward it with a smile, piece of candy, or other reinforcer. Susan would eventually learn that leaving you resulted in something positive and would let go of your leg to enter into school activities.

The final stage of behavior modification is evaluation. You must continue observing and recording the children's behavior so you can adjust and modify your schedule of reinforcement and rewards to obtain success (Madsen & Madsen, 1980).

Focus on the Positive

Not only does behaviorism work, but it is also very positive. By focusing your attention on children who are behaving well, you catch children being good rather than rewarding children with attention for undesirable behaviors. Early childhood educators have always recognized the power of rewarding positive behavior and extinguishing undesirable behaviors by ignoring them. Read (1976) discusses the value of ignoring the preschoolers' temper tantrums. These tantrums impress other children, and your attention to them can only serve to reinforce the behaviors, thus accelerating them. The best approach, Read (1976) claimed, is simply to ignore the tantrum, care for the other children, and remove the acting out child as necessary without any emotion or attention.

Another plus to behavior modification is that punishment is avoided. Behaviorists have shown that punishment is negative and its effectiveness limited (Skinner, 1974; Adler, 1964). Punishment simply doesn't work either to promote positive behaviors or to eliminate negative ones. First, using punishment often serves to suppress desired behaviors. If a child is punished for talking out in class, she may stop speaking entirely, and her communication skills would be reduced. Second, punishment may lead children to avoid situations entirely. A child who is punished in school may wish to avoid school. Rather than growing to love learning, the child may become a truant.

Then too, punishment often serves to increase other undesirable behaviors than the ones being punished. Behaviors that are punished reappear, often in more negative and stronger forms than the original. Finally, punishment may increase children's negative behavior. As long as you pay attention to the negative behavior, it will continue to appear. If you act aggressively and punitively toward children, they'll imitate these behaviors and will become more aggressive themselves.

Use with Caution

As with any other technique that is used to control children, behaviorism must be used cautiously. Anyone using the technique should have a clear understanding of how to do so, but also of why the technique is being used. Sometimes children's behaviors are so out of control that they can only be eliminated through a behavioral program.

Usually, everyone who comes in contact with an overly aggressive child—one who bites, spits, or kicks—feels a great deal of emotion. The child, teacher, and other children have probably built strong feelings about the child and his or her behaviors. These emotions can get in the way and interfere with attempts to help the child gain control. At these times, the use of behavior modification can permit both child and teacher to gain emotional control. Once progress is made, then the causes of the child's behavior can be examined, and other techniques may be employed to help the child gain control.

The critical thing is that no one wants to be controlled by another person. Teachers, even though they are the authority, will want to develop techniques of guidance that enable children to develop their own autonomy and become responsible for their own behavior. If children are controlled only with the use of external rewards, they'll have little chance of developing their own controls and becoming self-disciplined.

Children also quickly resent being manipulated. In one classroom, teachers were instructed to give children a small piece of candy every time they responded correctly or behaved appropriately. One child had just finished a painting and was observing the bright colors and designs with obvious self-satisfaction when the teacher gave her a candy. The child frowned, took the candy, and crushed it under her foot. Receiving the candy interfered with the child's intrinsic sense of satisfaction, and she resented it (Morgan, 1984).

Failure to praise or reinforce children presents still other problems. Many children are insecure and need the teacher's reassurance that they are valued. If these children fail to receive attention from the teacher or other rewards, they may become resentful and hostile (Read, 1976).

Psychoanalytic Approaches

Like the behaviorists, the psychoanalytic theorists view punishment as not only ineffective but also even responsible for increasing negative behaviors. On the other hand, while the behaviorists believe children's behavior can be guided through a series of rewards, the psychoanalysts see rewards as bribes. Rather than bribing children for good behavior, those endorsing psychoanalytic theories believe that because all behavior is caused, discipline begins with understanding the causes of behavior.

Four-year-old Christopher suddenly began biting other children. His bites were so vicious that most of the children refused to play with him or permit him to join their group. Finally, Christopher bit a child so violently that the teachers had difficulty stopping the bleeding.

At this point, the child-care director called a meeting of the staff and said, "Christopher cannot bite other children. We'll have to find out the cause of his biting." One of the teachers talked with Christopher's mother and the next day told the director, "Well, Christopher's biting is cleared up. You know his parents are divorced, and next Saturday his father is remarrying. We'll have to find some way for Christopher to express his anger in ways that are safe for both him and the other children."

It's easy for teachers to assume that a divorce and father's remarriage "caused" Christopher's biting, but psychoanalytic theories are much more complicated than this. Looking for the cause of children's behavior is not so simplistic.

According to the psychoanalytic theories of discipline, the adult's role is to understand that behavior is caused by the goals of the child, not necessarily by a divorce or other trauma.

The primary goal is that of seeking perfection, and, the theory states, all humans are driven to perfect themselves. A person's own style of striving for perfection is the basis for the way that person deals with problems. Children, like all humans, are more than passive recipients of stimulations: They actively create their own style of striving.

The psychoanalysts advocate that adults first observe a child to determine the goal of the disruptive behavior and then react in such a way that the child will cease that disturbing behavior (Adler, 1964; Mead, 1976; Weber-Schwartz, 1987). Instead of trying to change the child's behavior, the theory advocates that adults must change their way of reacting to the behavior.

If the psychoanalytic theorists are correct and children's behavior is caused by their goal of striving for perfection, then it is up to the adults to

According to the psychoanalytic theories, behavior is caused by children's goals.

identify the children's goal. Children are believed to seek perfection typically through one of four goals:

1. Getting attention
2. Achieving power
3. Getting revenge
4. Displaying inadequacy (Dreikurs, Greenwalk, & Pepper, 1982)

Christopher's teachers may have been correct. His biting may have been caused by his parent's divorce and father's remarriage. But what was Christopher trying to achieve? What was his goal? Was Christopher feeling powerless? Was his goal to get attention? Was his father neglecting him in the midst of wedding plans? Or was his goal that of getting revenge or achieving power?

If seeking power was his goal, then it would be important for the adults to understand this and not fight back. If Christopher's teachers had tried to fight Christopher, through some form of overt punishment, they would only be helping Christopher achieve his goal of getting power. Christopher would feel very powerful indeed if he had caused adults to lose control and fight back. Achieving his goal, his behavior would become more and more defiant.

If over the years, Christopher did not achieve his goal of getting attention or power, he might become like other children who have failed to gain power or attention and display inadequacy. Children who have been ignored or who failed over and over in their attempts to achieve their goals may become so discouraged that they expect only failure and defeat. These children typically pretend to be incompetent.

What are Christopher's teachers to do? They obviously cannot permit him to continue to bite other children. But they can't fight back or give him any type of attention for his misbehavior. They can, however, change Christopher's behavior by letting him experience the logical consequences of his behavior.

In Christopher's case the logical consequences might be that he would have to work and play alone for some period of time, or, perhaps, a neutral person could volunteer to stay by Christopher's side to prevent him from biting other children. So that the volunteer does not satisfy Christopher's need for power or attention, the volunteer's only contact with Christopher would be to prevent biting.

Biting, although common among young children in groups, is a special problem. Although Christopher's teacher may have been right about the reason for his biting, generally it is believed to be caused by inadequate supervision, crowded conditions, or permitting children to get overtired and not by something internal to a child. Christopher's biting may, in fact, have been caused by lack of adequate supervision instead of some internal striving for perfection. Thus, it may be difficult for Christopher to experience the logical consequences of biting.

Yet letting children experience the logical consequences of their behaviors is an efficient and effective means of guiding children to self-control.

Five-year-old Colin was alone in the block area, busily stacking blocks on the shelves. All the other kindergarten children were gathered on the rug watching a videotape of a popular movie. When asked why he was alone picking up blocks while the others were enjoying a segment of the movie, Colin replied, "It's logical consequences." When asked what in the world logical consequences were, he said, "Well, I didn't pick up the blocks during clean-up time, and the logical consequences of not doing it then is I have to do it now and miss the movie."

What are the logical consequences of typical misbehavior?
For the child who:

- Spills milk on another child, the consequences are to help clean up the spilt milk
- Leaves a mess at the easel, the consequences are to clean up the easel
- Dawdles and delays getting dressed, the consequences are to miss an outdoor activity

A teacher who implements logical consequences will:

1.   *Express the reality of the social order.* The social order represents a body of rules that operates on an impersonal level and must be learned in order for children to function adequately in a group (Dreikurs, Greenwalk, & Pepper, 1982). This social order is communicated to children clearly and consistently. For example, "It is time for lunch. We will eat now. Because we need to clear the tables for nap, everyone must eat now. We will not be able to wait for anyone." When the social order is clear and a child understands it, then it is logical that the child who doesn't get ready for lunch and arrives late will find that lunch is cleared away.

2.   *Relate to the misbehavior.* The teacher will make certain the child sees the relationship between the act and the consequences. Punishment will not be necessary because the consequences of behavior are so clear. A child who dawdles, like Colin, misses out on the next activity. A second-grader who squirts water on another is responsible for cleaning and drying the other child as well as the floor.

3.   *Be nonjudgmental.* Misbehavior is just that. Misbehavior. It is not a sin. Rather than preaching, scolding, or threatening the child who bites, the teacher neutrally removes the biter while attending to the child who was bitten. Following the incident, however, measures are taken to prevent future biting. The social order, "no one is permitted to bite another," is made clear. The consequences of biting, "no one will play with you because no one wants to be bitten."

4.   *Focus on what will happen, not on what did.* Punishment is concerned with the past, while logical consequences are concerned with the

present and the future. "Now what will you do?" "Now what can we do to help you so you won't bite again?"

A group of three-year-olds went wild during clean-up time. Instead of putting blocks on the shelf, they dumped all the blocks on the floor. A book was thrown at the book shelf, and baby dolls began flying in the housekeeping corner. The teacher sat on a small chair in the middle of the floor, and as children ran past her she calmly grabbed them and had them sit with her. She called a few others to come and soon the entire group was with her. She said, "This is a mess! Whew! Now who will put the blocks on the shelf? Good, Jose, Pam, and Anne, you will be in charge of the blocks. Juan, pick another child to help you put the books on the shelf, and who will be responsible for the housekeeping area?"

The purpose of logical consequences is to help children become more effective, to learn effective and appropriate ways of obtaining their goals.

5. *Eliminate anger, either open or concealed.* John stumped into his classroom and tossed his coat on the floor. Before the teacher could greet him, he took the aluminum pans of paint that were on a table for an art project, and flung them one by one across the room. One pan hit the floor near the teacher and paint splashed on her legs and dress.

It is hard not to express anger, either open or concealed, when you and the room have been sprayed with paint. Yet, if logical consequences are to be used effectively, teachers must not express anger, either open or concealed.

Catching her breath, the teacher said, "John, you are angry. Let's begin by helping me wash the paint off my shoes and stockings. Get the paper towels, and I'll get the soap and water." After some attempts with mopping paint off the teacher, John was then directed with a bucket of soapy water and sponge, to "wash all the paint off the floor."

Still showing no anger, the teacher washed her legs. She then joined John in washing paint off the floor. As they tackled the job together, she spoke quietly to John, encouraging him to express his feelings.

Later that morning, the teacher continued to encourage John to find productive ways to express his anger or to control his temper. The teacher continued working with him the next day and throughout the year. When she saw him beginning to lose control, she would intervene. A psychologist was consulted, and John and his family received support as they worked with the teacher to help John gain control.

Social-Cognitive Approaches

Ann stood alone watching the other children playing house. After watching for a time, she picked up a bucket of Legos and, walking into the housekeeping area, tossed the toys all over, laughing and yelling, "Cheerios for you! Cheerios all over you!" Of course, none of the other children thought the act as funny as Ann seemed to think. Chasing Ann out of the area, they resumed their play and Ann resumed watching from the sidelines.

Those endorsing cognitive views of guidance claim that children's ability to relate socially is associated with their cognitive understanding of the situation. Ann wanted to play with the others but had an inadequate understanding of how to enter into a play group. Linked to cognitive theories of development, the belief is that children's behavior reflects their thinking.

Rather than reprimanding Ann or passing judgment, the teacher would work with Ann and the others to develop social skills and an understanding of social situations. To do this, the teacher would try to increase Ann's social skills. Increasing social skills would enable Ann to be accepted by others, which would, in turn, enhance her self-esteem.

With the goal of developing social cognition, the teacher would ask Ann to think about the incident and engage in a problem-solving activity related to the incident. Viewing the whole situation, the teacher would see social-emotional issues, clearly evident in Ann's interaction in the housekeeping area, as an important part of intellectual development and would integrate these issues into the curriculum and classroom management.

The teacher might ask Ann to describe what had happened. Then she would encourage Ann to think of other ways she could enter the group. The teacher would consider that Ann is in the preoperational stage of thinking, in which she can keep in mind only one idea at a time. In discussing the situation with Ann, the teacher would try to understand the child's perspective and to use this understanding as a basis for her interactions. The point is that the teacher would try to help Ann to understand why the children were angry with her when she tossed the Legos on them and then help her to develop the skills needed to enter into a group. Direct teaching, in which the teacher explains the situation to Ann, would not be effective, but teachers can arrange situations that would offer children opportunities to practice and develop role taking and social skills.

Role Taking

Role taking might have its roots in sociodramatic play activities in which children play as if they were mothers, fathers, doctors, or teachers. Creative dramatics offer children yet another opportunity to learn the skills involved in taking on the roles of others (Ishee & Goldhaber, 1990). In creative dramatics, children act out, by themselves or with others, the role of another person, animal, or thing. Younger children may be given stories, poems, or songs to act out that have parts for all. For instance, all children can be either kings or horses, and take turns being Humpty-Dumpty, or all can be either Jack or Jill, or Little Nancy Etticoat.

Children in kindergarten or the primary grades may take turns being the actors or the audience. The folktales "Three Billy Goats Gruff," "Goldilocks," and "The Three Pigs" are good beginners for creative dramatics, but many other familiar stories and poems could serve as well.

Naturally occurring events also provide opportunities for children to practice role-taking. You can help children grow in taking on the role of others by:

Teachers try to understand the child's perspective.

- Asking them to imagine how someone else feels: "How do you think Sarah and Marria felt when the Legos hit them?" "How would you feel?" "Have you ever had someone say something to you that hurt you?"
- Helping children to connect their own feelings with the things that happen to them or that they are otherwise involved in. You can ask: "How do you feel when . . .?" "Why were you angry?" "Did it make you feel good when . . .?"
- Communicating to the children your understanding of the context of their experiences, what children are feeling, and the reasons for it: "You feel very angry now because you didn't get to paint." "You're happy because your block building is tall and sturdy." "You feel sad because they didn't ask you to play with them."

As children role play, they have a chance to gain insights into the feelings of others, think about alternatives for action, and explore consequences of their actions.

Children can be given "what if" problems and situations to act out. Young children, who cogently cannot put themselves in the role of others, are asked "what if" in connection with actual events. "Nancy, what if Steve took your car while you were looking for a place to park it?" "Steve, you pretend to take the car. Nancy, what would you do? What other ways could you act?"

Some other kinds of questions that might be asked about real situations are "What if you want to play in the housekeeping area, but children there say NO, you can't come in?" "What if there is only one wagon, but two children who want to ride in it?"

Social Skills

The social skills of sharing and cooperating can be taught through children's play and social interactions. Direct statements might be made. "We do it this way in school," or "Take two more turns, and then it's Aletha's turn" (Curry & Johnson, 1990).

Explicit coaching may be helpful. Successful coaching techniques include the following:

- Clarify the concepts and behaviors that need to be addressed, such as the idea that hitting is not going to solve the problem
- Discuss the idea and behavior with children and ask them to think about alternative ways for relating with others
- Practice social skills through role play with others
- Coach children in the use of concepts and behaviors in real situations

Books are also useful when teaching older children. Reading Aliki's *We Are Best Friends*, in which a boy makes new friends, can be followed with discussions about how children could make new friends. One second-grade teacher asked each child to write a personal letter to a friend.

It's George, by Miriam Cohen—the story of a boy who is not appreciated by other first-graders until he becomes a hero—illustrates a number of ways to make friends. Elizabeth Winthrop's *Lizzie and Harold* shows children that friends can be younger or older than oneself and of the opposite sex. After reading the book, teachers of primary children can discuss who can be a friend, list games friends play together, and even put children in pairs to learn to play Cat's Cradle and The Mattress, which are described in *Lizzie and Harold.*

Balancing Authority with Children's Autonomy

Understanding theories of discipline and knowing how and when to use them to guide children's behavior is but one step in the process of effective discipline. To guide children's behavior effectively, teachers must balance their own authority with the need for children to develop their own autonomy.

If you are not clearly in charge and children do not understand the guidelines of living and working with one another, they will never be able to develop autonomy and self-discipline. Likewise, if you are too much in charge, if you hold too tightly to your authority and impose too many rules on children's behavior, it will be unlikely children will ever be able to develop a sense of autonomy and self-control. When adults tell children what to do, how to behave, and when to act, it is difficult for them to learn to think, make decisions, and be autonomous. Democracy cannot survive with citizens who only know how to obey others, who act like puppets, and look to others to do their thinking and decision making.

This is why early childhood educators have embraced theories of guiding children's behavior that they believe to foster children's self-understanding and self-discipline and enable them to develop control that comes from within rather than depending on others to impose control over them. This discipline and guidance revolve around the principles of our democratic way of life, by:

- Focusing on the inherent dignity and rights of each human being instead of humiliation of the undisciplined.
- Basing discipline and guidance on humanitarian principles and ideals. In a democratic society, this means guidance based on loyalty to the principles of freedom, justice, and equality for all, rather than a narrower, more egotistical affiliation with "my group."
- Understanding of the goal in view, that of promoting each child's independence, rather than on taking someone else's word for specific appropriate behaviors (Redl, 1966).

There are no easy rules for creating a balance between your necessary authority when working with young children and children's need to develop autonomy. A lot will depend on:

- Your personality and value system
- The nature of the children you will be teaching
- Developing careful plans

Personality Considerations

"I was so angry with her I couldn't see straight, and I just hauled off and hit her." Children are frequently the recipients of actions stemming from some deep, and perhaps little understood, emotions of an adult. To be able to guide children with authority that leads to children's development of autonomy, you must get to know yourself and be clearheaded about your own value systems.

This gives you the opportunity to think and reflect about children's behaviors rather than react in anger or without reflection. Understanding yourself permits you to determine the degree to which your prejudices or viewpoints determine your actions toward children (Johnson, 1936).

First, examine your ideas about how children should behave. Accept that there are certain behaviors you find annoying and hard to tolerate. Then communicate them to children. If you cannot accept children's chewing gum or making noise above a certain level, let them know. When you respect children fully, they will respect you and accept whatever quirks you might have.

Do, however, accept the inevitable characteristics of young children. Infants and toddlers will naturally eat with their hands and smear food around, because this is the way they learn about their world and gain autonomy and control over meeting their own needs for food. Know and accept that four-year-olds will use a lot of "bathroom" language. Five- and six-year-olds can be cruel, calling one another horrendous names. Be prepared for the normal, natural behaviors of children. This doesn't mean you

Be prepared for the normal, natural behaviors of children.

have to accept all actions without reproof because "that's the way children act." Instead you need to understand children's viewpoints and teach them new ways of responding without getting upset and losing control over your own emotions. Seriously think about:

1.   How do I feel about children? Some people believe that children are really rather sinful beings in need of tight control and discipline (*Mission Life,* 1976). You may have been taught that children are instinctively evil, governed by internal drives (especially sexual), and that they must be controlled, usually through harsh punishment and at least some suffering (Howard, 1975, p. 63). Then, perhaps, you need to think about the source of these ideas, how you developed them, and whether they are appropriate to your teaching role.

Or you may believe, as did Rousseau and Froebel, that children unfold and develop their full potential without adult control and that guidance isn't necessary because children are naturally good and will follow basically good instincts. Or perhaps you, like the behaviorists, believe that external conditions are necessary for the development of self-discipline.

2.   What kind of children do you expect? Do you want instant obedience, or do you want children to think for themselves (Johnson, 1936)? What does it mean to you, as a teacher of young children, if children are encouraged to think for themselves? Children who think for themselves may say no to you or may suggest ways other than those you had in mind of behaving or acting.

3.   Which behaviors can you tolerate, and which are unacceptable? Are these behaviors the normal, natural behaviors of children: "I wouldn't expect a three to explain why she hit another, it's unrealistic" (Wolfgang & Glickman, 1980, p. 14). Can you adjust your thinking to accept some behaviors while helping children develop new ways of acting?

Think about the source of these ideas, how you developed them, and whether or not they will get in the way of your acceptance of the childish, spontaneous nature of all children.

The Nature of the Children

There are techniques that you can use to establish your own authority that also permit children to develop self-control and become independent. Some of your authority grows from your self-understanding. You have a clear idea about which decisions you are going to make and which are made by the children. In addition,

1. Think about the needs of individual children.
2. Take time to make careful plans.

3. Set limits.

4. Develop a "withitness" (Johnson, 1936; Kouin, 1970).

5. Learn techniques of involving children in group work.

Individual Needs

The individual isn't sacrificed for the good of the group, or the group for an individual (Redl, 1966). "There is no way out but to always consider both issues at once" (Redl, 1966, p. 262). Effective teachers are those that pay attention to individuals. They are proficient at diagnosing children's needs, know what is likely to be confusing or distracting, and focus children's attention on the work at hand (ERIC, 1981; National Association for the Education of Young Children, 1987).

Recognizing an individual's needs can head off disruption of the total group. One child may need encouragement, another a chance to work off anger, and another a quiet time alone (Murphy, Snyder, & Snyder, 1985).

Leanita, who had returned to the center from a rather extensive illness, was busy playing with her friends in the housekeeping corner. The noise level rose, and Leanita started to race around the corner. The teacher walked over to her, handed her a doll, and suggested, "Your baby is so tired, sit here and rock her to sleep." Leanita gratefully took the suggestion as a way of saving face and regaining her composure.

Other children may need to be redirected to another activity. "Sit here and work this puzzle until you feel ready to go back to playing without throwing the blocks." How you recognize an individual's needs is important as well. Kouin (1970) believes that a teacher's actions toward one student affect not only that student but the group as well. Asking children to stop a certain action in a task-focused way ("You'll be able to build with the blocks if you put the truck down") rather than in an approval-focused technique ("I like children who let others play with the truck while they build blocks") is more effective in fostering responsible behavior in the whole group.

Careful Planning

It was near the end of the school year in a primary classroom. The children were working at tables and some were at the computers. When the teacher was finishing working with a reading group, she said, "It's time to put our work away and get ready to go to the cafeteria. Sallie, collect the blue books. Give the black computer disks to Tim, and all of you get your lunch bags." Tim didn't stop work at the computer and with his laughing and comments drew a group of children around him. Sallie started to collect books, but she and Sonia began arguing about which color books to collect. Some of the children got their lunch bags and sat down but most roamed around the room.

The teacher sensed the chaos but said, "OK, Sallie, collect any books and get someone to help you. Sonia, you collect the computer disks." This time the children paid no attention at all. The teacher then walked around and picked up books, and one by one got children in line with their lunch bags, saying "We won't go until we're ready." But then the second bell rang, and the children ran down the hall without her to the cafeteria.

It was truly chaotic. When asked what happened and why the children were so out of control, the teacher said, "Well, I asked them to put their things away, but they didn't so I asked them to do something else instead."

If the teacher does not have a clear idea of what behavior she expects from the children, how will the children? Young children become frustrated, insecure, and difficult when they do not know what is expected, or what will happen next. Many problems are avoided when teachers plan carefully for routines and smooth transitions.

Routines.   Clear, consistent routines are the foundation. Routines help children know what behaviors will be expected and what behaviors are acceptable in different situations. Routines help make limits clear and ease life for the group. Further, the dependable, clear routines of work/rest, nap/lunch, and indoor/outdoor play enable children to develop independence and autonomy. With a clear idea of what they will do, children can carry on independently, without adult assistance.

Transitions.   With a dependable schedule and consistent routines, transitions usually occur efficiently and automatically, without disruption. Still, research suggests that the greatest source of discipline problems occur during times of transitions, especially when children must wait for the next activity.

To avoid problems during transitions, eliminate wait times and think ahead. Effective teachers rehearse every move they and the children will make, thinking ahead to avoid confrontations. If children will have to wait, teachers keep a variety of activities, finger plays, songs, games, stories, or other activities handy to keep children involved while waiting.

Setting Limits

Children have a great deal of choice in an early childhood program, but there are certain limits to these choices that are understood by everyone. Sometimes the children set the limits.

In Ms. D.'s kindergarten class the children were having difficulty adjusting to the group and to the constraints of a school setting. There were fights, hitting, screaming, and temper tantrums. Ms. D. called the children together for a meeting. She informed them that their behaviors were unacceptable and that they couldn't work together as a group unless something was done about the situation. She told the children they would have to set limits and rules for their behaviors. Her five-year-olds dictated a long list of behaviors they would not permit. It was almost a catharsis for them as each child told of the behavior that most upset them. As the list grew, one child said, "I know, let's have a rule to be nice. That's all we need, nice children." The teacher posted this rule, and for the rest of the year, when misbehavior was about to occur, she referred the children to it: "Remember our rule, *be nice!*"

In a group of four-year-olds, limits were established for woodworking. The children dictated them with the teacher adding some of her own. The rules were posted over the woodworking bench. Even though the children couldn't read the rules, they referred to and maintained them: "Put the tool down before you argue."

One teacher and his group of four-year-olds decided that they would forbid:

- Throwing or destroying toys
- Breaking or defacing furniture or walls
- Interference in another child's play
- Playing with food
- Throwing sand, stones, or other objects
- Biting, spitting, hitting, pushing, or otherwise trying to hurt another

These limits were consistently enforced. Often the teacher found that a look, raised eyebrow, or shake of the head was enough to remind the children. If this wasn't enough, this teacher would:

- Follow through on enforcing the rules. Speaking clearly, and in positive ways, he'd say, "Ride your bike here," "Put your food down," "Remember the rule, 'no hitting,'" or "Ask for it instead of pulling."
- If the request was refused, he would repeat it, and give reasons why it should be obeyed.
- Physically stop the child. Remove the object about to be thrown or take the child by the hand to another place in the room.

Talking in a quiet, calm voice, using clear statements so there is no confusion, and addressing the child by name are believed to be helpful in maintaining limits (Goffin, 1987).

These steps indicate a progression of adult control. The child is first offered suggestions and help in taking control, but if the child isn't ready or able to assume this control, the adult does intervene.

"Withitness"

Harriet Johnson (1936) wrote of the early childhood educator's need to "be with it." By this, she meant that the teacher is aware of each child's emotions and needs as well as those of the whole group. She thought this understanding necessary in order to know when and how to intervene in children's play and interpersonal relationships without destroying their opportunity to develop autonomy.

Teachers will find a sense of humor, lightheartedness, and ability to laugh with the children helpful. Johnson recommends a light touch in offering assurance to others and developing a genuine relationship with children as a senior partner in the cooperative enterprise of the school program (1936, p. 27).

Kouin (1970) identified another kind of "withitness" that effective teachers develop. This is awareness of the total group. Effective teachers really do seem to know everything and everyone in the room. They are alert to danger signals—perhaps a heightened noise level or a very still feeling in the room. They observe individuals and the group carefully and intervene with

Teachers who are "with it" are aware of children's needs.

a song, poem, or statement that stops trouble or misbehavior before it can occur. Unsuccessful teachers are not so aware, and they let misbehavior go on too long before intervening. Once having waited too long, they face difficult situations that often call for drastic measures.

Working with Groups

At times you will want the children to come together as a group. Children in the primary grades receive a great deal of instruction in groups and will work together to complete projects or work in small groups. Yet even two-year-olds can benefit from some group activities. It is worthwhile even for the youngest to develop the skills of being with a group to build a sense of camaraderie. A number of guidance techniques for helping young children develop the skills necessary for group living have been identified by early childhood educators (Clewett, 1988).

Two-year-olds will gather with you one or two at a time to listen to a story, sing simple songs, or listen to music. By three years of age, children will enjoy coming together to listen to a record, story, or finger play or even to enter into a discussion. With two- and three-year-olds, keep the group times very informal and short. Children are usually free to come and go as they wish, and you should be ready to change the activity to meet their interests. Be prepared for individuals to enter the group, stay a few minutes, then leave to play with something else and return again. Involving children in some physical activity, such as finger or hand actions done to a story or poem or movements to accompany a song, holds their interest and meets their need for activity. When you accept the childishness of two- and three-year-olds, you avoid the need for discipline, nagging, or even pleading for attention during short activity times.

Four-year-olds will probably be able to spend more time in groups. They still can't sit still for long or concentrate on group discussions and long stories or music sessions. Through kindergarten, group times are short, flexible, and informal.

Five-year-olds and those in the primary grades are able to participate more fully in groups and attend to more abstract work and group dialogue. Sitting with children in close physical proximity permits you eye and physical contact with each child. You can, when sitting close to the children, place a hand on a shoulder or touch or hug a child in order to gain and maintain attention.

Don't try to wait for the group to get ready. If you're working with a group of preschoolers, it would take you all day if you waited for everyone. You would eventually have to begin the activity when some of the children weren't ready, and that action would communicate your inability to take charge. The children would sense that you didn't have a clear idea of the behaviors you expected of them, and that would tell them that you really didn't mean what you said.

Rather than waiting for everyone to get ready, begin immediately with a finger play, song, puppet action, game, or a story. Use a quiet, low voice that makes children curious to come to find out what is happening.

Involve children as they come to the group, and you may encourage those who haven't yet finished a project to join you. "Rachel, Moritz, why don't you put that away now and join us. You can finish that after story time."

When children are in the group, encourage them to participate. Ask the most verbal children, "Hold that idea while we listen to Andrea," or "What did you think of that?" so all will be able to participate. Redirect children's conversations to focus on the group's task: "Yes, Allison, we'd like to hear about your new pony, but now we're reading this book about astronauts. Do you have something to add to the discussion?" Lead the group with a light, humorous touch, knowing that as the children mature, they will develop increasingly complex abilities to attend when in a group and interact with others in a group setting.

Applying the Approaches

Vignettes of children who had problems developing self-control follow. After the vignettes are ideas teachers used successfully to help these children develop control. As you read the vignettes, think about the approaches, combinations of approaches, and theories that were applied in helping these children resolve their difficulties and develop self-control.

The Negative Child

Joel opposes you with his every action. He never does what he's asked. A sure way of setting him off is to suggest he "put the block down," or "use the rope around the waist, not the neck." He antagonizes both you and the other children with his taunts, threats, and physical attacks. Yesterday, when you suggested Joel ask Clifford for a turn at the easel instead of pushing Clifford away, Joel threw a can of paint at you, covering you and several children with red paint. As you approached him, he threatened to "kill you because my father has a gun." Two children cried at this outburst, and the other children were subdued and withdrawn the rest of the morning. You really have to do something if you want five-year-old Joel and the other children to have a successful kindergarten year.

A number of techniques and approaches will probably be necessary with a child as negative and disruptive as Joel. As Adler and Dreikurs et al. might recommend, you could look at the causes of the behaviors. Physical causes should probably be the first to be ruled out. Does Joel suffer from fatigue, hunger, or some other physical problem that could result in his inability to handle the group situation?

Next, look to Joel's goals. Is he seeking to become a member of the group or to gain attention and power? His behavior may very well be caused by feelings of inadequacy and low self-esteem. Or Joel may be receiving rewards for negative behaviors, never having had a chance to be reinforced for appropriate behaviors. Perhaps he simply hasn't been taught how to enter a group. You could:

- Observe Joel over a period of time, or ask a volunteer to observe him and keep a record of his outbursts and negative behaviors. You might be able to identify some of the factors that trigger his behaviors and remove them. If Joel's behaviors seem to be triggered by small failures or even fear of failure, you can build successful experiences for him.
- Get a volunteer to help you with Joel. Either you or the volunteer can stay with him and help him achieve success by stopping him from acting out, either by physically removing him from a situation or holding onto him. Continual negative behaviors only increase his sense of failure, guilt, and inadequacy, so you'll want to stop him before he acts out. Explain your actions to Joel, if possible.
- Ignore the threats Joel shouts at you. Help the others model your behavior and ignore Joel as well. Children as young as three have been taught to ignore classmates' negative behaviors to help extinguish them. You might make statements such as "When Joel calls you 'stinky,' and says he'll beat you up, he's only trying to make you cry. If you don't cry, and walk away, Joel will stop. I won't let him hurt you."
- Avoid confrontations with Joel. Plan the environment and the program to limit confrontations. Walk away, change the topic, offer some other appealing activity, but don't respond to his taunts.
- Provide situations in which Joel can work and experience success. It may be a special task that only he can do. Do whatever you can to help him increase his feelings of importance and self-worth.
- If Joel seems confused by too many choices, organize the day for him, reducing stimulation and choices. Instead of asking him to work his way through the entire day, or with the whole group, structure a task for him, perhaps something he can do with one or two others.
- Continue to provide a model for Joel. Remember that his outbursts are emotionally upsetting to you as well as to the children. Model calm, rational behavior, never reacting with anger, and offering explanations for behaviors.

Remember that it took Joel years to develop his mode of behaving and reacting to others, and it will take time to change. Know that there are occasions when you must have the help of another adult, and don't be afraid to ask someone to help you with children who, like Joel, have developed a firm oppositional behavior pattern (Carberry, 1983).

The Passive-Dependent Child

First-grader Rosa doesn't do anything. She'll complete a task if you sit with her and continually tell her it is correct. She won't continue working after you've left, however. She sits on the playground bench while the others are involved in any variety of activities. During free time she sits at her desk, staring into space. If you ask her what she'd like to do or choose, she just smiles sweetly at you and shakes her head negatively. You're getting more and more concerned. Soon the accountability testing will take place, and you wonder if Rosa is getting anything at all out of first grade. How can she when she's never really participated in the activities and gives up before facing any real challenge?

As with Joel, you should try to find out some of the causes of Rosa's behaviors. Don't think of yourself as a psychologist. Your responsibility is to find out if Rosa is physically well, overtired, or hungry. Then too, Rosa, like Joel, may be hiding feelings of inadequacy, but instead of acting out as Joel does, she may find withdrawing a comfortable way of dealing with fear of failure. You might try:

- Getting a volunteer or someone to work with Rosa on a one-to-one basis, helping to give suggestions for completing tasks or entering into group activities. Because she is six years old, she may respond to being taught new behaviors.
- Slowly and gently try to get to know her. Sit with her and initiate conversations, giving her time to respond. Sit with her without saying anything, or read a story to her. Don't demand that she engage in conversation. If she does offer something, be certain to listen carefully. If she expresses fears, guilt, or inadequacy, don't make light of them. If you say, "Oh, that, everyone knows that's the smoke detector," she'll think you're unconcerned about her real feelings. Let her know you can be trusted to understand.
- Talk with her parents to discover activities Rosa enjoys doing at home or with other children. When you can identify something that interests her, provide materials on the topic to foster this interest.

- Lower your expectations for Rosa. Present her with small tasks that can result in immediate and gratifying success. Structure many successes. Limit choices for Rosa as well. Instead of asking her to find something to do, you might give her a specific simple task and support her attempts to complete it.
- Continue to reward and reinforce any behaviors that approximate independence. A reward may be a wink, smile, or something tangible.
- Review Rosa's history and records, and if possible, refer her for psychological testing to determine her strengths and weaknesses. Focus on the strengths as you plan activities that will enable her to eliminate weaknesses.

As with Joel, be prepared for small gains and uneven growth. Be there to support her as she attempts to reach out, gradually building a helping relationship with her.

The Child Who Steals

The other four-year-olds were the first to notice missing items. Gretchen brought a heart-shaped locket to school, and it was gone before the morning was over. Mike lost his basketball-shaped eraser, and your ceramic frog paper-clip holder has disappeared. Yesterday, as you came back into the room for some tissue during outdoor play, Julie was busily going through the cubbyholes, stuffing "treasures" into her snack box. Julie cried when you found her and said she never has taken anything. But the next day she returned the locket and your frog.

Stealing is upsetting to adults as well as children. With Julie, a four-year-old, try to find out if she understands the concept of ownership. Children under the age of six or seven do not always have fully developed concepts of ownership. The fact that they want something is the only thing that counts. They don't realize that taking something they want is stealing. Once you find out Julie's concept of ownership, you can look to other causes of behavior. Does she feel that she is an important part of the group? Is she taking things to be noticed or to receive attention? Observe her to find out when, why, and under what circumstances she steals. Consider the following:

- Does Julie have unmet needs? Does she have the things she wants, and does she receive attention for good behaviors? Give her tasks that enable her to gain the other children's attention and respect.

- Limit the potential for her to steal by removing trinkets and keeping someone in the room when the children are elsewhere.
- Try to have Julie understand the other children's feelings. For example, "Gretchen felt very sad when she lost her locket."
- Reward and reinforce Julie when she does do well, giving her attention.
- If Julie continues to steal, have her experience the logical consequences of returning the items, but support her as she does this.

As with all children, it is important to work closely with her parents and other professionals. Teachers, parents, and others in the school can work together to help Julie feel accepted, important, and self-assured.

The Child Who Lies

Susan lies constantly. None of the other kindergarten children even listen to her anymore. Now she's increased the number and intensity of her lies. She falsely claims she has a new swimming pool and that she and her family went to Disney World over the weekend. She has not actually upset anyone, but her ability to relate with the other children has deteriorated so much that they walk away from her when she tries to enter a group, and they have forcefully kept her from joining them in the block and housekeeping areas.

At five, Susan may not understand the difference between lies and truth. Try to foster an understanding through discussions, language arts activities, and stories: "This part is pretend, and this is not"; "It's fun to pretend." Sendak's *Where the Wild Things Are* (1969) is an example of a story useful in helping children separate fact from fantasy. As you work with Susan, continually teach her the difference between fact and fantasy. Try the following actions:

- Calmly introduce Susan to the idea that her Disney World story was exciting to listen to: "It's fun to make up stories. Why not dictate the story, and I'll write it in this book?" Let her tell stories to the other children, but be clear that both you and the children know her stories are pretend: "like the 'Three Billy Goats Gruff,' and we all enjoy pretending sometimes."
- Observe Susan to see if she's using lies to be accepted by the others. If this is the case, teach her some social skills and techniques for gaining

children's attention and entering and staying with the group without having to try for attention through stories.
- Rebuild her confidence: "You don't have to make it up, I'll understand how it really was."
- Ignore small lies and teach the others to ignore these as well. When she doesn't receive attention for lying and realizes she can get attention for more positive behaviors, the lies will disappear.

Maturation may work. As Susan grows, she may outgrow the need to tell stories. Be pleased with small gains, recognizing and rewarding them. Continue to build her confidence by teaching her to receive attention and power in positive ways.

The Child Who Swears

First-grader Henry swears! And how! His outbursts are colorful, descriptive, and shocking. Now the other children are beginning to use his vocabulary, and one of the parents has gone to the principal complaining that her child used a "disgusting" word she had learned at school.

Young children may use inappropriate language because of the shock value it holds. Everyone is shocked to hear an innocent young child use an obscene word. Most of the time the children haven't the slightest idea what the word means. They just know it receives a great deal of attention. Some children may swear because they're imitating the behavior of their neighbors or older siblings. For Henry, you can:

- Recognize that attention to the swearing will only increase the behavior. Set up a systematic schedule of behavior modification, and reward him for not using the words, ignoring the times he uses offensive language. Teach the others to ignore him as well, so he is not reinforced by the group.
- Give him alternative words to express his feelings. At six, he can learn that words have power, but some are more descriptive than others. Help him to increase his vocabulary so he'll continue to command power in expressing emotions, feelings, and ideas.
- Provide him with models, perhaps from the entertainment or sports areas, as well as yourself and other impressive figures in the school who express themselves fully without using shocking language.

The Show-Off

Just when you've prepared the children for your supervisor's visit, Aletha begins showing off. As the principal steps into your second-grade classroom, Aletha is on top of the desk completing her very best imitation of Donald Duck. The other children are delighted, clapping at her performance. It's bad enough to have this happen when the principal has come to observe you, but Aletha is constantly showing off, interrupting the children with noises, jokes, and antics. It is time she learned other ways of getting attention.

Perhaps Aletha has never received attention for appropriate behavior and is attempting to gain attention through showing off. Ask a volunteer to observe her or set up your own schedule to determine when, why, and under what circumstances she shows off. You might very well find out that Aletha is receiving attention only when she acts out. If this is the case, you can do the following:

- Establish a schedule of rewards and reinforcements for correct, acceptable behavior, and teach yourself and others to ignore the showing-off behaviors.
- Try to increase her feeling of importance. If she's good at impressions, perhaps she could have a spot in the school variety show or entertain children at some other appropriate function. Since she is in the second grade, Aletha should be able to develop an understanding of the time and place for different kinds of behaviors.
- Give her plenty of tasks she can complete successfully or put her in charge of some important function to increase her feelings of adequacy and diminish the need to show off.

Summary

In the small democracy of the early childhood program, the goal of guidance is to enable children to develop self-control and discipline themselves. Nevertheless, children do need limits and someone who will help them negotiate the complex rules of living together. Still, this guidance is always directed toward enhancing the inherent worth and dignity of the children, not in teaching them to obey an authority blindly in order to receive some reward or other.

A good test of how effective discipline in an interactionist framework is in helping children to gain control is to refrain from stepping in to solve children's problems, giving them the chance to develop their own skills of negotiating. When children are able to work together without the continual intervention of an adult, then you know that your techniques of guiding children's behavior have reached perfection.

Projects

Continuing Case Study

Observe your case study child, and note the number of times his or her behaviors are recognized by the teacher with rewards or some type of praise. How many times does the teacher recognize negative or inappropriate behaviors, and how many times does the teacher reward positive or appropriate behaviors? Keep a record, noting how the teacher's actions affect your child.

1. Ask each member of the class to write an anonymous definition of guiding children's behavior on a card. Compile these definitions to find out how many different definitions of guidance your group has. As a group, discuss where your ideas came from. Do they stem from your experiences in church, the family, or the community?
2. At the library, identify and list children's books that could be used as tools for teaching children how to enter a group, solve problems, deal with their feelings, or accept and understand the behavior of other children.
3. Children respond to statements that direct their behavior in positive ways. These statements make clear the behaviors that are acceptable, while letting children know what is unacceptable. They avoid negatives like "stop," "don't," and "no." Try writing statements that are positive and informative and could be used to stop children who are: throwing sand at one another, hitting each other, wiggling and fidgeting at story time, banging blocks on the floor instead of building with them, or splashing water on the floor.

Resources

Marion, M. (1992). *Guidance of young children* (3rd ed.). New York: Merrill/ Macmillan. This book blends child guidance theory and research with specific, positive, and useful guidance strategies.

Hildebrand, V. (1990). *Guiding young children* (4th ed.). New York: Merrill/Macmillan. This is a complete guide to managing young children's behavior, especially the very young.

Stone, J. G. (1991). *A guide to discipline.* Washington, DC: National Association for the Education of Young Children. This publication offers teachers and parents a sound guide for learning to help children discipline themselves by their words, manner, and avoiding problems in advance.

References

Adler, A. (1964). *Social interest.* New York: Capricorn.

Aliki. (1982). *We are best friends.* New York: Greenwillow.

Bandura, A. (1986). *Social foundations of thought and action.* Englewood Cliffs, NJ: Prentice Hall.

Carberry, H. H. (1983). Behavioral block busters. In J. S. McKee (Ed.), *Annual edition: Early childhood education* (pp. 167–169). Guilford, CT: Duskin.

Clewett, A. S. (1988). Guidance and discipline: Teaching young children appropriate behaviors. *Young Children, 43*(4), 26-31.

Cohen, M. (1988). *It's George.* New York: Greenwillow.

Curry, N. E., & Johnson, C. N. (1990). *Beyond self-esteem: Developing a genuine sense of human values.* Washington, DC: National Association for the Education of Young Children.

Dreikurs, R., Greenwalk, B., & Pepper, F. (1982). *Maintaining sanity in the classroom.* New York: Harper & Row.

ERIC Clearinghouse on Elementary and Early Childhood Education. (1981). *Classroom management.* Urbana, IL: Author.

Goffin, S. (1987). Cooperative behaviors: They need our support. *Young Children, 41*(2), 75-81.

Howard, A. E. (1975). When children talk back—listen! In J. D. Andrews (Ed.), *Early childhood education: It's an art! It's a science!* (pp. 58–75). Washington, DC: National Association for the Education of Young Children.

Ishee, N., & Goldhaber, J. (1990). Story reenactment: Let the play begin! *Young Children, 39*(3), 70-75.

Johnson, H. (1936). *School begins at two.* New York: New Republic.

Kamii, C. (1984). Viewpoints: Obedience is not enough. *Young Children, 39*(4), 11–13.

Kouin, J. (1970). *Discipline and group management in classrooms.* New York: Holt, Rinehart & Winston.

Madsen, C. H., & Madsen, C. K. (1980). *Teaching/discipline.* Boston: Allyn & Bacon.

Mead, D. E. (1976). *Six approaches to child rearing.* Provo, UT: Brigham Young University Press.

Mission Life. (1976). St. Louis: Concordia.

Morgan, M. (1984). Reward-induced decrements and increments in intrinsic motivation. *Review of Educational Research, 54*(1), 5-31.

Murphy, M., Snyder, M., & Snyder, R. (1985). *The young child as a person: Toward the development of a healthy conscious.* New York: Human Science.

National Association for the Education of Young Children. (1987). Good discipline is in large part the result of a fantastic curriculum. *Young Children, 41*(3), 49-51.

Piaget, J. (1932). *The moral judgment of the child.* New York: Harcourt Brace & World.

Read, K. B. (1976). *The nursery school.* New York: Saunders.

Redl, F. (1966). *When we deal with children.* New York: Free Press.

Sendak, M. (1964). *Where the wild things are.* New York: Harper.

Seefeldt, C. (1991). *How can I get the kids to behave?* Springfield, MO: Missouri State Department of Education.

Skinner, B. F. (1984). *About behaviorism.* New York: Alfred A. Knopf.

Weber-Schwartz, N. (1987). Patience or understanding. *Young Children, 42*(3), 52–54.

Winthrop, E. (1986). *Lizzie and Harold.* New York: Lothrop, Lee, & Shepard.

Wolfgang, C., & Glickman, C. (1980). *Solving discipline problems.* Boston: Allyn & Bacon.

Yarrow, M. R., Scott, P. M., & Waxler, C. E. (1973). Learning concern for others. *Developmental Psychology, 3*, 240-260.

8 Play: The Integrator of the Curriculum

"Play is necessary to affirm our lives."

(Levy, 1978, p. 1)

After you read this chapter, you should be able to respond to the following questions:

1. Explain the common elements of play and discuss the importance of the play experience for children.

2. Describe the historical differences in children's play.

3. Discuss how different theorists explain children's play.

4. What are the different stages of children's play, and how can teachers integrate play into the classroom for infants, toddlers, preschoolers and kindergartners, and primary-age children?

5. What does a teacher do to facilitate play for children? What is her or his role as an observer, planner, supervisor, and evaluator?

Why Children Play

A group of three-year-olds is seated around Mr. S., anxiously waiting to see the something special he has brought. Mr. S. pulls out a milkweed pod and holds it up as all the children stare in fascination. Then he says quietly, "This is called a milkweed pod, and inside are seeds. Watch." He opens the pod gently, takes out a few seeds, and says, "See, the seed is at the end of this soft silky thread. When the wind comes, they fly through the air." He then tosses the seeds in the air as the children watch, entranced. Some reach up with their hands, others lean forward with their bodies.

Mr. S. then says, "Listen to this poem about the milkweed pod." Using appropriate gestures, he recites a poem about a milkweed pod that opens and sends its seeds into the air. The first time the children listen and watch, intrigued. A few partially imitate his actions. Then he repeats the poem and the children close their hands like the milkweed pod, slowly open them, and then toss their hands in the air and watch as imaginary seeds fall to the ground.

Later Mr. S. puts the pods on a table, and several children pick them up, open them, and take out the seeds. They feel the seeds, rub them across their cheeks, and some even gingerly stick out their tongues as if to taste them.

For outdoor play, the pods are taken outside. Again the children open them, take several of the seeds, and toss them into the air. As they fall, the children run to catch them. They return laughing to the table to find more seeds to throw as they themselves twirl, whirl, laugh, and fall down.

This group of three-year-olds was involved in learning and playing in an activity that completely absorbed their attention from the time they were first shown the milkweed pods. Their involvement continued in a symbolic way as they heard the poem. Later they touched, smelled, and even attempted to taste the seeds. On the playground, they continued their involvement in what appeared to be only play.

How much of this activity was play and how much were the children learning? It is difficult to determine exactly. There is no doubt that at least part of this activity was not play because it was planned and directed by the teacher. And part of it was pure play activity in that it was child initiated, sustained, and very pleasurable. A combination of a teacher-planned activity and child-initiated play undergirds this simple science lesson for three-year-olds. A new concept, "milkweed pod seeds," appears to take on meaning for the children in their sensory and motoric play. And a teacher plans so that play is integrated as a part of the curriculum.

Because this was a lesson for three-year-olds, the activity followed by play perhaps seems reasonable. Still, play is a valuable activity for people at any age. Often adults do not understand the significance of play in children's academic and intellectual learning. Too frequently the thinking is that play is what you do after work or what happens at recess time or at home after the children have learned at school. The importance of play to academic learning and intellectual development is too often underestimated.

Psychologists, anthropologists, and educators have observed children in play situations in an attempt to understand the significance of these experiences for children's development. Yet no all-encompassing definition or justification of play has been forthcoming. If Dewey's explanation of play as "activities performed which are enjoyable, performed for their own sake and with no end result in mind" is correct, then the children in the above episode were playing (Dewey, 1913, p. 725). The children were totally engrossed, and the play was neither frivolous nor lacking in purpose, yet there seemed to be no particular end result. This play was serious business, and the children's exuberance indicated the great pleasure they were experiencing. The play certainly enriched and extended the children's learning, enabling them to explore and test their understanding of the milkweed pod.

For the young child, play is believed to be the basis for learning (Bredekamp, 1987; Cheyne & Rubin, 1983; Moyer, Egerston, & Isenberg, 1987; Piaget, 1962). As children engage in feeling, tasting, and smelling new objects, they gain a personal knowledge of objects like milkweed pods that no amount of telling or instruction can give. Play provides children with the opportunity to make sense of their universe. It helps them to discover and develop their own bodies, to discover others and develop interpersonal relationships, to recreate familiar roles, and to discover new modes of operating.

Play has vital significance in the curriculum as children progress through the grades. Researchers have linked the play experience with a wide range of psychological functioning, including:

1. Creative thinking
2. Problem solving
3. The ability to cope with tensions and anxieties
4. Acquiring new understandings
5. The ability to use tools
6. Development of language (Christie & Johnson, 1983)

Seemingly it's the playful attitude, which allows children to examine known facts in different ways, that leads them to discovering new combinations of ideas (Lieberman, 1977, p. 128).

Because play is pleasurable, children often stay with a task longer when they are playing. Teachers, of course, can make use of the playful mode to enable children to reinforce skills already learned, to discover new combinations, and to remain involved for longer periods of time in an activity (Iverson, 1982, p. 693). Playful practice accompanying activities related to the curriculum, however, must be under the control of the child. Adult-enforced activities tend to deprive the child of inner motivation and may take away the pleasure that child-controlled activities provide (Rogers & Sawyers, 1988, p. 15). Play is the integrator of the curriculum. Basic skills in mathematics, science, and language arts, in addition to social studies, can all be learned as children play with materials and ideas. Art, music, and movement education are perhaps even easier to adapt to a play approach because these subjects provide children with the opportunity to explore materials, place, and arrangement without rigid standards and criteria.

Play is not important just for the young child but for children of all ages. The 1990 International Association for the Child's Right to Play presented the importance of play to the educational process. Participants from fifteen countries agreed that: *(a)* play was important throughout the entire educational process, *(b)* spontaneous play was important to children's development, *(c)* natural, cultural, and interpersonal play environments needed to be improved and expanded to facilitate play, and *(d)* adult-child interactions in appropriate child play activities were an important component of learning (Jambor, 1990).

For centuries writers, artists, philosophers, educators, and psychologists have been intrigued by the phenomenon of children's play.

Although the views of childhood have changed over time and the importance of play to the education of the child has had different emphases, many of these early views persist. A review of some of these perspectives may help to clarify varying adult viewpoints toward children, childhood, and play in today's society.

Historical Perspective

People have always distinguished between children's play and adult play (Singer, 1973). Generally, the early Greeks, Romans, and Egyptians did not view children as innocent but did view them as helpless, cheerful, affectionate, and playful and thus needing play and guidance to become useful and responsible citizens. The early Christians maintained a similar view but their view originated in the belief that the child had a soul, was important to God, and therefore was to be carefully nurtured (Hughes, 1991, p. 4).

In the Middle Ages, knights spent their leisure time in tournaments and jousting, keeping skills honed and practicing through "play" for the real thing. Young people who wanted to become knights engaged in similar activities. Wandering minstrels called adults and children together to hear tales of ogres and dragons, stories of the feats of knights, and romantic tragedies. During the Middle Ages, play was a means of practicing skills as well as relaxing and learning about the world for both adults and children.

In the eighteenth century, Rousseau emphasized that it was important for children to develop their natural instincts. He said, "A child's play is his natural occupation and . . . he does not sense any difference" (Rousseau, 1947, p. 561). He saw children's learning taking place through the freedom and spontaneity that play provided. At the end of the eighteenth century, Pestalozzi, following this idea, started the first outdoor education school, emphasizing that children should continue playing as they did at home in order to learn.

During the nineteenth century, more people had more leisure time. Social consciousness was developing, and greater interest and notice were taken of childhood as a discrete and important period of development. Childhood play was seen as distinct, important, and different from adult play. Growing interest in child development focused attention on children. This resulted in study of the way that children play and how their play affects children's development.

In contrast to these ideas, the Puritan ethic in our country established a dichotomy of work and play: Work was viewed as serious and the means of getting into heaven, while play was considered frivolous and the work of the devil. In the United States, even as late as the mid-1800s, books for children encouraged piety, hard work, obedience, and humility. There was little encouragement to play (Lystad, 1977, p. 16).

At the same time, however, social reformers like Friederich Froebel, John Dewey, Patty Smith Hill, and Maria Montessori were stressing the importance of children's play for social, emotional, and intellectual development. Froebel and Montessori emphasized children's play by developing materials for children to use in prescribed ways. Dewey and Hill thought children should have the opportunity to learn through free play.

Dewey believed that play is of great educational value and that children first learn about their world through it. As play becomes more sophisticated, he noted, it provides opportunity for the playful attitude to emerge. The development of this playful attitude is what keeps one continually growing and learning (Dewey, 1913).

Patty Smith Hill (1970) freed children's play from the restrictions of the Froebelian structured program. She developed large blocks for children's play and emphasized their need for space and freedom in order for full development to occur.

The Puritan dichotomy of work and play has not been resolved. In defense of play, Frank (1968) states:

> During the first five or six years of life, the child is expected to learn to cope with the world, natural and human. . . . No program of teaching and adult instruction could adequately provide for his own personal observation and

Play, a seemingly nonpurposeful activity, is actually the most fruitful activity of the whole life cycle.

knowing. But he will master these many experiences through continued play, as we call this seemingly non-purposeful activity which is actually the most intensive and fruitful learning in his whole life cycle. (pp. 434–435)

Today our society is facing pressures to preserve its power as society changes from an industrialized world to an information-processing culture. This pressure reaches children as parents, educators, and legislators push for greater academic achievement and excellence. Some educators have interpreted these pressures to mean the elimination of play from the early childhood program, a practice that many see as harmful to children's total development and contrary to what has been documented about the early experiences of high achievers. Elkind (1987) points out that "the parents of people who have attained eminence were careful not to impose their own priorities on their children, but instead to follow each child's lead" (p. 19).

The benefits of play are linked to children's cognitive, creative, social, linguistic, and affective development (Dyson, 1990; Isenberg & Quisenberry, 1988; Johnson, Christie, & Yawkey, 1987; Pepler, 1986; Rubin & Howe, 1986). Rather than pressuring for academic achievement, these researchers point out that play provides the foundation for skills necessary for achievement and excellence in life. It is important for children of all ages to practice in order to perfect skills and gain confidence in their ability. Play provides this opportunity. Children gain social skills as they learn to negotiate roles in sociodramatic play, to share toys or materials with a partner, and to obey the rules of a game. Some researchers suggest that play and children's intellectual aptitudes are related (Christie, 1983; Levenstein, 1985; Lieberman, 1977). Perhaps further research will substantiate an even more direct link between play and IQ, but at present it is known that play does enhance children's cognitive and creative development. As children play, they are often forced to view events from another's perspective and to solve problems they encounter in what are real situations for them by experimenting and finding novel approaches to situations or interesting uses of materials.

Theories of Play

"Play, like love, defies description" (Tyler, 1976, p. 225). As with love, there is something almost magical about children's play that mystifies even intellectuals. Various definitions of play have been offered, and many theories about its nature and purpose have been advanced. Each theory explains something about it, yet no one is completely adequate. "Play appears in so many guises and a great variety of forms. Its results are so subtle and far reaching that any one definition or explanation will of necessity be partial and incomplete" (Perryman, 1962, p. 146).

Although there is no all-encompassing definition of play, there is some agreement about its common elements.

1. Play has intrinsic motivation. Children play as a result of some inner drive and not from external pressures. Activities are pursued for their own sake or for reasons determined by the individual.
2. Play is enjoyable. The child takes pleasure in the activity, though the outward manifestation of this pleasure can vary.
3. Play is flexible and free from externally imposed rules. It varies from situation to situation and person to person.
4. Play is nonliteral. It requires players to realize that what is happening is not what seems to be happening. In play children are not bound by reality, but act as if the events were real or exhibit a "what-if" attitude regarding the situation.
5. Play requires verbal, mental, or physical activity. Garvey (1977, p. 4) makes a point that lounging, though perhaps pleasurable, is not active and thus does not fit into a definition of play.
6. Play is freely chosen. Children's participation in the activity is from their own choice. If coerced by the adult, then the activity may not be seen as play. (Garvey, 1977; Rubin, Fein, & Vanderberg, 1983; Sutton-Smith, 1986)

Hughes (1991, p. 3) points out that not all of children's play is positive. Children may engage in play that is cruel, unkind, and perhaps even brutal to others. In this type of play, children are seeking dominance over others, and those being dominated may not be engaged in play although the episodes are happening in a play situation.

Play and work are often viewed as opposing activities. Although there are differences in work and play, work often becomes play and play becomes work. When play is an integrator for curriculum, then classroom activities will contain elements of both.

Krasnor and Pepler (1980) suggest that pure play is a combination and overlapping of several elements. Any activity a person engages in may be play, more or less, depending on the combinations of these elements manifested in the activity (p. 86).

To understand how powerful play can be in a child's development and how important it is in educational experiences, it is helpful to review the theories of play. No one of the theories completely explains play, but viewed together they give insights into play and its importance for both children and adults. The major themes of play fall into the following four basic categories (Ellis, 1973; Gilmore, 1971; Levy, 1978; Mitchell & Mason, 1948):

1. Classical
2. Psychoanalytical
3. Cognitive-developmental
4. Ecological

Classical Theories

The classical theories of children's play are concerned with the causes and consequences of play. These theories include the surplus energy theory, the recreation/relaxation theory, the pre-exercise theory, and the recapitulation theory.

The Surplus Energy Theory.   According to the surplus energy theory, humans are naturally active. They store up energy, and when they no longer need it for survival, they use it in pursuit of pleasure. Teachers often exclaim about the excessive amount of energy children seem to have and are anxious for them to get on the playground in order to exercise and "let off steam." When you observe children bursting from classrooms and running in all directions on a playground, the idea of surplus energy seems realistic.

The Recreation/Relaxation Theory.   This theory is the direct opposite of the surplus energy theory. While the surplus energy theory suggests that people have extra energy and need to release it, the recreation/relaxation theory suggests that people are depleted of energy and must find ways to restore it. In modern society, excessive strain is put on the brain tracts and fine-muscle coordination. Because work causes strain on physical and psychological energy, play is necessary to refresh and restore this energy. Recreational/relaxation theorists believe that gross-motor activities are appropriate for this release, because the body becomes more relaxed from them.

The Pre-Exercise Theory.   This theory postulates that children play in order to practice and perfect their instincts for survival. Upon entering the world, children's sensory organs are not perfect, and they must proceed in playful experimentation to develop the rudimentary senses necessary for later development of intellect and emotions. Practice and experimentation prepare and equip children with the skills they need to survive, as well as those required for maintaining life.

The Recapitulation Theory.   As in the pre-exercise theory, this theory is related to humans' innate instincts. In recapitulation, however, children's play is the reenactment of the activities of their ancestors. Children progress through play activities in stages similar to the cultural stages in human evolution. This theory suggests that through play the undesirable traits of humanity can be eliminated. Children's play prepares them to move beyond primitive stages of play to more sophisticated activities necessary in the modern world.

The surplus theory of play suggests that people have extra energy and need to release it.

Psychoanalytical Theories

The psychoanalytical theory of play, based on Freud's work and revised and extended by others (notably Erikson), focuses on the content of children's play. Play behavior is explained as a combination of the child's biological need to grow and the desire to be grown up. Play is a catharsis for the child. It is a means by which children relieve the anxieties they feel about situations in real life to which they cannot safely react (Levy, 1978, pp. 100-101).

Through play, children are able to create their own world (Jalongo, 1984). Play allows children to practice being grown up by letting them be boss, adult, doctor, or teacher. They are able to change the course of events and alter the outcome of situations if they wish. By doing so, they are able to reduce feelings of anxiety and move toward feelings of mastery and pleasure.

In a cooperative nursery, four-year-old Jamie finished listening to a story on a record. He asked his mother to put on another record, and she obliged. He listened briefly and then said, "I don't want that one. I want another one." His mother replied, "You have to finish listening to this one before you can have another." Jamie yelled, "I don't want this one. I don't like it!" Jamie's mother calmly insisted, "You have to finish with this record first." Jamie jumped up, threw off his earphones, and marched to the clay table. There he grabbed some of Chan's clay. When Chan screamed, "That's mine," and scrabbled for it, Jamie held on tightly. The assistant gave another batch to Jamie, saying, "There's plenty for all. Give Chan's back." Jamie looked at the new clay and slowly relinquished his to Chan.

Jamie picked up the ball of clay, and with a scowl on his face and body tensed he punched the clay, pounded it, and rolled it out. He made a long thin roll and several small balls, saying, "This is the momma snake, these are her babies." Suddenly he gathered all the clay together, saying, "Bam! They're all smushed up." He giggled. He pounded the clay hard, punched, pressed down on it, and then rolled it out once more into long thin rolls and small balls. He continued punching and rolling, gradually smiling more and occasionally chuckling, until cleanup time was announced.

In the manipulation of the clay, Jamie seemed to be able to control the situation. No adult intervened to limit or control his activity. The punching, pounding, and rolling seemed to relieve the anger he exhibited over his frustration with his mother's unwillingness to change the record. Jamie, through his play with clay, relieved anxieties, controlled the situation as he wanted, and eventually began to derive pleasure from the activity (Genta, Constabile, & Bertacchini, 1983).

In practicing being grown up, children will choose types of roles to model, especially in dramatic or fantasy play. The role they select is not chosen at random but reflects the control they wish to exert or the mastery they wish to attain. Peller (1971) maintains that the role chosen reflects certain basic principles. Some children choose to model people whom they wish to resemble; they play this out in a "wishful anticipation." Others assign a role to an inanimate object or imaginary playmate. In these children's minds, that object or playmate depends on them to be in control of the situation. Another common role is "deflected vengeance." In this role children vent anger and frustrations on a toy, as Jamie did on the clay (Peller, 1971, pp. 110-125).

Erikson (1950) extends the Freudian concept of play and emphasizes the growth processes that take place as children play. In *Childhood and Society*, he states that "the playing child advances forward to new stages of mastery. . . . Child's play is the infantile form of the human ability to deal with experience by creating model situations and to master reality by experiment and planning" (p. 186).

Cognitive-Developmental Theories

Cognitive-developmental theories of play focus on its content, emphasizing the different aspects of play as children grow and develop. Piaget (1962) is the major theorist in this area.

Piaget's view of child's play reflects his view of the child's developing intellect: Development is accomplished by the assimilation-accommodation process. In the assimilation process, children view their external environment and fit information gleaned from it into their established cognitive level of functioning.

If children's concepts are inaccurate or incomplete, then the children will alter their organized thinking patterns by the accommodation process so that they fit reality more closely. In this context, assimilation dominates in play, for play is the method children use to practice, consolidate, and elaborate what they know and understand of their environment.

In play, children can safely test new patterns of behavior. They can practice new forms of physical, social, intellectual, and emotional modes of behavior without having to suffer the consequences they might face in reality. In real life, they run the risk of being wrong, uncoordinated, angry, or confused, but play provides an opportunity to experiment with a role or activity. The children can revise or change the direction of the activity so they can be right, or they can gradually develop necessary coordination for the task at hand. In play children can order events in order to experience pleasure and satisfaction in their accomplishments.

Play, according to Piaget, has three distinct categories. The first stage is *practice play* and is seen predominantly as the sensorimotor stage of development. At this stage, the child performs and practices newly acquired motor skills with evident pleasure. *Symbolic play* is the second stage and develops during the preoperational period. During this stage children are able to suspend reality and pretend that one object is another. A doll becomes the baby brother who needs changing and feeding. A stick becomes a magic wand. In symbolic play, children build their own reality by taking on the roles of another person.

Piaget's notion of symbolic play is expanded by other researchers. When the pretending becomes more elaborate with the child sustaining the role for a longer period of time and using gestures to represent objects, then the play is called *dramatic play.* When children begin to interact with others and carry on a dialogue, then play is often referred to as *sociodramatic play* (Smilansky & Shefatya, 1990; Wolfgang & Wolfgang, 1992).

To Vygotsky, play is both pleasure and development.

During the symbolic stage of play children begin to build, construct, model clay, or use writing or painting tools to represent known objects. Piaget believed that the *constructive play* was a bridge from practice play to symbolic play to play using rules. Other researchers view constructive play as a distinct stage where children progress through identifiable developmental levels (Goodnow, 1977; Kellog, 1970; Smilansky, Hagan, & Lewis, 1988).

The final stage is *games with rules,* which flowers during the concrete operations stage. Play becomes subject to the rules and order of the real world. Children learn to follow and make up rules, and they reach agreements for their play. They enjoy a variety of games, and as they mature they are able to follow more complicated directions. They are able to engage in fantasy play where they take on specific roles and act out a story together. The story may be made up or may be an enactment of a television show, a movie, or a storybook (Christie, 1987).

For Piaget, play has two important by-products. One is pleasure or joy. The infant or child will often spend long hours playing with a toy or throwing rocks into a puddle with deep satisfaction. The second is the adaptive role that play provides. As children play, they eventually become better able to adjust their behavior to meet the demands of the real world (Morrison & Kuhn, 1983; Piaget, 1962).

Vygotsky (1978) agrees with Piaget that play is pleasure and is developmental. Both Vygotsky and Piaget perceive that play for infants results because of a basic need of wish fulfillment. During infancy, children discover that play with objects in their immediate environment gives satisfaction and pleasure. When an infant's immediate needs and desires are not met at once by an adult, the infant is distressed, but discovers that this distress diminishes and pleasure results when she plays with her hands, her feet, or objects that are nearby. For preschoolers, play becomes generalized and imaginary situations are set up with rules established by children themselves. Older children, recognizing that games are governed by rules, begin to play by external rules.

Vygotsky does not agree with the Piagetian beliefs that play reflects past experiences and that children's egocentric thoughts simply atrophy and have no useful purpose as children grow older. For Vygotsky, egocentric thought reflected in play is a bridge to more advanced cognitive development. It is the frustrations and difficulties, he notes, that children encounter in their play that enable them to solve problems and connect their actions with more developed thought processes (Vygotsky, 1962, pp. 16-17). As an example, he cites the incident of a five-year-old child who was drawing a streetcar when his pencil broke. The child tried to draw the wheel by pressing down harder on the pencil, but no line appeared. He then discovered watercolors and saying, "It is broken," proceeded to paint a broken-down streetcar. As he drew, he muttered to himself about the changes in his picture. For Vygotsky, such play activity demonstrates how the child is able to put an end to one activity and begin to plan and direct another related task, thus moving to a higher level of thinking (p. 17).

In play, children are learning the rules of behavior and start to subordinate their own desires to these rules. Such subordination requires self-control and allows children to act in more sophisticated ways, reflecting future development rather than past experiences. Because play contains all "developmental tendencies in condensed form" (Vygotsky, 1978, p. 102), play creates the zone of proximal development that allows children to develop higher levels of thinking. Through play, children's interactions with their peers and adults determine the direction of this development, as the rules of behavior in the game are spelled out and agreed upon.

Other theorists have developed or expanded on the idea of hierarchies for play forms. Parten's (1971) classic study identified the following six stages of social play:

1. *Unoccupied behavior*. A child moves from one activity or situation, watching but not becoming involved.
2. *Onlooker*. A child watches other children play for long periods. Sometimes the child asks questions or makes suggestions, but does not become involved.
3. *Solitary play*. A child spends time playing alone with toys the child selects. The child does not seem interested in other children or their play.
4. *Parallel play*. The child enjoys playing with toys near another child. The child may build a block structure beside another child in the block area, but each child is involved with his or her own play.
5. *Associative play*. Children play with others, engaged in some activity. They may be playing in the housekeeping corner, cooking, or dressing up. They tend to exclude others in this and limit play to two or three others. The play progresses according to each child's wishes with little or no negotiation.
6. *Cooperative play*. Children organize their play, assigning roles, dividing responsibilities, and negotiating terms. Often one or two children dominate in this.

Parten sees such earlier stages as unoccupied behavior or solitary play as immature behavior and cooperative play as more developed behavior.

Smilansky (1968), from her studies with Israeli children, expanded the Piagetian cognitive stages of play to four progressive stages:

1. *Functional play*. In this type of play, children practice physical and language skills that allow them to explore the environment and lay a foundation for the next stage of development.
2. *Constructive play*. Children progress from manipulating objects and language to building and creating things.
3. *Dramatic play*. From constructive play, children progress to symbolic play, a part of dramatic play. During this period they engage in activi-

ties or use materials to represent the real world as they act out their needs and desires.

4. *Games with rules*. In this type of play, children learn to adapt to prearranged rules and to act in accordance with defined limits.

More recent research suggests that symbolic play and games with rules can be found in rudimentary form in infants and that solitary and parallel play may not necessarily be immature behavior. But this does not necessarily negate the hierarchies. There appears to be a difference in the quality of the type of play at different age levels (Krasnor & Pepler, 1980, pp. 89-90).

Ecological Theories

Ecological theories of play are concerned with the structure and conditions that differentiate children's play. Researchers in this field are interested in discovering how play settings and attributes affect children's behaviors. Some early research indicated that materials or activity type would affect children's attention span, interactions, and amount and type of conversation (Herron & Sutton-Smith, 1971, pp. 78-82).

For example, Parten (1971) noted that playhouse equipment, such as a toy store or refrigerator, elicited twice as many complex interactions as did clay, blocks, or sand. Bender (1978) indicated that by doubling the number of blocks in the play area, cooperative behavior in that area was greatly enhanced. Hartley, Frank, and Goldenson (1952) noted that dramatic play "reflects and encourages changes in attitude and adjustment and supplies a laboratory in which the child may experiment with possible solutions" (p. 54). McLoyd (1986) summarizes the research on the effects of different types of toys on children's pretend play. He notes that younger children need high-realism toys, such as dolls, trucks, or different animals, to support their pretend play, but as they mature children should be encouraged to use low-realism toys, such as blocks, blankets, and ladders, to extend the imagination.

Cultural and socioeconomic studies reveal that environmental factors do play a significant role in how children play. Smilansky & Shefatya (1990) noted from an analysis of cross-cultural research that level of parental educational background was a common factor that made a difference in children's ability at pretend play (p. 90). From their own work, these researchers found major socioeconomic differences in parental interactions with and attitudes toward their children's play. They found upper socioeconomic parents tended to buy toys for their educational value. They viewed play as important for emotional and cognitive development and would therefore join in their children's play, listening appropriately to their children's pretend conversations and offering assistance when their children requested it. These parents also encouraged and supported their children's desire to have friends come to play in their homes. Lower socioeconomic parents, on the other hand, tended to buy children's toys for fun with little or no attention given to any educational value the toys might have. These parents tended to distance themselves from their children's play and to discourage any play that involved children's interruptions of adult activity. Finally, other children were welcomed in their homes only for family-related activities (Smilansky & Shefatya, 1990, pp. 132-134).

Literacy has been enhanced by the types of materials, environmental designs, and interactions of children in a play environment. Neuman & Roskos (1992) noted that putting literacy materials in familiar play settings resulted in children using more challenging language interactions about literacy and enhancing the quality of their literacy-based play. Dyson (1990) notes that children's stories and drawings are richer and more elaborate when children have the opportunity to play and interact with peers as they engage in writing activities. Undoubtedly, children learn about the functions of print in literacy-enriched play environments, and such an environment provides teachers the means for assessing children's literacy growth (Vukelich, 1992).

Frost (1992) researched outdoor play environments and found that creative and open, well-equipped playgrounds with multipurpose materials support richer experiences in play than do playgrounds with less versatile equipment. And there are more social interactions, greater use of language, higher quality of dramatic and constructive play, and greater persistence and duration of play in these types of playgrounds.

Castle and Wilson (1992) found that children of different ages invent games in creative outdoor play environments. These inventions allow children to solve problems as they learn math, science, social studies, and greater language skills. For example, children learn about physics and math as they invent a game of who can keep a hoop rolling down a path the longest (Maxwell, 1983). They develop social studies concepts as they play in a special spot in the woods, reenacting a scene from a story they read that morning—how the Native Americans taught the Pilgrims to plant corn. Children figure out math concepts as they invent a game of sticks and stones, gathering these materials, laying them out on the pavement, trying to see who can get the "right" number of stones to match the sticks. Such play allows children to develop intellectual competence while playing primarily for pleasure.

Play as Education: Foundation for Curriculum

The relevance of play in children's lives is documented by theorists and researchers. They demonstrate that important cognitive, creative, and social learning takes place as children play. Dewey (1933) notes that work and play are not dichotomous but that human beings follow a continuum from drudgery to work to play to fooling around. He points out that neither drudgery nor fooling around can be maintained for a very long period of time if there is to be productive enterprise.

Children learn as they move between work and play. Some researchers maintain that meaningful learning occurs mainly in play situations or in situations where children transform nonplay situations into play (von Aufshnaiter & Schwedes, 1989). Balancing play with work, therefore, becomes an important framework for developing curriculum and learning environments for children. With an understanding of the theories and stages of children's play and the interaction of adults in this play, a teacher has the tools to use play as the basis for curriculum.

Although the stages of play overlap as early play behaviors continue in qualitatively different forms into adulthood, particular types of play are more prominent at a given period of life. Infants, toddlers, preschoolers, and primary-age children play differently. The infant's play is predominantly practice play, while the toddler begins manipulating objects and language during play. The preschooler's and kindergartner's play is dominated by symbolic play. (They move from sociodramatic play to taking on roles in dramatic presenta-

Children learn as they move between work and play.

tions.) Children in the primary grades, although still engaging in practice, *manipulative*, and symbolic play, find games with rules highly interesting.

Infants (Practice Play)

The infants' "curriculum" is their growing awareness of themselves and their environment. Infants' early play consists of a series of movements that they try out and repeat over and over again. This practice play helps infants to develop reflexes and also gain a sense of self and an increasing understanding of their environment. Infants' play and work are intertwined and consist of a wide range and variety of activities. At times, infants will merely look and watch; their eyes may follow an object or focus with intense interest on another object. They may focus attention on a person and then avert their attention from that person. By playing with focusing this way, babies may be discovering that they can control to some degree the amount of attention directed to them.

As infants move and encounter objects, they will playfully explore them. They explore their caregiver's body by touching, pulling, squeezing, or even biting. They will lie in their crib examining their hands or feet and eventually will examine their eyes, nose, and mouth in a mirror held by an adult. Babies will shake a rattle or bang it for the pleasure of the movement or hearing the sound. Also, they experiment with the sounds they can make. When they begin to imitate sounds they hear, adults may respond to the imitation, causing a playful interaction. Infants may imitate gestures even the day after they see them, which supports the idea that symbolic play has its roots in infancy (Meltzoff, 1985).

Although infants explore and play by themselves, it is adults or older siblings who extend or give meaning and direction for the children's development. Vygotsky (1978) says that a child first gestures and continues to gesture in a playful manner, but it is the parent who interprets the gesture as pointing out something and thus directs the action and gives it meaning. Infants' play has been found to be more rich and varied when adults structure, interpret, and redirect this play (Hughes, 1991, pp. 59-60).

This early play between an infant and caregiver may be the basis on which later social interactions in dramatic play rest. In simple games like peek-a-boo the baby is not only learning about object permanency but is also learning give-and-take interaction, an important beginning concept in learning games with rules. Practice play allows babies to gain knowledge of their environment and to understand their own capabilities. It prepares them for the next stage of development.

Adult-Infant Interactions

The baby's most intriguing plaything is probably a caring adult. The caregiver provides basic security, meeting the infant's needs as well as interacting and playing with the infant.

Productive early interactions result as infants react to adults' tones and facial expressions and as they respond to being held, rocked, and stroked. According to Garvey (1977), when an adult elicits a smile from a baby, social interaction has begun. A baby first smiles upon hearing a human voice and later responds to face and body movements in this way.

Playing with an infant provides opportunities for the child to use and coordinate eyes, hands, and ears. The baby is also able to interact socially with others. Variations of traditional body games like peek-a-boo and pat-a-cake are examples of games that promote coordination as well as social interaction.

"Find the toy" games are also enjoyable and productive when they are played in a way that matches the child's development. As the baby begins to grasp toys, place a toy nearby, and see if he or she will find it. Saying "take the rattle" provides the baby with the beginning of object identification. Later, encourage the baby to move it from one hand to the other. As the infant becomes more mobile, you can attach a string to the toy and encourage the baby to pull it toward herself or himself.

Other games include:

- Hiding a toy under a piece of paper or a sheet and encouraging the baby to find it
- Shaking a small bell or other object beside, over, or behind the baby so the baby will have to turn his or her head to find it
- Dropping an object that makes a sound on the floor so the baby will look to see where it went
- Placing sound-producing objects in a box and then opening it with surprise and delight to see what is there

Infants can observe how objects go together as well as discover whole-part relationships, so games where the infant and you build and take apart are important. Use stacking blocks, and after placing them inside each other, take them out. Turn them upside down and build with them, then take the tower apart. Put lids on and take them off various types of boxes, containers, and pots. As you dress the baby, tie and untie the shoes, take off and put on the shoe or the sock, or zip and unzip the baby's suit in a playful manner.

Toddlers (Manipulative Play)

The toddler's curriculum, like the infant's, is based on play. The toddler is playing and learning at the same time. Toddlers are still involved in some practice play as they continue to exercise emerging skills. Toddlers take joy in experimenting and practicing their new walking, climbing, and running skills. As their fine-motor skills develop, they can stack blocks and place objects in and out of containers.

Toddlers, however, extend this practice play to manipulative play. In manipulative play, children are creators who enjoy their own creations. They are involved in intense exploration of objects and their uses. They begin to arrange things on their own (O'Brien, 1983). Toddlers may stack objects vertically or horizontally and may begin to experiment with new language patterns and enjoy listening to the sounds they make. The basis for the toddlers' understanding of mathematics, science, social studies, and language concepts is developed in their play as they explore and examine their world by experimenting and manipulating. Symbolic play has its beginnings at this stage with simple parent-baby themes. The child gives dolls and stuffed animals a symbolic significance and gently cuddles or rocks them as if they were a baby.

Adult-Toddler Interactions

Toddlers are developing autonomy and need to do many activities by and for themselves. But they still need an adult to supervise them and their play. Sometimes the adults will play with the toddlers, while at others they'll just be there to provide security or to keep the play from getting unruly or unsafe.

As symbolic play develops, toddlers can benefit from playing with an adult. Toddlers are just beginning to attach symbolic representation to objects and may need an adult to model behaviors. For example, you could sit in the housekeeping area and with a toy cup and saucer pretend to drink a cup of tea with the child. As the child plays with the toy animals, you can pretend to make the sheep's baa sound or the cat's meow.

While permitting toddlers to explore and experiment for themselves, adults can help them extend their observations and experimentations with a question, a word, or new materials. For example, you might label what they are doing or comment on the color they use or the size of the object. You could tell them they have a lot of blocks or only a few. You might add wooden animals to the blocks. You must use sensitivity to balance your involvement with toddlers' play with the time they need to discover for themselves.

Toddlers begin to enjoy playing with others, although they tend to play alongside rather than with one another. Interactions in this type of play occur as the toddlers touch each other as they would a toy—reaching, grabbing, pushing, pulling, and even biting. When their peers protest, they learn that playing with others requires rules of behavior. Adults have a definite role in helping toddlers develop skills of social interaction. They should encourage the children to use words to say what they want instead of shoving or grabbing. They should acknowledge that it hurts to be hit or that it is hard to wait a long time for a turn.

Toddlers' curiosity is boundless. In order to encourage this curiosity, the curriculum for two- and three-year-olds should allow for the exploration of their environment. If a child is intrigued with a caterpillar that is crawling alongside the outdoor sandbox, observe it with the child, noting some of the insect's actions. It is important to follow the child's lead. Your interest will reinforce the child's involvement. Later you might read Leo Lionni's *Inch by Inch* helping the child to recall the caterpillar you both observed.

It is difficult for toddlers to sustain interest in one topic over long periods of time, but some child-care providers have developed themes around which to engage children in a variety of activities (LeeKeenan & Edwards, 1992). For example, water is a part of their everyday life. Children enjoy playing in water and observing it from many perspectives. They can pour water, drink it from different containers, wash themselves and their toys, and paint with it while watching their creations disappear. Your responsibility as teacher is to observe, comment at times, and vary the environment to extend the child's understanding.

Preschoolers and Kindergartners (Symbolic Play)

The preschooler's and kindergartner's primary occupation remains play. By now children have acquired many motor skills—walking, running, jumping, climbing. Children of this age also are refining gross-motor skills as they skip, hop, climb, balance, and tumble. Preschoolers are often interested in both open-ended and structured types of materials like puzzles that require them to refine motor skills and meet the demands of the materials.

These children continue to learn about their world as their manipulative play becomes more elaborate. They can build structures that represent a house, a farm, or a fire station. Their artistic creations have more detail and may portray an experience, feeling, or event (Truhon, 1983).

The third stage in play development, symbolic play, appears with increasing complexity in the preschooler's sociodramatic play. In symbolic play, an object, action, gesture, or verbal substitution is used to represent the real situation (Shugar, Gepner-Wiecko, & Zamecka, 1983). The child takes on roles, pretending to be someone or something else. Dramatic play features:

- An imitation of some action or verbalization
- A certain persistence to the play
- Gestures or verbal substitutions for either objects or actions and situations

For example, a child pretending to be a waitress might hold up one hand and make writing motions with another, as if she had a pad and pencil in her hand. Or in another situation, a child may say, "Pretend I'm the mother and I'm fixing lunch," yet no objects or gestures accompany the words. A child may actually imitate adult language and actions by turning to a doll, putting her hands on her hips, and exclaiming: "Now, honey, eat your veggies like a good girl."

Sociodramatic play encompasses the features of dramatic play but also involves social interaction and verbal communication. Two or more children are involved in the play situations. Verbal communication during sociodramatic play serves to maintain the play as children explain, negotiate, argue about, or command what the roles are to be. This speech is reality-oriented and is a mechanism for solving problems in the play situation.

In this make-believe play, preschoolers and kindergartners can expand their physical prowess. They learn to cope with their feelings as they act out being angry, sad, or worried in a situation they control (Jalongo, 1983). Pretend play allows them to "think out loud" about experiences charged with both pleasant and unpleasant feelings (Fein, 1985). They can try to change unpleasant situations into pleasant ones in a "what-if" play situation (Bretherton, 1984). While elaborating on reality and rearranging what they know of the world, children develop their creative ability. In play, children gradually sort out fantasy from reality. Also, by experimenting with the various roles of the people in their home, school, and community, they come into contact with the needs and wishes of others.

As children negotiate the roles they will play, they begin gradually to accommodate differing viewpoints. In one play episode, two children with different experiences have to resolve a father's role.

In play, children gradually sort out fantasy from reality.

Bob: "I'll be the daddy, and I'll fix the pancakes."
Susan: (Indignant) "Daddies don't do that!"
Bob: "Uh, huh! My daddy makes pancakes every Saturday morning."
Susan: (After some thought) "Well, we'll have to pretend it's Saturday, then."

Play also allows children to increase their knowledge of the world by doing. They need to continue exploring, testing out their environment, and perfecting skills by repeating activities they feel are important. One preschooler, intrigued with making a Thanksgiving turkey, asked if she could make another one. After the sixth turkey, she took off her apron and announced, "There, I'm done!" Perhaps she felt some need to practice, achieve mastery, and repeat the task until fully satisfied with her performance.

Adult-Child Interactions

Adults support children's play in many ways (Christie, 1982). Perhaps the most important element they provide is time. Preschoolers and kindergartners need large blocks of free activity time if they are to become totally involved in constructive and symbolic dramatic play.

In addition to time, they also need materials, well-arranged space, and a background of experiences from which to draw for their play. These experiences can come from field trips, stories, films, or observations of animals, insects, and people at home, work, and play.

It may be helpful at times to enter into children's play. Smilansky (1968) suggests the following ways for a teacher to enhance preschoolers' dramatic play.

1.   *Enter into the play as a participant.* If children are having difficulty extending a play sequence or reenacting some event, you might enter into the play briefly. The amount and type of interaction is determined by observing and listening attentively to the children. If children have started to reenact an experience in a restaurant, you might extend and enrich their play by saying, "I'll be the customer. Will you take my order?"

2.   *Enter into the play as an outside observer.* At times, you can offer children vocabulary as they play, such as saying, "This is called an order." Or you might extend their play from the outside with the use of a question, such as "What will you do now? Where do you get the coffee?" Suggestions ("Put the food here") or feedback ("You're an excellent waiter, you asked so many good questions") are other ways of fostering children's play.

3.   *Continue to structure the environment.* Provide new materials, equipment, and challenges by removing props and toys that are no longer used or of interest to the children and adding those that will enable them to continue their dramatic play (McLoyd, 1983). One teacher added a type-

writer, pencils, rubber stamp pads, and an old telephone to the housekeeping area, extending homemaking play to office play.

Johnson, Christie, and Yawkey (1987) discuss the advantages and disadvantages of teacher intervention in children's dramatic play. Intervention seems most beneficial for children who have not begun to play in the manner characteristic of sociodramatic play. For these children, suggesting certain actions as an outsider or modeling actions as a full participant seems helpful. Studies have indicated that children who are guided in that way have richer conversations, greater cognitive gains, and more opportunities to learn how to learn from adults (p. 36).

Too much intervention or poor timing, however, may result in children's stopping their play. They might continue their activity for a while to please an adult, but because the intrinsic motivation, the special quality of play, has ceased, the play loses its meaning and richness.

Primary-Age Children (Games with Rules)

Play continues to be important for children through the primary grades, although it changes in a number of important ways. During the primary years, children's play continues to involve perfecting physical skills. Important play activities include skating, bicycling, throwing and catching balls, and learning to play musical instruments.

Rules are increasingly a part of primary-age children's lives. Interest in rules and the ability to follow them seem to dominate their play. Children now enter into organized games with rules that are either physical or academic in nature. Board or card games interest these children. Creative or manipulative play results in products that often have a purpose and function and may have been created with rules in mind. Primary-age children's sociodramatic play becomes more formal and organized and is often based on rules that children make up as they go along.

Piaget (1962) believed that children's ability to play games is due to their increasing ability to decenter or to take the viewpoint of another into consideration, as well as their increasing ability to accept and understand rules. At around six or seven years of age, children can also plan their actions and strategies within the framework of rules, taking into consideration others' views and ideas. Physical games like "Duck, Duck, Goose," "King of the Mountain," "Mother, May I," and musical chairs are just a few games that require physical skills as well as learning to play with the constraints of rules and considering others.

Purchased or constructed board or card games offer children additional opportunities to play using rules. These games give children practice in the academic skills of counting, matching, reading, and solving problems. Bingo can be varied in a number of ways to emphasize recognition or recall skills, such as matching words with pictures, recognizing initial sounds, or recalling number facts. Board games can be as simple as Candyland, which reinforces color matching, or as complicated as Probe and Monopoly, which require strategy-forming skills.

Constructive, creative play for the primary-age child is also influenced by a growing concern for rules. Sometimes "rules" inhibit and constrain children's creativity. Children may believe they're unable to draw, construct, or build because their creations do not compete with the real model. Nevertheless, they now develop the ability to construct objects that have a function or use, such as a rabbit hutch; puppets and a puppet stage; or curtains and shelves for the dramatic play area. Constructive play also exhibits itself in such group projects as building a fort, rocket ship, police car, ship, airplane, or other large object.

Fantasy continues throughout the primary years in sociodramatic play. This play, however, is more formal and often takes the form of real drama. Often primary-age children will gather their own props and prepare an entire play. They may write a script and make costumes and scenery for their play or puppet show. At other times, their fantasy play is spontaneous and begins with improvisation. These play themes may last for weeks, with events and characters changing over time. Children might build a fort, set up housekeeping, or form rival clubs.

Adult-Child Interactions

Play in the primary classroom can yield valuable dividends because it appears to affect divergent thinking and problem-solving skills (Christie & Johnson, 1983, p. 112). Play is pleasurable, and for the primary-age child it can serve as a great motivator for learning. If children need skills and knowledge for success in play, they may be more motivated to learn facts and acquire skills. Manning and Sharp (1977) relate how two seven-year-old girls were unconcerned with their mistakes in figuring out measurement problems, but when it came to making a puppet theater, they were quite careful to be sure they measured the materials correctly. They realized that the theater would collapse if they miscalculated.

Play can also enhance the creative process. A playful attitude in dealing with curriculum content helps the child "draw upon previous knowledge, play with existing ideas, and relate them to new facts" (Lieberman, 1977, p. 131).

Butler (1989) and Verriour (1989) point out the value of drama to academic learning. Butler (1989) maintains that children in science classes who enacted drama presentations around the newly acquired scientific content integrate their knowledge and concepts of a particular topic with the objective world while interacting with their peers. They test out their values and attitudes against those of others and analyze social implications of scientific concepts.

In many classrooms children experiment with planting flowers, tend these plants, and compare results. As a culmination experience, a second-grade group developed a musical presentation of their planting. Some children were farmers and others the flowers, as they reenacted what they had discovered about how their plants grew best. Their discussions the rest of the year indicated that they had gained a deep appreciation of what plants need to grow.

When drama is a part of an academic activity, tension is heightened and children derive a deeper meaning of the concept. Verriour (1989) cites an incident where second and third graders reenacted two shipwrecked immigrants facing a harsh New England winter after a Native American had stolen their belongings. Heated discussion followed about ownership of personal belongings and of land stolen from the Indians. Children in such roles are not only discovering and inventing but they are also negotiating and sharing meaning related to scientific, linguistic, and social concepts (pp. 284-286).

The primary child's classroom tends to be more structured than that of younger children, and often mathematics, reading, science, and the other subjects are taught separately. Having interest centers is helpful in uniting these separate subjects. With interest centers, children can use play as a bridge for integrating the curriculum content areas. The centers offer equipment and props that children can use as they choose projects that will enhance academic skill learning. Barbour, Webster, & Drosdeck (1987) demonstrate how a sandbox was used in a primary classroom to become an integral part of the language arts curriculum.

Play in the centers becomes more focused and is likely to involve writing, mathematics, and reading. Children may plan, write, and perform a play. Or they may select an art project to illustrate a story from one of their reading lessons. The sand and water tables may be used to create different geographical areas or imaginary planets. Scientific concepts can be explored as children add buildings, streets, rivers, and bridges to the sand table or design industrial areas and farmlands.

Using projects and encouraging playful experimentation in the primary classroom requires careful planning and a firm grasp of your goals for the children. Play doesn't guarantee learning. Play and work are structured and integrated to achieve the program's goals and derive maximum benefits.

The Teacher's Role in Play

Children's play is naturally spontaneous, pleasurable, and nongoal-directed. But the teacher still has important roles in children's play as:

1. Observer
2. Planner or organizer
3. Supervisor
4. Evaluator

Observer

Through observation, teachers can understand the meaning play has for children. As you observe, reflect on the stages of development and types of play. Careful observation can help you determine if a child is having real difficulty with a problem and needs help or if the child is momentarily stuck and will be able to resolve the problem alone (Udin, 1983). Observation gives clues to a child's level of thinking. Teachers may be able to discover if toys or materials are beyond a particular child's ability or if a situation doesn't provide enough stimulation for thinking, socializing, or expanding motor skills. Teachers who do not take the time to observe children's play carefully often disrupt productive play or fail to give the guidance needed.

During free play, three-year-old Timmy had come to the table where children were cutting and pasting pieces of colored paper. He watched for a while, then picked up some scissors and a piece of construction paper and tried desperately to cut it. He yelled, "Hey, teacher, these scissors won't work." The teacher found him a new pair of scissors and then walked away, feeling her task was done. Timmy tried to cut the paper using both hands on the scissors. He then put the scissors in his right hand and whacked away at the paper. After a few moments of unsuccessfully trying to cut his paper, he dropped his scissors, frowned, and in a whiny voice said, "I'm done."

If the teacher had taken a moment to observe Timmy's struggle, she would have noticed his desire to use the scissors as well as his inability to do so. With a few suggestions or a bit of appropriate assistance on how to hold the scissors and paper, Timmy might have gained enough skill so that he could have pursued his activity with pleasure.

Planner or Organizer

The classroom setting needs to be organized so play can proceed naturally and without too much disruption. The variety, amount, and range of materials in each interest center should be carefully chosen. Too many materials can be distracting, but too few will not provide enough interest for a center to be useful. When play in a certain area comes to a standstill, determine which materials to remove and what new stimuli to add. For example, new colors added to the easel, or different-textured papers to paint on, can evoke new enthusiasm or insights into children's creative expression. Some materials, such as table games, dictate the process and manner of play; others, such as art materials, are open-ended and allow children to impose their own order (Wasserman, 1984).

Providing availability and storage of materials allows children to learn concepts of size, color, and shape as well as classifying and organizing. Haphazard arrangements will not allow the productive learning that happens as children find materials and later put them away in an orderly fashion.

When planning and organizing, it is also important to consider time. Some activities take more time than others. Children need to be free to spend as much or as little time as they wish with their chosen activity. If they're asked to move from center to center or to change activities every ten or fifteen minutes, they may not be able to become fully involved in their play. If they are required to select a particular center for a certain amount of time they may become bored, and behavior problems might occur as they use materials improperly or annoy others.

Children need to be free to spend as much or as little time as they wish in a center.

Supervisor

As you observe children's play, you also act as a supervisor. You should be available to recognize children, offer feedback, or give support with a nod or a smile. Occasionally it may be appropriate to make comments to support their play or keep it in bounds: "You stopped carefully at the intersection," "Keep the blocks here."

Individual needs should be considered as you supervise. You may help a shy child enter into play by saying, "Pretend you're the baker, and sell these cookies to them," or "Ask them if you can have the shovel." Perhaps you can even enter with the child into the group's play. Children who have trouble controlling their behaviors may need a different kind of help during play. You can, with a smile, a nod, or some other action, let them know you are firmly in control and ready to help them.

Continually checking your classroom's physical arrangement is also part of your job. You must be concerned with safety, always removing broken objects from play areas and clearing pathways. You should help to leave the housekeeping area in order so that other children will want to play there. You should check that table games and puzzles are returned to the shelves, blocks put back, and paintbrushes washed and returned to the easels.

Evaluator

While observing and supervising children's play, you should continually evaluate it. Because play is a primary learning mode for children, observing them as they play is a means of assessing their social, intellectual, emotional, and physical skills and growth. Some examples of questions to focus your observing are:

- Are children showing progress in relating with one another?
- Are they expressing joy, anger, jealousy, or fear in their play in ways that allow them to cope more effectively with their feelings?
- Do they run, skip, climb, and move with greater ability?
- Can they handle scissors, pencils, and tools more efficiently?
- Do they show increased knowledge about their world?
- Are they using language effectively?
- How do they solve problems?
- What new concepts do they seem to be exhibiting through their play?

The quality of play is also assessed. Some questions to ask are:

- Does the play seem rich in ideas?
- Is the play flexible and fluid?

- Do children find new ways of using their bodies or of expressing themselves in their art or language?
- Do shy children find ways of entering into dramatic play?
- Do aggressive children share ideas and cooperate in play?
- Can children sustain play episodes for longer periods of time?
- Do the play themes become more varied and complex?

Progress and growth in and through play vary for each child. In order to validate and assess growth through play, you can use a formal observation device such as the Transdisciplinary Play-Based Assessment (Linder, 1990), or you can keep charts for each child, noting growth in different curriculum areas or attainment of different skills.

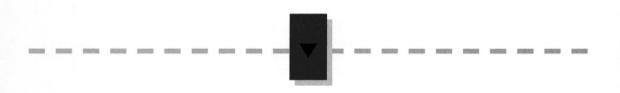

Summary

Play, as love, may defy description, yet there is no doubt that play is the integrator of the curriculum. The major portion of any school day is spent in play. Through play, children learn about themselves, others, and their world. Through play, they gain concepts from every curriculum area. There really is no other way for children to learn than through their play.

The idea that play is the integrator of the curriculum, if not the curriculum, stems from the first nursery schools, child-care programs, and kindergartens. From the very beginning of early childhood education, teachers learned to use the natural play activities of children to foster intellectual, social, physical, and emotional growth. Today we can document with solid research the power of children's play in promoting cognitive growth and learning.

Teachers have the responsibility of fostering productive play. Through their interactions with children, their use of observations of play,

how they plan, organize, and supervise children's play, teachers will be integrating important concepts into the total curriculum.

Projects

Continuing Case Study

Observe your child during a designated play time. Record the activity, the child's physical and emotional behavior, and the interaction (both social and language) that he or she has with other children. Note any teacher interaction. As you record your perceptions, note the developmental stage of play for your child. Compare your child's play with the textbook description of that developmental stage. From your observation, can you determine whether your child is involved in creative thinking, problem-solving, coping with tensions or anxieties, learning or practicing language, perfecting skills, or acquiring new understandings? What role, if any, does the teacher have in the above?

1. Read a fairy tale to a group of primary-age children. After reviewing the story with them and talking to them about setting and characters, suggest that some children might like to create a story setting in the sandbox. (It may be wise to set some guidelines for using the sandbox and have only two children at a time engage in the activity.) Record the children's play behavior, including their language, as they create the setting. What learning (if any) seems to be taking place? (You may want to review the role of the teacher as evaluator before doing the observation.)

2. Review the teacher's role as supervisor, as well as Smilansky's suggestions for teacher participation in children's play. As you observe children playing, take some steps at intervening. Note what happens to the children's play. Write your perceptions of what happened as a result of this interaction and your reactions to the results.

3. Observe a group of children in block play. Describe each child's behavior, including how he or she builds and interacts with others. Which types of play behavior as defined by Parten do you see children exhibiting?

4. Prepare materials for encouraging different types of dramatic play. Consider not only the different types of materials for the dramatic play area, but any rearrangement of space and motivating activity that might help.

5. Observe one child for a morning in a classroom of three-year-olds and one in a classroom of second graders. Record the activities and time that each child seems to play in each classroom, keeping in mind that play encompasses activities that are pleasurable, self-selected, and nongoal-directed. Compare the type of activity and the time involved in play. Does the play for each child observed reflect Smilansky's stages of play development?

Resources

The following are examples of the many books and pamphlets available to help teachers understand children's play as the basis for education. These books offer practical suggestions for fostering and guiding children's play.

Bergen, P. (1988). *Play as a medium for learning and development*. Portsmouth, NH: Heinemann.

Bloch, M., & Pellegrimi, A. D. (Eds.). (1989). *The ecological context of children's play*. Norwood, NJ: Ablex.

Curry, N. E. (1971). *Play: The child strives toward self-realization*. Washington, DC: National Association for the Education of Young Children.

Frost, J., & Sunderlin, S. (Eds.). (1985). *When children play*. Wheaton, MD: Association for Childhood Education International.

Goldberg, S. (1981). *Teaching with toys*. Ann Arbor, MI: University of Michigan Press.

Hirch, E. (Ed.). (1984). *The block book* (Rev. ed.). Washington, DC: National Association for the Education of Young Children.

Isenberg, J. P., & Jacobs, E. (1982). *Playthings as learning tools: A parents' guide*. New York: John Wiley.

Kamii, C., & DeVries, R. (1980). *Group games*. Washington, DC: National Association for the Education of Young Children.

Klugman, E., & Smilansky, S. (Eds.). (1990). *Children's play and learning*. New York: Teachers College Press.

McKee, J. S. (Ed.). (1986). *Play: Working partner of growth*. Wheaton, MD: Association for Childhood Education International.

McNanee, G. D. (1983). *The meaning and function of early childhood play*. Urbana, IL: ERIC Clearinghouse on Elementary and Early Childhood Education (ED 227 952).

Oppenheim, J. F. (1984). *Kids and play*. New York: Bettanline.

Sawyers, J. K., & Rogers, C. S. (1988). *Helping young children develop through play: A practical guide for parents, caregivers, and teachers*. Washington, DC: National Association for the Education for Young Children.

Singer, D. G., & Singer, J. L. (1990). *The house of make-believe: Play and the development of imagination*. Cambridge, MA: Harvard University Press.

Sponseller, D. B., David, J., Levadi, B. L., & Saaz von Hipple, C. (1981). *Your child and play.* Washington, DC: Government Printing Office.

References

Barbour, N., Webster, T. D., & Drosdeck, S. (1987). Sand: A resource for the language arts. *Young Children, 42*(2), 20-25.

Bender, J. (1978). Large hollow blocks: Relationship of quantity to block building behaviors. *Young Children, 33*(6), 17-23.

Bredekamp, S. (Ed.). (1987). *NAEYC position statement on developmentally appropriate practice in programs for 4- and 5-year-olds.* Washington, DC: National Association for the Education of Young Children.

Bretherton, I. (1984). Representing the social world in symbolic play: Reality and fantasy. In I. Bretherton (Ed.), *Symbolic play: The development of social understanding* (pp. 1-41). New York: Academic.

Butler, J. E. (1989). Science learning and drama processes. *Science Education, 73*(5), 569-579.

Castle, K., & Wilson, E. (1992). Creativity is alive in outdoor play! Children solve problems as they invent games. *Dimensions of Early Childhood, 68*(4), 11-14, 39-42.

Cheyne, J., & Rubin, K. H. (1983). Playful precursors of problem solving in preschoolers. *Developmental Psychology, 19*, 577-584.

Christie, J. R. (1982). Play training strategies. *Canadian Journal of Early Childhood Education, 2*, 47-52.

Christie, J. R. (1983). The effects of play tutoring on young children's cognitive performance. *Journal of Education Research, 53*, 93-115.

Christie, J. R. (1987). Play and story comprehension. A critique of recent research and training research. *Journal of Research and Development, 21*, 36-43

Christie, J. R., & Johnson, E. P. (1983). The role of play in a social-intellectual development. *Review of Educational Research, 53*(1), 93-115.

Dewey, J. (1913). Play. In P. Monroe (Ed.), *A cyclopedia of education.* New York: Dutton.

Dewey, J. (1933). *How we think.* Boston: Heath.

Dyson, A. H. (1990). Symbol makers, symbol weavers: How children link play, picture, and print. *Young Children, 45*(2), 50-58.

Elkind, D. (1987). *Miseducation.* New York: Alfred A. Knopf.

Ellis, M. J. (1973). *Why people play.* Englewood Cliffs, NJ: Prentice Hall.

Erikson, E. H. (1950). *Childhood and society.* New York: Norton.

Fein, G. G. (1985). The affective psychology of play. In C. C. Brown & A. W. Gottfried (Eds.), *Play interactions: The role of toys and parental involvement in children's development* (pp. 19-28). Skillman, NJ: Johnson & Johnson.

Frank, L. K. (1968). Play is valid. *Childhood Education, 44*(7), 434-450.

Frost, J. L. (1992). Reflections on research and practice in outdoor play environments. *Dimensions of Early Childhood, 68*(4), 6-10.

Garvey, C. (1977). *Play.* Cambridge, MA: Harvard University Press.

Genta, M. L., Constabile, A., & Bertacchini, P. A. (1983). Aggression, competition and play. *Eta Evolutiva, 15*, 5-14.

Gilmore, J. B. (1971). *Child's play.* New York: John Wiley.

Goodnow, J. (1977). *Children drawing.* Cambridge, MA: Harvard University Press.

Hartley, R. E., Frank, L. K., & Goldenson, R. M. (1952). *Understanding children's play.* New York: Columbia University Press.

Herron, R. E., & Sutton-Smith, B. (1971). *Child's play.* New York: John Wiley.

Hill, P. S. (1970). *Children and space.* Ottawa, Canada: Central Mortgage and Housing Corporation of the Federal Government Housing Agency.

Hughes, F. P. (1991). *Children, play, and development.* Boston: Allyn & Bacon.

Isenberg, J., & Quisenberry, N. L. (1988). Play: A necessity for all children. A position paper of the ACEI [Association for Childhood Education International]. *Childhood Education, 64*(3), 138-145.

Iverson, B. K. (1982). Play, creativity, and schools today. *Phi Delta Kappan, 63*(10), 693-694.

Jalongo, M. R. (1983). Promoting peer acceptance of the newly immigrated child. *Childhood Education, 69*(2), 117-124.

Jalongo, M. R. (1984). Imaginary companions in children's lives and literature. *Childhood Education, 60*(3), 166-172.

Jambor, T. (1990, June). *Why play is the fundamental right of the child.* Paper presented at the 11th annual world conference of the International Association for the Children's Right to Play, Tokyo, Japan. (ERIC Document Reproduction Service No. Ed 337 284)

Johnson, J. E., Christie, J. F., & Yawkey, T. D. (1987). *Play and early childhood development.* Glenview IL: Scott Foresman.

Kellog, R. (1970). *Analyzing children's art.* Palo Alto, CA: Mayfield.

Krasnor, L., & Pepler, D. (1980). The study of children's play: Some suggested future directions. In K. H. Rubin (Ed.), *Children's play: New directions for child development* (pp. 85-94). San Francisco: Jossey-Bass.

LeeKeenan, D., & Edwards, C. P. (1992). Using the project approach with toddlers. *Childhood Education, 47*(4), 31-36.

Levenstein, P. (1985). Mothers' interactive behavior in play sessions and children's educational achievement. In C. C. Brown & A. W. Gottfried (Eds.), *Play interactions: The role of toys and parental involvement in children's development* (pp. 160-165). Skillman, NJ: Johnson & Johnson.

Levy, J. (1978). *Play behavior.* New York: John Wiley.

Lieberman, J. N. (1977). *Playfulness: Its relationship to imagination and creativity.* New York: Academic.

Linder, T. (1990). *Transdisciplinary play-based assessment.* Baltimore, MD: Brookes Publishing.

Lionni, L. (1960). *Inch by inch.* New York: Astor-Honor.

Lystad, M. (1977). Adolescent image in American books for children: Then and now. *Children Today, 16*(10), 38-41.

Manning, K., & Sharp, A. (1977). *Structuring play in the early years of school.* London: Ward Lock Educational.

Maxwell, W. (1983). Games children play. *Educational Leadership, 40*(6), 38-42.

McLoyd, V. C. (1983). The effects of the structure of play objects on the pretend play of low-income preschool children. *Child Development, 54*, 626-635.

McLoyd, V. C. (1986). Scaffolds or shackles: The role of toys in preschool children's pretend play. In G. G. Fein & M. Rivkin (Eds.), *The young child at play. Reviews of research, vol. 4* (pp. 65-79). Washington, DC: National Association for the Education of Young Children.

Meltzoff, A. N. (1985). Immediate and deferred imitation in fourteen and twenty month old infants. *Child Development, 56*, 62-72.

Mitchell, E. D., & Mason, B. S. (1948). *The theory of play.* New York: Barnes.

Morrison, H., & Kuhn, K. (1983). Cognitive aspects of preschoolers peer imitation in a play situation. *Child Development, 54*, 1054-1063.

Moyer, J., Egerston, H., & Isenberg, J. (1987). The child-centered kindergarten. *Childhood Education, 63*(4), 235-242.

Neuman, S. B., & Roskos, K. (1992). Literacy objects as cultural tools: Effects on children's literacy behaviors in play. *Reading Research Quarterly, 27*(3), 203-223.

O'Brien, M. (1983). Sex-typed play of toddlers in a day care center. *Journal of Applied Developmental Psychology, 4*, 1-9.

Parten, M. B. (1971/1933). Social play among preschool children. In R. E. Herron & B. Sutton-Smith (Eds.), *Child's play* (pp. 83-95). New York: John Wiley.

Peller, L. E. (1971). Models of children's play. In R. E. Herron & B. Sutton-Smith (Eds.), *Child's play* (pp. 110-125). New York: John Wiley.

Pepler, D. (1986). Play and creativity. In G. G. Fein & M. Rivkin (Eds.), *The young child at play. Reviews of research, vol. 4* (pp. 143-155). Washington, DC: National Association for the Education of Young Children.

Perryman, L. C. (1962). Dramatic play and cognitive development. *The Journal of Nursery Education, 17*, 183-188.

Piaget, J. (1962). *Play, dreams and imitation in childhood.* New York: Norton.

Rogers, C. S., & Sawyers, J. K. (1988). *In the lives of children*. Washington, DC: National Association for the Education of Young Children.

Rousseau, J. J. (1947). *Emile ou l'education* [Emile or education]. In O. E. Fellows & N. L. Torrey (Eds.), *The age of enlightenment* (pp. 554-574). New York: Crofts. (Original work published in 1762)

Rubin, K. H. (1980). *Children's play: New directions for child development*. San Francisco: Jossey-Bass.

Rubin, K. H., Fein, G. G., & Vanderberg, B. (1983). Play. In P. Mussen & E. M. Hetherington (Eds.), *Handbook of child psychology, vol. 4. Socialization, personality and social development* (pp. 693-774). New York: John Wiley.

Rubin, K. H., & Howe, N. (1986). The social coordination of pretense in preschool children. In G. G. Fein & M. Rivkin (Eds.), *The young child at play. Reviews of research, vol. 4* (pp. 113-127). Washington, DC: National Association for the Education of Young Children.

Shugar, G. W., Gepner-Wiecko, K., & Zamecka, J. (1983). Speech variation and the realization of social roles by preschoolers. *Psychology: Bimonthly of the Polish Teachers Union, 25*, 386-397.

Singer, J. (1973). *The child's world of make believe*. New York: Academic.

Smilansky, S. (1968). *The effects of socio-dramatic play on disadvantaged preschool children*. New York: John Wiley.

Smilansky, S., Hagan, J., & Lewis, H. (1988). *Clay in the classroom: Helping children develop cognitive and affective skills for learning*. New York: Peter Long.

Smilansky, S., & Shefatya, L. (1990). *Facilitating play: A medium for promoting cognitive, socio-emotional, and academic development in young children*. Gaithersburg, MD: Psychosocial-Educational Publications.

Sutton-Smith, B. (1986). The spirit of play. In G. G. Fein & M. Rivkin (Eds.), *The young child at play. Reviews of research, vol. 4* (pp. 3-17). Washington, DC: National Association for the Education of Young Children.

Truhon, S. A. (1983). Playfulness, play and creativity. A pathoanalytic model. *Journal of Genetic Psychology, 143*, 19-28.

Tyler, B. (1976). Play. In C. Seefeldt (Ed.), *Curriculum for the preschool/primary child: A review of research* (pp. 225-249). Columbus OH: Merrill.

Udin, O. (1983). Imaginative play training as an intervention method with institutional preschool children. *British Journal of Educational Psychology, 53*, 32-39.

Verriour, P. (1989). "This is drama": The play beyond the play. *Language Arts, 66*(3), 276-286.

Von Aufshnaiter, S., & Scheweds, H. (1989). Play orientation in physics education. *Science Education, 73*(4), 476-479.

Vukelich, C. (1992). Play and assessment. Young children's knowledge of the functions of print. *Childhood Education, 68*(4), 202-213.

Vygotsky, L. S. (1962). *Thought and language*. Cambridge, MA: The MIT Press.

Vygotsky, L. S. (1978). *Mind in society. The development of higher psychological processes*. Cambridge, MA: Harvard University Press.

Wasserman, S. (1984). Promoting thinking in your classroom: Inconsistencies between means and ends. *Childhood Education, 60*(4), 229-234.

Wolfgang, C. H., & Wolfgang, M. E. (1992). *School for young children. Developmentally appropriate practices*. Boston: Allyn & Bacon.

9 The Language Arts

"First language learning is . . . a highly active, creative process rivaling the productions of the poet and artist in subtlety and originality."

(Slobin, 1966, p. 132)

After you read this chapter, you should be able to respond to the following questions:

1. What are the elements of language that young children acquire?

2. How do different theorists explain how children learn language?

3. What is the adult's role in fostering language in infants?

4. How would you respond to a toddler's curiosity about language, and how would you provide for prereading and prewriting opportunities?

5. What are the developmental factors that affect preschoolers' and kindergartners' progress in reading and writing? How do you integrate language arts experiences for preschoolers?

6. How would you describe the variety of speaking and listening activities for primary-age children? How would you describe the types of writing and both formal and informal activities that promote literacy skills?

7. What are the opposing views of how to teach children to read? Explain the differences.

Basic Levels of Language Learning

Humans use a variety of methods to communicate with one another. Verbal and written language forms are the most effective tools of communication. Through the development of these skills, children gain a deeper understanding of the complexity of their world. Language provides them with the means of understanding their role and significance in society. It becomes the major vehicle for expressing their wants and needs, for giving and getting information, and for expressing feelings and understanding of how others feel. It is also through language that children are controlled and learn to control others.

With little or no formal teaching, children of all cultures gradually acquire the means of communicating with significant others in their environment. Infants' differentiated crying, cooing, and verbal play, together with responses from linguistically competent others, are the beginnings of an interactive process in which children learn the five basic levels of language learning: *phonology* (sound system); *morphology* (rules regarding words); *syntax* (grammatical structure); *semantics* (meaning of words); and *pragmatics* (appropriate usage). By four or five years of age children, unless they are suffering from physical or emotional impairments, have learned to use the rules of their language environment effectively. Whether they speak the dominant language of the school that they enter or a dialect or another language, they have acquired the basic skills of language acquisition upon which to build further literacy skills.

Phonology (Sound System)

During the babbling stage, infants have the capacity to produce a wide range of sounds. The sounds babies produce gradually become closer to the sounds they hear in the adult language environment. As infants begin to put sounds together to make meaning, as in *mama, mik* (milk), or *baw* (ball), they are beginning to develop mastery over the phonetic system of their language.

By five years of age, many children have mastered most of the sounds of their language, although some children of seven or eight years of age are still struggling with the *r* or *l* sounds in clusters and say *pwease* for *please* or *cwy* for *cry* (Tompkins & Hoskisson, 1991, p. 21).

Morphology (Rules Governing Words)

As children begin to realize that combinations of sounds have meaning, they begin to learn new words. By eighteen months, children may have a vocabulary of twenty to fifty words, and by four years, they frequently are able to produce over 2,000 words. Even before entering school, children are beginning to understand morphemic rules. They can correctly make words plural and use the past tense of verbs. When children begin to over-generalize and say "sockez" for the plural of "socks" or "wented" instead of "went," it is evident that they have become aware of a rule and are not thinking of words that are plural or in the past tense as new and different. Although many of the rules for changing words are learned early, some are not acquired until six to ten years of age (Wood, 1976, p. 124).

Syntax (Grammatical Structure)

Children begin learning the syntax, or the grammar, of the language as soon as they begin to join words into sentences. They understand grammatical structure as soon as they understand multiple-word sentences. One toddler correctly brought his father's slippers when told to "go get Daddy's slippers." Another found her milk bottle in her crib when asked, "Where's your bottle?" The development of syntax proceeds through specific stages (Braine, 1963). As early as twelve to eighteen months of age, children use words in different grammatical functions. For example, they may say "mama" with different intonations meaning, "Here is Mama," "This is Mama's hat," or "The dog hurt Mama" (Bloom, 1976). At eighteen months, children speak in two-word sentences, and by two to three years of age, children can correctly use multiple words in different types of sentences: declarative (Daddy's home), negative (Daddy's not there), interrogative (Where is Daddy?), and imperative (Don't do that, Daddy!) (Menyuk, 1971, p. 103).

By five to seven, children are mastering the correct usage of pronouns, nouns and their modifiers (for example, this child, these children), and verb tenses. They use adverbial phrases, prepositional phrases, and conjunctions in correct sequence and form (Menyuk, 1969, p. 30). While this development seems impressive, complex structures of language may not be mastered until children are ten years of age (Kessel, 1970). Chomsky (1969) discovered that children still have trouble using and responding correctly to grammatical structure when terms like *promise, ask,* and *easy to see* are used.

Semantics (Meaning of Words)

While children learn the sounds and patterns of their language, they must also learn that words convey meaning depending on the context in which they are used. Semantic development is a long and complicated process, and it relates closely to the Piagetian stages of intellectual development. Wood describes the four stages of semantic development as: sentence dictionary, word dictionary-abridged, word dictionary-unabridged, and semantic dictionary (Wood, 1976).

At the sensorimotor stage, children at first use single words as if they were entire sentences. They form a sentence dictionary in which "meanings [are] tied to functions that words perform" (Wood, 1976, p. 150). For example, Chan, a young toddler, ran around the house looking for his daddy. He first said "Daddy?" meaning "Where is Daddy?" Then, looking in the bathroom and shaking his head, he said, "Daddy," meaning "Daddy's not in the shower"; finally, he went to the back door, opened it, and with hands on hips, yelled "Daddy!" meaning "Daddy, come here!"

Between two and seven, during the preoperational stage, children are forming "word dictionaries-abridged." Children are separating the words from the sentence and are attaching meanings to the words; the meanings are tied to concrete actions. A house, for one five-year-old, was "where Mommy, Daddy, my cat, and me live," and an apartment was "where Grandma lives with Pukey" (the canary). During this stage, children become aware that language is ambiguous in that terms may convey more than one meaning. They can deal with this ambiguity on the concrete level but not yet on the abstract. They can understand that a cold person could mean something other than that the person felt cold to the touch (Schickedanz, York, Stewart, & White, 1983).

From ages seven to eleven, children are at a concrete operational stage of thinking and are expanding their ability to discern meaning. Children are still tied to direct experiences and processes, but they are developing "word dictionaries-unabridged." A child at this stage understands the function of a house and may give it a definition as a place where you sleep, eat, and have your friends visit.

Pragmatics (Appropriate Usage)

Pragmatics is the ability to adapt one's speech patterns and word usage to differing social contexts (Bernstein, 1970; Sapir, 1929; Whorf, 1956). Children learn the rules of conversation from the communities in which they live (Heath, 1983; Labov, 1970; Tizard and Hughes, 1984; Vygotsky, 1962), but the specific rules of conversation and the way these rules are taught vary in different social and cultural milieus (Snow, 1989). The schools most children enter use the syntactic rules of Standard American English and the politeness rules of middle-class society.

Appropriate usage not only means that children must learn different word or grammatical usage but also that they must learn to whom they can speak, how they are to respond, under what circumstances they can speak and in what tone of voice, and which movements are appropriate (Ferrara, 1982). Learning the social conventions for proper usage starts early. Toddlers learn that certain intonation patterns, gestures, body movements, and persons involved in the conversation may signify different things even though the grammatical pattern may be the same. For example, when Josh wanted to be picked up, he raised his arms and demanded of his mother, "Mommy, up," placing an emphasis on the word "up." But earlier in the day, wanting to know if his mother was out of bed yet, he had asked, "Mommy up?" with his head cocked slightly as if listening, and using a rising inflection after the word "up."

By four years of age, children demonstrate amazing skill in using the proper conventions. Jalongo (1992) describes a group of children who changed roles frequently while at play. First one child was the teacher with an authoritative voice: "OK, children, . . .no gum chewing in school." Then she became the child in a submissive role: "Teacher, I have to go home now." Finally, she was a peer with equal status: "Let's pretend they are talking to each other." Body movement and tonal expressions rather accurately portrayed the "person" she was at any given moment in the play. The children in this brief play episode switched in and out of roles, at times in the same sentence (pp. 15–16).

Even fairly young children, as they move from one milieu to another, begin to learn that there are "proper" ways to say things depending on where they find themselves. One five-year-old announced to her friend who had just said, "I ain't goin' to the circus," "You aren't 'spose to say 'ain't' at school. You say, I'm going, I'm goin', I am goin'."

Another four-year-old, when corrected by his grandmother on how to express his need to use the bathroom, shook his head and said, "Oh, Grandma, I forget. I 'pee' at home but 'erinate' here."

The rules for social behavior can vary from one culture to another. Young children who have not had experiences changing milieus may have difficulty at first adjusting to the social rules of the school. In one classroom with children of many different ages, older children helped the teacher to communicate with new children not familiar with the school language and culture. Ms. D, a white teacher, wasn't successful in getting Philip, an African-American five-year-old just entering school, to join the other children in a circle. She first used a polite invitation to call all the children. When Philip didn't move, she said a more stern and specific command to Philip. Then, Greg, a seasoned African-American eight-year-old, raised his hand and asked quietly, "Do you want me to get him for you?" Upon receiving a polite "yes, thank you, Greg," he yelled to Philip, "Boy, get yo'r butt over here, yu' hear!" When Philip came immediately to sit beside Greg, Greg bent to him and continued, "When she say 'Boys and girls join me in the circle,' she mean come here. And when she say, *Philip*, it's time for circle! she mean get yo'r butt *here* (pats a spot beside himself) NOW!" Greg had learned not only the correct language patterns of the school but also the politeness rules. He first raised his hand and then asked permission to call Philip. Given permission, he used language and tonal patterns familiar to Philip. Greg was even skillful at switching between the two patterns in order to explain to Philip what the teachers' words meant.

Children like Philip and Greg can adapt and learn new speech patterns and word usage, but when the school-language expectations are too different from the minority-child's language learning patterns, respect for that child's language needs to be accompanied with help in learning new sets of rules for different contexts. Greg has learned to code switch, or use two language patterns in appropriate ways and at appropriate times. In the supportive environment of Ms. D's classroom, he helps others to adapt to the language and culture patterns of the school.

In most schools today, there are children from a variety of linguistic and cultural backgrounds whose phonology, syntax, semantics, and pragmatics are different from those of Standard American English, but who have indeed mastered the language rules of their own communities. It is important in schools that children's home language be respected while they hear and gradually learn Standard English.

Language learning is an ongoing process. The oral aspect and rule formation of the phonology, morphology, syntax, semantics, and pragmatics are learned early as children interact with significant adults in their environment. Some refinements and changes may take place as they progress in school, but new learning and refinements will be built on the basic language structures that children have learned much earlier in their own community of speakers.

How Children Learn Language

A great deal of research in language acquisition, from various fields of inquiry, has been conducted over the century. The richness of this research is apparent from the amount of knowledge available about when children acquire particular language skills. However, there still is debate about how language is acquired (Ingraham, 1989). Researchers from such various fields as education, psychology, ethnography, sociology, and linguistics have advanced different explanations.

No single theory explains the complicated process of language development. Many theorists have contributed to our overall understanding. Knowledge of the many different points of view can help as you interact with children and design a program to foster language growth.

The Nativist View

The nativist, or maturational, view is that children are "prewired" for language and that language is a process of normal maturation. Chomsky (1965), Lenneberg (1967), and McNeill (1966) are strong proponents of this theory.

Lenneberg (1967) maintains that language development is biologically determined and that its onset is regular and consistent with all children in all cultures. Chomsky (1965) explains children's ability to produce and understand novel sentences as an innate capacity. Children do not just repeat expressions they've learned, but they also test the rules they've formulated about their language. Children refine and generate a wide range of expressions from the particular sentences or expressions they hear.

McNeill (1966) believes children instinctively understand that there are basic structures or kernel sentences from which all other sentence types are generated. Through early hypothesizing and trial and error, children formulate the rules for transforming the basic structures into all sentence types.

The Behaviorist View

Behavioral theorists believe that significant others in children's lives model language behavior and reinforce children's responses through various reinforcing strategies until the responses resemble the model. According to Skinner (1957), language is a collection of verbal operants acquired through stimulus-response-reward conditioning and emitted as a function of various sorts of stimuli.

Habituated to the use of language, children recognize its use as a means of gaining control over their environment and of receiving constant reinforcement (Mowrer, 1960). The child's novel language behavior is "as though he had learned the rules" as a result of this generalized imitative repertoire (Peterson, 1971). Parents and teachers continually reinforce children by using language to control the environment, so children continue to become habituated to the language and learn its more complex structures (Staats, 1971).

The Interactionist/Constructivist View

In recent years greater emphasis has been placed on an interactionist/constructivist view stressing the social context of language development. The interactionist/constructivists acknowledge that certain functions of language are genetically determined, but maturational changes occur as children learn how to use language appropriately within their culture. Language and reasoning skills develop as children interact and respond to the language that is part of their environment. This interaction enables them to formulate rules for communicating in that environment. Vygotsky's (1962) and Piaget's (1955) views of language development reflect this theory. Both see language and thought as related developments that occur during different stages of development: sensorimotor, preoperational, concrete operations, and formal operations.

According to Piaget, language develops along with children's capacity for logical thought.

Piaget (1955) maintains that language develops along with the child's capacity for logical thought, judgment, and reasoning, and that language reflects these capacities. He notes that children have certain biological capacities for language learning, but as these internal structures grow and develop, children must interact with their environment and absorb these elements into their internal structure before the next stage takes place. Children need a language-rich environment in order to be able to construct the phonetic, morphemic, syntactic, and semantic rules of language. They also need to practice language in a variety of ways and for a variety of purposes.

According to Vygotsky (1962), children develop external speech, apart from thought, during the sensorimotor stage. Speech may accompany action, but it is not connected to an understanding of speech as communication. During the preoperational stage, this egocentric speech becomes inner speech, a sort of unconnected talk that one hears in one's head. At the same time, children become conscious that, through speech, they can communicate ideas and concepts. Vygotsky maintains that human consciousness develops through words. This awareness becomes apparent in children's language development as they become interested in learning the names of things and constantly ask to be informed.

Vygotsky places great emphasis on the adult role in this language development. He maintains that children develop their understanding of the rules and function of language from the adults who use that language in consistent and stable ways. In the beginning, children have vague notions of the meanings of adults' overt language even before they can say the words. These vague concepts or ideas come closer to adult meanings in a series of more complex ways (not unlike Piaget's stages) as the child interacts with the adult. During these stages, adults supply more context for concepts as children build and refine their own meaning. Although the children construct meaning, the adults determine the direction of their thinking process. "Verbal intercourse with adults becomes a powerful factor in the development of the child's concept" (Vygotsky, 1962, p. 69).

In the last two decades, ethnographic research on children's developing literacy (both oral and written) has added to our understanding of the sociocultural effect on language development. Some of the research has emphasized how the adult language environment can affect the more complex development of children's language and thus children's capacity for thought (Tizard, 1981).

Other researchers point out that children learn not only the structure of the language in a particular culture, but as they interact with parents and important people from their community, they also learn modes of communication and values related to differing literacy events (Heath, 1983; Teale, 1986). Different parental language styles, interactions, and values attached to reading and writing also affect children's literacy development (Bernstein, 1970; Elardo, Bradley, and Caldwell, 1977; Honig, 1982; Teale, 1986). Parental styles that include such characteristics as reading to children, mealtime conversations, role playing in pretend games, expanding children's language, engaging children in several verbal interchanges, responding to children's questions about reading and writing, and encouraging children's attempts at "pretend" writing and reading are related to children's more extensive use of oral and written language and problem-solving ability (Adams, 1990; Clay, 1991).

In addition, much research focuses on the interrelatedness of oral and written language development and on the importance of the social milieu—not only at home and in the community but also at school—in fostering that development (Hepler, 1991; Kantor, Miller, & Fernie, 1992).

Developing Goals

Broad goals for a language program will focus on increasing children's skills in listening, speaking, reading, and writing. It is neither advisable nor possible to separate the learning of one skill totally from the learning of another; however, at times you will focus more on one area of language than another. Four broad goals for the language arts curriculum may be developed: listening, speaking, reading, and writing.

Goal 1: Listening. Children will develop the ability to listen so they can make sense of their environment. They will be able to vary their listening strategies appropriately.

The National Council of Teachers of English has identified four types of listening: marginal, appreciative, attentive, and analytical (National Council of Teachers of English, 1954). When people listen as they perform other tasks, they are only marginally hearing what is being said or what is happening. People who listen for entertainment or pleasure can develop an appreciation for language and environmental sounds. People may listen carefully and attentively to gain information. Lastly, people may listen to figure out and analyze how what is happening or is being said will affect their own situation.

Goal 2: Speaking. Children will develop the ability to speak clearly, correctly, and distinctly so they can be understood at school, home, and in the larger community. They need experiences to help them make their needs and wants known, to give directions to others, to influence others, and to speak so as to interpret a story, a poem, and characters in a play.

Children need to learn that the manner in which they speak depends on the situation. Informal speech is appropriate with friends and family, but more precise speech is appropriate at school. Very clear and often formal speech is required in giving directions or a report. Speech used in interpreting dramas takes on different expressive qualities and intonations.

Goal 3: Writing. Children will develop the ability to write in an increasingly complex and precise manner in order to show appreciation, share information, request things, and give pleasure and amusement.

In children's early school and home environments, they need experiences in making marks on paper and in pretending to write. As these scribbles become more like letters, and the nonsense letters come closer to phonetic spellings, children discover that these marks have meaning. The first discovery is often their own name, and they become fascinated with the results, as did four-year-old Sammy, who spent an entire afternoon writing and rewriting his name when he discovered that SAM meant him.

From these beginnings, children learn the often difficult, but exciting, task of putting their words and thoughts on paper. They eventually learn that there are different purposes for writing and that the style of writing changes with the purpose.

Goal 4: Reading. Children will develop the ability to read increasingly difficult material and a variety of materials in order to gain and interpret information, follow directions, locate materials, and derive pleasure and enjoyment.

The young child first learns to gain information and interpret signs from the environment. It may be that children first notice changes in the faces of their caregivers and interpret their moods. They may notice the sky and know when they must wear a raincoat. Children also learn that pictures give meaning and that they can gain information and pleasure from them.

Children progress to understanding that what seems like scribbles have meaning. They will begin to understand that the person reading is getting words from those scribbles and that the sound ends when the print ends. In a print-rich environment, children learn to recognize letters and words and eventually become aware of the relationships of sounds to letters and words. Finally, they learn a system for figuring out the unknown parts of a passage and discover that they are reading and comprehending a new story. As they progress in reading, they learn to read different types of texts and establish different reasons for reading.

Providing Learning Opportunities

Even though children seem to learn language as naturally as they grow, the adults around them can foster this growth. Specific experiences within a language-rich environment can be planned to foster language growth.

Infants

Babies hear and respond to sounds in their environment, but all communication with infants isn't verbal. A great deal of language play goes on as infants are picked up, stroked, and receive eye-to-eye and cheek-to-cheek contact. Babies in turn touch, stroke, and pull at you as you interact nonverbally or talk with them.

When you bathe, feed, change, or dress infants, talk with them about what you are doing and call them by name. If they coo or babble, imitate these sounds. Babies will then imitate the sounds you make. Vary the sound slightly to see if the baby will imitate the new sound. Hum, sing, and recite nursery rhymes when you're around the baby.

Speech with an infant should be natural for you. Nevertheless, this speech will be altered somewhat by the use of shorter sentences and by speaking somewhat slower and using simpler terms. Low and Moely (1988) have found that children whose mothers changed the complexity of their speech, yet used adult labels and not baby talk, developed vocabulary earlier than other children.

Even though you're not speaking baby talk to infants, altering speech may be necessary. "It may be that children cannot learn to talk without [this]" (Schachter & Stage, 1982, p. 70).

As you feed the infant, talk about the food: "Oh, peas for lunch. . . ." "Open wide your little mouth, and *do* put it in." As you dress a baby, name and label the infant's actions and yours. "The head goes in first. Peek-a-boo!" "I can find your arm and then your other arm. Two arms."

Although the human voice is most important to the infant, babies also learn about their environment from other sounds they hear. As a baby stays awake longer, you can take the child to different rooms, outdoors, and even on trips.

When the baby starts to become aware of the sounds from the environment, you can reinforce them. For example, an infant may turn toward the ticking clock, and you can remark, "The clock makes a pretty sound—tick, tock." The infant may be startled if someone bangs the door. You may need to comfort the child by saying, "That was an awful bang." The sound of your voice is soothing and reassuring, and at the same time you have imitated the sounds the child hears in the environment.

Infants can also be introduced to literature. Their experiences with literature are out of the oral tradition. What baby doesn't delight in "This is the Way the Lady Rides," while being jounced on someone's knee, or doesn't giggle while being swung up high to the tune of "Dickery Dickery Dare"? The rhythmic flow of the English nursery rhyme "Rock-a-Bye Baby" or the Puerto Rican nursery rhyme "*Que linda manito*" (What a pretty hand) (Delacre, 1989) is soothing and calming and introduces children to the sounds and patterns of their language.

Infants are not too young to be exposed to books. The baby can be held in your lap and you can point to the pictures in a book. A nine- or ten-month-old may be able to point to the picture when you ask, "Where's the ball?" or "Where's the mommy?" If babies are exposed to books and pictures, by the time they are a year old they may be interested in turning the pages of the book themselves, even jabbering away in imitation of your reading.

There are excellent books made of sturdy cardboard with thick pages for the very young child. These usually portray everyday objects simply drawn and are very colorful. Examples are Tana Hoban's *What's That?* and a series of books by such authors as Dick Bruna, Helen Oxenburg, Jan Ormerod, and Rosemary Wells. Children enjoy looking at these books, patting them, and having an adult share the experiences with them.

Toddlers

Toddlers' curiosity about the world is boundless. To know about things is to name them, and children of this age demand words and labels for everything. Through this labeling, children are crystallizing their vague impressions of objects into firmer concepts (Cassirer, 1984; Taylor and Gelman, 1988). As toddlers' worlds expand, their vocabulary will increase rapidly. In an early childhood program, these children need many opportunities to solidify their concepts by engaging in listening, speaking, prereading, and prewriting activities with a concerned adult.

Speaking

Adult-child interactions include an adult who expands and elaborates on the language of the toddler and encourages speaking. Reinforcing the toddler's language and providing language models can extend vocabulary. When the toddler remarks, "Mommy gone," you might respond "Yes, mommy has gone, but she'll be back after your nap." Your reply extends the sentence the child has given. If the child notices the bunny in the classroom and says, "Bunny eat," you might respond, "Yes, the bunny is eating carrots. Do you eat carrots too?"

Children don't need to be with a constantly talking adult, but they do need interested people to notice what they are doing and to comment on it. You could comment on a picture a child has painted: "You used a lot of red paint," or "Let's see how many blocks you have on your tower," or "Your new shoes are the same color as mine."

Listening

As toddlers move about the environment, they can be encouraged to listen as well as talk. Beginning attending skills and critical listening skills are established by calling attention to and naming sounds both indoors and outdoors. The crunch of leaves, patter of rain, buzz of a bee, whistle of a teakettle, shout of a friend, or sound of footsteps on the stairs can all be used to foster listening skills.

Prereading

For toddlers, speaking, listening, reading, and writing are interrelated. Daily routines and activities provide them with "reading" opportunities. Pictures on cubbyholes can eventually help toddlers to find the place to put their belongings. As you play records, look at the title and read the name of the song. Some children may be able to pick out their favorite record by "reading" some distinctive mark on the cover. Covers of books become familiar if the story is read over and over, as do labels on food containers or other objects.

Books are enjoyed on a one-to-one basis or in small groups. You can plan at least one special story time each day. Introduce old favorites, folktales, and nursery rhymes as well as new books. Books selected for toddlers should have a simple text. Toddlers enjoy books that provide a feeling of security, such as Kay Chorao's *Baby's Lap Book*, Ruth Krauss's *Bundle Book*, or Margot Zemach's *Hush Little Baby*.

Other books that can help toddlers understand about themselves are Pat Hutchins' *Titch*, Ruth Krauss's *Carrot Seed*, and Anne Rockwell and Harlow Rockwell's *Can I Help?* Children's expanding language is stimulated by books such as Leo Lionni's *Little Blue and Little Yellow*, Nancy Carlstrom's *Jesse*

Bear, What Will You Wear? and Bruno Munari's *Who's There? Open the Door*. The world is full of experiences, and the toddler enjoys hearing that others may have similar experiences or feelings. Robert McClosky's *Blueberries for Sal*, Ezra Jack Keats's *Peter's Chair*, and Charlotte Zolotow's *William's Doll* delight children as they identify with the feelings of wanting a mother near, jealousy of a new baby, or wanting a special toy.

Toddlers should have access to some of the books because they often enjoy hearing the same story read over and over again. From being read to, children develop their own understandings of literacy, such as: books have a beginning, even if one holds them differently from the adult's way of holding them; one turns pages, moves one's head, and talks, then turns more pages until the last page of the book, when the cover is closed and the book is put away. When books are familiar enough, some toddlers may even begin to notice if a page is skipped or words are left out. They may begin to *pretend read* by copying the adult's gestures, turning pages, and speaking with a different intonation.

Poetry for the toddler may be recited rather than read. From the nursery rhymes and Mother Goose tales children hear the first of many stories that have a beginning, middle, and end. They delight in hearing what happened in "Humpty-Dumpty," "Little Jack Horner," "Hickory, Dickory, Dock," and "Jack and Jill." Daily experiences are enriched as poetry is recited while toddlers are involved in some activity. "One, two, buckle my shoe" or "There was a little girl who had a little curl," or "This is the way we brush our teeth" are introduced as children put on shoes, comb hair, or brush their teeth. Children may chime in or begin to repeat some of the phrases on their own, modifying the text.

Prewriting

Prewriting begins with fine-motor skill development. Providing children with many experiences to manipulate objects, touch and feel things, pick up beads, work switches, turn things, and operate locks is helpful in fostering small-muscle development. Pegboards, blocks, puzzles, and art materials offer children other means of developing fine-motor skills that will later be used for writing.

Toddlers are also interested in making marks on paper. Their scribbles with crayon, pencil, or magic markers are often accompanied by talk. These drawings are their first incursions into writing. The explanations they make or the labels they give these early marks are their beginning experiences with getting and giving meaning to symbols.

Although children may not become independent readers or writers until they are seven or eight years of age, informal and relaxed literacy experiences start early and lay the foundation for the enjoyment of reading and writing in later years.

Preschoolers and Kindergartners

Preschoolers' and kindergartners' language flourishes. They talk on and on about anything and everything, jumping from one topic to the next. Many will talk about an event saying "and then . . . and then . . . and then . . ." They delight in playing with language and will make up silly jingles, rhymes, and songs. Four- and especially five-year-olds use language correctly—making only a few pronunciation errors or pronoun and verb tense errors. They are beginning to use pencils and crayons in a more controlled fashion. A few may be able to write the letters of their name, and some are aware of sound-letter relationships and may recognize that the marks on a page give a message. Very few four- and five-year-olds are able actually to read.

Speaking and Listening to Each Other

Preschoolers and kindergartners are expanding vocabularies, using more elaborate sentence structure and refining the proper use of indefinite adjectives and pronouns. They are better able to participate in all four types of listening: marginal, appreciative, attentive, and analytical. The program for these children, therefore, permits opportunities for them to do a great deal of talking and listening.

Work in interest centers is conducive to conversations among small groups of children as they figure out how to build something, who will be the mother, or how they can work together. Adults continue to be resources for children's language and play by entering into the play at appropriate times or adding props if play is faltering.

Listening to and Discussing Literature

New and exciting worlds are opened to children through good literature. Kindergartners and preschoolers listen attentively to literature and are able to understand that other children have feelings similar to theirs. They are comforted to know that others can imagine the same or more horrible monsters than they do but that life is firmly planted in reality. They enjoy a wide range of books, but the books should be read more than once. New depths of understanding can be seen, and children can make the story truly their own after becoming familiar with it.

Choose a variety of books portraying people of all cultures and life-styles. Share with children the delightful books about African-American characters such as Lucille Clifton's *Everett Anderson's Nine Month Long*, Faith Ringgold's *Tar Beach*, and John Steptoe's *Daddy Is a Monster*. Hispanic characters are portrayed in Marie Hall Ets and A. Labastida's *Nine Days to Christmas* and Leo Politi's *Three Stalks of Corn*, and Asian characters in Taro Yashima's *The Village Tree* or Yoshiko Uchida's *The Rooster Who Understood Japanese*.

Books portraying Native Americans include Byrd Baylor's *Hawk, I'm Your Brother* and Paul Goble's *Death of the Iron Horse.*

Children also need exposure to books portraying imaginative, capable women, who can do any number of tasks, such as Margaret Mahy's *The Horrendous Hullabaloo*, Eve Merriam's *Boys and Girls. Girls and Boys*, and Natalie Babbitt's *Phoebe's Revolt.* "Ebonee," a delightful poem in Sharon Bell Mathis' *Red Dog. Football Poems. Blue Fly.*, extols the virtues of a female football player.

When reading to preschoolers and kindergartners, think about how you will present the story. You might read the title and ask them to guess what the story will be about. Or you could tell them the story is about someone like themselves who wants something very much. As you draw the children into the story, you are giving them a purpose for listening. After the story has been read, allow time for discussion. You could begin with one or two questions that recall parts of the story, but you also want to develop analytical, as well as attentive, listening skills. Help children translate the story into their own experiences and feelings with questions like "Which person did you like the best?" "How would you feel if you lost your tooth?" "What do you suppose Archie and Peter saw through the goggles?" If children have difficulty responding to your questions, model your own responses to the text. "I remember when I lost my first tooth, I put it right under my pillow" or "I don't know if I'd have been smart enough to wish on a feather if I lost my tooth, as Sal did."

Poetry continues in the lives of four- and five-year-olds, who enjoy and will recite a wide range of poetry. They like lyric poetry because of the special sounds or the imagery it brings to their everyday experiences.

Christina Rossetti's poems, such as *Who Has Seen the Wind?*, Mother Goose tales, and the humorous poetry of A. A. Milne, Edward Lear, Rachel Field, and Jack Prelutsky are all appropriate for children of this age. M. H. Arbuthnot and Shelton Root's *Time for Poetry* contains a collection of well-known poems for children of all ages. *Talking Like the Rain. A First Book of Poems* by X. J. and Dorothy Kennedy is a collection of poems for preschoolers and kindergartners and includes the work of many modern poets.

Finger plays are a type of poetry. Some finger plays are of limited literary quality, but others are appropriate because they are useful in teaching children language patterns or counting. Many Mother Goose rhymes as well as poetry of high literary quality can be introduced as finger plays, with children creating their own motions to go with the poem.

Introducing folk rhymes or poetry of different cultures allows children to share the special quality and rhythm of differing language patterns and gestures. Marc Brown's *Finger Rhymes* and *Hand Rhymes*, Barbara Michels and Bettye White's *Apples on a Stick: The Folklore of Black Children*, Isabel Schon's *Doña Blanca and Other Hispanic Nursery Rhymes and Games*, and Demi's *In the Eyes of the Cat: Japanese Poetry for All Seasons* are examples of such collections. Inviting parents to come to class and share folk stories, finger plays, songs, and nursery rhymes or poetry that have been a part of their culture ensures more accurate rhythmic and tonal expressions and increases the range of language experiences for all children.

Reading and Writing: Developmental Factors

The answer to the question the five-year-old asks in Miriam Cohen's story *When Will I Read?* depends on many factors.

Learning to read is not something that happens overnight. It takes place gradually in the context of total language experiences. Developmental factors may affect the learning process: physical, perceptual, cognitive, language, affective, and environmental/experiential. Having developed or not developed any one of these factors does not necessarily determine a child's ability to learn to read. Reading is a complex process, and the interrelatedness of the components seems to affect a child's progress in reading as much as anything.

Physical. A child who is in poor health and whose needs for proper nutrition and rest have not been met may have difficulty learning to read. Children who have hearing or visual impairments, or those with delayed speech or some other physical problem, may require special attention in learning to read and write.

The answer to the question "When will I learn to read?" depends on many factors.

Perceptual.   In order to read, it is necessary to associate the printed language with the spoken language. In order to write, it is necessary to translate oral sounds into graphic representations. These associations require the child to discriminate among letters and sounds. Although children may be able to see and hear without difficulty, they may have problems distinguishing similarities and differences in sounds and words. Some children may need practice focusing attention, attending to details, and developing observation skills.

Cognitive.   Reading and writing are cognitive processes, and such components as comprehension, problem-solving, and reasoning require intellectual capacities. Severely retarded people do not learn to read. A high IQ, however, is not a prerequisite for the process. At one time, it was determined that children should have a mental age of six and a half before being introduced to reading (Morphett & Washburne, 1931). Durkin (1966), summarizing other studies, suggests that the type of instruction is more important than the specific mental age.

Language.   Preschoolers are usually skillful users of oral language. Many have had experiences in drawing and labeling and talking about their drawings. This skill is important because it serves as the basis for children to understand the printed word. Some children will have less advanced language fluency because they may not have had the opportunities for speaking, listening, and drawing that other children have had. As these children become involved in the reading process, they may need more opportunities for dialogue with adults and peers regarding their in- and out-of-school experiences.

Affective.   Just as you consider children's physical well-being and cognitive development, you also should be concerned with their affective development. Children may be linguistically capable, intellectually ready, and physically capable—but still have difficulty adjusting to reading and writing. How children feel about themselves, school, and others can have an effect on their ability to learn to read.

Some children come to school believing that they can read and write because they know their favorite stories by heart or because their markings on paper have meaning for them. Teachers who prize and encourage these early attempts at literacy provide an important affective climate for children's progress toward reading and writing. Teachers who tell children by word or by deed that they are not reading the words correctly or not writing according to an adult's standard discourage too many children. Unfortunately these discouragements affect how children view their ability to master the steps toward literacy.

Environmental/Experiential Readiness.   In order to give meaning to children's early reading and writing experiences, it is important to provide pre-reading materials and prewriting experiences that match children's concepts. All children come to school with a variety of experiences. Some may have broader and more varied experiences than others, but all children's concepts can be extended through trips within the community, through books, films, and pictures that provide different cultural experiences, through cooking and sampling known and unknown foods, and through playing with new and old friends in blocks, in the housekeeping or dramatic play area, with sand and water, and at the woodworking bench. Special art, music, science, or social studies projects provide additional content from which they will learn new concepts.

Developing Literacy Skills

Important literacy skills are being developed in these preschool/kindergarten years: interest in reading and writing; recognition of the relationship of print to the oral rendering of that print; knowledge of the conventions of print and a beginning awareness of the terms that describe those conventions; concept of story.

Interest in Reading and Writing.   As children listen to stories and poems from the wide selection of good children's books, they begin to enjoy the special pleasure of sharing an experience with an imaginary character or discovering new information. Preschoolers' and kindergartners' developing interest in writing and reading is evident when they ask for special books to be reread, select a variety of books, experiment with writing, and are curious about the printed materials in their environment.

Recognition of the Relationship of Print to the Oral Rendering of That Print.   When children first hear stories, they do not realize that the print and the telling of the story go together. Often they believe that the story is from the pictures. Occasionally pointing to the text as you read and indicating where you start to read will help children grasp that the markings in the text are what you are reading, not the pictures. As children "pretend read" back to you and to each other, ask them to point to where they are reading. From stories read and reread, children become adept at "reading" the story, beginning at the top and turning the page at the correct words.

Knowledge of the Conventions of Print and a Beginning Awareness of the Terms That Describe Those Conventions.   From experiences with books and from following along during the rereading of dictated stories or Big Books, children learn the convention of the directionality of print: Reading starts at the top of a page, the left page is read before the right page, and reading starts from the left of the page and goes to the right. When you reach the end of the line, you move down a line but back to the left-hand side.

Further experiences in these conventions are provided as children watch you write their dictated stories. As you write, occasionally remark that a word needs a capital letter or a period is needed at the end of that thought. As you reread these stories with the children, move your hand along under the print in order to reinforce how the reading moves along.

Eventually children learn other conventions of print: that there is a relationship between sounds and letters, that several sounds make up a word, that spaces exist to separate words, that several words make up a thought or sentence, and that there are punctuation conventions to indicate different types of sentences. Kindergartners and preschoolers may become aware of only a few of these conventions, but in their various experiences with print, some of them will begin to sort out sound/letter relationships at the beginning and ending of words. Middle sounds are usually the last to be distinguished. Children will begin to point to words that begin with the same letters or sounds as their names. The difference between letter names and letter sounds can be confusing to children just learning the relationship between letters and sounds. It is important that you, as the teacher, are sure which you are talking about as you discuss letters with children.

As children dictate their special words or phrases to you, they should watch you write and spell the words. Have them trace the letters and talk with them about the parts of the words. For example, you might ask them if they recognize any letters or if the word has a beginning sound like one of their other key words. When they give a phrase, such as *pumpkin pie*, you might note that it is really two words and that there is a space between *pumpkin* and *pie*. They may note that the beginning of both words is the same or may be able to find all the *p*'s in the phrase. The discussion must be at each child's level of awareness and interest. From the discussion and from children's explorations in writing, be aware of the conventions that each child is discovering. Keeping notes on these discoveries will help you know how to proceed according to each child's interest and involvement. Children do not develop in the same way or at the same rate while learning these concepts. They need many experiences with the printed environment and many opportunities to ask questions, make hypotheses, and confirm their perceptions both with peers and with adults.

Concept of Story.   Applebee (1978, 1980) and Whaley (1981) have noted that many preschoolers and kindergartners have a sense of what makes a story. These children know that markers indicate the beginning and ending of a story, such as "once upon a time" and "the end." This concept is an important beginning in developing literacy, for children must come to understand that a written story has a different organization and structure than oral text (Halliday & Hasan, 1976).

Researchers have found that various ways of interacting with children increase their memory and concept of story. Several researchers maintain that children who have a sense of story are able to understand and remember details and events from the story much better than those who do not (Bower, Black, & Turner, 1979; Mandler & Johnson, 1977; and Rumelhart, 1978). You can help children acquire this essential insight by reading aloud to them from a wide range of good children's literature (Teale, 1984; Wells, 1985). Morrow (1985) has found that helping children retell stories by prompting their memory with such questions as "What happened next?" or "Did that happen first or last?" extend their comprehension. Children's comprehension can be further developed as you encourage them to read the same story with you several times, answering questions about any confusion over the story as you share a reading and retelling experience (Pappas & Brown, 1987).

Integrating the Language Arts into the Curriculum

During the preschool and kindergarten years, literacy events should be integrated into the entire curriculum. Children are laying important foundations for reading and writing as they are involved in the formal and informal activities of each day.

Formal *prereading* activities for four- and five-year-olds should be provided as you read stories and poetry to them. Time should be provided in the schedule to read to students individually or in small groups as well as in large groups. Children's favorite books should be read over and over again. Encourage them to read along with you. As they become familiar with the author's language and begin to say the words of the text as the pages are turned, they are taking the first steps toward literacy by pretending to read. Some of the stories and poetry may be copied onto large chart paper or selected from Big Books and read together as a class or privately, as in a "shared book experience" (Holdaway, 1979, 1984).

The best type of books to read for these shared experiences are those known as *predictable stories.* These books offer clear, repetitive story patterns, have repetitions of lyrical language, or have familiar sequences, such as counting or the days of the week. The concepts and themes are those familiar to young children. Folktales like "The Three Bears" and "The House That Jack Built," storybooks like Pat Hutchins' *The Doorbell Rang* and Larry Brimmer's *Country Bear's Good Neighbor*, and counting books like Eric Carle's *The Very Hungry Caterpillar* and Molly Bang's *Ten, Nine, Eight* are examples of predictable books.

Informal prereading takes place throughout the curriculum in such activities as "reading" one's favorite story to a peer or to a favorite doll; "reading" along with a taped story; "reading" recipes for cooking, labels and signs in dramatic play activities, directions for an art or woodworking project; and "reading pictures or signs" to find out where to put things or whose job it is to clean up.

Formal or informal reading activities may also be conducted as children "read" their own or another's dictated key words or stories (Ashton-Warner, 1986; Johnson, 1987; Veatch, 1979).

The writing process evolves during the preschool and kindergarten years as well. Researchers maintain that drawing is a part of the writing strategy (Baghban, 1984; Dyson, 1986; Graves, 1983). As children draw, they create imaginary worlds, often labeling and talking about their drawings as part of the creative process. Students' formal writing activities may be copying of labels or the story dictated from their drawings. Informal activities take place as they "pretend write" a grocery list for shopping, a note to leave for their mother, a letter to send by post, or the steps for making popcorn.

Children's early writings move through scribblings and attempts at making letters to attempts at matching letters to the sounds they hear in the words or phrases. They are also developing concepts about their own writings. Clay (1991) points out that children first make marks or scribbles for the enjoyment of seeing these marks on paper. Later children develop the concept that these marks have meaning even though they cannot decipher them. At this stage, it is not uncommon for a child to bring these scribblings to an adult and ask the adult to read it. If the adult responds by asking the child what he or she has written, the child is likely to say "I don't know, I can't read." In the final scribbling stage, children become aware that they can "write" a message and "read" it for a friend or an adult. These concepts are important steps before the child moves on to writing strings of letters and matching letters to sounds.

Then students should be given many opportunities to write using their own inventions for making letters and for spelling. As their fine-motor skills become better developed, their letters will be better formed. As they become more aware of conventional print, their spelling will come closer to conventional spelling (Bissex, 1980; Temple, Nathan, & Burris, 1982). In the process of writing children reveal their awareness of sound/letter relationships as well as their understanding of the conventions of print.

Discussion is an integral part of both the reading and the writing processes. As students share a book or read each other's *invented spellings,* they challenge the assumptions that each has made about the print. Throne (1988) points out the intense involvement children sustain as they discover how the written language works.

Although some children may appear to learn the reading and writing process naturally and move smoothly through each of the stages, not all children will (Hayes, 1990). As you surround children with books and prints, you also are an active writer, reader, and discussant—modeling how letters are made, pointing out where the message is, and discussing how you make letters or make sense of a text. You must become observant of the children who are grasping the concepts about print and those who do not seem to be progressing as well. The children who are moving more slowly may need you to work with them more directly in talking and pointing out the elements of the written text.

Setting the Environment

Children in preschool and kindergarten settings need a print-rich environment. The books that are available should be selected from the excellent offerings in children's literature. Print that is functional and gives messages to children should be on the bulletin boards, chalkboards, and in play areas. Children's own messages, labels, lists, and beginning writings should be part of these postings. Writing and art centers should contain a variety of papers, pencils, crayons, paintbrushes, and magic markers. Four- and five-year-olds do not need formal phonics lessons or formal lessons in writing letters, but they do need time and opportunity to discover what makes reading and writing work.

Listening and speaking become a part of the reading and writing process when schedules and space are organized to permit different kinds of interaction.

Schedules should be arranged so that there are several short periods of time in the day for such formal group activities as listening to stories; reading poems, stories, or directions for making things; discussing events; and writing experiences, stories, lists, or class letters. Large blocks of time should be scheduled for informal activities in which children can explore personal literacy activities that may have been prompted by a group activity or by dramatic play, science experiments, block play, cooking experiences,

Listening is a part of the reading and writing program.

listening to tapes, or painting. Classroom space must be organized so that children can come together as a group, but there should be smaller spaces for sharing learning with one or more peers or with an adult and space to work quietly alone.

Primary-Age Children

Six-, seven-, and eight-year-olds have good control over their language. For the most part, they can articulate well and are able to give directions, be critical, and use language creatively. In these years children are acquiring much larger vocabularies, new meanings for words, and more complex thought and language structure. As children develop and expand literacy skills, the language arts curriculum should provide purposeful and functional activities that reflect the interdependence of listening, speaking, writing, and reading skills.

Listening and Speaking

In the primary years, children can develop their abilities to:

- Listen attentively for longer periods
- Follow a topic and contribute ideas to that topic
- Gain information and share understandings
- Be critical of what they hear and express reasons for their criticism
- Appreciate creative language expression

Opportunities for children to express themselves should be created in the classroom. A variety of strategies and questioning techniques can foster children's speaking and listening skills. It may be helpful to wait a few moments to allow children time to think of their responses. You can encourage children to expand on their responses. For example, if, during a discussion of a story, children respond "bad" to the question "How would you feel if someone did that to you?" you can extend their thinking, vocabulary, and language structure by asking "What other words can you use to express *bad?* Can you say how you would feel with two or three words?" or "How would you finish the sentence: I would feel so bad I . . . ?"

Group Discussions.   In group discussion, you can encourage children to listen to one another, to keep to the topic, and to ask each other questions. The topic for discussion should be clear, perhaps announced or decided upon ahead of time so children can "research" or think about the ideas they wish to share. You shouldn't expect children automatically to keep to the topic; adults do not. At first allow some diversions, and as children become better able to express themselves, work toward keeping the children on the subject. Encourage them to ask each other questions. These can be used to extend or clarify the original statement. Young children's questions can become repetitive. If this happens, model new types of questions and encourage children to use other types.

Full group, as well as small group, discussion times are possible. One first-grade teacher structured his science activities to include small group discussions. He first did demonstrations with the whole class, for example, planting seeds and stating hypotheses about their growth. In groups of three or four, children were to carry out the procedure for planting, set up their experimental conditions, and make their recording charts.

Informal talk was required, and children were encouraged to keep this talk related to the task. When a group had finished setting up an experiment, the children in it were expected to examine books about seeds and growing things. The children were encouraged to share what they had discovered in their books and to ask each other questions. The teacher circulated, helping, listening, and joining in as appropriate. The small groups then reported to the total group the results of their experiments as well as discoveries from their reading.

Dramatics.   Reading, writing, speaking, and listening are all language arts skills used and applied as primary-age children become involved in dramatic activities. Children will learn lines from predetermined stories, plays, or poems and will interpret dialogue and action. They may create their own dramas as productions to present to the class, to others in the school, and to parents.

Television.   Because most children watch a great deal of television, you can use this medium for developing listening and speaking skills. Use children's home viewing as the focus of discussions. You could ask them to compare programs or discuss different television characters and how real they are. Characters on one show can be compared with those on another.

Older children might discuss how a character like Superman changes before one's eyes, which can lead into an exploration of television's techniques for creating fantasy. Or you could ask children to listen carefully to an advertisement for one of their favorite products and then have them compare the real product with the advertisement's claims.

Other children might note the adjectives or verbs used in a particular advertisement or some of the expressions of a television character. Both younger and older children can retell the events of a particular show or describe the setting of a program. If programs are taped, it is easier to control and schedule viewing so all children can have a common experience. Parts of a tape can be viewed to check initial conclusions.

Projects.   Craft, cooking, social studies, and science projects all provide children with opportunities for extending their listening and speaking skills. As projects are completed, children can share them with a small group or the total class. You can show children how to make a presentation interesting and to the point. One first-grade team role played making pretzels. Children became bowls, ingredients, rolling pins, and twisted pretzels as a narrator told the story.

Writing

Writing in the primary grades is a continuation of the preschool and kindergarten experiences. From early writing experiences—drawing, list-making, labeling, experience stories, and compositions with invented spellings—children progress to writing more complex texts. Britton (1970) has identified three functional categories of writing: *expressive, poetic,* and *transactional.*

Expressive writing is the way children usually begin their first experiments with writing. They write about themselves, their actions, their feelings, and their ideas.

Poetic writing begins as children become aware of the conventions of stories and poetry. They begin to use some literary elements in their writing. They write about the princess or the wise man who occupied the castle. The castle might be in the forest or beside a lake. They will have become aware that there are three parts in storytelling: a clear opening statement, for example, "One time there was this big volcano"; a series of events; and a resolution, with an ending like "They all lived happily ever after," or even "They all sat down to lunch." Thus, children are beginning to recognize that stories have characters, a setting, and a plot. As they become more aware of the rhyme and rhythm of poetic language, their own attempts at writing will be to make their story sound more "like book words."

Transactional writing is the expository writing of explanations, arguments, instructions, and persuasions. It can be quite a challenge for children to share in writing information about different breeds of dogs or to persuade others by means of the school newspaper that the schoolyard should be kept clean. Yet children in the primary years can learn the different types of writing, or these various "voices." Their first efforts may not be clearly in one category, but as they gain experience and share their writing with others, they will become more skilled in writing for different purposes (Salinger, 1988).

Writing should be an integral part of the total curriculum. You may have a writing center, but that should be the place where writing materials are stored for easy access. Dictionaries, all kinds of paper and writing implements, and children's work folders may be kept there. You will want to plan writing as part of children's daily experiences, both informal and formal.

Informal Activities.   A variety of writing materials should be available to children in various places in the classroom. Children should be encouraged to draw/write ideas even when they are involved in other work activities or in play. Messages can be written, lists can be made, labels can be attached to projects, newly discovered words can be jotted in notebooks. You need to model such writing and spontaneously respond to children's attempts at extending their writing competencies. Children should come to view writing as a natural means of communication.

During these informal times, you should not make any judgments about form or substance because children need some opportunities to practice and experiment with written language without the imposition of adult standards. As children gain confidence in their ability to use writing as a means of communication, you can devise more formal types of instruction to encourage them to attend to the mechanics of writing.

Messages.   Questions on the chalkboard or at various work areas in the room can encourage children to write comments and responses. The message may be a question encouraging them to puzzle something out, for example, estimating: "How may blocks will fit along this line?" Children could write their guess with a signature beside it. Older children could write how they came to guess that number. As children gain confidence about spelling and simple punctuation, a message might be written with deliberate errors asking, "Who can correct THIS?" A note to complement group projects might read, "How did you get the light to turn on?" A reminder that classroom jobs need doing could say, "The fish need to be fed today. Write and tell me who fed them and how much was given to the fish."

A message center could be established in the classroom where children could leave notes for each other. If there is a parent bulletin board in your room, you could encourage children to leave a note for a parent or caregiver there. It might be important to establish how long a note should stay up.

Lists.   As children plan special events, projects, or assignments, you can have them make lists to practice the mechanics of writing and to help them organize their ideas. The list of groceries to buy for the soup-making event will ensure that nothing is forgotten. Lists of people and their assignments for a project could keep the project moving. Ideas for building a rocket ship could serve as a reminder of what needs doing next. You could encourage children to make lists of things they need to bring from home the next day or questions to ask or important things to tell their parents. One second-grade teacher asked children to watch the moon rise each night for two weeks and draw what they saw, noting the position in the sky and the time when they looked. The drawings served as a graphic reminder of the changes that were occurring. Their informal jottings were the basis for informal and formal discussions during the two-week period.

Labels.   As children draw, create, or make materials during work or recess time, different sizes and shapes of stiff paper need to be available for making labels. The post office needs letter boxes with names on them. The village will need street signs. Labels on the geographic representations in the sandbox will identify the rivers, the peninsula, and the harbor. Creative titles for painting or wood and clay sculptures can be attached to children's work for display or simply to be put on a shelf to be found again before taking home.

Newly Discovered Words. Encourage children to jot down words whose sounds they like. Each student may have to keep a small notebook handy. They may choose words that they read, hear people say, or see or hear on television. You may need some occasional reinforcing activities to encourage the habit. One teacher had a "stump the teacher" day. Third-graders would write a word on the chalkboard from their list in hopes of having discovered a word the teacher did not know. The child writing the word had to spell it correctly and know its meaning and how to use it. Often a search in the dictionary was necessary to affirm the authenticity of the word. For more common words children can pantomime or draw and have others guess their special word.

During a more relaxed time, children can share a special word and explain where they found it and why they like it. The students' notebooks should be handy as they do their formal writing. By looking at it, they may get ideas or find a more descriptive word for their stories. Children should be encouraged to share lists.

Through such informal writing, children begin to develop a habit of extending their thoughts through writing.

Formal Activities. Students' experiences in formal writing allow them to learn that journals, stories, and expository writing use different styles. The mechanics of writing are important, but they should be taught in context and not as a separate subskill. You can help children develop their writing through individual teacher-child conferences and through peer conferences in which two children work together.

Journal Writing. Journal writing extends children's expressive language by letting them experiment in explaining what they have done, how they feel about it, and what new ideas they have. You may want to respond to what they write about. It is important, though, that you take the time to read the journals and respond to their experiences. Responses should be positive, and you should pose questions or reflect on their thoughts. Do not make comments on the mechanics of writing. Children should feel free in journal writing.

Writing Stories. Students' story writing gives opportunities for them to use their imagination. From their early experiences of hearing stories, children begin to develop an ear for the lyrical quality of language as well as a concept of story patterns. In many ways, you can help students' development.

It is important to read good literature to children several times a week. Hearing rich and vivid language will expand their knowledge of words.

Some teachers have found that using story starters helps children break the barrier of writing the first sentence. Other teachers have found that, after reading several opening sentences from well-known children's books, students may use the opening of a favorite story to begin their story. As they gain confidence, however, they begin to use their own creations. When students write daily, you may want to encourage them to focus on a particular part of the story, such as characters, plot, or setting. After reading passages describing settings from several different authors, you might ask children to experiment with writing more detailed settings. As you read stories that have a similar plot structure, ask children to plan stories that follow that pattern. Children can also try to write character descriptions that clarify not only a physical appearance but also a personality.

Expository Writing.   Children should write nonnarrative texts for many reasons. You might start by having them write a report of a trip or a special event and read it to you, the parents, the principal, or another teacher. As children progress, social studies and science can serve as the basis for a topic for which they become the expert. Remember that children need some guidance and choices in this type of study and reporting. Children can decide what they want to find out and how they want to represent what they have learned. You may need to help them sort through materials, discover the important points, and find ways to note the points they want to discuss. When children have their own ideas about how they want to proceed, it is wise to allow them to experiment with their strategies. Later, discuss with the entire group their successes and difficulties. Explore ways they might do things differently next time.

Mechanics of Writing.   The first and most essential objectives for beginning any writing are getting ideas to flow and putting those ideas in writing. The mechanics of writing come later. Children master the mechanics of writing as they learn to revise and rewrite ideas and correct syntax. It is not always easy to convince primary-age children of the importance of rewriting and revision. As children recognize themselves as writers, they need to realize that writing is a process of planning, writing a draft, and revising, sometimes several times before the final version is ready for the public. Children can be helped in this process by the notion of publishing their final draft as a book, for the school bulletin board, or for the school newspaper. You can use both teacher-child conferences and peer conferences in helping children do these rewrites.

Teacher-Child Conferences.   It is important that you establish a routine in the classroom so that each child has a private time with you for conferences. Daily conferences for each child are not necessary, but two or three a week can help to keep students' interest high. Conferences should follow some sort of routine and have a clear purpose; they should change as children develop greater skills (Graves, 1983; Johnson, 1987).

In conferences, students share their writing with you, and you ask questions and make comments to extend their thoughts. In the early stages of writing, you should ask about any misspellings and incorrect grammar or punctuation only when the writing does not communicate students' meaning. As children practice writing and try out the phonetic spellings of words, their spelling and punctuation should improve. Some teachers have found that encouraging children to underline words they are not sure are spelled correctly permits them to reread their writing and do some critical assessment before the conference. As good rapport and enjoyment of writing develop, students can be challenged to improve spelling, punctuation, and handwriting skills for the purpose of presenting their writing for publication.

Peer Conferences.   In the primary grades peer conferences must be handled with care. You may want the first peer groups to consist of two compatible students who share their ideas for stories or reports in "prewrite sessions." Later you can redirect these experiences by changing the focus from one in which children just share ideas to encouraging one child to share ideas and the other to question or challenge them. Use peers to extend thinking. In these dialogues, students are developing important negotiating skills that help them to think, reconsider, and defend their ideas. As the comfort level of sharing with a partner increases, students can be encouraged to share what they have written. For primary-age children, it may be wise for you to establish a beginning protocol of things to be checked by the partner, for example:

- One thing I liked in the story and why.
- Something I didn't understand in the story.
- Words I couldn't read.
- Are all the punctuation marks in place?

It may be wise to model the procedure and questions to be asked by partners. Group discussions about things that are helpful and not helpful in the peer conferences can lead to changing the protocols. In productive peer conferences, children are learning to improve all language arts skills: listening, speaking, reading, and writing.

Reading

The primary purpose of learning to read is to be able to comprehend a variety of written messages. During the primary years, children's comprehension grows as they learn how and where to get different types of information, how to read texts that have a specialized vocabulary, how to read more complicated directions, and how to read in order to expand personal pleasure. In this process children also extend their knowledge and understanding of *cue systems:* graphophonic cues (letter/sound relationships), syntactic cues (order and patterns of words), and semantic cues (how words are used for meaning). During this century, there has been a lot of controversy about the best way to teach reading. Yet in spite of vast amounts of research, no definitive means has been found (Barbour, 1992). The present controversy presents two opposing views of how children learn to read. One perspective maintains that children must first learn the *subskills* of the linguistic system by progressing from letters and the sounds these letters make, to figuring out words from the sounds of the letters, to making sense of these words in sentences. As they learn these subskills, they are expected to develop comprehension skills. Phonic rules assist the children in acquiring these subskills.

The *whole language philosophy* (sometimes referred to as emergent literacy or literature-based approach) is a belief that children learn to read and write in the same natural way that they learn to walk and talk (Smith, 1992).

Goodman, Smith, Meredith, and Goodman (1987) point out that reading is a constructive process and that children get meaning from symbols in context by using inferring, predicting, confirming, and correcting strategies. Linguistic principles are not learned as isolated units but are learned as children use these strategies to figure out and construct the meaning of any given text. Adults and older children in a print-rich environment provide models and facilitate the process. Teachers at some point "hand each child over to authors" (Smith, 1992, p. 435). The child learns to read as more skilled readers read with the child and then children themselves begin to "read" familiar text. Authors incorporate meaning through pictures and context. By encouraging and facilitating the reading and rereading of favorite sto-

Reading is learned as naturally as children learn to walk and talk.

ries, adults help children recognize that authors convey their meaning in the text (Smith, 1992, pp. 435–436).

Subskills Approach.   Although some *basal readers* use a whole language approach to reading, most are based on a subskills approach. Most elementary classrooms use at least one basal reading series. Such series provide children a reading text with controlled vocabulary and syntactic structure. A teacher's manual gives ideas and suggestions for teaching the lesson as well as for independent activities children can complete to reinforce the lesson.

All reading series have books designated for a particular grade level. Within each grade level are subdivisions, so children can read texts of increasingly difficult content.

Because basal texts are graded, they lend themselves to the formation of subgroups in the classroom. Often classroom teachers using these texts place children in groups based on reading level, and they select texts from a given series that seems to be at the most appropriate level for each group.

The basal text is a useful tool for instruction, particularly for new teachers. The vocabulary is controlled and has enough repetition of new words and phrases so children get practice and experience in reading these expressions. Skills are developed sequentially. The drawbacks to the approach are that lessons can be monotonous if they are always conducted in the same way. Also, the basal requires that all children in a particular group be at the same level of competence and be taught the skill in the same fashion. The usefulness of phonics rules and children's knowledge aren't always taken into account when using the basals. In spite of the research that indicates that only about 18 of the 45 phonic generalizations are useful (Clymer, 1963), most basal texts provide lessons for all 45 (Barbour, 1992). Taylor, Frye, and Goetz (1990) found that phonics lessons were taught successfully only to children who already knew the phonic skill, and those who didn't know it tended not to learn it.

If teachers do use a basal series, then flexibility in its use, creative approaches, and individualizing the instruction for each child will enhance the learning-to-read process.

Whole Language Philosophy.   Whole language is a philosophical view of how children learn both oral and written language. Learning to read and write as well as learning to speak is achieved by observing the process used by those who have acquired the skills, by experimenting, and finally by figuring out the cue systems in order to extract meaning and to communicate. This approach emphasizes the interrelatedness of the language arts skills—listening, speaking, writing, and reading—and the interrelatedness of learning to read in all curriculum areas.

In classrooms where teachers adhere to a whole language philosophy, there is a print-rich environment. Themes or special topics form the unit of study for the reading of literature and for reading in content areas.

Teachers personalize and individualize the instruction. Skill lessons are taught as children need skills to figure out the meaning of a passage or the way to express themselves in writing. The physical and emotional environment of the classroom supports the notion that all children can learn to read, even if the rate of progress and the manner in which a child learns to read are different.

Print-Rich Environment.   A print-rich environment offers children a wide selection of both fiction and nonfiction books and stories. With some teacher guidance, children are given the freedom to select their own texts. Having outstanding children's books in the classroom gives children both a taste of good literature and a chance to develop lifelong reading habits.

Themes or Special Topics.   At times you may want to select a class topic, have children read different books, and discuss various concepts or points of view about the topic. One primary classroom teacher chose the life of Helen Keller to enrich children's interest in knowing more about different handicapping conditions. Another used mysteries as a topic, including different children's mystery stories while introducing the concept of using clues in science class to unravel some of science's mysteries. Writing stories, making oral or written reports, and designing an art project using these themes integrates the language arts program.

Personalized, Individualized Instruction.   A personalized and individualized program enables students to build on prior knowledge and strengths as they improve their reading/writing skills. Teachers guide and facilitate the process, holding frequent conferences with each child and observing each child's strategies for getting meaning. Linguistic principles are discussed as children make discoveries about the rules of written language from both reading and writing.

Individual or Group Skills Lessons.   The teacher may present individual or group skills lessons from time to time, depending on students' needs. Assessment of such needs may be made in the formal reading time with the teacher or as students are reading in other areas of the classroom. In one first-grade classroom a teacher discovered that one child had theorized that the letter *c* had only one sound—that of *k*. As he tried to make this reasoning work, he sounded out the word *cinnamon* that was in the recipe he was using as "kinaman." Up to this point his theory had worked, so he had not realized that the letter *c* had more than one sound. As he began comparing words beginning with *ci* and *ce* with those beginning with *ca, co,* and *cu,* he became aware that the letter had two sounds, and he quickly discovered the "rule."

An Environment that Prizes Differences.   Although children may be grouped from time to time for different instructional purposes, a teacher espousing a whole language philosophy would not group children in set reading groups. Rather, children would read in different types of groups for different purposes. Children might listen to stories being read or shared in a whole class setting. They might read with or to a few friends who share an interest in a similar topic. They might practice oral or choral reading or work on particular skills with those who are at their skill level. They would spend much time in silent reading, gleaning information for science, social studies, math, or literature topics as well as finding new sources of pleasure.

In such a classroom, children aren't measured by the "grade level" at which they are reading, but rather on the progress they are making as they read and discuss different types of text. Reading is not viewed as an isolated subject but is facilitated as part of literacy development. Reading materials are discussed, listened to, and written about. The skills developed in one area of literacy reinforce and enhance the entire process.

Teachers using the whole language philosophy must be organized. They must also be adept at keeping records on children's progress, recognizing children's competence levels, and organizing a group of children to work independently. But more important, they must be knowledgeable about language and how it is learned. A teacher's viewpoint can affect how well a child learns to read. Strict adherence to a belief system that maintains that there is only one way to teach reading will result in many children not "joining the literacy club" (Clay, 1991; Smith 1992).

Summary

Language is an important part of young children's lives. Without a facility in language, children are limited intellectually as well as socially and emotionally. Without the ability to manipulate and understand words, they are restricted in their ability to receive information from others, from books and other printed materials, or to develop ideas and communicate them to others.

Whether in a child-care center, kindergarten, preschool, or primary grade, the entire day's program is directed at fostering children's ability to use and understand language in a manner that respects regional, cultural, and socioeconomic differences in family backgrounds.

Language begins with experiences. When a program is based on experiences, children have feelings and ideas to express and communicate to others. Children gain a common base for learning and using language when they join together in wondering how a moth emerges from a cocoon, in building a police car out of boxes and blocks, or in listening to firefighters tell about their work. As children grow in their ability to speak and listen, their need for written language emerges and they begin to invent ways to use writing to record and communicate their ideas and experiences.

From the base of listening, speaking, and prewriting experiences, children gain a readiness for reading. Each experience with language helps to foster children's ability to perceive the connection between the printed and spoken word, as well as decoding abilities, necessary for learning to read.

Projects

Continuing Case Study

Collect samples of your case study child's drawing, painting, and writing. Ask the child to "read" or explain to you what he or she has written or drawn. In your report, write your perceptions of the literacy skills this child has "mastered." Ask the child's teacher about the child's literacy skills and compare perceptions.

1. Ask a five-year-old to select a picture of a person or object from a book or magazine. Then you choose a picture. Using the two pictures, have the child talk about them while you record what the child is saying. Compare the number of words, the descriptive adjectives, and the complexity of sentence structure the child uses in describing each picture. Determine which picture elicited the more complex speech.
2. View the film *Foundations of Reading and Writing* (available from Campus Films, 20 East 46th Street, New York, NY 10017). List the activities shown and indicate whether they develop prereading, writing, listening, or speaking skills, or some or all of these skills. Compare these activities to those you observe in a preschool or kindergarten program.

3. Select a poem appropriate for choral recitation. With a group of third graders, rehearse and practice the poem for presentation to the entire class or to other children.
4. Walk the route a child would take to school. Record all the written words or letters you observe, such as those on signs, posters, and shop windows as well as words or letters on trucks that pass. Take that walk again with a five- or six-year-old, and as a game point out some of these words or letters to see if the child recognizes any. Later make flashcards of the words or letters that the child seemed to recognize to determine if any are recognizable without the object.
5. Create a card file of books and poems that you have read or shared with children. Note the age of the child and the child's reaction. Your collection should include books and poems that are appropriate for various ages and are representative of different cultures and both genders as positive role models.

Children's Books

Arbuthnot, M. H., & Root, S. (1968). *Time for poetry* (3rd ed.). Glenview, IL: Scott Foresman.

Babbitt, N. (1977). *Phoebe's revolt*. New York: Farrar, Straus & Giroux.

Bang, M. (1983). *Ten, nine, eight*. New York: Greenwillow.

Baylor, B. (1976). *Hawk, I'm your brother*. New York: Scribner's.

Brimmer, L. D. (1988). *Country bear's good neighbor*. New York: Orchard Books/ Franklin Watts.

Brown, M. (1980). *Finger rhymes*. New York: Dutton.

Brown, M. (1985). *Hand rhymes*. New York: Dutton.

Bruna, D. (1978). *I can dress myself*. New York: Methuen.

Carle, E. (1969). *The very hungry caterpillar*. New York: Philomel.

Carlstrom, N. W. (1986). *Jesse Bear, what will you wear?* New York: Macmillan.

Cauley, L. B. (1981). *Goldilocks and the three bears.* New York: Putnam.

Chorao, K. (1977). *The baby's lap book.* New York: Dutton.

Clifton, L. (1978). *Everett Anderson's nine month long.* New York: Harper & Row.

Cohen, M. (1977). *When will I read?* New York: Greenwillow.

Delacre, L. (1989). *Arroz con leche: Popular rhymes from Latin America.* New York: Scholastic.

Demi. (1992). *In the eyes of the cat: Japanese poetry for all seasons.* New York: Holt, Rinehart & Winston.

Ets, M. H., & Labastida, A. (1959). *Nine days to Christmas.* New York: Viking.

Goble, P. (1987). *Death of the Iron Horse.* New York: Bradbury.

Greenfield, E. (1991). *Night on neighborhood streets.* New York: Dial.

Hague, M. (1984). *Mother Goose: A collection of classic nursery rhymes.* New York: Holt, Rinehart & Winston.

Hoban, T. (1985). *What's that?* New York: Greenwillow.

Hutchins, P. (1977). *Titch.* New York: Greenwillow.

Hutchins, P. (1986). *The doorbell rang.* New York: Greenwillow.

Keats, E. J. (1981). *Peter's chair.* New York: Harper & Row.

Krauss, R. (1945). *The carrot seed.* New York: Harper & Row.

Krauss, R. (1951). *The bundle book.* New York: Harper & Row.

Leaf, M. (1987). *Eyes of the dragon.* New York: Lothrop.

Lear, E. (1980). *A book of nonsense.* New York: Viking.

Lionni, L. (1959). *Little blue and little yellow.* New York: Astor-Honor.

Kennedy, X. J., & Kennedy, D. M. (1992). *Talking like the rain: A first book of poems.* Boston: Little Brown.

Mathis, S. B. (1991). *Red dog. Football poems.*

Blue fly. New York: Viking.

Mahy, M. (1992). *The horrendous hullabaloo.* New York: Viking.

McClosky, R. (1948). *Blueberries for Sal.* New York: Viking.

Merriam, E. (1972). *Boys and girls. Girls and boys.* New York: Henry Holt.

Michels, B., & White, B. (1983). *Apples on a stick: The folklore of black children.* New York: Coward-McCann.

Milne, A. A. (1958). *The world of Christopher Robin.* New York: Dutton.

Munari, B. (1980). *Who's there? Open the door.* New York: Philomel.

Ormerod, J. (1985). *Messy baby.* New York: Lothrop.

Oxenburg, H. (1983). *The birthday party.* New York: Simon & Schuster.

Peppe, R. (1985). *The house that Jack built.* New York: Delacorte.

Pretusky, J. (1984). *The new kid on the block.* New York: Greenwillow.

Politi, L. (1976). *Three stalks of corn.* New York: Scribner's.

Ra, C. F. (Comp.). (1987). *Trot, trot to Boston: Play rhymes for baby.* New York: Lothrop.

Ringgold, F. (1991). *Tar Beach.* New York: Crown.

Rockwell, A., & Rockwell, H. (1982). *Can I help?* New York: Macmillan.

Schon, I. (1983). *Dona Blañca and other Hispanic nursery rhymes and games.* New York: Denison.

Steptoe, J. (1980). *Daddy is a monster . . . sometimes.* New York: Lippincott.

Uchida, Y. (1976). *The rooster who understood Japanese.* New York: Scribner's.

Untermeyer, L. (1959). *The golden treasury of poetry.* New York: Golden Press.

Wells, R. (1985). *Max's breakfast.* New York: Dial.

Yashima, T. (1953). *The village tree.* New York: Viking.

Zemach, M. (1976). *Hush little baby.* New York: Dutton.

Zolotow, C. (1972). *William's doll.* New York: Harper & Row.

Resources

The following books give additional ideas about promoting literacy. Also see the books listed under Reference.

Bosma, B. (1987). *Fairy tales, fables, legends, and myths: Using folk literature in your classroom*. New York: Teachers College Press.

Geller, L. G. (1985). *Word play and language learning for children*. Urbana, IL: National Council of Teachers of English.

Hansen, J. (1987). *When writers read*. Portsmouth, NH: Heinemann.

Johnson, K. (1987). *Doing words: Using the creative power of children's personal images to teach reading and writing*. Boston: Houghton Mifflin.

Loughlin, C. E., & Marin, M. D. (1987). *Supporting literacy: Developing effective learning environments*. New York: Teachers College Press.

McCracken, R., & McCracken, M. (1986). *Stories, songs, and poetry to teach reading and writing: Literacy through language*. Chicago: American Library Association.

Moffett, J., & Wagner, B. (1992). *Student-centered language arts, K-12*. Portsmouth, NH: Boynton/Cook Heinemann.

Naremore, R. C., & Hopper, R. (1990). *Children learning language: A practical introduction to communication development*. New York: Harper & Row.

Niles, J. A., & Harris, L. A. (1984). *Changing perspectives on research in reading and language processing and instructions*. Rochester, NY: National Reading Conference.

Ollila, L. O., & Mayfield, M. I. (Eds.). (1992). *Emerging literacy: Preschool, kindergarten, and primary grades*. Boston: Allyn & Bacon.

Smith, F. (1988). *Joining the literacy club*. Portsmouth, NH: Heinemann.

Willinski, J. (1990). *The new literacy: Redefining reading and writing in the schools*. London: Routledge.

References

Adams, M. J. (1990). *Beginning to read: Thinking and learning about print*. Cambridge, MA: The MIT Press.

Applebee, A. N. (1978). *The child's concept of story: Ages two to seventeen*. Chicago: University of Chicago Press.

Applebee, A. N. (1980). Children's narratives. New Directions. *The Reading Teacher, 34*, 137–142.

Ashton-Warner, S. (1986). *Teacher*. New York: Simon & Schuster. (Original work pub. 1963)

Baghban, M. (1984) *Our daughter learns to read and write*. Newark, DE: International Reading Association.

Barbour, N. (1992). Reading. In C. Seefeldt (Ed.), *The early childhood curriculum. A review of current research* (pp. 118–151). New York: Teachers' College Press.

Bernstein, B. (1970). A sociolinguistic approach to socialization with some reference to educability. In F. Williams (Ed.), *Language and poverty: Perspectives on a theme* (pp. 25–62). Chicago: Markham.

Bissex, G. L. (1980). *Gnys at wrk: A child learns to read and write*. Cambridge, MA: Harvard University Press.

Bloom, L. (1976). *Language development: Form and function in emerging grammars*. Hawthorne, NY: Mouton.

Bower, G. H., Black, J. B., & Turner, T. J. (1979). Scripts in memory for text. *Cognitive Psychology, 11*, 177–220.

Braine, M. (1963). On learning the grammatical order of words. *Psychological Review, 70*, 345–348.

Britton, J. (1970). *Language and learning*. New York: Penguin Books.

Cassirer, E. (1984). An essay on man. In A. Berthoff (Ed.), *Reclaiming the imagination* (pp. 107–113). Montclair, NJ: Boynton/Cook.

Chomsky, C. (1969). *The acquisition of syntax in children from five to ten*. Cambridge, MA: The MIT Press.

Chomsky, N. (1965). *Aspects of the theory of syntax*. Cambridge, MA: The MIT Press.

Clay, M. M. (1991). *Becoming literate: The construction of inner control*. Portsmouth, NH: Heinemann.

Clymer, T. (1963). The utility of phonic generalizations in primary years. *Reading Teacher, 16*, 252–258.

Durkin, D. (1966). *Children who read early*. New York: Teachers College Press.

Dyson, A. H. (1986). Transitions and tensions: Interrelationship between the drawing, talking and dictating of young children. *Research in the Teaching of English, 20*(4), 379–409.

Elardo, R., Bradley, R., & Caldwell, B. M. (1977). A longitudinal study of the relation of infants' home environments to language development at age three. *Child Development, 48*, 595–603.

Ferrara, A. (1982). Pragmatics. In T. A. van Dijk (Ed.), *Handbook of discourse analysis: Vol. 2. Dimensions of discourse* (pp. 137–159). Orlando, FL: Academic Press.

Goodman, K. S., Smith, E. B., Meredith, R., & Goodman, Y. M. (1987). *Language and thinking in school: A whole language curriculum*. New York: Richard C. Owen.

Graves, D. (1983). *Writing: Teachers and children at work*. Portsmouth, NH: Heinemann.

Halliday, M. A. K., & Hasan, R. (1976). *Cohesion in English*. New York: Longman.

Hayes, L. F. (1990). From scribbling to writing: Smoothing the way. *Young Children, 45*(3), 62–68.

Heath, S. B. (1983). *Ways with words: Language, life and work in communities, and classrooms*. New York: Cambridge University Press.

Hepler, S. (1991). Talking our way to literacy in the classroom community. *The New Advocate, 4*(3), 179–191.

Holdaway, D. (1979). *The foundations of literacy*. New York: Ashton Scholastic.

Holdaway, D. (1984). *Stability and change in literacy learning*. Portsmouth, NH: Heinemann.

Honig, A. S. (1982). Language environments for young children. *Young Children, 38*, 56–57.

Ingraham, D. (1989). *First language acquisition*. Cambridge, MA: Cambridge University Press.

Jalongo, M. R. (1992). *Early childhood language arts*. Boston: Allyn & Bacon.

Kantor, R., Miller, S. M., & Fernie, D. E. (1992). Diverse paths to literacy in a preschool classroom: A sociocultural perspective. *Reading Research Quarterly, 27*(3), 185–201.

Kessel, F. (1970). The role of syntax in children's comprehension from ages six to twelve. *Child Development, 35*(6), 48–58.

Labov, W. (1970). The logic of nonstandard English. In F. Williams (Ed.), *Language and poverty: Perspectives on a theme* (pp. 153–190). Chicago: Markham.

Lenneberg, E. (1967). *Biological foundations of language*. New York: John Wiley.

Low, J. M., & Moely, B. E. (1988). Early word acquisition: Relationships to syntactic and semantic aspects of maternal speech. *Child Study Journal, 18*(1), 47–54.

Mandler, J. M., & Johnson, N. S. (1977). Remembrance of things passed: Story structure and recall. *Cognitive Psychology, 9*, 111–151.

McNeill, D. (1966). Developmental psycholinguistics. In F. Smith and G. Miller (Eds.), *The genesis of language: A psycholinguistic approach* (pp. 15–82). Cambridge, MA: The MIT Press.

Menyuk, P. (1969). *Sentences children use*. Cambridge, MA: The MIT Press.

Menyuk, P. (1971). *The acquisition and development of language*. Englewood Cliffs, NJ: Prentice Hall.

Morphett, M. V., & Washburne, C. (1931). When should children learn to read? *Elementary School Journal, 29*, 497–503.

Morrow, L. M. (1985). Retelling stories: A strategy for improving young children's comprehension, concept of story structure and oral language complexity. *The Elementary School Journal, 85*, 648–661.

Mowrer, O. H. (1960). *Learning theory and the symbolic process*. New York: John Wiley.

National Council of Teachers of English. (1954). *Language arts for today's children*. New York: Appleton-Century-Crofts.

Pappas, C. C., & Brown, E. (1987). Learning to read by reading. Learning how to extend the functional potential of language. *Research in the Teaching of English, 2*(2), 160–177 .

Pellegrini, A. D., & Galda, L. (1986). The role of theory in oral and written language curriculum. *The Elementary School Journal, 87*(2), 201–208.

Peterson, R. (1971). Imitation: A basic behavioral mechanism. *Journal of Applied Behavioral Analysis, 4*, 1–9.

Piaget, J. (1955). *The language and thought of the child*. New York: Noonday.

Rumelhart, D. E. (1978). Understanding and summarizing brief stories. In D. Laberge and J. Samuels (Eds.), *Basic processes in reading: Perception and comprehension* (pp. 265–305). Hillsdale, NJ: Erlbaum.

Salinger, T. (1988). *Language arts and literacy for young children*. New York: Macmillan.

Sapir, E. (1929). The status of linguistics as a science. *Language, 5*, 207–214.

Schachter, F. F., & Stage, A. A. (1982). Adults talk and children's language development. In S. G. Moore & C. R. Cooper (Eds.), *The young child: Reviews of research* (pp. 79–97). Washington, DC: National Association for the Education of Young Children.

Schickedanz, J., York, M., Stewart, L., & White, D. (1983). *Strategies for teaching young children*. Englewood Cliffs, NJ: Prentice Hall.

Skinner, B. F. (1957). *Verbal behavior*. New York: Appleton-Century-Crofts.

Slobin, D. (1966). The acquisition of Russian as a native language. In F. L. Smith & G. C. Miller (Eds.), *The genesis of language: A psycholinguistic approach* (pp. 129–149). Cambridge, MA: The MIT Press.

Smith, F. (1992). Learning to read: The never-ending debate. *Phi Delta Kappan, 76*(6), 432–441.

Snow, C. E. (1989). Understanding social interaction and language acquisition: Sentences are not enough. In M. H. Bornstein & J. S. Bruner (Eds.), *Interaction in human development* (pp. 83–105). Hillsdale, NJ: Lawrence Erlbaum.

Staats, A. (1971). Linguistic-mentalistic theory versus an explanatory s-r learning theory of language development. In D. Slobin (Ed.), *The ontogenesis of grammar: A theoretical symposium* (pp. 103–153). New York: Academic Press.

Taylor, B. M., Frye, J. B., & Goetz, T. M. (1990). Reducing the number of reading skill activities in the elementary classroom. *Journal of Reading Behavior, 22*(2), 167–179.

Taylor, M., & Gelman, S. A. (1988). Adjectives and nouns. Children's strategies for learning new words. *Child Development, 59*, 411–419.

Teale, W. H. (1986). Home background and young children's literacy development. In W. H. Teale & E. Sulzby (Eds.), *Emergent literacy: Writing and reading* (pp. 173–207). Norwood, NJ: Ablex.

Teale, W. H. (1984). Reading to our children: Its significance for literary development. In H. Goelman, A. A. Oberg, & F. Smith (Eds.), *Awakening to literacy* (pp. 110–121). Portsmouth, NH: Heinemann.

Temple, C. A., Nathan, R. G, & Burris, N. A. (1982). *The beginning of writing*. Boston: Allyn & Bacon.

Throne, J. (1988). Becoming a kindergarten of readers? *Young Children, 43*(6), 10–16.

Tizard, B. (1981). Language at home and at school. In C. B. Cazden (Ed.), *Language in early childhood education* (pp. 17–28). Washington, DC: National Association for the Education of Young Children.

Tizard, B., & Hughes, M. (1984). *Young children learning*. Cambridge, MA: Harvard University Press.

Tompkins, G., & Hoskisson, K. (1991). *Language arts content and teaching strategies* (2nd ed.). New York: Merrill/Macmillan.

Veatch, J. (1979). *Key words to reading: The language approach begins*. Columbus, OH: Merrill.

Vygotsky, L. S. (1962). *Thought and language*. New York: John Wiley.

Wells, G. (1981). *Learning through interaction: The study of language development*. New York: Cambridge University Press.

Wells, G. (1985). Preschool literacy-related activities and success in school. In D. R. Olson, N. Torrance, & A. Hildyard (Eds.), *Literacy, language and learning* (pp. 229–255). New York: Cambridge University Press.

Whaley, J. F. (1981). Reader's expectations for story structure. *Reading Research Quarterly, 17*, 90–114.

Whorf, B. L. (1956). Science and linguistics. In J. B. Carroll (Ed.), *Thought and reality: Selected writings of Benjamin Lee Whorf*, (pp. 207–219). Cambridge, MA: The MIT Press.

Wood, B. S. (1976). *Children and communication: Verbal and nonverbal language development*. Englewood Cliffs, NJ: Prentice Hall.

10 Art

Children and art seem to go together.

After reading this chapter, you should be able to respond to the following questions:

1. What are the major theories of art? How do these theories influence the practice of teaching art?

2. Describe the stages of children's art. How will your knowledge of the stages of the development of art affect your teaching of art?

3. Why is art important in the curriculum?

4. What role does the teacher plan in:

   a. Determining goals for the visual arts?

   b. Motivating children to produce art?

   c. Selecting appropriate materials?

   d. Instructing children in art?

5. How is appreciation for art fostered?

"Look what I made," exclaims three-year-old Schwana excitedly, almost as if she is surprised at her power to leave marks on paper as a result of her scribbles.

"This is my daddy on his horse," four-year-old Mike tells his mother, interpreting his scribble.

"Not yet, not yet. I'm not done with my painting," five-year-old Andrea begs for more time.

Children and art seem to belong together. Wherever groups of children gather, whether at home or at school, there is art. Across the nation in Head Start and child-care centers, preschools, and public school kindergarten and primary classrooms, children are intent on scribbling designs on paper with large chunky crayons, engrossed in spreading bright-colored tempera paint over large sheets of newsprint, or patting, pushing, and pounding moist clay.

World over, children are fascinated by making art, as though they are driven to leave their mark. Whether in the high mountains of Peru, deep in the Amazon rain forests, or on New York City sidewalks, children can be observed creating art—making marks with sticks on sand, mud, or concrete.

Art and young children are a natural combination. Uninhibited children, anxious to explore their environment, to experiment with materials, to understand their world, and to communicate ideas and feelings, find making art an intriguing and gratifying experience (McWhinnie, 1992).

Children's attraction to the arts may come from the fact that no matter how primitive or simplistic their work may appear to someone else, it gives them the opportunity to express their ideas and thoughts, reflect on and make sense of their experiences, and release emotions and feelings, all in a unique and personal way.

Theories of Art

Adults have always found children's art fascinating. For years psychologists and artists have questioned why children draw as they do, what their art means, and how their art progresses from the abstract to the realistic.

Theories have been advanced to explain children's art and provide insights into the meaning and value that art has for children. Each theory has influenced the teaching of art, and each is useful in explaining the nature of children's art.

Cognitive Theories

"Look outside," a first-grade teacher tells the children. She then asks, "Do you see the sky just above you, like the blue line you've drawn on the top of your paper? Of course not. Look, the sky goes all the way down and touches the ground. Now draw the sky all the way down on your paper. Not just at the top," she commands.

Some of the children fill in their paper with blue, but Kate does not. Walking around the room, the teacher sees Kate's picture with the sky depicted as a line at the top of the paper and says, "Kate, I told you, the sky goes all the way down and touches the ground. Why haven't you filled in the sky in your picture?" Kate, shaking her head explains, "But the sky doesn't come all the way down. It's only on top of us. If it came all the way down we couldn't breathe."

Kate's drawing with the baseline of grass at the bottom and the sky line at the top of the paper illustrates the cognitive theory of art. The child draws what she knows, not what she sees (Luquet, 1913).

This phrase—that children draw what they know and not what they see—is most often used to describe cognitive theories of art. Children's art differs from adult art because children just don't know as much as adults. Because children's art reflects their thinking and knowledge, they omit parts of the body they don't know about or draw the sky as a blue line overhead because they think of it that way. As children grow in knowledge and understanding of the world and as they increase the number and complexity of their concepts, their drawings change and become more realistic and adultlike. The accuracy, detail, and complexity of their work increases in direct relation to their knowledge.

Piaget and Inhelder (1969) agree. They relate children's thought processes to the stages of their art. During the sensorimotor period of thought, children scribble. Moving into preoperational thought, children's art is preschematic, with circles, squares, and lines used to represent objects and things. When they are in the concrete period, children's art becomes more representative and they use schema. Realism appears as children reach the stage of formal abstract thought.

The idea that children's art is related to their level of intellectual functioning was validated by Florence Goodenough (1926). Goodenough collected children's drawings of a man and showed that these drawings increased in detail and realism as children's knowledge increased. She argued that children's drawings of any object reflect their concept of that object.

Psychoanalytic Theories

Painting at the easel, Roberto first draws a house. Then he paints a small figure in a corner of one room of the house. Next he adds large figures that are painted over the house with red paint. Finally he covers the entire picture with a coat of black paint and stomps away.

According to adherents of the psychoanalytic theory of art, Roberto, whose parents were in the middle of a bitter divorce, was using art to express what he felt, not what he knew. Those endorsing the psychoanalytic view of art believe that art is a mirror of children's emotions, subconscious thoughts, and feelings. These theorists believe that children draw people as a circle with sticks representing arms and legs not because they don't know people have bodies with neck and shoulders, but because the circle represents a force deep within the child that is used as a symbol to represent the womb, breasts, or other emotionally loaded objects. Cole (1966) titled her book *Children's Art from Deep Down Inside* as an illustration of this idea. Children's art is a reflection of unconscious feelings not intelligence (Feldman, 1970). Psychoanalytic theorists explain the progression from the circle to a more realistic representation of the human figure as a growth process. As children grow, conscious thoughts suppress the powerful force of the unconscious, and children can then draw and paint more representationally.

The pioneers in psychoanalytic approaches to early childhood education, Anna Freud, Lois Barclay Murphy, Katherine Baker Read, and Rose Alschuler, all accepted the idea that children's art was related to their unconscious thought and was a form of nonverbal expression. They advocated providing children with free-flowing tempera paints, finger paints, clay, and other materials that would permit freedom of expression. They regarded small crayons and paper, pencils, and fine paintbrushes or pens as too restrictive and constraining for children to use in expressing unconscious feelings and emotions.

Supporters can be found for the psychoanalytic theory. Psychologists who agree that children's art is related to the psychological, not cognitive, growth of the child use their patients' drawings of the human figure as indicators of their personality or to analyze those who have psychological problems.

Perceptual Theories

Mike had often watched his father, a jockey, racing on a horse. Mike drew a flurry of scribbles, faster and faster. When he finished, he said, "There, my daddy won." To those endorsing the perceptual theories of art, Mike's drawing, depicting action and motion, illustrates that children do not draw what they know or feel, but rather what they see. They believe children see perceptual wholes; that is, they do not just see the sum of the parts, but a total image structured by an active brain. Being active, the brain organizes the images that the eyes receive. Individual brains organize these perceptions differently. Children's drawings are influenced by the organization their brain imposes on incoming images.

Children probably see more than they draw, but their drawings are limited by their inability to represent images on paper. Paintings and drawings do not include all of the details they see because the younger the child is, the less able she or he is to recreate a perceived object on a piece of paper. So the child invents.

> Thus, seeing the shape of the human head means seeing its roundness. Obviously, roundness is not a tangible perceptual thing. It is not materialized in any one head, or in a number of heads. There are shapes, such as circles or spheres, that represent the roundness of an object, such as a head. (Arnheim, 1954, p. 134)

When a child makes a circle for a head, that is the inventive part of drawing.

Developmental Theories

Although other theories of art have been used to guide teachers as they work and plan for children's experiences with art and explain children's art, the developmental theory may be the most familiar and widely accepted. Anyone who has observed children and their growth in artistic depiction recognizes the developmental stages of children's art (Golomb, 1992).

Developmental Stages of Art

Lowenfeld (1957) described children's progress in art as the unfolding of a genetic program. He believed each stage was a part of the natural and normal aspects of children's growth and development. These stages were sequential and hierarchical, and each was characterized by increasing progress. Even though stages have been identified and accepted, the age at which children progress through them varies.

Infants and Toddlers (0–2 Years).   Between birth and the age of two, children are in the sensorimotor stage of development. Lowenfeld (1957) called this the stage of scribbling. Piaget and Inhelder (1969) describe this period as particularly important because "during this time . . . the child constructs all the cognitive substructures that will serve as a point of departure for later perceptive and intellectual development" (p. 1). The child's grasping, manipulation, and other tactile and kinesthetic sensations are the beginning of thinking.

If you watch a baby draw or a toddler scribbling, you know art is a sensorimotor activity. As a child draws or paints, every part of his or her body moves, all working to move the crayon or brush across the paper. Once the child begins the movement, it's difficult to stop. As a consequence, whatever surface the child is working on often becomes covered with paint and crayon.

Because it is the sensory experience of making marks that's important, the child doesn't even recognize the scribbles. In fact, these children receive

Children recognize the marks they make and begin to name them.

so much satisfaction from just handling the materials—dumping the crayons out of the box, putting them back in again, rolling them across the table or in their hands—that they may not even begin drawing.

Art is such a sensory experience at this age that children may use crayons in both hands as they draw, singing in rhythm to the movements they are making. They may not even notice that the pen they're working with isn't leaving marks on the paper (Goertz, 1966).

Because it is the process that is important to children when they're toddlers, there's no need to label their scribbles with their names or ask for stories or titles to accompany them. You will, however, want to save samples from time to time to keep a record of children's progress.

It is not necessary to hurry the toddler into new or different materials or to try to interrupt the process by introducing new techniques. You won't need many art supplies. Toddlers will need large, chunky crayons that won't break in their tight overhand grasp and a supply of newsprint or other large sheets of inexpensive paper. Other art materials you might make available are one color of tempera paint, large brushes, and paper. Paper for painting may need to be heavier than newsprint because children will paint the paper until it disintegrates. A soft clay or bread dough for pulling, punching, poking, and rolling is the only other art material necessary.

Preschoolers–Primary Grades (2–7 or 8 Years).   Piaget and Inhelder (1969) describe the stage from age two to five as one of symbolic function. At this stage, children can think about an object even if it's not present and may begin to find representations of objects in their scribbles. The children's products are still scribbles, but the nature and function of the scribbling have changed. This is the *preschematic* stage.

Children begin to recognize the marks they've made and to name their scribbles. A change from kinesthetic activity to representational attempts occurs. Children realize that there is a relationship between the objects they've drawn and the outside world and that drawing and painting can be used to record ideas and express feelings.

During this stage, children hold their implement more as an adult does and have increasing control over the materials. They can control their scribbles, making loops, circular scribbles, and lines that are distinguishable and can be repeated at will. As they draw, they begin to name scribbles as some shape, line, or form reminds them of an object: "This is my dog." "I'm making a swing set." If, however, the adult asks the child to tell what he or she is drawing or to name the scribble, the response is often, "I don't know yet, I'm not finished."

Children of this age value their scribbles. Teachers can put the children's names on their work so they can be taken home or displayed in the room. The work of Goertz (1966), who found that by age three or four children won't draw if their pen is out of ink, supports the idea that preschoolers value their scribbles.

At this stage, wide individual differences exist in drawing. Children who have had experience with drawing at home or in the preschool will be more advanced (Goertz, 1966). Individual differences in the ability to control the media, as well as to represent ideas, are also present. Children in kindergarten and the primary grades continue developing control over materials. Their schema become increasingly representative. (See Figure 10–1.)

The Values of Art

"If only I had more time," a teacher offered in explanation for the elimination of art from the curriculum. "If drawing were on the tests we have to give, you'd be sure we'd have art every day, but it isn't on any test of basic skills I know of!"

Under pressure to account for children's achievement through standardized tests, art is becoming an endangered species for young children in too many schools. To many educators, parents, and other taxpayers, art is a frill, something you do if there is time left after real work. "Some adults

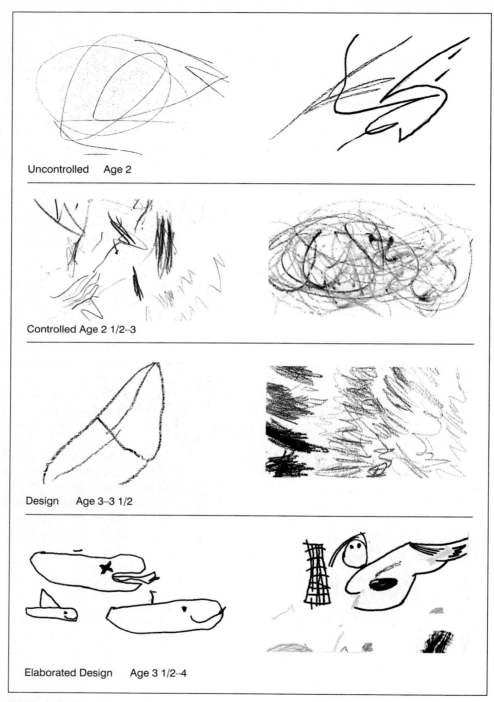

Uncontrolled Age 2

Controlled Age 2 1/2–3

Design Age 3–3 1/2

Elaborated Design Age 3 1/2–4

Figure 10–1
Children's scribbles

Adapted from *Children's Drawings from Lines to Scribbles* by Barbara Biber, 1962, New York: Bank Street Publications.

dichotomize children's academic and artistic achievement, as if the former were nutritious vegetables and the latter, a rich dessert" (Jalongo, 1990).

Other people believe art is only for the gifted and talented. As one teacher said, "I'd include more art activities, but none of my children are going to be artists, so why bother."

It may be, however, that art is neglected because many people are unaware of how basic art is to the growth, development, and learning of young children. Even when teachers themselves value children's art, they may be ill prepared to articulate these values to others.

Once you understand and believe in the values of art, you'll be able to protect children's time for art and select goals, plan and implement art.

Art is basic! It is valuable to children in and of itself. It is also critical for children's intellectual growth and academic achievement. Its contribution to the whole child can't be ignored.

Art for Art

"The prime value of art lies in the unique contribution it makes to the individual's experience with and understanding of the world. The visual arts deal with an aspect of human consciousness that no other field touches on: the aesthetic contemplation of the visual form" (Eisner, 1972, p. 9). Art is a part of the curriculum for its own sake (Bruner, 1990). No other part of the curriculum introduces children to an understanding and appreciation of the visual arts. Children need to develop awareness and knowledge of color, form, line, shape, and texture in their environment and in artworks. They need to create their own art and to appreciate the work of others. No other subject area meets these needs.

Art Is Cognitive

Creating in the visual arts involves the use of symbols. This ability to represent one's experiences with symbols is a major cognitive stage for young children (Golomb, 1992; Raines & Canady, 1990). As children create art, they must organize their thoughts and actions into patterns and symbols. They reason, invent, create, and solve problems. For example children must decide how to fit two pieces of wood together, which colors to use to express an idea, or how to make a piece of paper stand up. They give concrete representation to abstract ideas, thoughts, and feelings.

The expressive arts enhance children's ability to interpret symbols (Jalongo, 1990). It is the "symbolic ability of the child on which everything which is distinctly human will develop" (Smith, 1984, p. 28).

Concept formation is also enhanced through the visual arts. The act of drawing forces children to develop perceptual sensitivity to their world, perceiving likenesses, differences, shapes, sizes, textures, and colors. Research (Forseth, 1980; Lansing, 1981) has shown that experiences in art foster children's ability to observe and discriminate between observations, skills that are prerequisites for concept formation. This research has led Lansing (1981) to conclude, "Art—drawing in particular—should no longer be viewed as a frill in our schools" (p. 22).

Art Is Emotional

"The expressive arts foster learning from the inside out" (Jalongo, 1990, p. 196). The psychoanalytic theorists endorse art because it is emotionally satisfying. According to them, through the visual arts, a certain amount of tension can be released while allowing expression of thoughts, ideas, and emotions. Feelings that cannot be identified or named find expression. Anger and frustration can find healthy release as one works with clay, paint, or wood; joy and happiness can be expressed with crayons, paints, and paper.

Children's feelings of competence and self-esteem increase as they create a product. The sense of accomplishment that arises from creating art supports children's emotional development.

Art Is Social

Returning from a field trip to the firehouse, Juan paints a truck with huge black tires, filling the paper. Susan fills her paper with yellow paint because "That's the way it was. The truck was yellow, the boots were yellow, it was really yellow!" Andrea builds a structure from boxes and blocks and announces, "There, that's the firehouse. Who wants to play firefighter?"

When art is a part of the curriculum, children learn from firsthand experience to value diversity. They learn that each person is unique and that although they may have shared the same experience, each one expresses that experience in a different way. Art helps children develop respect for other peoples' opinions and value diversity.

Art also helps children develop skills of working together, cooperating, and sharing. Children share materials and space, and they learn to leave their work space and materials ready for another person to use. Because art is an emotionally satisfying experience for young children, children feel comfortable working with others. Children with special needs or who are new to the American culture may find working in small groups as they create art a safe, nonverbal way to become a part of the group.

Art Is Academic

But will they learn to read and write if they spend so much time with art? The answer is a definite YES! In fact, children who do not experience art do not achieve as well as those who have had many art experiences. The power of art to foster children's academic skills has been fully documented (Green & Hasselbring, 1981; Lansing, 1981; Lewis & Livison, 1980).

Because art requires children to think of an experience, idea, or feeling and then find symbols to express it, art is a highly symbolic activity. Every academic skill requires that students have the ability to think about something not present and then represent the thought in symbolic form. Art is learning and thinking itself.

Art activities are especially helpful in promoting writing and reading skills. "While early childhood teachers are aware that children's drawings are representations of their real world, they often fail to recognize the significance of drawings that are symbols of symbols" (Raines & Canady, 1990).

Art is now believed essential for learning to read and write (Raines & Canady, 1990; Schickedanz, 1986). As children scribble, they use all of the strokes needed to write. Their scribbles are, in fact, the beginning of written language (Clay, 1975). Drawing may be the single most important readiness activity for writing (Klein, 1985).

Art is also related to mathematics skills and achievement. Children who have measured materials, created different shapes, and counted art tools and materials appear to have an advantage in mathematics skills over children who have not had these experiences.

The Role of the Teacher

No one can visit the infant, toddler, and preschools in the city of Reggio Emilia, Italy, or view the exhibit, The Hundred Languages of Children, without being awed by the beauty and wonder of the children's art (City of Reggio Emilia, 1984). The art of the children of Reggio stuns all who view it!

Whether paintings, drawings, collages, constructions, or sculpture, the art products of Reggio's children are replete with details. Bright, rich, colored paints fill large easel paper. Colorful, composed, stylish drawings are executed on paper of all sizes and types. Clay sculptures, with joined pieces, stand everywhere. Someone who was magically transported to a classroom in Reggio without being told what it was no doubt would conclude that the classroom was some type of art museum.

Observing the wondrous art children produce in Reggio, people immediately begin to question the following:

- Are the children in Reggio Emilia, Italy, somehow different than those in the United States?
- Are they more advanced artistically?
- Is the culture of Italy so different?
- Why, why, why do young children in Reggio Emilia, Italy, paint, draw, and sculpt as they do?

The children of Reggio really are no different than young children anywhere. And although the cultures of Italy and the United States are different, the real difference in schools for young children in Reggio and other schools is found in the role of the teacher.

Teachers, their directors, the parents, and the community play an active and critical role in fostering children's art. Teachers, and the strategies they use, are responsible for the wonders of art the children produce.

The art products of the children are stunning because teachers care about the process of creating art. Teachers in Reggio see no difference between process and product. If the process of producing art is flawed, the product is flawed as well. It is not a question of process over product, but the fact that process and product are one and the same.

Teachers anywhere, not just in Reggio Emilia, Italy, can become skilled in the process of fostering children's art. Like the teachers there, you can develop the skills and understandings of the process of teaching art to young children.

Regardless of where you live or the characteristics of the children you teach, you can promote their artistic abilities by:

- Becoming knowledgeable of the goals of art education
- Understanding how to motivate children's art
- Developing appropriate teaching strategies
- Appreciating art yourself in order to foster children's art appreciation

Deciding on Goals

The National Art Education Association (NAEA) (1992) asserts that art brings the personal dimension of feeling, sensitivity, empathy, and expression to the curriculum. The visual arts help involve children in perceiving the world, reacting to things they see and feel, and in interpreting emotions, feelings, and insights. The association states that art is a body of knowledge, as well as a series of activities, organized to provide experiences that are related to specific goals.

Teachers must have a clear understanding of these goals if they are to prepare a successful art program. When the goals are internalized, they can serve as guidelines for selecting materials, planning activities, and evaluating children's progress. Specific goals can be determined for individual children and activities. The National Art Education Association suggests the following overall goals:

Goals for Making Art

Through their experiences in the visual arts, children should:

- Increase their skills in the use of and mastery over art materials
- Learn to use materials in ways that are innovative and unusual
- Become intensely involved in making art
- Show a progression through the stages of art. They should develop the ability to work with intent and purpose and to organize and express ideas and feelings through the visual arts.

Goals for Looking at Art

Through their experiences in looking at visual art, children should:

- Recognize and respect their own and others' artwork
- Understand the concept of "the artist"
- Show appreciation for differing viewpoints in art products
- Perceive visual relationships within their environment
- Become familiar with the content of art—line, balance, color, shape, form, texture—by perceiving it in the environment and in artworks

Goals for Talking About and Evaluating Art

Children should appreciate their own and others' art. They should grow in the ability to:

- Discuss how artists create their products
- Name and discuss the content of art: line, color, texture, form, and shape
- Perceive aesthetic relationships and develop aesthetic awareness

Motivation

"I can't draw," says four-year-old Sandra. "Show me," demands Vanessa. "Do it for me, I can't," pleads another.

When children whine or cry, claiming they can't draw, or if they only produce the stereotypical house, tree, or flower picture over and over again, they are not demonstrating lack of artistic talent, but rather the need for motivation.

The National Art Education Association is developing standards for the visual arts. These include standards for kindergarten through grade 4.

Creation and Performance
- Children use art media, tools, techniques, and processes skillfully.
- Children organize elements using principles or structures.
- Children effectively communicate ideas, attitudes, and feelings through a visual arts form.
- Children innovatively express idea(s) with visual arts forms.

Historical and Cultural Context
- Children engage in art historical inquiry.
- Children describe themes and other commonalities that cross cultural and time boundaries in art.
- Children develop elementary skills to effectively compose and contrast works of art by different artists.
- Children describe influences on art styles, forms, and media.

Perception and Analysis
- Children differentiate and describe complex and natural or geometric shapes or combinations of shapes.
- Children describe underlying principles, structures, or organization of visual characteristics.
- Children categorize visual and other sensory characteristics.
- Children respond appropriately to aesthetic characteristics.
- Children interpret the meaning of works of art.
- Children describe the characteristics of works of art aesthetically.
- Children compare, contrast, and judge works of art.

Figure 10–2
Art standards
National Art Education Association. (1992). Working draft of visual art standards. *NAEA News, 34*(6), 1–24.

Art, as an expression of a feeling, an experience, idea, thought, or image, cannot be produced without first feeling, experiencing, thinking, or imagining. What can children draw if they have nothing to express? If they have nothing to think about, to feel, or dream about?

If children are to produce art, they must be motivated. Without sufficient psychological, experiential, or vicarious motivation, children will not be able to express themselves through art, and they may even lose interest in producing art.

Psychological Motivation

Brittain (1979) believes that teachers must provide the psychological motivation that makes creating art possible. If children do not feel secure, safe, and comfortable with you, the other children, and themselves, they will not be able to risk or meet the challenge of producing art. They must know that they and the art they produce, whether scribbles or representational, will be accepted and respected.

Teachers should first be able to accept each child as he or she is, believing fully that "each child has something valuable to offer" (Moyer, 1990, p. 130). It is easy for teachers to recognize children who are artistically talented.

One teacher, when complemented on the beauty of the paintings and drawings on a bulletin board replied, "I know! These children really know how to draw. They're wonderful. Fortunately you're not seeing what the others do, or more to the point, what they can't do! Their work is so embarrassing I would never display their work."

Another teacher in the same school demonstrated the ability to accept and give recognition to each child. This teacher arranged a bulletin board of children's art that included a variety of tempera paintings, watercolors, pencil sketches, crayon drawings, torn paper pictures, and collages. The work of each child was represented. When questioned, this teacher's response was, "Children chose the medium to use. Each child has something valuable to offer. Isn't this a wonderful variety of art" (Moyer, 1990, p. 130).

Freedom and choice are also involved in children's psychological safety. Children have to know they are free to choose both the materials to work with and the way to use them. Giving children the freedom to choose and the time to create affirms for them that they are respected and accepted as individuals.

Each day, children should find a variety of readily available art materials. "Presenting a variety of materials to children gives them a measure of control in a world where they have little control. Children may choose the material with which to work, decide on the topic and proceed at their own pace" (Moyer, 1990, p. 130).

Giving children time for art production demonstrates another kind of respect. First, children are given time to grow. Two- and three-year-olds, barely out of the sensorimotor stage of development, are given the time to be two and three. They are expected to explore art materials, to scribble, mess around, and try to find out how paint feels, what they can do with clay, and how to use paste and scissors. They are not hurried into or pressured to represent their ideas through art, to be interested in a product, and much less to produce one.

Older children who are beginning to represent their ideas, are also given time for exploration. If children over four or five have had plenty of time to find out how the materials feel, what they can do with them, and how to control them, they are ready to develop skilled use of materials. Children are given time to use the same art materials over and over again so they can control a material and fully utilize it to express themselves.

Time is also given so children can work on a project for as long as they wish. A five-year-old, following a visit to Sea World, began to make a book

Children are given time for exploration.

about the ocean. The teacher permitted the child not only to work on the book the entire morning, even during story hour and snack, but also arranged for her to continue work on the book for the next several weeks.

Perhaps nothing undermines children's sense of psychological safety and demonstrates disrespect of them more than asking them to complete patterned artwork or to copy adult models. Children who are given patterns to cut out or outlines to color in are being told that they and their art are worthless. A pattern of a dog for children to color in or cut out says to children as clearly as words could that, "This is what your drawing should look like. This is the RIGHT way to make a dog. You and the way you draw are wrong. Really wrong."

Some teachers, believing they are not destroying children's psychological safety, direct children in art activities. They say to the children, "Here is this paper plate, and these are the eyes, ears, nose, and mouth for you to use in 'creating' a space man." Then they direct children where to paste the paper nose, ears, and eyes. They explain to the observer, "You see, children need to experience and express their own ideas. That's why they are creating a space monster for themselves." These teachers' only purpose is to undermine children's sense of competence and self-worth. Actually, activities like these are neither art nor craft, but simply a waste of children's time and talent as well as a waste of paper.

Respect for children means giving them responsibility. When children are responsible for themselves, others, and the materials they use, they know you respect them and their abilities. Teaching children how to prepare art materials, mix paint, and clean up after themselves communicates respect. Even two-year-olds can wash paint brushes and return them to the easel so others can paint, hang up their own paintings to dry, and clean tables after painting or making collages.

Experiential Motivation

Psychological safety, freedom, and time are not enough to motivate children's art. For children to produce art, which is an expression of an idea, thought, feeling, or imagination, they must have something to express. To create art, children must first think, feel, or imagine. Without motivation, children eventually deplete their store of ideas, feelings, and imagination. The role of teachers is to replenish children's storehouse of feelings, ideas, and imagination through firsthand experiences.

True, children experience all of the time (Dewey, 1944). But in order for an experience to motivate children to thought and then art, it must be firsthand and demand reflection.

"When we experience something, we act upon it, we do something with it" (Dewey, 1944, p. 139). A true experience involves both active and passive elements. Instead of having children just walk in the rain, play on the grass, or look at a spider, ask them to observe. Try to open them up to using all of their senses as they look at a raindrop or spider, and to think about and describe the experience.

A teacher had asked all the children to draw their Thanksgiving. Paul sat there with a blank sheet. The teacher, walking around the first grade, noticed he was having trouble and asked what was wrong. He said he didn't know how to draw. She asked what he had to eat for Thanksgiving, and he replied, "A turkey." The teacher asked, "What was the turkey like?" Paul puffed himself up and said, "Full, it was full, just full." After the opportunity to think about the experience, Paul was able to draw a full, stuffed turkey.

Only after children have observed and talked about their observations should they be asked to draw.

Ask the children to look again, to look another way. Have them look at a raindrop through a magnifying glass. Try to catch a raindrop in their hands. Watch a raindrop as it falls on the window. How does it look? How does it feel? Why?

As children encounter raindrops or spiders, ask them to think about their experience. Describe the raindrop. What colors did you see? What might be in the raindrop? Look at the photographs we took of you playing in the rain. Remember how the rain felt on your face? Where could we find more about the rain?

The point is, children cannot be asked to draw without having something to think about, without having experienced something. Two first-grade classrooms in the same school illustrate this.

In this school, the principal suggested that the first-grade teachers open the school year by initiating a theme of myself and my friends. This theme, the principal explained, would help children to feel at home and enable them to become acquainted with one another.

Both first-grade teachers in the school agreed and decided to begin the unit by making murals for the hall titled "Our New Friends." One teacher told the children they were to draw a picture of their friend for the mural. She gave the children paper and new marking pens. They went to their tables and in less than a minute most had completed a stick figure of a new friend which they pasted on the mural paper.

The other teacher read a poem about friends. She then led the group in a game that involved calling children's names. Next she asked each child to pick a child they did not know. When all the children had partners they didn't know, or did not know very well, she asked them to find out something about each other. She gave them a list of questions to ask each other including what they liked to eat and play, whom they lived with, what TV shows they watched, and so on.

Then she gave the pair of children a mirror and asked them to examine and compare their facial features. Walking around the room, she helped children talk about the shape and size of their eyes and mouth, look at the way their eyelashes curled or were straight, and describe the color of their eyes, hair, and skin. She asked them to trace the shape of their face with their hands, to feel the shape of their eyebrows, their cheeks, and then to compare their own features with those of their new friend.

Only after children had observed and talked about their observations, did she hand out paper and pens and direct them to draw their new friend. Even after the children began drawing, she encouraged them to look again, to continue to observe their new friend, to recall the shape of the child's eyes, nose, and so on. It was nearly twenty minutes before this group of first graders finished and was ready to begin assembling the portraits of their friends into a mural.

Given the fact that the two groups of children were homogeneous, the differences between the two murals were astonishing. One displayed drawings that were full of details, individualized, colorful, and complete, and the other showed weakly drawn stick figures. The only explanation for the difference in the two murals was the difference in children's experiential motivation.

Artistic Motivation

Another form of motivation is found in art itself. Art materials and artworks can serve to motivate children to produce art.

In Reggio Emilia, even the way the art materials are arranged motivates. Stored in clear plastic bins or open baskets, the brightness and shine of materials, organized by color, type, size, and texture, entice children to try color combinations or create collages. Having children involved in mixing their own paints, in watching colors run together, and in feeling the smoothness of paint also can motivate.

Different textures of paper, colors, and size motivate. After a trip to visit a high-rise college dormitory, a group of children in a campus child-care program were given long paper, a variety of construction papers, paints, marking pens, and paste. They were not told to draw the dormitory, but a number of children found the long paper useful in representing their experience of visiting the dorm.

The art of others motivates as well. For example, by examining the illustrations in children's literature (Szekely, 1990), children can see some of the many different ways artists use materials to express feelings, ideas, and emotions. For example, you can introduce children to new ideas for using paper and paste by asking them to look at the illustrations of Ezra Jack Keats and think about how he created the pictures and how they could use the same techniques. You can also have children look at other children's and teachers' works.

Social Motivation

Children involved in a theme or project are motivated to express their experiences. A group project focusing on moths led a group of second-graders to create a mural of moths, a large paper maché and tissue paper moth for the hall, and mobiles of moths for their own rooms.

A group of five-year-olds enjoyed listening to nursery rhymes. Picking up on the group's enjoyment, the teacher led the children in creating several group murals. She provided a panel of brick wallpaper and asked children to add Humpty-Dumpties, all the king's men, and all their horses. The teacher started another mural with a shoe shape, and the children added pictures of themselves to represent all the children who lived in the shoe.

Four-year-olds in a synagogue nursery school created a mural titled "And God created the heavens and the earth." The teacher directed them in painting the heaven on a large sheet of brown wrapping paper using large sponges and brushes with blue paint, and the earth with green. After the paint dried, the group was asked to think about the things God created and to select one either to paint, cut out of paper, or draw and then to place it on the part of the mural depicting the heaven or the earth.

Vicarious Motivation

Not all motivating experiences need to be firsthand. Some can be vicarious and involve imagination. A poem, nursery rhyme, or story that can be read and thought about may be motivational. These are more successful as motivators when children are able to associate themselves with the story, poem, or song. You can ask them to think about the character they liked the best, a new ending for the story, or the part that frightened them or pleased them the most. Then ask the children to draw or paint what they thought about.

Teaching Strategies

The teacher plays an active role as children create art. What this role is depends on the children's previous contact with the media, their developmental stage, and the type of artistic experience they are engaged in. "We need the series perspective, the context, and the preschooler's spontaneous verbalizations and verbal responses for an essentially neutral observer to adequately grasp what has been done" (Beittel, 1973, p. 141).

Just being there to serve as a sounding board (Brittain, 1979, p. 142) may be sufficient to produce art. After all:

> No first grader, engrossed in painting a picture of her pet rabbit, is going to be helped by being asked whether the line she is about to put around her rabbit should be light or heavy. As the brush touches the paper, the proper weight of lines for HER rabbit emerges as the child, paint, brush, paper, and the memory of the rabbit unite in a natural gestalt. (Leeds, 1986, p. 19)

A more direct role is suggested by those endorsing cognitive theories of art. If art truly is an expression of an idea, feeling, or image, it is a form of communication. Children, especially preschoolers of four or five years who are in the preschematic and schematic stages of art, often offer narrative accounts to accompany, explain, and supplement their drawings. They seem to benefit from the presence of an adult who engages them in a conversation about their art, which lets them expand on and share their unique perspectives of the world (Thompson, in press).

But what do you say to children? The answer to this question depends on the age of the child, the context, as well as theory. Sparling and Sparling (1973) suggested that for children under the age of two or three, adult talk should focus on the process: "You covered the paper." "Your whole body moved as you worked." "You moved your crayon so fast over the paper." They reduced the guiding principles for talking to a scribbling child to gearing what you say to the developmental level of the child and being specific.

The Sparlings (1973) also suggest that adults can describe children's art products in terms of visual forms. Discuss the lines, texture, colors, shapes, and forms. When the work becomes representational, recognize the theme with comments like the following: "Your painting is about the trip we took to the farm." "Here are your mother and your sister." "This part of your drawing makes me feel calm and happy."

Thompson (in press) says, "Talking to children about their art enriches their immediate experience and expands their understanding of the nature of visual forms and of their own activity as artists. . . . Clearly, any work of art represents merely a fragment of the work of the artist, but this observation is far from trivial in the case of a young child. Adults who would understand the nature of children's art and further their development must recognize and join in the dialogue through which children name and ponder, initiate and pursue, the creation of visual forms."

In addition to talking to children as they produce works of art, the role of the teachers includes:

What do you say to children as they paint?

1. Selecting materials for children's artistic expression
2. Fostering appreciation for art

Selecting Materials

"When teachers understand how children develop, and when they are sensitive to their role in helping children learn through art, then they have a foundation for developing the content of a good art program for children" (Lasky & Mukerji, 1980, p. 49). The content and the materials selected for the art program must encourage children to express ideas, experiences, and feelings at the sensorimotor and symbolic stages.

Young and inexperienced children have simple desires and needs. They prefer paints, crayons, and paper. At the same time, they enjoy construction materials and dough for modeling (Gaitskell & Gaitskell, 1952). There is no need to focus on the new, the different, or the innovative when selecting materials for children. Each day children should have a choice of selecting something with which to paint, draw, cut, paste, construct, model, or sew.

Painting.   Paints are probably the most popular art material for young children. Children find using bright, fluid paints pleasurable and satisfying. Even though children progress through the same stages of artistic development with paints as they do with other media, going from manipulation to representational work, paints foster a different kind of expression.

It's not unusual for children who draw representational pictures to paint a sheet of paper repeatedly, covering it with one shiny coat of paint after another, or to paint scribbles that run and flow together. The medium seems to lead children into longer periods of experimentation, exploration, and manipulation.

Paints can either be mixed from dry tempera or purchased in liquid form. Mixing small amounts of paint daily ensures freshness and limits waste. Involving children in the mixing can help them to increase confidence and develop independence.

It's important to keep paints fresh and strong. Weak, watery paint holds little appeal, and those that are moldy or dried are worthless. Primary-age children may enjoy a variety of colors. The primary colors, red, yellow, and blue, can be toned by adding black or white. Other colors, such as avocado green, turquoise, lavender, beige, and gray can be mixed. These will stimulate the older children to a renewed interest in paints.

Make paints, brushes, and easels easily accessible and arrange them so that children will need only a little help to use them. Store paper near the easel or painting area, and use large thumbtacks or clips on the easel so that children can manage it by themselves. Store a variety of brushes, some wide and others narrow and pointed, all with points up, in a can next to the paints (Seefeldt, 1973). For children under age four, the long-handled brushes can be cut, with ends sanded or protected with masking tape.

Even though paints continue to be the most popular medium throughout early childhood education, giving older children a variety of paper to work with may sustain this interest. Paper should be large, at least eighteen by twenty-four inches. Children in kindergarten sometimes enjoy pastel newsprint as well as paper of different textures.

After painting, children should also be able to clean up by themselves with little direct assistance. Place a can of water at the easel or table for children to use in soaking brushes, or have them carry the brushes to a sink. Provide a place for children to dry their paintings—either on the floor, the table top, or a clothesline stretched across the room.

Do not limit children's paintings to easels. Only a few easels can be available in any room at any one time, and most primary classrooms will not have them at all. Arrange to have children paint on table tops or on the floor. A six-pack holding cans of paint and brushes can be carried anywhere in the room or even outdoors. Children seem to spend more time on their paint-

Figure 10–3
Materials for painting

Paint with

- Tempera paint, premixed or ready to mix
- Strong watercolor paints
- Finger paints

Paint on

- Paper on easels
- Paper on table tops, floor
- Different colors of construction paper
- Newspapers
- Computer printout paper
- Opened-up paper bags
- Discarded paper from shirts, clothing
- Boxes
- Shelf paper
- Wood
- Paper attached to the play yard fence
- Paper plates
- Different-shaped paper: tall and thin, round, square, or wide

Paint using

- Brushes
- Gadgets or all kinds and shapes of brushes
- Fingers, hands, fists
- Water

ings when the paper is placed on a flat surface like a table top. Such paintings often include more details and are more complex than those done at an easel (Griffin, Highberger, & Cunningham, 1981). (See Figure 10–3.)

Watercolors are rarely recommended for use with young children. They are hard to use, and the colors are thin, weak, and runny. Nevertheless, purchasing good quality watercolors (in individual cakes or tubes) and good quality brushes permits children to enjoy and express themselves in another medium. When working with watercolors, children need smaller pieces of paper, probably nine by twelve inches. Textured watercolor papers offer the best results. The fine colors, small brushes, and water seem to calm young children, and they become intensely involved with watercolors, especially on rainy days.

The use of finger paints in the early childhood program is traditional and springs from the psychoanalytic theory of art. The fluid, messy paints are viewed by educators who advocate the psychoanalytic theory as freeing the children's feelings and permitting them to give free rein to expression without being inhibited by tools. Those who endorse a cognitive view of art do not advocate using finger paints. Their view is that just when children are learning to use a tool for drawing and are trying to represent ideas and experiences with the tool, the school asks them to revert to the primitive use of

*Children should have a concept
of printing before it is introduced.*

hands with a material that doesn't lend itself to details and realistic representations.

Yet finger paints do seem to be a part of the curriculum. Finger paints
can first be introduced on table tops without paper. Let children explore the
medium, just smearing and smearing the paint on the surface. If children
want to save their paintings, you can show them how to take monoprints of
the paintings by carefully spreading a piece of newsprint over the painting
and lifting the paper off the table, taking the paint with it.

Once children are over the manipulative stage of finger painting, they can
use glazed finger-paint paper. They can also use shelf paper or any other
paper with a shiny surface.

If children have enough experience using finger paints, the teacher can help
them develop techniques and styles in order to express ideas. Using a fist,
several fingers, and tools (combs, tongue depressors, or templates) enables
them to include some details and representation in their finger paintings.

Introduce children to the concept of printing by having them observe the
prints on clothing, wrapping paper, wallpaper, or stationery. Teach the idea

Finger Paints

Finger paints can be purchased or made. You can make finger paints by mixing liquid starch with dry tempera. It is handy to give it to children in squirt bottles. Paints can also be made by mixing flour and cold water and cooking until a gel forms, then adding food color or tempera.

Tempera

Add a small amount of liquid detergent to paints, and they'll adhere to waxed surfaces or glass. Add sand or sawdust for textured paints. Add liquid starch to stretch paint. Remember, if you add other substances to paint, you'll change the chemical composition, and they may become toxic.

Figure 10–4
Paint variations

that whenever we want to repeat a pattern or create a design using a repeated pattern, we can do it by printing. Give children a purpose for printing, perhaps making wrapping paper or stationery. Printing stationery is a favorite of primary-age children, and the results are excellent gifts for parents at holidays. Children can make designs on the paper by printing with their fingertips or with the eraser at the end of a pencil. They can even cut the eraser into a shape to make prints of leaves or other geometric shapes. The stationery can be bordered or printed with a design in one corner. A smaller repeat of the pattern can be printed on the envelope to complete the set.

Children can make prints with almost anything. Place a variety of gadgets on the printing table, mix paint to a heavy consistency in a shallow tin dish, and saturate a sponge or folded paper towel with heavy paint, placing it in the bottom of a shallow tin to form a print pad. The teacher can teach the children to press their objects lightly into the paint and then stamp the object on their paper or other surface.

Spools, cookie cutters, hair rollers, tin cans, forks, box lids, and many other everyday household items can be used for printing. Children's first attempts at printing will not result in any planned pattern or design, but will be random. Later attempts will have designs and patterns.

Figure 10–4 gives information on how to make two types of painting materials.

Drawing.   You should have crayons and paper available to help children fulfill their need to represent ideas and feelings through drawing. When the materials are stored on open shelves, the choices are clear and children have ready access to them. Store some sets of crayons in their original boxes of eight colors each, and put others in color-coded boxes with red in

For Primary Children

- Draw on two-by-two-inch blank slides with small felt-tip pens and have a slide show.
- Draw on larger transparencies and have a transparency show. Use permanent magic markers to draw on fabric. Use the fabric to make curtains, aprons, skirts, or other items to give as gifts or for use in the room.
- Draw with yarn. Dip yarn in liquid starch or heavy white glue that's been diluted with a bit of water. Then draw with the yarn, draping it in shapes on the paper.
- Remove the balls from discarded plastic roll tubes of deodorant, fill the tubes with bright liquid tempera paint, and replace the balls so children can draw with them.

Figure 10–5
Drawing projects

one box, blue in another, and so on. It is useful to have another box of scrap crayons to take outdoors. Multicolored chunk crayons can be made by melting bits and pieces of scraps together and then hardening them in a muffin tin. These are fun to use outdoors or on large mural paper for scribbling, but they do not lend themselves to representative, symbolic drawing.

Crayons, felt-tip pens, paint crayons, and other drawing tools should also be available. For children five years of age or older, you can provide colored pencils, ballpoint pens, and lead pencils.

Chalk can also be used for drawing. Children under four need large chunks of chalk that will not break in their overhand grasp. Older children can use finer chalk. Chalk used on colored construction paper interests children. You can spray the chalk painting with fixative or cheap hair spray in a pump bottle. Five-year-olds can dip pieces of chalk into water that's been mixed with a bit of liquid starch or glue for binding, and then draw with the dampened chalk. Wetting a piece of paper and then drawing over it with dry chalk is another technique.

Crayons and other media can be used in combination. Children can combine chalk and crayons or crayons and paints. For older children who can cover paper with a heavy coat of crayon, crayon resist can be fun. Have them draw a picture, perhaps of Halloween night, then show them how to wash over the crayon drawing with a thin coat of dark paint. The paint must be thin enough to let the crayon resist it and show through. Children should probably be nearing six years of age for this.

Show children how they can use their crayons in different ways to obtain different effects. Crayons can be used on their side, tapped on paper to leave dots, or used with pressure to leave shiny marks or tap lightly to leave feathery marks.

Children can construct with paper, wood, or other materials.

Any kind of paper is appropriate for crayon drawing, although it should be smaller than that used for printing. You can purchase manila paper, colored construction paper, and newsprint.

Figure 10–5 gives examples of art projects for children.

Constructing.   Construction offers another dimension for artwork. As with drawing and painting, children's first attempts at construction are exploratory. The thrill of putting items together without any intent to represent anything intrigues them.

First, they'll find out what they can do with scissors, paper, paste, wood, hammers, saws, and junk. They will cut paper into bits with no concern for an end product. They will smear paste around as if it were paint with no thought of joining two pieces of paper. Only after such attempts will children use paper and paste to produce something.

Give children scissors that actually cut. There's no place for plastic scissors that are useless or for blunt scissors that won't work. Teach them how to use scissors and supervise them when they are first learning. Demonstrate how they should hold scissors and offer help to beginners. You may have to hold a child's hand as the child masters the task of cutting. Purchase left-handed scissors for left-handed children and scissors created especially for children who may have a physical disability.

Paper can be cut and curled, cut into fingers, or made into any other shape. Five- and six-year-olds can be taught to fold paper and produce paper cuttings and to cut out the important part of a crayon drawing for emphasis.

All types of papers and paste are useful. Regular library paste is stored in small jars that have lids children can manage. Glue in bottles with rubber tops is also useful, as is the strong white liquid glue that permits children to paste together a wide variety of materials with success.

Collage is a form of paper and paste satisfying to young children. In a collage, bits of flat objects are pasted onto a surface, and the surface can be built up into a three-dimensional work of art. Anything can be used to make collages. Collage-making is more purposeful when the materials are organized by categories and stored in clear containers. Such categorization of buttons, beads, feathers, and seeds in separate, clear containers gives children an experience with classifying and lets them examine the material available. Feathers, straws, toothpicks, shells, shiny paper bits, stars, pieces of dried flowers, carpet scraps, and fabric scraps, each in its own clear container, can be stored near the scissors, paste, and paper.

Children can also collect collage materials. Take a walk around the school to gather materials to make a fall or spring collage. A trip to the office, kitchen, or machine room might yield other scraps for collages.

You can also introduce primary-age children to mosaics, another type of collage. Perhaps you can take the children on a field trip to examine a mosaic on a sidewalk, on the side of a building, or in a museum. After doing so, they can create mosaics by arranging bits of materials to make a design or picture. Small bits of colored construction paper, shells, kitchen tiles, or small stones can be used to make mosaics.

For other mosaics, they can use brightly colored tissue paper cut into pieces. Children dip the pieces into liquid starch or diluted mucilage and arrange them on their paper in a design. A light-colored background, white or pastel, is essential for the tissue to retain transparency. When the tissues are pasted on top of each other, new colors result and an attractive product emerges. Children under age seven find it too tedious to cut many pieces of paper, so cut the paper for them before the pasting begins.

For junk construction, you will need boxes, paper, cans, and other containers. You can get hundreds of them from local factories and packaging plants. You can also use cleanser cans, cracker or toothpaste boxes, and discarded egg and berry cartons. Supply the children with unlimited masking tape, plastic-coated wires, hole punches, brads, and strong glue for joining, and children will construct marvels. (See Figure 10–6.)

Kindergarten children may be given a theme around which to center their construction. They might be asked to build a machine, a spaceship, a robot,

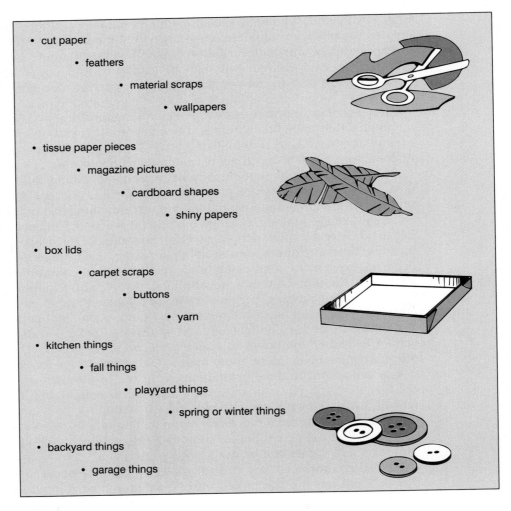

- cut paper
    - feathers
        - material scraps
            - wallpapers

- tissue paper pieces
    - magazine pictures
        - cardboard shapes
            - shiny papers

- box lids
    - carpet scraps
        - buttons
            - yarn

- kitchen things
    - fall things
        - playyard things
            - spring or winter things

- backyard things
    - garage things

Figure 10–6
Materials for collage

an animal, or anything else. Sometimes children can work together in small groups on one large product.

Figure 10–7 gives two construction projects for children.

Creating with Wood. What could be more satisfying than creating with wood? The joining of two pieces of wood and the physical release of hammering nails into a board or sawing a rough piece of wood gives children a sense of accomplishment. The products, even though they will not be representational, have weight, height, and depth, and children value them highly.

Mobiles

Mobiles are difficult for young children to make. A mobile should hang free so the air can breeze through it and move its parts. Balance is required. Children, however, can attach things to a coat hanger for a type of mobile. A theme should direct the project and focus children's intentions, such as creating a mobile for spring, night, or Halloween. Children can think of objects or people dealing with the theme, make pictures of them, cut them out, and hang them on a coat hanger with a piece of string. Adults will probably have to attach the drawing to the hanger because children have difficulty making knots. Children can also use soft pipe cleaners to attach objects to a frame. A group project creating a large mobile around some theme is appropriate for children five years old or older.

Stabiles

Stabiles are another type of construction. Any kind of junk can be used, but the purpose of the stabile is to create a form that has a fixed base and is upright. Using soft clay that will harden, wood, or styrofoam as a base, children arrange sticks, straws, weeds, flowers, or other materials in the base to form a stabile. A stabile is the opposite of a mobile. It's stable, and firmly planted on a surface.

Figure 10–7
Construction projects

Soft wood and high-quality tools are required for safety. Accidents occur when tools are inadequate. Steel tools are a good investment and will last for years. C clamps or vises, fifteen to twenty inches, medium-sized hammers, sandpaper, and nails are necessary to begin woodworking. You can get wood scraps from lumberyards or carpentry shops.

Teach children how to hold and use each tool. As a group, decide on rules for the workbench area. Show children where to place their hands when sawing and using the hammer. Demonstrate the power of the hammer by smashing a can in front of them. Remember that a young child has enough strength to hammer a nail into a finger or saw deeply into flesh. You might ask a parent, teenager, or volunteer to supervise at all times at the woodworking bench. Children need individual attention to gain control over the materials and make things with wood.

After a lot of experience with wood in the kindergarten or primary grades, children can follow templates to create actual objects. Children can measure wood to make a roof for the rabbit hutch or the sides of a bookshelf. Balance these more structured activities with free woodworking.

Modeling. Clay to squish between fingers, roll around in your hands, or pound on a table is satisfying and pleasurable. You can provide many types of clay. Potter's clay in red, gray, or white is available ready-mixed or in

Salt Dough
Salt
Flour
Water

Mix equal parts of salt and flour. Add enough water to moisten well. Knead until a uniform, pliable dough is formed. Add a few drops of food coloring if desired. All dough will harden if left in the air. If you do not want the dough to harden, add a few drops of cooking oil. Keep stored in a refrigerator, for children's use.

Baking Dough
4 cups flour
1 cup salt
1/2 cup water (approximate)

Mix to a pliable form that doesn't stick to the hands. Knead for a few minutes until smooth. Children create all sorts of shapes with the dough. Then bake 1 hour in a 325°F oven.

Sawdust Dough
Sawdust
Wallpaper paste
Water

Mix equal parts of sawdust, wallpaper paste, and water. If mixture is sticky, add more sawdust. Mixture will harden as it dries.

Figure 10–8
Modeling materials

powdered form, as is self-hardening clay that doesn't require firing. Nonhardening clay, play dough, and other materials are also useful.

Store clay in containers that will keep in moisture. Prepare the clay by making small fistfuls out of the large chunk. A small indentation in each chunk can be filled with water to keep clay fresh and pliable enough for children's hands. Keep Masonite boards covered with nonstick fabric or squares of nonstick cloth as working surfaces for clay. Children can then take some clay and a mat and work wherever they wish.

As children work with clay and dough, demonstrate various techniques. For example, to attach parts of clay to one another, a small piece of clay can be dissolved in a small amount of water to form a mudlike fluid called slip. Slip is used like glue to attach pieces of clay. Smoothing the two edges with fingers or tools completes the joining process.

The only tools children usually require when working with clay are their hands. But tools can help five-year-olds and primary-age children add texture and interest to their products and develop the skills of a ceramist. Figure 10–8 gives directions for making three types of modeling dough.

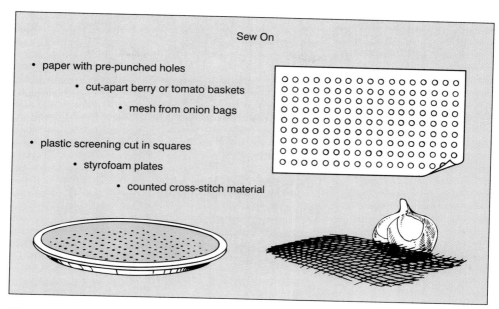

Figure 10–9
Materials for practicing sewing

Sewing.   Sewing requires an amazing degree of small-muscle coordination. Children four years of age or older enjoy it. Each room should have its own sewing box, equipped with large-eyed blunt needles, thread, scissors, scrap materials, and buttons. The sewing box is useful for making repairs on children's clothing, dolls, or puppets, but it can also be available for children's use. Children might use material to sew a dress for a doll, a cover for the housekeeping area, or an entire puppet.

Large darning needles, yarn, and sewing bases that allow the needle and thread to slip through easily should also be handy. Plastic screening cut into small pieces with edges bound with masking tape to form a frame is inexpensive and appropriate for children's first sewing attempts. Children can easily push the needle and thread through the holes. Once they get the idea of sewing, children can create patterns and designs. Usually one or two children will master the ability to thread needles and knot when finished, and they can help teach other children.

Burlap is another material children handle easily if it is placed in some frame for support. Onion or potato sacks with large netting are useful. Styrofoam meat trays or containers might also be used as a base for sewing. Primary-age children are able to learn a few simple stitches, for example, running stitch and cross stitch. They may design a sampler or picture as a gift. (See Figure 10–9.)

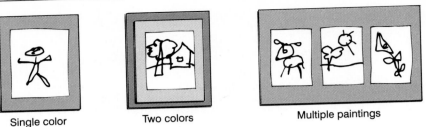

Single color   Two colors   Multiple paintings

Paste painting on contrasting colors of construction paper.

Paste frame over painting. On very special occasions, to create a gift for parents, cut a shape in the frame.

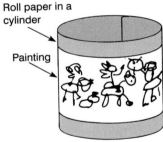

Roll paper in a cylinder

Painting

Triangle—fold paper in thirds

Fold heavy paper or cardboard to make 3-D frames.

Painting

Box lid   Styrofoam tray   Paper plate

Paste painting, drawing, or scribble in box lid, styrofoam tray, or on a paper plate for a different frame.

Figure 10–10
Suggested frames for children's art

Fostering Appreciation of Art

"In the literal sense of the term, it's doubtful if appreciation can be taught . . . we can set the conditions under which appreciation can develop" (Riston & Smith, 1975, p. 188). Fostering appreciation of art involves at least three elements:

1. Surrounding children with beauty and works of art
2. Demonstrating respect and appreciation for children's art products
3. Introducing children to the concept of the artist and to the idea that they can discuss the qualities of art in their work and the works of others

Fostering appreciation takes place throughout the day in subtle but tangible ways (Broudy, 1970). (See Figure 10–10.) Parents can also show their appreciation for children's art by providing experiences, time, and space for art at home. You can suggest to parents that they try some of the following:

- Take trips to art galleries and shows with their children
- Keep drawing, collage, and painting materials available for children to use at home
- Find places to display children's art
- Borrow prints of art from the library to display at home
- Wonder with children over the beauty in their environment, examining the colors of a moth's wings, a rainbow, the weeds growing in the cracks of the sidewalk
- Talk with children about their art

Surrounding Children with Beauty

Children's classrooms are their homes away from home, where they spend the greater part of their waking hours. Classrooms should, therefore, surround children with beauty. Teachers should keep their rooms clean and orderly and demonstrate to the children that they respect them by creating an aesthetically pleasing environment.

The teachers of the British Infant Schools and the child-care centers in Reggio Emilia are convinced that children's behaviors, as well as their art, are affected by the quality of the classroom environment. Every corner of the room, the hallway, and the building holds something of beauty. In these schools, it may be a plant, a branch of spring flowers just about to burst into bloom, or a lovely vase placed on a table draped with an interesting piece of fabric. At other times, displays are more elaborate, based on some theme or unit of work (rocks, shells, dinosaurs) that children have studied.

Sometimes children arrange the displays, and sometimes teachers take charge.

Plants, flowers, and prints of famous paintings are in every room. Rather than decorating the room with trite cutout pumpkins or stereotypical representations of bunnies or flowers, teachers find prints of works of art for children to enjoy. It is possible to borrow prints from the local library or to purchase inexpensive prints or postcards of famous works of art from your local museum. Sometimes magazines and newspapers contain prints suitable for display.

Display the children's works as well. At around age five or six, children will want their work displayed. Four-year-olds and young five-year-olds still want to take their work home immediately. For these children, it may be appropriate to tack their artwork on a bulletin board from which they can remove their picture when it's time to go home. When children are able to leave their works for others to enjoy, more permanent displays can be arranged.

One teacher installed two strips of balsa wood in the hall at two levels. Children displayed their paintings, murals, and other artworks by tacking them to these strips (Cohen & Gainer, 1976). Kindergarten and primary-grade children can be responsible for arranging their own displays. Show children how to use a staple gun as well as thumbtacks, tape, and other materials for mounting and display.

Small tables should be available in order to permit children to display three-dimensional artworks. An attractive cloth can be draped over the display table. You might label these displays to inform others about the media, theme, or techniques used.

Appreciating Children's Work

Respect for children's products starts by providing them with freedom and choice of materials and time to master the media, and it continues with your treatment of their products. Even when children aren't actively interested in their product, you should treat their work with respect. Don't act as if each scribble is a masterpiece, but you can store samples in a folder or portfolio as a record of children's progress.

At times, you can cut parts of children's scribbles or paintings and frame them to send home to parents or for display in the room. Select contrasting colored construction paper for the frames.

Help parents to understand and respect the work of their children. Appreciation requires knowledge. Even before school begins, hold a meeting for parents to show them samples of typical art products of children at that stage. Explain what the stages mean and why each is important to the child's developing artistic skill and academic achievement. Prepare a booklet for parents explaining the types of art activities you'll be including in the program and why. You could include examples of art in the booklet, so parents know what to expect.

Continue informing parents about their child's artwork by attaching explanatory notes to children's products. You might note that a drawing is the child's first attempt to use geometric forms to represent reality or that the child is now selecting realistic colors. For scribblers, tell something of what the child sang while painting or how involved she was in the process.

Suggest ways parents can display their children's artwork at home, and encourage home art production. Some teachers are able to give each child an art kit to use at home, which includes some crayons, paper scraps, paste, and scissors.

Concept of the Artist

Begin by letting children know they are artists. They create a product and express their ideas and feelings through their artwork. Children might discuss their work by telling you the title or something about the meaning of their drawing. Start by discussing the concepts of art and the artist, using the children's works: "How did you do this?" "What were you thinking of when you decided to build this?" These questions introduce children to the idea that art expresses some idea or feeling.

Look at the artwork of others. Ask children to think of a name for another child's painting, and see if they can guess the name the artist gave it. This introduces the concept that the same work of art may hold different meanings for different people.

Asking children to guess the title of a painting or a print by a famous artist introduces art history. Discuss why the artists selected the name they did, where they lived and when, and what life was like for them when they were the same age as the children.

Discussing what life was like when the painting was created introduces the idea that art has a history and that there are differences as well as similarities in artworks. There is no "correct" way to do this. Some questions that might stimulate children's thinking are: "What is this?" "Can you tell what you see?" "What does it make you think about?" "Why do you think the artist made it?" "What was she trying to say?" "How does it make you feel?" "Do you like it? Why or why not?" "What colors, shapes, forms, lines, circles, or squares did the artist use? Why?"

Children over age five could be given two paintings to compare. They might be asked, "Which would you hang in your room? Why?" "Look at how the artists worked. Which do you think took a long time? Was the artist careful when working? Which didn't take long to paint? How can you tell?" "Are these both good ways to work? Why or why not?"

Take the children to visit museums to observe art or to visit artists in their studios. Artists might also come to visit the class and discuss their work or demonstrate techniques for children. The goal is to develop the ideas that:

- Art is a means of nonverbal communication.
- Art is the product resulting from the idea of the artist.
- Artists use what they see, think, and feel to create art with a wide variety of materials (Schwartz & Douglas, 1967).

Don't forget to include discussion of art in children's literature. Use illustrations of the works of Leo Lionni, Ezra Jack Keats, Virginia Burton, Marcia Brown, José Aruego, Donald Crews, Molly Bang, Beatrix Potter, and others to communicate ideas and feelings.

Summary

Art is serious work. Through the visual arts, children express their ideas, thoughts, and feelings using symbols. Because art is a symbolic process, it demands careful thought on both the part of teacher and child. The teacher's role is a serious one. The teacher is responsible for understanding the theories and values of children's art as well as being able to articulate them to others. Like the teachers in Reggio Emilia, teachers in our nation should carefully plan to motivate children before expecting them to express themselves through visual art forms. Teachers should also develop skills in selecting appropriate art materials for children's use and in guiding children in the process of creating art.

By considering their own art products and the artworks of others as serious work, children can appreciate them. A part of this appreciation is being able to talk about art, describing, comparing, and contrasting elements in artworks.

When art is considered seriously, children's creative expression can thrive and "there is great pleasure, the compulsive satisfaction obtained from a constant involvement in the process of art. There is the willingness to disregard what others are doing, to flout convention, and to pursue one's own ideas and goals, however formulated, to their graphic conclusions" (Gardner, 1980, p. 268).

Projects

Continuing Case Study

Collect samples of your child's drawings and paintings over a period of time. Analyze them to determine the stage of art your child is in. Do you observe any changes in the child's art over a period of time? How would you use this knowledge in planning for this child's experiences with the visual arts?

Observe your child when given choices of media. What media does the child most often select? Can you ask the child why? How long does the child spend with a specific medium? How does the child's use of this medium differ from other types of media?

1. Make a list of children's books with outstanding illustrations that could be used to introduce children to the concept of the artist as well as to different techniques and a wide variety of art materials.
2. Observe children making art. Which materials do children choose most frequently? How much time do children of different ages spend with these materials? How do they use them?
3. Interview teachers in a primary school, and ask them how they manage to protect children's time with art and integrate art into regular classroom activities.
4. Work with a small group of children (or even one child) to try to motivate art by a firsthand experience, such as touching a tree or a kitten or observing a moth. Then ask the children to draw a picture. Identify how this experience influenced the drawings.

Resources

Edwards, C. (1990). *Affective development and the creative arts: A process approach to early childhood development.* New York: Teachers College Press. A resource for teachers, it is full of ideas for children's art activities.

Golomb, C. (1990). *The child's creation of a pictorial world.* Berkeley, CA: University of California Press. An outstanding book, it describes how children depict their world. It is a conceptual book, yet offers insights into practice.

Mary Renks Jalongo's article "The child's right to the expressive arts: Nurturing the imagination as well as the intellect" in *Childhood Education, 1990, Volume 66* (pp. 311–317) is a good resource for documenting the power of arts for children.

Sources of slides, prints, and art reproductions can be obtained from your local museums, art galleries, or bookstores. The following supply prints as well.

Art Institute of Chicago
Matching and Adams Street
Chicago, IL 60603

National Gallery of Art
Department of Extension Programs
Washington, DC 20565

Smithsonian Institution
Washington, DC 20560

References

Arnheim, R. (1954). *Art and visual perception: The psychology of the creative experience.* Berkeley: University of California Press.

Beittel, K. R. (1973). *Alternatives for art education research.* Dubuque, IA: Wm. C. Brown.

Brittain, W. L. (1979). *Creativity, art, and the young child.* New York: Macmillan.

Broudy, H. S. (1970). Quality education and aesthetic education. In G. Pappas (Ed.), *Concepts in art and education* (pp. 66–81). New York: Macmillan.

Bruner, J. (1990). *Acts of meaning.* Cambridge, MA: Harvard University Press.

City of Reggio Emilia. (1984). *The hundred languages of children.* Reggio Emilia, Italy: Author.

Clay, M. M. (1975). *What did I write?* Auckland, New Zealand: Heinemann.

Cohen, E. P., & Gainer, R. S. (1976). *Art: Another language for learning.* New York: Citation.

Cole, N. (1966). *Children's art from deep down inside.* New York: John Day.

Dewey, J. (1944). *Art and experience.* New York: Macmillan.

Eisner, E. (1972). *Educating artistic vision.* New York: Macmillan.

Feldman, E. B. (1970). *Becoming human through art.* New York: Macmillan.

Forseth, W. D. (1980). Art activities, attitudes, and achievement in elementary mathematics. *Studies in Art Education, 21,* 22–27.

Gaitskell, C., & Gaitskell, M. (1952). *Art education in the kindergarten.* Peoria, IL: Charles A. Bennett.

Gardner, H. (1980). *Artful scribbles.* New York: Basic Books.

Goertz, E. C. (1966). *Graphomotor development in preschool children.* Unpublished master's thesis. Cornell University.

Golomb, C. (1992). *The child's creation of a pictorial world.* Berkeley, CA: University of California Press.

Goodenough, F. (1926). *Measurement of intelligence by drawings.* New York: Harcourt Brace Jovanovich.

Green, J. C., & Hasselbring, T. S. (1981). The acquisition of language concepts by hearing impaired children through selected aspects of an experimental core art curriculum. *Studies in Art Education, 23,* 22–31.

Griffin, M. E., Highberger, R., & Cunningham, J. L. (1981). Young children's paintings: A comparison of horizontal and vertical painting surfaces. *Studies in Art Education, 23,* 46.

Jalongo, M. R. (1990). The child's right to the expressive arts: Nurturing the imagination as well as the intellect. *Childhood Education, 66,* 195–203.

Klein, M. L. (1985). *The development of writing.* Englewood Cliffs, NJ: Prentice Hall.

Lansing, K. M. (1981). The effects of drawing on the development of mental representation. *Studies in Art Education, 22,* 32–37.

Lasky, L., & Mukerji, R. (1980). *Art: Basic for young children.* Washington, DC: National Association for the Education of Young Children.

Leeds, J. A. (1986). Teaching and the reasons for making art. *Art Education, 39,* 130–132.

Lewis, H. P., & Livison, N. (1980). *Art: Basic for young children.* Washington, DC: National Association for the Education of Young Children.

Lowenfeld, V. (1957). *Creative and mental growth* (3rd ed.). New York: Macmillan.

Luquet, G. H. (1913). *Three drawings of a child.* Paris: F. Alcan.

McWhinnie, H. (1992). Art for young children. In C. Seefeldt (Ed.), *The early childhood curriculum: A review of current research* (2nd ed.), (pp. 262–286). New York: Teachers College Press.

Moyer, J. (1990). Whose creation is it, anyway? *Childhood Education, 66,* 130–132.

National Art Education Association. (1992). *Art education: Elementary guidelines (draft version).* Washington, DC: Author.

Piaget, J., & Inhelder, B. (1969). *The psychology of the child.* New York: Basic Books.

Raines, S., & Canady, R. J. (1990). *The whole language kindergarten.* New York: Teachers College Press.

Riston, J. E., & Smith, J. A. (1975). *Creative teaching of art in the elementary school.* Boston: Allyn & Bacon.

Schickendanz, J. (1986). *More than the ABCs.* Washington, DC: National Association for the Education of Young Children.

Schwartz, J. B., & Douglas, N. (1967). *Increasing the awareness of art ideas of culturally deprived kindergarten children through experiences with ceramics.* Washington, DC: Department of Health, Education, and Welfare.

Seefeldt, C. (1973). The use of wide paint brushes in the five-year-old kindergarten. *Studies in Art Education, 14*(3), 11–13.

Smith, F. (1984). *Creative teaching of art in the elementary school.* Boston: Allyn & Bacon.

Sparling, J., & Sparling, M. (1973). How to talk to a scribbler. *Young Children, 28,* 333–341.

Szekely, G. (1990). An introduction to art: Children's books. *Childhood Education, 66,* 132–139.

Thomas, C. M. (1990). "I make my mark": The significance of talk in young children's artistic development. *Early Childhood Research Quarterly, 5,* 215–232.

Thompson, B. (in press). *Art.* Washington, DC: National Association for the Education of Young Children.

Music

"Music is a joy. It sharpens and delights the senses."

(Kuhmerker, 1969, p. 157)

After you read this chapter, you should be able to respond to the following questions:

1. What are the traditional theories of music education?

2. What are the values of music education for young children?

3. Describe the role of the teacher in setting the stage and selecting the goals for music.

4. Discuss how you would plan and implement the goals of:

   a. Movement for infants and toddlers, preschoolers, and kindergartners and primary-age children

   b. Listening for infants and toddlers, preschoolers, and kindergartners and primary-age children

   c. Singing for infants and toddlers, preschoolers, and kindergartners and primary-age children

Music is a wonder in and of itself, and yet it is also much more. It is singing, dancing, and creative movement, and it can be used as a change of pace and a release for tension and energy. Music for young children can be a set of related, interdependent, or individual activities, either spontaneous or lasting for a few moments or hours. Music can involve one child or a whole group and can enhance the total curriculum. Music "is, and should always be, an enjoyable experience" (Comte, 1982, p. 38).

"Music learning is especially important during early childhood" (Music Educators National Conference [MENC], 1991, p. 3). During their early years, children can accomplish a great deal musically. Their natural abilities of moving rhythmically, playing, and singing can be expanded and developed.

Theories of Music

Songs, games, chants, and finger plays for mothers and children were among the gifts and occupations Froebel designed for the kindergarten. But even before Froebel, music was a part of the curriculum for young children. In early Colonial schools, children were taught the Psalms and the alphabet through song. By the 1900s, theories of music education were being developed. The theories of composers and music educators Émile Jaques-Dalcroze, Carl Orff, and Zoltán Kodály continue to influence music education today.

Émile Jaques-Dalcroze

Jaques-Dalcroze, an early twentieth-century Swiss educator, developed a system of music education that is still used today (Alper, 1992; Comte, 1982). He organized music education around the following:

- *Movement.* Development of bodily movement as the means of fusing the motor activities of the child with intellectual experiences.
- *Listening.* Developing an ear for sound, being able to sing a melody.
- *Creating.* The capacity for free invention, or piano improvisation, which would integrate movement, listening, and creating.

Jaques-Dalcroze believed in an integrated approach to music, one in which listening, moving, and creating would be related. Believing that the physical body was a musical instrument, Jaques-Dalcroze began by teaching movement to children about four years of age. To begin, he had children tiptoe around the room to piano accompaniment. When the music stopped, the children were to freeze. Jaques-Dalcroze believed that this helped children understand the difference between sound and silence (Jaques-Dalcroze, 1921).

As children progress, they learn to keep in step with the music and to adjust their steps to it. They can make their steps larger or heavier when loud music is played or smaller and quicker for soft music. When the tempo changes, children adapt by slowing down or speeding up. Legato, flowing music results in smooth movements, while staccato, detached music leads to quick, light movements.

The relationship between movement, listening, and creating makes the theories of Jaques-Dalcroze widely accepted today. "Viewed in retrospect, Dalcroze's objectives were always toward dual growth—cognitive and affective—through music. From the very beginning he emphasized the interrelatedness of time, space, and energy in movement" (Aronoff, 1969, p. 170).

Carl Orff

A twentieth-century German composer and educator, Carl Orff also believed that music education begins with movement. His imaginative and spontaneous approach to teaching music started with children's own body responses and actions. He based his teaching on the following:

- The idea that rhythm is represented in all living things
- That speech, movement, and music form an integrated whole in each person
- That no child, no one, is wholly nonmusical

Zoltán Kodály

Zoltán Kodály based his ideas of music education on singing. He developed his theories after Hungary came under Communist control in 1945. If people were really to be lifted from their misery, he believed, they should be given something permanent for themselves—something that could never be taken from them, that could bolster their morale in time of trouble and lift them in time of joy. To this end, Kodály developed a music curriculum that began with three-year-olds in nursery schools.

Instead of starting with rhythmic movement, Kodály taught children simple folk music. After the children were able to recognize and reproduce Hungarian folk tunes, they were introduced to the visual representation of music (Bacon, 1969).

Three- and four-year-olds sang nursery songs, stepped, clapped to the beat of songs, and played simple percussion instruments. They were taught to recognize differences between loud and soft and to identify familiar melodies. They were introduced to concepts of high and low pitch and fast and slow tempo. By the time children were four years old, they were expected to know more than twenty songs and to be able to identify known songs simply by hearing the clapped rhythm of the melody.

A Kodály curriculum spirals from very simple to more complex folk songs and concepts. As children grow, they are introduced to rhythmic clapping, hand signals (a different signal for each note of the musical scale), charts of rhythmic counting and clapping, and charts of hand signals.

After forty years of the Kodály method in Hungarian schools, Hungarians up to the age of thirty or so can usually read and write music as naturally as their own language. Children who have had Kodály music instruction as a daily activity show greater achievement in nearly all other academic fields, especially reading and mathematics (Bacon, 1969). And who could doubt the power of music to hold a nation together after watching the Hungarian people singing their country's songs in Freedom Square when freedom came to Hungary during the Velvet Revolutions of the late 1980s and early 1990s?

The theories of Jaques-Dalcroze, Orff, and Kodály continue to influence music education today. They each advocate that:

- Music is for everyone.
- Music instruction should begin early in life, during the critical preschool years.
- Teachers can design methods appropriate for the young child.
- Singing, listening to music, and moving to music are naturally related to the everyday experiences of young children.
- Creative responses to music should be fostered.
- Studying formal instruments should be delayed until musical skills and understanding are fully developed.
- Instruction can be designed that is appropriate for groups.

The different theories of Jaques-Dalcroze, Orff, and Kodály indicate that there is no best approach or program to teach music (Alper, 1992). The music program for young children must take the best from each theory to adapt every experience to the needs, maturity, and desires of the individual child. Each experience must be based not only on a theory, but also on the teacher's understanding of how each child perceives and understands the world.

The Values of Music

Music is valuable not only for itself, but also as an integral part of the curriculum. Music can enhance children's creativity and their social, physical, intellectual, and emotional development. In today's world of accountability, teachers need to recognize the value of music education and be ready to tell others how valuable music is for children's growth, development, and learning (Gardner, 1985).

Music for Music

Music exists in the curriculum for its own end, to give children the opportunity to learn about its meaning and implied emotionalism and its effects and values in relation to beliefs about reality and growth (Stinson, 1990). It provides children with the opportunity to reflect and gain new insights into life and to discriminate, perceive, and enjoy the beauty of art.

Part of the purpose of music in the curriculum is to acquaint children with the diversity of music. Children, even toddlers, enter the preschool with developed tastes in music. They know what they like. When Ms. S. asked a group of three-year-olds what their favorite Christmas song was, they responded with a commercial: "Shop at Big Store, Shop at Big Store, It's Your Christmas Town." Children's musical taste can be developed, but they can't do this by themselves (MENC, 1991). They need adults who will guide and introduce them to a variety of musical forms and styles. They need to gain the ability to recognize, discriminate, and judge music. This is a gradual process (Thomas, 1983). It is neither imposed on the children nor left up to chance. You should carefully plan opportunities for children to develop the ability to:

- Demonstrate preferences in music
- Differentiate characteristics of different types of music
- Gain the idea of what a composer is
- Learn the names and works of specific composers
- Relate to music with meaning and feeling

Creativity

Creativity is the power to produce something new and original. It is more than just daydreaming or thinking about things. It results in a product that is original and clever (Torrance, 1965). Creative persons are those who produce fluently, making a great number of new and original products, and who are flexible in their thinking. The arts, both visual and musical, offer children unique opportunities to create and to be fluent, flexible, and original in their thinking (Hoffman, Kantner, Colbert, & Sims, 1991).

Children are often naturally original in their response to music. They're inventive, and are so joyous and spontaneous in their approach to life that they often overwhelm adults with their expressive creativity. Children

Value the uniqueness of each child's response to music.

express their feelings and ideas freely as they pound on a drum or dance uninhibitedly in the light of a sunbeam. This inventiveness demands opportunities for expressive creativity in school.

Children's initial expressive creativity does not, however, meet the requirements of true or productive creativity. Children need time, maturity, skills, and knowledge to produce something new that will change the course of our thinking and way of life. But their original responses to music should be cherished, protected, and supported by the school.

Teachers who are spontaneous and who value spontaneity and originality of thought in others support children's creative responses. Those who are respectful of unusual ideas foster creative responses (Torrance, 1965). As children respond to music, you can support them by:

1.   Focusing on the different ways children respond to the same experience, valuing each response. Let children see that their uniqueness is valued. "Look, Jerry is moving his arms this way to the drumbeats. Who can find another way?" "What else can we sing?" "How can you dance to let others know you're sad?"

2.   Recognizing all children. Comment on the dance and musical expression of each child. "What a smooth dance, Linn." "Olivia, your song makes me think of Christmas bells." Let children know you've really thought about their creations and recognize them as individuals.

3.   Giving children the freedom, materials, and time in which to react. Creativity takes time, practice, and skill. Large blocks of time, along with freedom to use the time as children see fit, are necessary.

4.   Withdrawing judgment. Although creativity involves a product, young children's products cannot be compared to adults'. Don't direct the children, telling them how to move, sing, or produce, but let them express their ideas and feelings in their own way. Then let them do the evaluation. "How did it make you feel?" "Which way was the best?" "What would you do differently next time?"

Music Is Social

Music not only provides opportunities for aesthetic and creative development, but for social development as well. "Music is by its very nature a social art" (Leonhard, 1983, p. 23). As Kodály recognized, music has always held a significant place in society's rites and rituals. Music serves to unite social groups because it helps each person feel part of a group. Almost everyone can recall wonderful feelings of belonging that resulted from singing in a church or synagogue, at a sorority or fraternity meeting, or around a campfire with a scout group.

Social skills develop once children feel part of a group. Music requires the participation of all, which demands respect for one another's ideas and responsibilities. Children must wait their turn and cooperate with others if they are to strike a triangle only when appropriate and share instruments.

Self-esteem can be fostered through music (Brazelton, 1990). All children, but especially those with special needs, find music a nonthreatening and pleasurable experience. When carefully planned to meet the needs of individuals as well as the group, music permits all children to feel successful and important (Lewis, 1990).

> The basic elements of a music program—singing songs, playing instruments, listening to music, and rhythmic movement—can widen the horizons of the disabled child. Music can draw the shy, withdrawn child into a group, encourage spastic children to control their movements, and encourage all to come into closer contact with their peers and support social relationships. (Spodek, Saracho, & Lee, 1984, p. 294)

Music enables children to feel a part of their group, and at the same time it transmits the values of the larger society. Folk songs transmit the culture of one generation to the next (Bagheri, 1990; Eigan, 1988). "Through folk music we share in the culture of others, and glimpse an understanding of groups of people who shared common experiences, interests, skills, and aims" (Lloyd, 1978).

Music Is Physical

"Music needs to be a part of an infant's experiences from the very beginning of life . . . it helps develop balance, physical coordination, and control over muscles" (Brooks & Obrutz, 1981, p. 9). As children sway, clap, dance, and sing to music, they are developing muscular control and physical coordination. The ability to respond vocally to music, to control the muscles of the mouth, and even the ability to listen require physical control. Control over the larger muscles develops through moving to music, playing instruments, and observing others move or dance. Participation in music helps children develop an awareness of their own bodily capabilities and an awareness of their ability to master themselves.

Music and the Intellect

Music is an abstraction that requires perceiving, remembering, and conceptualizing. Bruner (1966) describes three different modes of understanding and processing information from the environment:

1. Through action and manipulation (enactive)
2. Through perceptual organization and imagery: aural, kinesthetic, and visual (iconic)
3. Through words and symbols (symbolic)

Music offers children the opportunity to use all three modes of cognition rather than just one (Alper, 1992). Before the child begins using language, he uses the enactive mode of knowing—moving to music and learning about the world through action and manipulation. The iconic mode of learning, which involves organizing perceptions and forming images, develops by listening to music. Children develop auditory discrimination as they distinguish between sounds, picking out those that are alike or different or recalling a series of sounds (Krumhansl & Keil, 1982; Gardner, 1985). The symbolic mode develops from the enactive and iconic modes of learning. All music involves symbols; notes, words, sounds, and movement are all symbolic. The pleasure of singing and creating notations for songs results in children's growing awareness and understanding of symbols.

Music and the Emotions

"Music is a joy. It sharpens and delights the senses. In the classroom teachers value music for creative movement, song and dramatics, expression, as a change of pace, and as a release for tension and energy" (Kuhmerker,

1969, p. 157). Music can ease a tense moment when tempers flare and tension mounts; a song can lighten the mood, enabling children and adults alike to release tensions and relax.

Music can help children identify, clarify, and structure their own feelings. "Music is one mode of understanding the world and our experience of it, it is a way of knowing the affective and knowing through feeling" (Swanwick, 1979, p. 39). It helps put children in touch with their own and others' feelings. Children find that music can be sad, happy, humorous, serious, thoughtful, or angry.

Objectives for Music Education

Establishing Goals

As a result of their experiences with music, including moving, listening, and singing, children should be able to:

1. Have intense involvement in and respond to musical experiences
2. Develop an aesthetic awareness of the value of music as a joy in life
3. Develop confidence in their own ability to express themselves creatively in movement, listening, and singing
4. Grow in the ability to express ideas, feelings, and attitudes through moving, singing, and listening
5. Through manipulation of and familiarity with music, be able to make discriminations among instruments, songs, and types of music

Setting the Stage

Create a musical environment in the classroom. Provide adequate space to move and enough time to explore, experiment, and grow. Also allow adequate space to move and enough time for planned musical experiences and freedom to play with music. An environment created for musical growth includes:

- A flexible schedule, so music can be integrated into every activity of the day and can be used on the spot for the moment. Each child's play, questions, or random investigations can be used as a basis for learning music.
- Keeping music informal and welcoming and building on children's ideas. Allow for repetitions.
- Designing activities for individual children, small groups, and the total group.

Statement of Goals

From
Teaching General Music: A Course of Study
Music Educators National Conference, 1991

Performing/Reading
During preschool and kindergarten, children will:
* use singing and speaking voice to demonstrate different vocal timbres
* select and play a variety of classroom instruments to indicate different timbres
* match given pitch patterns through singing within a comfortable range
* sing simple short melodies with a range of a fifth
* respond to a steady beat through clapping, swaying, walking
* sing or chant an example of loud and soft dynamics through alternating short phrases or echoing.
* move to indicate phrase changes in simple form
* play classroom instruments to demonstrate phrase changes
* sing a variety of simple folk songs and composed songs
* create visual representations to indicate formal structure
* create personal icons to represent simple pitch patterns or directions

Creating
During preschool and kindergarten, children will:
* invent simple sound patterns
* develop a system for communicating individual improvised patterns
* create or invent songs to accompany play or stories
* develop icons to communicate and record personal pieces
* sing or play invented endings to melodic phrase presented
* express mood through movement or classroom instruments

* Appreciating each child's ideas and accepting each at his or her own level of participation.
* Providing sensory experiences that will stimulate and challenge children to use higher levels of thinking and encourage them to perceive, associate, relate, and make value judgments.
* Offer children musical sounds, instruments, and records that are accurate and produce quality musical timbres.
* Plan for a balance of spontaneous, free exploration of music activities initiated by you or other adults.

The Role of the Teacher

Teaching children music depends on the teacher. It is not the method, theory, or even musical ability that counts, but the teacher (Andress, 1984). Teachers can:

Listening and describing

During preschool and kindergarten, children will:

- following teacher-guided experiences, listen to short compositions
- move to and discuss components that occur in listening examples
- expand attention to a variety of familiar and unfamiliar music through repeated listenings.
- indicate high and low pitches through listening
- move to express contrast of loud and soft dynamic levels
- demonstrate through movement and discuss style characteristics of marches and lullabies
- graphically represent "smooth and jumpy" stepwise movements or skips of a piece.
- visually and aurally identify instruments that represent different families such as string, wind, and percussion
- talk about musical sounds using simple vocabulary such as up/down, loud/soft, fast/slow

Valuing

During preschool and kindergarten, children will:

- discuss how music exists at home and school
- participate eagerly in classroom music activities
- spontaneously use music to accompany private tasks or games
- select from available recorded music
- recognize music as work or occupation
- discuss music events with their families

1. Familiarize themselves with a variety of theories
2. Recognize the values of music
3. Establish goals and objectives for the music curriculum
4. Set the stage
5. Develop an understanding of the three aspects of music: moving, listening, and singing

Three Aspects of Music

Moving, listening, and singing are all a part of the early childhood program. It's a good idea for you to understand how children develop skills in the three aspects of music so you can foster growth in them.

Moving

Movement Develops

"Movement is the infant's first instinctive reaction to life" (Sheehy, 1968, p. 97). Movement occurs even before a child is born. During the early months of life, movement begins with learning to control the muscles of the head. Control over movements progresses from the head downward to the shoulders, arms, trunk, and finally legs.

Motor development also proceeds from gross to fine. The first movements are large, with little control over finer muscles. Movement control proceeds from the central axis of the body outward. The baby's early movements are gross body actions, starting with the shoulders but without separate arm, hand, or finger movements. Over a year passes before the baby can make independent finger movements or oppose thumb and forefinger to grasp an object. The baby holds his head up and turns it before being able to sit up, stand, or walk, and progresses from grasping a block with the entire hand to being able to pick up tiny bits of lint with thumb and forefinger.

By two years of age, toddlers can crawl, slither, roll, clap, and push and pull (Stinson, 1990). Their rhythmic response to music increases dramatically. Two-year-olds enjoy bouncing, swaying, shaking arms, nodding the head, tapping feet, and clapping hands to music. They'll imitate others by running, galloping, swinging, and jumping to music (Bressan, 1990). Two- and three-year-olds vary widely in their rhythmic capacity. Their ability to keep time to a march doesn't depend entirely on age. Some two- and three-year-olds are able to tap a steady beat, while others are unable to do so. Some who have been able seem to forget, or regress, and are unable to repeat it until some time has passed.

Three-year-olds are able to keep fairly good time to music (Russell, 1975). They can move fast or slow with more smoothness and control over their bodies. They can stop and turn, yet they still have difficulty understanding that a relationship exists between the sound they hear and what their muscles do. It takes mastery of at least three skills before children can move in time to music. The skills are

1. Control over their own movements
2. Ability to listen to the music
3. Ability to put the two together

With additional experiences in music movement, as well as maturation, four-year-olds can make sustained smooth movements to music and can adapt their body movements to contrasting and changing accompaniments.

Repetition may account for some of this ability. Children have an instinctive tendency to reach out into the environment again and again. Once they've learned to walk backward, for instance, they continue to do so. Or they walk up and down the stairs endlessly, repeating a learned movement over and over (Flavell, 1963). A child who has moved to music over and over is able to move more skillfully.

Children five to eight years old have learned to move to music with smoothness, refinement, and rhythm. Functionally, these children's movements are efficient. They have a greater understanding of height, weight, distance, and depth. Their actions are more economical and appropriate. They use fewer unnecessary movements, merging separate movements into harmonious smooth motions. They can skip, run, and catch a ball or even something as delicate as a soap bubble without breaking it.

Expressively, children of this age group are able to use movement in symbolic ways. They can express an idea, a feeling, or an emotion through a movement. They can create a dance, a skit, or a play to symbolize their feelings and experiences. Their cognitive skills include imagination and their motor skills, control. Together these permit symbolic expression.

Fostering Growth in Moving to Music

Goals.   Experiences with music should help children to:

1. Develop an awareness and understanding of their own movement capabilities
2. Increase control over their movements, progressing from control of functional movements to that of expressive movements
3. Experience a wide range of movement moods
4. Learn to work together in shared dance and movement activities from functional to expressive movements

Infants and Toddlers.   A number of movement games can be played when babies are awake and in a playful mood, such as "This Little Piggy," "Rock-a-Bye, Baby," "pat-a-cake," or "So Big." Any games that involve the adult's moving increasingly closer to the baby, gathering force and speed, and culminating in a moment of impact and excitement, perhaps even touching or picking up the baby, offer another type of experience with movement.

Sometimes adults' movements with an infant are businesslike and abrupt, such as those made when diapering, dressing, or carrying the child to or from the car. Other movements are quieting and soothing, as when the baby is rocked to sleep or patted. Schemas build in the child based on the repetitious pattern of these various types of movement (Brearley, 1970).

The methods of Jaques-Dalcroze (1921) are appropriate for introducing toddlers and preschoolers to moving to music. Jaques-Dalcroze suggested beginning with children's own rhythmic movements. Rather than asking

Children explore and experiment moving to music.

children to make specific movements, such as moving across the room like bears or ducks, begin by building on children's natural movements. Say, "This is how your feet sounded when you ran across the room," and then repeat the rhythm or sounds with a drum or other instrument.

Beginning with children's movements means becoming an astute observer of them in order to report and describe them to the children. Name the movement and describe the body part making the movement as well as the type of movement it is. The movement could be running, striking, jumping, or gliding; the parts used to make the movement could be feet, arms, hands, or head; and the movement itself could be described as heavy, strong, light, fast, slow, high, low, smooth, or jerky. Concentrate attention on one or two movements at a time. For example, "your toes go so lightly over the floor," or "your feet glided smoothly." Comments that are specific and direct children's attention to particular aspects of movement heighten their awareness and clarify their movements (Stinson, 1977, p. 51).

Infants and Toddlers

Motor development from gross to specific. By two, can crawl, slither, roll, clap, and push and pull. Threes can keep time by moving to music, fast or slow.

Simple games, Pat-a-cake, enjoyed. Match children's natural movements with drumbeats or other instrument.

Preschoolers

Four- and five-year-olds can move to music with smoothness, refinement, and rhythm. Can walk, run, march, gallop, and skip to beat and can vary tempo and intensity.

Listen to music or beat, think and move to music. Props can be added. Represent rhythms on chart.

Primary-Grade Children

Move expressively in symbolic ways to express ideas, feelings, or emotions. Create dramas, tell stories through movement, act out stories using dance.

Figure 11–1
Summary of movement skills

Up to this point, your role as a teacher is to try to match the children's movements with specific instruments and rhythms. You are responding to the children's spontaneous movements, accompanying them with a drum, piano, or other instrument, and focusing their attention on what their bodies can do and how they can move. Music is introduced gradually and begins with children's establishing their own pace and using their own ideas. Sometimes you might introduce children to the sound of one instrument and have them explore and experiment with what they can do with their body to imitate the instrument's sound.

You might begin by sitting on the floor with a small group of children to introduce them to a maraca. Ask them to listen to the maraca's sound and say how they might move to that sound. Some might wiggle their arms and hands, while others jump up and down wiggling their entire bodies. Follow their actions with the maraca. You can ask three- and four-year-olds to stop when the maraca does, to wiggle their bodies while staying glued to one spot on the floor, or to wiggle different parts of their bodies (MENC, 1991). (Figure 11–1 charts children's development in moving.)

You can introduce other instruments in the same way. This exercise helps develop the concept that bodies can be moved in response to rhythm or music, which is believed to be a prerequisite for all later music development (Bibeau, 1982). Give verbal labels for the sounds of the instruments as well as for children's movements.

Next you can introduce children to the idea of moving to familiar songs. Some children will have experienced moving to "Ring Around a Rosy" or another traditional singing game. Cherry (1971) sees such singing games as "Picking Up Paw Paws," "Rock-a-Bye, Baby," and "Farmer in the Dell" as transitional for later expressive movement in time to music.

For children under age five, movement instruction should focus on experimentation and discovery. The Music Educators National Conference (1991) recommends:

- Allowing continuous opportunity to experience music, to move experimentally, and to discover what the body can do.
- Remembering that children's motor responses will be primitive and trying to avoid teaching a child how to keep perfect time to a specific meter, tempo, or musical pattern, but instead simply helping the child move spontaneously.
- Offering continual opportunities for children to get in touch with the feel of the rhythm and by doing so improve their balance and muscular coordination in response to a sound stimulus.

Preschoolers, Kindergarten, and Primary-Grade Children.   Children above age four continue exploring and experimenting with fundamental or functional movement. They need opportunities to respond freely, spontaneously, and expressively to music. Now, however, children can be introduced to the basic functional movement patterns. Keeping a balance between spontaneous and unguided movement introduces children to the patterns of walking, marching, and running to the beat of a drum or other instrument. As you introduce each movement, you should:

1. Give children a period of time to listen to the rhythm and think about how their feet could move.
2. Use the vocabulary of movement, such as the words *walk, run, skip,* and *gallop.*
3. Provide for individual differences.

Play a drum, beating out a walking pattern. Have the children listen to the beat and clap the pattern. Ask children to think about what they could do with their feet, then have them walk to the beat of the drum. Begin slowly in 4/4 time, and gradually increase the tempo. Or play the drum softly or heavily, and have them move their feet to match these sounds (Smith, 1970).

Children could draw a picture of the beat. You might provide them with a large piece of chart paper or an overhead projector. Children may use lines (— — —), circles, (O O O), or any other notation (Liddell, 1983).

Try a running beat in 4/4, 2/4, and 6/8 time. Again, ask the children to think carefully about the sounds they hear and move their body to these sounds. Ask how they could draw them. Skipping and galloping are more difficult for children to master. A skip is in 6/8 time and involves a step and hop, first on one foot, then the other. Children who can skip might demonstrate the step while others watch. Sometimes skipping with a child, repeating the beat of a skip, and chanting, "Skipping is fun, skipping is fun, skipping is fun for everyone" is helpful.

Galloping is also done to 6/8 time, except one foot is first in each step, and the second is brought up to meet it. In a gallop, children's heels never touch the floor. Again, ask the children to listen to the beat of a gallop, represent it by drawing it on a chart, and then move to the gallop.

When children have mastered these basic movements, they may take turns using the drum to beat out rhythms for others to follow. Don't expect children to keep perfect time. Continue practice with functional movements, introducing movement to bells, the piano, and other instruments. Vary the pitch and time, so children experience learning to walk, run, march, skip, and gallop to different tempos and intensities.

After children have many experiences with functional movements, ask them to move expressively. Perhaps children will experience initial success if you ask them to listen to a march and then respond with a bodily motion; perhaps they can listen to music that encourages running, hopping, and jumping. Next, proceed to music that requires more interpretation, such as waltzes or ballets. Again, have the children listen to the music first and think about how the music makes them want to move. Encourage them to think about the parts of the music to which they might move quickly, slowly, or smoothly, or those to which they would twirl, swirl, or tiptoe (Bressan, 1990; Cleland, 1990).

Props are useful. Children can use colored scarves that sway and twirl to help them interpret waltzes or other dances. Balloons, balls, and hoops provide children with more means for expressive movements. Hoops made from inexpensive plastic hoses stapled together with a dowel (a wooden stick that joins the ends) can be placed on the floor so the children can curl up inside them. Children can also use them to jump through, to twirl in the air or at their sides, all in response to music.

Observing moving things in the environment leads to other types of expressive movement. Have children watch falling leaves, snowflakes, or raindrops and then represent these movements with their bodies. Or have them observe animals as they move. The movement of snakes, turtles, kittens, elephants, grasshoppers, butterflies, or anything else the children observe can be rhythmically described and imitated by children's movement.

From these experiences, show children how you can tell a story through dance. The class might be able to observe a local dance troupe or watch a short portion of a ballet on television to introduce this concept. You can have children dance out a theme—Halloween night, going to the moon, a trip to the beach—all in time to music selected to reflect the theme.

Other stories can be reenacted through movement and dance. The story should have action, changes in feeling, and many characters, so that a group of

Listening is basic to all music activities.

children can participate. Stories that lend themselves to dance are "Sleeping Beauty," "Cinderella," and "The Three Bears," among other folktales.

Poetry is also a resource for expressive movement. The strong rhythms of Mother Goose or Robert Louis Stevenson rhymes offer a mood, action, and theme to interpret through movement. Following the dance, have children reflect on their experiences. Perhaps they can listen to the music again, repeat some of the movements, and think about other ways to express the idea through movement. They can decide which parts were the most successful and how they could change their dance the next time.

Listening

Listening is basic to all music activities. Even though this iconic mode follows the enactive, listening comes before all else. Children can't respond physically until they've learned to listen, and they cannot sing until they've listened to a song.

Listening involves more than just hearing. It is an active process involving perceiving and organizing. The ability to attend to and recall these organized perceptions is required.

Listening Develops

Infants are believed to possess the ability to listen at birth. Babies respond to sounds even before birth, and soon after they explore the environment in an attempt to locate the source of a sound. At two months, infants will lie motionless with their attention fixed on the sound of singing or an instrument. And although babies can't sing, they try to reproduce the sounds they hear at a very early age.

By two years of age, children enjoy listening to songs sung by others live or on a recording. Two-year-olds enjoy making their own music, either with objects like toys with sound devices, pots and pans, keys, and plastic containers or with their own voices. Orff and Keetman (1960) wrote that the making of rudimentary sounds with found objects should be encouraged. Every child needs to pound on something to make sounds because these experiences lead to the discovery of the beauty of tone, no matter how crude they may seem.

Three-year-olds can listen to a song or a musical selection for a short time. If they initiate the activity, they'll attend to songs sung by others in person or on records and may even be able to listen as someone plays a musical instrument in person or on a recording (Nye & Nye, 1977).

Listening is one musical activity that a child of any age can enjoy.

> While he may not be able to perform the music of Bach he is able to listen to compositions of the well-known baroque composer and to become aware of the many characteristics of music of this period. Through attentive listening he may respond to many other compositions that are beyond his capacities as a young performer. (Smith, 1970, p. 122)

Regardless of the degree of maturity or understanding of music, everyone is able to enjoy and benefit from listening to music. You don't need to reproduce or perform to any acceptable standards—just attend, perceive, relax, and enjoy.

If four-year-olds have had sufficient background experiences with music and movement, they'll be able to listen attentively. They can pick out sounds of specific instruments from a recording if they've been introduced to the instrument, and they enjoy making their own sounds as they listen to music, applying concepts of loud, soft, happy, sad, light, heavy, fast, or slow.

As children progress in listening experiences, they advance from making gross discriminations in sounds to making fine discriminations. Five-year-olds are able not only to listen to a story song, piano selection, or recording of an orchestra but they can discuss the performance and their listening experience as well.

By the time children are in the primary grades, they should be able to listen attentively to music, move to its rhythm, and dramatize the mood. They can distinguish between slow and fast, loud and soft, high and low, as well as identify familiar melodies and orchestra instruments (MENC, 1991).

Fostering Growth in Listening to Music

Goals.   Listening to music in the preschool/primary classroom will allow children to:

- Become acquainted with sources of environmental, mechanical, and musical sounds
- Discover the joy, satisfaction, and relaxation listening to music will provide
- Discriminate among the characteristics of music, including rhythm, melody, and dynamics
- Identify the mood communicated through music
- Develop and demonstrate their preference in music

Infants and Toddlers.   Sounds are all around children. It's up to you, however, to foster their ability to distinguish among the sounds and to discover the sources of environmental, mechanical, animal, human, and musical sounds. Build on infants' natural interest in sounds by helping them to produce, identify, and recognize the sounds in their environment as well as by introducing them to the pleasures of listening to music.

Orff suggested that adults begin children's music education by imitating the sounds infants and toddlers make. If they bang with blocks, you might repeat the rhythm, clapping your hands. Listen to the sounds children make with their bodies, such as slapping, clapping, and clucking, and label these sounds.

Focus on sounds children seem to be interested in. After toddlers have heard a dog, cat, or other animal or listened to an animal record, encourage them to make the animal's sounds. Let them experiment and explore without adult models.

Explore mechanical sound sources in the environment. Bring an alarm clock and have toddlers listen to the tick. Take time to stop and listen to the wheels creaking along when the tricycle is being peddled. Have children play with rhythm instruments and explore the sounds each one can make. Listen to the humming of a fly caught under the window shade, the gentle sound of rain, or the chirping of birds at the feeder.

Three-year-olds can begin to associate the sound with the object that makes it. With small groups or individual children, display a number of sound-making objects, perhaps a piece of crinkly paper, a bell, and a tone block. Hide the objects from the children behind a screen and produce one of the sounds. Ask the children to identify which object made the sound. They can play the game by themselves once they've been given the idea.

Arrange plenty of time for listening to music. The times should be short and informal, but they introduce children to the pleasures of music. Quiet, calm music can help children relax. Folk tunes, familiar songs, or songs that tell stories can encourage physical response. Whether for relaxing or physical activity, all music should be of high quality.

Preschoolers and Kindergarten Children.   Four- and five-year-olds will expand their abilities, skills, and preferences in listening. They'll enjoy listening to music for relaxation, daydreaming, and pleasure. Repeat children's favorite music. Just as adults enjoy listening to a familiar song, so do children. It's difficult to develop taste and value if you're exposed to a piece only once or twice.

Five-year-olds can begin to develop a more extensive understanding of the qualities of music. Concepts of loudness, duration, and pitch are difficult to develop. Preschoolers will confuse the terms *high, loud,* and *fast* as well as *slow, low,* and *long* (Laczo, 1983).

The concept of loudness develops first. Ask children to listen and identify the parts of a musical selection that are loud and those that are soft. Have them raise their hands first when they hear loud sounds, then when they hear soft ones. Beat a drum loudly, then softly. Play story games, discussing loud and soft in connection with the dramatization of the voices in the story.

Duration is the next concept that develops. Just as you had children identify loud and soft, ask them to identify the parts of the music that are fast and those that are slow.

The concept of pitch is most difficult to understand. Kyme (1974) found that having a child blow across the top of a bottle containing water can help develop the concept of high and low pitch. As the water level in the jar is lowered, the sound chamber becomes deeper, and the child discovers that the pitch of the sound is lower. The child is then better able to relate to the bassoon as an instrument with a low sound because it has the longest sound chamber. (You might also point out that the name bassoon contains the word *bass,* which means low pitch.)

Another way to show children the meaning of high and low sounds is to stand step blocks, a xylophone, or tone blocks on end, from top to bottom. When these instruments are on end, the top blocks produce higher tones than the bottom ones. Have the children explore other sources of high and low sounds in their environment.

Five-year-olds can be introduced to the variety of instruments. Ideally, a musician should play an instrument for the children and discuss and demonstrate it. As children examine and listen to the instrument, name it for them. Have them identify sounds that are loud and soft, high and low, or fast and slow. Perhaps children could begin to make a chart of instruments familiar to them or find references to specific instruments in library books, such as Kuskins' *The Philharmonic Gets Dressed* (1982).

Once children know a number of instruments, play musical selections that include them. Five-year-olds will be able to identify the sounds of spe-

---

Infants and Toddlers

Natural interest in sounds; recognizes sounds in environment and tries to find sound source; imitates sounds. By two, enjoys listening to songs.

Focus on sounds of interest to child, listening to rain, a cat, or a drum. Listen to music, folk tunes, chants, for short duration.

Preschoolers

Concept of loudness develops first, then duration. Pitch is most difficult to understand. Children confuse terms like *high, loud,* and *fast* as well as *slow, low, and long.* Fours and fives develop preferences in listening and enjoy music for relaxation, daydreaming, and pleasure.

By four or five years of age, children can identify sounds and have preferences in instruments. They have favorite musical selections and enjoy rhythm bands.

Primary-Grade Children

Can recognize a variety of instruments; request well-known, well-liked music; understand the character of music; recognize the name and the composer of a work; listen with appreciation.

Listening to all types of music attentively, move to rhythm, distinguish fast and slow, loud and soft, high and low.

Figure 11–2
Summary of listening skills

---

cific instruments. Encourage children to develop and demonstrate their preferences for instruments: "I like the violin, it sounds like real music." "There's the trumpet, you can always tell the trumpet." (See Figure 11–2 for a summary of listening skills.)

Rhythm bands and instruments have a long history in early childhood education. Patty Smith Hill, one of the pioneers of the nursery school, introduced the idea of making music with found instruments. In a rhythm band, children select different instruments and together beat time to a song. When four- and five-year-olds are introduced to the concept of a band, they should be creating music, not just noise.

First, children need time to explore the instruments. Perhaps you can use a sound carrel. You can create a carrel out of a discarded cardboard box big enough for one child to sit in, a tent for children to crawl inside, or an empty laundry cart with a hole cut in one side. Place rhythm instruments in the carrel, and have children enter it to explore the sound of a specific instrument. After children have had a period of exploration, introduce each instrument. Start by selecting a specific instrument to accompany a part of a song. For instance, you might give children sand blocks to use as they sing "Scraping Up Sand—Little Liza Jane" or a triangle when singing "Rig a Jig, Jig."

Rhythm bands have a long history in early childhood education.

Only after the instruments have been used and are familiar to the children should you plan a band. Even though the early childhood pioneers used and advocated found objects, it is now possible to offer children instruments that are accurate in tone and provide pleasing sounds. You can purchase good drums, flat bronze bells, maracas, rhythm sticks, sand blocks, gongs, cymbals, and a triangle. A tone block, step bells, and a xylophone are also valuable.

After the band has played, ask the children to evaluate their music. Use a tape recorder so children can listen to their own music. Discuss with them the parts of the band they found most pleasing to listen to, the parts they would change, and those they would like to repeat.

Children in the Primary Grades. Listening experiences for primary-grade children are built on preschool experiences and continue children's expansion of skills. If primary-age children haven't had the opportunity to listen to sounds and music, then the prerequisite skills can be developed. With a background of listening, primary-age children can:

1. Recognize a variety of instruments in recordings and learn the names for groups of instruments
2. Develop preferences for instruments and music, requesting liked and known music
3. Understand the character of music, selecting from music a personal, subjective message
4. Recognize names and composers of works, and begin to develop the concept of the composer
5. Listen appreciatively to music (Laczo, 1983)

Singing

Just as moving and listening are natural parts of children's growth and development, so is singing. Whether they are two-year-olds or third-graders, children sing happily, without following an example, making it an integral part of every day. Teaching singing comes only after children have developed the spontaneous, natural ability to sing.

Singing Develops

Singing is so natural that some music educators believe children sing before they talk (Baldwin & Stecher, 1925; Bentley, 1969). The infant's babblings and cooings do seem to be more song than words or phrases. By the end of the first year, babies have experimented with different pitches and voice inflections. Eventually these result in words as well as imitations of sounds from the environment.

By two years of age, most children chant a kind of singsong speech. These chants consist of minor thirds and have been labeled the natural chants of childhood. These chants seem to express a fact or a thought and imitate the imaginary part of a child's play. For instance, children like to repeat the same sounds over and over (Moorehead & Pond, 1941), singing, "slippery, slippery, slippery, jug, jug, jug," while playing with plastic cups and water. "Hippety, hop, hippety, hop, blump, blump, blump, blump" was one chant of a four-year-old overheard on a busy sidewalk (Shelley, 1976).

Chants consist of a repeated tone, or they begin with a repeated tone and end with a descending third. The rhythm begins in 2/4 time and ends in 6/8. Chants are generally accompanied by physical rhythmic movement, such as walking, hopping, pounding, rocking, or splashing water.

There is more to this primitive egocentric chanting and playing than adults may first perceive. Moorehead and Pond (1941) remind us that this same chant is that associated with "Unison Dervishes, . . . American Indian Dance rituals, . . . Haitian voodoo chants, and . . . litanies of the Christian church" (p. 41). By three years of age, children may be able to listen to a song sung by another and might sing along. Three-year-olds are rarely able to match pitches when they first begin to sing (Smith, 1970). Sometimes they try to move their voice up or down in an approximate outline of a melody.

Between four and eight years of age, children are considered middle-range singers and have difficulty carrying a tune. But they do enjoy singing with others. Typically, children in this age range will be able to match some of the pitches, and some can sing alone, especially if the song is of their own making. Five-year-olds have favorite songs that they recognize and request. Children in kindergarten and primary grades develop a repertoire of songs they can sing, although childhood chants continue.

Fostering Growth in Singing

Goals.   Experiences with music will encourage children to:

- Be able to create pleasing sounds with their voices, singing naturally and in tune
- Create, sing, and enjoy chants
- Develop the ability to match pitch and increase singing range
- Develop vocal independence, singing with or without accompaniment
- Enjoy singing alone or with others
- Learn a repertoire of songs, selecting and recognizing them

Infants and Toddlers.   Infants' babbling and toddlers' chants are the foundation for instruction in singing. Use these natural chants as the beginning of singing instruction. You can either repeat the chants to children, by singing "swinging up, swinging down," or respond with a new chant. To encourage a child who is having difficulty, you might sing: "Yes, you can, yes you can, try, try, try." Or you can make up a chant to go with the children's actions using the same sol-mi chant or tone and rhythm of the children: "Susan is rocking, up and down, back and forth, up and down," or "jumping up, up, up, jumping down, down, down."

Two- and three-year-olds are especially responsive to hearing their teacher repeat their chants. You can sing them back to the children on the spot or during a group singing time. You might even be able to capture a chant on a tape recorder for later listening.

The chant can be used throughout the day. Anything that can be spoken can be sung. Chanting children's names, giving feedback through song, and singing about daily routines are natural ways to teach singing. "Sing your day," advise the music educators (MENC, 1991, p. 42). Chanting or singing your day lets children see that the voice is a natural way of expressing ideas and that ideas can be expressed through song.

Even if you're a little hesitant about making up songs to accompany children's activities, you can still adapt their chants to fit a special occasion. If the children chant "squishy, squishy, dough, dough, dough" while playing with clay, you might adapt the words when making pudding, mixing paints, or washing table tops.

Two- and three-year-olds will be able to participate in brief group singing sessions. Whether coming together as a group to sing, chant, or just move to songs, toddlers find singing enjoyable. Familiar folk tunes like "Twinkle, Twinkle, Little Star," "Mary Had a Little Lamb," "Open, Shut Them," "Skip to My Lou," "London Bridge," and "Johnny Had One Hammer" are examples.

You may do most of the singing because two- and three-year-olds are just experimenting with the idea of song. These group times will be short, with children free to come and go as they wish. Group times should build on children's interests as well as actively involving them in the song.

Preschoolers and Kindergarten Children.   Four- and five-year-olds enjoy singing together in small groups or with the full group. Singing times are still brief and rather informal, continuing throughout the day, but children of these ages are able to sing songs that are increasingly complex and of greater variety. When selecting songs for preschoolers, find those that:

- Range from above middle C to middle B, as suggested by Kodály
- Are directional in tone, going either up or down
- Include a lot of repetition, such as echo or cumulative songs like "Old MacDonald"
- Match children's interests so that they revolve around their lives
- Have action, are easy to dramatize, or result in some game

Introduce new songs to children gradually. You might sing the song several times during the day informally and spontaneously to accompany some occasion. Perhaps when the first snow of the season falls you could begin singing, "Snow is falling, in my garden, lightly dancing on the ground," or when a child brings in a branch of pussy willows, sing the pussy willow song. At other times, you might introduce the song using a recording. Play the record at story time, rest time, or lunchtime.

When introducing the song to the group, you might use a prop—perhaps a puppet or something that relates to the song's content—and then sing the entire song to the children. Ask the children to listen to the song or to respond as you sing it by making hand or body motions. You might even ask a group of children to become pumpkins, birds, or whatever the song is about and act it out as you sing. Repeat the song again, singing it all the way through. This time, ask the children a question designed to focus their attention and thinking: "When I sing, listen to find out what Ms. O'Leary

Infants and Toddlers (Birth to Age Three)

Hush, Little Baby	Little Sally Waters
All the Pretty Horses	Head and Shoulders
Jim Along, Josie	Clap Your Hands
Twinkle, Twinkle, Little Star	Hickory Dickory Dock
Ring Around the Rosy	

Preschoolers (Four to Five Years Old)

This Old Man	The Muffin Man
Mary Had a Little Lamb	London Bridge
Rain, Rain, Go Away	Skip to My Lou
Open, Shut Them	Old MacDonald Had a Farm
B-I-N-G-O	

Primary-Grade Children

Six Little Ducks	There's a Little Wheel
The Ants Go Marching	Frère Jacques
One Elephant	Alouette
My Dog Rags	Ojo Ma R Q
I Had a Cat	

Figure 11–3
Songs for young children

ate," or "This time, listen and remember what the cow did." As you sing, encourage the children to join in or fill in for you when phrases are repeated. If you are teaching "Rig a Jig, Jig," stop singing, and have the children sing the repetitive lines. Or divide the group, asking only those children who have something blue on to sing with you, then the other children. In this way, you repeat the song a number of times and encourage children to become involved.

Children won't learn a new song after one introduction. Plan to introduce the song again the next day and the next, informally as well as formally. Sometimes you may use a recording of the song or an instrument to accompany your singing. Following the ideas of Kodály, perhaps you can use a simple percussion instrument, such as a hand drum or step block, to accompany you, or have the children clap the melody as you sing. It's not necessary to play the song on the piano; some music educators, like Kodály, even discourage this practice (Kodály, 1964) believing that the use of instruments produces out-of-tune singing. (See Figures 11–3 and 11–4.)

"But I can't sing!" This is a familiar and common lament of beginning teachers. Let's observe in a kindergarten classroom for a moment.

Mr. M. is sitting on a low chair and calls children to him. They come into the room ready for a quiet activity, sitting around him on the rug. He doesn't

---

Infants and Toddlers

By two, children chant a singsong speech of repeated tones. Threes can listen to a song and sing along, are rarely able to match pitch.

Repeat child's chants to child. Using child's chants, sing new words. Group singing is short, chanting folk tunes, with active involvement.

Preschoolers and Kindergartners

Children sing in middle range, from middle C to B. Voices are directional, not just repetitious. Group singing periods are short.

Introduce whole song, with props or actions, and repeat several times. Children respond with hand or body motions and sing along. Songs with repetition and folk songs are favorites.

Primary-Grade Children

Large repertoire of songs, sing in lower ranges, able to expand range, most can sing in tune.

Correlate singing with widening range of interests and skills.

Figure 11–4
Summary of singing skills

play the piano, although there's one in the room, but he does use an auto-harp that he keeps in tune. He begins, using one chord of the autoharp, singing the children's names as they join the group. His singing is more of a chant: "Here comes Allison, here is Paul, how are you today?" "Sing about me, sing about me," calls out Andrea. Mr. M. makes up a song about Andrea using the sol-mi chant. Next he and the children sing a few folk tunes. Mr. M. doesn't sing loudly, but rather keeps his voice and the autoharp soft. The children do most of the singing.

Today he's introducing a new song. He's been singing it to himself for several days and has sung it during activity time. Now he sings it again. Instead of using the autoharp, he uses the tone blocks to help keep his voice in tune. The song is sung all the way through, then repeated once again. Children begin to sing with him. Tomorrow he's planning to sing the song again.

If you're unsure of your own singing ability, you can:

- Use a tape recorder to introduce the song
- Practice before presenting it to the children, learning it carefully so you can sing it with confidence
- Teach the song to a child or a few children who can carry a tune, and use them as helpers when you introduce the song to the class
- Use a rhythm instrument, step blocks, or an autoharp to keep your voice on pitch

Children in the Primary Grades.   Children in the primary grades continue to build their repertoire of songs. They prefer folk songs, songs about their own lives, and action songs, and they sing in the lower ranges. But they are ready to begin to expand this range. For them, singing is a time to enjoy the companionship of others while expanding skills. The goals of the program are to enlarge children's repertoire *and* skills, correlating singing activities with their ever-widening range of interests and knowledge.

Representation of music, which started when children used their bodies to move to music, expands to include pre-music-reading activities. Pictorial representation of music can begin with the use of hand signals. Or children's hands can follow the pitch of the music, moving up and down to follow the direction of the notes. At other times, you might write the notes to a song on the overhead projector as children sing or learn to sing a new song.

Most children will be singing in tune by the primary grades. Some primary children, however, still have difficulty carrying a tune. The role of voice training has been highly debated (Shelley, 1976). Nevertheless, Smith (1970) concludes that children can be trained to match their voice to the music. Response songs such as "Sing Your Name" have been suggested as a means of helping children reproduce tunes.

You might also specifically ask children to use their singing voice, because some children do not realize that they sing in a voice different from the one they speak with. Lifting of hands to follow the song or asking children to sing high like a bird, the wind, or a siren, may be helpful in encouraging some children to use their voice differently as they sing.

For children who have difficulty singing:

- Encourage them to improvise, singing about the activities they are doing in school or anything that interests them.
- Provide opportunities for them to listen to their own voice.
- Help them write charts of original melodies, using their own ideas.
- Select songs within the comfortable range for children. Middle C, although used occasionally, tends to be a bit low for young children, while F or G at the top of the treble staff may be too high.
- Allow children to begin a song at their own pitch.

Summary

Music is an integral part of children's growth, development, and learning in early childhood education. A number of theories of music education have been advanced and continue to influence music education today. The theories of Jaques-Dalcroze, Orff, and Kodály continue to influence music education for each of them believed that music was for everyone and should be taught early in children's lives.

You will want to be aware of the values of music, not only to defend its place in the curriculum, but also to be able to select goals and objectives for children's learning. Music is valued for itself and to foster children's creativity, feelings of belonging to a group, physical and intellectual skills, and emotional growth.

It is you, the teacher, who will set the stage for children's learning to move to music, to listen to music, and to sing. By understanding children's development in each of the areas of music—moving, listening, and singing—stating learning objectives and planning activities for each area, you, as the teacher, can develop balanced, comprehensive, enjoyable, and worthwhile music for young children.

Projects

Continuing Case Study

Observe your child as she or he listens to music. Take note of the type of music being listened to, and describe your child's behavior to the music. What behaviors suggest the child is, or is not, engaged in pleasurable listening? Is the child developmentally ready for the experience? How could you determine what she or he is getting from the listening experience?

1. Review curriculum guides for music education from your local school system or state department of education. What goals and learning objectives are stated? How are these to be achieved, and how is children's growth evaluated? Take a specific age level (perhaps kindergarten) and note how objectives and activities are sequenced to achieve these goals.
2. Find a familiar folktale or story such as "The Three Pigs," and create a sound story using rhythm instruments, the piano, song, or other sound-producing objects to represent the action in the story. If you can, tell the story with the sounds to a group of children.
3. Compile a file of recordings for use in teaching concepts of rhythm.
4. Create a collection of songs that will appeal to young children. Find songs that are in the ranges of toddlers, preschoolers, and kindergarten and primary-grade children.
5. Take advantage of free or inexpensive musical events on your campus or in the area. Attend as many of these as you can to familiarize yourself with music.

Resources

The following record companies are excellent sources for children's records.

Bomar Records, Inc.
  622 Rodier Drive
  Glendale, CA 91201

RCA Victor Dance-a-Story Records
  Ginn and Company
  Boston, MA 02117

Children's Record Guild and Young People's
  Record Guild
  Franson Corporation
  225 Park Avenue South
  New York, NY 10033

Folkways Records
  701 Seventh Avenue
  New York, NY 10035

Percussion instruments can be obtained from:

Continental Music
  150 Aldredge Blvd.
  Atlanta, GA 30366

Music Education Group
Garden State Road
Union, NJ 07083

Rhythm Band, Inc.
P.O. Box 126
Fort Worth, TX 76101

The fourth editions of Bayless and Ramsey's book, *Music: A Way of Life for the Young Child* (1991), and Haines and Gerber's *Leading Young Children to Music* (1991), both published by Macmillan, are classic resources for teachers of young children and musts for every teacher's library.

The Music Educators National Conference, based in Washington, DC, publishes an annual yearbook. The yearbook puts teachers in touch with the most current thinking in the field of music education.

References

Alper, C. D. (1992). Early childhood music education. In C. Seefeldt (Ed.), *The early childhood curriculum: A review of current research* (pp. 237–264). New York: Teachers College Press.

Andress, B. (1984). Music is beginning. In M. E. Ramsey (Ed.), *It's music* (pp. 15–18). Washington, DC: Association for Childhood Education International.

Aronoff, F. W. (1969). *Music and young children.* New York: Holt, Rinehart & Winston.

Bacon, D. (1969). Kodály and Orff: Report from Europe. *Music Educator's Journal, 55*(8), 53–56.

Bagheri, H. (1990). Dance as a multicultural education for young children. In W. J. Stinson (Ed.), *Moving and learning for young children* (pp. 189–200). Reston, VA: National Alliance for Health, Physical Education, Recreation, and Dance.

Baldwin, B. T., & Stecher, L. I. (1925). *The psychology of the preschool child.* New York: Appleton-Century-Crofts.

Bentley, A. (1969). Measurement and development of musical abilities. *Journal of Research in Music Education, 17*, 41–46.

Bibeau, M. J. (1982). Acquisition of pulse response. *Journal of Music Education, 30*(2) 107–127.

Brazelton, A. E. (1990). The development of self-esteem in children. In W. J. Stinson (Ed.), *Moving and learning for young children* (pp. 77–83). Reston, VA: American Alliance for Health, Physical Education, Recreation, and Dance.

Brearley, M. (1970). *The teaching of young children.* New York: Schocken.

Bressan, E. S. (1990). Movement education and the development of children's decision making ability. In W. J. Stinson (Ed.), *Moving and learning for young children* (pp. 67–73). Reston, VA: American Alliance for Health, Physical Education, Recreation, and Dance.

Brooks, R. J., & Obrutz, J. E. (1981). Brain lateralization: Implications for infant stimulation and development. *Young Children, 36*(3), 9–17.

Bruner, J. (1966). *Toward a theory of instruction.* Cambridge, MA: Harvard University Press.

Cherry, C. (1971). *Movement for the developing child.* Belmont, CA: Fearon.

Cleland, F. (1990). How many ways can I . . .? Problem solving through movement. In W. J. Stinson (Ed.), *Moving and learning for young children* (pp. 73–77). Reston, VA: National Alliance for Health, Physical Education, Recreation, and Dance.

Comte, M. M. (1982). Music in the early childhood years. *Australian Journal of Music Education, 30*, 33–39.

Eigan, K. (1988). *Primary understanding.* London: Routledge.

Flavell, J. H. (1963). *The developmental psychology of Jean Piaget.* Princeton: Van Nostrand.

Gardner, H. (1985). *Frames of mind.* New York: Basic Books.

Gantley, N. (1983). Music, movement in the kindergarten curriculum. *Canadian Music Educator, 24*(2), 6–12.

Hoffman, S., Kantner, L., Colbert, C., & Sims, W. (1991). Nurturing the expressive arts. *Childhood Education, 68*, 22–27.

Jaques-Dalcroze, E. (1921). *Rhythm, music and education.* (H. F. Rubinstein, Trans.). New York: C. P. Putnam.

Kodály, Z. (1964). *Choral method.* 15 Vols. Oceanside, NY: Boosey & Hawkes.

Krumhansl, C. L., & Keil, F. C. (1982). Acquisition of the hierarchy of tonal functions in music. *Memory and Cognition, 10,* 243–251.

Kuhmerker, L. (1969). Music in the beginning reading program. *Young Children, 24*(3), 157–163.

Kuskins, K. (1982). *The philharmonic gets dressed.* New York: Harper & Row.

Kyme, G. (1974). The appropriateness of young audiences' music program for primary grade children. *Journal of Research in Music Education, 1*, 366–372.

Laczo, Z. (1983). Listening to music in primary grades: Curriculum reform and experience. *Canadian Music Educator, 24*(3), 7–19.

Leonhard, C. (1983). Music education. A socially significant enterprise. *Canadian Music Educator, 24*(3), 23–27.

Lewis, E. G. (1990). Children with special needs: Mainstreaming with movement. In W. J. Stinson (Ed.), *Moving and learning for young children* (pp. 135–137). Reston, VA: National Alliance for Health, Physical Education, Recreation, and Dance.

Liddell, C. (1983). Rhythm for the young child. *Music Teacher, 62*(10), 17–18.

Lloyd, A. L. (1978). The meaning of folk music. In R. Leach & R. Palmer (Eds.), *Folk music in school* (pp. 76–83). London: Cambridge University Press.

Michael, P. (1972). The optimal development of music abilities in the first years of life. *Psychology of Music, 4*, 8–13.

Moorehead, G. E., & Pond, D. (1941). *Music for young children, I. Chant.* Santa Barbara, CA: Pillsbury Foundation Studies.

Music Educators National Conference. (1973). *Music in early childhood.* Washington, DC: Author.

Music Educators National Conference. (1991). *Music in early childhood.* Washington, DC: Author.

Nye, R. E., & Nye, V. T. (1977). *Music for young children* (2nd ed.). Dubuque, IA: Wm. C. Brown.

Orff, C., & Keetman, G. (1960). *Music for children.* (Adapted by D. Hall and A. Walter.) New York: Associated Music.

Ostwalt, P. F. (1972). Musical behavior in early childhood. *Developmental Medicine and Child Neurology, 15*(1), 367–375.

Russell, J. (1975). *Creative movement and dance for children.* Boston: PLAYS.

Sheehy, E. (1968). *Children discover music and dance.* New York: Teachers College Press.

Shelley, S. (1976). Music. In C. Seefeldt (Ed.), *Curriculum for the preschool-primary child: A review of the research* (pp. 201–225). Columbus, OH: Merrill.

Smith, R. B. (1970). *Music in the child's education.* New York: Ronald.

Spodek, B., Saracho, O., & Lee, D. (1984). *Mainstreaming young children.* Belmont, CA: Wadsworth.

Stinson, S. W. (1977). Movement as creative interaction with the child. *Young Children, 32*(6), 49–51.

Stinson, W. J. (Ed.). (1990). *Moving and learning for the young child.* Reston, VA: American Alliance for Health, Physical Education, Recreation, and Dance.

Swanwick, K. (1979). *A basis for music education.* Windsor, Berkshire, England: NFER.

Thomas, R. (1983). Music, school, and society. *Music Teacher, 63*(8), 15–17.

Torrance, R. E. (1965). *Rewarding creative behavior.* Englewood Cliffs, NJ: Prentice Hall.

12 Mathematics

"The three year old is ready to begin counting. He knows we have three rabbits, for he feeds them and watches them in their house. He counts the shelters too, and the birds in the aviary—and there are only three."

(McMillan, 1919, p. 123)

After reading this chapter, you should be able to respond to the following questions:

1. What understanding of mathematical concepts do children have?
2. Describe the principles of teaching mathematics to young children.
3. What are the goals for mathematical learning?
4. How are these goals achieved in the areas of:
   a. Number
   b. Geometry
   c. Measuring
   d. Probability and graphing

"And how are you?" the adult asks. The child, with all her egocentric thought showing, replies with the answer closest to her at the moment: "I just turned four!" She holds up four fingers, as if to help you understand, and says, "It's this many!"

Young children are interested in mathematics and numbers. They count and use numbers. "Hey, you gave him one more than me." They compare ("You're higher up"), classify ("All of those are mine," "I get the round ones"), and order ("Let the little car go first, then the next biggest, and the next").

At a very early age, children demonstrate their knowledge of mathematics. Children's natural curiosity about their world leads them to explore concepts of mathematics and the science of pattern and order. By the time children are five, they are using concepts of pattern and order. They recognize shapes and size, most of them can count to ten, and many of them can write a few numerals.

This initial knowledge of mathematics is informal and personal knowledge. Informal knowledge is "made up of intuitions, perceptual information, invented strategies, and other knowledge that has been acquired in dealing with everyday quantitative situations" (Hiebert & Lindquist, 1990, p. 19).

Formal knowledge differs from personal or informal knowledge. Formal knowledge is acquired largely through interaction with adults, usually in the school setting. It is "knowledge that consists of methods, procedures, or rules for solving school mathematics problems" (Hiebert & Lindquist, 1990, p. 19). Formal knowledge tells children how to manipulate written symbols according to rules and step-by-step prescriptions.

Researchers are beginning to distinguish between conceptual knowledge and procedural knowledge. "Conceptual knowledge refers to the knowledge of relationships. Mathematical concepts—that is, principles and constraints that define or characterize ideas and experiences—are relationships between pieces of information. Procedural knowledge entails (a) the written symbols that are used to represent mathematical ideas, and (b) the rules and procedures that are used when solving mathematics problems" (Campbell & Carey, 1992, p. 154).

During the period of early childhood, children will be developing a foundation of informal and formal mathematics as well as conceptual and procedural knowledge.

This foundation of knowledge:

1. Is centered on the goals and objectives for mathematics learning

2. Is based on teachers' understanding of how children develop mathematical concepts

3. Is implemented through sound principles of teaching

Goals for Mathematics Learning

Mathematics during early childhood encompasses a broad range of content. This content has been divided into the categories of attitudinal, conceptual, and procedural goals by the National Council of Teachers of Mathematics (NCTM) in the document *Curriculum and Evaluation Standards for School Mathematics* (1989). These standards list five general goals that reflect the importance of mathematical literacy for all students. It states that all students should:

1. Learn to value mathematics
2. Become confident in their ability to do mathematics
3. Become mathematical problem solvers
4. Learn to communicate mathematically
5. Learn to reason mathematically

The document identifies curriculum standards for kindergarten through the fourth grade. Four of these standards look at the following aspects of mathematical thinking:

1. Mathematics as problem solving
2. Mathematics as reasoning
3. Mathematics as communication
4. Mathematical connections

Eight of these standards deal with the following content of mathematics:

1. Number sense and numeration
2. Estimation
3. Concepts of whole number operations
4. Whole number computation
5. Fractions and decimals
6. Geometry and spatial sense
7. Measurement
8. Graphing and probability

Development of Mathematical Concepts

Piaget (1963) has outlined the development of number concepts in children. He traces the beginning of number concepts from birth at the sensorimotor stage through formal thought at around age 11 or 12.

Sensorimotor Period (0–2 Years)

Piaget's observations of children suggest that infants come into the world with only a few reflex actions—cooing, sucking, and moving the tongue. Through their actions on the environment and the sensations they receive, they begin to impose organization or structure on what they do. Concepts of mathematics are believed to develop as children grasp small and large objects, touch a variety of blocks, or move objects of different shapes around on the floor.

Piaget believed that mathematical understandings begin when infants develop object permanence, the realization that an object exists even if it is not present. When children can think about something not in their environment, they can use symbols, imitate, and use words to represent objects in the environment.

Classification skills are also believed to have their beginning in infancy. That children use words means they are putting objects into categories and classifying. When they recognize that a dog is different from a horse and put the dog into the category "dogs" and not "horses," they are classifying. They've gained the ability to take a newly introduced object and put it into some category they have previously discovered or identified.

Preoperational Period (2–7 or 8 Years)

The preoperational stage, ages two through age seven or eight, is characterized by the development of preconcepts. Children in this age group can manipulate symbols or representations of the physical world. During this period, children learn to conserve, which is necessary for all later mathematical understanding.

> Our contention is merely that *conservation* is a necessary condition for all rational activity, and we are not concerned with whether it is sufficient to account for this activity or to explain the nature of reality. This being so, arithmetical thought is no exception to the rule. A set or a collection is only conceivable if it remains unchanged, irrespective of the changes occurring in the relationships between the elements. (Piaget, 1964, p. 3)

Children have developed the understanding that materials or objects stay the same regardless of how they are changed in form or arranged differently

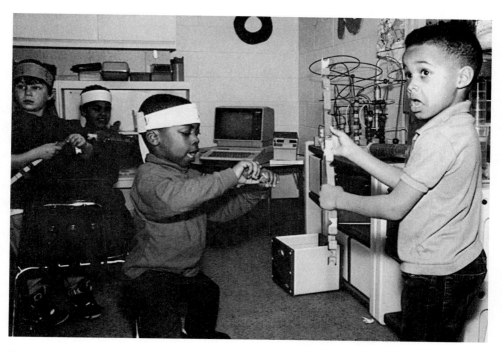

Children develop the understanding that materials stay the same regardless of how they are arranged differently.

in space. Without this ability to conserve, children may be able to learn simple mathematical skills or routine calculations, but they will be constrained in developing mathematical understandings and will be unable to solve more complex problems or tasks.

There are three levels of conservation:

1. Children consider it natural for the form or number of materials to change or vary according to their arrangement, shape, or the container they are in.

2. Children develop the idea that the amount of matter stays the same, even if arranged differently.

3. Children are able to conserve quantities, volume, discontinuous quantities, and mass. They will tell you, "It's still the same, you just moved them around," or "You didn't take any away or add any, you only put them closer together."

Through the age of seven or eight, children's mathematical thinking is called *semilogical*. Because they can't keep in mind more than one relationship at a time, they have difficulty making comparisons and seeing relationships. They are unable to use the reversible thought processes that would permit them to think logically.

Concrete Operations (7 or 8 to 11 or 12 Years)

During the concrete operations stage, children continue to expand logico-mathematical thought. They are operational in their thinking. They still need objects to handle and manipulate as they think (hence the term *concrete operations*), but they are no longer overwhelmed by the perceptual or sensory cues they receive from the environment. Even though children still base their ideas on observations of and experiences with objects, they are beginning to break away from the manipulation of objects as a way of knowing (Copeland, 1974).

Children are ready to think about classes, seriations, and numbers. By age 11 or so, they can reverse thought, complete calculations, and develop logical ideas of number, weight, area, and time.

Formal Operations (Age 11 to Adult)

The ability to use logical thought and deductive reasoning is possible at the formal operational stage. Children can establish any relation between classes and use combinations and permutations. They are able to consider powerful mathematical ideas or problems, make maps, and deal with problems concerning time and distance, probability, and geometry.

Principles of Teaching Mathematics

"In reality, no one can teach mathematics. Effective teachers are those who can stimulate students to learn mathematics . . . students learn mathematics well only when they construct their own mathematical understanding" (National Research Council, 1989, p. 58).

Mathematics is an example of logical thought or knowledge. *Mathematical knowledge* is different from social or physical knowledge. Social, or conventional, knowledge is arbitrary—today is Friday; the name of this is *chair*. The source of social knowledge is people, their customs, and ways of doing things. Social knowledge is dictated, like the knowledge to stop on red (Kamii & DeVries, 1978). Physical knowledge is different. The source of physical knowledge is in the object itself. The chair is hard, the pencil is smooth. The pencil will roll when pushed and break when bent. Physical knowledge is the nature of materials and things (Piaget, 1969). One gains physical knowledge by experiencing and acting on objects in the environment.

On the other hand, mathematical knowledge doesn't exist in objects or in external reality. It doesn't have an external reality, but is a relationship (Kamii, 1982). When a child is given three pencils, the social or conventional knowledge is that they are called pencils, and the physical knowledge is that they will roll and break if bent. But the idea that there is more than one pencil is constructed by the child. The relationship "three" isn't in the pencils or in arbitrary knowledge given by society, but in the mind (Kamii, 1982, p. 5).

Because mathematical knowledge is a relationship constructed by the mind, direct teaching alone will not build it. Children have to develop or construct it for themselves through their own experiences and reflections on them (Forman & Kuschner, 1983; Baroody, Ginsburg, & Waxman, 1983). No amount of verbal instruction or drill will enable children to construct the idea of number (Lemoyne & Favreau, 1981). Knowledge of number is acquired through action with the physical world and from the coordination of actions on objects that lead to the process of reflection, which is the basis for logical thinking (Thorlindsson, 1983).

"Children construct their own knowledge and understanding of mathematical concepts and procedures" (Payne, 1990, p. 10). Construction of knowledge requires that children be actively involved in learning through:

1. Firsthand experiences
2. Interaction with others
3. Use of language
4. Reflection

Firsthand Experiences

Children need a variety of materials to manipulate and the time and opportunity to sort, classify, count, weigh, measure, stack, and explore them if they are to construct mathematics knowledge, both formal and informal. "It is impossible to keep children from doing things with manipulative materials. Some of these actions may be cognitively constructive, some not. Nevertheless, there is an action, and it is this action that forces some kind of thinking and reaction" (Payne, 1990, p. 11).

Children's firsthand experiences with materials serve a number of purposes. First, as children manipulate materials, they are forced to think and react. Children are active physically as well as mentally. They are doing the thinking, seeking relationships, making patterns, counting, and sorting. "It is not the pretty colors or the feel of manipulatives that makes them valuable; rather it is that manipulatives help to promote and focus the reflective thought of the young child—and even the adult" (Payne, 1990, p. 11).

Then, too, materials permit children with a wide range of interests and abilities to enjoy success. When children work with open-ended materials that have no preset goals, they offer a wide range of difficulty, complexity, and challenge that involve all children regardless of their cognitive maturity.

Further, firsthand experiences stem from every area of the curriculum and serve to integrate children's mathematical learning with every other type of learning. The firsthand experiences of setting tables, feeding the fish, measuring salt to make salt dough, building a city of blocks, playing board games with others, putting puzzles together, sewing, or knitting that take place throughout the day and across the curriculum require children to count, reflect, estimate, measure, and lead to the construction of mathematical knowledge.

Interaction with Others

As Piaget pointed out, children need interaction with others as well as with their physical world in order to construct knowledge (Piaget, 1963). Through interaction with peers, children's ideas about the way things are bump head on into other people's ideas about the world. It's through this bumping together of differing ideas that children are able to question their own view of the world, and make adjustments to their own thinking. "It has been hypothesized that construction of understandings may be facilitated when students share their interpretations or conjectures, offer verification or explain their reasoning, or, if necessary, justify their perceptions (Lampert, 1990; Resnick, 1988).

Group projects facilitate children's social interaction and can be a vehicle for mathematics learning. Working together to build a bus with blocks or create a fast-food restaurant out of a box, children will have to count, measure, and compare as they exchange ideas, correct one another, and adjust their thinking to take into account that of other children.

Mathematics can be the focus of group projects. For example, a primary class might try to guess the number of buttons in a container or the number of words in a reading passage. Also, surveys of the class can take place. Children can describe their class in terms of the students' height, weight, hair color, length, likes, and dislikes and graph their results.

Project work motivates children to share ideas, argue, and discuss approaches or strategies. Teachers should withdraw judgment. "The teacher or other children may raise questions, but, in order to enhance children's trust and willingness to talk about mathematics and to support their confidence to investigate further problems, the teacher does not judge the correctness of the understandings constructed by the children" (Campbell & Carey, 1992, p. 156).

Yet, teachers' informal social interactions with children enable them to construct mathematical knowledge. If teachers do not guide, question, react, or respond to children as they manipulate materials or interact socially with other children, the desired mathematical learnings may not result. "Usually manipulatives require that a teacher or knowledgeable

Children need interaction with others in order to construct knowledge.

adult interact with the learner; otherwise, the manipulatives become nothing more than pieces of wood or plastic" (Payne, 1990, p. 11).

Teachers can focus children's attention or thinking by demonstrating a skill or procedure, making a statement, or asking a question. For example, "You put all of those together," or "Why do those belong together?" "Which is greater, this group or that?" Teachers might ask children to try something another way: "What would happen if . . . ?" "Can you do it another way?" It would be impossible to list all the types of questions or verbal interactions possible. The idea is for the teacher to listen to children, observe them as they work and play, and then reply in a way that will enable children to clarify their thinking and extend it.

Using Language

Playing and working together, children will naturally talk about what they are doing. Their talk is essential to learning, whether they are arguing, seeking solutions, or just chatting about what they are doing. The process of speaking and listening is the first step in the representation of mathematical ideas through language. "In our mathematics classroom, children talk, listen, write, and read. Along with the visual or perceptual images they build with physical materials, they develop a language to describe mathematical concepts and procedures" (Hiebert & Lindquist, 1990, p. 30).

Children's talk and informal conversations lead to the development of a language that can be used to describe mathematical concepts and procedures. Language helps children organize their thinking and experiences, moving children from the physical world into the abstract world of numbers. Language also acts as a tool for future learning. With the ability to describe relationships and ideas, children are better able to learn new concepts.

Reflection

Children must think about their actions on the world. They need to reflect on the things that they experienced and to draw abstract patterns and see regularities from these experiences (Cobb & Steffe, 1983). The key is to help children recall past experiences to use as materials for thinking and to help them learn to monitor their own thinking.

Young children probably aren't aware of the limits of their own knowledge and thinking, and do little monitoring of their own memory, comprehension, or thinking. Thinking about thinking, called metacognition, is seen as holding promise for increasing children's ability to think and learn. According to Flavell (1979), metacognitive knowledge is "that segment of your (child and adult) stored world knowledge that has to do with people as cognitive beings and with their diverse cognitive tasks, goals, actions, and experiences" (p. 906). These metacognitive experiences are defined as any conscious cognitive or affective experience that pertains to thinking.

Adults monitor their thinking constantly. You may be thinking as you read this, "What parts do I understand?" or "Which should I review for the exam?" Children are less attuned to their own thinking. Yet Flavell (1979) suggests that it is possible to help children think about their thinking, reflect on things they know and don't know, and realize when they're confused and when they have a clear idea of what to do next.

Achieving the Goals and Objectives

The goals and standards of the National Council of Teachers of Mathematics suggest that mathematics is not a set of skills and procedures that children must acquire, but rather a way of thinking about "relationships among mathematical entities and between mathematical statements and situations involving quantities, relationships, and patterns" (Resnick, 1988, p. 33). If mathematics instruction is to foster thinking, then the focus should be on problem-solving tasks "because problem solving is the context for developing children's mathematical thinking. Therefore, in designing an appropriate mathematics curriculum for young children, a critical factor is the creation of a problem-solving environment from which mathematical ideas can emerge" (Campbell & Carey, 1992, p. 152).

To teach children mathematical relationships involves introducing them to the following concepts:

1. Number

2. Geometry

3. Measuring

4. Probability and graphing

Number

Parrots, horses, and dogs count. They peck, tap, or bark, respectively, a number of times on command. But animals do not have any concept of number. They are only repeating a pattern that has no meaning to them and bears no relation to mathematical concepts. Very young children also count. They sign "This Old Man," or chant, "one, two, three, four, five . . . I caught a fish alive." But their counting, like the animals', is without meaning. It is based on rote learning and memorization, and does not indicate that children have an understanding of number or number operations. "The development of number concepts involves much more than the ability to count by rote or recognize numerals" (Richardson & Salkeld, in press).

A sense of number is more than rote counting. It involves developing an understanding of one-to-one correspondence, being able to pair the term "one" with the first object counted, and the term "two" with the second, and so on (Fuson, 1988). Only when children compare the number of members in two sets directly has one-to-one correspondence taken place.

Understanding number also involves knowledge of counting strategies, including an understanding of counting by groups, and an appreciation for the structure of the place value system as a way of dealing with counting large numbers of objects. Concepts of adding, subtracting, multiplying, and dividing are also necessary.

Number concepts have been found to develop best "in situations that have meaning to children, number sense must be an integral part of classroom routines" (NCTM, 1991, p. 7). Whether in a preschool, kindergarten, or the primary grades, numbers must be an integral part of the day. Try to think of all the ways children will need to use numbers in the school day. The list would be endless, but might include:

• Only five children can work together with the blocks today

A sense of number is more than rote counting.

- Counting themselves for attendance
- Selecting four children to purchase a new fish for the aquarium
- Setting the table with one napkin and glass at each place
- Balancing blocks
- Estimating the number of times they can jump in place
- Using a timer to clean up, counting the number of minutes it takes
- Play a game taking turns and using dice

Preschoolers Experience Numbers

Children will not achieve the ability to count rationally until they are seven or eight years old. This doesn't mean that you should delay introducing counting, the number names, or experiences with numbers until children reach that age. You can provide many opportunities with numbers and rote counting in connection with actual experiences.

Beginning with infants in cribs or playpens, take every opportunity to count and use the number names. Children should hear over and over the folk rhymes and nursery tunes, "One, two buckle my shoe," "Two Little

Blackbirds," "This Old Man," "Five Little Chickadees," and so on. They can play games such as "In a Spider's Web," and hear many stories that use counting. (See Resources at the end of this chapter.)

Children also see and experience number names in their classroom and play yard. There may be numerals on the mailbox or on or near the telephone, or their classroom may be numbered. Children see numbers on the recipes they use when they cook, and they observe cooks in the school using numbers as they measure the flour to make biscuits.

Children watch with interest as you write the numeral telling how old they are, or the numerals that describe their weight, height, or the number of fingers they have on each hand. They can dictate an address to you and find the numerals on the mailbox. When they have a birthday, they count four candles on their cake, put four raisins on each cupcake, count four chairs, and wear a birthday hat with the numeral 4 on it (Nixon & Nixon, 1971).

Rote counting is meaningless unless it is related to some function or purpose. The number of children who want to work at the workbench at any one time can be counted, as can the number sitting at a table who need juice.

Depending on the children's interests and needs, they may count the number of round blocks, the number of books returned to the playroom, the number of boys or girls, the number of children who have a birthday during any one month, or the number of times someone can bounce and catch a ball.

Children's sociodramatic play is rich with potential for mathematical learning. You can stimulate children's counting while promoting awareness of the integral use of numbers in daily life by including timers, clocks, calendars, calculators, and other number items as a part of the sociodramatic play area.

In the Kindergarten

Informal counting activities continue in the kindergarten. You can also plan some counting activities, such as the following:

1. Name the number of objects they've counted.
2. Match numerals to objects, and match sets with equivalent and unequal numbers.
3. Record the number counted, representing the number of objects in writing by a picture or some other means.
4. Reproduce a number, by showing, illustrating, drawing, or constructing the correct number when given a number name (Hollis, 1984).

Some other very specific kindergarten activities are given in the box.

Mystery Boxes

A set number of boxes is prepared by placing a different number of small objects in each and cutting a hole in one side of the box. Children reach in, feel, and count the objects in the box. Then they tell the number of objects they felt. Begin with only one to three objects, and increase the number as children gain counting skills. By the end of kindergarten, children may be able to match the number of objects they feel in the box with the numeral representing that number.

Bowling

Children roll a ball to knock down a group of objects: empty milk cartons, plastic squirt bottles, or empty juice cans. They then count how many have been knocked down and how many are standing. Again, by the end of kindergarten, they may identify the numeral and even write it.

Collections

Children make collections of objects to fit in a number box. Boxes are labeled with the numeral, and children match the number of objects with the numeral. The objects in a set do not have to be the same or even belong to the same category to make a set.

Dominoes

Demonstrate how to play dominoes, matching the domino with a given number of dots with another of equal dots.

Calendar Bingo

For one child or even a small group of children, match numerals cut and mounted on small cards with those on a calendar mounted on heavy paper.

Button, Button

Working with one child or a small group, give each a handful of buttons of the same size, color, and shape. Then say, for example, "Move two buttons," and allow the children to follow the direction by moving two buttons away from the others. Children can give directions to you or the others.

Matching Cards

Children play any kind of game with a set of cards marked with the numerals one through ten. "Go Fish," matching games, or any invented games can be played.

Board Games

"Candyland," "Chutes and Ladders," "Cherry Tree," and other board games are excellent for fostering counting skills. When children play any kind of board game, they gain an understanding of the rules embodied in mathematical concepts and develop a better memory for the rules, retaining and being able to apply them in other situations (Hollis, 1984).

Numbers in the Primary Grades

Through ages seven or eight, children are able to count by rote and have developed a partial understanding of numbers, but they are still confused if objects are rearranged. They are unsure of conservation and are not firmly in the stage of thinking without concrete representation. This means that they require objects to manipulate as they learn mathematical skills, and they haven't yet achieved an understanding of number on an abstract level. In the primary grades, children will:

- Recognize and say the names of the numerals.
- Be able to place numerals in order.
- Understand what the symbol stands for.
- Be able to associate the numeral with a set: The numeral 3 goes with a set of three objects.
- Know that each number in order stands for one more than the number that comes before it.
- Learn to match each number to any set of the size that number stands for and to make sets that match the number.
- Be able to write the numerals.
- Begin operations on whole numbers.

Liedtke (1983) suggests the following steps in teaching children to associate numerals with sets and to write the number names. She begins by creating groups of dissimilar objects on a felt or magnetic board. There may be several different sets of five. Children are asked to describe how the sets are alike and how they differ. The idea is that although each set is created of dissimilar objects, each is similar because each has five objects. Children could reproduce or represent this number using their fingers or other body parts and saying the number. You may write the numeral on the board, and children could identify other numerals that are the same in the room, as well as other sets that contain the same number.

Next, Liedtke gives children a sheet of construction paper and toothpicks. Children are to take a certain number of toothpicks, say, five, and create a design with them on their paper. Children compare the designs to find in what ways they are similar (that is, that they all have five toothpicks) and in what ways they are different.

The teacher uses the overhead projector to give the children more practice in writing the numeral 5. Children can trace the numeral after the teacher makes it and practice writing it unaided. The teacher can introduce the numerals 1 through 10, and 11 through 20 can be introduced in similar fashion.

When introducing addition and subtraction, the major goal is "to provide the child with many experiences involving both physical representations of the operations and the properties of a given operation so that he has the basis needed for abstracting the mathematical ideas. . . . Proficiency with computing is not the goal of early instruction" (Folsom, 1975).

Through the primary grades, regardless of instruction, children appear to add and subtract using counting (Houlihan & Ginsberg, 1981). They count to find the sum in addition and to use the difference in subtraction. Most frequently, children use their fingers for counting, adding, and subtracting. Teachers can introduce objects, like flannel boards with cutouts, chalkboards with chalk, and rods, chips, or small blocks, to help children substitute them for fingers.

Physical representation is also possible with a calculator. "Children should use calculators throughout their school work, just as adults use calculators throughout their lives" (National Research Council, 1989, p. 47). Calculators help children learn to count orally and focus on problem solving rather than merely on computation.

Using a calculator, children will be able to count forward and backward, recognize the value of digits in multidigit numbers, practice basic facts, search for patterns, and solve problems (Payne, 1990). Children can:

The potential for microcomputers has been recognized.

- Find out how many numbers they can count between 13 and 25, identifying the first and last number counted.
- Skip count, exploring number patterns by counting by 2, 3, 4, 5, and 10 using different starting points. You may ask, "What numbers do you say when counting by 2 from 11 to 21?"
- Find any number. "What number will appear if you enter 10 + 1 and press the equal key 10 times?" (Worth, 1990, p. 51).

The potential for microcomputers has also been well recognized (Campbell & Clements, 1990). All types of software are available for children's mathematics learning. There are programs designed to promote problem solving or drill and practice. While these do not replace active teaching and learning (Campbell & Clements, 1990), they can be used to reinforce skills or present challenging problem-solving tasks in a motivating fashion.

"The number of mathematical concepts, operations, symbols and algorithms introduced, developed, and supposedly mastered by primary school children is of large magnitude" (Folsom, 1975, p. 189). You can obtain curriculum guides from the local school system and state department of education to guide you in the selection of goals and activities. Textbooks also offer a progression of concepts and experiences to introduce primary children to number concepts. But it is crucial to remember that children in the primary grades are still in the period of concrete operations and will continue to require physical representations from which they can abstract ideas of number and operations on numbers.

Geometry

Our world is made of spatial patterns, shapes, and movement. We are in fact, a "world of geometry" (NCTM, 1991, p. 19). Because we live in a three-dimensional world of shapes and figures, children have informal knowledge of principles of geometry and space and an intuitive feel for their surroundings and the objects in them (NCTM, 1989). As children grow, this intuitive feel of geometry is formalized. Through hands-on experiences in an early childhood program, children will begin to identify similarities, differences, and relationships among the shapes found in their world and to develop spatial awareness.

Like all the other knowledge children construct, much of their geometric knowledge will take place in connection with their ongoing, naturally occurring experiences in the classroom. To turn children's ongoing activities into learning experiences, however, requires a teacher who has internalized the goals of teaching geometry and who can interact sensitively with children, using the vocabulary of geometry in ways that extend, clarify, and expand children's existing informal knowledge.

While children build with blocks, arrange shapes of paper to create a collage, or play with board games, they will be using principles of geometry. They will be asked to handle, name, and describe shapes. Teachers may question, "What shape will fill this space?" Or comment on the shapes of the blocks, "Use this yellow hexagon so you can join this line of blocks."

Children's attention can be focused on the shapes around them. The teacher could take the children on a field trip to note all the shapes on the outside or inside of the school building or to a building site and observe, over time, the changes in the shape of the building and the materials used. In the preschool, kindergarten, and primary grades, teachers should extend these informal experiences with specific experiences planned to introduce principles of geometry and enhance children's spatial awareness.

The experiences should introduce children to four sequential levels of understanding of geometric concepts (van Hiele, 1986):

- Level 0. *Visualization*. Identification of figures as wholes. "This is a square, circle, triangle."
- Level 1. *Analysis*. Children focus on specific properties of figures. "There are three sides."
- Level 2. *Informal Deduction*. Children organize discoveries about properties of figures and see how definitions are used. "All triangles have three sides."
- Levels 3 and 4. *Deduction and Rigor*. These levels refer to the more formal and abstract study of geometry typical of high school and college courses.

Preschool and Kindergarten

Most preschool and kindergarten children are generally at level 0. Preschool and kindergarten teachers should focus children's attention on the appearance of shapes. In the preschool, teachers develop children's awareness of shapes and space. Children play group circle games like "Duck, Duck, Goose"; Ring Around a Rosy"; "Farmer in the Dell"; "Did You Ever See a Lassie"; and "Round and Round the Village."

In "Round and Round the Village," for example, children stand in a circle, with their hands joined. One or more children walk around the circle as the group sings or chants, "Go round and round the village" three times and then "As we have done before."

Then at the next verse, children raise their arms and "It" goes in and out under their arms. The chant this time is "Go in and out the windows," repeated three times, and then "As we have done before."

On the last verse "It" stands in front of another child, who becomes "It." The chant becomes, "Now stand before your partner," repeated three times, then "As we have done before."

Other games, such as the "Noble Duke of York," "Looby Loo," and "Simon Says," introduce children to the terms up/down, top/bottom, and left/right. Children also have opportunities to explore shapes and space by sorting, classifying, and comparing with board games, geoboards, and tangram pieces.

Exploration of space continues in the kindergarten. Large shapes can be made on the floor by taping masking tape in the shape of a triangle, square, or rectangle. Ask children to identify the shapes on the floor and to walk on the shapes. As they walk along the shapes, have them count the sides (NCTM, 1991). While they are walking, also ask them the following:

- How many steps do you take on each side as you walk around the triangle? How many corners do you meet?
- How many of you fit inside the triangle? On the triangle? Outside the triangle? (NCTM, 1991, p. 22)

On another day, four children are given a large loop of yarn. If each child holds the yarn to make a corner, what figures can they make? (NCTM, 1991, p. 22)

A mystery bag or box is also useful. Place attribute blocks in the box and ask children to feel inside without looking. As they feel the objects or object, ask them to describe the shape of the object and guess what it is.

As with preschoolers, use geoboards with kindergarten students. Children can copy patterns or figures or be asked to create specific patterns. You can draw sample figures on an overhead and ask them to copy the figures. You can also have children use their visual memory by asking them to duplicate three-dimensional patterns using blocks. Show the children a block pattern, remove it, and then ask the children to replicate it. Children could work in pairs, with one child building a model and the other replicating it.

Primary Grades

"A powerful way for children to think about geometric objects is in the form of paths, as records of movement" (Campbell & Clements, 1990, p. 269). Children first investigate paths. Stories, such as *Hansel and Gretel*, can be read and children can create their own path. They might record the path they take to get to the office, play yard, or home from school.

After children have explored paths and walked paths, they can use the computer program Logo. Using Logo, children are able to learn about geometric shapes not so much from their perception of objects as from the actions they perform on these objects. When children have themselves moved on paths, they can "learn to think of the turtle's actions as ones that they can perform. We see evidence of this when in trying to figure out what a given set of directions will make the turtle draw, children turn their bodies in an attempt to figure out a turn" (Campbell & Clements, 1990, p. 269).

Measuring

Children's ability to use measurement develops from experiences with classifying, comparing, and ordering. As children actually compare the weight of an apple and a pear, find a block as long as their box, or see that the blue bucket holds as much sand as two of the red buckets, they're using the concepts of measurement.

Before children do any formal measurement, they need to be able to conserve and understand that the length of an object remains the same whatever changes occur in its position. This involves the ability to understand that measurement can be expressed as a multiple of any number of units.

Preschoolers

Just because children are not able to understand formal measurement, however, doesn't mean you should delay experiences with measurement. Babies, toddlers, and preschoolers all experience measurement. From birth until seven years of age, children make comparisons, order, and imitate adults' measuring. They play as if they're measuring feet for new shoes, or they measure their block buildings or fort.

In the Kindergarten

From ages five to seven, children measure using arbitrary units, saying, "It takes four footsteps. Find one four footsteps long." During the concrete operational stage, after age seven, children see the need for standardized measures and can use them. Do not hurry to move children into the use of standardized measuring units during the early childhood years, but provide them with experiences that involve measurement (Lovell, 1971). The sequence of measuring activities is:

1. Experiences with comparing, ordering, and seriating
2. Measuring with several variable units to develop the idea that there is a need to measure with a standardized unit
3. Measuring with original, arbitrary units to clarify the need for standard units
4. Practice using standardized measuring units

Robinson, Mahaffey, and Nelson (1975) point out that children in sixth grade do not have accurate concepts of measurement. Over 60 percent of the sixth graders they questioned were unable to complete accurate measurements of length, area, volume, or weight. Robinson, Mahaffey, and Nelson concluded that the early years in school should be used to provide children with a base of informal, spontaneous experiences with measurements. Spontaneous, informal measurement activities might include:

- Finding out how long (or tall) each child is using a piece of cash register tape.
- Using a trundle wheel to find out how long the play yard is.
- Finding out the length of the room, using a child's foot as the unit of measure. Trying to measure the room using another child's foot.
- Having children determine how many blocks or pieces of paper it takes to cover a desktop, a table top, a section of garden, or the floor of the block house.
- Counting the number of cups of water it takes to fill a bucket or the number of paper cups it takes to fill a bottle with sand.
- Finding all the objects in the room too small to hold the baseball.
- Using balance scales to measure all sorts of materials—shells, rocks, bolts, pine cones. Ask children to find how many objects it takes to balance a weight, a bolt, a pine cone, a cotton ball, or a paper clip. Teach the idea that big in size may not be the same as heavy.

Children can count the number of cups of water they pour.

In addition to playing with materials and scales, plan measuring activities that have a real purpose, such as the following.

- Pick up children's interest in building a fort or house. Use this opportunity to have them measure. They might use a piece of rope to measure the area they wish to cover or how high the wall is.
- Make puppets. Children may need to measure how much material they need to make a sash for the puppet or the material to make a skirt.
- Measure materials needed in cooking or those needed to make paints, play dough, or salt dough.
- Measure shelves, boxes, or cupboards to see if they're large enough to store specific materials.

Primary Grades

In the primary grades, opportunities to measure using arbitrary units eventually lead to the recognition that a standard unit is required. As different children get different results by using their feet as the unit of measure, they may recognize that a standard unit of measure is necessary.

A transition from arbitrary units occurs after plenty of opportunities to measure in kindergarten or the primary grades. Create rulers by giving each child a piece of cardboard and a number of paper clips. Paste the clips end to end on the top of the cardboard, and have children mark off the length of one clip, two clips, and so on. Any object can be used. This type of ruler can serve as a transition to real rulers and introduces standard units of measuring like inches, feet, and yards (Robinson et al., 1975).

Children in the primary grades continue measuring in relation to actual experiences. Teachers will introduce standardized units, but formal work with standard units should begin only after children have reached the end of preoperational thought (Hiebert, 1981).

Probability and Graphing

Probability and graphing are closely related. "Graphs can be used to estimate the likelihood of an event. The likelihood of an event occurring is the probability of that event and is represented by a number from 0 to 1 inclusive" (Leutzinger, 1990, p. 253). Concepts of probability and graphing, which begin with classifying, sorting, and counting activities, also involve the use of number and number comparison.

Classification, putting together things that are alike or that belong together, is one of the processes necessary for developing the concept of number. In order to classify, children must be able to observe an object for likenesses and differences as well as for attributes associated with purpose, position, location, or some other factor. Children progress through the following stages as they develop classification.

1.   Sorting into graphic collections without a plan in mind. Children may put all of the blocks with a letter on them together and then, ending with a blue letter, continue by putting all blue blocks with the group. When the grouping is complete, they won't be able to tell you why the blocks belong together, only that they do.

2.   Grouping with no apparent plan. When asked why all the things go together, children respond with some reason, but one not immediately clear to the adult: "Well, all these are like Grandma."

3.   Sorting on the basis of some criterion. Children proceed to being able to sort a group of objects on the basis of one criterion. All the green things or all the round things go together, but not all green *and* round objects.

4.   Next, children can create groupings on the basis of two or more properties, putting all the green *and* round objects together in a group.

5.   Finally, children sort objects or events according to function, use, or on the basis of a negative concept, such as all the things that are not used in the kitchen.

Preschoolers

Before children can classify, they must have some concept of "belonging-ness," "put together," "alike," and "belong together." Concepts and labels for identities, attributes, purposes, locations, positions, and so on are required. The acquisition of these concepts and verbal labels for them becomes an integral part of the mathematics program in early childhood (Gibb & Castaneda, 1975, p. 98).

The role of the adult is to enable children to gain these ideals through experiences and manipulation of materials. Time for play with a wide variety of materials selected specifically for classifying activities should be provided.

Materials for children's classifying may be kept together on a shelf in the manipulative toy or game area of the room. Boxes or sorting trays are kept with the materials. A sorting tray can be constructed by attaching a series of metal jar lids to a board or piece of cardboard, mounting a number of clear plastic cups on a board, dividing a board or tray into sections with colored pieces of tape, or mounting small, clear plastic boxes onto a board. Egg cartons, plastic sewing boxes, toolboxes (such as those for storing nuts or bolts), and fishing boxes are useful as sorting trays and stimulate children to use materials mathematically. Provide children with:

- Boxes of scrap materials—velvet squares, tweeds, and net—cut into uniform sizes and shapes for feeling, sorting, and classifying according to texture. A large collection of materials may lead children into setting up and playing store.
- A box or shelf of bells—cow bells, Christmas bells, decorative bells, sleigh bells—all inviting children to sort and classify on any basis they decide, perhaps size, color, shape, or sound.

- A box of greeting cards—Easter, Valentine's Day, Chanukah, birthday, get well, Christmas. Children use pictures, symbols, size, shape, color, or texture to decide which cards go together.
- An old-fashioned button box, with many buttons, all too large to be stuffed into ears or noses. Children sort buttons into groups on the basis of the attributes they choose.
- A box of various textured papers, cut into uniform shapes and sizes for the younger children, and then into a variety of shapes for older children. Smooth papers, watercolor paper, textured papers, and others can be obtained from a local print shop. (Give the print shop a cardboard box with your name and phone number in large print on the side. Ask them to fill the box with scraps and call you when it's filled.) Children sort the paper according to texture, color, and then on the basis of more than one attribute.
- Individual boxes of shells, beans, macaroni, seeds, beads, or rocks. Again, all should be too large to find their way into children's ears or noses.
- Collections of nuts, nails, screws, and bolts to classify according to shape, size, or function. (Be certain all are safe for children's handling.)

If children lose interest in sorting and classifying, put some of these materials away for a while and bring out others. Or you might motivate them toward classifying activities by putting some items in a basket on the top of a shelf along with a sorting board. The basket might contain items of clothing, which could be sorted according to color or function, or it might contain seashells, leaves, or other items that reflect the children's current interests.

In the Kindergarten

Kindergarten children enjoy sorting and resorting the same materials. They still need time for manipulation and free play, but at this age they can begin sorting on the basis of a given criterion. You might ask a child or small group of children to "Put all the blue ones here," "Find all the square ones," "Put all the things you see on a farm together." Other groupings can be made on the basis of function or association: "Find all the things a firefighter would use." "Put all the adult animals with the baby animals." "Find all the things that do not belong inside." The words *some, none, one,* and *all* can be added to children's play.

You can also introduce group activities. Put children into pairs, and give each group a basket or box of found, unrelated objects, with the following directions:

- Sort all of these so you have two piles. Each group should contain things that go together.

- Now put these things into three groups, being sure each group has things in it that belong together.
- Play "one different." The first person to take a turn picks out one object. The next must find an object that is different from the first in some way. Next, pick an object different from the last object selected. (Charlesworth & Radeloff, 1978)

Primary Grades

In the primary grades, classification of objects leads to the concept of sets. Children probably don't use the terminology of sets in their everyday life, but they do have experiences with sets of objects. Plan initial experiences with sets to introduce children to the idea that a group of objects can be described as *a set*. You can ask children to locate a set of animals or make a set of things you wear. You can also show them an object, for example, a plastic bird, and ask them to create a set of objects starting with it.

Children can learn that:

1. A set can be named by describing or listing its members.
2. The name of a set determines its membership.
3. The phrases "a set of" and "the set of all the" can name different sets.
4. An object can be a member of more than one set. (Gibb & Castaneda, 1975, p. 99)

Children familiar with the idea of sets can match sets on the basis of number. Having two children work together to create matching sets is a useful activity. Give each child a plastic sandwich bag and a set of small blocks. Ask the first child to put a set of blocks in the bag. The partner must match the set, placing the same number of blocks in the other bag. Then they switch. Throughout their work, you and the children should use the terminology *number* and *set* to describe the activity.

You and the children can create other sets using flannel boards and pieces of yarn. Give the children a group of unrelated, dissimilar items. Within the loops of yarn or on the board sets, have the children create sets that match on the basis of number, that do not match on the basis of number, that have no more than the other, or that have fewer than another. Have them create an empty set.

As preparation for addition, children can be given opportunities to separate sets of up to ten members into subsets and name the numbers of members in each of the subsets. Finally, they will be able to relate a set of objects with the oral numeral name and the written symbol to show how many members are in each set.

"*Comparing* is the process by which the child establishes a relation between two objects on the basis of some specific attribute" (Gibb & Castaneda, 1975, p. 102). Children seem to make comparisons easily and naturally, especially when the comparisons involve them personally. "My shoes are newer than yours," "I've got the biggest," "My sister is little," "You've got more."

Preschoolers

In the preschool, children's natural interest in comparing can be extended. When children build with blocks, they may be asked to make additional comparisons: "Which tower is the tallest?" "Pick up the heaviest blocks first." "Build something as tall as this." Have children identify parts of their buildings using the vocabulary of comparison.

When containers of different sizes and shapes are used in sand and water play, children can make comparisons based on volume. In the preschool, these are informal and related to children's actual experiences. "How many blue cups of water will it take to fill this bucket?" "How many red?" "Which is the heaviest?" "This doesn't hold as much."

You can find good opportunities for informal comparisons in the stories, poems, and folktales that children are already familiar with. "The Three Billy Goats Gruff," "The Three Bears," and others offer comparisons on the basis of differing attributes.

In the Kindergarten

Throughout the preschool years and into kindergarten, ask children to observe and note differences in the objects in their environment, to name them, and to discuss them with one another. The following materials can be used to aid children in comparing.

- String, ribbon, pencils, rulers, clay snakes, lines, or strips of paper. Ask children which is longest, longer; shortest, shorter.
- Buttons, dolls, cups, plastic animals, trees, boats. Have children identify the biggest one, or one bigger than another.
- Containers and coffee cans filled with various materials and sealed, buckets or bags of items. Ask which is the heaviest or the lightest; which is heavier than another.
- Toy cars, trucks, swings. Ask which is the fastest, slowest; which is faster than another.
- Paper, cardboard, books, pieces of wood, food slices, cookies. Have children make or find one that is thick, thicker, thickest, or thinnest.
- Voices, musical instruments, drums, or other noisemakers. Pick out the loud or soft sounds; the loudest and softest. (Charlesworth & Radeloff, 1978)

Asking children to observe fosters mathematical knowledge.

Primary Grades

More formal comparisons are made in the primary grades. Children should be moving from making comparisons based on attributes and identities known to them, such as color and size, to making comparisons based on height and width, and finally to comparisons based on number.

Daily classroom routines are still important for making informal comparisons. You can add more formal, structured activities to lead children to the ideas of equivalence and making comparisons on the basis of number. Children must be able to pair the members of two sets and establish a one-to-one correspondence between them. The ability to conserve and to understand that sets can be quantitatively the same shows that children have achieved reversibility of thought (Lemoyne & Favreau, 1981).

At first, you can use complementary sets to establish the idea of equivalence. Asking children to match sets of doll clothes to dolls, glasses to bottles, cups to saucers, or one blue chip with one red chip offers initial experiences with equivalence. Until children have achieved the ability to conserve, however, they'll still be confused if the sets of cups and saucers, for instance, are spread out or placed closer together. **They'll claim that** there are more cups than saucers because they are spread out.

Children can create equivalent sets out of marbles, plastic chips, small blocks, or other objects. Children five years or under do so by counting aloud, matching one object to another in another set. As they are unable to conserve, they will claim that one set has more or less if the objects are rearranged.

Using dominoes or large sets of dice that are either made from blocks, small boxes, or other objects offers additional opportunities for making comparisons of number. Games can be created to match one of the dominoes or dice with another that has the same, more, or fewer dots than another (Horak & Horak, 1983).

Ordering is a higher level of comparing. "It involves comparing more than two things or more than two sets, and involves placing things in sequence from first to last" (Charlesworth & Radeloff, 1978, p. 97). The ability to *seriate*, or order, follows children's development of conservation and classification. Even before age three, children will be able to make spontaneous seriations. They will nest blocks, build towers, or place rings in graduated sizes on a post. This ordering, however, is based on trial and error and doesn't constitute true seriation, which is based on operational thought.

Next children are able to place a pattern in one-to-one correspondence with a model, then to place objects in rows on the basis of length, width, height, and size. First attempts at ordering involve just two objects, but with practice and maturation, children can make comparisons of more than two objects and seriate or order these on the basis of some attribute. The ability actually to seriate, to order from the smallest to the largest or to count "with true understanding of the inclusion relations involved, develops usually at around seven to eight years of age" (Copeland, 1974, p. 80).

Preschoolers

Children under age four are unable to conserve or classify with accuracy. They are not ready for formal work and need many readiness activities in grouping sets of objects and comparing them to determine relations such as "same," "more than," or "less than." This requires that children match using one-to-one correspondence. Preschoolers are able to do this only in a very limited way.

Ordering activities follow the same procedures and use many of the same materials as classification and comparing. Some materials that can be used for ordering are sets of rods of differing lengths; Montessori-type materials that require ordering of pegs, colors, or sounds; blocks; and Tinkertoys.

After children have had a period of free exploration and play, you might have them do the following:

- Find the shortest or longest rod or Tinkertoy.
- Pick from three objects of differing heights the one that is shortest and describe the remaining two objects.
- Describe how the objects in a series, arranged from shortest to longest, differ from one another.

In the Kindergarten

The vocabulary of ordering can be used when children are in kindergarten. Label children's actions using words like *last, first, biggest, fattest, next, before, after.* Also use ordinal numbers—first, second, third, and so on—as they relate to children's experiences. Children should not be expected to develop a true understanding of these terms until around age seven or eight.

Primary Grades

To perform simple ordering tasks, children do not need to understand either cardinal or ordinal numbers; they can arrange a series of sticks in order from shortest to tallest without using either. An ordinal number refers to the position of an object in a set. When counting children in a line, you say "four" when pointing to a given child. The number four refers to the total number of children in that set, so it's the cardinal number. But when you say the child is fourth in line, you are using the ordinal number, which describes the position of the child in the line.

Piaget maintained that even though ordination and cardination are different ideas, they involve each other. Ordination always involves cardination, and cardination always involves ordination (Piaget, 1964). Payne and Rathwell (1975) suggest that children can learn the names for third through tenth because these are the same as the cardinal names of the numerals three through ten. The term *first* is usually easily related to children's actual experiences, as is *last*, but *second* has to be learned separately.

Children can count off in line, using the terminology *first, second, third,* and so on, or they can count crackers, books, or any items that are ordered using the ordinal numbers. Copeland (1974) cautions that it is important to keep in mind the following mental abilities that children need before they can successfully order or seriate:

1.   Reversibility of thought or ability to order in two directions, such as forward and backward.

2.   Transitivity—if B is greater than A, and C is greater than B, then C is also greater than A. This entails coordinating a series of relations and doesn't appear until around age seven or eight.

3.   The dual relations involved for a given element in determining its position, that is, that it must be larger than the preceding element and yet smaller than the element that follows.

Graphing is one way to present a great deal of information. Graphs are a major means for organizing, displaying, and comparing information and are a useful tool for communication. You can see at a glance which child is tallest, which cup holds the most, or how many buckets of water the aquarium holds.

Graphing is a complex activity involving communication, classification, one-to-one correspondence, symbolization, spatial constancy, and measurement. Graphs may be in the form of pictures, like line or bar graphs or circle or pie graphs, which illustrate relationships or percentages.

In the Preschool and Kindergarten

Graphing begins with making graphs. Perhaps the first graphs will be life-size, with children taping the piece of cash register tape used to determine how tall they are to the wall or a chart. At a glance, children can see who is tallest or shortest, and which children are the same size (Shaw, 1984). The same technique can be used to illustrate how far each child can jump, how much the plants grew, or how long children's feet, arms, and hands are.

Floor graphs can introduce children to the idea that they can represent themselves using a symbol. Give each child a piece of construction paper of the same color and size. Select a problem, perhaps whether children will select milk, juice, or chocolate milk for snack or what name they will choose by vote for the guinea pig. The choices can be pictures on the wall. Children can take their piece of paper to the picture of their choice and sit on it. These papers will form the floor graph. The number of children in line for milk or juice can be counted, or the number voting for the name Christina or Julia for the guinea pig can be counted. The children leave their papers on the floor, creating a bar or block graph to represent their choices.

Graphs can also be used to illustrate children's ages, weights, favorite TV shows or sports, shoe sizes, birthdays, and hair or eye colors. For example, one graph illustrated the number of children who were over age five, those under age five, and those who had just turned five that month.

Primary Grades

Making graphs continues in the primary grades. As children experience graphing in the second and third grades, they can begin to interpret graphs. Graphs might be used for prediction, to record an experience, or for measuring. Give each child a clip or clothespin. Have each child place the clip on the side of the graph they select. The graph might be designed to answer the question, "Will it rain tomorrow?" with one side marked *Yes* and the other *No*. Children might also use clips to vote for such decisions as whether to make pudding or gelatin for the next party.

Another activity relates graphing to measuring activities. Graph how many cups it takes to fill the bucket, how many boxes of sand to fill the sandbox, or how many containers of water to fill the aquarium.

Summary

"Pattern is a unifying theme that weaves mathematical topics together. The study of patterns supports children in learning to see relationships, to find connections, and to make generalizations and predictions" (National Council of Teachers of Mathematics, 1991, p. 1). Whether children are counting, graphing, classifying, or measuring, the search for patterns and relationships will take place. All of mathematics is the search for order, pattern, and relationships.

The search for patterns begins in teaching mathematics through children's firsthand experiences, which include children's social interactions with peers and with other adults. These experiences are covered with language and demand that children think and reflect about them.

Projects

Continuing Case Study

Observe your child as he or she plays outdoors. Record every time he or she uses a concept from mathematics. How does the child use the natural environment, and what is the role of other children? How could an adult capitalize on one of these encounters and use it to expand children's understanding of mathematical concepts?

1. Design a number game for children in the primary grades. This could be a board game, matching game, or other, but it should foster recognition of numerals and counting and matching symbols to sets or sets to symbols.
2. Develop a file of activities that would be useful in helping children in the preschool and primary grades classify, compare, order, measure, graph, and count.
3. Obtain several early childhood education supply catalogs. Identify toys or items that children could use to advance number concepts and facilitate their understanding of numerical operations.
4. Review several commercial mathematics textbooks for children in kindergarten and primary grades. Note the sequence of skills required. Which are congruent with Piagetian theory and which are not?

Children's Books

These children's books can be helpful in reinforcing mathematical ideas.

Anno, M. (1977). *Anno's counting book.* New York: Crowell.

Bang, M. (1983). *Ten, nine, eight.* New York: Greenwillow.

Behrens, J. (1975). *The true book of metric measurement.* Chicago: Children's Press.

Bitter, G. (1981). *Exploring with computers.* New York: Messner.

Carle, E. (1971). *The very hungry caterpillar.* New York: Crowell.

Feelings, M. (1971). *Moja means one.* Illustrated by T. Feelings. New York: Dial.

Fey, J. (1971). *Long, short, high, low, thin, wide.* Illustrated by J. Russell. New York: Crowell.

Froman, R. (1973). *Less than nothing is really something.* Illustrated by Don Madden. New York: Crowell.

Grossman, V., & Long, S. (1991). *Ten little rabbits.* Illustrated by Sylvia Long. San Francisco: Chronicle Books.

Hort, L. (1991). *How many stars in the sky?* Illustrated by James E. Ransome. New York: Morrow.

Hussey, L. (1992). *Animaze! A collection of amazing nature mazes.* Illustrated by Lorna Hussey. New York: Alfred A. Knopf. Beautifully illustrated mazes display a delightful variety of animals and their natural habitats.

Keats, E. J. (1972). *Over in the meadow.* New York: Scholastic.

Lobel, A. (1981). *On Market Street.* Illustrated by Anita Lobel. New York: Greenwillow.

Milne, A. A. (1982). *Pooh's counting book.* Illustrated by E. H. Shepard. New York: Dutton.

Nedobeck, D. (1981). *Nedobeck's number books.* Chicago: Children's.

Testa, F. (1983). *If you look around you.* New York: Dial.

Watson, C. (1977). *Binary numbers.* Illustrated by Wendy Watson. New York: Crowell.

Resources

The National Council of Teachers of Mathematics in Reston, VA, publishes excellent books on teaching mathematics to young children. Among these are J. M. Payne's *Mathematics for the Young Child* (1990) and *The Kindergarten Book* (1991).

The outstanding Science 5/13 teaching units are now available in the United States. The series, ideal for the teacher who wants to focus on critical thinking skills, were developed in England. The books, *Early Explorations, Investigations, Early Experiences,* and *With Objectives in Mind,* $10.75 each, are available from Teachers' Laboratory, Inc., P.O. Box 6480, Brattleboro, VT 05302.

References

Baroody, A. J., Ginsburg, H. P., & Waxman, B. (1983). Children's understanding of mathematical structure. *Journal for Research in Mathematics Education, 14,* 156–168.

Campbell, P., & Carey, D. (1992). New directions for the early childhood mathematics curriculum. In C. Seefeldt (Ed.), *The early childhood curriculum: A review of current research* (pp. 152–175). New York: Teachers College Press.

Campbell, P., & Clements, D. (1990). Using microcomputers for mathematics learning. In J. N. Payne (Ed.), *Mathematics for the young child* (pp. 265–285). Reston, VA: National Council of Teachers of Mathematics.

Castaneda, A. M. (1987). Early mathematics education. In C. Seefeldt (Ed.), *The early childhood curriculum: A review of current research* (pp. 165–183). New York: Teachers College Press.

Charlesworth, R., & Radeloff, D. J. (1978). *Experiences in mathematics for young children.* New York: Delmar.

Cobb, P., & Steffe, L. P. (1983). The constructionist researcher as teacher and model builder. *Journal for Research in Mathematics Education, 14,* 83–85.

Copeland, R. W. (1974). *How children learn mathematics*. New York: Macmillan.

Flavell, J. H. (1979). Metacognition and cognitive monitoring. *American Psychologist, 34*, 906–911.

Folsom, M. (1975). Operations on whole numbers. In J. N. Payne (Ed.), *Mathematics learning in early childhood* (pp. 161–191). Reston, VA: National Council of Teachers of Mathematics.

Forman, G. E., & Kuschner, D. S. (1983). *The child's construction of knowledge: Piaget for teaching children*. Washington, DC: National Association for the Education of Young Children.

Fuson, K. C. (1988). *Children's counting and concepts of number*. New York: Springer.

Gelman, R. (1979). Preschool thought. *American Psychologist, 34*, 900–905.

Gessell, A., Illg, F. L., & Ames, L. B. (1974). *Infant and child in the culture of today*. New York: Harper & Row.

Gibb, E. G., & Castaneda, A. M. (1975). Experiences for young children. In J. N. Payne (Ed.), *Mathematics learning in early childhood* (pp. 95–125). Reston, VA: National Council of Teachers of Mathematics.

Hiebert, J. (1981). Cognitive development and learning of linear measurement. *Journal for Research in Mathematics Education, 12*, 197–211.

Hiebert, J., & Lindquist, M. M. (1990). Developing mathematical knowledge in young children. In J. N. Payne (Ed.), *Mathematics for the young child* (pp. 17–39). Reston, VA: National Council of Teachers of Mathematics.

Hollis, M. L. (1984). Teaching rational numbers: Primary grades. *Arithmetic Teacher, 31*(6), 36–39.

Horak, W. M., & Horak, W. J. (1983). Dice have many uses. *Arithmetic Teacher, 30*(6), 4–6.

Houlihan, D. M., & Ginsberg, H. P. (1981). The additive methods of first- and second-grade children. *Journal for Research in Mathematics Education, 12*, 95–106.

Kamii, C. (1982). *Number in the preschool and kindergarten*. Washington, DC: National Association for the Education of Young Children.

Kamii, C., & DeVries, R. (1978). *Physical knowledge in preschool education: Implications of Piaget's theory*. Washington, DC: National Association for the Education of Young Children.

Lampert, M. (1990). When the problem is not the question and the solution is not the answer: Mathematical knowing and teaching. *American Educational Research Journal, 27*, 29–63.

Lemoyne, G., & Favreau, M. (1981). Piaget's construction of number development: Its relevance to mathematics learning. *Journal for Research in Mathematics Education, 12*, 179–196.

Leutzinger, L. P. (1990). Graphical representation and probability. In J. N. Payne (Ed.), *Mathematics for the young child* (pp. 251–265). Reston, VA: National Council of Teachers of Mathematics.

Liedtke, W. (1983). Young children—small numbers: Making numbers come alive. *Arithmetic Teacher, 31*(1), 34–40.

Lovell, K. (1971). *The growth of understanding in mathematics: Kindergarten through grade three*. New York: Holt, Rinehart & Winston.

McMillan, M. (1919). *The nursery school*. London: J. M. Dent.

National Council of Teachers of Mathematics. (1989). *Curriculum and evaluation standards for school mathematics*. Reston, VA: Author.

National Council of Teachers of Mathematics. (1991). *Kindergarten book*. Reston, VA: Author.

National Research Council. (1989). *Everybody counts*. Washington: National Academy Press.

Nixon, R. H., & Nixon, E. C. (1971). *Introduction to early childhood education*. New York: Random House.

Payne, J. N., & Rathwell, E. (1975). Number and numeration. In J. N. Payne (Ed.), *Mathematics learning in early childhood education* (pp. 251–265). Reston, VA: National Council of Teachers of Mathematics.

Payne, J. N. (1990). New directions in mathematics education. In J. N. Payne (Ed.), *Mathematics for the young child* (pp. 1–17). Reston, VA: National Council of Teachers of Mathematics.

Piaget, J. (1963). *The origins of intelligence in children.* New York: Norton.

Piaget, J. (1964). Cognitive development in children: Development and learning. *Journal of Research in Science Teaching, 21,* 176–196.

Rea, R. E., & Reys, R. (1971). Competencies of entering kindergartners in geometry, number, and money. *School Science and Mathematics, 41,* 389–482.

Resnick, L. (1988). *Learning to think.* Washington, DC: National Academy Press.

Richardson, K., & Salkeld, L. (in press). Developmentally appropriate curriculum. In S. Bredekamp (Ed.), *Reaching potentials: appropriate curriculum and assessment for young children. Volume 2.* Washington, DC: National Association for the Education of Young Children.

Robinson, G. E., Mahaffey, M. I., & Nelson, I. D. (1975). In J. N. Payne (Ed.), *Mathematics learning in early childhood* (pp. 227–251). Reston, VA: National Council of Teachers of Mathematics.

Shaw, J. M. (1984). Making graphs. *Arithmetic Teacher, 31*(5), 7–9.

Thorlindsson, T. (1983). Social organization and cognition. *Human Development, 26,* 289–317.

van Hiele, P. M. (1986). *Structure and insight.* New York: Academic Press.

Wheeler, B., & Wheeler, M. M. (1981). The calculator for concept formation: A clinical status study. *Journal for Research in Mathematics Education, 12,* 323–339.

Wilder, R. R. (1968). *Evolution of mathematical concepts: An elementary study.* New York: John Wiley.

Worth, J. (1990). Developing problem-solving abilities and attitudes. In J. N. Payne (Ed.), *Mathematics for the young child* (pp. 39–63). Reston, VA: National Council of Teachers of Mathematics.

"Science is thinking and doing and making the two come together."
(Holt, 1977, p. 2)

After you read this chapter, you should be able to respond to the following questions:

1. What are the processes of science?

2. Give a definition for thinking. What processes are involved in thinking?

3. Give a definition of concept formation. What processes are involved in concept formation? Give an example of how children develop concepts.

4. What are the goals for teaching thinking and for fostering concept formation?

5. What are the biological sciences? How are these best introduced to young children?

6. What are the physical sciences? How are these introduced to young children?

Young children are natural scientists. They are curious, interested, into everything, always questioning, and trying to find out what will happen if. With their abundant curiosity, they are eager to discover all they can about the world in which they live. As they poke, take apart, and mess around with mud, sand, and water, they are like scientists. As they try to understand the nature of their biological and physical world, they think and do at the same time.

Science, one of the most important areas in education (Rutherford & Ahlgren, 1990), has its foundation in programs for young children. For example, children playing with magnets at age three are not really learning theories of magnetism, but they are becoming aware of magnets. By exploring what magnets do, they are constructing their own personal knowledge of magnetism. This experience and the personal knowledge that results will serve as the children's basis for conventional knowledge of magnetism when they reach the stage of formal operations. When children observe guppies being born and chart their development, they are not learning the theories of biology, but they are becoming aware of, and inquiring into, the nature of

Children act as scientists, observing, collecting information, and advancing hypotheses.

life, growth, and development. This awareness will lay the foundation for formal learning experiences in biology.

Most important, perhaps, as children play with science during their early years, they are developing the ability to think, to sense problems, and to find ways of solving them.

Like scientists, children think, form concepts, and solve problems. In *How We Think*, Dewey (1910) likened children's thinking to that of scientists trying to solve problems. Both children and scientists observe, infer, classify, and reach conclusions. These processes, which children use unconsciously, "are the methods that a scientist uses consciously" (*Science 5/13*, 1976, p. 1).

But science is not just processes; it is products as well. Knowledge of living things—plants and animals—and of the physical sciences—astronomy, chemistry, meteorology, and physics—is the product of science. Children learn both the processes—thinking, forming concepts, and problem-solving—and the products of science—knowledge of the biological and physical sciences—as they explore and experiment with their environment.

The Processes of Science: Thinking and Concept Formation

Humans think. Our ability to think, to create, and to think about our own thinking separates us from other animals. Thinking means action. When we think we are active in: *(a)* organizing, manipulating, and interrelating facts and concepts; *(b)* forming and testing hypotheses; and *(c)* evaluating and interpreting evidence (Dewey, 1910).

Thinking seems to involve a state of doubt or mental difficulty that results in a solution to a problem. For Dewey, thinking and problem solving were much the same thing. Thinking has no age limits. Infants, kindergarten and primary children, fifth-graders, and adults all think in the following several steps:

1. Recognizing that a problem exists.
2. Identifying the problem and surveying what one knows about it. During this step the thinker is gathering data.
3. Formulating hypotheses or tentative solutions to the problem. The thinker makes some tentative statement about events or relationships, which is provisionally accepted as valid for purposes of reasoning, experimenting, or investigating.
4. Testing the hypotheses. A person cannot know which hypothesis or tentative solution is valid until all are tested.
5. Collecting additional data. Sometimes the first hypothesis proves wrong. Additional information is needed to permit new hypotheses to be tested and others to be confirmed, checked, or verified.

6. Summarizing and drawing conclusions. Based on testing hypotheses, the thinker draws conclusions and summarizes findings.

7. Finally, formulating new generalizations, principles, or a plan of action for applying what has been learned.

Eighteen-month-old Shawn is playing with her toys on a rug. She is pushing blocks around, piling them up, and then knocking them down with glee. As she plays, now and then she takes a sip of juice from a plastic bottle her mother has handed her. Excited by her play, she drops the bottle on its side, and juice spills out on the rug. By accident Shawn puts her hand on the wet spot on the rug. The wetness puzzles her. She looks at her hand, noticing that there is a problem.

Shawn feels the rug once more. Looking again at her hand and the rug, Shawn takes her bottle and drinks from it, then looks at it and back at the rug. She feels the wet spot on the rug again, appearing to formulate tentative solutions to the problem.

Next Shawn tests her hypothesis by deliberately spilling some of the juice on the rug and feeling the new wet spot (testing the hypothesis). She does this again, feeling the wetness she's just created on the rug, and once more feels the original spot (collecting additional data). Then she smiles and drinks the remainder of juice in the bottle, as if satisfied at her conclusions.

A group of third-graders who are going over their mathematics papers also demonstrates thinking. Dannie says, "Hey, I got better this time. I got four more done." Phil responds, "I remembered my eights better," and Tommie chimes in, "I didn't get any more done—I don't know why," identifying a problem.

"When did you do your practice, Dannie?" asks Tommie. "I did it in the morning," replies Dannie. "Well, so did I, but I didn't get better. How did you do your practice? Maybe I didn't do it right," says Tommie, advancing a tentative idea about his problem.

"Phil, how did you practice your math?" "Just like Mrs. B. said. I went up one row, then down the other," answers Phil. "Did you do it in the morning?" asks Tommie. "No, I did it after school."

Going around the room, Tommie, Phil, and Dannie ask the other children not only when they practiced but also how. Tommie sums up their findings. "You could study in the morning, the afternoon, or you can go up the row first, or you can do those you know first," testing the hypothesis that when and how one studies is related to the number of problems correctly solved. "I'm going to try doing the practice after school, but I'm going to do it the way Phil did. If that doesn't work, then I'll do all the rows up first."

Table 13–1   National science projects

Project and Director	Address	Description
Science—A Process Approach American Association for the Advancement of Science	Ginn & Co. Xerox Distribution Center Carlstadt, NJ	Emphasizes the laboratory method of instruction and focuses on ways of developing basic skills in observing, classifying, measuring, predicting, and other skills needed for scientific investigation.
Elementary Science Project Joseph C. Paige	Department of Education and Physics Howard University Washington, DC 20001	Compensatory science experiences for disadvantaged children and their parents.
Elementary Science Study Randolph Brown	55 Chapel Street Newton, MA 02160	Child-centered science material designed around open-ended investigations.
Science Curriculum Improvement Study Robert Karplus	Lawrence Hall of Science University of California Berkeley, CA 94720	To develop in children an investigative attitude and a functional understanding of fundamental concepts in the physical and biological sciences.
Science 5/13	Macdonald Educational 850 Seventh Avenue New York, NY 10019	To help teachers aid children in learning science through firsthand experiences, using a variety of methods.

Whether they involve a toddler trying to figure out how the wet spot got on the rug or third-graders who are pondering the effectiveness of their strategies for learning, the processes of thinking and solving problems are the same.

Thinking, an active process that takes place within an individual, is difficult to measure. You can infer that thinking is taking place only by observing behaviors. Often, as in the case of Shawn or the third-grade boys, you wouldn't be able to say that thinking resulted in new learning. You would have to observe the children later, as they applied some principle related to spilling liquids or developing strategies for memorizing number facts. Fostering children's ability to think through their own activity and action continues to be a primary goal of all education, one that is especially important in science.

Science and Thinking

Science programs in early childhood education build on the idea that children have many opportunities to think, which promote observing, inferring, classifying, advancing hypotheses, and communicating them to many other people. Many science curricula focus on these processes, as Table 13–1 shows.

Observing

When observing, a child learns to use all or as many senses as possible: seeing, hearing, smelling, tasting, and feeling. Forman and Kuschner (1977) have suggested four stages to have children follow in observing: *(a)* identify parts of the thing or object, *(b)* look at it from the other angles, *(c)* contrast the thing they are observing with other things, and *(d)* relate the structure of the object or thing to its function. "Look at its eyes—it can see all around, even in back of its head."

Psychologists seem to agree that children need many things in their environment to see, hear, touch, smell, and taste (Denner & Sheldon, 1976; Macbeth & Fowler, 1972; Offenback, 1983). In addition to a stimulating environment, rich in sensory experiences, interaction with a caring, sensitive, and supportive adult is necessary.

The adult's role is not only to provide things to observe, but also to focus children's observations, using language to describe and label them. Words are useful in fixing observations and in enabling children to perceive similarities and differences in the things they're observing as well as in reaching conclusions and forming concepts.

As children observe, try to focus their attention on a specific detail. Perhaps they are observing a melting ice cube or a jack-o'-lantern that is growing mold. They can be helped with questions and comments to concentrate on specific details and observe with more than one sense. "Look at the legs" or "How many colors do you see in the dragonfly's wing?" Also try to get children to focus observations for extended periods of time so that they notice details, similarities, and differences.

You can give primary-grade children a piece of red yarn and ask them to make a circle on the sidewalk with the yarn. Then ask them to observe all the living and nonliving things in that circle (Jones, 1987). Or give children magnifying glasses and a variety of cut flowers. Looking through the glasses, children will observe the flowers' differences in a new way.

Some activities that might be used to help children observe and understand the use of observation are:

• *Seeing.* Look at a lima bean growing; see the fish swim; watch the shadows on the play yard; observe the shape, color, and movement of the clouds each day.

- *Smelling*. Cut open a pineapple, and smell the fruit; smell pine needles gathered on a walk; identify the vanilla the cook is using; smell the spices or the baking bread.
- *Touching*. Touch the rough skin of the pineapple, and feel the prickly leaves; touch the different textures at the woodworking bench—the cold steel of the hammer, the rough sandpaper, the boards; feel the smooth plastic and the fuzzy leaf.
- *Tasting*. Taste the sweet pineapple, the vanilla cookies, and the baking bread; put a drop of a spice on your tongue, and tell how it tastes; close your eyes, and taste a bit of onion, apple, pear, and radish, then guess what they are.
- *Hearing*. Listen to the wind outside or to the sounds of traffic in the street; listen to your own voice on a tape recorder; listen to the sounds in the kitchen, the center, and the play yard.

Inferring

Inferring involves suggesting explanations, reasons, or causes for past events. It requires that the individual think and reason about what has occurred. It differs from predicting because predicting involves something that might happen in the future. Inferences are like hypotheses in a way because they are based on judgment and evaluation, and they may not always be valid.

When children are observing, ask them to make judgments, hypotheses, or inferences about their observations. "What does it mean?" "Why do you think?" "How does it . . . ?" Because inferences are often incorrect, children must feel free to make mistakes (Burton, 1983) and to try again.

Some activities that help children understand the meaning of inferring appear in the box.

A Mystery Box

Seal an object inside a box and pass the box around. Have children guess what's inside the box without being able to look inside. Why did they make the guesses they did? Which were correct?

Hands Behind Back

Ask children, one at a time, to put their hands behind their back. Place a small object in their hands—a button, spool, pen, bead, figurine—and have the children identify it without looking at it. Discuss why their inferences were accurate. What additional information was required to make more accurate inferences?

Look Outside

Look outside and ask children to tell whether it's hot or cold, windy or quiet. Have them identify the reasons they think so.

Classifying

In order to classify, children must not only observe, but also think. They have already had many opportunities to observe and classify their environment before they come to school. At home they put the forks together in a compartment separate from the spoons; put all the cookies on one plate; all their toys in a box; all their socks in one drawer.

Children could classify in the following ways:

- Seeds by size, shape, or means of travel
- Insects by type, with or without wings
- Pictures of animals as wild, domestic, or living in a zoo
- Properties of objects—hard, smooth, soft, large, rough, bright, fat, thin, wide, narrow, shiny, sticky, loud, hot, and cold
- Toys as wheel toys, wind-up toys, or toys to build with.

Communicating

Children should be encouraged to tell how and what they have observed, inferred, or classified in order to clarify their own thinking and to build social interaction skills. Teachers can plan opportunities for them to communicate with peers, as well as with teachers and other adults.

As children work on the processes of science and thinking, they may tell how one object or idea is like or not like another, how it feels, what they can do with it, or what it makes them think of. Communicating can include verbal discussions, drawing, painting, dancing, moving, or dramatizing ideas. Some ideas to encourage children's communication are:

- *Living things.* Ask children, "How is a turtle like a fish?" "How is the kitten just like you?" "What do they make you think of?"
- *Properties of objects.* Have children describe objects using words like *hard, smooth, wide, hot,* and so on.
- *Feelings.* Encourage children to describe their feelings, giving names to their emotions. "How did you feel when you saw the birthday cake?" "How did you feel when that spider was on your arm?" Or give names to children's feelings: "I'll bet you were frightened when . . ." or "You looked so happy when . . ."

Science and Concept Formation

Concepts, described as classes of events or objects and the relationships among them, are "generally what we think about" (Gleitman, 1986, p. 315).

Having a store of concepts means being able to respond in consistent ways to classes of objects or situations. The "thinking, doing, and making" of science are seen in the relationship among the processes of thinking—observing, inferring, and communicating—but one cannot engage in these until a store of concepts and broad principles has been created (Finley, 1983).

Concepts serve as a mental filing cabinet. Children can use concepts to reorganize and categorize their experiences into meaningful wholes. Even infants are believed to begin to understand their world by categorizing early experiences (Benham, Hosticka, Payne, & Yeotis, 1982). Broad categories are learned first, proceeding from the general to the specific. Children first learn the broad category, *dog*, then classify dog into big and little, barking and quiet, and so on. Next, they group dogs into breeds, such as dalmatians, spaniels, and so on, finally making finer and finer distinctions among breeds.

Through identifying similarities and differences, children learn by process of elimination that some things are included in a category and others are not. After concrete concepts have developed, such as *dog, man, smooth, insect*, abstract ones evolve such as *truth, beauty, kindness*, and *love*.

With a store of concepts, children do not have to process each encounter with their environment separately. This enables them to learn more about their world more efficiently. Once they have developed a store of concepts and see relationships among the concepts, children can begin to make generalizations. A *generalization* is a statement of a general law or principle that might be applied to several situations having common characteristics. Generalizations are the guidelines by which we govern actions, and they are much more complex than a simple statement of fact. The formation of concepts is believed to consist of three processes: differentiation, grouping, and labeling.

Differentiation

Perception is involved in differentiating properties or characteristics of objects and events. Perceptions are "what is known of an object, a quality or a relation as a result of a sensory experience" (Russell, 1956). You know something is red, hot, or sweet because of your sensory experience. But perception involves more than just taking in information through the senses. An individual must be able to identify distinctive features as the result of sensory experience.

Grouping

Grouping is the ability to abstract certain common characteristics in an array of dissimilar objects or events. Children must have experiences with the environment and concrete objects in order to be able to group their perceptions. Telling a child that one object is heavy and another light doesn't help that child group objects on the basis of heavy or light. Only through experience, repetition, and practice is there "an increased ability of the organism to get information from its environment, as a result of practice with the array of stimulation provided by the environment" (Gibson, 1969, p. 77).

Labeling

Categorizing and labeling entail being able to use verbal labels that encompass and organize diverse objects and events. Language is important to concept formation. Once children have a word or a label, they can associate that word with the object or thing it stands for. Words represent concepts that evoke words, making the process of concept formation and language development integrated (Carroll, 1964). Once children have words, they can communicate concepts to others and use language to assist them as they form new concepts.

The foundation for all concept formation is in children's hands-on encounters with the environment. All concept formation begins in acting on objects—feeling, tasting, smelling, seeing, and hearing them.

Children cause objects to move—throwing, banging, blowing, pushing, and pulling them, and they observe changes that take place in objects when they are heated, cooled, mixed together, or changed in some other way. As physical knowledge develops, children become better able to establish relationships (comparing, classifying, ordering) between and among the objects they act

---

Science Curriculums

Science—A Process Approach (SAPA, 1975).
Emphasizes the laboratory method of instruction and focuses on ways of developing basic skills in observing, classifying, measuring, predicting, and other skills needed for scientific investigation.

Elementary Science Project (EEP, 1985)
Compensatory science experiences for disadvantaged children and their parents.

Elementary Science Study (EES, 1985)
Child-centered science material designed around open-ended investigations.

Science Curriculum Improvement Study (SCSS, 1988).
To develop in children investigative attitudes and a functional understanding of fundamental concepts in the physical and biological sciences.

Science 5/13 (1973).
A series of booklets designed to help teachers aid children in learning science through firsthand experiences using a variety of methods.

upon. Such relationships are essential for the emergence of logical, flexible thought processes. (Smith, 1987, p. 35)

Informal encounters with the environment provide the building blocks for science concepts. "Informal experiences, at the water table, or in the animal center, sandbox, or block corner, allow children to explore objects freely and to discover their properties, what they are made of, and how they react when acted on in various ways" (Smith, 1987, p. 35).

Teachers should:

- Be aware of daily experiences that involve science and capitalize on them.
- Encourage and facilitate children's explorations in science.
- Remember that meaningful learning is an active, self-regulated process. (Smith, 1987, p. 36)

The criteria given in Figure 13–1 are useful in selecting experiences and materials to promote concept formation and thinking.

Are the materials selected those that:

- Children will naturally gravitate to for play?
- Provide opportunities for the development of perceptual abilities through total involvement of the senses (perception of color, size, shape, texture, hardness, sound, scent, etc.)?
- Encourage self-directed problem-solving and experimentation?
- Children can act upon—cause to move—or that encourage children's observations of changes?

Do the experiences that evolve from children's play with the materials:

- Provide opportunities for the teacher to extend the child's learning by asking questions or making suggestions that stimulate children's thinking?
- Allow for additional materials to be introduced gradually to extend children's explorations and discoveries?
- Allow for differences in ability, development, and learning style?
- Allow children to freely interact with other children and adults?
- Encourage children to observe, compare, classify, predict, communicate?
- Allow for the integration of other curriculum areas?

Figure 13–1

Criteria for selecting science materials and activities that foster children's thinking processes

From "Theoretical framework for preschool science experiences" by R. F. Smith, 1987, *Young Children, 42*(2), p. 35. Reprinted by permission.

The Product of Science: Knowledge

Children need something to think about. Science introduces children to knowledge from both the biological and the physical realms. Selecting goals for this knowledge base requires understanding of the children, the content of science, and the community.

The Children

Knowledge of children's thinking comes first. Piaget (1964) documented that children's understanding of both biological and physical sciences develops gradually. First, children attribute life to anything that has an activity or function of any sort. Piaget termed this *animism* and *artificialism*.

Children need to think about something.

Through age six or seven, children believe that every object has a force. According to children, engines, air, and the clouds move because *they* want to. Poison is alive because it could kill you, and rain is alive because it falls when it wants to or because it doesn't want you to play outside.

From about six to eight years of age, children still confuse movement with life. Anything that moves must be alive. The difference between mechanical movement and biological life is very confusing. After age eight, children believe that only those things that can move spontaneously are alive. The sun, the stars, and the wind, they think, are alive and conscious. Only after age 11 do children restrict life to animals alone or to plants and animals.

Children younger than 11 or 12 also believe that every object, including natural bodies, is "made for" a purpose (Piaget, 1964). They believe a natural object is made for the purpose for which we use it, and because it has been made for humans, it is closely related to them. For instance, children believe a mountain is made for climbing or a lake for boating. They believe things are either made by humans or that things create themselves for humans.

Attempting to change children's understanding of the world through direct instruction does not seem to work (Lemoyne & Favreau, 1981). It seems that children younger than 11 or 12 distort what an adult tells them to make it fit their ideas of living and nonliving. If told the vacuum sweeper isn't alive and can't hurt them because you have to push a button and turn on the electricity to make it work, children just believe that the button or the electricity is alive. Similarly, ten-year-olds, who have been taught about evaporation in school, use this information to support their *animistic* or *anthropomorphic* thinking. They will claim that the clouds get a bucket to fetch the water from the rivers to take back with them to the sky to make rain.

The Content

Science is a large field. Think of all of the content of the biological or physical sciences. The role of the teacher is to select from the sciences those things that are closest to the children, that interest them the most, and that are from their past experiences. The things that are closest to them physically are natural choices.

Balance is necessary, however. Children's interests in the biological sciences can overwhelm you. You may become so enthralled with the things that interest them that you neglect to introduce them to the physical sciences. Keep your program balanced.

Remember, too, that it is not necessary to present young children with everything at once. Each teacher is responsible for only a small part of children's learning. The science experiences children will have in an early childhood program are just the beginning and will serve as a base for later understandings. Early childhood education need only present an introduction and not a complete, in-depth study of the biological and physical sciences.

The Community

In selecting content, you will also find it helpful to look at the community and identify the resources that are available there. Take an inventory of the resources in the school that the children can use. Find out about the museums in your area or other interesting places where children could observe the processes of science and come into contact with its content (Holt, 1977).

Consider children's safety. When science is conceived of as a process and children are encouraged to observe actively using as many senses as possible, they can encounter dangerous situations. Science materials should be safe for children to handle. Teach children to approach strange objects and substances with caution. Train them to observe with caution, for example, sniffing substances cautiously and touching and tasting only under adult supervision.

The Biological Sciences

The biological sciences involve the study of living organisms and their activities. They include botany, the study of plants, and zoology, the study of animals.

Goals

As children use the processes of science—observing, inferring, classifying and communicating—they should be thinking, solving problems, and developing concepts of:

- Living and nonliving things
- The variety of living things on the earth (name and describe)
- Categorizing living things
- Why and how living things act as they do; the interdependence of life
- The way humans use living things and their products and respect for living things

Indoor and outdoor environments are filled with plants and animals for children's observation, thinking, and problem solving. The room is full of plants, insect or animal cages, aquariums, and terrariums. The outdoors is also a "workshop" in which children can learn about the biological sciences (Williams & Sherwood, 1983; Ziemer, 1987).

Biology, the study of living things, demands respect for living things. If you do plan to keep plants or animals, be certain you do so properly, demonstrat-

Show respect for life by making sure any caged animals are well cared for.

ing respect for life. Show the need to protect and care for the total environment through attitude and actions: "We'll keep the grasshopper in the insect cage this morning so you can observe it. Does the grasshopper have wings? How does it use its legs? When we finish observing, we'll release it."

In deciding to keep living things:

- Ask yourself if there are animals or plants in the natural environment that could be used instead of caged animals for children's firsthand experiences.
- Be certain that caged animals are well cared for.
- Be aware of the health hazards for children. Birds can carry psittacosis, and turtles and other animals can carry salmonellosis (Holt, 1977). Dogs, rabbits, and other animals may have parasites. Some children may be allergic to animal dander or harmed by molds or plants.

Fostering Concepts

Direct instruction (Lemoyne & Favreau, 1981) appears futile in science; children need actual experiences with living things. Use many of the plants and animals in the natural environment as the focus of children's study. Become familiar with these living things, and be able to identify those that may present health hazards to children. Some insects, such as mosquitoes, houseflies, and cockroaches, may carry dangerous diseases and infections (Holt, 1977). Some plants or plant parts may be poisonous. Know which can be handled and examined closely, and which should be observed at a distance.

Plants

Three-year-olds may enjoy planting seeds and watering them once or twice. They can also be asked to observe the growing plants. But these children soon lose interest in the garden and move on to other activities (Forsom, 1971). If working with toddlers, it helps to find seeds that are large enough for children to handle and that sprout quickly, such as scarlet runner bean seeds.

Children over the age of four or so may be interested in observing seeds sprout on a dampened sponge or wet paper towel. As they observe seeds changing, name the parts of the plant and discuss the changes that occur as the plant grows. Even at five years of age, children are confused about which parts of the plant are roots, leaves, stem, buds, and blossoms.

Be prepared to plant seeds that children bring to school. Children often present teachers with the seeds from their orange, apple, avocado, grapefruit, or other food they have eaten. Flat wooden, metal, or heavy cardboard boxes can be used for flats when filled with potting soil. Clear plastic sandwich boxes are good containers for sprouting seeds. Recommendations for usage of different types of plant containers appear in the box.

Do not try to experiment with the amount of light, food, or water that plants need until children are in the upper primary grades. It's enough for children under age six or so to observe seeds sprout and grow and become familiar with the names of the parts of plants. If plants turn yellow or die from excess or insufficient sunlight or water, draw children's attention to the plants' needs. Ask children to draw their own inferences: "Why do you think . . . ?" "What happened . . . ?" You might point out the needs of all living things for proper amounts of light, food, and water.

Animals

Animal life can be observed in the classroom environment. Animals like guinea pigs, hamsters, and mice adjust to life in the classroom and offer children extended opportunities to observe, make inferences, and communicate with others. Children will frequently bring you insects that they captured on the way to school or at home. You can construct a cage for insects

Plant Containers

Ordinary Clay Pots

Porous and ideal.

Wooden Containers

Drill drainage hole in bottom of any wood container, and place layer of coarse gravel in bottom before adding soil.

Styrofoam Containers

Not water permeable, so less frequent watering is required. Add drainage holes and gravel to the bottom of the container.

Plastic Containers

Not porous; drainage hole required. Fill bottom with coarse gravel before adding soil. Because plastic containers are not porous, less frequent watering is required.

Plastic Baskets

Plastic berry and vegetable baskets can be used as plant containers. Cover inside with sphagnum moss, spanish moss, or other moss. Water will run through, however, so something to catch excess water is required.

Plastic Bags

With bottoms filled with gravel for drainage, plastic bags can be used as containers for plants. Water less frequently than plants in clay pots, more frequently than plants in styrofoam or plastic containers.

using the bottoms of two plastic bottles. Cut the bottom inch or two from the bottles. Take a piece of plastic screening, roll it up, and place one of the bottoms at each end of the rolled-up screen. Let the screen unroll and you have a cage for insects. You can place branches, leaves, or plants at the bottom to permit insects to perch and maintain life in their temporary home. (See Figure 13–2.)

Animals that exist far away also interest children. Books, filmstrips, pictures, slides, stories, and poems about animals may be useful in expanding children's interest in and understanding of animal life.

The Great Variety of Life

Children's initial experiences observing plant and animal life are an introduction to the concept of the variety of living things. No one knows exactly how many different kinds of plants and animals exist. When classified, there appear to be nearly a million different kinds of animals. Children five and over may begin to observe and study the variety of life in their environment. Activities to foster the understanding of the variety of life are listed in the box.

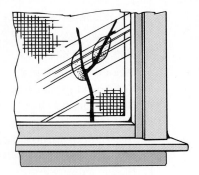

Screen cylinder   Screened window

Screen cylinder

Roll a piece of window screening into a cylinder, clip the sides together, and place it between the tops of plastic coffee can lids or two plastic bleach bottle bottoms. Some teachers like to place a piece of clay or plaster of paris at the bottom to stabilize the cage and to hold twigs for insects to sit on.

Screened window

An ideal place for cocoons is a screened window. Cocoons kept between a window and screen all winter are subject to the same moisture and temperature and will emerge where children can observe them in the spring.

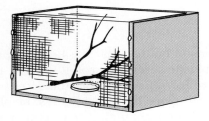

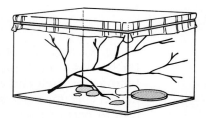

Wooden box and screening   Insect terrarium

Wooden box and screening

Replace two adjoining sides of a wooden box, leaving two sides and two ends, with window screening. Hinge the screening as a door on one side.

Insect terrarium

Some insects, such as grasshoppers and crickets, may be kept in a terrarium with a gauze or screen top. Plants and animals that live together in similar habitats out-of-doors should be selected. Aeration and drainage are important. A bowl of water, with stones or a twig over it, completes the insect terrarium.

Figure 13–2
Insect cages

Ant observation nest

A large fruit jar with a lid is all that's required. Place a block or cylinder of wood in the center of the jar and fill the space between the wood and the glass with a mixture of soil and sand. When you find a colony of ants with eggs, larvae, and pupae, scoop them and the young into the cage. If you dig deeply, you may find the queen, who is larger than the others.

To maintain moisture, keep a small set sponge in the jar. Feed once a week by placing sugar or a small piece of bread soaked in honey water in the jar. After a few hours, remove food the ants have not eaten.

Fasten opaque paper around the jar with a rubber band and remove when observations are being made.

Some ants, while fascinating to observe, can inflict very painful, severe bites. Be aware of this variety of ant, and limit the ants kept to those that do not injure humans.

Categorizing the Variety of Life.   Children over five will be able to begin categorizing plant and animal life. The first categories you might want to focus on are "living things" and "nonliving things." Next you can move to the categories "plants" and "animals." As children mature, you can develop finer classifications of plant and animal life.

For children in kindergarten or the primary grades, you may construct learning stations. Children can sort pictures of objects into correct categories by separating living and nonliving things or by categorizing pictures of plants and animals. Individual booklets, made of a few pieces of paper stapled together, can be used to make scrapbooks. Children can fill these booklets with pictures cut from magazines, pictures they draw, or stories they dictate or write. The theme of each booklet would be a category: living things, nonliving things, plants, animals, animals that live on land, plants that live in water, and so on.

Wall charts might be constructed as well, each chart for one category of plant or animal life. Titles might include "Plants with Seeds," "Animals in the Woods," "Farm Animals," "Plants We Eat," "Plants We Do Not Eat," and so on. Children place pictures they create or cut from magazines on the appropriate wall chart.

A Nature Walk

A nature walk, perhaps around the block or just a few blocks from school, is helpful in learning about the variety of life. Prepare children for the purpose of the walk: "We're going to look at different plants growing from cracks in the sidewalk." "Today, count the number of flowers you see." "Listen for the songs of the birds, how many can we hear?" "As we walk, look for insects." On the walk:

- Let children stop whenever they want to examine insects, plants, animals. Follow up on their interest with questions, provide verbal labels for things they're observing, and engage them in discussions. When you can, ask questions that call for them to make inferences or hypotheses about the plant or animal they're observing.
- Record the number and type of life you are observing. Children in the primary grades may be responsible for this. With preschoolers, you can have children observe as you keep count or in some other way record the life you observe.
- Take only those things back to the classroom that can be cared for properly.
- Control enthusiasm by taking only one specimen and leaving the rest. Take one seed pod, for instance, in order to protect the balance of nature.
- Show respect by only observing and not interfering with nests, plants, or animal habitats.
- Ask children to listen, as well as look (Holt, 1977).

Walking field trips can be taken to identify:

- Plants with flowers, seed pods, pointed leaves, leaves that are not green, and smooth leaves; those with berries and thorns; or those growing in trees, on the ground, or near a pond (*Science 5/13*, 1976).
- The three most common plants found in the shade, sun, or swampy area.
- The three most common plants found within a block.
- The plants that are tallest, shortest, heaviest, lightest, most spread out, and so on.
- All of the insects under a log, rock, or piece of bark.
- The animal life found in a bucket of pond water.
- Animals that have 2, 4, 6, or 8 legs.
- Animals that are helpful or harmful to humans.
- Large or small animals, those covered with fur or feathers, or those covered with scales.

Why and How Living Things Act As They Do.   Observations of plant and animal life are valuable not only to identify and categorize the variety of life on earth but also for finding out how plants and animals adapt to their environment. Why and how living things act as they do provides focus for other observations of living things in the environment. Concepts of the interrelatedness of life and of the life cycle can be introduced.

Adaptation.   Adaptation is the process of change in plants and animals that results from interactions with the environment over a period of time.

Animals and plants adapt in order to survive and reproduce. Those that do not adapt are unable to meet their needs and do not survive.

Children also adapt. They wear raincoats and boots on a rainy day, a snowsuit or a heavy coat on a cold winter day, and light clothing in the summer. They observe adults preparing for changes in seasons—weather-proofing homes, cleaning furnaces, removing air conditioners, and drawing drapes to keep the heat and light out or in.

Focus children's attention on the ways they adapt, and then shift the discussion to how plants and animals in their environment adapt. Watch a chameleon change color to match its surroundings, the rabbit's coat thicken as winter approaches, or the toads burrow underground. Follow the observations by asking children to make inferences about the changes they observe, encouraging discussion and communication.

Study the mouth parts of animals. Focus attention on the woodpecker's pointed bill cutting through the bark of the tree to capture insects or the duck's wide bill skimming the pond for plant life. Compare the beaks of birds that come to the feeder and record which seed each bird prefers. Find books that illustrate the beaks of birds, and have children note similarities and differences in the pictures. Again, ask them to make inferences about the nature of the type of beak and method of feeding.

Observe other body parts of animals—feet, fur, legs—to identify the specialized features of each group of animals in relation to the environment it lives in. Also study the leaves, roots, or flowers of specific plants in relation to their environment. How do thorns protect a plant? Why does one plant have thick, waxy leaves, while another has thin, fine needles? What kinds of roots do different plants have, and why?

Interrelatedness.   All life is interdependent. Virtually nothing exists independent of other living or nonliving matter. As children observe and study living things, they'll certainly come across the idea that many animals survive at the expense of others.

You do not need to experiment with feeding living things to other animals; however, if pets and animals are kept at school, children will be involved in feeding whether the animal eats other living things or prepared food.

Children in kindergarten or the primary grades can keep a record of their pets and the foods they eat. List the pets, and record the type and amount of food each consumes. Discuss and compare the variety of foods that different animals eat. Record the amount of water each consumes, and discuss the shelter, light, and air each requires.

The Life Cycle.   The study of living things leads to the concept of life cycle. All living things have a beginning and an end. Children may observe beginnings as they watch guppies being born or a moth laying eggs. The birth of a brother or sister naturally leads to asking how life begins. Or the death of a fish, insect, or rabbit leads to questioning the how, why, and what of death. When introducing concepts of life and death:

1. Face your own feelings and attitudes first. Examine how you feel about birth and death. Children will unconsciously model your attitudes. If they see you shy away or become embarrassed or frightened by their questions, they'll pick up on your discomfort. If you're able to accept the facts of reproduction, birth, and death in a matter-of-fact manner, children will as well.

When dealing with life and death, be truthful and factual as you communicate with children, and use accurate vocabulary. Become as knowledgeable about the reproductive process, birth, and death as you can, and relate these to both plants and animals.

2. When children question you about reproduction, birth, or death, begin by asking them what they know. Children receive a great deal of information about how life begins and ends, but it is confused, disjointed information that leads to inaccurate concepts. One child in a discussion of how babies are born said, "I don't know everything, I only know that you need a lot of eggs to get a baby."

Once you have an idea of what children are thinking, you can answer their questions by either clarifying or adding information that will help them develop a more accurate understanding of the topic. Further, asking children what they know gives you some indication about the specific information they are requesting.

3. Talk with parents. Find out what parents have told their children about life and death, the types of experiences children have had, and the information parents believe appropriate for the school to provide. Inform parents of your plans for handling the topics of birth and death when these subjects arise.

4. Provide children with additional experiences with the life cycle. Give them time to digest and assimilate their experiences. Don't try to present everything at once. Answer frankly, but "do not burden them with more information than they want to know at any one point . . . make sure that they're given information when they want it. The information is needed in small doses, with time to digest it, and with many repetitions" (Read, 1976, p. 253).

Humans Use Living Things.　Humans not only depend on living things but control them as well (Lubbers, 1982). Children can experience control over living things by planting and maintaining a garden. As children dig, plant, and nurture their own garden, they can experience the satisfactions of controlling and using living things. Perhaps insects will take over the garden, and problems of how to control other living things will become personal to the children. Eliminating the pests without upsetting the balance of nature or damaging other living things—birds, beneficial insects, or other animals—becomes a problem to be solved.

You might take children on trips to a hatchery, tree farm, animal farm, bird sanctuary, game preserve, greenhouse, or other place in your area to observe how humans control and use living things. Children might interview a farmer, the county agriculture agent, or a horse trainer to find out other ways in which humans use living things for their own benefit.

Children over age five can think of ways they use living things. They may chart the plants they eat or use in some other way.

Social consciousness and possible solutions to problems arise as children come into contact with specific situations. Awareness of a forest fire, a flood, or endangered plants or animals in a specific area of the country could lead children to explore how people care for and protect the living things in their environment. Children can begin to build an awareness of their responsibility to protect living things.

The Physical Sciences

Goals

The physical sciences involve the nature of the universe and include the following:

- Astronomy—the study of heavenly bodies and their motion
- Chemistry—the study of the materials found on the earth and changes that occur in them
- Meteorology—the study of weather and air
- Physics—the study of matter and energy

By using the processes scientists use—observing, inferring, classifying and communicating—children will think, solve problems, and develop concepts of:

- The sun, moon, and stars, noting the regularity of changes that take place as time passes
- The different qualities and properties of materials and changes that occur in common substances around them
- Weather conditions and the changes that occur in weather
- Sound, heat, and electricity, and sources of each, as well as the concept that to move or cause movement requires energy

Fostering Concepts in the Physical Sciences

Providing opportunities for children to act on objects and see how things react is the purpose of science instruction in the preschool or primary classroom (Kamii, 1982). Activity and action are necessary (Thorlindsson, 1983). Two kinds of actions are required. The first comes from throwing, pushing, kicking, and touching objects and things in the world and is called *simple abstraction*. The second kind of action required for children to learn is *reflective abstraction*, or mental activity. Children need to learn to think, or reflect on, the action or activity that has taken place.

Your role is to construct experiences for children with their physical world and help them to integrate and organize thought based on their actions. Kamii and DeVries (1978) suggest that the only study of the physical world appropriate for young children is based on their own actions and reactions to things they can push, pull, roll, twirl, spill, suck, kick, drop, or jump on. They suggest four levels of planning for the teaching of physical science:

1. Acting on objects. Seeing how objects react and what they can do with these reactions.
2. Acting on objects to produce a desired effect.
3. Becoming aware of how the desired effect was produced ("I sawed this wood so long, my saw is hot").
4. Offering explanations of causes and then drawing conclusions ("When you rub things together a really long time, they get hot"). (Kamii & DeVries, 1978, p. 12)

Consider the children when determining the experiences you will plan. Ask them what they already know about astronomy, chemistry, meteorology, and physics. Minstrell and Smith (1983) suggest that the teacher should:

1.   Find out what children are thinking, ask them about their ideas, and continue to ask why until you uncover children's thought processes.

2.   Listen to children's explanations and ask additional questions until you really understand what children are saying.

3.   Act on children's explanations. Guide them into additional experiences based on discussions you've had. Plan experiences that will extend their ideas, giving them other opportunities to test hypotheses, make observations, or experiment.

4.   After these additional experiences, ask children about their ideas again, listening carefully in order to plan still more opportunities for observing, advancing hypotheses, and solving problems.

Astronomy

Children believe the sun and moon have been made by a man who lights a match and that they are alive. The true study of astronomy seems unrealistic. Things in the sky are far from us, so obviously you can't give children direct contact with them. They can't reach up and grab a piece of the sun, star, or the moon for study (Slavin, 1983). But you can ask children to observe the sun, moon, and stars and make inferences based on their observations to use as a basis for instruction.

If you work with infants or children under three years of age, all you will want to do is to establish a predictable schedule for each day. In this way, the very young child can become familiar with the routines associated with day and night. Three-year-olds will enjoy books about their day. The book *Good Morning, Good Night* (Martin, 1969) is an example of a picture story-book designed to familiarize toddlers with the idea of day and night. As they enjoy the book, children can tell what they do to get ready for bed, whom they say good night to, and what they do when they get up in the morning.

Preschoolers can take part in making plans for the activities they'll do during the day and discuss the routines associated with night. Four- and five-year-olds will be able to observe differences in the sky during night and day. Five-year-olds can draw one picture of their room at night and another to represent their room during the day.

Primary-age children may make wall charts titled "Night" and "Day" and categorize pictures by pasting them on the appropriate chart. Pictures might include things they see or things that happen during the day or night. People who work at night, such as firefighters, clerks, and police officers, could visit and tell about the tasks they do as children sleep.

Five-year-olds can observe changes in the sky. They might be asked to observe the color of the sky during sunrise or sunset or to describe the sky at night. Remember that observing the sun can be dangerous. Looking directly into its glare can cause eye damage. Instead of asking children to observe the sun directly, have them record the earth's position around the sun by keeping a record of the sun's position on a window over a period of a day, marking the position with masking tape.

Observation of shadows is another way of introducing children to changes that occur during the day as the earth rotates on its axis. In the primary grades, children might relate changes in shadows to the time of the day. Mark the shadow of the school building on the play yard at various times of the day. At times, there will be no shadow at all; at others, large shadows will be present. Children won't relate these changes to the position of earth and sun, yet as scientists, they'll observe, make inferences, and absorb different understandings from their experiences that will form the building material for later concept formation.

Children in the preschool could:

- Find out what kinds of shadows they can make with their body.
- Make shadows with different objects—umbrellas, boxes, wheel toys.
- Outline shadows at different times of the day and compare drawings.
- Play shadow tag.
- Play "Simon Says" with shadows. Simon says, touch your shadow, stand with your shadow in front of you, hide in your shadow, step on someone else's shadow, and so on.

Realistically, however, children's experiences with astronomy will continue to be limited throughout the early childhood years. Observing the sky and the things in the sky, describing and comparing observations, and communicating these to others verbally or through drawing or painting may be appropriate.

Meteorology

Children don't separate the study of sun, moon, and stars from that of the weather because it's really all the same to them. Piaget (1964) reports that children see rain and snow as made by humans and clouds as made either by humans or by God. Clouds are regarded as solid, probably made of smoke or stone, and they make rain, thunder, and lightning.

Children do, however, experience changes in the weather. These changes can be observed, described, and discussed. Observations can lead to making inferences and drawing conclusions. You can have children observe the following weather changes and draw conclusions about how they affect them:

- Try standing in the sun on a hot day. How does it feel? Now move from the sun into the shade. Where are you more comfortable, and why? Which place would you prefer to stand or be in longer?
- Explore the wind. Take kites or pinwheels outside on a windy day. Blow soap bubbles in the wind. Walk with your back against it. How did it feel? Walk facing the wind. Walk with the direction of the wind. Stand in the wind, and then in a protected spot in the play yard. What is different?
- Find out what the wind can do. Look for things the wind holds up—gliders, parachutes, birds; for things it blows along—paper, clothes on a line, kites; and things that dry in the wind—clothing, hands, the sidewalk.
- Watch cloud formations and play "Do you see what I see?" Once back inside, make cloud pictures. Read a poem about clouds, or write or dictate poems about clouds. For children in the primary grades, name the clouds. Cumulus clouds are shaped like cauliflowers; cirrus clouds are high, thin, and wispy; and nimbus clouds are those that are dark and that bring rain and storms.
- Wash doll clothes, and dry them in the shade, sun, and wind. Where did they dry the fastest, and why?
- Examine clothing worn in different weather conditions. Why are boots, hats, wool clothing, sun hats, snowsuits, or shorts worn? Make booklets called "Clothes I Wear in Summer" "Clothes I Never Wear" (Allen & Allen, 1961).
- Catch snowflakes on dark pieces of construction paper.
- Count and record the seconds between lightning and thunder.

Children in the primary grades can begin long-term recording of weather conditions in the form of a time line, using symbols for sunny, cloudy, cold, or warm days, and other seasonal weather conditions. One first-grade teacher used a large monthly calendar in her classroom for recording daily weather conditions and events. Instead of discarding them at the end of the month, she placed them on a wall in the back of the room. At the end of the school year, the first-graders were able to look at the calendars and recall the activities they had taken part in during the year, as well as the history of the weather. They discussed how the weather affected their lives and activities and how they adapted to changes.

Chemistry

Chemistry is the study of the properties of materials and the changes that occur in them. Children believe that magic causes these changes, that substances change because they want to, or that humans create the changes, so it is not wise to introduce children to experiments or other experiences that might serve to reinforce this thinking. Rather, begin by exploring what materials in the environment are like and how they can be changed.

Infants delight in watching soap bubbles blowing in the wind. Toddlers can blow soap bubbles or paint the yard and building, using a paper carton full of water and a paintbrush. Both infants and toddlers can play in the water, sand, and mud. They can also experience being pushed through space or can push and pull objects, perhaps cardboard boxes, across the yard.

Three- and four-year-olds can focus their attention on the properties of things in the room and play yard. How does the table feel? Which is the roughest stone? What happens to the chalk when you rub it on the sidewalk? These initial explorations are based on children's interests and spontaneous activities.

Children may find crayons melted by the sun and might experiment by trying to find other things that will melt when placed in the sun. Children under five will try things at random and lose interest in the project, abandoning their collections of objects. By the age of five, more systematic explorations of the nature of substances can be arranged. Children can begin to chart the objects or substances they find that melt in the sun and those that do not.

This experiment can lead to others. Children might find out what and how other materials change, and make a table like the following.

Object	How Changed	Can You Recognize It?
ice	melted	no
sugar	pounded	yes
salt	dissolved in water	no
rocks	crushed	no

Primary-age children can explore other materials. They can be given many different types of liquids and asked to explore their nature and record findings. Be prepared for a certain amount of mess with newspapers and mops. Bring in water, cooking oil, vinegar, liquid detergent, glycerin, and other liquids; dishpan-sized containers, buckets, and small containers of various sizes; sponges; paper towels; newspapers; eye droppers; food coloring; and styrofoam egg cartons. Ask the children to experiment to find out:

- What liquid makes the largest spot when dropped on waxed paper?
- What happens if two liquids are mixed together?
- What happens when food coloring is added to various liquids?
- Will all of the liquids freeze?
- Which will run the fastest when placed on waxed paper? (Good, 1977, p. 266)

Or children may try to find all the substances that will freeze, dissolve, or mix together. Provide a variety of materials for children to explore. You could, for example, give them small amounts of instant coffee, tea leaves, sugar, sand, and glycerin so they can find out which will dissolve when placed in water and which will freeze.

These experiences are not meant to teach children any formal principles of chemistry, only to provide opportunities to use the methods of the scientist and to build an openness to finding out about materials and substances in their environment (Osborne & Cosgrove, 1983).

Physics

The study of physics for children is confined to making and doing. Children's experiences with physics begin by:

1. Doing things
2. Lighting things
3. Listening to things
4. Finding out how things react on land and water, and in the air (*Science 5/13*, 1973)

Doing Things.   As children play outdoors, riding their bikes, swinging, climbing, or using the seesaw, focus their attention on their actions. How fast does the tricycle go? How do you make it stop? What makes it move? How can you make it go faster or slower? These questions can be explored with interested three- or four-year-olds spontaneously as they play. With children five or older, questions might lead to drawing inferences and forming conclusions or to finding out more about the nature of motion through the use of reference materials or other resources.

As children play outdoors, focus their attention on their actions.

The same type of discussion can take place in connection with other things the children do. As they play with blocks, ask: "Who can build the tallest tower?" "Why is it difficult to get the tower as tall as you?" "When the tower falls, which way will it fall?" Introduce a ramp to block play, and have children try to build using the ramp, or experiment by rolling different objects down it. Have them observe which objects roll fastest, slowest, and not at all. Ask them to infer why this occurs and to draw conclusions.

Find other activities for children to do and objects for them to push and pull, roll and twirl, and move through space.

Lighting Things.   In the kindergarten and primary grades, children can explore making light. All they need are a flashlight bulb, bulb holder, battery, and single-strand bell wire. Using these simple materials, they can discover that when the bare wire end is screwed under the battery's terminal, the other bulb will light. They can then make light circuits for their car made of blocks or wood, or light up the eyes of a robot they've made. Once they've mastered lighting things, they can use the same principle to make a bell ring in the housekeeping area, their car, or a play phone.

Listening to Things.   Children have listened to music, stories, poetry, and song. Now ask them to find out how to make sounds, and relate their experiences to the concept of vibrations. Every sound made involves vibrations, but when you can't see the vibrations, it's difficult to understand the concept that movement is associated with sound.

Find objects that children can see vibrate. You can use objects like elastic bands, metal rulers, and drumheads (place seeds or sand on a drumhead so children can see the vibrations).

Make telephones by stretching a wire or string between two tin cans. Have the children explore how long the string can be before they lose the sound. Experiment with different kinds of cans. Will a paper carton or plastic cup serve as efficiently? Which holds the sound better, a string or a piece of wire?

Experiment with ways to make sounds softer. Bring a small transistor radio to school, and try to find the best way to muffle the sound of the radio (*Science 5/13*, 1973). Children might hide the radio in a drawer, cabinet, or styrofoam-filled box, wrap it in cloth, or put it into a large glass jar.

As with all experiences, ask children to observe carefully, make inferences, and record their observations. Finish the projects by having them reach conclusions about the nature of sound.

Things on Land and in the Air and Water.   Use children's toys to explore how things travel on land. How many of them roll? Which rollers are most efficient: wheels, marbles, or pencils? Give children a box filled with something heavy, and have them find a way to move it across the floor. Provide rollers to aid their explorations.

You can use a dishpan of water and a number of objects that will float or sink to help children experiment with how things travel on water. Again, the concept of floating will not develop until much later in children's lives; these activities are only laying the foundation of experiences required for later concept formation.

Making paper airplanes is an appealing activity. Explore different methods of folding paper to produce the best glider. Make parachutes from a handkerchief or a piece of plastic or paper tied to a wooden spool. Explore different materials for the parachute, and make some with a hole in the center and others without. Observe which materials hold the parachute up the longest.

Remember that it is not only children's actions on the things in their environment that are important, but also their ability to reflect and think about their actions (Linn, Clement, & Pulos, 1983). Using a variety of questions may foster children's reflective activity. Questions may be descriptive, definitive, operational, or causal (Nevborig & Klausmeier, 1969).

A descriptive question asks children to give details of an object or an event based on their observations. These questions are factual, and they are important because they lead children to focus their attention on their actions and to describe these actions. They may have to make comparisons as they describe their actions, and they will find the need to learn more descriptive language. Examples of descriptive questions are "What is it made of?" "What kind of roller is it?" "How did it fly?"

Definitive questions are more complex. They focus on the general characteristics of objects and events and the means by which they are classified. Asking "What is heat?" "What is friction?" "What is vibration?" leads children into not simply defining but defining in relation to a class or category. Children cannot answer these questions unless they've had a great many experiences with actual materials and the opportunity to observe and then describe them.

Summary

Science is doing and thinking and making the two come together. Children, inherently interested in learning about themselves and the world in which they live, find science compelling. Their natural curiosity leads them to try to find out why, to explore what they can do, and to learn about their world.

As they explore their world, children act like scientists. They use the processes of science and thinking to make observations and inferences about the things in their world. They classify, group, and reach conclusions. The process of thinking is not separated from content; children need to think about something. Those things that the biological and physical sciences study provide the content for children's explorations and thought.

It still takes a teacher who is knowledgeable of the physical and biological sciences and of children's thought processes to give meaning to children's explorations. The teacher, by structuring the environment, questioning, and offering information, leads children to expand their ideas of the scientific world into more conventional ways of thinking.

Projects

Continuing Case Study

Interview your child and another child who is either younger or older than your case study child. Ask both children to tell you about the origins of the sun, the moon, and the stars. Pick out a number of objects in the environment—such as a river, stone, clouds, or tree—and ask them to tell you whether these things are living or nonliving, and why they answer as they do. Record their answers. Discuss in class what understanding of children's thought processes means to teaching both the biological and the physical sciences.

1. Write a lesson plan designed to teach four-year-olds about plants. Give your overall goal as well as specific objectives. What experiences will you arrange to foster these goals?

2. Observe children playing with wheel toys, wind-up toys, or blocks. Record each instance of their exposure to concepts from the physical sciences.

3. Obtain a flashlight bulb, a bulb holder, battery, and a single strand bell wire. Try to discover how to make the bulb light. Relate your own experience to that of children under age eight.

4. Create a file of resources in the community that could be used to expand children's experiences of the physical or biological sciences.

Children's Books

Arnold, C. (1980). *Five nests*. Illustrated by Ruth Sanderson. New York: Dutton.

Atsushi, K. (1983). *Animal mothers*. Illustrated by Masayuki Yabuuchii. New York: Philomel.

Branley, F. (1973). *Eclipse: Darkness in daytime*. Illustrated by D. Crews. New York: Crowell.

Cole, S. (1985). *When the tide is low*. Illustrated by Virginia Wright-Frierson. New York: Lothrop, Lee & Shepard.

de Paola, T. (1975). *The cloud book*. New York: Holiday.

Ehlert, L. (1990). *Color Farm*. New York: Lippincott.

Ehlert, L. (1990). *Feathers for lunch*. New York: Lippincott.

Fleming, D. (1991). *In the tall, tall grass*. New York: Henry Holt.

Flower, P. (1978). *Barn owl*. Illustrated by Cheryl Pape. New York: Harper & Row.

Gans, R. (1977). *Caves*. Illustrated by Giulo Maestro. New York: Crowell.

Garelick, N. (1973). *Down to the beach*. Illustrated by Barbara Cooney. New York: Four Winds.

Greeley, V. (1990). *White is the moon*. New York: Macmillan.

Hader, B., & Hader, E. (1948). *The big snow*. New York: Macmillan.

Hopkins, L. B. (1984). *Crickets and bullfrogs and whispers of thunder: Poems and pictures by Harry Behn*. San Diego: Harcourt Brace Jovanovich.

Hutchins, P. (1971). *Changes, changes*. New York: Macmillan.

Keats, E. J. (1982). *Clementina's cactus*. New York: Viking.

Keller, H. (1992). *Furry*. New York: Greenwillow.

Lauber, P. (1979). *What's hatching out of that egg?* New York: Crown.

Lionni, L. (1959). *Little blue and little yellow*. New York: Astor-Honor.

Martin, B. (1991). *Polar bear, polar bear, what do you hear?* Illustrated by Eric Carle. New York: Henry Holt.

Nakatani, C. (1973). *The zoo in my garden*. New York: Crowell.

Nardi, J. (1988). *Close encounters with insects and spiders*. Ames, IA: Iowa State University.

Pringle, L. (1973). *Twist, wriggle, and squirm: A book about earthworms*. Illustrated by Peter Parnell. New York: Crowell.

Provensen, A., & Provensen, M. (1978). *The year at Maple Hill Farm*. New York: Atheneum.

Selsam, M. (1982). *Cotton*. Photographs by Jerome Vexley. New York: Moria.

Simon, S. (1979). *Animal fact/animal fable*. Illustrated by Diane deGroat. New York: Crown.

Spier, P. (1972). *Crash! Bang! Boom!* New York: Doubleday.

Spier, P. (1977). *Noah's ark*. New York: Doubleday.

West, D. (1992). *Why is the sky blue—and other answers to all of the questions you always wanted to ask*. New York: Barron's Educational Series.

Resources

The Science 5/13 series, developed in England during the 1970s, is available in the United States through Teacher's Laboratory, Inc., P.O. Box 6480, Brattleboro, VT 05302. This excellent series offers teachers of young children excellent, practical ideas for implementing a science program that involves children in critical thinking skills. The series is based on Piagetian theory and is clearly a must.

Helping Children Explore Science (1992), by M. J. P. Cliatt and J. M. Shaw, and *Science Experiences for the Early Childhood Years*, by H. Harlan, are classics available from Macmillan.

References

Allen, R. V., & Allen, C. (1961). *An introduction to language experience programs*. Chicago: Encyclopedia Britannica Press.

Benham, N. B., Hosticka, A., Payne, J. D., & Yeotis, C. (1982). Making concepts in science and mathematics visible and viable in the early childhood program. *School Science and Mathematics, 15*(2), 49–56.

Burton, G. (1983). Being a real teacher. *Arithmetic Teacher, 30*(8), 4.

Carroll, J. B. (1964). Words, meanings, and concepts. *Harvard Educational Review*. New York: Harper & Row.

Denner, B., & Sheldon, C. (1976). Sensory processing and the recognition of forms in nursery school children. *British Journal of Psychology, 48*, 101–104.

Dewey, J. (1910). *How we think*. New York: D. C. Heath.

Finley, F. N. (1983). Science processes. *Journal of Research in Science Teaching, 20*(1), 147–155.

Forman, G. E., & Kuschner, H. (1977). *The child's construction of knowledge: Piaget for teachers*. Monterey, CA: Brooks-Cole.

Forsom, M. P. (1971). *Three year olds' knowledge of plants*. Unpublished manuscript, Florida State University, Tallahassee.

Gibson, E. J. (1969). *Principles of perception, development, and learning*. New York: Appleton-Century-Crofts.

Gleitman, H. (1986). *Psychology* (2nd ed.). New York: Norton.

Good, G. R. (1977). *How children learn science*. New York: Macmillan.

Holt, B. G. (1977). *Science with young children*. Washington, DC: National Association for the Education of Young Children.

Jones, C. B. (1987). Simple science. *Science Teacher, 25*(2), 32–33.

Kamii, C. (1982). *Number in the preschool and kindergarten*. Washington, DC: National Association for the Education of Young Children.

Kamii, C., & DeVries, R. (1978). *Physical knowledge in preschool education*. Englewood Cliffs, NJ: Prentice Hall.

Lemoyne, G., & Favreau, M. (1981). Piaget's construction of number development: Its relevance to mathematics learning. *Journal for Research in Mathematics Education, 12*(3), 179–197.

Linn, M. C., Clement, C., & Pulos, S. (1983). Is it physics if it's not formal? *Journal of Research in Science Teaching, 20*(3), 763—771.

Lubbers, J. D. (1982). Justifiable consumerism. *Journal of Research in Environmental Education, 14*(1), 24–26.

Macbeth, D., & Fowler, S. (1972). The extent to which pupils manipulate materials and attainment of process skills. *NARST Abstracts, 55*. Columbus: Ohio State University.

Martin, B. (1969). *Good morning. Good night*. New York: Holt, Rinehart & Winston.

Minstrell, J., & Smith, C. (1983). Alternative concepts of a strategy for change. *Science and Children, 21*(3), 31–33.

Nevborig, M. H., & Klausmeier, H. J. (1969). *Teaching in the elementary school* (3rd ed.). New York: Harper & Row.

Offenback, S. I. (1983). The concept of dimension in research on children's learning. *Monographs of the Society for Research in Child Development, 48*(6, Serial No. 204).

Osborne, J. R., & Cosgrove, M. M. (1983). Children's concept of the change of states of water. *Journal of Research in Science Teaching, 20*(9), 225–257.

Piaget, J. (1964). *The child's conception of the world* (J. A. Tomilson, Trans.). New York: Harcourt Brace Jovanovich.

Read, K. B. (1976). *The nursery school: Human relationships and learning* (6th ed.). Philadelphia: W. B. Saunders.

Rebok, G. W. (1987). *Life-span cognitive development*. New York: Holt, Rinehart & Winston.

Russell, D. (1956). *Children's thinking.* Waltham, MA: Blaisdell.

Rutherford, F. J., & Ahlgren, A. (1990). *Science for all Americans.* New York: Oxford University Press.

Science 5/13. (1973). *Change.* New York: Macdonald Educational.

Science 5/13. (1976). *Using the environment.* New York: Macdonald Educational.

Slavin, L. (1983). The sky's the limit. *Science and Children, 20*(6), 20–22.

Smith, R. F. (1987). Theoretical framework for preschool science experiences. *Young Children, 42*(2), 34–40.

Thorlindsson, T. (1983). Social organization and cognition. *Human Development, 26,* 289–317.

Williams, R., & Sherwood, E. (1983). Activities in math and science for young children: Using the school yard. *School Science and Mathematics, 71*(1), 76–82.

Ziemer, M. (1987). Science and the early childhood curriculum: One thing leads to another. *Young Children, 42*(6), 44–52.

14 Nutrition, Safety, and Health

"Make health an aim; normal development cannot be had without regard to the vigor of the body."

(Dewey, 1944, p. 115)

After reading this chapter, you should be able to respond to the following questions:

1. How can you integrate nutrition, safety, and health education into the total curriculum and routines for the daily program?

2. What goals will you select for nutrition education? How will you achieve them?

3. The fact that accidents are a leading cause of death in young children suggests that one should teach children about traffic, fire, and poison safety. Describe how you will plan and arrange a safe physical environment in an early childhood program as well as teach children principles of safety.

4. Describe the ways you will teach children concepts of physical health as well as provide for their health and physical safety.

Health

Good health for children was an aim of the pioneers in early childhood education. It had to be. Without antibiotics, with polio, whooping cough, and diphtheria, children in groups were at risk for infection and serious, life-threatening illnesses. With medical advances, we have become somewhat more relaxed about children's health and safety when in a group situation. This, however, does not mean that children are not at risk when in groups. They still are. "Children under three years of age are especially vulnerable to disease because their immune systems are not fully developed and they have not developed resistance to infection" (Kendall & Moukaddem, 1992, p. 72).

Just as in the past, early childhood educators are diligent about providing a safe and healthy environment in which children can grow and learn. They must satisfy children's needs for rest, exercise, nutrition, and dental and medical care. Children must learn health concepts as well as sound attitudes and skills that will last them a lifetime.

Providing for the health of children and teaching health cannot be separated. Participation in ongoing health and safety routines at school are the means by which concepts of health are fostered. Health and safety lessons are not scheduled for every other week, every other day, or even daily, but are integrated with the ongoing health services and activities of the school.

For example, as children brush their teeth after lunch, giggling with one another as the toothpaste foams inside their mouths, they are participating in a daily, common health routine. At the same time, however, teachers can use this experience to teach one child how to hold the toothbrush, to introduce vocabulary to others: "brush over your gums"; "brushing your teeth makes your mouth feel fresh, but it also keeps your teeth and gums healthy."

Health has been defined as a complete physical well-being, not merely the absence of disease or infirmity (World Health Organization [WHO], 1980). Therefore, the goals of health education include teaching concepts, attitudes, and skills in the areas of:

1. Nutrition

2. Safety

3. Hygiene and physical health

4. Physical activity

To be effective, health and safety education should be based on the following principles:

1.   Health education should be directed to children and parents, as well as to the early childhood staff, health professionals, and the community.

2. The focus of the goals should be action. Goals can be defined in terms of what children or adults will do as a result of their experiences in school.

3. Health education should emphasize skills that children can develop immediately. Knowledge children gain should not apply to only a few situations, but should be general enough to lead to future learning.

4. Experiences should be selected with children's cognitive abilities in mind. Children cannot understand causality. The relation between hand-washing, nutrition, safety measures on the playground, and good health is beyond their cognitive skills. They cannot anticipate the effects of dangerous situations, poor nutrition, and unsound health practices.

Nutrition Education

"Food—and the attitudes, values and behaviors related to food—plays a basic part in everyone's life—each and every day" (National Dairy Council, 1979, p. 2). Food is necessary not only for physical health and growth but also for intellectual development and social well-being. How children feel, behave, look, and learn is affected by what they eat.

How we feel physically affects our behavior and growth. A hungry or malnourished child will not have the energy to attend to the academic tasks of school. If children's attention is focused on hunger and their total health is diminished by an inadequate diet, they will have difficulty learning. The link between nutrition and intellectual growth has been firmly established.

> From the day a poor child is conceived by his poorly nourished mother, he is probably unequal. His growth is likely to be slower; he is more likely to be assaulted by infections and prenatal complications, and he is all too likely to be born in a premature state, which exposes him to enormous risks of brain damage. (Winick, 1969, p. 667)

Food is also closely related to children's social and cultural life. Think of your own family and the link between food and your celebrations of religious and cultural holidays: the turkey at Thanksgiving, the special breads for Passover or Easter, and the traditional birthday cake. All hold deep personal, psychological, and cultural meanings. Children's attitudes, as well as likes and dislikes of food, will reflect their geographical, sociological, and religious heritages.

Education about food and nutrition makes a basic, important contribution to children's total welfare. Early experiences with food and nutrition are designed to establish attitudes, foster concepts, and develop behavioral patterns that will have a lasting effect.

You cannot teach children about nutrition without having them experience food.

Goals for Nutrition Education

The White House Conference on Food, Nutrition, and Health emphasized the following four concepts of nutrition education:

1. Nutrition is the food we eat and how the body uses it. We eat food to live, grow, keep healthy, and have energy for work and play.
2. Food is made of nutrients. Each nutrient has a specific use; the four basic food groups give a balance of food.
3. All people throughout life need the same nutrients but in differing amounts.
4. The way food is handled influences the amount of nutrients and the food's safety, appearance, and taste. Food is grown, processed, and prepared.

The conference identified the following goals for nutrition education. Children should develop the following attitudes toward food:

1. Willingness to accept and try foods not known to them, developing acceptance of a variety of foods.
2. Awareness of food dislikes, likes, and an understanding of why they select certain foods above others.
3. Wholesome response toward food. Children need to develop the attitude that food is to nourish and sustain and is not a substitute for love, affection, attention, or friendship.

The conference identified the following behaviors as goals in nutrition education:

1. Children should develop the ability to use utensils in a manner that pleases them and others, and the skills of eating while enjoying the company and conversation of others.
2. Children should select a variety of foods, balancing food choices among the four basic food groups.
3. Children should establish orderly meal patterns.

Achieving the Goals

Children achieve the concepts, attitudes, and behaviors of nutrition education directly by preparing, producing, and consuming food. One cannot teach children about nutrition without allowing them to experience food. The first prerequisite of any early childhood program is to provide children with food that meets their nutritional requirements and is appropriate for their developmental needs. Meals and snacks in an early childhood program account for one-third to one-half of a child's daily nutrients. Communication with parents is necessary in order to plan for snacks and meals that will complement and balance the child's food intake at home. Table 14–1 gives suggested meals for different programs.

Appropriate menus consider not only the child's intake of food at home, but also likes and dislikes. Children enjoy foods that have bright colors and crunch. They prefer finger foods to those that require utensils. Raw carrot

Table 14–1   Number of meals served

Length of Program	Minimum Number oт Snacks and Meals
Four hours or less	One snack, midway through
Five to seven hours	One midday meal, and a midmorning and afternoon snack
Eight hours or more	Two meals and two snacks

Snowballs

4 cups mixed dried fruit
Rind of 1/2 orange
1 1/2 cups almonds or any grated nut or coconut
Toss together fruit, rind, and 1/2 cup nuts or coconuts. Prepare meat grinder by pouring hot water through to prevent sticking. Force mixture through grinder. With clean, moistened hands, children shape into 3/4-inch balls. If using nuts, chop the remaining ones; if coconut, grate finely. Roll balls in nuts or coconut to coat. Store in covered jar. Makes 6 dozen.

Coconut-Raisin Drops

11/2 cups chunk-style peanut butter
3 tablespoons maple syrup
3/4 cup dark seedless raisins
Flaked coconut
Blend together peanut butter and maple syrup. Stir in raisins. Drop by rounded teaspoonfuls into the flaked coconut. Roll mixture in coconut to coat, and then shape with hands into balls. Chill until firm.

Peanut Butter Banana Pops

1 cup milk
1 ripe banana, cut into chunks
1/2 cup creamy peanut butter
1/2 teaspoon vanilla
In a blender, puree milk and banana until smooth. Add peanut butter and vanilla. Blend well. If a blender is not available, mix ingredients together and mash and blend with an eggbeater. Pour into freezer mold and freeze until firm. Unmold.

Orange Juice Pops

1 can frozen orange juice concentrate
1 can water
Mix concentrate and water. Pout into molds or small paper cups. Insert straw or stick for handle. Freeze. Remove mold by dipping in warm water.

Walking Salads

Prunes stuffed with peanut butter
Cheese sticks wrapped in lettuce leaves
Fruits on toothpicks: melon balls; prunes, melons, and pineapple wedges stacked; pineapple wedges and melon balls stacked.
Vegetable sandwiches: cucumbers spread with cream cheese; carrot curls spread with peanut butter; celery stuffed with cheese.

Stuffed Celery

Stuff celery with peanut butter, creamy cottage cheese, mashed pineapple and cream cheese, or avocado cheese spread.

Figure 14–1
Recipes for children's snacks
From *Individual Child Portion Cooking: Picture Recipes* by B. Johnson and B. Plemons, 1984, Mt. Rainier, MD: Gryphon House. Adapted by permission.

radishes	cucumber wedges	tomato wedges
raisins	grapefruit wedges	cauliflower bits
nuts	lettuce leaves	green peppers
strawberries	turnip sticks	dry Chinese noodles
grapes	banana slices	pitted ripe olives
pea pods	graham crackers	blueberries
croutons	broccoli bits	trail mix
muffins	plums	crackers to spread
fruit kabobs	cabbage leaves	with tuna, cheese, etc.
pretzels	pineapple cubes	tangerines
peas in pod	dry cereals	
orange segments	cinnamon toast	

Figure 14–2
Nutritional snacks children over age three enjoy

sticks, cucumber cubes, and tomato and orange wedges appeal to children more than cooked carrots or tomato juice. Figure 14–1 gives recipes for children to make, and Figure 14–2 lists nutritional snacks for children.

Health professionals recommend limiting children's intake of sugar (Rogers & Morris, 1986) because excess sugar causes dental caries and supplies too many empty calories. Fresh fruits, peanut butter on apples or celery, and vegetables with dip are recommended in place of sugary snacks.

Introduce new foods slowly, one at a time (see Figure 14–3). Involve children in preparing the food, and never force them to eat it. Let them see others tasting and enjoying the food. They might be able to taste a small portion of it by putting a drop on their tongue. If they don't like it, they should not have to eat it. When children consistently refuse a food, whether it's new or familiar, it's often because of an allergy or other physical reason. So it's best not to force a child to eat anything.

The Emotional and Physical Climate

Create a pleasant emotional and physical atmosphere for eating to foster sound attitudes toward food. Meals and snacks should be served in an attractive, clean, bright, and well-ventilated environment. If you are teaching in a public school, request that the meals be served family style, with a few children and adults sitting around a table passing dishes of food. Often principals or supervisors do not know the values of family-style service and are pleased to be able to help you establish it in your kindergarten or primary classroom.

The physical environment can be improved by setting the tables with cloths and asking the children to make centerpieces from found objects or artwork. Perhaps they could decorate the table with an item representing the current holiday season.

New foods should be introduced gradually. Specific experiences can be planned and might include:

1. Involving children in the preparation of new foods prior to presenting them at mealtime. Peas can be shelled, beans cut, corn husked, and cauliflower washed and broken into pieces.

2. Use snack time to introduce food. Let children test bits of turnips, brown bread, oranges, or whatever during snack.

3. Encourage children to taste new food through tasting parties. Present the food in bite-sized pieces on a fancy party tray.

4. Use a mystery bag. Pass around a sealed bag containing a new fruit or vegetable. Have children in turn feel the bag and whisper to you what food they think is inside. Then open the bag, examine the fruit or vegetable, and prepare it for tasting.

5. Have children share in the preparation of a special holiday or seasonal food. Cranberries can be washed and cooked at Thanksgiving, or asparagus prepared in the spring.

6. Give children the responsibility of preparing the snack for the day—fixing enough of the new food for everyone to have a taste.

7. Ask parents or neighborhood volunteers to share their cultural or ethnic dishes with the children.

Figure 14–3
Introducing new foods

The emotional climate is as important as the physical environment. "It is important that children and food come together in a happy pleasant way" (National Dairy Council, 1979, p. 11). Unfavorable attitudes toward food may stem from unpleasant experiences with eating. Try to provide a quiet time before meals so children can calm down. Children may wash their hands, listen to a story, or find a quiet activity—either reading to themselves, listening to a record, or resting—before lunch or snack. If children are too tired, they won't enjoy eating.

By adult standards, children dawdle and seem to eat very little. You should remember that a child's stomach is small and accept the fact that children need to eat little. Provide small servings, with the clear understanding that more food is available if desired. Don't bribe children with treats if they eat or threaten to remove privileges if they don't eat. Accept the fact that children may go on food jags, eating only one food for a time while rejecting all others.

Introducing Food Concepts

While children are preparing snacks, setting tables, or eating lunch, informally introduce them to concepts from nutrition: "I'm glad it's time to eat. I

Children can help prepare a clean environment for eating.

need energy to finish this day." "Eating grapefruit sections helps keep our skin and gums healthy." "Cheese and milk both have calcium. We need some calcium to help us grow each day." Don't expect children to develop complex understandings of chemistry, digestion, or the physiology involved in the utilization of vitamins or minerals. But if television advertisements are able to attract children to foods because of "sweetness" or "richness," it seems appropriate to begin exposing children to the need for specific nutrients (National Dairy Council, 1979).

Discuss other qualities of food as well. Some discussions may center around the variety of food textures ("This is smooth, crispy, crunchy"); colors ("This is red, green, what else is orange?"); flavors ("This is bland, tart, spicy"); where and how food is grown; and how it was processed, marketed, and prepared.

Children over age five may be introduced to other concepts. They might begin informally to categorize foods into the four basic groups by making a scrapbook of foods that belong to a specific group. Or they could contribute pictures of food to charts, using a different chart for each of the four food groups. Lotto games or learning stations based on the idea of the four food groups could be constructed.

Table 14–2   The four basic food groups

1. *Dairy:* Milk, whole, evaporated, or skim, and cheese or cheese products
2. *Meat:* Meat, poultry, fresh eggs or alternatives of beans, peas, cheese, or peanut butter
3. *Vegetable/Fruit:* Fruits and vegetables of any kind
4. *Bread/Cereal:* Whole-grain or enriched breads and cereals

Structure other experiences to teach the concept that food is necessary for everyone regardless of age. Arrange to have infants, toddlers, and older persons eat with the children. Introduce the idea that everyone requires the same nutrients, but perhaps in differing amounts.

Have children discuss their favorite foods, how they learned to eat them, and how they became their favorites. Find out the origin of the foods, where they were grown, and how they are prepared. Table 14–2 describes the basic food groups.

Children can:
-   Make ice cream with a hand-operated freezer
-   Shell and cook peas
-   Prepare apples to make applesauce
-   Squeeze oranges or other citrus fruits
-   Peel carrots or cucumbers with hand peelers
-   Mix packaged gelatin dessert
-   Spread cheese, peanut butter, butter on bread to make toast.
-   Stuff celery
-   Cut fruit for salad
-   Wash vegetables for salad
-   Shape bread dough
-   Mix pancake mixes
-   Roll cookie mix
-   Cut out cookies
-   Roll meatballs
-   Sprinkle cinnamon and sugar on bread for cinnamon toast
-   Create their own pizzas by putting cheese and tomato sauce on halved English muffins
-   Stuff pita bread with any filling

Figure 14–4
Children can prepare food

Children Prepare Food

Children can become active participants in producing their own food and preparing their own snacks or meals. They can grow their own garden; shop for raw, frozen, or canned peas; or visit a farm or food-processing plant to see how food is grown, packaged, and prepared for sale. A visit to the supermarket in the early morning shows them how different foods are delivered. Have children observe refrigerated trucks and bread and dairy trucks, and find out how the food gets from the truck to the shelves.

Children enjoy cooking and preparing food. (See Figure 14–4 for some examples.) They feel responsible as they participate in an "adult" activity and competent in preparing something for members of their group. Many concepts in addition to those from nutrition are introduced as children cook (see Figure 14–5).

Although educators believe that preparing food is a valuable experience for children, before you undertake it, be certain that it's appropriate for the children you are working with. Cooking is not valuable if the teacher stands in front of the group performing the steps as children watch, or if only a few children can participate. Nor is it appropriate if the experience doesn't fulfill the goals and objectives of the program, but is presented because "it's a lot of fun." Ask yourself:

1.   What is the age and level of maturity of the children? What skills of coordination do they have? Will they actually be able to stir, cut, pour, and measure? What knowledge of food do they currently have on which to base this new experience?

2.   How many children can take part in the activity at one time? Pick recipes that permit a number of children to work at one time, or arrange activities so children can work in small groups. One teacher brought five

---

Physical Change: Foods melt, liquefy, and solidify.

Mathematical: Food is measured and weighed; cooking is timed.

Language: New vocabulary is introduced as food simmers, dissolves, boils, and is kneaded, chipped, or flaked.

Reading: Children read recipes or follow a large picture recipe as food is prepared. Booklets of their favorite recipes are sent home.

Cultural awareness: Cooking introduces children to other people's customs. Matzos can be made for Passover, stollen or Mexican Christmas cookies for Christmas, or black-eyed peas for good luck on the New Year.

Cooperation: Children work together as a team to produce a concrete product, and together they enjoy the results.

Figure 14–5
Concepts developed during food preparation

Health and Safety Tips

Preventing Food Poisoning

To prevent food contamination, food prepared on the premises or brought from home should comply with state requirements for food service preparation. If the state does not have food preparation requirements, the center should strive to comply with NAEYC's Guidelines for Food Preparation and Service (see *Accreditation Criteria and Procedures of the National Academy of Early Childhood Programs,* rev. ed. [1991], p. 71).

or

To prevent food contamination, all food shall be from health authority approved sources, and shall be transported, stored, prepared, and served in a sanitary manner and approved by regular inspections from local health authorities.

Refrigeration and storage

- All readily perishable or readily contaminated food or drink shall be refrigerated at or below 45°F (7° C) except when being prepared or served.
- Frozen foods shall be stored at 0°F (–17°C).
- Prepared foods shall be stored in plainly labeled and dated containers.
- All containers and utensils shall be stored off the floor. Dishes and utensils shall be stored in closed storage space. Cupboards shall be clean.
- All refrigerators, stoves, and other equipment used in connection with the operation of the kitchen shall be so constructed and arranged as to be easily cleanable, and shall be kept in good repair.

Staff health and safety

- Cooks and assistant cooks shall meet state or local medical requirements.
- All staff shall wash hands before and after handling and/or preparing food.
- Cooks and assistant cooks shall refrain from smoking during food preparation and serving.
- All staff shall wash their hands with soap and water after using restroom facilities.
- Cooks and assistant cooks shall wear hair restraints as necessary.

Vermin control and sanitation

- Kitchen facilities shall be maintained in a sanitary condition, free of dust, flies, vermin, rodents, overhead leakage, condensation, sewage backflow, residual pesticides, and other contamination.
- All chemicals and potentially dangerous products, such as medicines or cleaning supplies, shall be stored in original, labeled containers in locked cabinets inaccessible to children.

This safety and loss prevention tip is offered as a service of CIGNA Care Providers Insurance, which brings you the Safety Group Program endorsed by NAEYC.

Reprinted with permission from National Association for the Education of Young Children (1992). *Young Children,* 47(5), 50.

small pumpkins to her third-grade classroom and arranged for volunteers from the eighth grade to work with the children. The group was divided into five committees, each having the responsibility of deciding how to carve the pumpkin, carving it, and preparing the seeds for toasting. With one volunteer assigned to each group of four or five children, each child had an opportunity to participate fully.

3. How safe is the activity for children? Any time heat or cutting tools are being used, safety is primary. Children should be told in a matter-of-fact manner of the dangers and of the safety measures they should follow. Remember that steam is a major cause of burns that occur while cooking. To prevent burns from steam, never let children lift lids from electric frying pans or other utensils.

Sanitation is equally important. Be certain that children wash their hands and that utensils and work surfaces are disinfected.

4. What follow-up activities will be implemented? You might read stories that involve food preparation, send recipes home, or find out how the food you've prepared is processed. These follow-up activities will bring more meaning to the cooking activity.

Little research has been done on the effectiveness of nutrition education. From the limited studies, indications are that training without practical experiences at home and school has short-term effects (Blackeway & Knickrehm, 1978). This lack of effectiveness suggests that nutrition education must take place through children's actual experiences and should focus on attitudes and feelings as well as development of concepts. The importance of parental involvement is also clear. Without a total, continual approach to nutrition education that is integrated between home and school, children's behaviors will probably not change.

Safety Education

Accidents are the leading cause of death for children under age fourteen. When children become mobile around one year of age, motor vehicle accidents are the major cause of death. Drownings, fires, and ingestion of poisons follow motor vehicle accidents in killing more children than all diseases combined (National Safety Council, 1980). Because accidents are so common, it is imperative to teach children the skills, attitudes, and knowledge that could lead to saving their lives.

The importance of providing children with an environment prepared for their experimentation and exploration cannot be overstated. Accidents most frequently occur to children who have had little opportunity to explore, find out for themselves, or experience minor scrapes and bumps and who therefore feel no responsibility for their own safety (Seder, 1974).

- Create an emergency plan and practice it. Define the roles of each teacher and staff member and the children.
- Post the emergency plan.
- Post emergency phone numbers.
- Teach children what to do if the teacher becomes ill or is injured.
- Teach children to use the phone, dialling either 911 or 0 for operator.
- Know who will transport an injured or ill child.
- Have parents list their preferred doctor and hospital. Keep a record of these numbers, but with the understanding that in an emergency you may call any doctor or hospital.
- Determine precautions for special needs children.
- Keep an updated first-aid kit.
- Be certain staff members are trained in CPR and first aid. (Aronson & Pizzo, 1977)

Figure 14–6
How to be prepared

When children do not have a safe environment in which to practice safety skills or the opportunity to face challenges, they're more likely to be involved in some type of accident. They have no idea of the consequences and no experience in making decisions or judging hazards. Such children are most likely to experience serious injury or death from accidents.

A safe environment is not only free from hazards but contains a diligent, observing, supervising adult. As a teacher, you must check the safety of the play yard and playroom before the children arrive, and then you must be continually alert for potential hazards. As children play, you reinforce safety rules. Rules have been decided by you and the children and might even be posted as a reminder. But you will have to keep on reminding, in a positive yet firm way, as children play: "Ride your bike here"; "Climb the tree with your hands free"; "Remove the truck from under the climbing bars."

Always Be Prepared

Being prepared is a must. Aronson and Pizzo (1977) found that few child-care teachers, staff members, or children had any idea of what to do in an accident. It was rare to find anyone who knew what his or her responsibility was. Emergency phone numbers were not posted, and children did not know what to do if the adult became ill or injured.

You, the other adults who work with you, and the children should practice a prepared emergency plan. The plan should be written and posted.

Reprinted with permission from National Association for the Education of Young Children (1992). *Young Children, 46*(4), p. 64.

Decide who will stay with the children, what the children will do, and what the other adults will do. Teach children to use the phone. Have them practice dialing the emergency number, and teach those two or under how to obtain the operator. Even two-year-olds can find the "0" for operator, especially if a red dot is painted over the number.

Think ahead. Who will transport an injured or sick child to the doctor or hospital? Have parents record the numbers of their preferred doctor and hospital, but inform them that in an emergency you may call the doctor or hospital nearest to the school. (See Figure 14–6 for how to be prepared.)

Decide about the precautions required for special needs children. Who will stay with the child with a visual or hearing impairment, or what will you do with the child in a wheelchair should you need to evacuate the building?

Keep a first-aid kit ready, freshened periodically and within easy access in the classroom and the play yard. The kit should include, at the minimum:

- A box of assorted Band-Aids
- A box of three-inch sterile gauze squares
- Sterile gauze bandages, both two-inch and one-inch sizes
- A roll of one-inch adhesive tape
- Absorbent cotton
- Antibacterial soap
- Petroleum jelly
- Cloth or absorbent sanitary pads for application of pressure

At least one permanent staff person should be trained in first aid and cardiopulmonary resuscitation (CPR). Your local Red Cross or other health agency offers free courses in accident preparedness and first aid. This training needs to be updated regularly.

All children should feel responsible for their own safety and share responsibility for the group's safety. Plan to include material about traffic, drowning, fire, and poison safety in your curriculum. Remember that traffic accidents, drownings, fires, and poisonings are the four leading causes of injury and death among children.

Traffic Safety

You share in the responsibility of helping children learn to cope in traffic. Real experiences are required. Teaching children to sing songs about traffic safety or to recite poems or rhymes is of little use and may even promote injury. Pease and Preston (1967) found that children used these rhymes almost superstitiously, as if saying the rhyme before they darted into the street would somehow magically protect them. Perhaps the teacher had said, "If you sing this song, you'll be safe in traffic."

The most common cause of traffic accidents for young children is darting out in front of cars. Children, intent on play or crossing the street to join a friend, dart into traffic at midblock. Drivers, unable to see the small child and unprepared for a pedestrian in the middle of the block, simply do not see the child in time to stop. Most of these accidents happen on residential streets. The traffic is usually moving slower than 35 miles per hour, the child is within a few blocks of home, and the weather is usually pleasant. The goals of traffic safety, therefore, should address the midblock or "dart-out" accident.

1. Stop before stepping into the street.
2. Listen and scan for traffic before crossing.

Practice crossing streets with children.

3. Walk across residential streets with deliberation.

4. Interpret traffic signals and signs correctly. (Ross & Seefeldt, 1978, p. 69)

Stop Before Stepping into the Street

For children under age five, or those who have not been involved in learning traffic safety, the first step in teaching is to develop the habit of stopping before walking into a street. Two-year-olds begin by going outdoors and identifying the different surfaces of the school and play yard and stopping every time the surface changes. Next children are taken to a quiet, residential street or on a walk around the block and are asked to identify places where surfaces change, stopping at each place.

The curb is another place to stop, since the surfaces change there. Learning and practicing stopping when the surfaces change or when there is

Learning Signs

Make two sets of traffic signs out of cardboard. Place one in a "feeling box" and the other on a table next to the box. Have children select a sign from the table and try to find the same one in the "feeling box" using only their sense of feel and trying to identify the sign's shape.

Show and Tell

Instead of a show and tell time, set aside one day to have children tell how they come to school. Have them name one safety rule they followed and describe hazardous or unsafe practices they've observed as they travel to school either walking, riding the school bus, or in a private car.

Streets and Sidewalks

Construct a learning station called "Streets and Sidewalks" from two cardboard box lids. Label one box *Streets* and the other *Sidewalks*. Cut a number of pictures of various vehicles from magazines—bicycles, toy cars, wagons, tricycles, trucks, cars, and so on. Mount them on cardboard. Place a red dot on the backs of those that are to be driven in the street; a blue dot on the backs of those to be driven on the sidewalk. Children sort pictures into appropriate boxes and discuss their choices.

Cross at Corners

As a homework activity, ask children to count the number of streets they cross between home and school. Construct a class graph with the information. Tape numerals—1, 2, 3, 4, 5, 6, and 7—to the top of the edge of a table. Have each child place a small block over the numeral that represents the number of streets between home and school.

Follow the Signs

Reinforce outside sign and signal traffic experiences with this game. Make simulated traffic signs and signals and play "Follow the Sign." Children march around the room, stopping to follow the sign the leader holds up.

Figure 14–7
Traffic safety activities

a curb establishes the habit of stopping before entering a street. Parents should also be involved in practicing this habit. Write a brief letter informing parents of your goal, and how they can practice at home with their children.

Listen and Scan for Traffic

Once children learn to stop before going into the street, they need to learn to listen and scan for traffic before crossing the street. With adequate adult supervision, take children on a field trip to learn to listen and look for traffic. Children under age five are confused whether traffic is traveling toward or away from them. They need to practice observing traffic and identifying its direction and also the speed cars are traveling.

Crossing a Residential Street

Construct a pretend street with crosswalks and corners using masking tape or chalk on the play yard surface. Have children use this street to practice crossing. They use their tricycles or other wheel toys to role play pedestrians and drivers. They are first reminded to stop when the tape indicates that the surface of the yard changes and the street begins, and to listen and look for oncoming traffic. Additional practice can be structured using a table-top street with toy cars and people.

With trained, adequate adult supervision, you may be able to take a small group of children to a corner and practice crossing the street. When you focus on crossing, children often get the idea that this is a very dangerous business and it's best to run across the street as fast as they can. Running to cross is another major cause of traffic deaths. Children, who are typically uncoordinated, trip and fall in front of oncoming traffic. Teach children to walk with deliberate speed as they cross. Ask them to focus on the task of crossing, not playing, thinking about anything else, or running.

Interpreting Traffic Signals and Signs Correctly

Instead of easing the task of crossing streets, traffic signals and signs make it more difficult for children. Often children will elect to cross midblock in order to avoid signs and signals that they do not understand.

Children can be taught to interpret the meaning of the lights and signals found at intersections. First, they need to learn that red is used to symbol-

---

- Do I have a written plan for a fire drill?
- Do I conduct monthly drills based on the plan?
- Have I had the plan reviewed by the fire department?
- Have I held a meeting with the center staff to discuss the plan?
- Do I review the plan for a new member?
- Does everyone know where the fire extinguisher is and how to operate it?
- Have I practiced fire drills during nap and mealtimes?
- Do I have an assembly point outside of the building?
- What method do I have for accounting for the children once outside?
- Have I held fire drills with different exits blocked?
- Have I given the children and their parents information about fire and smoke accidents?

(Collins, 1977, p. 29).

Figure 14–8
Plan for fire drills

ize danger and means stop. Use a red tag on objects that may be hazardous in the room and play yard. Ask children where red flags should be placed.

Play follow-the-leader games, with children stopping whenever a leader holds up a red flag. Once children understand the meaning of red, play the same games using green and yellow flags. Practice crossing a pretend playground street following the signals given by one of the children, with others role playing pedestrians and drivers.

Do not attempt to practice crossing streets at an intersection without the aid of a police officer and other well-prepared, trained adults. Police officers can take small groups of children to the intersection to explain the traffic signal lights and to help the children use the lights as they practice crossing. Children should be at least five years of age before you expose them to this activity.

Protecting children in traffic is the responsibility of teachers, parents, and the community alike. All adults and older children will serve as models and should practice traffic safety themselves at all times. The community should take action to arrange for traffic signs, signals, or crossing guards where needed. The goals of the school must be reinforced at home by the parents.

Figure 14–7 gives five traffic safety activities for the teacher to do with students.

Fire Safety

Project Burn Prevention (1978), funded by the U.S. Consumer Product Safety Commission, is a program designed to provide schools with fire prevention information. It conducts a mass media campaign to prevent injury from burns to children across the country. The program helps prepare children for fires by outlining the procedures to be followed in case of fire. Your goals for fire safety education can include:

1. Teaching children to approach fire with caution and respect
2. Involving children in practice fire drills
3. Teaching children to drop and roll if they are involved in a fire
4. Teaching children where the fire extinguisher is and how to use it, as well as how to call the fire department

The Firefighter's Visit

Invite a firefighter to the classroom to introduce children to fire safety practices. The firefighter can teach children the habit of dropping and rolling if they or their clothing catches on fire. They can also demonstrate precautions to take when using fire or heat. Follow this demonstration with teaching respect for fire. Even if it's just the candle for the Halloween pumpkin, keep a bucket of sand and water nearby whenever handling fire. You don't have to frighten children, just teach them the potential dangers of fire.

Firefighters also need to show children that they are helpful, friendly, trained people who can be trusted. Often firefighters are unable to rescue children in burning buildings because children are frightened of their full gear and equipment. During the visit, the firefighter can show the children each piece of equipment, explaining its purpose and then putting it on. While dressing, the firefighter can continually remind children that he or she will look different when dressed in full gear. Once dressed, the firefighter might shake hands with each child as a means of demonstrating trust. Next, the firefighter should take off each piece of gear, again explaining its purpose (Maryland Community Association for the Education of Young Children, 1988).

Plans for a Fire Drill

While the firefighter is visiting, show children where the fire extinguishers are and how they are used. Have them practice dialing the number to reach the fire department, and hold a fire drill. A fire marshall in Georgia (Collins, 1977) has developed the questionnaire in Figure 14–8 to assist early childhood educators in training children and staff for fire emergencies.

Poison Safety

More than 117,000 children a year experience accidental poisoning in our country, as reported to clearinghouse control centers in forty-five states. The development of poison control centers and placement of the "Mr. Yuk" sticker on dangerous substances have helped to eliminate many cases of accidental poisoning. Yet children in an early childhood setting are just as susceptible to poisoning as they are at home. In the school, it becomes your responsibility to protect children from possible poisoning accidents. Your goals are to teach children to:

1. Recognize the Mr. Yuk symbol and understand what it means.
2. Take medications only from adult family members, parents, physicians, or health personnel.
3. Understand that some things are to eat, while others are not. Using food for art confuses children on this point. Clear lines should be drawn: Food is to eat; other substances—berries found on the playground, art materials, toys, leaves, flowers—are not for eating.

Your Responsibility

When you work with children under age five, it is your responsibility to watch them carefully and prevent them from putting anything into their mouth. You can't expect babies to do this as they try to find out about their world. However, you are responsible for observing the children, freeing the environment from poisonous substances, and removing nonfood objects that do find their way into children's mouths.

Check your room and play yard for all poisonous substances, and remove all that you find. Ascertain what cleaning supplies and other toxic materials are stored in any place the children might encounter accidentally. If you serve meals, be certain that food items are stored separately from nonfood items. There have been tragic mistakes of hurried cooks or teachers confusing bags of flour with cleaning products when poisons were not stored in separate rooms or in places away from food.

Keep the number of your nearest poison control center posted by the phone. If you don't know this number, write to the U.S. Government Printing Office, Washington, DC 20013, and obtain a directory of poison control centers.

Things We Eat and Things We Do Not

Teach children to recognize the Mr. Yuk symbol and understand its meaning. Obtain Mr. Yuk stickers from your local health department. With the children, place Mr. Yuk on things in the classroom that could harm them if

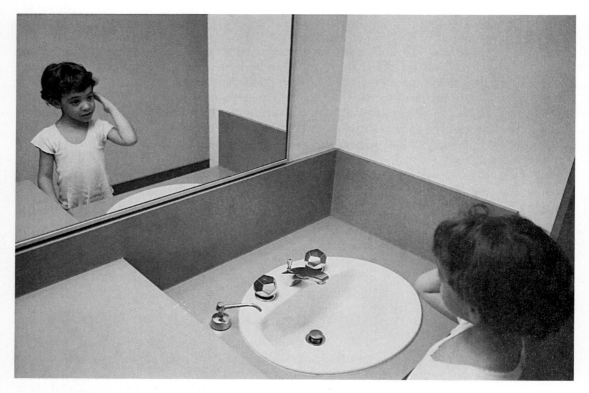

Each school will have routines for washing, eating, and resting.

eaten. Teach recognition of the sticker by playing matching or bingo games. Older children enjoy making their own Mr. Yuk stickers.

To assess children's understanding of things that are not to be eaten, create a learning station sorting game. Have children sort pictures of things to eat and things that are not food. Include pictures of hand lotions, bleach, wild trees with berries, flowers, and other things.

Stop children from putting anything into their mouth or tasting substances as they explore their environment. Remind them to ask an adult before smelling or tasting anything. Use children's encounters with the environment to reinforce their understanding of poison. For instance, on a walk through the neighborhood, identify different berries and flowers, pointing out those that birds and animals eat but humans do not and why.

Water Safety

The American Academy of Pediatrics (1988) offers reminders for water safety. The academy believes that adults are responsible for monitoring and protecting children when they are around water. Adults must always keep toddlers and preschoolers in sight when they are near swimming pools, lakes, or other bodies of water. It is adults' responsibility to supervise children, and no child should ever be left unattended when alone near a pool or other body of water. No child is drownproof because he or she has had swimming lessons, and no child should be allowed to swim alone.

Toys and other floating devices are not substitutes for supervision. Parents and caregivers should learn CPR and should know the special techniques for infants and children.

The academy recommends that swimming lessons be reserved for children older than age three. Paul Dyment, chairman of the American Academy of Pediatrics Committee on Sports Medicine, also cautions against swimming classes for children under age three. Children may swallow too much water, which can dilute the sodium content in their blood and cause convulsions. Swallowed water may also transmit viruses, causing infectious diarrhea in small children. Swimming classes give parents and caregivers a false sense of security, for it is unlikely that any child can be made water-safe.

Physical Health and Activity

Education for physical health and activity arises from children's needs and actual experiences. It cannot take place without involving them directly in health routines, activities, and exercises. Goals for health education are integrated and overlapping. They might include:

All About Me

Make a scrapbook for each child called "All About Me." Include the height and weight of the child in the book as well as pages for the child to describe his or her physical features in words or pictures.

I Will Grow

Have first or second graders divide a piece of paper into three parts. In the first part they will draw a picture of something they did when they were a baby, labeling this "I DID"; in the second, something they do now, labeling this "I CAN"; and in the third space, something they will do in the future, labeling this "I WILL."

Wearing Clothes

Collect pictures of different types of clothing—work, play, swimming, winter, and summer. Have children categorize these pictures according to when they wear them. Discuss why they wear the clothing they do.

Hidden Dirt

Have children wash their hands. Then take small pieces of cotton dipped in rubbing alcohol. Rub the back of each child's hand with the moistened cotton. Look at the dirt on the cotton and discuss what it means. Even when you think you've washed your hands, there still may be dirt present.

We All Need Sleep

Check the number of children who have siblings who are younger than they and those who have siblings older. Find out how long babies sleep, the children sleep, and how long the older brothers and sisters sleep. Discuss why the infants sleep longer than older children.

Make Toothpowder

Have each child mix 1 part of salt to 3 parts of baking powder. Put a few drops of wintergreen extract into this. Let it dry. Then try it out. Compare this toothpowder with commercial toothpaste. Which do the children like the best and why? Which does the best job and why?

Figure 14–9
Health activities

Concepts

1. Development of an understanding of human growth and development
2. Knowledge of body functions and parts
3. An understanding of the purposes of medical and dental examinations and care

Attitudes

1. A respect for one's body
2. Willingness to take responsibility for the care of one's body

Behaviors
1. Development of healthy habits and practices
2. Ability to care for one's own health
3. Developing the habit of physical exercise and activity

"The health teaching shall be largely done by guiding children in developing desirable health behaviors, and knowledge through their every experience in a healthy environment. This guidance shall include systematic practice of health habits and needs" (Willgoose, 1974, p. 127). Just as the goals of health education cannot be separated from one another, neither can routines or activities be specified as unique to any one goal. The routines of bathing, rest and exercise, dental and medical checkups, hand-washing, and toothbrushing develop concepts of health as well as attitudes of respect for one's body. Figure 14–9 gives examples of various health activities.

Hygiene and Physical Health

The routines of dressing, washing, eating, and resting will take up a great deal of your time with young children. In fact, you will sometimes think of yourself as a caregiver and not a teacher. You have to develop the understanding that these activities, while essential for health, are equally essential for teaching about health. All of the daily routines serve as the basis for teaching children the concepts of body functions and parts and the habits of caring for themselves.

Each school will have routines for body care. If you're working with children under age five, it is probably mandated that child-sized toilets, sinks, and mirrors be available. If they are not, arrange for the use of platforms or small, sturdy benches or stools so children will be able to reach sinks, get their own toothbrush, and turn on faucets for themselves.

Washing hands before and after using the toilet and before eating, as well as washing faces and brushing teeth after eating, are routines that should be established and followed. When children participate in routines, you introduce them to the purpose and objective of these activities.

Brushing teeth leads to discussions of teeth or to naming of mouth parts. A nurse, dental hygienist, or dentist might visit and demonstrate correct toothbrushing and flossing techniques to the children. Or you might take the class to visit a dentist's office and examine the chair, mirror, and other equipment. You can also have the dentist demonstrate how to brush and care for teeth and gums.

You can follow up routine toothbrushing and the visits to the dentist by reading books, role playing, and finding out more about how teeth grow and develop. Provide children with props that will foster dramatic play. A flashlight, white shirts, and a simple chair are all that are necessary to stimulate dental play.

Losing a tooth is an occasion to focus on concepts of growth and development. The lost tooth can be examined and discussed: "Why did the tooth come out?" "What will happen next?" "How else will you grow and change next year?"

Dressing and undressing routines, like toothbrushing and face- and hand-washing, are used to introduce vocabulary and concepts of growth. When working with children under age five, you'll want to develop skills of dressing and undressing. Harriet Johnson (1936) encouraged her teachers to get children past the "meal-snack stage," where children are passively stuffed into clothing, to the stage where they complete the task for themselves.

Break dressing and undressing into small steps. "First roll your sock, now put it over your toe, now pull it here, over your heel." Offer children help with the first button of a coat or a sweater: "I'll do the first, you do the rest." "I'll put the boot over the toe of your shoe, then you can pull it over the rest."

Help is supportive and informative. As you begin a task, explain how the children can complete it independently. Give them the opportunity to struggle for a while and accomplish it for themselves, but be observant and ready to step in if frustration occurs. Don't do for the children what they can do for themselves. "It's ridiculous to see a five-year-old with an easily handled fat zipper being zipped by a hovering adult. An observant teacher can see when frustration is about to set in and offer a little help or word of advice and demonstration" (Hildebrand, 1975, p. 189).

When at home, children adjust their daily schedule to their body rhythms. They rest when tired and are boisterous and active when refreshed. When in a group, the same balance must be found. Boisterous, active times must be balanced by quiet, restful periods. Primary-age children will need a quiet time following recess or periods of high activity just as children in the preschool or child-care center do.

Kindergarten children and those who are younger do need a time to relax in whatever manner they choose. Some children in full-day programs will actually nap, and they need a quiet room with a cot. Others will be content to pursue a quiet activity as they rest on a cot. Every child should be able to select the type of resting situation desired, as long as it doesn't disturb the others and offers a truly relaxing time for the child.

Rest routines should lead to the recognition of the relationships between rest and health. A nurse or doctor might be invited to describe how the body changes when at rest and the need for rest.

Body care and grooming should be designed to introduce children to their own growth and development. As they notice changes in growth while they dress, undress, or brush their teeth, introduce them to body structure and function, developing the following concepts:

1. Changes in height and weight are called *growth*.
2. Different rates of growth are normal.
3. As people grow, they develop skills.
4. The body has many parts, each serving a function.

Full-length mirrors in the dressing area and dramatic play areas will draw children's attention to their bodies. As children play with their reflection in the mirror, ask them: "How does your arm move?" "How many parts of your body move?" "How many ways can you move?" Give children names for body parts: *waist, hips, calves, shoulder,* or *joints*. "Simon Says" games, played while looking in a mirror, are fun with an individual or a few children. Give such directions as "Simon Says touch your toes (your elbow, eyebrow)."

Fun with mirrors and reflections can also lead to a discussion of the function of body parts. "What does your nose do?" "Your ears?" "Eyes?" Or you might discuss physiology. "Breathe in. Look at your chest. What happens? Now breathe out." As children observe their own chests expand and contract, you can introduce them to the concept of breathing. Have children find their heart with their hand and feel its beat.

When children have scrapes or bruises, you can examine the wounds as you wash and disinfect the area. "This part of your skin will hurt a bit; look how bruised it is." "Underneath the skin are blood cells." The direction of the discussions depends on your sensitivity and the children's interest, as well as your specific objectives.

Measuring and weighing children enable you to discuss concepts of growth. Without making comparisons that place children in competition from tallest to shortest or thinnest to fattest, in a matter-of-fact manner present the idea that children grow, and at different rates.

"Where's the bathroom?" asks four-year-old Chan on his first day in the early childhood program. The bathroom is an important place for young children. Toileting, as with every other routine, is an individual matter. No two children, like no two teachers, can schedule their needs to use the bathroom at the same time. Ideally, bathrooms should be located in the classroom, so young children will not have to travel through long hallways to reach them. Although preschoolers can "go to the bathroom" without direct supervision, they must feel secure in the knowledge that a concerned adult is nearby, ready to help if necessary.

Busy bathroom times occur before and after lunch and again after a nap. These are almost social occasions, with children soaping hands, playing in the water, and sitting on toilets while chatting. Such times provide further opportunities to discover and name parts of the body, and begin to note sex differences. Under age five or six, boys and girls will be comfortable using the same bathroom facilities, and they will note differences in a natural way. Comments and questions that children have should be handled perfunctorily with statements like "Boys stand to urinate, girls sit"; or, "Girls have vulva, a clitoris, and a vagina, boys have a penis." Adult terminology should be used in reference to sex organs. But when working with very young children, those just learning to use the toilet, you'll also want to know the terminology they use at home, so you'll be able to communicate with them.

After age five or near the end of the fifth year, a natural modesty sets in. Children are no longer comfortable using the same bathroom. In one

Physical exercise is easily justified in schools today.

kindergarten there were two bathrooms. The teacher propped the doors of the two rooms open, not only for supervision, but also to use children's experiences with the bathroom to teach sex differences and positive attitudes toward body parts. The children accepted this, and throughout the year used either bathroom. But toward the end of the kindergarten year, the girls requested a sign that said "GIRLS ONLY," and asked to have it posted on "their" bathroom, so one would be for boys and one for girls.

If you're working with toddlers, toilet learning will be a part of your job. It's usually good to begin this when children are around the age of two. Toilet learning, as with all other health care and teaching, is coordinated with the parents' efforts. It doesn't make much sense to begin in the school if work is not coordinated with that at home. Discuss your methods with the parents, and ask them how they are teaching their child to use the toilet.

In an early childhood setting, peer modeling is usually effective. Younger children, seeing older ones use the toilet, model this behavior. Learning seems to occur naturally. Watch, however, for signs that the child needs to use the toilet, and place the child on it for a few minutes. A few words of encouragement or praise will be reinforcing.

Accidents happen and should be accepted as a normal course of events with a quick cleanup, a change of clothing, and some comforting words to the child. Even when teaching five- and six-year-olds, you'll want to keep a complete set of clothing handy for emergency changes. Children become so involved in their work and play that they leave toileting to the very last moment. Then, much to their chagrin, they're too late. Never shame them; rather, take a comforting, accepting attitude, and help them regain composure and confidence.

Physical Activity

Physical activity in the schools is easily justified. The benefits of physical activity, as well as establishing attitudes toward fitness and activity that will continue throughout life, are clear and well understood (Bailey, 1973; Donaghue, 1977; Russell, 1981). Despite knowledge of the benefits of physical activity for children, there is little evidence to suggest that children in kindergarten and the primary grades experience daily, vigorous physical activity (Manitoba Department of Education, 1978).

Young children need time as well as space and equipment for both small- and large-muscle exercise. A lot of exercise is provided as children play indoors or outdoors. Additional experiences, however, should be planned to help children become more aware of their bodies and how they move them, as well as to provide a period of vigorous physical activity on a daily basis (Javernick, 1988).

Movement exploration provides children with this opportunity. Movement exploration is based on the original work of Laban (1948) and begins when children become aware of their bodies and of what they can do with their bodies in space. It teaches concepts of body awareness and knowledge of body parts and functions, as well as offering physical exercise (Sullivan, 1982). Movement exploration is based on the following elements:

- *Body awareness.* The shape of the body in space; where different parts are; how the body moves and rests; the body's behavior when combined with other bodies; and how the voice is a part of the body.
- *Force and time.* Being limp, energetic, light, fluid, staccato, slow, or quick.
- *Space.* Where the body is in a room. The level (high—erect posture, or in the air; middle—crawling or stooped; low—on the floor); direction (forward, backward, sideways); size (bigness, smallness); path through space (extensions of the body parts into space); locomotion—movement through space at various levels (lowest—wriggling, rolling, scooting; middle—crawling, crouching, using four limbs; highest—walking, running, skipping, galloping, sliding, leaping, hopping, and jumping); weight relationship of body to ground, ways to manage body weight in motion and in relationship to others.
- *Working with others.* Combining with others to solve problems, develop trust, explore strength and sensitivity; to feel a sense of union with others.
- *Isolation.* How various individual body parts—head, shoulders, arms, hands, elbows, wrists, neck, back, upper torso, ribs, hips, legs, knees,

ankles, feet—can move. These can swing, jerk, twist, shake, lift, tense, relax, become fluid, press, glide, slide, float, flick, slash, punch, or dab.
- *Repetitions.* Getting to know a movement and how it feels when repeated often; being able to repeat a shape or action. (Sullivan, 1982, pp. 3–4)

Teachers act as guides and offer children challenges or problems to solve. Two types of problems are involved: those designed to encourage each child to explore continuously and discover a variety of movement responses; and those designed to encourage explorations and discovery of limited movement responses. The first type, free exploration, is more appropriate for the very young. The second, guided exploration, is centered around you and the child and involves promoting and refining skills. Guided exploration can be introduced to children who are four or older.

Problems or tasks can be stated in a number of ways in order for children to grasp their meaning. Each child's response is correct and can be reinforced with praise. Praise and comments are designed to help children analyze their own movements and become aware of:

1. Their relationship to the physical environment.
2. Their body and what it can do.
3. The components of movement, speed, direction, and force. Comments such as "OK," "great," "José ran fast," "Kim jumped high," and "Watch Allison's knees when she jumps. Can you see how they bend?" help focus children's attention on their activities and reinforce their efforts. Examples of problems are:

   a. Can you walk in place (forward, sideward, backward)?
   b. Walk on tiptoes and then on your heels.
   c. Walk without touching anyone else. How would you walk up a hill? On a rainy day? Snowy day? Hot day?
   d. Walk with a partner. Now walk with your partner without touching.

Children select their own level of participation or creativity as they respond. If the exercise becomes too physical, they're free to withdraw or rest. As each solves a problem in a way that demands more or less physical effort, each can succeed at his or her own level.

Summary

Providing for the health, safety, and well-being of children must be a goal of every early childhood program. Not only is providing for children's health a goal, but teaching children principles and practices of health and safety is also a goal.

These two goals, which cannot be separated from each other, cannot be separated from the total curriculum. Teaching takes place as children practice good health and safety practices. Still, because young children are not in a position to care for themselves, the adults around them are ultimately responsible for ensuring children's safety in their school and community.

Parents and other community agencies and associations share in your responsibility for providing for children's health and safety. Involving others will help you achieve the goals of promoting children's total health, well-being, and safety.

Projects

Continuing Case Study

Interview your case study child by asking questions like the following: What happens when you get a cut? How do you breathe, and why? Where is your heart? Why do we eat?

Record your child's knowledge of health and body functions as well as any attitudes he or she reveals about health. In class, discuss what children's understanding means for planning and teaching health, safety, and nutrition.

1. Observe in a child-care center during nap, lunch, and outdoor play. How do teachers use these routines to teach health concepts? Make a list of the experiences you observe.
2. Now observe the same routines in a preschool program located in a local elementary school. Do the routines differ from those of the child-care center?
3. Tour a grade school. Note the way the environment is arranged. What indicates to you that the children and staff are prepared for accidents? What indicates unpreparedness?
4. Conduct a cooking experience with a small group of children. First cook the food yourself, so you'll know what to expect. Then introduce the experience to the children. Identify key concepts you will introduce as well as your goals and objectives. Evaluate the project.
5. Interview children to find out what they know of the traffic system. Ask them what traffic lights mean and where, how, and why they should cross streets. Design a lesson to promote traffic safety based on their responses.

Children's Books

These children's books might be used in connection with food preparation or for reinforcing concepts in nutrition.

Bang, M. (1980). *The gray lady and the strawberry snatcher*. New York: Four Winds.
Birdwell, N. (1979). *Kangaroo stew*. New York: Scholastic.
Brown, M. (1947). *Stone soup*. New York: Scribner's.
Couzyn, J. (1990). *Bad day*. Illustrated by Paul Demeyer. New York: Dutton.
de Brunhoff, L. (1978). *Babar learns to cook*. New York: Random House.
Heller, N. (1991). *The tooth tree*. New York: Greenwillow.
Hoban, R. (1964). *Bread and jam for Frances*. Illustrated by L. Hoban. New York: Harper & Row.
Krauss, R. (1945). *The carrot seed*. New York: Harper & Row.
McCloskey, R. (1952). *One morning in Maine*. New York: Viking.
Miller, V. (1991). *On your potty*. New York: Greenwillow.
Pinkwater, M. (1974). *Fat Elliot and the gorilla*. New York: Four Winds.

Potter, B. (1902). *The tale of Peter Rabbit.* New York: Frederick Warne.

Robinson, B. (1969). *The fattest bear in the first grade.* New York: Random House.

Selsam, M. (1972). *Vegetables from stems and leaves.* New York: Morrow.

Sendak, M. (1962). *Chicken soup with rice.* New York: Harper & Row.

Resources

The organizations below will provide you with free or inexpensive materials to use with children as you teach concepts, attitudes, and behaviors in nutrition, safety, and health. Send them a postcard requesting either information about their organizations or a list of publications and materials.

U.S. Department of Health and Human Services
Washington, DC 20201

Your state department of education

Your state department of motor vehicles

U.S. Department of Transportation

Federal Highway Administration
Washington, DC 20590

Consumer Product Safety Commission
Washington, DC 20207

National Safety Council
425 North Michigan Avenue
Chicago, IL 60611

National Dairy Council
6300 North River Road
Rosemont, IL 60018

Traffic safety teaching materials are available from the National Association for the Education of Young Children, 1509 16th Street, NW, Washington, DC 20036. These include a multidimensional curriculum packet, *Walk in Traffic Safely* and *CROSS-Children Riding on Sidewalks Safely.*

References

American Academy of Pediatrics. (1988). *Water safety.* Washington, DC: Author.

Aronson, S. S., & Pizzo, P. (1977). Health and safety issues in day care. In *Policy issues in day care: Summaries of 21 papers.* Washington, DC: Department of Health, Education and Welfare.

Bailey, D. (1973). Exercise, fitness, and physical education for the growing child. *Canadian Journal of Public Health, 64,* 13–22.

Blackeway, S. F., & Knickrehm, M. H. (1978). Nutrition education in the Little Rock school lunch program. *Journal of the American Dietetic Association, 78,* 389–391.

Collins, R. H. (1977). Planning for fire safety. *Young Children, 32,* 22–33.

Dewey, J. (1944). *Democracy and education.* New York: Free Press. (Originally published 1916)

Donaghue, S. (1977). The correlation between physical fitness, absenteeism, and work performance. *Canadian Journal of Public Health, 68,* 201–203.

Hildebrand, V. (1975). *Guiding young children.* New York: Macmillan.

Javernick, E. (1988). Johnny's not jumping: Can we help obese children? *Young Children, 43*(2), 18–23.

Johnson, B., & Plemons, B. (1984). *Individual child portion cooking: Picture recipes.* Mt. Rainier, MD: Gryphon House.

Johnson, H. M. (1936). *School begins at two.* New York: New Republic.

Kendall, E. D., & Moukaddem, V. E. (1992). Who's vulnerable in infant child care centers? *Young Children, 47*(5), 72–77.

Laban, R. (1948). *Modern educational dance.* London: Macdonald & Evans.

Manitoba Department of Education. (1978). *Manitoba schools physical fitness survey.* Winnipeg: Author.

Maryland Community Association for the Education of Young Children. (1988). *Fire safety for young children.* College Park, MD: Author.

National Association for the Education of Young Children. (1992). Health and safety tips. *Young Children, 46*(4), p. 64.

National Association for the Education of Young Children. (1992). Health and safety tips: Preventing food poisoning. *Young Children, 47*(5), p. 50.

National Dairy Council. (1979). *Food: Early choices*. Chicago: Author.

National Safety Council. (1980). *Accident and safety statistics: 1979*. Washington, DC: Author.

Pease, K., & Preston, B. (1967). Road safety education for young children. *British Journal of Educational Psychology, 37*, 305–313.

Project Burn Prevention. (1978). *Protect someone you love*. Washington, DC: Consumer Product Safety Commission.

Rogers, C. S., & Morris, S. S. (1986). Reducing sugar in children's diets: Why? How? *Young Children, 41*(5), 11–20.

Ross, S., & Seefeldt, C. (1978). Young children in traffic: How can they cope? *Young Children, 33*, 68–74.

Russell, R. D. (1981). *Education in the '80s: Health*. Washington, DC: National Education Association.

Seder, S. (1974). *Teaching about safety. Vol. 3: Pedestrians*. Chicago: National Safety Council.

Sullivan, M. (1982). *Feeling strong, feeling free: Movement exploration for young children*. Washington, DC: National Association for the Education of Young Children.

White House Conference. (1969). *Food, nutrition, and health: Final report*. Washington, DC: Government Printing Office.

Willgoose, C. E. (1974). *Health education in the elementary school*. Philadelphia: W. B. Saunders.

Winick, M. (1969). Malnutrition and brain development. *Journal of Pediatrics, 74*, 667–679.

World Health Organization. (1980). *Research in health education*. (Tech. Rep. Series No. 432.) Geneva: Author.

Social Studies

"We are both social and individual beings, connected with others in a multitude of ways, as well as ultimately alone in the world."

(Damon, 1983, p. 1)

After reading this chapter, you should be able to respond to the following questions:

1. How can children's knowledge of self form the foundation for the social studies?

2. What do teachers do to foster self-esteem?

3. How do children learn about others?

4. How do you help children develop skills in communicating, sharing, and cooperating?

5. What are the developmental stages in children's learning about other cultures?

6. How do teachers foster children's understanding of other cultures?

7. What is the knowledge base of the social studies?

8. How are field trips related to fostering knowledge of the social world and concepts of the social studies?

9. Describe how you will plan for a field trip.

The Social Studies

> Three-year-old Jack nestled close to his mother, who was reading to him. "Oh, oh!" said Jack, pointing to a picture of a whale illustrating the page. "Bad whale, bad whale, whale didn't go home—he stuck in ice."
>
> "Hey—watch out! You almost knocked over the space ship. Sit here," Kim commands. "Now—blast off—1, 2, 8, 9!"
>
> "We'll need two more dollars if you want ice cream," explains seven-year-old Vanessa to the group planning refreshments for a class party.

Whether pondering the plight of whales trapped in ice off Port Barrow, Alaska, or determining how much money is needed to buy ice cream for a party, children are engaging in the social studies, those studies that concern the nature of people and their world, the heritage of the past, and all of contemporary social living (National Council for the Social Studies, 1989).

The social studies are both integral to children's lives and of high interest to them. Driven by a desire to know and achieve mastery over self and their environment (Maslow, 1968), children are eager to gain an understanding of many aspects of their political, economical, cultural, and environmental world. They want to learn all they can about the world in which they live.

Not only are the social studies integral and interesting to children, but they also are essential to the perpetuation of our democratic way of life. All of education has the goal of preparing children to become members of a society, yet the social studies are uniquely suited to fostering the knowledge, skills, and attitudes necessary for participation in a democracy. The knowledge, skills, and attitudes that make up the field of social studies enable children to participate in the small democracy of their classroom today and prepare them to take their place as fully functioning citizens of a democracy when they are adults.

Goals for the Social Studies

The National Council for the Social Studies (NCSS) and the National Commission on Social Studies in the Schools (NCSSS) have suggested goals for the social studies. They include:

1. *Knowledge.* Embracing all of the disciplines of the social sciences, everything concerning the nature of people and their world, the heritage of the past, and all of contemporary social living.

The National Council for the Social Studies suggests that children learn:

- A sense of history
- Concepts of geography
- Concepts of economics

2.   *Attitudes and Values.* Social studies for children are more than a collection of separate though related understandings of the social sciences. For a society to perpetuate itself, its young must clearly understand the values and attitudes of that society (NCSS, 1989; National Commission on Social Studies in the Schools, 1989). The democratic beliefs drawn from the Constitution and the Declaration of Independence, such as due process, freedom of speech and expression, equal protection, and civil participation, are rooted in the concepts of respect for self and others and for the equality of others.

3.   *Skills.* The survival of a democratic society is possible only when its members are able to think and make decisions. The social studies teach the social skills of cooperating and relating with others and participation in a democratic society.

Knowledge

"Children are born into a world of complex human relations where grown-ups love and hate, help and fight one another, where people live and work in groups," wrote Lucy Sprague Mitchell (1951, p. 32). Because children's social world expands beyond that of the classroom, teachers of young children have the responsibility of helping children develop knowledge of the wider world. Children who have knowledge of their complex world feel more secure and can reach out to others, those near to them and those far away.

Children are born into a world of complex human relations.

Field Trips

Through trips into the community to see and observe the adult world, children can become aware of and explore their immediate world. In 1889, Froebel wrote:

> Parents and teachers should remember this—take the little ones at least once a week for a walk—not driving them out like a flock of sheep, nor leading them out like a company of soldiers, but going with them as a father with his sons, and acquaint them more fully with whatever the season or nature offers them. (Froebel, 1889, p. 163)

To Mitchell, the field trip was the base of the social studies program. "The social studies program for kindergarten, grades one and two, is based on trips" (Mitchell, 1951, p. 204).

Trips provide children with firsthand opportunities to learn about their world. Through trips children:

- Have contact with adult models in the world of work
- Observe social systems, such as banking, garbage collection, traffic control, fire and police protection, and other systems
- Use the methods of the scientist as they gain skills in observing, collecting information, inferring, and drawing conclusions
- Use the methods of the historian as they examine traces of the past
- Have a mutual experience that can later be recreated in dramatic play or expressed through music, dance, art, or literature
- Are stimulated to gain new ideas and motivated to further learning

Almost every social studies concept can be fostered through the field trip, either within the school or in the immediate community. For the key concepts from geography, field trips could be taken to observe weather conditions or changes that occur with the seasons, as well as the earth's surfaces—lake, grassy field, or sandy beach. As you take the trip, children organize themselves in space, locate various places, and use maps.

Other trips might be taken to foster history concepts, such as a walk through the neighborhood to note any changes. You might watch as people build or tear down a house, build a road, or fill in a pond. You may take a walk to a historic marker in the community, a museum, or a very old building to study traces of the past. Visiting an older person in the community can foster concepts of the past and of the continuity of human life. Children could find out how the older person lived when he or she was the same age as they are now.

Concepts from economics might be fostered through field trips to stores to make purchases, introducing the idea of being a consumer, or to someplace where goods are being produced. A trip to the supermarket or airport can introduce the idea of diversity of jobs as children list and observe the variety of positions people hold.

Be certain to visit service providers in the community, such as physicians and dentists, the library, and the county clerk, to foster the idea that we consume services as well as goods. A trip to a farm might be taken to find out more about how a farmer balances consumers' wants and needs.

Figure 15–1 summarizes the places to which field trips can be taken.

Before the Trip

Field trips are a serious commitment of time and money for you, the children, the parents, and the community. Before planning any trip, evaluate it in terms of your goals for children's learning. Then establish specific objectives for the trip. You might select any of the key concepts from the social sciences as objectives or focus on concepts from another area of the curriculum.

Assess the children's experiences. Find out which places they've been to many times, which they'd like to learn more about, and which their parents would like them to visit. Remember, however, that just because children have been someplace many times doesn't rule it out as an excellent field trip. Returning to a familiar place gives children a common interest to foster dramatic play or another creative enterprise. Also, you may as a group be able to go "behind the scenes" and see things denied to the general public. Also very young children feel a sense of comfort when they are familiar with a place and can focus their attention on the goals of the trip.

Check with your school or program to determine the rules and regulations concerning field trips. Such things as insurance coverage for drivers, safety restraints for children, and permission slips may be required. Also note that permission slips inform parents of your plans, but they may not legally protect you or the school from liability.

Permission may also be required from the principal or director, or in some cases, the parent advisory board. If you're planning a number of trips during the year, you might get permission for all of them at one time.

First, take the trip without the children so that you can plan how you will get there with the children and so you will be acquainted with the place. Talk with the people, informing them of the goals of the trip and the children's nature and interests. After you've seen the place, you'll be in a better position to determine what learning will result from the visit.

Walking field trips are the most valuable for young children. They are short, matching children's attention span. Also because children are at least partially familiar with the places they are walking to, the trips offer them more opportunities for learning. Walking trips are inexpensive, and can be taken more frequently than those requiring a bus or other form of transportation. Yet even a walking trip demands careful planning. What streets

Walking Field Trips

Don't overlook the interesting things right in the school or neighborhood. Walking field trips are popular with children.

Within the School

Many possibilities exist within the school for field trips. Children can:

- Visit the nurse's, principal's or director's, or custodian's offices within the school
- Trace the route the contents of the trashcan take when they leave their room
- First find all of the signs without words in the school, and then those with words
- Record all of the different materials in the school building: the tile in the bathroom, wood flooring, tile on the floor or walls, plaster and wood, glass and metal
- Count the number of doors on a given floor
- Listen to the footsteps of people going downstairs
- Identify all of the machines in the office, kitchen, and engineer's room
- Observe repairpersons at work
- Record the colors they find in school materials
- Go to different sides of the school building, look out the windows, and record what they see from the four sides of the building
- Count the number of people who work in the school, and record the diversity of jobs
- Trace the pipes from the bathroom to the basement
- Record every sound they hear in the office, hallway, or lunchroom
- Wait for the letter carrier

Outside the School Building

Go outside and staying within the play yard focus children's attention on:

- The shapes they see on the building
- Locating their room from the outside
- The wind in the trees
- Counting the number of surfaces on the play yard
- Locating and recording the address of the school
- Recording the sounds they hear
- Identifying the materials on the outside of the school building
- Finding out what they see from the different sides of the building
- Watching the traffic, counting the number of trucks, cars, buses, and other vehicles passing by
- Identifying the trees on the play yard
- Locating the principal's or director's office from different spots on the play yard
- Finding out how their feet feel on different surfaces of the play yard
- Recording all of the colors they see on the building
- Observing deliveries to the school, perhaps milk, food, or supplies

Figure 15–1
Summary of field trips

Around the Block

A number of valuable trips can be taken by walking around the block or within a few blocks of the school. These include:

- Observing a neighbor's flower or vegetable garden
- Identifying street signs and traffic signals
- Observing different clothing people walking on the street are wearing
- Counting the number of red lights
- Seeing how many different types of flags they can find
- Locating signs without words, and then those with words
- Imagining the whereabouts of the people whose cars are parked along the road
- Counting the number of houses on a hill
- Visiting local shops or stores, the gas station, firehouse, library, shoe repair store, or other places nearby
- Going to the nearby park to have a picnic
- Watching electrical wires being repaired

Must Places to Visit

Your Home

Children are amazed to find out you have a home other than the school. You actually have a TV, a bathroom, and a bed!

Places Their Parents Work

If at all possible, arrange for individual children to visit their parents at work. This is especially important for children in an all-day child-care program.

Behind the Counter Trips

Threes and fours, just as older children, enjoy seeing what goes on behind the scenes at stores, gas stations, bakeries, hamburger stands, or camera, paint, or photographer's studios.

A Field

Open fields for running, picking wild flowers, resting under a tree, or having a picnic make excellent places to visit.

The Homes of Neighbors

When your school or center borders on the homes and yards of neighbors, ask if you can bring the children to the yard to visit with them and ask them about their life.

The Principal's, Director's, or Religious Leader's Office

Visit the office of the person who is viewed as the authority by the children. If your center is located in a religious facility, visit the sanctuary and have the religious leader describe what happens during the services.

will you cross? How many adults will be needed to make the trip safely? Will the children need a rest stop, and where would this be?

Prepare the Children

Once you are ready for the trip, prepare the children. Children need some background information about the place they'll visit and some indication of what to look for once there. Have them list the questions they have or what they want to find out about, either dictating them to you or writing them. Have them think about the kind of behavior that will be expected both on the way to the place and during the visit. If there are restrictions on their behavior, perhaps touching equipment or talking during certain parts of the trip, you'll want to talk about these restrictions and perhaps even role play the situation. Preparation may take several days, as children role play going to the site, decide on the questions they'll ask when there, and read books or look at pictures about the place before going.

Prepare the Adults

Adults who will go with you also need careful instructions and preparation. They need to know the behavior expected of them, how the children are supposed to behave before and during the trip, where and how you'll reassemble when they arrive at the site, and other procedures for the trip. Children assigned to each adult should be carefully identified. Name tags with a type of identification for each accompanying adult are helpful.

Because you can't be with all the children at all times during the trip, share with the parents some of the points of interest you expect children to observe. Suggest questions they might ask to help children to focus their attention or give them a list of questions the children have prepared.

Prepare the people at the site. They need to know the goals of your trip and the children's interests. Let them know how long the children's attention spans are and how great their ability to understand different concepts.

Taking the Trip

Even though you've made careful plans for the trip and you, the children, and the assistants are well prepared, you must be flexible. One class on a walking field trip to the post office became so interested in observing a cherry picker and workers fixing telephone wires that they never made it to the post office. One of the parents went to the post office to inform the postal workers of the change in plans, and the trip was rescheduled.

Flexibility is necessary when using bus transportation as well. More than one trip has ended unsuccessfully because the bus driver wasn't there when expected. Have materials available to keep children productively involved if there are unexpected delays. Crayons and paper are good standbys, as are finger plays and songs.

Always consider toileting and providing for drinks of water when planning any field trip. Be sure children have used the bathroom before leaving on the trip, and check out bathroom facilities at your destination. Allowing time for toileting and drinks should be part of your plan. Carry a canteen of water and paper cups with you, as well as moist towelettes, tissue, and first-aid supplies. If at all possible, take a camera or ask a parent to bring one. Photos of the children while on the trip help children recall their experiences later.

On the trip, share the questions the children want answered with your hosts. You can help enrich the trip by giving the host a printed list of questions and things the children want to find out about.

After the Trip

Have plans ready for your arrival back at the school. Children are likely to be tired, so low-key activities are best. Allow time for children to relax and wind down before trying to talk about the trip.

Follow-up activities help children to clarify their experiences. Add appropriate equipment to the play areas that will encourage children to role play their experiences. Additional colors of paint and crayons as well as other art materials may be useful in helping children recreate their experiences. A trip to a chicken hatchery, for instance, might call for addition of yellow paints and papers, and perhaps even soft, yellow materials to the art supplies. A trip to the post office might be followed by the addition of a table with envelopes, rubber stamps, pencils, papers, and stamps, fostering post office play.

One kindergarten group requested "a really whole lot of boxes" following a trip to the hospital. From these boxes they built a miniature hospital. Their hospital rooms were well equipped and even included the physical therapy room and operating rooms.

Thank you letters to the host are a must. Not only do these promote cooperation in the community, but also they give children experience in functional writing and reading. Include information about the trip in the newsletter to the parents, letting them know how the children are using this experience in their learning.

A Reverse Field Trip

A well-planned trip into the community gives children a more in-depth understanding of their world. However, it can also be advantageous to bring community resources into the classroom. Children can take nature walks, but you can also bring in specimens for them to examine more closely. The

After the trip children can reenact their experiences.

acorns from a tree, an abandoned bird's nest or beehive, and plant life from a nearby pond all make learning within the classroom reality-based.

You can ask community representatives to visit the school as well. Fire and police departments commonly have trained representatives who will discuss safety with you and the children in the school. Plumbers might be willing to bring tools and demonstrate fixing a leaky faucet. Or a local puppeteer or theater group can recreate their art in the classroom.

Printed materials, audiovisual materials, and special models or exhibits prepared by industries or businesses in the area can also be used effectively. A local television station may have taped a special program on the community and let you play it in your school.

Prepare children for these visitors in much the same way you plan for a field trip. Provide them with background information, have them draw up questions to ask the visitor, and be sure they understand the kind of behavior they should extend to the guest who will make the visit rewarding for all. Some teachers appoint a host or hostess to greet the visitors and thank them as they leave. Role playing the situation gives children greater confidence when the time comes.

The guest also needs to be prepared in terms of understanding the children's level of interest, maturity, and excitability. One amateur archeologist visited a first-grade class with specimens of dinosaur bones found in the area. He put them on a table to display, but was horrified when the children went to handle them and began to play "dinosaurs" with them.

Bringing visitors and resources to the classroom serves to foster children's understanding of their world just as the field trip does. Both expand the children's world and introduce them to social-science concepts. So that the trip and the resource visit promote children's thinking skills and are of the highest value, find ways for children to relate the experiences from one trip to another. You might do this through questioning, providing props in the dramatic play areas, or through the use of audiovisual aids, books, or other materials. Ask the children to describe their experiences, categorize and classify them, and communicate them through drawing, painting, dancing, dictating, writing, or some other form of expression.

History

As children explore their immediate environment, key concepts from the study of history can be fostered. Through field trips, you can introduce children to the concepts of the past, change, and the continuity of life.

Change occurs right within the school. As children walk through the school, their attention can be focused on the things that change and on the immediate past. Room arrangements, decorations, art displays, and the building itself change. You can help children to recall the immediate past and to discuss the changes that occur.

Walking through the neighborhood, children can observe signs of change with the seasons or changes that people make. With each change—a house being painted, roads built, buildings renovated—you and the children can discuss what is happening, why, and how things change.

Visits to historic markers in the community, to museums, older homes, or other places of interest may be possible. Some museums will send traveling exhibits to the school.

Visiting an older person in the neighborhood can foster concepts of the past, change, and the continuity of human life. Kindergarten or primary children could interview the older person to find out the games they played and toys they liked best when they were young. Because these often are similar to the ones children enjoy today, you can help children to see that although things change, many human things—feelings, likes, dislikes—stay the same. There is a continuity to human life that children experience as they visit older people. Children might speculate on the changes that will occur as they grow. The fact that they will still be the same person, only older, will be stressed (Seefeldt & Warman, 1990).

Economics

The concepts of scarcity and plenty, the meaning of producers and consumers, and the advantages of division of labor have been identified in the field of economics education (Minneapolis Public Schools, 1967). Field trips into the community will offer children an opportunity to become aware of and explore these economic concepts.

Although they will not have developed a complete understanding of producer and consumer until after age twelve or so (Bent & Bombi, 1988), children become aware of the meaning of being a consumer by going to stores to make purchases. If children are producing something together, perhaps a playhouse or police car, a trip can be taken to a hardware store to purchase needed supplies. Groups of children will be given responsibility for one purchase. One group can purchase nails, another the wood siding. In this way, children become aware of the relationship between consumer and producer because they play both roles.

Other trips can be taken to doctors, dentists, or to the library so children become aware of the fact that people produce services as well as goods. With primary age children, you can discuss how people pay for the doctor, dentist, librarian, or teacher. It's difficult for children to conceive of service providers as receiving a salary.

When children are consumers, they must make choices. Knowing what things they want and which they need helps them to make wise decisions. Many times during the school day, as children are given choices, teachers might remind the children to ask themselves if this is something they want or really need. "Which things are necessary?" "Is this something you really must have or just want?"

Geography

Location is one of the major concepts identified by the Joint Committee on Geographic Education and the National Council for Geographic Education for study by young children (Fromboluti, 1991). Concepts of location go hand in hand with concepts of direction. Children will use directions to locate themselves in space and to locate their homes and school. Beginning with trips taken within the school building, ask children to do the following:

- Walk to the cafeteria or office and tell how they would locate their room from this point in the school.
- Take a walk around the school building to find the signs and numbers that tell where things are located. Have them look for signs and symbols on streets and buildings.
- Go outside, cross the street, or walk far enough from the school so children can view the entire building. Ask children to locate their room from

this viewpoint. Or have them point out the office, director's office, or other parts of the building.

- Locate stores and other landmarks in the neighborhood in relation to the school. Take a walk to the park, or any nearby place of interest. Draw a simple map to follow and have children note the signs and landmarks that tell them where they are as they walk along.

Maps are one tool people use to locate themselves and others on the earth. Maps, however, are an abstraction of reality and constitute an extremely complex idea for children. Nevertheless, by using maps in connection with field trips, children's awareness of maps and their use can be fostered.

Attitudes and Values

The democracy of an early childhood program supports and fosters the attitudes and values of equality and respect for others. It seems that, for the egocentric young child, the fostering of these attitudes and values begins with a focus on development of the attitude of respect for self. Without first respecting oneself, it seems unlikely that one can respect others.

The democracy of an early childhood program supports respect for all.

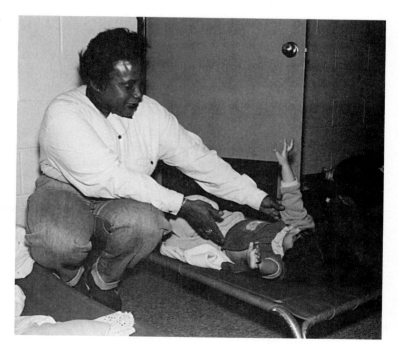

The idea that respect and love for others begins with first learning to love yourself stems from the Bible and the Talmud. The biblical command to love your neighbor as yourself suggests that in order to love your neighbor, one must first develop love of self. The Talmudic sage Hillel questions, "If I am not for myself, who is for me; and being for my own self, what am I? If not now, when?"

A child's self-concept, or self-image, is the foundation on which she or he will build all future relationships with others and the world. The more adequate children feel about themselves, the better able they are to reach out and relate to others and to feel a sense of oneness with people and the things in their world. Permeating the entire early childhood program will be concern for fostering a sense of self-worth, dignity, and a healthy self-concept in each child. From this base, children learn to relate with others and gain knowledge of their world.

Fostering a Good Self-Concept

The enhancement of *self-concept* is a valued goal of education. Although the words are not strictly synonymous, self-esteem, self-concept, and self-image can be broadly defined as a person's perceptions of self. It is formed by experiences with and interpretations of one's environment. It is something that is greatly influenced by others (Shavelson & Bolus, 1982). Although definitions of self-concept vary, Shavelson and Bolus describe it as:

- Having an organization or structure. People categorize vast amounts of information about themselves and relate categories to one another.
- Multifaceted—particular facets reflect the category system adopted by a particular individual or that shared by a group.
- Hierarchical—moving from the development of a perception of behavior to inferences about one's self.
- Generally stable—as children grow, the self becomes increasingly situation specific and somewhat less stable (in school I'm a good reader, at home I'm the baby sister).
- Growing in complexity from childhood to adulthood.
- Consisting of both a descriptive (I have brown hair and eyes) and an evaluative component (I am good).
- Something that is different from such constructs as cognition, intelligence, and creativity.

The Physical Self

How our bodies move and interact with objects, how we think we look, and the kinds of things we can do with our physical bodies, all influence our self-concept. Self-awareness is thought to have its origin when infants begin to discover themselves as physical beings, separate from the rest of the environment. The seemingly aimless flinging about of babies' arms and hands is believed to be attempts to determine the boundaries of physical self and the environment. Sensations of cold, hunger, and warmth all work together to help infants learn about body and self. During the entire sensorimotor period, children use their bodies to learn more about the physical self. Recognizing the importance of children's perceptions of their physical self for the development of a good self-concept, you might:

- Take photos of children for scrapbooks, bulletin boards, or gifts.
- Provide full-length, magnifying, and hand mirrors for children to see themselves. Give them feedback as they observe themselves: "You have black hair and eyes," "Look at your shoulders," or "You're growing each day, look how tall you are."
- Play games that emphasize body parts, such as "Looby Loo" or "Simon Says" as well as using movement exploration activities.
- Make booklets or charts of activities children can do. A booklet called "I Can Run" could begin with the main sentence, "I can run . . ." that serves as a base for other pages, such as "I can run quickly," "I can run on tiptoe," or "I can run with my hands in the air." Children dictate the text and illustrate the pages.

Understanding, accepting, and having a clear sense of self include gender identity, gender role, and sexual orientation. Gender identity is believed necessary in order for children to make sense of their world. Once children construct a stable gender identity, they develop gender-appropriate values and standards. Some theorists use the Freudian social learning and cognitive developmental view of how children learn psychosexual identification.

In the Freudian framework, a boy's desire for his mother leads to fear of the father's retaliation, then to identification with the father, and finally to sex-typed identity. Social learning theory sees the boy's attachment to the father stemming from the fact that the father is the major rewarder and punisher-controller of behavior. After attachment, the boy identifies with and models his father and takes on a sex-typed identity.

Cognitive theorists believe gender identity begins as children develop categories, or concepts, for the words *male* and *female*. Once the concept has been developed, children begin to model the parent of the same sex: Boys take after their fathers and girls after their mothers.

Gender identity seems a necessary stage of development. Stereotyping on the basis of sex, however, is inappropriate. Teachers are powerful reinforcers of stereotypes. They have been found to interact with girls in ways that differ from their interactions with boys, which leads to the perpetuation of stereotyping and negates development of a positive self-image for both sexes (Sheldon, 1990).

Observing nursery school teachers, Serbin and O'Leary (1975) found that boys were valued for what they would be and girls for what they would give. Girls seems to be aware of their lower status and tried harder to please and to be attentive and well behaved; boys, however, were rewarded more for their potential than their good behavior.

Serbin and O'Leary (1975) have also observed that teachers interact with boys and girls differently. They found that teachers rewarded girls for dependent behaviors, repeatedly paying attention to girls who clung to them, stood near them, or waited for directions. At the same time, the teachers praised boys for the tasks they did on their own and for being independent.

Teachers have also been found to challenge boys to try harder and to repeat tasks in order to achieve mastery. Perhaps this is because boys weren't as neat in their work or too obedient. Girls, on the other hand, were never challenged toward greater achievement. This challenge differential may be related to women in our society having achieved far less than men in many fields. Fewer than 18 percent of all doctorates awarded in our nation go to women. Teachers of young children might ask, "Could it be that women achieve less in our society because they aren't being rewarded for their achievement in school, are not being challenged, or not asked to try harder?"

Girls, because of this type of differential treatment, may become alienated from themselves and distrustful of their own intuitions and affirmations. They learn to fit themselves into the mold of society, and as adults, may know something is wrong, but "will continue their anxieties by continuing to settle for the security of society's prevailing patterns" (Riley, 1984, p. 16).

The Psychological Self

We know ourselves as physical beings, but self-esteem involves more than recognition of the physical body. It also deals with self-knowledge, self-perception, and our attitudes and emotions. Bem (1972) believes we know ourselves only indirectly as we interpret events and others, and as we follow our emotions and attitudes.

Emotions.   As children grow and mature, their emotions grow. Emotions proceed through a series of stages from the infant's relatively undifferentiated emotional responses to what is termed emotional maturity. By the age of three months, infants seem to be able to differentiate between distress and delight, and by two years of age a child can express a full range of emotions, including fear, disgust, anger, jealousy, distress, delight, elation, and affection.

Children, like adults, have ways of handling emotions and expressing feelings. In an early childhood setting, children learn new ways of expressing emotions and feelings that are socially accepted and will not interfere with their own or others' learning. Help children develop an understanding of their emotions by:

1. Recognizing and naming their feelings
2. Understanding and accepting them
3. Helping them to find wholesome outlets for their feelings

Attitudes.   Attitudes and values are another part of the psychological self. Our attitudes are believed to influence how we feel about something and to affect the way we respond, behave, and act. An opinion is simply a verbal expression of belief, but attitudes imply an emotional liking or disliking of something.

Everything in an early childhood program is bound up in and influenced by attitudes and values. Even the very act of attending school reflects our attitude toward education. Because attitudes and values are a part of the school situation, you have the responsibility to help children understand and clarify their attitudes and beliefs. Asking children the following questions is believed helpful in promoting self-understanding (Raths, 1962, p. 35).

- Are you glad you feel that way?
- Have you thought of any other ways of doing that?
- Have you felt this way for some time?
- What are some examples of what you have in mind?
- What are some things that are good about the way you feel?
- Is this idea so good that everyone should feel the same way?
- Who else do you know that feels that way?

Making choices and decisions fosters an understanding of one's attitudes and belief systems. "One of the major responsibilities of adults is to give children freedom to learn from their own experiences and to shoulder the consequences of making choices" (Riley, 1984, p. 7). As children weigh the alternatives involved in making choices, they are learning something about themselves and developing a psychological understanding of self.

Children's names are very much a part of the psychological self. Allport (1958) believes "the sense of self depends on more than the bodily me" and that self-concepts depend heavily on labels for self and others. By the second year of life, children are beginning to use their name in reference to themselves and their possessions.

> The most important linguistic aid of all is the child's own name. He hears it constantly. "Where is Johnny's nose? Where are Johnny's eyes? Good Johnny." By hearing his name repeatedly, the child gradually sees himself as a distinct and recurrent point of reference. (Goodman, 1976, p. 26)

Each child entering a school group needs to feel the sense of self that comes when others use his or her name. Teachers who call children by name are helping them to differentiate self from group, as well as to integrate individuals into the group. The name lets children sense their distinctiveness, helping them establish their independent status within the group and at the same time permitting entry into it.

Children model a teacher's use of names. Gentle reminders to children to use each other's names as they play or in conversations is appropriate. "This is Taro," "Juan didn't know you were talking to him. Use his name so he'll know you mean him."

Children enjoy singing name songs like "Here Is a Friend," "Get on Board," and "Mary Wore a Red Dress." Occasionally substituting children's names for those of characters in stories, poems, or songs also gives children knowledge of the importance of their names and their presence within the group.

Some teachers make a class booklet at the beginning of school. They take a photo of each child, paste it in the scrapbook, and label the picture with the child's name. Five- and six-year-olds can be given ditto masters and asked to draw a picture of themselves on the sheet. Depending on the children's skills, the teachers or the children can write their names under the picture. The ditto masters are then run off and stapled together to form booklets that each child gets.

Other teachers make a mural of children's photos and names titled "We Are in Room 1." Experience stories about each child in the class can be written. Place a photo of the child along with a story dictated or written by the child on a wall chart. The charts decorate the hallway or the room.

The use of names alone, however, will not create a strong self-concept. Showing respect for the individuality of children and others through the use of names fosters only the beginnings of self-esteem and confidence. This is followed by permitting children to express individuality, making choices about what and how they will learn, whom they will learn it with, and finding freedom to express their own ideas, attitudes, and emotions through play, art, literature, and movement.

Fostering Respect for Others

When children are valued and respected within the democracy of an early childhood program, they are able to respect others, both those who are similar to themselves and those who differ. America is truly a nation of many cultures. The different cultural groups that have made up our nation have not blended into one, but have survived and remained to enrich and beautify our lives (Hornbeck, 1984). We need to teach children to embrace and value the many cultures that make up our nation not only for their beauty, but because "we can't afford the cost in terms of human potential that any other course would demand" (Hornbeck, 1984).

The general goals of multicultural education are to develop an understanding of and appreciation for all racial, ethnic, and cultural groups. Specific goals are to provide information on:

Valued and respected, children value and respect each other.

- The history and culture of racial, ethnic, and cultural groups in the community, the nation, and the world
- Historical events, situations, and conflicts—interpretations of these from diverse ethnic perspectives
- The contributions that racial, ethnic, and cultural groups have made to the development of American civilization
- The social and economic conditions that racial, ethnic, and cultural groups have experienced and continue to experience in the United States
- The nature of racism, bias, and prejudice as these affect the behavior and experience of racial, ethnic, and cultural groups (Maryland State Department of Education, 1980, p. 5)

Multicultural education, with its broad and specific goals, "requires that the total school environment be changed so that students from diverse ethnic and racial groups will experience educational equality" (Banks, 1982, p. 592). At the same time, children learn specific information about other groups and begin to value diversity. Because such learning cannot be accomplished with a separate subject matter curriculum, an infusion model has been suggested. These goals are consciously incorporated, or infused, into the total curriculum. Education that is multicultural should not be an

> add on to an already overcrowded curriculum. Rather, it should be an on-going, ever-present attempt to promote among our students a recognition and understanding of the similarities and differences among people. A sense of self-esteem and a genuine respect for other individuals and groups are encouraged at all times. (Curriculum and Instruction/Charles County Public Schools, 1984)

Developmental Stages

An understanding of how children develop concepts of other cultural, ethnic, and racial groups is necessary in order to infuse a multicultural curriculum into the total program. Children form concepts of others in the same way they form concepts of their own group. Lambert and Klineberg's study (1967) provides the most complete explanation of how children learn about others. From their study of children in a number of different nations, Lambert and Klineberg concluded that the manner in which the concept of "own group" is taught has important consequences. The process of establishing this concept apparently produces an exaggerated and caricatured view of one's own nation and people. The stereotyping process appears to start in the early concepts children develop of their own group; children do not begin stereotyping foreign peoples until age ten.

Early training in national contrasts appears to:

- Make certain foreign groups outstanding examples of peoples who are different.
- Give children the impression that foreign people are different, strange, and unfriendly. Children stressed the differences of foreigners, which suggests an overall orientation of suspicion.
- Affect children's self-concepts. Children in some nations think of themselves in racial, religious, or national terms. Self-concepts of certain groups of children reflect what Lambert and Klineberg (1967) presume to be the culturally significant criteria used in their training to make distinctions between their own group and others.

The study made clear that parents and other significant people in the child's environment transfer their own emotionally colored view of others to the child. Significant others seem to assign specific attributes to members of particular groups during the period of cognitive development when the child has not fully differentiated one group from another or his own group from others.

Children's self-concepts, the way they are taught about others, and their parents and significant others who do the teaching are all important factors in children's gaining international understanding. In planning to teach young children, it is critical to know that the child will naturally recognize the focus on people's differences more easily than on their similarities.

Significant Others

"Let's begin with ourselves" (Pellowski, 1969). Teachers, as well as children, bring to their classrooms a decided set of values, attitudes, and understandings. Before attempting to teach multicultural education, you must first examine your own understandings, feelings, and attitudes.

Many Americans believe, rather chauvinistically, that our country is superior to all others. Perhaps children have picked up these attitudes before they enter the classroom. You must try to show children why this attitude is not necessarily accurate. Ask yourself:

- What have I read from each country? Did this reading present an accurate point of view? Was it current? Was it written by someone of that nationality?
- Am I familiar with any of the country's films? What do I know of the art of the country? Have I read a current novel?
- What do I know of the religious customs of the country? The government? The economy? Is my current information up-to-date? Is it free from stereotypes?
- Are my background materials relevant to the culture as a whole, or do they represent just one portion of the people?
- Have I talked to anyone who is a native of the country or who has lived there for some length of time? (Pellowski, 1969)

Focus on Similarities

You should always try to focus on similarities rather than differences among people. Very young children are able to identify differences and begin to stereotype others by focusing on them. Therefore it seems feasible to begin by focusing on the similarities among people everywhere, regardless of culture.

People the world over are alike in many ways. Children who understand the similarities among people are able to move to recognizing the uniqueness of each cultural group without fear, distrust, or stereotyping. In all cultures, people have the following features, although the specifics vary:

- Art forms
- Group rules
- Social organization
- Needs for food, shelter, clothing, and other materials
- Language

Art Forms.   Children who are encouraged to create their own poetry, paintings, dance, literature, or crafts can readily understand and appreciate the art of others. Art from all nations helps children discover people's common heritage. Children can:

• Visit museums and display art from all over the world
• Begin an exchange of their paintings, drawings, or creative writing with a school in another country
• Invite visitors to tell folktales from their nations and compare the tales with those of the United States
• Listen to poetry from other lands—perhaps some haiku from Japan—and dictate or write their own

The visual arts and music allow for personal expression, communication, and tangible achievement without depending on words. They provide a comfortable means for valuing similarities among peoples, as well as for recognizing the uniqueness of groups. As you study the art of other nations, compare it with the art of the children, artworks of others, and art products unique to cultures of America.

Group Rules.   As children begin to realize that rules are necessary to live together effectively, they can understand how groups function more successfully when the rights of each group member are recognized. Children who can establish their own rules for using playground equipment or for behaviors in the classroom are beginning to learn that people everywhere use a system of rules.

The school has rules as well. Children in the primary grades may relate the rules of their school to those of their classroom, home, and community. Perhaps the rules of the city, state, and nation can be identified and related to children's experiences with school rules. The fact that all people everywhere have rules can be pointed out.

Social Organizations.   Although family and social group composition changes dramatically from place to place, all human beings live in some type of group or social organization. To comprehend similarities among social groups, children in the primary grades can:

• Graph their families' composition to show how many different kinds of family units are represented in their classroom. You'll want to point out how all units are, at the same time, similar and different.
• Exchange letters with a family in some other nation to learn how the family is the same as their own family.
• Invite some visitors from other countries to tell about their own families, the activities family members do together, and how they share work or celebrate holidays.

Similar Needs.   People have similar needs. The universal needs for food, shelter, clothing, and other materials can be introduced. Explore the things children in the kindergarten or primary grades need to live.

- Have them draw a picture of the house they live in. Classify the pictures by type of home. Discuss the need for homes. Find pictures of homes in other places. Avoid stereotyping by making certain these homes represent current living conditions as well as the variety of homes found in any given country.
- Make booklets titled "Things My Family Needs." Compare children's booklets. Relate these needs and wants to those of people in other countries.
- Discuss the foods children like to eat, why they eat, and find out what foods children would like to try. What foods do they eat on special occasions? Chart them and trace these preferences to the children's cultural, ethnic, or racial background.
- Everyone needs clothing. Discuss clothing children need and clothing they would like to have. Find out how people dress in different parts of our nation, such as Florida, Alaska, or in the Southwest. Find out how people dress in other nations and why. Again, be certain not to stereotype groups. Present current, factual representations of clothing, not only clothing worn in the past, such as wooden shoes from Holland or kimonos from Japan.

Language.   People everywhere communicate verbally and nonverbally. Children can learn that both verbal and nonverbal communication skills are involved as they express feelings, ideas, attitudes, and knowledge. Verbal communication may involve many different languages; nonverbal communication is useful when you do not understand the verbal communication of others. Children can be given many opportunities to communicate in the classroom on a one-to-one basis or in large or small groups. Methods might include using a telephone or tape recorder or dictating to you. Draw children's attention to the use of nonverbal communication and extend the concept by introducing sign language, role playing, and dramatizations.

Listen to someone speaking another language. You, a visitor, or one of the children might teach a few phrases of the language. The children might learn a simple folk song using the language or listen to songs sung in another language.

By emphasizing the things that bind people together and helping children see the similarities that exist among all people regardless of culture, you introduce them to the multicultural nature of the world. As children learn about their own country, they also learn about other countries and cultures. A child's self-concept, as well as the attitudes and values of significant others, plays an important role in developing multicultural understandings.

With a strong sense of self, children are ready to live with others.

Skills

The entire early childhood program and curriculum is designed to foster children's social skills and ability to participate in a democratic society. With a strong self-concept, children are ready to develop the skills of communicating, sharing, cooperating, and participating in a social group.

Social Skills

Children who have a strong sense of self are ready to learn to live with others. The ability to communicate is basic to living and working with others.

> Men live in a community [by] virtue of the things they have in common, and communication is the way in which they come to possess things in common. Without communication to insure the participation in a common understanding to secure similar emotional and intellectual dispositions, there could be no community, no group with which to relate. (Dewey, 1944, p. 7)

Communicating

Not all communication is verbal. Children are quick to read one another's emotions, feelings, and attitudes through nonverbal means of communication. One kindergartner was overheard telling another, "Don't be scared, I've been there before. It's O.K., it just smells funny" as they walked through the hall on the way to visit the engineer's room. No one had said a word about being frightened, but as the children descended into the dark basement, surrounded by strange smells and sounds, one child sensed another was afraid of the unknown.

Communication demands the ability to put oneself into the role of another. Social communication is based on this ability and requires:

• An understanding that there is a perspective other than one's own, and that not everyone sees, feels, or thinks alike

Children are expected to have emotions and express them.

- A realization that an analysis of another's perspective would be useful
- The ability to carry out the analysis as necessary
- Knowledge of how to translate the results of analysis into effective social behavior: that is, in terms of getting along better with persons whose viewpoints are under consideration (Flavell, 1979)

These abilities grow and develop with time, maturity, and practice. Dramatic play offers children experiences with taking on the role of another. In it, children act as if they were the mother, baby, father, or teacher. Other experiences can be arranged to give children the idea that successful communication requires knowledge of other's viewpoints. Direct teaching isn't profitable, but you can:

- Help children connect their own feelings with the actions and things they're involved in. When opportunities arise, you can ask them, "How did you feel then?" "What made you so angry?" "What made you so happy?"
- Communicate to children your understanding of the context of their experiences. "You feel angry now, because . . ." "You're happy because . . ." "I think Booketee is sad because . . ."
- Suggest problems for children that they can solve through role play: "What if you're waiting for your turn on the slide, and . . ."

Sharing

Learning to communicate is, in part, learning to share. Children communicate by sharing ideas, taking turns listening and speaking, and sharing their time and interests. Learning to share is an important goal of the preschool and primary classroom, because children begin to realize that the welfare of society depends on the willingness of its members to share.

Everyone finds it a little difficult to share because it means you must give up some of your ideas, interests, and time, as well as sacrificing something of yourself for the good of others. Before children can share, they must first feel secure. If children have enough for themselves—whether it is attention, security, love, or toys—they are better able to share with others.

Most sharing occurs when there are small groups of children and high teacher- or adult-child ratios. Small groups allow for:

- More teacher-child interaction, which appears to let children know they are valued and respected and helps to eliminate unnecessary frustrations.
- Increased recognition. Children can share their ideas and feelings more readily in smaller groups. They have more opportunities to participate in activities such as taking the lunch money to the office, carrying the flag, or having the teacher read their story.
- The development of feelings of social adequacy. When children are just learning to relate with others, large groups may produce feelings of inad-

equacy. But children will usually find it easy to handle small numbers of others and will feel more adequate and competent (Ladd, 1990).

Models.   As early as 1937, Murphy observed that in preschool groups where teachers are noticeably spontaneous, warm, and responsive, children show more sympathy and understanding toward one another. Prescott, Jones, and Kritchevsky (1967) found that teachers who deliberately try to respond to children's needs serve as models for behavior. Further evidence suggests that more sharing takes place in groups where the teachers make the effort to work closely with individuals and to help individual children enter into social groups.

Direct Teaching.   At times, direct instruction in sharing might be used. Some teachers have children practice sharing by using dolls in role-playing situations that may arise in the group. Giving children a doll, you might say, "Pretend both of the dolls want the car. What will they do?" Information on how to go about taking turns and informing another of your intentions and desires can be communicated as the children play with their dolls.

Cooperating

Cooperating is another skill that means becoming less egocentric, so that you give something of yourself and become less concerned about yourself and more about the welfare of the group. Guidance and support in learning to cooperate are necessary as children balance the task of developing a strong sense of self with learning to become a member of the group. Not all cooperation is democratic. When individuals lose too much of themselves to follow the will of the group, democracy isn't the end result. Democratic cooperation means that an individual's desire to be with others and belong to a group is integrated with the desire to retain individuality. Reinforcement, lessening competition, and planning group activities all work to foster the behaviors associated with cooperation (Kemple, 1991).

Reinforcement.   Children will be more cooperative when they are rewarded. Weingold and Webster (1964) asked two groups of children to work on a mural. In one group, each child was rewarded for the group product. In the other, children were told that only the child doing the best job would receive the reward. In the first group there was an increase in friendly, cooperative behaviors and peer interactions; in the other group, less attention was given to the product, and boasting and other depreciating behaviors increased.

Eliminating Competition.   Competition is the opposite of cooperation. In many classrooms, competition is fostered because of the belief that it's good for children and consistent with the values of our society. Competition is natural, but it can destroy cooperation, and it is especially damaging to children's self-identity in a group. To encourage cooperative behaviors, you can reduce competition. You might:

- Play games without winners or losers
- Continue to recognize and reinforce children for their individuality
- Ask each child to take part in special tasks
- Compliment and reward children for cooperative actions
- Model cooperative behaviors

Participating in a Democracy

From the base of social interactions in the classroom, children learn to value participation in a democratic society. The ability to be responsible for oneself and to participate fully in the welfare of a group is an asset in any society, but in a democratic society, it is a requirement for citizenship. The disposition to work for the common good and to participate in joint efforts begins early.

For young children, under the age of seven or eight, participation begins as they assume responsibility for themselves. Rooms for three- and four-year-olds are arranged not only to permit but also to promote children to take responsibility for their own dressing, toileting, and washing. These very young children may begin to assume responsibility for others and the group by joining in small groups for brief discussions, to dictate thank you notes or other letters, or to listen to stories and sing songs together. With adult assistance, three- and four-year-olds can participate in setting tables, serving food, clearing up after play and work, or caring for plants and animals that belong to the group.

Early on, children without disabilities learn to participate in enabling children with special needs to function fully in the group. In one group of four-year-olds, Kathy, a girl with spina bifida, received regular and casual help from her classmates who did not have special needs. They handed her crutches to her, helped her on with her coat, carried things for her, and waited patiently for her as they played together.

Over the age of five or six, children participate in other group activities. They can plan together and divide up responsibilities. Sharing ideas, children in the primary grades are able to solve problems and make plans for their own learning. Children who are given responsibilities they can fulfill within the group are learning to participate in a democratic society. Experiences with voting and following the will of the majority give children opportunities to experience democracy in action.

With very young children, everyone can have her or his own way. For example, children can vote to make either gelatin or pudding, with each group being allowed to make and then eat what they choose. Or the class may be divided for games, those voting for "Simon Says" playing in one area of the room, and those for "Looby Loo" in another area. After a number of experiences with voting, the entire class may follow the will of the majority.

Learning to live and participate within the group means setting rules and following them. Children should take part in establishing rules in the class. They can contribute to the rules for woodworking, block building, use of the bathroom and water tables, and so forth.

Other rules are made for children, and children learn to value them as well. Everyone must participate in a fire drill, for example. Because there is little opportunity for them to contribute to the rules of the drill, the children can use this occasion to discuss why it is important to follow certain rules, why rules are made, who makes them, and how they are made. Children can also become aware of other rules they must follow: the traffic laws, rules for riding the bus, and rules for home. These questions might be discussed: "What would happen if no one followed the rules?" "Do you think everyone should obey traffic rules?" "Why?"

Experiencing rules and discussing the purposes for them can help children realize that rules are made to protect them and others. Children should also realize that they have the responsibility to follow the rules, to make rules that are needed for living within a group, to change rules that no longer function to protect them or others, and to adjust the rules to fit changing situations.

Children's ideas should continually be moving toward conventional knowledge.

Children should be moving from:

- Perceiving rules as coming from "on high"
- Thinking of rules as unchanging
- Perceiving people as powerless before the law
- Being egocentric, self-centered, and indifferent to others

Children should be moving to:

- Knowing that rules and laws are established by people
- Realizing that rules and laws are always changing
- Understanding that they have control over their own lives
- Being empathic, socially responsible, and considerate of others

Valuing Democracy

The knowledge, attitudes, and skills of the social studies prepare children to take their place as productive citizens of a democratic society. In an early childhood program, however, children are not just preparing to become members of a democracy, but they also are citizens of the democratic society of the classroom and school. Within the democratic environment of the early childhood program, children practice principles of democracy. Daily they contribute to building and fostering a democratic society, and daily they receive the benefits of belonging to this society.

Through every experience in the program, young children learn that they are worthy, valued, and respected. They know that their individual needs and wants will be met and that their rights to freedom of speech and pursuit of happiness and other rights will be protected. At the same time, they are learning to expand their concerns and give up some of their egocentrism for the good of others and the group. As members of a democratic community, children develop a sense of shared concern, recognizing that their interests overlap with the interests of others and that their welfare is inextricably entwined with the welfare of others.

It is the teacher who establishes and maintains the basic principles of democracy in the classroom. The way the teacher establishes control, deals with individual children and their interactions with one another, and teaches sends a powerful message to children about the values of a democracy. Although there is no one right or wrong way for a teacher to do this, when observing in a democratic classroom, one immediately becomes aware of how teachers actively support individual worth and dignity while at the same time protect and nurture the welfare of the total group. In a democratic group, certain tenets are consistently followed:

1. *Teachers share control.* Teachers do not give orders and expect children to follow their directions blindly. Rather than emphasizing the task or skill to be learned, teachers focus on how children are feeling, reacting, and interacting with one another.

2. *Children make choices.* Instead of the teacher prescribing work to be done, how, and under what time constraints, children make choices about what they will learn, how, and with whom. Cookbook approaches, filling in the blanks, and following prescribed lesson plans are replaced with centers of interest, learning stations, and other materials for children to explore and use as tools for learning. Rather than solo learning, group work and projects are fostered.

3. *Discipline is firm and consistent, but does not revolve around force, coercion, or threat.* Already believing that rules come from authority and that being good means following orders, children need to participate in setting and following rules and begin the long process of being able to separate intent from action.

4. *Freedom of thought and speech are fostered.* Children are expected to have opinions and express them. This expectation governs every area of the curriculum. Instead of giving children duplicated sheets to color or patterns to trace around for art, children are asked to express their own ideas, thoughts, and feelings in drawings, paintings, or their constructions. In language arts, they are asked to discuss, write, and express what they know and feel and how to make choices about how they will learn math and science skills.

5.   *Children are never overwhelmed by the power of others.* Teachers are not power figures in the classroom, nor do they permit individual children to govern through power assertions, bullying, or threats.

6.   *A sense of community is built.* A classroom is a group of individuals. The teacher develops this group into a community by helping children share goals. Even young children can begin to see that they are a part of, and share in, the common goals of their family, their own group of friends, the class, and the school. Not only are children encouraged to see themselves within the context of the total group, but small groups within the total group are fostered (Au & Kawakami, 1991).

7.   *Teachers model respect for others.* A teacher who cares about and respects each child in the group and each adult who works with the children serves as a model for the children. Teachers model and encourage mutual respect. They let children know in a number of very explicit ways that each person is respected and cared for.

8.   *Teachers elicit respectful, caring behaviors from the children.* Teachers model respect and caring for other children but they also teach children how to care for and respect others.

Summary

The social studies, that part of the curriculum concerned with the study of people and their interactions with others and the environment, transmits a culture or way of life to the young. Through social studies, children begin to develop the self-understanding that will serve as a foundation for learning about others and the world.

Children gain knowledge of social studies as they live, grow, and experience. Developmentally, learning about self, others, and the world go hand in hand. Interactions with others provide knowledge of self. And these interactions promote knowledge of the world and one's place in it.

A child's self-image or self-concept is the foundation on which she or he will build all future relationships with others and the world. The more adequate children feel about themselves, the better able they are to reach out and relate to others and to feel a sense of oneness with people and the things in their world. Permeating the entire early childhood program will be concern for fostering a sense of self-worth, dignity, and a healthy self-concept in each child. From this base, children learn to relate with others and gain knowledge of their world.

Projects

Continuing Case Study

Observe your case study child interacting with others. What evidence of cooperation, communication, and sharing do you note? How do the ages of the other children relate to any differences in the way your child interacts with others?

Now complete your case study. You should have records of your child's interactions with all areas of the curriculum in a variety of situations. Taking the information on self-concept in this chapter and your records, can you make some judgments about the educational status of the child? How does the child feel about himself or herself? What are the child's strengths in relating with others, both children and adults? Which are his or her favorite subjects? What can she or he do best? What areas are weak? If you were to teach this child, what educational plan would you develop in order for him or her to reach full potential?

1. Write to embassies of different countries requesting free materials that present current information about the country. You can get embassy addresses from your school or public library. Some of the material will be appropriate to use with young children; some will be useful for you as you build your own understanding of other countries.
2. Begin a resource file of children's games from around the world. Teach one game to a small group of children, explaining the origin of the game. I. Vinton's book *Folkways Omnibus of Children's Games* (New York: Stackpole, 1970) is one resource for games from around the world.
3. Within the classroom, college, or university, many nationalities and ethnic groups will be represented. Interview someone from a culture other than yours. Ask what elements of the culture he or she would like children to understand and how this could best be presented to children.

4. Plan a lesson to develop social skills for a group of six-year-olds. If possible, try your lesson out with a group of children.

Children's Books

Analyze materials for use with children to be certain they reflect the many groups in our nation in a balanced way. For instance, if girls or women are presented as passive in one story, balance this with a story of girls or women who are active, aggressive, and forceful. Find books that accurately represent minorities and the multiethnic composition of our nation. Remember that minorities comprise many different cultures that can be found in books. For instance, blacks may be portrayed in the culture of the inner city, suburbs, Africa, Caribbean Islands, or the rural South.

This list of books offers an indication of the resources available that do not omit, distort, or present with a lack of sensitivity any group of people, and that reflect the pluralistic nature of our culture and the world.

Historical

Anno, M. (1978). *Anno's journey*. New York: Philomel.

Brenner, B. (1978). *Wagon wheels*. Illustrated by Don Bolognese. New York: Harper & Row.

Clifton, L. (1973). *All of us come across the water*. Illustrated by John Steptoe. New York: Harper & Row.

Fritz, J. (1973). *And then what happened, Paul Revere?* Illustrated by Margot Tomas. New York: Coward-McCann.

Fritz, J. (1980). *Where do you think you're going, Christopher Columbus?* Illustrated by Margot Tomas. New York: Putnam.

Goodall, J. (1979). *The story of an English village*. New York: Atheneum.

Gray, G. (1978). *How far Felipe?* Illustrated by Ann Grifalconi. New York: Harper & Row.

Haley, G. E. (1973). *Jack Jourett's ride*. New York: Viking.

Hall, D. (1983). *Ox cart man*. Illustrated by Barbara Cooney. New York: Viking.

Houston, G. (1992). *My Great-Aunt Arizona*. Illustrated by S. C. Lamb. New York: Harper-Collins.

Lankford, M. D. (1992). *Hopscotch around the world*. Illustrated by K. Milone. New York: Morrow.

Lobel, A. (1971). *On the day Peter Stuyvesant sailed into town*. New York: Harper & Row.

Provensen, A., & Provensen, M. (1983). *The glorious flight: Across the channel with Louis Berliot*. New York: Viking.

Rylant, C. (1982). *When I was young in the mountains*. Illustrated by Diane Goode. New York: Dutton.

Sandin, J. (1981). *The long way to a new land*. New York: Harper & Row.

Spier, P. (1973). *The Star-Spangled Banner*. New York: Doubleday.

Spier, P. (1981). *The legend of New Amsterdam*. New York: Harper & Row.

African American

Bang, M. (1983). *Ten, nine, eight*. New York: Greenwillow.

Carew, J. (1980). *Children of the sun*. Illustrated by Leo Dillon & Diane Dillon. Boston: Little, Brown.

Clifton, L. (1979). *The lucky stone*. Illustrated by Dale Payson. New York: Delacorte.

Everett, G. (1991). *Li'l Sis and Uncle Willie*. Illustrated by W. H. Johnson. New York: Rizzoli.

Jaquith, P. (1981). *Bo Rabbit smart for true: Folktales from the Gullah*. Illustrated by Ed Young. New York: Philomel.

Jordan, J. (1975). *New life: New room*. Illustrated by Ray Cruz. New York: Crowell.

Mathias, S. B. (1975). *The hundred penny box*. Illustrated by Leo Dillon & Diane Dillon. New York: Viking.

Musgrove, M. (1976). *Ashanti to Zulu*. Illustrated by Leo Dillon & Diane Dillon. New York: Dial.

Scott, A. (1967). *Sam*. Illustrated by Symeon Shimin. New York: McGraw.

Steptoe, J. (1966). *Stevie*. New York: Harper & Row.

Ward, L. (1978). *I am Eyes Ni Macho*. Illustrated by Nonny Hogrogian. New York: Greenwillow.

Asian

Estes, E. (1978). *The lost umbrella of Kim Chu*. Illustrated by Jacqueline Ayer. New York: Atheneum.

Hoyt-Goldsmith, D. (1992). *Hoang Anh, a Vietnamese-American Boy*. Illustrated by L. Migdale. New York: Holiday.

Mosel, A. (1976). *The funny little woman*. Illustrated by Blair Lent. New York: Scribner's.

Pattison, D. (1991). *The river dragon*. Illustrated by Jean & Mou-sien Tseng. New York: Lothrop.

Uchida, Y. (1976). *The rooster who understood Japanese*. Illustrated by Charles Robinson. New York: Scribner's.

Yagawa, S. (1981). *The crane wife*. Illustrated by Suekichi Akaba. (Trans. Katherine Patterson). New York: Morrow.

Yashima, T. (1953). *The village tree*. New York: Viking.

Yashima, T. (1955). *Crow boy*. New York: Viking.

Yolen, J. (1977). *The seeing stick*. Illustrated by Remy Charlip & Demetra Maraslis. New York: Crowell.

Hispanic

Aardema, V. (1979). *The riddle of the drum: A tale from Tizapan, Mexico*. Illustrated by Tony Chen. New York: Four Winds.

Behrens, J. (1978). *Fiesta!* Photographs by Scott Taylor. Chicago: Children's.

de Paola, T. (1980). *The lady of Guadalupe*. New York: Holiday.

Mohr, N. (1979). *Felita*. Illustrated by Ray Cruz. New York: Dial.

Politi, L. (1978). *The nicest gift*. New York: Scribner's.

Sonnebon, R. (1970). *Friday night is Papa night*. Illustrated by Emily McCully.

Interracial

Bang, M. (1983). *Dawn*. New York: Morrow.

Isadora, R. (1983). *City seen from A to Z*. New York: Greenwillow.

Native American

Baker, O. (1981). *Where the buffaloes began.* Illustrated by Stephen Gammell. New York: Frederick Warne.

Baylor, B. (1975). *The desert is theirs.* Illustrated by Peter Parnell. New York: Scribner's.

Baylor, B. (1982). *Moonsong.* Illustrated by Ronald Himler. New York: Scribner's.

Bulla, R. C., & Syson, M. (1978). *Conquista!* Illustrated by Ronald Himler. New York: Crowell.

Dodge, N. C. (1975). *Morning Arrow.* Illustrated by Jeffrey Lunge. New York: Lothrop, Lee & Shepard.

Goble, P. (1978). *The girl who loved wild horses.* Scarsdale, NY: Bradbury.

Jeffers, S. (1991). *Brother Eagle, Sister Sky.* New York: Dial.

Locker, T. (1991). *The land of the gray wolf.* New York: Dial.

Miles, M. (1971). *Annie and the old one.* Illustrated by Peter Parnell. Boston: Little, Brown.

Scott, A. (1972). *On Mother's lap.* New York: McGraw-Hill.

Resources

Each state department of education and local school system should have guidelines for teaching social studies. Write for information on these guidelines as well as those for multicultural education and eliminating sex discrimination in your school. For general information write to:

Resource Center on Sex Equity
Council of Chief State School Officers
400 North Capitol Street, NW, #379
Washington, DC 20001

Women's Educational Equity Act
Publishing Center
55 Chapel St.
Newton, MA 02150

Connecticut Project on Global Perspectives
218 E. 18th St.
New York, NY 10003

Social Science Education Consortium, Inc.
ERIC Clearinghouse for Social Studies/Social Science Education
Boulder, CO 80302

Every school and teacher's library should have Derman-Sparks and the A.B.C. Task Force's *Anti-Bias Curriculum: Tools for Empowering Young Children*, (1989), Washington, DC: the National Association for the Education of Young Children.

References

Allport, G. (1958). *The nature of prejudice.* New York: Anchor.

Au, K., & Kawakami, A. J. (1991). Culture and ownership: Schooling of minority students. *Childhood Education, 67,* 280–292.

Banks, J. A. (1982). Multiethnic education and the quest for equality. *Phi Delta Kappan, 12,* 592–685.

Bem, D. J. (1972). Self perception theory. In E. Berkowitz (Ed.), *Advances in experimental social psychology* (vol. 6). (pp. 74–91). New York: Academic.

Bent, A. E., & Bombi, A. S. (1988). *The child's construction of economics.* New York: Cambridge University Press.

Bruner, J. (1960). *The process of education.* Cambridge, MA: Harvard University Press.

Curriculum and Instruction/Charles County Public Schools. (1984). *Education that is multicultural: A curriculum infusion model.* College Park: University of Maryland.

Damon, W. (1983). *Social and personality development.* New York: Norton.

Dewey, J. (1944). *Democracy and education.* New York: Free Press. (Originally published 1916)

Flavell, J. H. (1979). Metacognitive and cognitive monitoring. *American Psychologist, 34,* 906–911.

Froebel, F. (1889). The education of man. New York: E. Appleton. (Original work published 1826)

Fromboluti, C. S. (1991). *Helping children learn geography.* Washington, DC: Department of Education.

Goodman, M. (1976). *The culture of childhood*. New York: Teachers College Press.

Hornbeck, D. W. (1984). *Guidelines for multicultural education*. Baltimore: Maryland State Board of Education.

Kemple, K. M. (1991). Preschool children's peer acceptance and social interaction. *Young Children, 45*(3), 70–75.

Ladd, G. W. (1990). Having friends, keeping friends, making friends and being liked by peers in the classroom: Predictors of children's early school adjustment. *Child Development, 61*, 1081–1100.

Lambert, W., & Klineberg, O. (1967). *Children's views of foreign people: A cross-cultural study*. New York: Appleton-Century-Crofts.

Maryland State Department of Education. (1980). *Guidelines for multicultural education*. Baltimore: Author.

Maslow, A. (1968). *Toward a psychology of being*. Princeton, NJ: Van Nostrand.

Minneapolis Public Schools. (1967). *Economic education*. Minneapolis: Author.

Mitchell, L. S. (1951). *Our children and our schools*. New York: Simon & Schuster.

Murphy, L. (1937). *Social behavior and personality*. New York: Columbia University Press.

National Council for the Social Studies. (1989). *Social studies for early childhood and elementary school children: Preparing for the 21st century*. Washington, DC: Author.

National Commission on Social Studies in the Schools. (1989). *Charting a course: Social studies for the 21st century*. New York: Author.

Pellowski, A. (1969). Learning about present-day children in other cultures. In *Children and international education: Portfolio No. 6* (pp. 1–3). Washington, DC: Association for Childhood Education International.

Prescott, E., Jones, E., & Kritchevsky, S. (1967). *Group day care as a child rearing environment*. Pasadena, CA: Pacific Oaks College.

Raths, J. (1962). Clarifying children's values. *National Elementary Principal, 42*, 34–39.

Riley, S. S. (1984). *How to generate values in young children*. Washington, DC: National Association for the Education of Young Children.

Seefeldt, C. (1993). *Social studies for the preschool/primary child* (4th ed.). New York: Merrill/Macmillan.

Seefeldt, C., & Warman, B. (1990). *Young and old together*. Washington, DC: National Association for the Education of Young Children.

Serbin, L., & O'Leary, D. (1975, December). How nursery schools teach girls to shut up. *Psychology Today*, 57–63.

Shavelson, R. J., & Bolus, R. (1982). Self-concept: The interplay of theory and methods. *Journal of Educational Psychology, 74*(1), 3–17.

Sheldon, A. (1990). "Kings are royaler than queens": Language and socialization. *Young Children, 45*(2), 4–10.

Vinton, I. (1970). *Folkways omnibus of children's games*. New York: Stackpole.

Weingold, H., & Webster, R. (1964). Effects of punishment on cooperative behavior in children. *Child Development, 35*, 1211–1216.

Glossary

accommodation.   Changing an already existing mental structure to include information.

AIDS.   Acquired immune deficiency syndrome.

animistic or anthropomorphic thinking.   Attributing life and intention to things that are not alive.

assimilation.   Absorbing new material into already existing mental structures or schemata.

autonomy.   Development of a sense of self and pride in achievement.

basal readers.   Reading books that are graded, with controlled vocabulary and syntactic structure.

basic trust.   Development of a sense of inner security; determined by the outer predictability of the environment.

behavior modification.   Process of guiding behavior through a series of rewards and reinforcements.

behavioristic.   Based on the belief that learning occurs because of rewards or reinforcement.

big books.   Books in large print, either teacher or commercially made.

bilingual.   Fluent in two languages.

"blended" families.   Families that result from remarriage.

British Infant Schools.   Programs based on Dewey's and Piaget's philosophies (term used in Britain).

child abuse and neglect.   Maltreatment of children.

child care.   Generic term for programs available for children ages two to five.

child-initiated approaches.   Program approach in which the child initiates the learning activities, and the teacher responds to the child's cues.

classification.   Mental process of placing objects, events, and things in categories.

cognitive development.   Changes in a child's way of knowing about the world that result in the growing ability to acquire and use knowledge.

comparing.   Process by which one establishes a relation between two objects on the basis of some specific attribute.

concepts. Classes of events or objects and the relationships among them; generally, what we think about.

concrete operational period. Piaget's term for the third stage of mental development of children (ages seven to eleven years); characterized by the ability to think logically while manipulating objects—or from a base of concrete reality.

concrete operations. Children's process of thinking abstractly as long as they have objects or things to manipulate as they think.

conservation. Ability to understand that materials or objects stay the same regardless of changes in form or arrangements in space.

constructionism. The belief that children, as all humans, construct their own knowledge as opposed to being taught knowledge by another.

creativity. Power to produce something new and original.

criterion-referenced test. Test designed to assess how well the taker has mastered a set of instructional goals and objectives with specified criteria.

cue system. Strategy used to discover how to read.

cursive writing. A way of writing in which letters are joined together in a flowing manner.

day care. Programs designed to provide care for children whose parents are employed outside the home.

decoding. In this context, analyzing graphic symbols of printed language in order to elicit meaning.

developmentally appropriate practice. Learning activities suitable for a child's age, stage of development, and interests.

disabled. Those who fall below the range of normal functioning.

DISTAR. A model program with a structural behavioral approach, designed by C. Bereiter and S. Engelmann.

dramatic play. Play in which children engage in activities or use materials to represent the real world as they act out their needs and personal desires.

emotional development. Changes in the structure of such feelings as sadness, fear, and joy.

encoding. In this context, expressing ideas, thoughts, and feelings in written or spoken language.

equilibration. Organism's tendency to bring about a dynamic balance between already existing structures and new events.

ESL. English as a second language.

evaluation. Judgment of the teaching/learning process.

expressive writing. Communicating with graphics and written expressions of oneself.

family day care. Care provided in a home by a parent or other adult.

field trip. Learning excursion into the community.

Follow Through. Government-sponsored project expanding the ideals and practices of Head Start to include kindergarten and primary-grade programs.

formal operational period. Piaget's term for the final stage of mental development of children age eleven to adult-hood; characterized by movement from concrete operations to abstract thinking.

formative evaluation.   Systematic, ongoing evaluation that leads to refining or reformulating plans.

games with rules.   Play subject to rules and order, as in the real world.

gifts and occupations.   Froebelian term for a curriculum including balls, blocks and cubes, and paper folding.

gifted.   Describes children who surpass the range of normal intelligence.

goals.   Broad aims of a program. Goals form a framework for specific objectives.

handicap.   General term to describe physical, emotional, or mental impairment.

Head Start.   Government-funded special program designed for young children in poverty; the goals of the program are to increase children's opportunity for achievement.

IEP.   Individualized education program; mandated by law for handicapped children.

industry.   Developing a sense of adequacy in dealing with the environment.

infancy.   Birth through twelve months of age.

inferring.   Suggesting explanations, reasons, or causes for events; based on observation.

informal evaluation.   Judgment made at the moment of teaching about the worth and value of the teaching/learning act.

initiative.   Ability to plan and undertake one's own actions.

instructional objectives.   Specific statements that guide the teacher's daily interactions with children.

integrated.   In this context, refers to an approach that presents content as a unified whole. Opposite is *separate-subject approach.*

intentionality.   Ability to aim to make things happen.

interactionist.   Perspective that learning takes place as the result of interactions between maturational development and environmental stimuli.

interest centers.   Areas for learning organized around some theme and designed to foster the broad goals of the total early childhood program.

intrinsic.   Describes an inner drive uninfluenced by external pressures.

invented spellings.   Children's written versions of ideas or thoughts. They may be shapes as well as letters and do not confirm to prescribed orthographies.

key concept.   Organizing idea identifying the structure of content.

kindergarten.   German word meaning children's garden (Froebel). In our country today kindergartens are usually sponsored by the school system and are designated for five-year-olds.

Lanham Act.   Act passed during the Second World War to provide funds to establish child-care centers in factories, so mothers could work for the war effort.

learning stations.   Designated areas containing specific materials and designed to teach specific learning objectives.

least restrictive environment.   Environment that suits the particular needs of children with handicapping conditions without constraining them.

LEP. Limited English proficiency.

lesson plans. Directions for specific activities; usually include a statement of goals, activities, materials, and evaluation.

mainstreaming. Placement of handicapped children in regular classrooms.

mandates. Programs, plans, goals, and objectives that teachers are required to follow.

manipulative play. Play in which children engage in intense exploration of objects and arrange things in their own way.

mathematical knowledge. Knowledge that does not exist in objects or in external reality but in relationship.

modeling. Observational learning, for example, as children imitate the behaviors of others.

morphology. Rules regarding single words.

movement exploration. Activities that entail becoming aware of one's body and its capabilities.

multicultural. Describes a program that incorporates appreciation for differing cultures and settings.

nativist. Learning perspective that heredity determines development.

nongraded primary. Age-grade placement from kindergarten through grade three is eliminated. Children move at their own pace through the kindergarten and primary grades. Also called ungraded primary.

norm-referenced test. Standardized test that gives a score indicating a child's performance on the test compared to other children of the same age or grade.

nursery school. Usually, a school for children between two and five years of age; may be half day or full day; typically sponsored by private groups.

nurturist. Learning perspective that humans are essentially passive and receptive to environmental stimuli.

object permanence. Idea that an object exists even if not present; mental imagery.

observing. Learning about the world through the senses: seeing, hearing, smelling, tasting, and feeling.

ordering. Higher level comparing involving two or more things or sets; involves placing things in sequence from first to last (*seriation*).

phonology. Sounds and sound system of a language.

physical development. Growth in size and weight, body growth, and control over motor abilities.

poetic writing. Writing that expresses thoughts following conventions of meter, structure, rhyme, and so on.

practice play. Stage of play in which the child performs and practices newly acquired skills with pleasure.

predictable stories. Tales with repetitive story patterns or language.

preoperational period. Piaget's term for the second stage of internal development of children ages two to seven or eight years; characterized by children's ability to use mental symbols and imagery.

preschematic. State of art between two and five years of age; characterized by scribbles that children recognize, name, and repeat.

preschooler. Child three to four years of age.

primary grades. Grades one to three, for children ages six to eight; usually part of a school system.

project method. Teaching through themes and group projects.

psychoanalytic theories. Theories of education based on Freud's assertions about emotions, motivation, and personality development.

punishment. Any action that suppresses behavior.

reinforcement. An event following a behavior that encourages recurrence of that behavior.

rhythm band. Collection of instruments such as blocks, bells, triangles, or home-made instruments used for making music.

schemata. (plural of *schema*) Mental organizational patterns.

schematic. Describes drawings and paintings characterized by the beginnings of realism.

self-concept. Broadly defined, a person's perceptions of self.

semantics. Meaning of words.

sensorimotor period. Piaget's term for the first stage of intellectual development, characterized by the individual's learning about the world through sensory input and motor actions.

separate-subject approach. In this context, refers to presenting material as specific academic content, for example, numbers are taught as math and during math period.

social development. Children's growth in becoming able to relate with others effectively.

social studies. That part of the curriculum concerned with the study of people and their interactions with others and the environment.

sociodramatic play. Dramatic play that includes two or more children in the play situation; verbal communication maintains play.

special needs children. Children whose development or capacity to perform does not fall within the normal range.

standardized tests. Tests given under specific conditions and following a manual for exact directions and timing.

subskills. Underlying skills that form part of a larger category of skills.

summative evaluation. Objective judgment of the value and worth of a program.

symbolic play. Play in which children suspend reality and pretend that one object is another.

syntax. Grammatical structure of language at the level above morphology.

systematic observation. Long-term or intensive observation to access or evaluate behavior.

teacher-child-initiated approaches. A program approach in which both child and adult initiate learning activities; sometimes called an *open framework*.

teacher-initiated approach. A program approach in which the adult is the initiator and clearly in charge.

thinking. Mental deliberation that results in a solution to a problem.

toddler. Child one to three years of age.

transactional writing.   Expository writing; writing that explains.

Transition Demonstration.   A program designed to follow Head Start children and their parents with Head Start like services and curriculum from children's transition from Head Start through grade three.

unit plans.   Plans for children's learning that encompass a relatively long period and are unified around a theme.

ungraded primary.   Age-grade placement from kindergarten through grade three is eliminated. Children move at their own pace from kindergarten through grade three. Sometimes called nongraded primary.

whole language approach.   Approach to teaching reading that emphasizes the natural way children learn to read.

WPA.   Works Progress Administration. During the Great Depression, the WPA funded nursery schools in order to provide employment for unemployed teachers.

zone of proximal development.   The distance between the ability to perform a task independently and the ability to perform a task under guidance of a more skilled person.

Index

The Authors

Carol Seefeldt, professor, teaches undergraduate and graduate child development courses at the University of Maryland in College Park. She has worked in the field of early childhood education for more than thirty-five years, first as an assistant in a child-care center and then as a primary school teacher in Milwaukee, Wisconsin; St. Louis, Missouri; and Granite City, Illinois. In Temple Terrace, she opened and directed a church-related preschool program. From 1969 to 1972, she served as regional training officer for the state's Project Head Start.

At the University of Maryland, Carol Seefeldt received the Distinguished Scholar Teacher Award for 1982–1983. She is active in the National Association for the Education of Young Children and has served as president of the Maryland Association for the Education of Young Children. She also has served on the board of directors of the Maryland Committee for Children and works with the Association for Childhood Educational International. She is a frequent consultant and speaker and conducts workshops and training programs for those working on the behalf of young children.

Dr. Seefeldt is the author of seventeen textbooks and numerous research and professional articles that have appeared in professional journals. Her research focuses on intergenerational attitudes, curriculum for young children, and the effects of competition on child growth and development. Currently, she is director of the evaluation for the Montgomery County Maryland Head Start-Public School Transition Demonstration.

Nita Barbour, associate professor, was the director of early childhood education and chair of the department of education at the University of Maryland-Baltimore County. Her experiences in early childhood education include her work in Maine, where she developed and implemented programs for teaching foreign languages to young children. She was awarded a Fulbright Fellowship to study literature and languages at the Sorbonne in Paris.

In Michigan, Nita Barbour taught four-year-olds and acted as coordinator of research and program development for preschoolers. She has taught at every level of education from preschool through high school.

She has been a teacher in Project Head Start and directed a Child Development Associate program for Head Start at the University of Maryland-Baltimore County.

She is active in the Association for Childhood Education International, where she serves as chair of the publications committee and developed the teacher education guidelines for its *Childhood Education's International Guidelines for Teacher Preparation*. She also served as president of Washington Metro's Association for Childhood Educational International. She is active in the Association of Teacher Educators and has served as regional officer for that association and as a training coordinator for the Maryland Committee for Children.

ISBN 0-02-408452-2

9 780024 084521